# Lecture Notes in Computer Science 980

Edited by G. Goos, J. Hartmanis and J. van Leeuwen

# Springer

*Berlin*
*Heidelberg*
*New York*
*Barcelona*
*Budapest*
*Hong Kong*
*London*
*Milan*
*Paris*
*Tokyo*

Afonso Ferreira  José Rolim (Eds.)

# Parallel Algorithms for Irregularly Structured Problems

Second International Workshop, IRREGULAR '95
Lyon, France, September 4-6, 1995
Proceedings

 Springer

Series Editors

Gerhard Goos, Karlsruhe University, Germany

Juris Hartmanis, Cornell University, NY, USA

Jan van Leeuwen, Utrecht University, The Netherlands

Volume Editors

Afonso Ferreira
CNRS — Laboratoire de l'Informatique du Parallélisme
Ecole Normale Supérieure de Lyon
46 Allée d'Italie, F-69364 Lyon Cedex 07, France

José Rolim
Centre Universitaire d'Informatique, Université de Genève
24, Rue General Dufour, CH-1211 Genève 4, Switzerland

Cataloging-in-Publication data applied for

Die Deutsche Bibliothek - CIP-Einheitsaufnahme

**Parallel algorithms for irregularly structured problems** : second
international workshop, IRREGULAR '95, Lyon, France,
September 4 - 6, 1995 ; proceedings / Alfonso Ferreira ; José
Rolim (ed.). - Berlin ; Heidelberg ; New York ; Barcelona ;
Budapest ; Hong Kong ; London ; Milan ; Paris ; Tokyo :
Springer, 1995
  (Lecture notes in computer science ; Vol. 980)
  ISBN 3-540-60321-2
NE: Ferreira, Alfonso [Hrsg.]; GT

CR Subject Classification (1991): F.1.2, D.1.3, C.1.2, B.2.6, D.4, G.1-2

ISBN 3-540-60321-2 Springer-Verlag Berlin Heidelberg New York

© Springer-Verlag Berlin Heidelberg 1995
Printed in Germany

Typesetting: Camera-ready by author
SPIN 10485642    06/3142 – 5 4 3 2 1 0    Printed on acid-free paper

# Preface

The Workshop on Parallel Algorithms for Irregularly Structured Problems –
Irregular '95 – is the second in the series, started in Geneva in 1994, that addresses issues related to deriving efficient parallel solutions to irregularly structured problems. This series of meetings is intended to foster cooperation between
theoreticians and practitioners of the field. The former study models and design
and analysis of parallel algorithms while the latter still face inefficient performance of parallel solutions to concrete problems in science and industry, mainly
because of irregular structures.

The scientific program of Irregular '95 consists of five sessions divided in
four main streams, namely, Programming Methods & Compiling Techniques,
Mapping & Scheduling, Applications, and Optimization. Each of the three days
of the workshop presents, in addition, an invited lecturer, expert on that day's
theme. The contributed papers published in these proceedings were selected by
the Program Committee on the basis of referee reports. Each paper appearing
in these proceedings was reviewed by at least three referees who judged the
papers for originality, quality and consistency with the themes of the conference.
Comments from the referees were sent to authors to aid in the preparation of final
manuscripts. Due to the high level of the submissions, eight short contributions
were accepted in addition to the twenty regular ones. We wish to thank all of
the authors who responded to the call for papers, our invited speakers, all of the
referees, and the members of the Program Committee:

A. Apostolico, Padova & Purdue    H. Burkhart, Basel
M. Cosnard, Lyon    A. Gerasoulis, Rutgers
T. Hagerup, Saarbrucken    V. Kumar, Minnesota
B. Monien, Paderborn    P. Panagiotopoulos, Thessaloniki
S. Ranka, Syracuse    J.-L. Roch, Grenoble
J. Saltz, Maryland    J. Szwarcfiter, Rio de Janeiro
P. Thanisch, Edinburgh    M. Valero, Barcelona

We are grateful to the European Association for Theoretical Computer Science, and to the Special Interest Group "Irregular" of the International Federation of Information Processing (IFIP) for their sponsorship, and to the PRC PRS
of the French CNRS, the CNRS, the Conseil Général du Rhône, the University
of Geneva, and the Laboratoire de l'Informatique du Parallélisme for financial
support. We would like to thank particularly the members of the Organizing
Committee consisting of P. Berthomé, T. Duboux, V. Roger and S. Ubeda; and
all of those who helped Irregular '95 to be a successful event. Finally, we are
grateful to the Laboratoire de l'Informatique du Parallélisme and the Ecole Normale Supérieure de Lyon for providing secretarial support and facilities for the
Conference.

September 1995                         A. Ferreira, J. Rolim

# Préface

Le colloque **IRREGULAR '95** sur l'Algorithmique Parallèle pour Problèmes Irréguliers est le second d'une série, débutée à Genève en 1994, qui s'intéresse à la production de solutions parallèles efficaces pour des problèmes à structure irrégulière. Cette série de rencontres a pour but d'augmenter la collaboration entre utilisateurs et théoriciens du domaine.

Le programme scientifique d'Irregular'95 comporte cinq sessions réparties dans quatre grands thèmes : Méthodes de programmation et techniques de compilation; Placement et ordonnancement; Applications; et Optimisation. De plus, chaque jour du colloque débute par l'exposé d'un conférencier invité, expert dans le thème du jour. Les contributions publiées dans ces actes ont été sélectionnées par le Comité de Programme au vu des conclusions des rapporteurs. Chaque article présent dans ces actes a été évalué par au moins trois rapporteurs qui ont jugé de l'originalité, de la qualité et de l'adéquation du texte avec les thèmes du colloque. Les commentaires des rapporteurs ont été transmis aux auteurs pour les aider dans la préparation des versions définitives. En raison du haut niveau des articles soumis, huit contributions courtes ont été retenues en complément des vingt articles principaux. Nous tenons à remercier tous les auteurs qui ont répondu à l'annonce du colloque, nos conférenciers invités, l'ensemble des rapporteurs ainsi que les membres du Comité de Programme qui était composé de :

| | |
|---|---|
| A. Apostolico, Padova&Purdue | H. Burkhart, Basel |
| M. Cosnard, Lyon | A. Gerasoulis, Rutgers |
| T. Hagerup, Saarbrucken | V. Kumar, Minnesota |
| B. Monien, Paderborn | P. Panagiotopoulos, Thessaloniki |
| S. Ranka, Syracuse | J.-L. Roch, Grenoble |
| J. Saltz, Maryland | J. Szwarcfiter, Rio de Janeiro |
| P. Thanisch, Edinburgh | M. Valero, Barcelona |

Nous sommes reconnaissants à l'EATCS (*European Association for Theoretical Computer Science*) et à l'IFIP (Special Interest Group Irregular of the *International Federation of Information Processing*) pour leurs soutiens, et au PRC PRS du CNRS, au CNRS lui-même, au Conseil Général du Rhône, à l'Université de Genève et au Laboratoire de l'Informatique du Parallélisme pour leurs apports financiers. Enfin, nous voulons particulièrement remercier les membres du comité d'organisation composé de P. Berthomé, T. Duboux, V. Roger et S. Ubeda ainsi que tous ceux qui ont permis à Irregular'95 d'être un succès, avec en particulier, le Laboratoire de l'Informatique du Parallélisme et l'Ecole Normale Supérieure de Lyon pour la mise à disposition des moyens logistiques nécessaires au colloque.

Septembre 1995                                          A. Ferreira, J. Rolim

# Contents

# IRREGULAR '95
## was supported by

Ecole Normale Supérieure de Lyon

Université de Genève

SIG Irregular of IFIP

European Association for
Theoretical Computer Science

PRC-GDR Parallélisme,
Réseaux et Systèmes

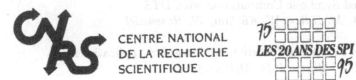

CENTRE NATIONAL
DE LA RECHERCHE
SCIENTIFIQUE

75 □□□□□
□□□□□
LES 20 ANS DES SPI
□□□□□
□□□□□ 95

## Applications

## Optimization

\* Invited speaker

# Regular versus irregular
# problems and algorithms

T. Gautier, J.L. Roch and G. Villard *

LMC-IMAG, 46 av. F. Viallet, F38031 Grenoble Cedex

**Abstract.** Viewing a parallel execution as a set of tasks that execute on a set of processors, a main problem is to find a schedule of the tasks that provides an efficient execution. This usually leads to divide algorithms into two classes: *static* and *dynamic* algorithms, depending on whether the schedule depends on the indata or not. To improve this rough classification we study, on some key applications of the STRATAGÈME project [21, 22], the different ways schedules can be obtained and the associated overheads. This leads us to propose a classification based on regularity criteria *i.e.* measures of how much an algorithm is regular (or irregular). For a given algorithm, this expresses more the quality of the schedules that can be found (irregular versus regular) as opposed to the way the schedules are obtained (dynamic versus static).

These studies reveal some paradigms of parallel programming for irregular algorithms. Thus, in a second part we study a parallel programming model that takes into account these paradigms to free the user from task scheduling. An implementation, PAC++, is presented.

## 1   Introduction

There are two main differences between sequential and parallel computers: in the latter, there are potentially very large overheads in communication (or memory accesses) and in task management. Independently of these overheads and beyond the NC class [12], the notion "amenable to a good parallel solution" may be captured by classifying problems and parallel algorithms with respect to their *nonoptimality* or *inefficiency*, *i.e* the extra amount of work done by the parallel algorithm as compared to a sequential algorithm [43, 45]. This can be also expressed using the concept of *scalability*, *i.e* the ability to provide a linear scaling of performance as function of the cost of the machine [65].

*Communications: locality.* The communication overhead may be modeled using various models of the parallel random access machine, PRAM, family [26, 43]. Much work has been done in this field. This has led to classify problems and parallel algorithms with respect to their *gross locality*, *locality* for short, *i.e.* the ratio of the computational complexity by the communication complexity [56]. Non local algorithms require high performance communication capabilities to

* The work presented here was in part supported by the STRATAGÈME project of the french *Ministère de l'Enseignement Supérieur et de la Recherche*.

be efficiently implemented. As long as communication overheads are significant on the existing parallel computers or in other words, as long as the PRAM cannot be efficiently simulated, to exploit locality will be a main issue to acheive high performance.

The notion of locality may also be understood as a notion of *irregularity*. Indeed, problems that have *regular*, oblivious or predictable patterns of memory accesses, give rise more easily to programs organized so that they have low communication costs. It may be argued that the more an algorithm is local the more it is regular. But this is not sufficient [13]: another relevant criterion for the irregularity of an algorithm is the irregularity of the communication patterns it involves: "a key factor success is the use of regular global communication patterns". The locality concept relies on the fact that models of parallel computation emphasizes that the tasks of computation and of communication can be distinguished [67].

*Scheduling: worst-case irregularity.* Obviously, task management is also a main issue toward efficiency of parallel programs. Optimal solutions for key problems such as *list ranking* may rely on task scheduling solutions [11]. There is also a context for parallelism where tasks have costs that cannot be determined in advance (*e.g.* indata dependent costs). From that angle, concepts are not so well established than concerning communication overheads. For instance, Brent's theorem does not handle the problem of assigning processors to their jobs. One can divide algorithms into two classes: *static* and *dynamic*. The former are characterized by that the structure of their executions is known in advance, the computational steps remain the same regardless of indata; on the other hand, the latter may execute differently depending on the indata. Dynamic algorithms often have static parts which may be referred as *basic blocks* [2]. But this division into static and dynamic algorithms is very poor and focus more on the way a schedule can be computed than on the quality of the executions that it provides.

Thus, since the scheduling is a key point for efficiency of executions, it is much interesting to try to classify algorithms with respect to the difficulty to schedule them finely *i.e.* in some sense, with respect to the cost-overhead due to scheduling. In this paper we are going to capture this by defining the *irregularity* of problems and algorithms. This will be done in a natural way, one may have an approach dual to the one used for communication overheads. Following the definitions of locality and informally, the more an algorithm is *irregular*, the more it must be difficult or costly to schedule the tasks it generates so that the resulting execution is efficient. Even if resources needed for executions may heavily depend on the indata, only worst-case executions are usually considered from a theoretical point of view: this first notion of irregularity will be called *worst-case irregularity* at section 2.

*Local efficiency and irregularity.* When measuring invariants of an algorithm, the yardstick that is used is either a sequential algorithm to capture the inherent parallelism, or a parallel algorithm to capture the communication complexity. Quite often, only worst-case execution times are considered. We think this can be far from reality when execution time varies a lot with the indata, and we will revisit the definition of efficiency at section 3. Indeed, from a practical point of view, one usually compare the parallel execution to the sequential one with the same indata. Limitations of worst-case definitions are crucial for NP-complete problems or algorithms that require exponential serial time. These latter may well be classified as "efficient algorithm" in the EP class (Efficient/Polynomially fast [45]), even if it is inherently difficult to dynamically load-balance their executions, so that, for any fixed indata, the implementation is efficient (we will speak of *local efficiency*). This is well known and has been also somehow illustrated by now anectotal superlinear speed-ups in various domains [46, 70, 57, 48]. This will lead to a second measure of irregularity in the definitions at section 3, where usual efficiency will be preferably computed for executions (local efficiency) than for algorithms (worst-case efficiency).

*Irregular algorithms versus irregular data-structures.* Irregularity is often considered in the literature. Two aspects of the notion appear: *irregular algorithms* and *irregular data structures*. As it can be underlined, we have chosen to measure irregularity on algorithms rather than on data structures. However we will consider both approaches to be equivalent. This is true in many cases, especially when a "satisfying distribution of the data structure" on which the algorithm operates is a "satisfying distribution of the work-load" and thus corresponds to a task scheduling with efficient execution. Indeed, a data structure is irregular when the cost to operate on parts of it is not exactly known or is unknown by advance. Parallelization approaches that are based on the splitting of such structures may consequently lead to a bad distribution of the load *a priori* and require dynamic load-balancing. Examples among various others can be found in [21, 22]. Especially for image processing [49], for a dictionary machine [15, 18] and for branch and bound algorithms [23], the irregularity of the data structure is an imbalance of the load.

*Organization of the paper.* The paper is organized as follows. We focus at section 2 on worst-case studies and try to define irregularity with respect to scheduling complexity. Regular and irregular strategies (or patterns) of scheduling will be associated to different costs. As noticed earlier by several authors we try to emphasize a duality between routing and scheduling. We believe that this leads to a better understanding of irregularity (at least in worst-case studies). This is formalized by the definition of *the parallel execution problem* [68]. Then at section 3 we recall well known facts on efficiency: from many practical points of view, when executions times are indata-dependent, a local efficiency (for fixed indata) better suits to measurements. Load-balancing will be necessary to have globally efficient algorithms (locally efficient everywhere): this will be another aspect of irregularity.

From these two first sections, some basic concepts will appear to be useful for parallel programming of irregular algorithms. We identify them at section 4 and show how they can be implemented using generic C++ classes at section 5.

# 2 Worst-case irregularity

The model of parallel computer we use consists of a set $\mathcal{P}$ of $p$ processors. A processor, at a first level, works sequentially with its local memory and, at a second level, communicates with other processors via a global memory. We consider that an execution of a parallel algorithm is a set $\mathcal{T}$ of tasks each executing on an indatum taken from a set $\mathcal{X}$. Let $\mathcal{O}$ be the subset of $\mathcal{T} \times \mathcal{X}$ of the couples $(t, x)$ such that $t$ executes with $x$ in input.

## 2.1 The parallel execution problem

Abstractions of the communication overhead is usually formalized as *routing problem* or *memory access scheduling problem*. The task management overhead leads to the *scheduling problem*. If we abstract the whole overheads as the *parallel execution problem*, a solution to this problem can be given as a solution to the routing problem and a solution to the scheduling problem. The quality of a solution to the routing problem governs the time needed to simulate a PRAM by other machines with communications like the DCM [44, 45], the LPRAM [1] or the XRAM [68].

Following [68] we propose a unique framework, and we formalize a solution to the *parallel execution problem* as a *parallel execution scheme* (PES). A PES is a couple $(\mathcal{P}, \mathcal{S})$ where $\mathcal{S}$ is a *scheduler* that handles objects in $\mathcal{O}$. An initialized PES is a quadruple $(\mathcal{P}, \mathcal{S}, \mathcal{I}, \mathcal{D})$, where $\mathcal{I}$ is the input specification *i.e.* a mapping $\mathcal{O} \subset \mathcal{T} \times \mathcal{X} \to \mathcal{P} \times \mathcal{P}$, this mapping indicates where the data and the tasks are initially situated. In the same way, $\mathcal{D}$ is the output specification. It is a mapping $\mathcal{O} \subset \mathcal{T} \times \mathcal{X} \to \mathcal{P}$ that specifies where the tasks in $\mathcal{T}$ will execute and thus where the data in $\mathcal{X}$ has to be routed. We assume that having started one task, a processor will complete it (we refer to [6] for a detailed discussion using process migration). We also assume that tasks are indivisible.

The two problems of routing and scheduling are often considered separately but have, at least from a theoretical point of view, remarkably similar properties and are handled in similar ways. For instance, when the model of machine incorporates barrier synchronization [39, 67], it is noticed in [67] that in a "general dynamic load-balancing situation there also exist phenomena that are compatible with barrier synchronization" (this is not clear from a practical point of view [8, 3, 29]). Similarities between the two problems may also be pointed out when load-balancing are characterized by the communication patterns they involve [25]; a scheduling overhead can be viewed as a communication overhead. Further, as surprisingly noticed in [66], "general many to many routing can be reduced to sorting plus load-balancing".

*The routing problem.* If routing problem is addressed alone, we have $\mathcal{O} = \mathcal{X}$ a set of packets. The scheduler $\mathcal{S}$ manages the transfers (or equivalentely the memory accesses). It consists of a routing algorithm which actually routes the packets that have been scheduled by the queing discipline [68]. The communication overhead is usually the cost of the communications themselves (on a real machine, links have a given bandwidth or accesses to a common memory can be quantified). It is unusual to associate an overhead to the computation of the specifications $\mathcal{I}$ and $\mathcal{D}$. When the routing problem is considered, these specifications are known. The problem of routing can be solved before execution (off-line) or during execution (on-line). An execution may consists of alternative phases of computations and of synchronizations [67] or such phases may execute asynchronously [13]. Every synchronization phase may consists in structured communication patterns like permutations or message may be generated dynamically and ask for unstructured patterns.

*The scheduling problem.* If scheduling problem is addressed, we take $\mathcal{O} = \mathcal{T}$ a set of tasks. The scheduler $\mathcal{S}$ handles the computational tasks generated by the algorithm. It consists of a load estimater that measures the load of the machine and of a decider that assigns a schedules to the tasks [72, 9]. As opposed to the routing problem, the scheduling overhead is usually the cost of measuring the load [24] and of deciding task creation and the schedule. In other words, at task creation, the input and output specifications has to be computed. This duality leads to formalize the irregularity (as it has been done by locality) of an algorithm as being related to a scheduling complexity. The more the scheduler is working, the more the algorithm is irregular. The problem of scheduling can be solved before execution (static scheduling) or during execution (dynamic load-balancing and load-sharing). An execution may consists of alternative phases of computations and of scheduling [11] or phases can be done asynchronously. Associated patterns may be regular (*e.g.* constant unit time tasks to distribute on processors at a given moment) or irregular if tasks are created dynamically with varying time requirements that cannot be determined in advance.

Routing and scheduling may be handled simultaneously. In static scheduling studies such as in [63, 20, 37, 71], the problem is to schedule tasks given that a communication between two tasks that are mapped onto different processors has a nonzero cost. There, the problem is to compute an output specification $\mathcal{D} : \mathcal{T} \times \mathcal{X} \to \mathcal{P}$ to minimize a given cost [52].

## 2.2 Worst-case irregularity

In the following we focus on overheads that take place during execution. Both communication and scheduling overheads have to be considered, the former usually corresponds to carry out the data exchanges whilst the latter corresponds to compute the specifications. In [56] the locality of a problem is the ratio of the parallel work of the best PRAM algorithm that solves the problem by the communication complexity on two processors. From there it will be easy to express the worst-case irregularity of algorithms and problems provided we can measure a scheduling complexity. The model of parallel machine we use for that will be a $p$-PRAM (CREW P-RAM with $p$ processors). The parallelism is usually achieved by the following statement:

for all $j \in J$ in parallel do instruction($j$)

this statement assignes to each element $j$ in $J$ the processor indexed code($j$) that is uniquely determined by $j$ in constant time.

Instead, generalizing the *fork* instruction [26, 4], a program will generate parallelism through statements of the following type:

$$\text{for all } t \in \mathcal{T} \text{ in parallel do schedule}(t) \tag{1}$$

Here the execution of the statement consists of scheduling the tasks in $T$ so that they are completed in optimal time. A task is a program to be run by one processor. The *length* of a task is its sequential time: it may not be known until the execution completes. Processors are chosen by a scheduling mechanism that solves the *Task Scheduling Problem*, TSP. This problems is defined as follows [11]. Polynomially many tasks are given, each of length between 1 and $c(n)$ and the total length of the tasks is bounded by $w(n)$ ($c(n)$ and $w(n)$ are at most polynomials in $n$). The problem is to schedule the tasks on a $p$-PRAM so that the tasks are completed in time $O(\max\{w(n)/p, c(n)\})$. If $p$ is upper bounded by $w(n)/c(n)$ the time is optimal.

We assume the TSP is solved in time the ratio of the number tasks $\#\mathcal{T}$ divided by the number of processors. We will say that the *scheduling complexity* of one call to the scheduler is $\max(1, \#\mathcal{T}/p)$; the *scheduling complexity* of an algorithm is the sum of the scheduling complexity of all the calls to the scheduler.

**Definition 1.** The worst-case regularity $\rho_w(n)$ of an algorithm on $p$ processors written with **schedule** instructions is the ratio: the parallel work $w(n)$ required to run the algorithm divided by the scheduling complexity. The worst-case irregularity $\iota_w(n)$ is the scheduling complexity.

This definition focus much more on practical algorithms than on problems. A dynamic algorithm, that can be easily expressed using dynamic scheduling and attain good efficiency, will be irregular if the scheduler contributes a lot to the efficiency. Solving the TSP it has been established in [11] that list ranking can be computed in optimal logarithmic time on a PRAM. We can easily write the corresponding algorithm using the scheduler, since only one call is sufficient to schedule $n$ tasks on $p = n/\log n$ processors, the irregularity is $\iota_w(n) = \log n$. Conversely, a static algorithm that is easily expressed using a static mapping will be regular. The computation of an $n$-point FFT graph is implemented with no effort with irregularity $O(1)$ on $n$ processors. To implement the time optimal list ranking with irregularity $O(1)$ (without calling the scheduler) using the rather sophisticated method in [11] would be tedious; but an inefficient list ranking on $n$ processors (see [38, 43] for instance) is obviously also of irregularity $O(1)$.

## 2.3 Granularity and irregularity

The irregularity of one call to the scheduler is the ratio of the number of parallel tasks generated by the number of processors. Consequently, for a given input size, if the number of task creations remains constant for a size-dependent algorithm (following the terminology in [45]), the irregularity may increase when the number $p$ of processors decreases. To make irregularity bounded independently of the number of processors, it is thus necessary to consider a size-independent algorithm such that the number of tasks is related to $p$.

For instance, let us consider the two previous examples on a $p$-PRAM with $p \leq n$ processors. The $n$-point FFT is easily implemented using $p$ parallel tasks, in time $\theta(n \log n/p)$: the irregularity remains $O(1)$. To modify the granularity allows to keep the same irregularity. More generally, for any given size of problem, if the algorithm is static (the execution graph remains the same regardless of indata), using clustering and scheduling techniques it is possible in a compilation phase, to produce a graph for a $p$ tasks parallel algorithm [37]. The irregularity is always $O(1)$. But the efficient list-ranking using the scheduler has irregularity $O(n/p)$ on $p$ processors. The number of tasks generated by the algorithms remains equal to $n$.

To conclude this section, we may point out that remarks in [13] may also be applied to scheduling: synchronizations should be avoided between computations and scheduling and it is important to distinguish between regular and irregular behaviours of the load-balancer itself. We above all suggest that load-balancing should not be considered separately but as part of the algorithm itself as it is done for communications.

## 3  Efficiency and irregularity

Dynamic algorithms are defined to be algorithms that execute differently depending on the input. It may be that only the execution graph depends on the indata with the execution time remaining constant, but in a more general context we must consider situations where also the execution time varies. Indeed, for instance for algorithms such as branch-and-bound, used to solve NP-complete problems, a worst-case execution can be efficiently parallelized (in EP). Instead, a main concern from a practical point of view is to ensure that, for fixed entries, the execution will be efficient and in particular to ensure that a good speed-up is obtained with respect to a sequential execution with the same entries. *How much the execution time depends on the indata* will be a measure of irregularity.

### 3.1  Local and global inefficiency.

In the following, we extend the definitions in [45] to take into account the above comments. For a sequential algorithm $\mathcal{A}$, we denote by $t(x, n)$ its sequential running time on an input $x$ of size $|x| = n$. For a parallel size-independent [40] algorithm $\mathcal{B}$ that solves the same problem, we denote by $t_p(x, n)$ its running time on a $p$-PRAM with $1 \leq p \leq h(n)$. Thus, $t_p$ is a function of $x$, $n$ and $p$, $p$ being a free parameter. As in [42], the parallel work $w_p(x, n)$ denotes the number of operations effectively performed by the algorithm $\mathcal{B}$. We have for all $x$:

$$w_p(x, |x|) \leq p t_p(x, |x|).$$

Let $t(n) = \max_{x, |x|=n} t(x, n)$ be the worst-case sequential running time and similarly define $t_p(n)$ and $w_p(n)$, the number $p$ of processors being constant for a constant input size $n$. We are interested in the performances of algorithm $\mathcal{B}$ with respect to the yardstick sequential algorithm $\mathcal{A}$ (which will be when possible the best known sequential algorithm). In this framework, we focus on parallel algorithms that are in EP when worst-case complexity is considered.

To take into account execution time variations, we define the *global inefficiency* $\eta_p(n)$ of $\mathcal{B}$ with respect to $\mathcal{A}$ to be the maximum of the local inefficiency:

$$\eta_p(n) = \max_{x, |x|=n} \frac{w_p(x,n)}{t(x,n)}.$$

Assuming that $\mathcal{B}$ is in EP and that the worst-case is attained, for all $n$ there exist $x_0$, $|x_0| = n$, such that $t(x_0, n) = t(n) = w_p(x_0, n) = w_p(n)$. If one assume that $t_p(x, n) \leq t(x, n)$ then $\eta_p(n) \leq p$; if $w_p(x, n) \geq t(x, n)$ then $\eta_p(n) = \Omega(1)$.

We have defined the global inefficiency as a maximum, this seems to be reasonable from a practical point of view [2]. For difficult problems or highly dynamic ones, difficulties arise when every particular case has to be handled efficiently. Despite the fact that often no analytic information on the variations of the execution time is available, the minimization of the global inefficiency is related to the scheduling mechanism, nothingly when speculative parallelism is involved. This makes that efficiency relies on frequent calls to a scheduler and thus increases the irregularity of the algorithm (following definition 1).

The main concern is then to build an algorithm that firstly minimizes the global inefficiency and secondly the irregularity in order to limit the use of the scheduler.

## 3.2 Iterative executions and highly unstructured problems

A similar model of execution than above, that breaks the distinction between static and dynamic approaches, is evoked in [36] for the N-body problem and can be generalized to many iterative solutions. The performances of a static scheduling deteriorates when the solved problem is dynamic, a "static scheduling" can be re-computed dynamically when needed. Examples also include back-tracking search and branch-and-bound optimization [17, 5, 66]: algorithms alternate between computational phases, "expansion phases", where the repartition of the load becomes skewed and load-balancing phases.

In many of these applications the duration of the tasks is not known, this information slackness makes that only heuristics can be developped. An interesting question that is often raised is *how frequent one need to call the load-balancer* (this frequency may vary dynamically). Following the definition, if on $p$ processors the load-balancer is called every $\nu(n)$ units of time on $\#\mathcal{T}(n)$ tasks for an algorithm with parallel time $t_p(n) = w(n)/p$, the irregularity could be defined as:

$$\iota_w(n) = (t_p(n)/\nu(n)) \times (\#\mathcal{T}/p)$$

---

[2] Other possible choices are to define an *average inefficiency* or to compute the *variance of the inefficiency*. Many strategies tend in fact to reduce these latter quantities.

but, as underlined previously, this is currently of limited interest since it seems difficult to establish such a formula for real highly unstructured problems. But if it is known that scheduling is called on tasks of equal size $s(n)$, *i.e.* on every task at a given level of granularity, then we deduce that $\iota_w(n) = t_p(n)/s(n)$.

## 3.3 Gaussian elimination

For an input square matrix $A$ of dimension $n$, we are going to consider parallel algorithms that implement the following one to compute the rank of $A$.

```
r:=n;
for k, 1..n
    if A(k,k) = 0 then search a row l such that A(l,k) != 0;
    if A(l,k) = 0 then r:=r-1
    else
        swap row k and row l;
        for i, k+1..n if A(i,k) != 0 then zero A(i,k) using row k; endfor;
enfor;
```

The sequential cost is at least $O(n^2)$ (number of tests if $A$ is a regular upper triangular matrix) and $O(n^3)$ in the worst-case. It is obvious to give a p-PRAM algorithm that runs in $O(n^3/p)$ using $p \leq n$ tasks, which is both efficient and polynomially fast following the classification in [45] and having irregularity $O(1)$. This is not satisfying from a practical point of view since such an algorithm may run in the same time $O(n^2)$ in parallel than in sequential for certain matrices in input (*e.g.* consider a row repartition of $A$ and a matrix having diagonal and lower diagonal unity with zeros elsewhere). Its global inefficiency is thus $\eta_p(n) = O(n)$.

Instead, the operations can be scheduled at each phase $k$ of the elimination. One will easily get convinced that a balanced load-distribution is obtained using $p$ tasks at each step. Since $n$ steps are performed this gives a satisfying algorithm with irregularity $O(n)$ and a global inefficiency $\eta_p(n) = O(1)$.

## 3.4 Array and lists redistribution

The *Task Scheduling Problem* and the *Object Redistribution Problem* as specified in [11] leads to useful and efficient practical implementations. We also refer to [53] for the *Token Distribution Problem* and for other formulations to [14] in the synchronous case and to [7] in the asynchronous case. A plethora of examples of such implementations could be chosen. Among them we find works for ray tracing [27, 51], image processing [49], particles movement simulation [54, 64] or for dictionary machine [15, 18]. These solutions consist in dynamically load-balance tasks in arrays or lists at barrier synchronizations, by solving in particular cases the two former scheduling problems, with irregularity $O(1)$ (the scheduler's job is hand-coded).

If we go back to Gaussian elimination, we have previously obtained a balanced load-distribution by scheduling $p$ new tasks at each elimination step. Instead, we may now use an array redistribution to balance "by hand" the tasks after each elimination step. Such a computation involves an $O(n)$ work overhead at each step, this does not affect the asymptotic cost of the whole algorithm. Moreover, we can write this new algorithm using $p$ tasks, each task performing a sequence of elimination steps, each followed by a redistribution step. The irregularity is now $O(1)$ with a global inefficiency remaining constant.

# 4 Parallel programmation of irregular algorithms

From the previous sections, some "paradigms" (key observations) for parallel programmation can be given if target algorithms are irregular:
- load-balancing should be considered as part of the algorithm itself,
- there is no major reason that lead to distinguish between static and dynamic scheduling, a mixed approach may be considered,
- the formalization mainly rely on the notion of task,
- attributes such as cost informations should be associated to tasks,
- attributes such as scheduling informations should be associated to tasks,
- even if highly irregular, many applications may execute efficiently with synchronized load-balancing.

These remarks have directed the design of the library *Parallel Algebraic Computing* ++, PAC++, that provides high level facilities to program and execute efficiently *irregular algorithms* on distributed memory machines [33, 34]. The library itself will be briefly described at next section. The main target application of the library is computer algebra [30, 58, 35], the example we have chosen to illustrate the PAC++ programming model is taken from this field. However, as it will be shown, the way PAC++ takes advantage of underlying automatisms such as *static scheduling* or *load-balancing*, can be used in various other areas involving algorithms which behaviours at execution cannot be statically predicted.

We now focus on main concepts only to provide a "high-level" description of the model which aim is to free the user from task scheduling. We rely in part on preliminary studies in [59, 60, 69] for the notions of *cost prediction informations* and of *poly-algorithm* and on [55, 10] for the run-time support ATHAPASCAN of PAC++ (this support provides a *fork/join* mechanism of *threads* and a load-balancer). The main objective is to write programs such that a description of the precedence graph can be easily computed (*e.g.* by a symbolic execution or by detecting static parts [47]) and scheduled (statically or during execution), or such that tasks are well specified so that they can be handled by a load-balancer [32]. Our purpose is not to give a model of a *scheduler* and of a *load-balancer*, but to see how they can be easily interfaced in a common framework.

## 4.1 Overview

We consider that an execution of a parallel algorithm is a set $\mathcal{T}$ of tasks (a task will be a function) that execute either sequentially or simultaneously on $n$

processors. Such an execution can be represented as a dependence directed graph, an *execution graph*, which vertices are sequential tasks and which arcs indicate precedence constraints between these tasks. If the graph does not depend on the values of the entries of the algorithm, it is viewed as a representation of the algorithm itself.

Given a set $\mathcal{T}$, if we assume that no task migration is possible, the problem of executing the graph on $n$ processors (of determining completely a parallel execution), reduces to specify a scheduling for each task of $\mathcal{T}$ (see section 2.1):

- *a date of execution* that indicates when the task will execute, this date can be for instance an absolute time if a clock is available or a relative time (*e.g.* task $T_j$ will execute when $T_i$ has completed),

- *a site of execution* that gives the processor that will execute the task.

Once the date and the site have been fixed we will say that the task has been *scheduled* for parallel execution, the couple (date, site) will be called a *schedule* of the task.

Various strategies can be used to schedule the tasks on a target parallel machine. But obviously the strategy that can be used heavily depends on the knowledge available on $\mathcal{T}$ before execution. A static scheduling can be used if the graph and the costs of the tasks are known. Conversely, any decision concerning the date and the site will be taken during execution by a dynamic load-balancer if no information is available before execution. Anyway, whatever the stategy that is used, the key objects are the tasks and their schedules. This appears directly in the model of programmation we propose, as explained at section 4.2 below, *functions* and *algorithms* will play the role of tasks. Since the notions naturally extend to graphs of tasks [7], we construct and use *weighted graphs* at section 4.3. Once these are defined, the job of either a static scheduler or a load-balancer is to assign values to schedules of functions, algorithms or graphs. In addition, a load-balancer also take structural decisions concerning the execution graph. Depending on the load of the machine and depending on the indata, a load-balancer will have to choose between several algorithms to solve the same problem, the one that is currently the best [65]. It may also indicate if a problem has to be splitted (and in how many parts) or not. These aspects will be developped at section 4.3.

The programming model is based on a C-like programming language: a sequential program is a function that may recursively call other functions. We assume the parallel machine to be a set of $n$ processors that work simultaneously. Since programs will reduce to $n$-ary *Remote Procedure Calls* each processor is viewed as a computational *server* and is associated to a unique identification $P_i$, $1 \leq i \leq n$. Each server is able to execute a given set of functions, this set may vary from a server to another. A server has its own memory that can be addressed by all the functions it executes. There is no global memory: a function cannot access the memory of a server but the one it executes on.

## 4.2 Functions and algorithms

Any function $f$ executing on a given server can ask for the execution of another function $g$ on another server. In a simple sequential framework such a request would be mainly characterized by the actual values of the arguments of $g$. From a parallel point of view, independently of the function and of its arguments a request will also be associated to a *site* and a *date*.

These informations will be given by a description $d$ of the request on $g$: a description of the actual execution of $g$. As said previously, such a description will be called a *schedule* of $g$. Once a schedule $d$ has been updated to give relevant informations it can be used to start a request Y:=g(X) where $X$ stands for values of the arguments of $g$ and $Y$ for the corresponding returned values. We use call as usually to manipulate threads in the following way:

- $Y := d.\text{call}(g(X))$, the function $g$ will execute as specified by $d$, the result is assigned to $Y$.

Parallelism between such calls will be generated by $n$-ary calls at next section.

Clearly for these calls, at least the site has to be known. We will see later how the updating of $d$ will be let to static schedulers and dynamic load-balancers, but we can notice that, using the statically known identifications $P_i$ of the servers to assign the site indicated by $d$, this yet gives us a standard model based on *Remote Procedure Call*, RPC.

To reach the notion of task, to a function must be associated characteristics understandable by the mechanism that will handle the tasks to schedule them. Further, we can assume that such a mechanism will take decisions considering only these informations *i.e.* without considering the function itself. For instance, using a *Unit Execution Time* model, graphs are scheduled independently of the operations that tasks actually realize. Consequently, to couple together informations and functions appears to be a key point. We introduce for that the notion of *algorithm*.

An algorithm is a couple formed by a function $g$ and an information concerning this function. To simplify, we will assume that this information is a cost information and is a function $C_g$ of the arguments of $g$, the values returned by such a function will be used as inputs of schedulers and load-balancers. These include *static informations i.e.* that do not depend on the values of the arguments of $g$ ($C_g$ is a constant function): for instance resource requirements (*e.g.* the subset of the servers that can execute $g$) or a static cost (all basic functions in a *Unit Execution Time* model).

More generally, the cost of a function may not be known as a constant value but may depend on its arguments. In this case $C_g$ may be a function that gives a cost *a priori* of the algorithm given by $g$ in terms of the sizes of the arguments [59, 60]. If $X$ is a value of the arguments of $g$, we will denote by $|X|$ its size then $C_g(|X|)$ is the algorithmical cost of the computation of $g(X)$. For instance, to formulate that the cost of a matrix product is $O(n^3)$, is an information that can be given statically and which can be relevant at execution and exploited automatically as soon as $n$ is known. We will say that such an information is *quasi-dynamic*: it depends on the sizes of the arguments but not on their values.

The updating of the static and quasi-dynamic informations will partly rely on the user; it may also be done by a symbolic execution.

Conversely, when an algorithm leads to highly dynamic executions, if no static or even quasi-dynamic information is known, the cost of the algorithm may be updated only by the load-balancer (for instance following statitics), in this case we say the information to be *dynamic*.

From now we will denote by $G = [g, C_g]$ the algorithm defined by functions $g$ and $C_g$. In the same way we have associated to a function a description of a request on it, we associate to an algorithm $G$ and values $X$ of the arguments of $g$, a schedule $D$ of a corresponding execution. Once $D$ is updated, the algorithm can be manipulated as follows:

- $Y := D.\mathtt{call}(G(X))$, the function $g$ will execute as specified by $D$.

We will refer to the information function $C_g$ concerning $G$ by:

- $G.\mathtt{cost}(|X|)$, returns $C_g(|X|)$.

The notion of algorithm corresponds to a task and its cost, we now construct graphs.

## 4.3  Scheduling and load-balancing

As specified above either a function, an algorithm and we will see, a graph of algorithms have their executions described by a schedule. This schedule can be assigned "by hand" by the users for instance if a description of the machine is known. In the general case this can be done automatically. A scheduler will take in input a static graph of algorithms. A load-balancer will manage expressions involving dynamic choices. In both cases they will be invoked using the instruction $\mathtt{schedule}$ (from the $p$-PRAM model at section 2.2).

For a graph of algorithms $\mathcal{G} = \{G_1, \ldots, G_k\}$ (each with input $X_k$), provided a corresponding weighted graph $\mathcal{C}|\mathcal{X}| = \{C_1(|X_1|), \ldots, C_k(|X_k|)\}$ of informations is known, a static scheduling can be computed. The execution will be directed by a graph of schedules $\mathcal{D} = \{D_1, \ldots, D_k\}$ that can be initialized using the instruction $\mathtt{schedule}$:

- $\mathcal{D}.\mathtt{schedule}(\mathcal{C}|\mathcal{X}|)$, computes a scheduling and assigns it to $\mathcal{D}$.

If we denote by $\mathcal{X}$ the inputs of the input nodes of $\mathcal{G}$ and by $\mathcal{Y}$ the outputs of the output nodes, then execution can be started using:

- $\mathcal{Y} := \mathcal{D}.\mathtt{call}(\mathcal{G}(\mathcal{X}))$, executes the graph $\mathcal{G}$ using sites and dates given by $\mathcal{D}$.

We can see that this reduces to $\mathtt{call}$ for functions if the graph $\mathcal{G}$ is simply a function $g$ with no informations attached to it and $\mathcal{D}$ is a schedule $d$ of $g$. Thus, before calling a function $g$, the site can be chosen automatically using $d.\mathtt{schedule}()$. In the same way, an $n$-ary call of functions corresponds to a special case of graphs, for any fixed $k$ the simultaneous execution of $k$ functions may be specified as follows:

- $\mathcal{Y} := \mathcal{D}.\mathtt{call}\ (g_1(X_1) \wedge \ldots \wedge g_k(X_k))$.

In the above we have asked for the execution graph to be known. We will see at section 4.4 that this can be overcomed in some cases when the graph is not known: an interpretation of the program can generate the graph for the scheduler.

When a static approach is not possible, a lack of **schedule** instructions will make decisions fall into the load-balancer hands. As underlined previously, another goal is to offer alternatives. We consider for that the two basic operations with choices *or* and *split*.

Given two algorithms $G_1$ and $G_2$ to solve the same problem, depending on the current state of the machine when the solution of the problem is needed, the best choice (the cheapest one for instance) may be either $G_1$ *or* $G_2$. For input costs $C_i(|X|)$, $1 \leq i \leq k$, we propose an *or* operator on the algorithms. Choices are made using the instruction **choose**:

- $G$.**choose**$(G_1 \vee \ldots \vee G_k, |X|)$, assigns $G$ to one of the $G_i$.

Then, as previously seen, we can schedule $G$ and execute it. This implements the notion of *poly-algorithm*.

In the same way, let $G$ be an algorithm to be executed with $X$ in input and let the potential degree of parallelism that can be generated by splitting $G$ be described by a set $K$ of integers. More precisely, we assume that for any integer $k$ chosen among $l$ values in $K = \{k_1, \ldots, k_l\}$ executing $g(k, X)$ ($g$ is the function given by $G$) consists of splitting $X$ into $X(1), \ldots, X(k)$, next of simultaneously executing algorithms $\bar{G}(X(1)), \ldots, \bar{G}(X(k))$ and finally of merging the results $Y_1, \ldots, Y_k$ to recover $Y = g(X)$, then the choice of the best value $k$ is let to the load-balancer using:

- $G'$.**choose**$(\wedge_K(G), |X|)$, assigns $G'$ to an algorithm which consists in executing $G$ with the chosen value $k$ for the splitting.

The cost information $C(|X|)$ of $G$ may indicate the overhead for the splitting and the costs of the sub-algorithm $\bar{G}$. Once the choice is made, we are led to the schedule and the execution of $G'$.

The principle that has been applied for any object is firstly to initialize a schedule of the object then to start the execution following indications of sites and dates given by this schedule. These phases can be done automatically once the user has described a graph or has written algorithms. Further, as briefly discussed below, mixed static/dynamic scheduling can be used by automatically constructing, at least partially, the execution graph

As announced, a preliminary version of a library using these concepts has been implemented under C++. This will be presented at section 5 where C++ classes lead to implementations of **Algorithms**, of **Schedule** representing the schedules and of **CostInfo** representing the cost informations. Further developments should be concerned with sequences of algorithms. Indeed, in the above we are limited to situations where cost information is related to the indata of a given algorithm. In general cases an algorithm may also give relevant informations on its outdata, that can be subsequently used as input cost of other algorithms.

## 4.4 Interpretation and execution

Once a program involving algorithms is written, it can be executed in a way mixing static and dynamic scheduling. A description of the execution graph may be obtained via a partial evaluation (symbolic unfolding) of the program. Two extreme cases may be distinguished. On the one hand, if the program is static, the obtained graph describes the whole execution, a unique schedule has to be computed. This schedule may be computed statically. On the other hand, when the program countains branching (resp. indirect accesses) where the conditions (resp. adresses) cannot be decided form the sole knowledge of the indata, the program is referred as *dynamic* [47]. In this case, a symbolic execution (also partial evaluation [47]) of the whole input program, generates a set of possible execution graphs, only one of them being valid for a given indata. In order to provide a valid graph, the execution of the program is dynamically splitted into successive static parallel steps. Each step firstly consists in building the graph description of the corresponding computations, then the scheduling of the graph is proceeded and the execution started.

At the highest level, the partial evaluation of a general program allows to build a graph, which nodes represent either elementary tasks, either nested sub-graphs which will be dynamically built before their scheduling. Following section 2, the irregularity of the program, related to the number of calls to the scheduler, here appears as a consequence of the dynamic behaviour of the program.

## 5 An application: Parallel Algebraic Computing ++

To illustrate this section we have chosen a central problem in computer algebra: the *manipulation of algebraic numbers*. Let us look at an example. Following [50] the matrix

$$A = \begin{bmatrix} -149 & -50 & -154 \\ 537 & 180 & 546 \\ -27 & -9 & -25 \end{bmatrix}$$

can be brought into Jordan normal form [28]:

$$J = \begin{bmatrix} 3 & 0 & 0 \\ 0 & 2 & 0 \\ 0 & 0 & 1 \end{bmatrix}.$$

Now how does $J$ vary under a small perturbation $A_\epsilon$ of $A$? We take

$$A_\epsilon = \begin{bmatrix} 130\,\epsilon - 149 & -50 - 390\,\epsilon & -154 \\ 537 + 43\,\epsilon & 180 - 129\,\epsilon & 546 \\ 133\,\epsilon - 27 & -9 - 399\,\epsilon & -25 \end{bmatrix} \approx \begin{bmatrix} -148.9999 & -50.0003 & -154 \\ 537.0000 & 179.9999 & 546 \\ -26.9999 & -9.0003 & -25 \end{bmatrix}$$

where $\epsilon \approx 0.000000784$ is such that

$$4 - 5910096\,\epsilon + 1403772863224\,\epsilon^2 - 477857003880091920\,\epsilon^3 + 242563185060\,\epsilon^4 = 0.$$

In this case it should be computed that two distinct eigenvalues have collapsed to a double eigenvalue with one unique eigenvector [50]. Such a result can be obtained by means of computer algebra provided one can manipulate $\epsilon$ as an algebraic number *i.e.* as a root of the above polynomial. This an example of application of computations with algebraic numbers. After a short presentation of the problem we show below how its directly enters the scope of PAC++ as an application of *algorithms* and *cost information* for irregular algorithms.

## 5.1 Computations on algebraic numbers

An algebraic number over a field $F$ is a root of a polynomial over $F$ [41]. As proposed in [16], a convenient way to manipulate these numbers with a computer is precisely to represent them by polynomials whom they are roots. For instance $\sqrt{2}$ can be represented by $\lambda^2 - 2 = 0$. Now consider the problem of triangularizing the following matrix by a Gaussian elimination:

$$A(\mu) = \begin{bmatrix} (\mu^2 + 1)(\mu - 3) & 1 \\ 1 & 0 \end{bmatrix}$$

where $\mu$ is an algebraic number such that $\chi(\mu) = (\mu^2 + 1)(\mu - 1) = 0$. The computation leads to a "discussion": the first entry of the matrix is zero if $\mu$ is such that $\mu^2 + 1 = 0$ and is nonzero if $\mu - 1 = 0$. These two cases may lead to two different upper triangular matrices:

$$T_1 = \begin{bmatrix} (\mu^2 + 1)(\mu - 3) & 1 \\ 0 & 1/((\mu^2 + 1)(\mu - 3)) \end{bmatrix}$$

by zeroing the entry $A_{2,1}$ with the nonzero pivot $A_{1,1}$ if $\mu - 1 = 0$ ($\mu^2 + 1 \neq 0$); or to:

$$T_2 = \begin{bmatrix} 1 & (\mu^2 + 1)(\mu - 3) \\ 0 & 1 \end{bmatrix}$$

after a column swap since the pivot is zero if $\mu^2 + 1 = 0$ ($\mu - 1 \neq 0$). Thus for a $n \times n$ matrix $A(\mu)$ with $\mu$ being the root of a polynomial $\chi(\mu)$ of degree $n$, the elimination may produce new branches each time an equality to zero has to be tested for a pivot. A step $k$ of the elimination, a test for pivoting may *split* the computation into two sub-computations that consist in continuing the elimination on two sub-matrices of dimension $n - k$ with respectively two polynomials $\chi_{k1}(\mu)$ and $\chi_{k2}(\mu)$ (divisors of the initial polynomial $\chi(\mu)$). These two branches of computations can be handled simultaneously and thus provide rough-grain parallelism:

- two tasks are created that have to be scheduled dynamically,
- two relevant cost information should be taken into account: the new tasks consist in triangularizing matrices of *dimension $n - k$*, the polynomials defining the algebraic numbers are of *new degrees $d_{k1}$ and $d_{k2}$*.

Since it cannot be determined in advance when splittings will occur, we see that algorithms using algebraic numbers in this way will be irregular. From a theoretical point of view, manipulating algebraic numbers and algorithms involving algebraic numbers may well be classified in complexity classes like NC [61, 62] (worst-case studies). But we think that efficient parallel algorithms will strongly rely on dynamic scheduling as it is presented below. Notice that if we refer to section 2.2, the triangularization above may lead to at most $n$ splittings since the degree of the polynomial $\chi(\mu)$ in input is $n$. In the worst-case these splittings may occur sequentially and give a worst-case irregularity $\iota_w(n) = O(n)$.

## 5.2 PAC++: Basic classes for parallel computation

We now describe an implementation of some of the concepts introduced at section 4. In two parts, we begin with the implementation of basic objects. Then at section 5.3 we focus on main features needed for parallel handling of algebraic numbers. For further insights the reader will refer to [33, 34, 31].

As shown with the examples above, data strutures and execution times may vary a lot: most of computer algebra algorithms are *irregular* but also provides *quasi-dynamic cost informations* (as defined at section 4.2). To take into account this irregularity and these informations, a set of C++ classes is offer to the user for developping portable programs that can be efficiently executed on different machines.

**5.2.1 Remote calls of functions.** A parallel program in PAC++ is written using a set of virtual processors mapped at execution on physical processors. Each processor is a server for algebraic computations: can execute a prescribed set of functions given by a library. This set is extended by the user's defined functions. The parallelism of an application is expressed through asynchronous or synchronous remote calls to these functions. The call of a function on a processor is executed by a thread using the above cited runtime support ATHA-PASCAN [55, 10]. ATHAPASCAN is a parallel extension of C which includes an adaptative granularity scheme and static/dynamic scheduling mechanisms.

A function that can be remotely called is called an *entrypoint*. This is implemented via the **EntryPoint** class of objects. To execute a remote call, the arguments of the function are bufferized in an object of type **iBuffer** (*input Buffer*). When the call is completed, the result is got out an object of type **oBuffer** (*output Buffer*). Thus an entrypoint has the following prototype:

```
void MyEntryPointFunction (iBuffer& , oBuffer& ) ;
```

**5.2.2 Algorithms.** An *algorithm* is an entrypoint plus quasi-dynamic cost informations. For most of parallel algebraic algorithms, the arithmetic and communication costs are known at certain levels of granularity [59, 60]. In our current implementation a cost information is couple formed by these costs:

```
class CostInfo {
public:
  // CostInfo cstor :
  CostInfo ( double ArithCost, double CommCost ) ;
} ;
```

All algorithms in PAC++ are objects rather than functions. They have in common the following main features:

(ı) informations to instanciate the computation for given input data depending on the algorithm;

(ıı) quasi-dynamic cost informations;

(ııı) a main function giving the task to perform;

(ıv) temporary data on which the algorithm works;

(v) output data.

Only features (ıı) and (ııı) are implemented as virtual member functions of the basic class **Algorithm** from which derive all other algorithms. Since data structures depend on the algorithm, four functions for *packing* (to put into an **iBuffer**) and *unpacking* (to get out an **oBuffer**) are purely virtual:

```
class Algorithm {
public:
  virtual void main( ) = 0 ;
  virtual CostInfo cost( ) const = 0 ;
  virtual packargs ( oBuffer& ) = 0 ;
  virtual packres  ( oBuffer& ) = 0 ;
  virtual unpackargs ( iBuffer& ) = 0 ;
  virtual unpackres ( iBuffer& ) = 0 ;
} ;
```

Two global operators are defined over algorithms that provide structured calls to parallel sub-algorithms:

- AND, indicates that several algorithms will be executed simultaneously;

- OR, indicates that a choice (which depends only on the cost information and on the load of the machine) will be made between several algorithms.

In the current PAC++ prototype of an interface for handling irregular algorithms no other operator (*e.g.* sequence, composition) is offered. Only expressions involving AND and OR operators are valid.

### 5.2.3 Schedules.

The schedules of functions and algorithms are implemented via the **Schedule** class. The member functions on an object of this type are **spawn**, **wait** and **call**. In addition, any object of the class must be initialized before used using the **schedule** member function. An outline of interface of the class **Schedule** is as following:

```
class Schedule {
public:
  // Initialization :
```

```
  void schedule ( const Algorithm& G ) ;
  // Asynchronous remote call
  Schedule& spawn( Algorithm& G ) ;
  // Synchronization
  void wait( Instance& Result ) ;
  // Synchronous call
  Schedule& call ( Algorithm& G ) ;
} ;
```

The implementation of this class relies on the tools available. The **schedule** function makes use of underlying static and dynamic schedulers. The three other functions are written upon the runtime support ATHAPASCAN.

**5.2.4   Execution of programs.** From the user point of view the different phases to initialize and start an execution should be gathered. Thus an important function is

```
Algorithm& Execute ( const Algorithm& G ) ;
```

This function executes an expression of algorithms and returns the result as an other expression of algorithms. The choices between algorithms, the initialization of the schedules and the execution itself are automatically performed.

Let us look at an example. We derive an algorithm to compute the rank of a square matrix from the basic class **Algorithm**. In particular, the virtual member functions are re-defined. The algorithm takes in input a matrix and returns an integer:

```
class RankAlgorithm : public Algorithm {
public:
  // Ctsor and initialization
  RankAlgorithm ( const Matrix& inputMatrix ) ;

  // Return the cost information (arithmetic and communication)
  CostInfo cost(  )
  { int n = indata.rowdim() ;
    return CostInfo( n*n*n,  n*n ) } ;

  // The main function
  void main(  ) ;

  // Packing and unpacking of argument and result
  packargs ( oBuffer& B ) {B << indata } ;
  packres   ( oBuffer& B ) {B << outdata } ;
  unpackargs ( iBuffer& B ) { B >> indata } ;
  unpackres  ( iBuffer& B ) { B >> outdata } ;

protected:
```

```
  Matrix A ;   // input: a matrix
  int Step ;   // internal variable: the current step
public:
  int rank ;   // output: the (current computed) rank of the matrix
} ;
```

To execute such an algorithm for computing the rank of a given matrix $M$ we proceed as follows. Firstly, an object **Rank** is declared and instanciated with the indata **M** (a matrix). Then, the above function **execute** is called:

```
Matrix M ;
// here some initializations of M
RankAlgorithm Rank ( M ) ;
Execute( Rank ) ;
if (Rank.outdata ==1) { .... }
else {....}
```

## 5.3  Parallel handling of algebraic numbers splitting

As described in introduction at section 5.1, in the example of the computation of the rank of a matrix $A(\mu)$ which entries are algebraic numbers, splittings during Gaussian elimination may occur when a nonzero pivot has to be chosen. If we denote by **Rank** the previous algorithm, then on a matrix $A(\mu)$ several values should be returned: each time a splitting occurs the number of returned values may be incremented by one. If $A(\mu)$ is given by

$$A(\mu) = \begin{bmatrix} 1 & 0 \\ 0 & \mu^2 - 1 \end{bmatrix}$$

where $\mu$ is an input algebraic number defined by $\chi(\mu) = (\mu^2 + 1)(\mu^2 - 1) = 0$, then the rank will be either equal to 2 if $\mu^2 + 1 = 0$ or equal to 1 if $\mu^2 - 1 = 0$.

Anyway, one may want to get *one of the possible results* or *all the results*. This choice is let to the responsability of the user. PAC++ offers two main managers of computation for this purpose: the computation with one root (arbitrarily chosen) and with all roots [19]. In this latter case, the whole computation (*e.g* the rank computation) is embedded in a manager which creates new parallel threads whenever a new splitting occurs. The completion is ensured by a synchronization barrier to recover all the results of the different parallel computations (the **AND** of algorithms provides such a synchronization).

In addition to the previously mentioned facilities, the implementation requires to spawn functions following the *fork* instruction of the PRAM model [26, 4]. Indeed, the *context* of the spawned function, *i.e.* the data needed to the computation following the splitting, must be recopied and associated to the spawned executions of the sub-algorithms. In the example of the rank, this context is essentially the sub-matrix that remains to eliminate after a nonzero pivot is found.

This context highly depends on the algorithm. In the current version of the library, this context is identified by the user-defined **restart** member function to *restart* the computation after a splitting. For such a type of algorithms, the class `ForkAlgorithm` is derived from the basic class `Algorithm`:

```
class ForkAlgorithm : public Algorithm {
public:
  virtual ForkAlgorithm* getstate() const = 0 ;
  virtual void restart() = 0 ;
} ;
```

When a splitting happens, the manager creates a copy of the current algorithm by calling the `getstate` member function and calls the `restart` function to continue the computation (on the same site or on another site depending on the scheduler answer).

On the rank example, the class `ForkRankAlgorithm` over algebraic numbers may be derived and implemented from the `RankAlgorithm`:

```
class ForkRankAlgorithm :
    public ForkAlgorithm, public RankAlgorithm
{
public:
    // Same ctsor than for RankAlgorithm :
    ForkRankAlgorithm ( const Matrix& M ) : RankAlgorithm (M) {} ;

    // getstate returns a copy at step k of the (n-k)x(n-k)
    // sub-matrix and save the current value of the rank
    ForkAlgorithm* getstate() const ;

    // restart the computation on a sub-matrix, at the end of
    // the computation, the returned rank if the one of the
    // input nxn matrix.
    void restart() ;

protected:
 int saved_rank ;
}
```

The example we have chosen demonstrates the use of algorithms and of cost informations for linear algebra. Notice that clearly, a cost information need not be complexity in terms of the input's size: a "cost" may be a priority, a statistical cost or any other relevant information on the computation. Together with schedules, this can implemented and used for a wide range of applications.

# 6  Conclusion

Inspired by the notion of locality we have proposed a definition of irregularity based on a scheduling complexity. By this preliminary study on the subject we want to emphasize that:

- routing and scheduling present many similar aspects and lead to somehow dual problems,
- scheduling should be considered as part of the algorithm itself.

This last point implies that no difference should be made between static or dynamic scheduling. In addition, while complexity definitions are usually given in a worst-case context, we believe that this is unappropriated to many irregular algorithms and other directions exist. Another way to define irregularity could have been to use task graphs. Intuitively, the irregularity of a nonstatic algorithm is related to the number of graphs corresponding to the possible executions and to the difficulty to compute these graphs. It seems harder to derive a satisfying definition from these aspects. This would need analysis tools and ways of comparing graphs and is an interesting direction for further studies.

# References

1. A. Aggarwal, A.K. Chandra, and M. Snir. Communication complexity of PRAM's. *Theoretical Computer Science*, 71:3–28, 1990.
2. A.V. Aho, R. Sethi, and J.D. Ullman. *Compilers: principles, techniques and tools*. Addison-Wesley, 1986.
3. S. Aluru and J. Gustafson. Subtle issues of SIMD tree search. In *Parallel Computing: Trends and Applications, Proceedings of PARCO'93, Grenoble France*, pages 49–56. Elsevier Science, 1994.
4. J.L. Balcázar, J. Díaz, and J. Gabarró. *Structural Complexity II*. Springer-Verlag, 1990.
5. Benaïchouche, M. Résolution parallèle de l'Affectation Quadratique (QAP) et de la Couverture Minimale d'un Graphe (VCP) par la méthode Branch & Bound. In *Proc. of FRANCORO, Rencontres Francophones de Recherche Opérationnelle*, 1995.
6. G. Bernard, D. Steve, and M. Simatic. Placement et migration de processus dans les systèmes reépartis faiblement couplés. *Technique et Science Informatiques*, 10(5):375–392, 1991.
7. D.P. Bertsekas and J.N. Tsitsiklis. *Parallel and distributed computation: numerical methods*. Prentice-Hall International, 1989.
8. Powley. C., C. Ferguson, and R. Korf. Depth-first heuristic search on a SIMD machine. *Artificial Intelligence*, 60, 1993.
9. T.L. Casavant and J.G. Khul. A taxonomy of scheduling in general-purpose distributed computing systems. *IEEE Transactions on Software Engineering*, (14):141–154, 1988.
10. M. Christaller. Athapsacan-0a sur PVM.3. Technical Report APACHE 11, IMAG Grenoble France, 1994.
11. R. Cole and U. Vishkin. Approximate parallel scheduling part I: the basic technique with applications to optimal parallel list ranking in logarithmic time. *SIAM J. Comput.*, 17(1), 1988.
12. S.A. Cook. A taxonomy of problems with fast parallel algorithms. *Inf. Control*, 64:2–22, 1985.
13. M. Cosnard. A comparison of parallel machine models from the point of view of scalability. In *proceedings of the 1rst Int. Conf. on Massively Parallel Computing Systems, Ischia, Italy*, pages 258–267. IEEE Computer Society Press, May 1993.

14. G. Cybenko. Dynamic load-balancing for distributed memory multiprocessors. *Journal of Parallel and Distributed Computing*, 7(2), 1989.

15. F. Dehne and M. Gastaldo. A note on the load-balancing problem for coarse grained hypercube dictionary machines. *Parallel Computing*, 16, 1990.

16. J. Della Dora, C. Dicrescenzo, and D. Duval. About a new method for computing in algebraic number fields. In *Proc. EUROCAL'85*, LNCS 204, Springer Verlag, pages 289–290, 1985.

17. S. Dowaji and C. Roucairol. Influence of priority of tasks on load-balancing strategies for distributed branch-and-bound algorithms. In *Proc. of IPPS'95, Workshop on Solving Irregular Problems on Distributed Memory Machines, Santa Barbara, USA*, 1994.

18. T. Duboux, A. Ferreira, and M. Gastaldo. MIMD dictionary machine: from theory to practice. In *CONPAR 92, Lyon, France*, LNCS 634, September 1992.

19. D. Duval. *Diverses questions relatives au calcul formel avec des nombres algébriques*. Thèse de Doctorat d'Etat, Université de Grenoble, France, 1987.

20. H. El-Rewini and T.G. Lewis. *Introduction to Parallel Computing*. Springer-Verlag, 1990.

21. G. Authié et al. *Algorithmes parallèles, analyse et conception I*. Hermès, 1994.

22. G. Authié et al. *Algorithmes parallèles, analyse et conception II*. To appear, 1995.

23. Cung V.D. *et al.* Concurrent data structures and load-balancing strategies for parallel branch & bound/A* algorithms. In *Third Annual Implementation Chalenge Workshop, DIMACS, New-Brunswick, USA*, 1991.

24. D. Ferrari and S. Zhou. An empirical investigation of load indices for load-balancing applications. In *Proc. Performance'87, 12th IFIP WG7.3 International Symposium on Computer Performance, Brussels Belgium*. Elsevier Science Publishers, 1987.

25. C. Fonlupt. *Distribution dynamique de données sur machines SIMD*. PhD thesis, Université de Lille 1, France, 1994.

26. S. Fortune and J. Wyllie. Parallelism in random access machines. In *Proceedings of the 10th ACM Symposium on Theory of Computing*, pages 114–118, 1978.

27. A. Fujimoto, T. Tanaka, and K. Iwata. Accelerated ray tracing system. *IEEE Comp. Graph. and App.*, Apr. 1986.

28. F.R. Gantmacher. *Théorie des matrices*. Dunod, Paris, France, 1966.

29. M. Gastaldo. *Contribution a l'algorithmique parallèle des structures de données et des structures discrètes : machine dictionnaire et algorithmes pour les graphes*. PhD thesis, ENS Lyon et UCB Lyon I, France, Dec. 1993.

30. J. von zur Gathen. Parallel arithmetic computations: a survey. In *Proc. 12th Int. Symp. Math. Found. Comput. Sci.*, pages 93–112. LNCS 233, Springer Verlag, 1986.

31. T. Gautier. PAC++: presentation and experiments. In *International Symposium on Symbolic and Algebraic Computation, Montreal, Canada - Poster session*, July 1995.

32. T. Gautier, F. Guinand, J.L. Roch, and A. Vermeerbergen. Régulation de charge et adaptation de grain : Athapascan. Preprint IMAG Grenoble France, (Journées de Recherche sur le Placement Dynamique et la Régulation de Charge, GDR PRS, Mai 1995).

33. T. Gautier and J.L. Roch. PAC++ system and parallel algebraic numbers computation. In *PASCO'94, Hagenberg/Linz Austria, Sept. 1994*.

34. T. Gautier, J.L. Roch, and G. Villard. PAC++ v2.0: user and developer guide. Technical Report APACHE 14, IMAG Grenoble France, 1994.

35. K.O. Geddes, R. Czapor, and G. Labahn. *Algorithms for computer algebra*. Kluwer Academic Press, 1992.
36. A. Gerasoulis, J. Jiao, and T. Yang. *Scheduling of structured and unstructured computation*. DIMACS Series in Discrete Mathematics and Theoretical Computer Science, to appear, 1995.
37. A. Gerasoulis and T. Yang. A comparison of clustering heuristics for scheduling DAG's on multiprocessors. *J. Par. Distr. Comp.*, Dec. 1992.
38. A. Gibbons and W. Rytter. *Efficient parallel algrithms*. Cambridge University Press, 1988.
39. P.B. Gibbons. A more practical PRAM model. In *Proceedings of the 1989 ACM Symposium on Parallel Algorithms and Architectures*, 1989.
40. A. Gottlieb and C.P. Kruskal. Complexity results for permuting data and other computations on parallel processors. *J. ACM*, 31:193–209, 1984.
41. N. Jacobson. *Basic Algebra I*. W.H. Freeman and Company, 1974.
42. J. Jájá. *An introduction to parallel Algorithms*. Addison-Wesley, 1992.
43. R.M. Karp and V. Ramachandran. Parallel algorithms for shared-memory machines. In J. van Leuwen, editor, *Handbook of Theoretical Computer Science Vol. A*, pages 869–941. North-Holland, 1990.
44. C.P. Kruskal, T. Madej, and L. Rudolph. Parallel prefix on fully connected direct connection machine. In *Proc. Int. Conf. on Parallel Processing, Illinois USA*, 1986.
45. C.P. Kruskal, L. Rudolph, and M. Snir. A complexity theory of efficient parallel algorithms. *Theoretical Computer Science*, (71):95–132, 1990.
46. T.H. Lai and S. Sahni. Anomialies in parallel branch-and-bound algorithms. *Communications of the ACM*, 27(6):594–602, 1984.
47. B. Lisper. Detecting static algorithms by partial evaluation. In *Proc. ACM Sigplan Symposium on Partial Evaluation and Semi-Based Program Manipulation*, 1991.
48. B. Mans and C. Roucairol. Parallel branch & bound for discrete optimization problems. In *Workshop on Parallel Processing of Discret Optimization Problems, Mineapolis*, 1991.
49. S. Miguet and Y. Robert. Elastic load-balancing for image processing algorithms. In Parallel Computation H.P. Zima, editor, *1rst International ACPC Conference, Salzburg, Austria*, 1991.
50. C. Moler, 1993. Communication about Mathlab test example *gallery(3)*.
51. K. Nemoto and T. Omachi. An adaptative subdivision by sliding boundary surfaces for fast ray tracing. *Graphics Interface*, 1986.
52. M. Norman and P. Thanish. Models of machines and computation for mapping in multicomputers. *ACM Computing Surveys*, sep. 1993.
53. D. Peleg and E. Upfal. The token distribution problem. In *Proc. of the 27th Annual IEEE Symposium on Foundations of Computer Science*, pages 418–427, 1986.
54. J.M. Pierson. A dynamic parallel implementation of a physically based particles models. In G. Hégron and O. Fahlander, editors, *Fifth Eurographics Workshop on Animation and Simulation, Oslo Norway*, 1994.
55. B. Plateau and al. Présentation d'APACHE. Technical Report APACHE 1, IMAG Grenoble France, 1993.
56. A. Ranade. A framework for analyzing locality and portability issues in parallel computing. In *Parallel Architectures and their Efficient Use*, LNCS 678, pages 185–194, 1993.
57. V.N. Rao and V. Kumar. Superlinear speed-up in ordered depth-first search. In *Proc. 6th Distributed Memory Computing Conference*, 1991.

58. J.L. Roch, F. Siebert, P. Sénéchaud, and G. Villard. Computer Algebra on a MIMD machine. *ISSAC'88, LNCS 358 and in SIGSAM Bulletin, ACM*, 23/11, p.16-32, 1989.

59. J.L. Roch, A. Vermeerbergen, and G. Villard. Cost prediction for load-balancing: application to algebraic computations. In *CONPAR 92, Lyon, France*, LNCS 634, September 1992.

60. J.L. Roch, A. Vermeerbergen, and G. Villard. A new load-prediction scheme based on algorithmic cost functions. In *CONPAR 94, Linz Austria*, LNCS 854, Sep. 1994.

61. J.L. Roch and G. Villard. Fast parallel computation of the Jordan normal form of matrices. *Parallel Processing Letters*. To appear.

62. J.L. Roch and G. Villard. Parallel computations with algebraic numbers, a case study: Jordan normal form of matrices. In *Parallel Architectures and Languages Europe 94, Athens Greece*, LNCS 817, July 1994.

63. V. Sarkar. *Partitioning and Scheduling Parallel Programs for Multiprocessors*. Pitman, 1989.

64. M. Smith and E. Renshaw. Parallel-prefix remapping for efficient data-parallel implementation of unbalanced simulations. In *Parallel Computing: Trends and Applications, Proceedings of PARCO'93, Grenoble France*, pages 215–222. Elsevier Science, 1994.

65. M. Snir. Scalable parallel computers and scalable parallel codes: from theory to practice. In *Parallel Architectures and their Efficient Use*, LNCS 678, pages 176–184, 1993.

66. R. Subramanian and I.D. Scherson. An analysis of diffusive load-balancing, 1995. Preprint - University of California, Irvine, USA.

67. L. Valiant. A bridging model for parallel computation. *Communication ACM*, 33:103–111, 1990.

68. L. Valiant. General purpose parallel architectures. In J. van Leuwen, editor, *Handbook of Theoretical Computer Science Vol. A*, pages 944–971. North-Holland, 1990.

69. A. Vermeerbergen. Les poly-algorithmes et la prévision de coûts pour une expression portable et extensible du parallélisme. In L. Bougé, editor, *Actes de RenPar'6, ENS Lyon, France*, pages 51–54, 1994.

70. G. Villard. Parallel general solution of rational linear systems using p-adic expansions. In *IFIP WG 10.3 Working Conference on Parallel Processing, Pisa Italy*, 1988.

71. M.-Y. Wu and D. D. Gajski. Hypertool: a programming aid for message-passing systems. *IEEE Trans. Soft. Eng.*, 1(3):330–343, 1990.

72. S. Zhou. A trace-driven simulation study of dynamic load-balancing. *IEEE Trans. on Software Engineering*, 14(9), 1988.

# Algorithmic Skeletons for Adaptive Multigrid Methods

George Horton Botorog          Herbert Kuchen

RWTH Aachen, Lehrstuhl für Informatik II
Ahornstr. 55, D-52074 Aachen, Germany
{botorog, herbert}@zeus.informatik.rwth-aachen.de

*Abstract.* This paper presents a new approach to parallel programming
with algorithmic skeletons, i.e. common parallelization patterns. We use
an imperative language enhanced by some functional features as host for
the embedding of the skeletons. This allows an efficient implementation
and at the same time a high level of programming. In particular, low
level communication problems such as deadlocks are avoided. Both data
and process parallel skeletons can be used, but the emphasis is placed on
the first category. By defining data parallel skeletons for dynamic data
structures, we obtain constructs for handling problems with irregular
and/or dynamic character. The implementation of an adaptive multigrid
algorithm illustrates how such problems can be solved by using these
constructs.

*Keywords:* Algorithmic Skeletons, Data Parallelism, Adaptive Multigrid, Imperative Host Languages, MIMD-DM computers.

## 1.  Introduction

Most languages employed today in the programming of MIMD computers with
distributed memory are imperative languages, like Occam, parallel C or parallel
Fortran. Here, the user must control the parallelism in his program on a rather
low level, by explicitly sending and receiving messages, synchronizing processes,
distributing data, balancing the load etc. This enables him to write efficient
programs, with a precise granularity of parallelism, but the price is high: such
programs are mostly non-deterministic, which complicates the task of testing and
debugging. Moreover, the use of low level features can easily lead to deadlocks
and decreases portability.

Another possibility is to use declarative, mainly functional languages. Functional programs contain implicit parallelism, since (sub)expressions can be evaluated independently of each other. Thus, a compiler can automatically parallelize
a functional program. Moreover, functional programs are high level and deterministic, then presenting advantages over their imperative counterparts: they
are easy to test and debug, portable and error or context deadlock. The drawback of the approach is that parallel implementations of functional languages is

_____

* The work of this author is supported by the "Graduiertenkolleg Informatik und
Technik" at the RWTH Aachen.

# Algorithmic Skeletons for Adaptive Multigrid Methods

George Horatiu Botorog*        Herbert Kuchen

RWTH Aachen, Lehrstuhl für Informatik II
Ahornstr. 55, D-52074 Aachen, Germany
{botorog,herbert}@zeus.informatik.rwth-aachen.de

**Abstract.** This paper presents a new approach to parallel programming with algorithmic skeletons, i.e. common parallelization patterns. We use an imperative language enhanced by some functional features as host for the embedding of the skeletons. This allows an efficient implementation and at the same time a high level of programming. In particular, low level communication problems such as deadlocks are avoided. Both data and process parallel skeletons can be used, but the emphasis is placed on the first category. By defining data parallel skeletons for dynamic data structures, we obtain constructs for handling problems with irregular and/or dynamic character. The implementation of an adaptive multigrid algorithm illustrates how such problems can be solved by using these constructs.

**Keywords:** Algorithmic Skeletons, Data Parallelism, Adaptive Multigrid, Imperative Host Languages, MIMD-DM computers.

## 1 Introduction

Most languages employed today in the programming of MIMD computers with distributed memory are *imperative* languages, like Occam, parallel C or parallel Fortran. Here, the user must control the parallelism in his program on a rather low level, by explicitly sending and receiving messages, synchronizing processes, distributing data, balancing the load etc. This enables him to write efficient programs, with a proper granularity of parallelism, but the price is high. Such programs are mostly non-deterministic, which complicates the task of testing and debugging. Moreover, the use of low-level features can easily lead to deadlocks and restricts portability.

Another possibility is to use declarative, mainly *functional* languages. Functional programs contain implicit parallelism, since (sub)expressions can be evaluated independently of each other. Thus, a compiler can automatically parallelize a functional program. Moreover, functional programs are high level and deterministic, hence presenting advantages over their imperative counterparts: they are easy to test and debug, portable and cannot contain deadlocks. The drawback of the approach is that parallel implementations of functional languages

* The work of this author is supported by the "Graduiertenkolleg Informatik und Technik" at the RWTH Aachen.

tend to be very inefficient. The main reasons lie in the fine granularity of parallelism, as well as in the heuristic task and data distribution, which usually lead to high communication overheads.

Given these two extremes, the next step would be to search for a solution somewhere in between. Such a solution are *algorithmic skeletons* [3]. A skeleton is an algorithmic abstraction common to a series of applications, which can be implemented in parallel. Skeletons are embedded into a sequential host language, thus being the only source of parallelism in a program. Confining parallelism to skeletons makes it possible to structure and control it. Moreover, the user must no longer cope with parallel implementation details, which are not visible outside the skeletons. On the other hand, skeletons are efficiently implemented on a low level. At the same time, they offer an interface which totally abstracts of the underlying hardware, thus making the programs portable. Classical examples of skeletons include map, farm and divide&conquer [4].

A common feature of most skeletons that have been defined is that, in order to provide the required *flexibility*, they have functions as arguments, i.e. they are higher-order functions. We shall illustrate this with the definition of *divide&conquer* (d&c), which can be expressed in a functional language as follows.

```
d&c :: (a -> Bool) -> (a -> b) -> (a -> [a]) -> ([b] -> b) -> a -> b
d&c is_trivial solve split join problem =
    if (is_trivial problem)
        then (solve problem)
        else (join (map (d&c is_trivial solve split join) (split problem)))
```

The skeleton gets four functions as arguments: is_trivial tests if a problem is simple enough to be solved directly, solve solves the problem in this case, split divides a problem into a list of subproblems and join combines a list of sub-solutions into a new (sub)solution.

Given this skeleton, the implementation of an algorithm that has the structure of *divide&conquer* requires only the implementation of the four argument functions and a call of the skeleton. For instance, a quicksort procedure can be implemented as follows

```
quicksort list = d&c is_empty identity (divide (hd list)) append list
```

Note that a similar flexibility cannot be achieved by first-order functions, i.e. functions without functional arguments. Besides the elegance of this style of programming, it is important that the skeleton is implemented in parallel[1], handling communication and synchronization as well as distributed data internally. Thus, instead of error-prone communication via individual messages, there is a coordinated overall communication, which is guaranteed to work deadlock-free.

As the example above shows, algorithmic skeletons can be represented in functional languages in a straightforward way as higher-order functions. It would therefore seem appropriate to use a *functional* language as host. Indeed, nearly all implementations of skeletons rely on functional hosts.

---

[1] The above definition of d&c only describes the overall functionality, it does not capture the parallel implementation.

There are currently a number of research groups working on the design and implementation of parallel functional languages with algorithmic skeletons. One could mention here the works of Darlington et al. [4], Bratvold [2], Rabhi [10], Pepper et al. [8], Skillicorn [11] or Kuchen and Stoltze [6].

On the other hand, few attempts have been made to use an *imperative* language as a host. One such attempt is P$^3$L [1], which builds on top of C++, and in which skeletons are internal language constructs. The main drawbacks are the difficulty to add new skeletons and the fact that only a restricted number of skeletons can be used, lest the language should grow too big. Another approach is taken in the language ILIAS [7]. Here, arithmetic and logic operators are extended to pointwise operators that can be applied to the elements of matrices. Furthermore, contiguous subranges of matrices can be specified. These operations are actually no skeletons in the sense of the former definition, but operations obtained through overloading of language constructs. Still, their internal behavior closely resembles that of some skeletons.

Depending on the kind of parallelism used, skeletons can roughly be classified into *process parallel* and *data parallel* ones. In the first case, the skeleton creates a series of processes, which run concurrently. Some examples include `farm`, `pipe` and `divide&conquer`. Such skeletons are used in [1, 2, 4, 10]. Data parallel skeletons, on the other hand, act upon some distributed data structures, performing the same operations on all elements of the data structure. Data parallel skeletons, like `map`, `shift` or `fold` are used in [1, 2, 4, 6, 8, 11].

A common feature of all data parallel approaches listed above, is that the underlying data structures are static, mostly arrays. The reason is that arrays are better suited for parallel processing than other data structures, as they can easily be distributed and most of the operations on them are easy to parallelize. Moreover, since the structure of an array remains unchanged, no dynamic remapping or load balancing are required.

In this paper, a new approach is presented. On the one hand, an imperative host language is employed. On the other hand, data parallel skeletons are defined for dynamic data structures. It is shown, how these data structures and skeletons can be used in solving irregular problems. The rest of the paper is organized as follows. Section 2 describes the imperative host language and the additional features that are needed to integrate the skeletons. Section 3 presents the types of skeletons we shall use. The emphasis is placed on data parallel skeletons, which are embedded into parallel abstract data types. Section 4 presents an irregular application, a full multigrid algorithm with adaptive grid refinement, implemented on the basis of skeletons. Finally, Section 5 concludes the discussion.

## 2 The Host Language

As already stated, most implementations today build upon functional hosts, since these allow a straightforward integration of the skeletons. The improvement over direct parallel implementations of functional languages is considerable, rising up to 2 orders of magnitude [6]. Nevertheless, programs written in these languages still run about 5 to 10 times slower than corresponding parallel C programs [6].

We choose our host language to be an imperative, C-like, one. This approach
has several advantages. On the one hand, the sequential parts of the program
are more efficient if written in an imperative language. Moreover, since host and
skeletons are both imperative, the overhead of the context switch, which is considerable in the case of a functional host, has no longer to be taken into account.
On the other hand, imperative languages offer mechanisms for local accessing
and manipulation of data, which have to be simulated in functional languages
[6]. This should lead to further gains in efficiency, bringing the performance of
our language close to that of low-level parallel imperative languages.

The question arising is what are the functional features needed for the integration of skeletons? We have already seen that most skeletons have functional arguments, so *higher-order functions* are surely among these features. Since
an implementation of these constructs is inefficient, they are eliminated by the
compiler at an early stage. This is done by instantiating calls to higher-order
functions to equivalent calls to appropriate specialized first order functions (see
[12] for details).

A second feature we need are *partial applications* of functions. Consider again
the definition of the skeleton d&c. We had defined the type of this skeleton as

```
(a -> Bool) -> (a -> b) -> (a -> [a]) -> ([b] -> b) -> a -> b
```

instead of

```
(a -> Bool) × (a -> b) × (a -> [a]) × ([b] -> b) × a -> b
```

This implies that d&c can be applied to its first argument, yielding a new function with the type (a -> b) -> (a -> [a]) -> ([b] -> b) -> a -> b, then
to its second etc., until the last application finally returns a value of type b. The
underlying idea is to consider the application of a n-ary function as a successive application of unary functions. This procedure is called *currying*, after the
mathematician H. B. Curry. See [9] for further details.

Partial applications are useful in a series of situations, for instance in supply-
ing additional parameters to functions. Consider the d&c call in the else branch
of the above example. On the one hand, the function map expects a functional
argument of the type a -> b. On the other hand, we want to call d&c and at
the same time provide it with the rest of the arguments it needs, apart from the
problem to be solved, i.e. is_trivial, solve, split and join. This can be done
by the partial application of d&c to these arguments, which yields a function of
the type a -> b.

Partial applications are one of the main reasons for the functional extensions
of the host language. If functional arguments with no arguments of their own
could be simulated in C by pointers to functions, this is no longer possible with
functional arguments yielded by partial applications. We do not consider here the
possibility to pass the additional parameters as global variables, since it is bad
programming style to simulate variables which actually have local scope by global
ones. This would introduce a source of errors, which are hard to find. Moreover,
this simulation is not always possible, e.g. if different partial applications of the

same function are given as parameters to the same skeleton, what should be stored in the global variables then?

The third feature we need is *polymorphism*, since we want to define functions that depend only on the structure of the problem, and not on particular data types. For instance, the skeleton d&c performs the same operations, regardless of the type of the problem and the solution. The advantage is that the same skeletons can be employed in solving similar or related problems.

*Polymorphic types* are either type variables[2], or compound types built from other types using the C type constructors *array, function, pointer, structure* or *union* and containing at least one type variable. Although polymorphism can be simulated in C by casting, this is nevertheless a potential source of errors, since it eludes type checking. Our approach leads however to safer programs, since a polymorphic type checking is performed[3].

To summarize, the functional features needed to facilitate the integration of skeletons are higher-order functions, partial applications and polymorphism. Note that the necessity of these features is *not* eluded by the possibility to implement skeletons as library routines. On the contrary, a library of sufficiently flexible skeletons is enabled by these features.

Concluding this section, we will briefly address some implementation issues. A program is processed by a front-end compiler together with the necessary skeletons. The main task of the compiler is to eliminate the functional features of the language. Higher-order functions and partial applications are translated by an instantiation procedure which resembles higher-order macro-expansion [12]. Since polymorphism is translated by instantiation too, a single transformation is employed. The front-end compiler generates parallel C code based on message passing, which can then be processed by a C compiler.

## 3 The Skeletons

We have seen that skeletons can be classified into data parallel and process parallel ones. Although both types can be used in our language, the emphasis is placed here on the first category. There are two main reasons for this. On the one hand, data parallelism seems to offer better possibilities to exploit large numbers of processors. On the other hand, data structures are central to our pursuit, since we aim at using dynamic data structures to solve irregular problems.

A problem that arises when using distributed data structures in an imperative language is that the programmer is able to access local parts of the data structure, for instance by pointers or indices. If this occurs in an uncontrolled way, heavy remote data accessing may cause considerable communication overhead. In order to control the access to data, we use abstract data types, which guarantee a clear interface to the data structures and the skeletons working on them, and hide implementation details. Data parallel skeletons are thus not stand-alone, but always part of an ADT. Since the underlying data structures of these ADTs

---

[2] Type variables are defined using the new keyword typevar.

[3] To quote Milner: "Well-typed programs don't go wrong".

are distributed, we will call them *parallel abstract data types* (PADTs). Apart from controlling data accesses, PADTs have some other important advantages:

- They allow regular and irregular problems to be equally dealt with. Irregularity is supported on the one hand by dynamic data structures and on the other hand by implicit or explicit operations for extending or restricting a data structure, for dynamic data re-mapping and for load balancing.
- They can be generic, thus allowing a systematic instantiation of the data structure and the operations.
- They group skeletons together, making their inclusion easier. This is very important, if a large number of skeletons is available.

A similar approach is taken by Skillicorn [11] with his *categorical data types*. The difference to the approach presented here is that the operations of a categorical data type must be homomorphisms, i.e. they have to respect the structure of the data type, whereas the operations of the PADTs must not. Our approach thus seems more flexible, since it allows the use of operations that are not homomorphisms, like for instance neighborhood operations (see Section 4.2).

In order to use PADTs, we need to enhance the language with two more constructs. On the definition level, the construct **pardata** allows the declaration of a PADT. On the application level, PADTs are included, and if necessary instantiated, by means of the **parinst** construct. We shall illustrate the way these constructs are used by a simple example. We shall define a generic data type **matrix** and show how it can be employed to compute the shortest paths in a graph by transitive closure.

The PADT **matrix** is parameterized by the type of its elements. The definition of the PADT, comprising only a selection of the skeletons, is given below.

```
pardata matrix (typevar elem_t)
   matrix mat_load (FILE *infile);
   void mat_dump (matrix m, FILE *outfile);
   matrix mat_gen_add (matrix m1, matrix m2,
                       elem_t gen_add (elem_t val1, elem_t val2));
   matrix mat_gen_mult (matrix m1, matrix m2,
                        elem_t gen_add (elem_t val1, elem_t val2),
                        elem_t gen_mult (elem_t val1, elem_t val2));
   ...
end
```

The skeleton **mat_load** loads the elements of a matrix from a file and distributes them onto the processors, while **mat_dump** does the opposite: it collects the elements of a matrix and dumps them to a file. **mat_gen_add** and **mat_gen_mult** perform a generic addition and multiplication of two matrices respectively. These generic skeletons can be instantiated to different operations. As an example, we shall compute the shortest paths between every two vertices of a graph represented by its adjacency matrix. For that, we have to define a matrix of integers and instantiate the functional arguments **gen_add** and **gen_mult** by min and +. The following program results:

```
parinst matrix (int) int_mat;

void shortest_paths () {
    int_mat a;
    a = mat_load (infile);
    for (i = 0; i < log2 (n); i++)     /* compute the transitive closure */
        a = mat_gen_mult (a, a, min (), plus ());
    mat_dump (a, outfile);
}

int min (int x, int y) {return (x < y ? x : y);}
int plus (int x, int y) {return (x + y);}
```

# 4 Adaptive Multigrid

In this section, we will show how skeletons can be used to implement irregular algorithms. As an example, we will use adaptive multigrid methods, since they are both appropriate for parallelizing and have a dynamic character. First, we will give a short description of the method[4] as well as of the internal representation of the underlying data structure. Then we will define the skeletons that perform the operations on the grid. Based on these operations, the implementation of a full multigrid algorithm will then be sketched. Finally, the process of adaptive refinement and its implementation with skeletons will be regarded more closely.

## 4.1 The Method

Multigrid methods are iterative solvers for systems of discretized (partial) differential equations on a grid hierarchy. The hierarchy consists of a number of grid levels, where each new level is obtained, depending on the chosen method, either by refining (i.e. by adding more points to), or by coarsening (i.e. by selecting some of the points of) the current level [5].

The main advantage of these methods is their efficiency: they require only $\mathcal{O}(n)$ operations[5], where $n$ is the number of points on the finest grid [5]. Another advantage of multigrid methods is that they can be used in relation with adaptive refinement techniques, such that a refinement is performed only in those areas, where this leads to relevant improvements of the accuracy of the solution.

The basic idea of multigrid methods is to eliminate the high frequencies of the error in relatively few relaxation steps on a fine grid, while the lower frequencies are eliminated by reducing the problem to coarser grids, on which they appear as higher frequencies and can be attenuated again by relaxation. This process can be continued recursively for a number of steps. Coarser grids are therefore viewed as correction grids. The opposite view, in which the finer grids are the correction grids, can also be employed [5]. This has the advantage, that it permits adaptive refinement, leading to finer levels confined to increasingly smaller sub-domains.

Although a series of multigrid algorithms has been defined, they all build on the same basic procedures, the differences consisting mainly in how the cycles

---

[4] We present here the general methodology, rather than a specific multigrid method.
[5] In the sequential case.

over the grid levels are organized. Regardless of the particular algorithm, the basic operations are:

- *refining* and *coarsening* of the current grid level, which can be done adaptively, based on the current approximation of the solution or of the error,
- *prolongation* and *restriction* of data when moving to a finer, respectively to a coarser grid level; these operations are usually applied to the solution, error, residual and right hand side,
- *relaxation*, which is performed on one grid level, and consists of a number of iterations of a certain solver, like Jacobi, Gauss-Seidel, SOR etc. [5].

Apart from these operations, some additional operations are needed to support parallelism:

- *distributing* data to all processors and *collecting* distributed data (for instance, for output),
- *environment* (or *neighborhood*) operations, which select for a grid point its neighboring points on one or more levels up to a given depth,
- operations for *load balancing*, necessary in irregular applications,
- *'map'-operations* which evaluate a function for all items of a distributed data structure.

The two categories of operations represent the basis for the multigrid skeletons, which will be presented in the next subsection.

Without getting into implementation details, we will shortly describe the internal representation of the grid. The entire grid consists of a series of levels, from which one is always the current level. A grid level is represented as a graph, thus allowing a unitary handling of irregular (locally refined) grids. The points of a level (i.e. the vertices of the graph) are defined by their coordinates in a $n$-dimensional space, where $n$ is usually 2 or 3. One or more distributed variables, representing the solution, the error etc. can be assigned to these points. Each of these variables is identified by a unique numerical id. Further, due to the distribution of the grid, overlap areas are defined. They represent extensions of the sub-domains that are placed on different processors and serve only to improve the efficiency of reading accesses to the neighborhoods of data items placed on the borders of sud-domains. If data values in the overlap areas are altered, then these areas are updated automatically.

## 4.2 Skeletons for Multigrid

We shall now present the skeletons needed in multigrid operations. As stated in Section 3, they will be embedded into a parallel abstract data type. We shall restrain the description of the PADT to its *interface*, as it represents the part of the PADT that is visible to the user. The implementation of the skeleton mg_refine and of a function that performs an adaptive refinement will be described more detailed in Subsection 4.4.

multigrid is a generic PADT, parameterized by dimension, type of the coordinates of the points, type of the distributed variables and horizontal and vertical overlap factors. The dimension is an integer value that is 2 or 3 for most applications. Single coordinates and data values at the grid points can be of different types, but mostly single or double precision reals are employed. The overlap areas serve only to improve the efficiency of reading accesses to the distributed data. Consider for instance the case of a 2-dimensional regular grid. If an interpolation operator uses the values at the 4 adjacent grid points, then a horizontal overlap factor of 1 is sufficient to avoid additional communication for the computation of the elements on the borders of sub-domains of the grid placed on different processors. The same applies on the vertical, if elements of one grid level are needed to compute elements on another grid level, like for instance in the prolongation and restriction procedures. Overlap factors should therefore be chosen at least 1. The interface of the PADT multigrid is given below. Due to lack of space, only a selection of the skeletons is presented.

```
pardata multigrid (int dim, typevar coords_t, typevar data_t, int hovl,
                   int vovl)
  multigrid mg_load_coords (FILE *infile);
  void mg_dump_coords (multigrid mg, FILE *outfile);
  void mg_destroy (multigrid mg);
  void mg_refine (multigrid mg, coords_t *refine_f (coords_t p));
  void mg_coarsen (multigrid mg, coords_t *coarsen_f (coords_t p));
  void mg_balance (multigrid mg);

  int mg_allocate (multigrid mg);
  void mg_deallocate (multigrid mg, int id);
  void mg_load_data (multigrid mg, int id, FILE *infile);
  void mg_dump_data (multigrid mg, int id, FILE *outfile);
  void mg_prolongate (multigrid mg, int id, data_t prol_f (coords_t p));
  void mg_restrict (multigrid mg, int id, data_t restr_f (coords_t p));

  coords_t *mg_coords_env (multigrid mg, coords_t p, int hrad, int vrad);
  data_t *mg_data_env (multigrid mg,coords_t p,int hrad,int vrad,int id);

  void mg_relax (multigrid mg, int *from_ids, int to_id,
                 data_t relax_f (int *ids, coords_t p));
  void mg_map (multigrid mg, int *from_ids, int to_id,
               data_t appl_f (int *ids, coords_t p));
end
```

The skeletons can be grouped into grid operations (the first six), data operations (the next six), selection operations (the next two) and computational operations (the last two).

*Grid operations* comprise the constructor mg_load_coords, which loads the coordinates of some points from a file, distributes them and builds upon them a one-level grid; the operation mg_dump_coords, which dumps the coordinates of the current grid level into a file and the destructor mg_destroy. Note that in the case of the first two skeletons an external data support is necessary, since it is possible, that the memory of one processor is too small to hold the entire data from one level of the grid. Finer or coarser grid levels can be derived from the current one by using the operations mg_refine, respectively mg_coarsen. The strength of these skeletons lies in their functional arguments, which create the single points of the new grid. By using partial applications, additional parameters can be supplied to these functions, thus providing the possibility to *adaptively* create a new grid, depending for instance on the data values on the old grid. An example of an adaptive refinement function is given in Subsection 4.4. In case of an adaptive refinement, the resulting grid is usually unbalanced. This can be evened out by calling the skeleton `mg_balance`, which tries to achieve a (nearly) equal load on all processors and at the same time to minimize the communication between them. The load balancing procedure is based on a dimension exchange algorithm, in which each processor exchanges load with its neighbors.

*Data operations* include the constructor `mg_allocate`, the destructor `mg_deallocate`, as well as operations for loading data items from a file and distributing them on the current grid level (`mg_load_data`), respectively collecting data from this level and dumping it to a file (`mg_dump_data`). The extension of data to a finer level is done by `mg_prolongate` and to a coarser level by `mg_restrict`.

The *selection operations* (`mg_coords_env` and `mg_data_env`) compute for a given grid point a list of neighboring points (environment), respectively of data placed at these points. The number of neighboring levels is given by the 'vertical radius' (`vrad`), whereas the depth of the area of adjacency is determined by the 'horizontal radius' (`hrad`). These operations are useful for grid refinement or coarsening, as well as for the prolongation or restriction of data from one level to another and for relaxation. In order to compute the neighboring points efficiently, care has to be taken, that the radii do not exceed the corresponding overlap factors given in the declaration of the multigrid type (or, to put it the other way around, that the overlap factors are upper bounds of all radii used in computations).

It is worth noting, that the selection operations are not parallel, but bound to a given grid point. Parallelism is achieved by using them inside map-like skeletons, for instance in the argument function of the refinement procedure (see Subsection 4.4 for an example).

Finally, *computational operations* comprise relaxation and mapping on a grid level. `mg_map` maps a given function to all points of the current grid level. It gets as argument a list with the id's of the variables to be used in the computation (`from_ids`), which it passes to the function to be applied (`appl_f`). The return value of this function is written into the variable identified by `to_id`. `mg_relax` works similarly to the map skeleton. In the following example, we will use the Jacobi relaxation procedure, but other methods, like Gauss-Seidel or SOR, can be employed as well.

The skeletons defined in this PADT represent the basic operations for multigrid [5], so that practically all (structured or unstructured) multigrid algorithms can be implemented with them. An example is given in the next subsection.

### 4.3 The Implementation of a Full Multigrid Algorithm

We will now present the implementation of a full multigrid algorithm (FMV) [5]. The algorithm is based on two ideas: *coarse grid correction* and *nested iteration*. The first idea was explained in Subsection 4.1, the second will be outlined in the following.

When using an iterative method to solve a linear system, an initial approximation of the solution is needed. This approximation can either be randomly chosen, or generated by some procedure. This procedure could be for instance a relaxation performed on the same problem on a coarser grid, followed by a prolongation of the solution. This leads to an improved initial guess for the fine grid problem. The initial guess on the coarse grid can be obtained by a similar procedure and so on, recursively, up to the coarsest grid.

Combining nested iteration with coarse grid correction, we obtain full multigrid algorithms. If we choose the simplest correction cycle, the V-cycle, then the FMV-algorithm results. This algorithm is described below.

We start on the coarsest level (0) and refine the problem to level 1. After that, a coarse grid correction is performed in a V-cycle between level 1 and level 0, with pre- and post-smoothing relaxations. The next step consists of a new refinement (to level 2) and a new V-cycle correction (between level 2 and level 0). Continuing this procedure yields a full multigrid V-cycle (FMV) algorithm (sketched in Figure 1).

The parameters of a full multigrid algorithm are the number of pre- and post-smoothing steps ($\nu_1$ and $\nu_2$), the type of the correction cycle (given by $\gamma$) and the number of correction cycles performed on each level ($\delta$). The FMV algorithm depicted in Figure 1 is characterized by $\gamma = 1$ (V-cycles) and $\delta = 1$ (one correction cycle per level).

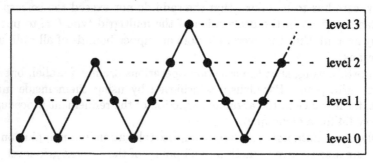

**Fig. 1.** Full multigrid V-cycle (FMV)

We will now present the implementation of the FMV algorithm based on the skeletons defined above. Some of the details have been omitted for simplicity, others are given only in pseudo-code. The notation [x, y, z, ...] is an explicit representation of the array or structure built with the listed components. The implementation is given below.

The first statement represents an instantiation of the generic PADT multigrid to a 2-dimensional grid whose points have real coordinates and double precision values. The vertical and horizontal overlap factors are both set to 1. The function FMV mainly contains the nested iteration, starting at level 0 and refining until some convergence criterion is fulfilled. Apart from that, this function also handles I/O and the allocation of the grid and of the variables. The function MV performs the coarse grid correction in a V-cycle with some pre- and post-smoothing steps on each level. On the coarsest level, an exact solution is computed, since this is usually cheap enough.

```
parinst multigrid (2, float[2], double, 1, 1) mgrid2;

void FMV () {
    mgrid2 mg;     int l = 1;
    load and distribute coordinates and data;
    while (! converge (id_u)) {               /* some convergence criterion */
        mg_refine (mg, local_ad_ref (mg, id_u)); /* adaptive refinement */
        mg_balance (mg);                      /* re-distribute the refined grid */
        mg_prolongate (mg, id_u, interpolate (mg, id_u));
        mg_prolongate (mg, id_f, interpolate (mg, id_f));
        for (i = 0; i < δ; i++)                         /* level iterations */
            MV (mg, l++, id_u, id_f);                   /* V-cycle on level l */
    }
    collect distributed data and output result;
}

void MV (multigrid mg, int l, int id_u, int id_f) {
    if (l == 0)                                         /* coarsest grid */
        compute exact solution of (u, f);
    else {
        for (i = 0; i < ν₁; i++)                        /* pre-smoothing */
            mg_relax (mg, [id_u, id_f], id_u, jacobi (mg, ω));

        id_r = mg_allocate (mg);                        /* residual variable */
        mg_map (mg, [id_u, id_f], id_r, residual (mg)); /* compute res. */
        mg_restrict (mg, id_r, inject (mg, id_r));
        id_v = mg_allocate (mg);        /* error variable, initialized to 0 */
        mg_restrict (mg, id_v, inject (mg, id_v));

        for (i = 0; i < γ; i++)                         /* coarse grid correction */
            MV (mg, l-1, id_v, id_r);

        mg_prolongate (mg, id_v, interpolate (mg, id_v));
        mg_map (mg, [id_u, id_v], id_u, minus (mg));            /* u = u - v */
        for (i = 0; i < ν₂; i++)                        /* post-smoothing */
            mg_relax (mg, [id_u, id_f], id_u, jacobi (mg, ω));

        mg_deallocate (mg, id_r);
        mg_deallocate (mg, id_v);
    }
}
```

## 4.4 Adaptive Refinement

In this subsection, we will show how the mg_refine skeleton is defined and how
a particular adaptive procedure can be implemented on its basis.

The grid refinement skeleton is a map-like function which is applied to all
points of the current (and at the same time finest) level. For each point of the
grid, one or more points of the new grid are generated, depending on the need
for local refinement. If the grid needs no refinement in an area, then only the
given point is returned. Otherwise, a list with additional points is generated.
The definition of the skeleton mg_refine is given below in pseudo-code.

```
void mg_refine (multigrid mg, coords_t *refine_f (coords_t p)) {
    for all points p of the current level of mg do in parallel
        newpoints_p = refine_f (p);
        build links between parent and children points;

        for all p' ∈ newpoints_p do
            if (∃ q, p' ∈ newpoints_q)          /* p' was already created */
            eliminate p' from newpoints_p;
    build graph of new level from all newpoints;   /* new grid is distributed */
    construct vertical and horizontal overlap areas;
}
```

The skeleton uses the local refinement function refine_f to generate for each point one or more new points and at the same time builds the links between parents and children. After that, the local results are merged to form one new grid (not necessarily connected), whereas duplicates produced by different local refinements are removed. Finally, data along the borders of the sub-domains of the grid placed on different processors are replicated to create the overlap areas.

We now want to take a closer look at the local refinement procedure. For that, we shall consider a simple locally refined nested grid. Let the coarsest level be a 2-dimensional regular grid, consisting of rectangles or even squares. The refinement is done by orthogonal recursive bisection, but only in those areas, where this leads to an improvement of the accuracy of the solution. If, for instance, the solution has a singularity in the upper right corner, then a sequence of grids like the one in Figure 2 is generated.

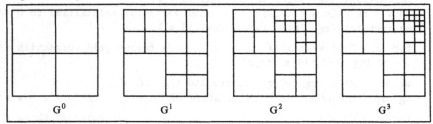

**Fig. 2.** Adaptive orthogonal recursive bisection

An example of how the local refinement is done, is shown in Figure 3. Here, the grid $G^l$ is refined to yield the grid $G^{l+1}$, whereby only some areas, like the hatched one, actually undergo a refinement.

The local refinement of the hatched square generates 9 new points in the grid $G^{l+1}$. Nevertheless, since the refinement function is mapped to all points of $G^l$, only the 6 white points in $G^{l+1}$ have to be generated by the refinement corresponding to $P^l_{i,j}$, the others being produced by the (trivial) refinement of the points $P^l_{i+1,j}$, $P^l_{i,j+1}$ respectively $P^l_{i+1,j+1}$. The white points can be computed for instance according to the equations:

$$P^{l+1}_{i,j} = P^l_{i,j} \quad (1)$$

$$P^{l+1}_{i+1,j} = \frac{P^l_{i,j} + P^l_{i+1,j}}{2} \quad (2)$$

$$P^{l+1}_{i,j+1} = \frac{P^l_{i,j} + P^l_{i,j+1}}{2} \quad (3)$$

$$P^{l+1}_{i+2,j+1} = \frac{P^l_{i+1,j} + P^l_{i+1,j+1}}{2} \quad (4)$$

$$P^{l+1}_{i+1,j+2} = \frac{P^l_{i,j+1} + P^l_{i+1,j+1}}{2} \quad (5)$$

$$P^{l+1}_{i+1,j+1} = \frac{P^l_{i,j} + P^l_{i+1,j} + P^l_{i,j+1} + P^l_{i+1,j+1}}{4} \quad (6)$$

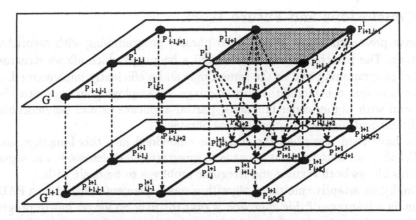

**Fig. 3.** Local adaptive grid refinement

As these equations show, all 4 vertices of the hatched square are needed to generate the white points in the finer grid. The dependencies are depicted in Figure 3 by dotted lines. Since the local refinement function is mapped to a single point of the old grid at a time (here to $P_{i,j}^l$), an operation is needed to compute the environment for a given point. This operation is `mg_coords_env`, which returns the 4 direct neighboring points of $P_{i,j}^l$. Calling this function again for some of the direct neighbors, yields the indirect neighbors, too. Moreover, the refinement can be performed depending not only on the coordinates of the points of the old grid, but also on certain values at these points, like for instance the solution approximation. This 'data environment' is computed by the operation `mg_data_env`. We can now define the local refinement function as follows.

```
coords_t *local_ad_ref (multigrid mg, id_u, coords_t p) {
    ps = mg_coords_env (mg, p, 1, 0); /*ps = [P_{i-1,j}^l,P_{i+1,j}^l,P_{i,j}^l,P_{i,j-1}^l,P_{i,j+1}^l]*/
    us = mg_data_env (mg, p, 1, 0, id_u);            /* us analog */
    ps = ps ∪ {P_{i,j+1}^l}        /* by calling mg_coords_env for P_{i,j+1}^l */
    us = us ∪ {u_{i,j+1}^l}        /* by calling mg_data_env for u_{i,j+1}^l */
    if (eval_sol (u_{i,j}^l, u_{i+1,j}^l, u_{i,j+1}^l, u_{i+1,j+1}^l) < ε) /* no need to refine */
        return ([P_{i,j}^l]);
    else {
        compute P_{i,j}^{l+1} ... P_{i+1,j+1}^{l+1} according to equations (1) ... (6);
        return ([P_{i,j}^{l+1}, P_{i+1,j}^{l+1}, P_{i,j+1}^{l+1}, P_{i+2,j+1}^{l+1}, P_{i+1,j+2}^{l+1}, P_{i+1,j+1}^{l+1}]);
    }
}
```

The examples given in the last two subsections illustrate the way higher-order functions and partial applications can be used to enhance the expressive power of skeletons. The call of the skeleton `mg_refine` inside the body of the procedure FMV gets as functional argument a partial application of the function `local_ad_ref` to its first two arguments (`mg` and `id_u`). This yields by currying a new function with one argument, which has exactly the type expected by `mg_refine`. The skeleton supplies in its body the last argument needed by `local_ad_ref`, namely (the coordinates of) the point p.

# 5 Conclusions and Future Work

We have presented a new approach to parallel programming with algorithmic skeletons. The principal aim was to design a language which allows structured parallel programming and at the same time can be efficiently implemented.

We have first considered the host language. By employing an imperative host enhanced with higher-order functions, partial applications and polymorphism, an efficient and high-level language was obtained.

We have then described the skeletons embedded into this language, using parallel abstract data types as a means to integrate the skeletons. It was argued, that this allows both regular and irregular problems to be dealt with.

Finally, an adaptive multigrid algorithm was implemented based on a PADT. The main advantage of this approach is that the user no longer has to program global procedures for the whole grid, but only local ones for single grid points. As the grid is distributed, this is a considerable simplification, since it frees the user from the burden of accounting for the explicit aspects of parallelism.

We are currently working on a prototype implementation of the language. Future plans include using skeletons in other application areas of parallel computation, like computational geometry or the N-bodies problem.

## References

1. B. Bacci, M. Danelutto, S. Orlando, S. Pelagatti, M. Vanneschi: $P^3L$ : a Structured High-level Parallel Language and its Structured Support, Technical Report HPL-PSC-93-55, Pisa Science Center, Hewlett-Packard Laboratories, May 1993.
2. T. A. Bratvold: Parallelizing a Functional Program Using a List-Homomorphism Skeleton, in H. Hong (ed.) Parallel Symbolic Computation PASCO '94, Lecture Notes Series in Computing, Vol. 5, World Scientific, 1994.
3. M. I. Cole: Algorithmic Skeletons: Structured Management of Parallel Computation, MIT Press, 1989.
4. J. Darlington, A. J. Field, P. G. Harrison et al: Parallel Programming Using Skeleton Functions, in Proceedings of PARLE 93, LNCS 694, Springer-Verlag, 1993.
5. W. Hackbusch, U. Trottenberg: Multigrid Methods, Lecture Notes in Mathematics 960, Springer-Verlag, 1982.
6. H. Kuchen, R. Plasmeijer, H. Stoltze: Efficient Distributed Memory Implementation of Data Parallel Functional Languages, in Proceedings of PARLE 94, LNCS 817, Springer-Verlag, 1994.
7. L. D. J. C. Loyens, J. R. Moonen: ILIAS, a Sequential Language for Parallel Matrix Computations, in Proceedings of PARLE 94, LNCS 817, Springer-Verlag, 1994.
8. P. Pepper, M. Südholt, J. Exner: Functional Programming of Massively Parallel Systems, Technical Report No. 93-16, Technische Universität Berlin, 1993.
9. S. L. Peyton Jones: The Implementation of Functional Programming Languages, Prentice-Hall, 1987.
10. F. A. Rabhi: Exploiting Parallelism in Functional Languages: A "Paradigm-Oriented" Approach, in T. Lake, P. Dew (Eds.) Workshop on Abstract Machines for Highly Parallel Computers, Oxford University Press, 1993.
11. D. Skillicorn: Foundations of Parallel Programming, Cambridge Univ. Press, 1994.
12. P. Wadler: Deforestation: Transforming Programs to Eliminate Trees, in Theoretical Computer Science, No. 73, 1990, North-Holland.

# Run-time techniques for parallelizing sparse matrix problems *

**M. Ujaldon [†], S. D. Sharma [‡], J. Saltz [‡], E. L. Zapata [†]**

[†] *Computer Architecture Department*
*University of Malaga*
*Plaza El Ejido, s/n. 29013 Malaga, Spain*
*{ujaldon, ezapata}@atc.ctima.uma.es*

[‡] *Computer Science Department*
*University of Maryland*
*College Park, MD 20742*
*{shamik, saltz}@cs.umd.edu*

**Abstract.** Sparse matrix problems are difficult to parallelize efficiently on message-passing machines, since they access data through multiple levels of indirection. Inspector/executor strategies, which are typically used to parallelize such problems impose significant preprocessing overheads. This paper describes the runtime support required by new compilation techniques for sparse matrices and evaluates their performance, highlighting optimizations and improvements over previous techniques.

## 1  Introduction

A significant number of scientific codes use sparse matrices. Such applications are hard to parallelize efficiently, particularly for a compiler. This is because sparse matrices are represented using compact data formats which necessitate heavy use of indirect addressing (through pointers stored in *index arrays*). Since these index arrays are read in at runtime, compilers cannot analyse which matrix elements will actually be touched in a given loop, making it impossible to determine communication requirements at compile-time.

To parallelize loops that use indirect addressing, compilers typically use an *inspector-executor* strategy [6]. Loops are tranformed so that for each indirect reference in the loop, a preprocessing step, called an inspector is generated. During program execution, the inspector examines the global addresses referenced by the indirection and determines which (if any) non-local elements must be fetched. The executor stage uses this information to fetch the data and to perform the computation in the original loop body. Such runtime preprocessing techniques have been fairly well studied and successfully incorporated into compilers [7, 1].

---

* This work was supported by the Ministry of Education and Science (CICYT) of Spain under project TIC92-0942 and by ONR under contracts No. SC 292-1-22913 and No. N000149410907, by NASA under contract No. NAG-11560 and by ARPA under contract No. NAG-11485. The authors assume all responsibility for the contents of the paper.

The inspector-executor paradigm incurs a runtime overhead for each inspector stage, which is greatly increased when multiple levels of indirection are used. To reduce these costs, Ujaldon et al. [8] proposed the *sparse array rolling* (SAR) technique, in which a data-parallel compiler can treat many common multi-level indirections as single-level indirections, thus greatly decreasing the amount of preprocessing required for a sparse code. This paper provides actual evidence of the performance benefits of sparse array rolling, reducing the costs of previous strategies by around 50% on a sparse-matrix vector product kernel. However, choices of how data is distributed, and how much preprocessing is carried out, can influence the performance of the inspector and executor stages in opposite ways. To study this tradeoff, we provide an overview of the runtime support of both schemes and evaluate the impact of various choices on both inspector as well as executor performance.

The paper is structured as follows. Section 2 provides a general overview of the sparse array rolling technique. Section 3 gives an overview of the SAR runtime support and points out the distinctions between it and the runtime support provided by CHAOS. Section 4 discusses the benefits and drawbacks of using the SAR approach. Experimental results are presented in section 5. The last two sections discuss related work and present the conclusions we drew from this work.

## 2 Sparse Array Rolling (SAR)

This section provides a brief overview of the sparse array rolling (SAR) technique. Among the different data distributions and storage formats over which SAR can be applied [9], we have confined the discussion in this paper to the CRS (Compressed Row Storage) format and the Multiple Recursive Decomposition (MRD) [9]. For a more formal characterization of types of references that can be optimized using SAR see [8].

### 2.1 Sparse Matrix Storage Format

The CRS format (e.g. Figure 1) represents a sparse matrix A using three vectors: the Data vector stores the non-zero values of the matrix, as they are traversed in a row-wise fashion; the Column vector stores the column index of each non-zero element in the Data vector; and the Row vector marks the beginning of each row in the Data vector.

The use of such compact representations necessitates the use of indirect addressing through the auxiliary index arrays, Row and Column. These index arrays also frequently appear in expressions for loop bounds. For example, Figure 3 illustrates a loop that multiplies a sparse matrix with a dense vector. The outer loop iterates over rows; while the inner loop iterates over the non-zero elements in each row. There are three indirect references in this loop; Data(J), Column(J) and X(Column(J)), where J, the loop counter, is based on values in the vector Row.

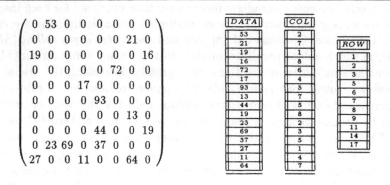

**Fig. 1.** CRS representation for a sparse matrix $A$

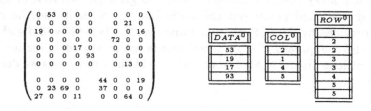

**Fig. 2.** MRD distribution for $A$ onto a 2x2 array of processors and local CRS vectors rebuilt on processor $P(0,0)$

## 2.2 Multiple Recursive Decomposition

The SAR technique relies on the decomposition of the sparse matrix into rectangular sparse submatrices, such that each submatrix can be represented using the same storage format as the original matrix. The Multiple Recursive Decomposition (MRD) [9] is one of the distribution schemes fulfilling these criteria.

MRD recursively decomposes the sparse matrix over $P$ processors performing a certain number of horizontal and vertical partitions until $P$ submatrices have been obtained. At each stage of the partitioning process, the nonzeros in the submatrix of that stage are divided as evenly as possible. This results in the mapping of a *rectangular* submatrix to each processor, preserving neighborhood properties that enable SAR optimizations as well as maintaining load balance (see Figure 2).

MRD determines a distribution for the non-zeros (the Data vector). The index arrays are *rebuilt* so that each processor has a complete set of data structures needed to access the local rectangular submatrix (see Figure 2)). Other dense vectors in the program can also be aligned with one of the dimensions of a MRD decomposition, which can cause a limited degree of replication of the elements of the vector.

## 2.3 Language Support

Using user-specified directives [9], a compiler can automatically insert the run-time calls necessary to distribute matrices and vectors as described earlier. To achieve this, the user has to provide the compiler the following pieces of information for each sparse matrix: the name of the matrix, its index domain, the type of its elements, the sparse storage format together with the names of the arrays responsible for representing such a format, and finally the data distribution selected for the matrix. The following set of directives show how data-parallel languages can convey this information to a compiler.

```
REAL A(N,M),  SPARSE (CRS(Data, Column, Row)),  DYNAMIC
DISTRIBUTE  A::(MRD)
REAL Y(N)  DYNAMIC, CONNECT (C) WITH A(C,:)
```

The keyword DYNAMIC indicates that the distribution will be determined at runtime as a result of executing the DISTRIBUTE statement. The CONNECT keyword is used to align a dense vector with one of the dimensions of the sparse matrix; here the vector Y is aligned with the columns of A.

---

```
        FORALL 10 I=1, M  ! iterate over rows
           Y(I) = 0.0
           FORALL 20 J= 0, Row(I+1)-Row(I)-1   ! iterate over nonzeros in row I
              Y(I) = Y(I) + Data(Row(I)+J)*X(Column(Row(I)+J)))  ! Reduction
20         CONTINUE
10      CONTINUE
```

---

**Fig. 3.** Sparse Matrix A (Data,Column,Row) is multiplied with dense Vector X and results stored in vector Y

## 2.4 Example

We use the loop in Figure 3, to discuss the preprocessing optimizations that can be performed by a compiler using SAR techniques.

There are six memory references in the loop body: Row(I), Row(I+1), Y(I), Data(Row(I)+J), Column(Row(I)+J)) and X(Column(Row(I)+J)). Using the terminology of [2], the first three references are classified as *level-1 non-local references*, the second two as *level-2 non-local references* and the last one as a *level-3 non-local reference*. A level-N non-local reference usually requires N preprocessing stages when applying inspector-executor, one for each indirection.

Compilers using the SAR technique can greatly reduce these preprocessing overheads. The Row(I) and Row(I+1) references do not require any preprocessing since the Row vector contains only local pointers. The Y(I) reference also does not require any preprocessing if the Y vector is aligned with the rows of the MRD distribution. For the level-2 non-local reference `Data(Row(I)+J)`, the compiler knows the J-th non-zero element in the I-th row of the sparse matrix $A$ is being accessed, which eliminates preprocessing for the intermediate `Row(I)` reference, since using only the indices `I` and `J` and a look up to a local *MRD-descriptor* [8] the runtime support can directly determine the owner processor. The same analysis could be resued for the `Column(Row(I)+J))` references if `Column` had appeared as a target array in the loop body (it does not). More importantly, the same analysis also applies to the level-3 reference `X(Column(Row(I)+J))` if the vector `X` is aligned with the columns of the sparse matrix $A$. This is because the alignment with columns ensures that element `X(Column(k))` is mapped to the same processor as `Column(k)` and `Data(k)`.

To summarize, the SAR technique requires only a single stage of preprocessing for the loop-nest in Figure 3 while standard compiler techniques would generate three preprocessing stages. The key idea behind these optimizations is that the compiler can use the semantic knowledge of the matrix storage format to skip over intermediate references to the sparse matrix index arrays, thereby rolling multi-level indirections into single-level indirections. For more details we refer readers to [8].

# 3 Run-time support

Compilers using SAR techniques can eliminate many levels of indirections using knowledge of the storage format and distribution of the sparse matrix. For the indirections that remain, the preprocessing must still be performed. The runtime support must provide mechanisms for performing such preprocessing. It also provides efficient communication mechanisms that utilize the results of such preprocessing, and perform the actual communication.

In this section we describe the runtime support that was developed to support the sparse array rolling technique. We use a sparse-matrix vector kernel to (SpMxV) to demonstrate standard runtime preprocessing techniques, and illustrate parallelization using SAR runtime support. In the SpMxV kernel, a sparse matrix is multiplied with an input vector, and the resulting output vector is used as the input vector in the next iteration over the product operation. This process is repeated until some convergence criteria are satisfied. Figure 4 shows the pseudo-code for this kernel.

---

```
DO k = 1, num_time_steps
    Y = A.X              ! Sparse Matrix Vector Product
    X = Y                ! Copy Y into X
ENDDO
```

---

**Fig. 4.** An outline of the SpMxV kernel

```
C   PARTITION ARRAYS                          C   PARTITION MATRIX and VECTORS

    ttable_rows = Partition_rows()                mrd_desc = MRD ( Row, Column, Data)
    ttable_nz = Partition_nzeros()                distribute( mrd_desc, Column, Data)
    distribute(ttable_rows, X, Y, Row)            rebuild( mrd_desc, Row)
    distribute(ttable_nz, Column, Data)           align_with_rows( mrd_desc, Y)
                                                  align_with_cols( mrd_desc, X)
C        INSPECTOR
C   1st PHASE (for Row(I) )                    C       INSPECTOR
                                              C   Everything's aligned
    rptr = Collect(all indices I)             C   so the gathers will not
    C1 = Translate( ttable_rows, rptr)        C   do any communication
    Gather( C1, remote Row )
                                                  rptr = Collect(index pairs I,J )
C   2nd PHASE ( for Column(Row..))                Comm1 = Translate(mrd_desc, rptr)
C   Since nonzeros are partitioned                Gather( Comm1, remote Data)
C   to match rows, the gathers
C   do not actually cause comm.                C   EXECUTOR
                                              C   Since Y and X are not aligned,
    cptr = Collect( all (Row(I)+J) )          C   Y must be redistributed to align
    C2 = Translate(ttable_nz, cptr )          C   with X before the copy
    Gather( C2, remote Column)
    Gather( C2, remote Data)                      DO k = 1, num_time_steps
                                                    Gather( Comm1, remote X)
C   3rd PHASE (for X(Column(..))                    Y = A.X
                                                    Accumulate( Y )
    xptr = Collect(Column(Row(I)+J))                Redistribute(Y, col_align)
    C3 = Translate(ttable_rows, xptr )              X = Y
                                                  ENDDO
C   EXECUTOR

    DO k = 1, num_time_steps
      Gather( C3, remote X)
       Y = A.X
       X = Y
    bfENDDO
```

**Fig. 5.** Parallelization of SpMxV using CHAOS and SAR : CHAOS code (left), SAR code (right)

## 3.1   SpMxV parallelized using CHAOS runtime support

Here we provide an overview of how a compiler would use CHAOS support to parallelize the SpMxV kernel. For details about CHAOS, see [7]. Figure 5 shows the kernel parallelized using pseudo-calls to the CHAOS runtime library.

**Partitioning:** Standard compilers would parallelize the sparse-matrix vector product loop-nest by distributing iterations of the outer loop using an owner-computes rule. This work distribution prescribes a row-wise distribution for the sparse-matrix data-structures. An irregular mapping of rows, such that an equal number of non-zeros are assigned to each processor, achieves the best load balance. The non-zero vectors ( Data and Column) are distributed such that each non-zero is assigned to the processor that owns the corresponding row. This distribution also optimizes the inspector since the indirect references to the non-zero arrays, Column and Data, do not need communication. Thus the gathers at the second inspector stage do not actually carry out any communication. The information about the mapping of rows and non-zeros to processors is stored in globally accessible data-structures called translation_tables.

**Inspector:** Multiple inspector stages are required to inspect the references in the loop-nest. Each CHAOS inspector examines the indirect references and looks up the translation_table to determine which remote elements need to be fetched. The CHAOS inspector also performs two communication optimizations

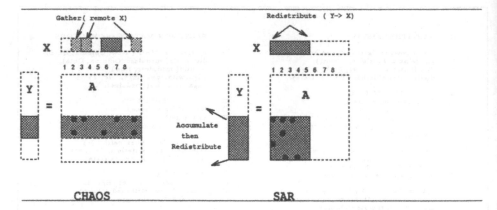

**Fig. 6.** Communication in executors

– duplicates in the remote references are removed so that communication volume is reduced and the requests for data are exchanged among processors in advance so that only actual data needs to be transferred in the executor.

**Executor :** The array X is updated inside the main loop and hence the remote elements of X must be fetched by using a call to a collective communication routine **gather**, in each iteration. Aligning X and Y to the same distribution ensures that elements of Y do not need to be redistributed for performing the copy from Y to X. Figure 6 gives an overview of the communication required in this executor.

## 3.2   SpMxV parallelized using SAR runtime support

SAR is a compile-time optimization and thus its benefits are largely orthogonal to those of CHAOS's optimizations. Unlike CHAOS, the runtime support developed to support SAR was focussed at reducing inspector costs and makes very minimal efforts to optimize the executor communication. However, it is useful to compare the runtime support for the two schemes so that the impact of preprocessing optimizations can be evaluated, and the best integration of runtime and compile-time support can be achieved. Figure 5 shows how the SpMxV kernel would be parallelized using SAR runtime support. These calls are explained in greater detail below.

**Partitioning:** The sparse matrix A is partitioned using MRD (see Figure 2); the X and Y vectors are aligned to the rows or columns of the MRD distribution respectively. As explained in Section 2, this distribution ensures that only a single stage of preprocessing is required to parallelize the loop. Also note that the *rebuilding* of the Row array during partitioning is akin to first aligning the array with the rows of the MRD decomposition and then localizing the indexes. The MRD decomposition of the matrix data-structures into local data-structures allows both iterations of both loops in the sparse-matrix vector product loop-nest to be distributed. The outer loop iterates over rows of the local submatrix and the inner loop over the local non-zeros in each row. This achieves good load balancing and locality. However, the alignment of Y to the rows of the MRD distributed sparse matrix $A$ implies that different processors upate different copies of the same Y element, and these copies must be merged after the computation.

**Inspector :** The MRD inspector stage is quite simple, and has already been discussed in Section 2. A single preprocessing stage is sufficient to determine the communication requirements for the `X(Column(Row(I)+J))` and `Data(Row(I)+J)` references. The remote elements are gathered using CHAOS like **gather** calls. Since both the X and the Data vectors are aligned using MRD, the preprocessing step discovers that there are no remote elements that need to be fetched; the gathers are therefore null function calls.

**Executor :** The executor for the SAR version is very different from the CHAOS version, mainly because of the differences in the way data is distributed. The first **gather** call will not perform any communication for SpMxV, since X is aligned to the columns of the MRD. After the computation of the product, local copies of the Y array are accumulated. This is a result of distributing the sparse matrix in a 2-dimensional fashion ( Using a row-wise 1-D MRD partition, as in the CHAOS, version would eliminate this accumulation ). Yet another stage of communication is required to align the elements of Y and X before they can be copied over. The last communication step can be optimized either by combining it with the accumulation step or by redistributing only those elements of Y that are accessed in the references to X, as in CHAOS. These first optimization could be performed with additional compiler support and the latter would require more preprocessing. Neither of these optimizations are currently implemented in the runtime support. Figure 6 gives an overview of the communication in the executor resulting from the mapping chosen in the SAR case.

To summarize, the SAR and CHAOS parallel versions of SpMxV use different inspectors. The difference lies mainly in the number of inspector stages rather than on the type of preprocessing done at each stage, thus reflecting the impact of the SAR optimization. The very different partitioning strategies chosen to optimize the preprocessing for each version necessitates different executor implementations.

## 4    A Theoretical Comparison

After presenting an overview of the two preprocessing schemes, we now analyse the strengths and weakness of each technique. For simplicity, we will use the SpMxV kernel presented in the previous section as an illustrative example for our discussion. The same kernel is used in the experiments.

### 4.1   Inspector Costs

SAR reduces many multi-level indirection to single-level indirections and requires fewer preprocessing steps. The cost of each stage of preprocessing is also lower than CHAOS. The main reason for this is that each CHAOS preprocessing stage makes accesses to the `translation_table`, which is a distributed data-structure storing the mapping of array elements to processors. [2] For our experiments, we used a replicated translation_table to store the mapping of rows and a distributed translation table to maintain the mapping of non-zeros. The SAR strategy of using compact and replicated MRD-descriptors to store the mapping information is more well-suited for sparse matrix problems. Such descriptors could also be used with CHAOS inspectors in the SpMxV kernel since the matrix was decomposed row-wise into rectangular submatrices.

Another distinction between the CHAOS preprocessing and SAR inspectors is in the determination of communication requirements. CHAOS analyses the communication exactly for each gather and accumulate. On the other hand, SAR relies on a complete redistribution when an array is copied into another array with which it is not aligned. With more preprocessing, the SAR runtime support could determine which elements are actually referenced in the new array and communicate only those elements. Our experiments show that this would be a worthwhile optimization in applications like SpMxV where the executor is performed many times.

## 4.2 Executor

The SAR technique was aimed at reducing inspector costs; it does not intrinsically perform any new optimizations on the executor. As with any parallel code, the communication overhead in the executor depends on the data distribution chosen by the user. Typically there are three sources of communication in sparse matrix codes — gathers, accumulates and redistributions. The sparse matrix distribution and the alignment of dense vectors should be chosen in a fashion that reduces all three types of communications.

For the SpMxV kernel, our choice of distributions had the following effects on executor communication. The alignment of X to columns eliminates the gather communication. Using a 2-D decomposition necessitates the acummulation phase and alignments of X and Y to different dimensions requires redistribution. The CHAOS implementation, on the other hand, uses a 1-D row-wise distribution of the sparse matrix and aligns the Y to the rows thus eliminating the accumulation phase. Aligning X with Y also eliminates the redistribution phase but introduces communication to gather X.

We will compare the effect of these distribution choices on the executor performance of SpMxV in Section 5 and recommend how to best optimize the inspector using sparse array rolling while still keeping executor communication costs low. We also note that the choice of distribution is often dictated by the structure of the entire application and a choice that is best for one loop-nest may not be optimal for another.

The distribution strategies by both the CHAOS and the SAR implementations, assign rougly an equal number of non-zeros to each processor, thus the

---

[2] This communication overhead can be reduced by replicating the *translation_table* on each processor; this however is not a scalable solution since to store the mapping of non-zeros would require a table with as many entries as there are non-zeros.

executor computation time executor is roughly balanced in both versions. Indeed during our experiments we found the load imbalance ( [max.time - avg.time]/avg. time ) to be less than 10%.

### 4.3 Memory overheads

CHAOS has two principal sources of memory overheads — *translation tables* and *communication schedules*. Translation tables in CHAOS keep track of the mapping of elements (rows or nonzeros for sparse matrices) to processors. For irregular mappings (i.e not block-cyclic) the table size is proportional to the number of elements being mapped. When replicated, these tables occupy considerable amounts of memory; when distributed, they require communication to perform lookups. The SAR scheme uses a specialized MRD-descriptor to represent the mapping of rectangular submatrices to processors. The size of this data-structure is proportional to the number of submatrices (i.e processors) and can be replicated across processors.

Communication schedules store the list of addresses that are determined to be remote during preprocessing and that must be communicated. Both SAR and CHAOS inspectors have to store schedules. However, the SAR technique has fewer inspector stages and constructs fewer schedules, thus reducing this overhead.

### 4.4 Matrix sparsity

The *sparsity rate* is defined as the ratio between the number of nonzero elements of the matrix, $\alpha$, and the number of total elements of the matrix $(m \cdot n)$. The sparsity rate as well as the the placement of the non-zeros in the matrix considerably influences the the communication volume in the executor.

SAR uses an approximated communication analysis in the preprocessing stage – it looks up the MRD descriptor and determines the regular section of the dense vectors ( X and Y ) that intersect with the local submatrix. CHAOS carries out an expensive and exact analysis to determine which elements should be communicated. When the matrix is very sparse, CHAOS's strategy can significantly reduce communication volume. On the other hand, if the matrix is relatively dense, the exact communication analysis performed by CHAOS is fruitless, since most elements in the regular section will be communicated anyway. Section 5 presents experimental results using two matrices having very different sparsity rates.

## 5 Experimental results

This section studies the benefits of the SAR optimization by evaluating the reduction in preprocessing time resulting from the optimization.

**Table 1.** Characteristics of benchmark matrices

| Matrix | Rows | NonZeros | Sparsity Rate | $X_{Chaos}$ | $X_{sar}$ | $Y_{sar}$ |
|---|---|---|---|---|---|---|
| BCSSTK29 | 13992 | 316740 | 0.0016 | 456 | 3146 | 1360 |
| PSMIGR1 | 3140 | 543162 | 0.0551 | 2912 | 751 | 311 |

## 5.1 Experimental Setup

As described in Section 3, the SpMxV kernel was parallelized using two different schemes. The first version of the code used calls to the SAR runtime support while the second used calls to CHAOS. Both codes were parallelized by hand, but used only those optimizations and runtime calls that a compiler would insert. The SAR version assumed compiler-support for sparse array rolling. Both parallel versions of the code were run on an Intel Paragon using two matrices from the Harwell-Boeing benchmark set. The matrices are BCSSTK29, a very sparse structures matrix and PSMIGR1, a matrix containing population migration data that is relatively dense. The column $X_{chaos}$ denotes the average number of elements of **X gather**'ed by each processor in the executor of the CHAOS code when running on 32 processors. $Y_{sar}$ and $X_{sar}$ provide the equivalent numbers for the two communication stages in the executor of the SAR version. These numbers reflect the impact that data distribution and the matrix's sparsity rate can have on executor efficiency.

In our experiments, we did not account for the time to do the initial redistribution of the sparse matrix. The time for this stage depends on the format of the input data file; in general an expensive distribution step is required by both versions.

## 5.2 Inspector costs

In Figure 7 we present the preprocessing costs for the two versions of the kernel on the two matrices. The SAR-optimized inspector overheads are consistently between 40 % to 60 % lower than those of the CHAOS version. We examined this reduction more closely, by tabulating the relative cost of each stage of the CHAOS inspector. Figure 8(a) shows the contribution of each stage of inspection in the CHAOS version. Note that the preprocessing eliminated by the SAR-optimization corresponds to the first and third stages (INSP-1 and INSP-3) of the CHAOS inspector, i.e roughly 40

Figure 8(b) shows a breakup of the costs of INSP-2 in terms of functions performed by CHAOS inspector. Collect refers to the cost of collecting all the indirect references in a temporary array prior to inspection. The SAR inspector performs an identical operation. Duplicate refers to the cost of removing duplicates from these references so that communication volume is reduced. The SAR inspector does not perform duplicate removal. XchngReq refers to the exchange of the list of requested addresses among processors. This cost is zero in INSP-2 since the row-wise partitioning of non-zeros ensures that none of the references are remote. SAR has similar functionality and its cost is zero too due to the

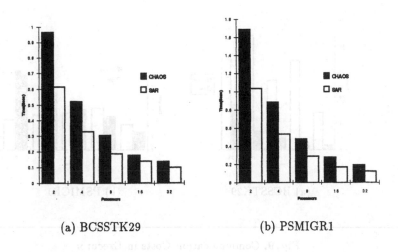

(a) BCSSTK29    (b) PSMIGR1

**Fig. 7.** Preprocessing Costs

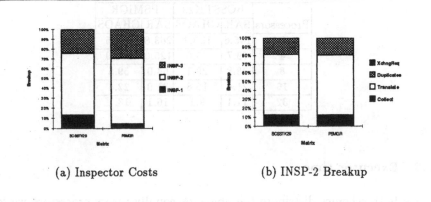

(a) Inspector Costs    (b) INSP-2 Breakup

**Fig. 8.** Breakup of Inspector Costs in CHAOS

alignments of Data and X. The main component of the inspector cost in both versions is in a Translate routine, which determines the processor to which a particular non-zero is mapped. In CHAOS, the translation_table that stores this information is distributed across processors necessitating a single collective communication step in which all the references are resolved. In the SAR version, the mapping information is stored in a replicated but compact data format which requires a binary search to determine the home processor for each reference. The overheads of performing the search for each reference seem to balance the cost of the extra communication to look up the translation table in CHAOS.

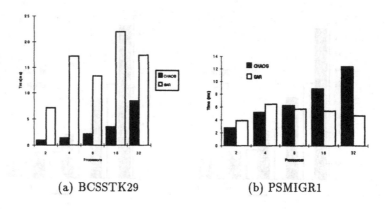

(a) BCSSTK29  (b) PSMIGR1

**Fig. 9.** Communication Costs in Executor

**Table 2.** Compute Time of executor (in ms)

| Processors | BCSSTK29 | | PSMIGR | |
|---|---|---|---|---|
| | SAR | CHAOS | SAR | CHAOS |
| 2 | 145.6 | 135.3 | 263.8 | 250.5 |
| 4 | 79.7 | 75.8 | 125.0 | 104.0 |
| 8 | 38.8 | 29.1 | 64.0 | 59.5 |
| 16 | 21.4 | 15.8 | 31.0 | 22.4 |
| 32 | 11.1 | 9.1 | 16.1 | 13.1 |

## 5.3   Executor time

Since both schemes distribute the nonzeros equally across processors we found that the computational section of the executor could be effectively speeded up by both schemes. Table 2 shows only the time taken for the computational component of the executor for the two matrices. As can be seen, the computation scales well with both schemes providing evidence of effective load balancing in both schemes.

Figure 9 shows the executor communication overhead for both schemes. The MRD distribution scheme proves helpful to the SAR code in PSMIGR, since each processor needs only those elements of X aligned to it. In the CHAOS version which uses row-wise distributions, a relatively dense matrix will require fetching almost the entire X array on each processor. For the larger and sparser matrix BCSSTK29, the opposite is true; the redistribution will require large subsections of Y to be sent to each processor, even though after the copy into X, only a few of the elements of X are referenced in each processor.

## 5.4 Discussion

Our experiments show that the SAR optimization is indeed very effective at reducing inspector costs. Its effectiveness depends on the original costs of the preprocessing steps that can be eliminated. We observe that the storage and lookup strategy used for the mapping of the non-zeros to processors is crucial for optimizing inspector peformance.

We also note that as expected, the executor performance is highly influenced by the data distribution used and the sparisty of the input matrix. For SpMxV and other kernels that have similar access patterns, we recommend using one-dimensional distribution mechanisms and CHAOS-line communication optimizations when the input matrix is large and sparse. For relatively dense matrices a two-dimensional distribution such as MRD, without sophisticated communication optimizations is better.

The ideal compiler-runtime strategy would be to use SAR-like optimizations at compile time and to use runtime support that can automatically determine the degree of communication optimizations appropriate for a particular matrix. The user should be responsible for choosing the right distribution strategy — this choice would be dictated by the sparsity of input matrices used in the application domain and the relative importance of the inspector and executor costs on the algorithm.

# 6 Related Work

There have been many efforts aimed at providing compile-time and run-time support for irregular problems such as [5, 4, 7]. Most of the research on irregular problems in Fortran has concentrated on handling single-level indirections. In practice, irregular application codes have complex access functions that go beyond the scope of current compilation techniques. Das et. al. suggested a technique using *program slicing* [1], that can deal with multiple levels of indirection by transforming code containing such references into code that contains only a single level of indirection. However, their technique will generate multiple inspector stages for multi-level indirections.

A significantly different approach is that followed by Bick and Wijshoff, who have implemented a restructuring compiler which automatically converts programs operating on dense matrices into sparse codes. This method simplifies the task of the programmer at the expense of losing efficiency, postponing the selection of the sparse storage format until the compilation phase.

# 7 Conclusions

In this paper, we have discussed the sparse array rolling (SAR) preprocessing technique, and have showed how it can significantly reduce the preprocessing overhead introduced by inspectors [6] in sparse-matrix codes. We have compared our runtime methods to previous techniques, particularly those implemented by

CHAOS, a standard runtime library. Using different input matrices from the Harwell-Boeing sparse matrix collection, we compared the performance of these techniques on SpMxV, a very common sparse kernel. The results demonstrate the benefits of the sparse array rolling technique. For the SpMxV kernel, SAR optimizations decreased the preprocessing overheads of CHAOS between 40% and 60%.

# References

1. R. Das, J. Saltz and R. von Hanxleden. *Slicing Analysis and Indirect Access to Distributed Arrays*, Proceedings of the 6th Workshop on Languages and Compilers for Parallel Computing, Aug 1993, pp 152-168. Also available as University of Maryland Technical Report CS-TR-3076 and UMIACS-TR-93-42.
2. R. Das, J. Saltz, K. Kennedy, P. Havlak. *Index Array Flattening Through Program Transformations.* Submitted to Supercomputing'95. San Diego, CA. Dic. 1995.
3. *High Performance Language Specification.* Version 1.0, Technical Report TR92-225, Rice University, May 3, 1993. Also available as Scientific Programming 2(1-2):1-170, Spring and Summer 1993.
4. A. Krishnamurthy, D.E. Culler, A. Dusseau, S.C. Goldstein, S. Lumetta, T. von Eicken, and K. Yelick. *Parallel Programming in Split-C*, Proceedings Supercomputing'93. Nov. 1993, pp 262-273.
5. P. Mehrotra and J. Van Rosendale. *Programming distributed memory architectures using Kali.* In A. Nicolau, D. Gelernter, T. Gross and D. Padua, editors, Advances in Languages and Compilers for Parallel Processing, pp. 364-384. Pitman/MIT-Press, 1991.
6. R. Mirchandaney, J. Saltz, R.M. Smith, D.M. Nicol and Kay Crowley. *Principles of run-time support for parallel processors.* Proceedings of the 1988 ACM International Conference on Supercomputing, pages 140-152, July, 1988.
7. S. D. Sharma, R. Ponnusamy, B. Moon, Y. Hwang, R. Das and J. Saltz. *Runtime and Compile-time Support for Adaptive Irregular Problems*, Proceedings Supercomputing '94, Nov. 1994, pp. 97-106.
8. M. Ujaldon and E.L. Zapata, *Efficient Resolution of Sparse Indirections in Data-Parallel Compilers.* Proceedings of the 9th ACM International Conference on Supercomputing. Barcelona (Spain), July 1995 (to appear).
9. M. Ujaldon, E. L. Zapata, B. Chapman and H. Zima. *Vienna-Fortran/HPF Extensions for Sparse and Irregular Problems and their Compilation*, Submitted to IEEE Transactions on Parallel and Distributed Systems. Also available as Technical Report,

# Fast Execution of Irregularly Structured Programs with Low Communication Frequency on the Hypercube

Vincenzo Auletta, Alberto Negro, Vittorio Scarano

Dipartimento di Informatica ed Applicazioni "R. M. Capocelli"
Università di Salerno, 84081 Baronissi (SA) – Italy
E-mail: {auletta, alberto, vitsca}@udsab.dia.unisa.it

Abstract. In this paper we study the problem of efficiently executing a parallel program composed of $N$ tasks on a $O(N)$-node hypercube, assuming that (a) communications between tasks are irregular, i.e. any pair of tasks may want to communicate at any step of the program and (b) communications between any two tasks occur with a low frequency, i.e. frequency $f = O(1/N \log N)$.

Our probabilistic technique emulates such programs with slowdown $O(\log \log N)$ with high probability.

The problem can be also seen as the problem of emulating a CRCW PRAM program on a distributed memory parallel machine whose interconnection network is the hypercube and our result can be equivalently used in this model.

As a part of the emulation technique, we develop a Distributed Random Function Algorithm that has independent interest, being an efficient way of clustering homogeneous information into a hypercube.

## 1. Introduction

The problem of efficiently executing a parallel program on a distributed memory parallel machine is approached in literature in two different, orthogonal ways. If the program has a particular, well-known structure, a solution can be obtained by using graph-theoretical results that allow one to embed the computation graph (i.e. the graph obtained by associating vertices to tasks and communications to edges) into the host graph (i.e. the graph obtained associating vertices to processors and edges to physical links) [1-4].

Different techniques have to be used when the parallel program has no structure at all, that is any pair of tasks may want, in principle, to communicate during the computation. In this case, in fact, graph embedding techniques are not helpful, since embedding the complete graph or (relatively) low bisection networks (such as hypercubes, meshes, etc.) produces poor results with respect to emulation efficiency.

One approach that is more useful in this case is to, first, to optimize communications requests by clustering tasks with a consistent communication requests by using well-known heuristics [6, 7, 8, 9]. Then, try to efficiently execute the resulting parallel program by making use of techniques that can take advantage of the limited communication frequency between pair of tasks.

# Fast Execution of Irregularly Structured Programs with Low Communication Frequency on the Hypercube

Vincenzo Auletta    Alberto Negro    Vittorio Scarano

Dipartimento di Informatica ed Applicazioni "R.M. Capocelli"
Università di Salerno, 84081 Baronissi (SA) – Italy
E-mail: {auletta,alberto,vitsca}@udsab.dia.unisa.it

**Abstract.** In this paper we study the problem of efficiently executing a parallel program composed of $N$ tasks on a $O(N)$-node hypercube assuming that *(a)* communications between tasks are irregular i.e. any pair of tasks may want to communicate at any step of the program and *(b)* communications between any two tasks occur with a low frequency, i.e. frequency $f = O\left(1/(N \log^2 N)\right)$.

Our probabilistic technique emulates such programs with slowdown $O(\log \log N)$ with high probability.

The problem can be also seen as the problem of emulating a CRCW PRAM program on a distributed memory parallel machine whose interconnection network is the hypercube and our result can be equivalently stated in this model.

As a part of the emulation technique, we develop a Distributed Recombination Algorithm that has independent interest being an efficient way of clustering homogenous information on a hypercube.

## 1    Introduction

The problem of efficiently executing a parallel program on a distributed memory parallel machine is approached in literature in two different, orthogonal ways.

If the program has a particular, well-known structure, a solution can be obtained by using graph-theoretical results that allow one to *embed* the computation graph (i.e. the graph obtained by associating vertices to tasks and communications to edges) into the host graph (i.e. the graph obtained associating vertices to processors and edges to physical links) [14].

Different techniques have to be used when the parallel program has *no structure* at all, that is any pair of tasks may want, in principle, to communicate during the computation. In this case, in fact, graph embedding techniques are not helpful, since embedding the complete graph on (relatively) low bisection networks (such as hypercubes, meshes etc.) produces poor results with respect to emulation efficiency.

One approach that is more useful in this case is try, first, to optimize communications requests by clustering tasks with consistent communication requests by using well-known heuristics [6, 7, 8, 10]. Then, try to efficiently execute the resulting parallel program by making use of techniques that can take advantage of the limited communication frequency between pair of tasks.

Our paper follows the latter approach: we study the problem of efficiently executing a parallel program composed of $N$ tasks on a $O(N)$-node hypercube assuming that inter-task communications are irregular and occur between each pair of tasks with a low frequency, i.e. with frequency $f = O\left(1/(N \log^2 N)\right)$. The technique here proposed is probabilistic and emulates such programs with slowdown $O(\log \log N)$ with high probability[1].

Our study represents a first step toward a better theoretical understanding and the formalization of the well-known mechanism of trading-off communications frequency with irregularity in executing a parallel program. As a matter of fact, our research can be seen as an attempt to quantify exactly the following (somewhat imprecise) statement:

*If a parallel compiler is able to keep inter-task communication frequency low in a parallel program (by using clustering heuristics) then consistent improvements in execution time can be obtained.*

Our emulation scheme achieves slowdown $O(\log \log N)$, i.e. below the diameter-based $O(\log N)$ lower bound for $N$-node hypercubes which would, otherwise, limit performances of emulation schemes based on graph embedding techniques.

The problem of efficient execution of irregularly structured parallel programs on a hypercube can be also formulated as the problem of emulating a CRCW PRAM program on a distributed memory parallel machine whose interconnection network is the hypercube. A PRAM can be seen as composed by $N$ processors, each with its own segment of the (global) "shared memory", communicating with one another through a complete network. A PRAM program has, therefore, a complete graph as a computation graph and any pair of tasks may want to exchange messages (i.e. read/write in the other's segment of the "shared memory").

Our result, rephrased in this context, becomes the following: we show how to emulate an $N$-task CRCW PRAM program on a $N$-node hypercube with slowdown $O(\log \log N)$ with high probability, provided that task $i$ accesses variables in the memory of task $j$ with relative frequency $f_{i,j} = O\left(1/(N \log^2 N)\right)$.

In a certain way, this result represents an extension (under limiting assumptions) of the previously known result by Ranade [15] who showed how to emulate an $N$-task CRCW PRAM program on an $N$-node butterfly (and with minor changes on an $N$-node hypercube [12]) incurring, with high probability, a slowdown of $\Theta(\log N)$.

As a part of the emulation technique, we also develop a Distributed Recombination Algorithm that has independent interest, since it can be generalized to problems where clustering of homogeneous information on a hypercube are to be obtained [3].

---

[1] In the following, an event $Q_N$ is said to happen with high probability (w.h.p.) if $\lim_{N \to \infty} \Pr(Q_N) = 1$.

## 1.1 The formal setting

The result is established in the framework of Parallel Random Access Machine for which an access frequency to external memory modules[2] is defined.

This model is used only as a well-known, archetypical model but the emulation technique can be immediately adapted to message-passing models. We believe that this model interchangeability of our technique represents an advantage and, for sake of clarity, we choose to present the result only in one model.

*The model.* A Parallel Random Access Machine (PRAM) is composed by a set of $N$ identical independent processors, each with its own private memory, communicating through a shared memory of size $M$ [11]. Any processor can access a location of the shared memory in unit time.

Several PRAM models have been described, having different rules on concurrency. The most powerful of them is the Concurrent Read Concurrent Write (CRCW) PRAM, where an arbitrary number of processors can read or write in the same memory location at the same time.

An alternative view of a PRAM is to consider the set of $N$ processors connected by a complete network, where each pair of processors is connected by a physical link, and the global memory is divided in *pages* of size $M/N$, each of them residing at one processor. The requests for a variable in a shared page are accomplished by exchange of messages (READ or WRITE messages) through the complete network interconnecting the processors.

We consider a PRAM program $\mathcal{P}$ as a set of $N$ identical tasks exchanging messages through a complete network and a distributed memory parallel machine $\mathcal{M}$ as a set of $N$ independent processors with an interconnection network (not a complete one).

The *emulation* of $\mathcal{P}$ by $\mathcal{M}$ is accomplished in a synchronous, pulsed fashion: we assume that in a unit time a processor of $\mathcal{M}$ can execute any instruction of $\mathcal{P}$ (execution step) and a message can travel through a single link of $\mathcal{M}$ (communication step). Communication between tasks that are executed by non adjacent processors is accomplished through *message passing*, where intermediate processors forward the message toward the destination. Therefore, the communication between a pair of non adjacent processors in $\mathcal{M}$ is performed by a sequence of communication steps. Processors not performing communication are forced to be idle until the machine executes the number of communication steps that are necessary to ensure the delivery of each message.

More formally, we associate a *computation graph* $G(\mathcal{P}) = (V_G, E_G)$ to the parallel program $\mathcal{P}$ (where the nodes $V_G$ are the tasks and an edge $(i, j) \in E_G$ if the tasks $i$ and $j$ exchange information) as well as a *host graph* $H(\mathcal{M}) = (V_H, E_H)$ to the parallel machine $\mathcal{M}$ (where the nodes $V_H$ are the processors and an edge $(i, j) \in E_H$ if a physical interconnection link[3] joins $i$ to $j$). Task $i$ of $G(\mathcal{P})$ is mapped onto processor $\phi(i)$ of $H(\mathcal{M})$ and a communication from task

---

[2] A task accesses an external memory module if it reads/writes a variable that does not reside in the processor where the task is mapped.

[3] We assume that the links of $\mathcal{M}$ are bidirectional, i.e. if $(i, j) \in E_H$ then $(j, i) \in E_H$.

$i$ to task $j$ is accomplished routing the message along a path connecting $\phi(i)$ to $\phi(j)$ in $H(\mathcal{M})$.

*The problem.* We investigate the problem of executing an $N$-task PRAM parallel program $\mathcal{P}$ on an $N$-node parallel machine $\mathcal{M}$. Each task of $\mathcal{P}$ can exchange information with any other task. Our goal is to execute $T_p$ steps of $\mathcal{P}$ with $T_m = S \cdot T_p$ steps of $\mathcal{M}$ where the slowdown $S$ is as small as possible.

The problem of emulation of PRAM programs on a distributed memory parallel machine has been extensively studied (in a different framework) in the past. In [1] it is proved that any deterministic emulation of an $N$-node PRAM parallel program by a bounded-degree network must incur in a slowdown $\Omega(\log^2 N / \log \log N)$ and a deterministic emulation is shown which takes time $O(\log^2 N)$. Ranade, in his seminal paper [15], showed a probabilistic emulation of a $N$-task CRCW PRAM program on an $N$-node butterfly with slowdown $O(\log N)$ with high probability. This technique can be easily generalized to an $N$-node hypercube [12].

Ranade emulation of PRAM programs has two components. First a hashing function is used to partition the shared memory among the processors of the butterfly; a processor will require access to a variable sending a message (either a READ message or a WRITE message) to the processor that has that shared variable. The second component is an algorithm for efficiently routing such messages among processors.

*Our result.* We show that it is possible to emulate a PRAM program with slowdown $O(\log \log N)$ with high probability if the relative frequency of access to the shared pages of memory is bounded. This can be considered as an extension (under certain limiting assumptions) to the $O(\log N)$ slowdown emulation of PRAM programs [15].

More formally, we propose an algorithm to execute an $N$–task PRAM program $\mathcal{P}$ on a $O(N)$-node hypercube $\mathcal{H}$ with slowdown $S = O(\log \log N)$, with high probability, if any task $i$ accesses variables in the shared memory page of task $j$ with relative frequency $f_{i,j} = O\left(1/(N \log^2 N)\right)$, where the *relative frequency of access* $f_{i,j}$ is defined as the ratio between the number of communications between tasks $i$ and $j$ in $\mathcal{P}$ and the number of instructions of $\mathcal{P}$.

The execution of $\mathcal{P}$ is divided in *phases* each consisting of $T$ steps[4]. Before the execution, each task $i$ is assigned to the processor $\phi(i) = i$ of the hypercube $\mathcal{H}$. We point out that during the execution of $\mathcal{P}$, the task $i$ will be always located at the processor $i$. At the beginning of each phase, a small part of the state of each task (called the *partial state* of the task) is delivered to a *temporary processor* in order to optimize the communications for the current phase. We can prove that, w.h.p., all the tasks requiring communications in a phase can be clustered in a $O(\log N)$-node subcube. The emulation of the $T$ instructions within the subcube is achieved using Ranade emulation with slowdown $O(\log \log N)$ (w.h.p.) and

---

[4] $T$ will be determined in the sequel.

then the partial state of the task $i$ is sent back to the processor $i$ that updates its state.

It should be pointed out that each communication link of $\mathcal{M}$ is supposed to carry only a constant amount of information and that tasks never migrate. The transmission of the partial state of a task to a temporary processor is pipelined taking into account the size of the partial state. Ranade emulation is based also on message combining: for example, READ messages to the same variable are combined in a single request when they meet at one intermediate processor $x$. When the required value is sent back through $x$ it is sent out along all the links where the request came from. However, as pointed out also in [12], the size of the message resulting from the combining is considered as having the same size of the original messages.

*Outline of the paper.* The main part of the analysis of the emulation algorithm is based on several well-known results from the theory of Random Graphs [5] that are briefly summarized in Section 2.

In Section 3, we will provide the general framework of the technique. Then, in Section 4, we will show the emulation under the assumption that all the necessary information about the memory accesses to shared pages is known at the beginning of the execution. In this case the delivery of the partial states is accomplished under central control.

Successively, we will consider, in Section 5, the more general case where the information about the memory accesses to shared pages required during a phase is known only at the end of the previous phase. In this section, we outline a Distributed Recombination Algorithm (DRA) that is used in order to evaluate locally the temporary processor for each task, more details can be found in [2]. Several proofs are omitted due to space limitations, see [2] for details.

## 2 Random Graphs

In the following we shall adopt the standard graph-theoretical terminology as in [4]. In order to describe our emulation technique it is necessary to introduce some results from the theory of Random Graphs (see [5, 4] for the proofs).

Let us consider the complete graph on $N$ vertices $K_N$ having vertex set $V(K_N) = \{1, 2, \ldots, N\}$ and edge set $E(K_N)$ such that $|E(K_N)| = \binom{N}{2}$. We consider the set $\mathcal{G}^N$ of all the subgraphs of $K_N$ having vertex set $\{1, 2, \ldots, N\}$ and define on it a probability measure.

**Definition 1** $\mathcal{G}(N, p)$, $0 < p < 1$, *is the probability space consisting of all the subgraphs of $K_N$ having vertex set $\{1, 2, \ldots, N\}$ and edge set obtained from $E(K_N)$ selecting each edge independently with probability $p$.*

**Definition 2** $\mathcal{G}(N, p_1, \ldots, p_k)$, $0 < p_i < 1$ for $1 \leq i \leq k$, *is the probability space consisting of all the subgraphs of $K_N$ having vertex set $\{1, 2, \ldots, N\}$ and edge set $E = \cup_{i=1}^{k} E(G_i)$ where $G_i \in \mathcal{G}(N, p_i)$.*

We point out that, in Definition 2, $G_i$ and $G_j$ are probabilistically independent for $1 \leq i \neq j \leq k$ and, therefore, a graph $G$ in the model $\mathcal{G}(N, p_1, \ldots, p_k)$ can be seen as a graph $G'$ in $\mathcal{G}(N, p)$, where $p = 1 - \prod_{i=1}^{k}(1 - p_i)$.

A subset $Q \subset \mathcal{G}^N$ is called a *property* if for any $G \in Q$ and for any $H \in \mathcal{G}^N$ isomorph to $G$ we have that $H \in Q$. If $\lim_{N \to \infty} \Pr(Q) = 1$ then we say that almost every (a.e.) graph in $\mathcal{G}(N, p)$ has a property $Q$.

As an almost direct consequence of several well-known results in Random Graph Theory (see [5]) we can prove the following two Lemmata (the proofs will appear in the final version, see also [2]).

Let us denote by $\mathcal{T}(G)$ the maximum size of a tree component of $G \in \mathcal{G}(N, p)$.

**Lemma 1** *Let $p < 1/2N$. Then a.e. $G \in \mathcal{G}(N, p)$ is such that $\mathcal{T}(G) \leq 2 \log N$.*

**Lemma 2** *For any constant $\kappa$ and any $g(N) < \left( 0.72 \frac{N(\log N - \log \log \log N)}{(\kappa - 1)^2} \right)^{-1}$, a.e. graph $G \in \mathcal{G}(N, g(N))$ has no more than $\log \log N$ nodes of degree greater than $\kappa$.*

Hence, we obtain that if $p < 1/2N$ then almost every graph $G \in \mathcal{G}(N, p)$ is such that the size of the maximum component is at most $2 \log N$ and all the components are acyclic; moreover, if $p < \left( 0.72 \frac{N(\log N - \log \log \log N)}{(\kappa - 1)^2} \right)^{-1}$ for a given constant $\kappa$, there are no more than $\log \log N$ nodes of degree greater than $\kappa$, w.h.p.

## 3 The Emulation Framework

In order to develop the algorithm to emulate a PRAM program $\mathcal{P}$ on a hypercube $\mathcal{H}$, we first provide the terminology and describe the general technique and some results, due to Ranade [15], that will be used in the following.

*The Parallel Program.* The CRCW PRAM program $\mathcal{P}$ is composed by a set of $N$ identical *tasks*. The shared memory of size $M$ is divided in $\frac{M}{N}$ equal sized *pages* that are assigned to each task of the PRAM. The requests for a variable in a shared page are accomplished by exchange of messages (READ or WRITE messages) between tasks.

The execution of any communication instruction is supposed to take unit time. In the following, if not differently specified, we will assume that the size of the message is constant.

The relative frequency of access from the task $i$ to the task $j$ is $f_{i,j} = O\left(1/(N \log^2 N)\right)$.

*The Parallel Machine.* A *hypercube* of dimension $d$ is composed by $N = 2^d$ processors each labelled with a distinct $d$-bit label and a bidirectional link joins every pair of processors whose labels differ on exactly one bit. The $N$ *processors* of hypercube $\mathcal{H}$ are identical, sufficiently powerful to simulate task instructions without a significant computational delay and have a common clock. The transmission of a message of unit size on a link takes a time unit and at most one message can use a link in each direction in the same step. A message directed to a non adjacent processor is routed to the correct destination by a message passing technique: each intermediate processor forwards the message toward the destination according to a routing algorithm (more details follow).

Each processor can be considered composed of two units: the *Processing Unit* (PU) that is responsible for the execution of task instructions, and the *Routing Unit* (RU) that is devoted to forwarding the messages that are not directed to its PU through the correct outgoing edge. We assume that, in each step, the RU is able to permute correctly the $\log N$ incoming messages to the correct outgoing edges and extract messages eventually directed to the PU (multiport model).

## 3.1 The general technique

The execution of $\mathcal{P}$ is subdivided in *phases* each consisting of $T$ steps. Before the execution of $\mathcal{P}$, each task $i$ is assigned to processor $\phi(i) = i$ of the hypercube $\mathcal{H}$.

At the beginning of each phase, the partial state of each task $i$ is delivered to a temporary processor $\mathcal{TP}(i)$ in order to optimize the communications for the current phase. The temporary processor $\mathcal{TP}(i)$ will take care of the execution of task $i$ during the $T$ steps of the phase. The partial state is composed by the local variables that are supposed to be accessed during the phase and by the values of the internal registers of the PU (program counter, etc.). In the following we shall assume that the *size* of the partial state is $O(T)$, that is in $T$ steps the program can access at most $O(T)$ variables, both local or shared ones.

The crucial observation is that, if a bound on the relative frequency of access is given, w.h.p. all the tasks that require communication with task $i$ in a phase can be delivered to temporary processors that are in the same $O(\log N)$–node subcube where $\mathcal{TP}(i)$ is and, therefore, the slowdown incurred by the Ranade emulation in the subcube is $O(\log \log N)$ w.h.p. Such phases are called *good*.

At the end of any good phase, the temporary processor $\mathcal{TP}(i)$ sends back to the processor $i$ (i.e. where $i$ is mapped) the updated values of the variables $\mathcal{TP}(i)$ received at the beginning of the phase, and the processor $i$ can update the state of the task $i$.

We will show in the analysis that, with very low probability, some phases are such that there is no gain in moving the partial state of the tasks to temporary processors. During such phases, called *bad*, no delivery of partial states is done, the computation of task $i$ will be executed by processor $i$ and Ranade emulation will take place in the whole hypercube $\mathcal{H}$ with slowdown $O(\log N)$.

Critical issue is how to evaluate $\mathcal{TP}(i)$ for each task $i$. For sake of clarity, we shall first describe, in Section 4, the technique in the simpler but unrealistic *off–line scenario* where all the communication requests are known before the execution of $\mathcal{P}$.

Then, in Section 5, we shall show a distributed algorithm that evaluates for each task $i$ the temporary processor $\mathcal{TP}(i)$, assuming the *on–line scenario* i.e. where each task knows the communications required in a phase only after the end of the previous one. The length of the phase will be different in the two scenarios: in the off-line scenario each phase will be $T_{\text{off}}$ steps long while in the on-line scenario will be $T_{\text{on}}$ steps long.

**The Routing Algorithm.** Some communications will be performed using the Ranade randomized routing algorithm for the $\log N$-level butterfly (see [15]).

**Theorem 3 ([15])** *It is possible to route at most $P$ packets originated in each processor of a butterfly to the correct destination in time $O(\log N + P)$, with probability greater than $1 - N^{-c}$ for any constant $c$.*

It is possible to use Ranade algorithm on a $N$-node hypercube $\mathcal{H}$ in the multiport model with a constant slowdown (see [12]).

Our *Routing Algorithm* (RA) consists of applying iteratively Ranade algorithm in $\mathcal{H}$ until all the messages have been delivered. At the end of each application if a node has non-delivered messages it broadcasts to all the processors that a new application of Ranade algorithm is necessary.

In Lemma 6 we shall prove that, using the RA, $T$ different instances of a routing problem can be solved in the hypercube $\mathcal{H}$ with high probability by $O(T)$ applications of Ranade algorithm.

**The Emulation Algorithm** We shall use Ranade emulation of PRAM programs [15] as an *Emulation Algorithm* (EA) in order to emulate good phases in the $O(\log N)$-node subcubes and bad phases in the whole $N$-node hypercube. His result is formally stated here.

**Theorem 4 ([15])** *For any constant $c$ and sufficiently large $N$, given an $N$-processors CRCW PRAM with shared memory of size $M$, $M$ polinomial in $N$, then one instruction can be emulated by an $N$-node hypercube with slowdown $O(\log N)$ with probability greater than $1 - N^{-c}$.*

As shown by the author in [15], Theorem 4 can be generalized in order to emulate any $T$ instruction CRCW PRAM program with slowdown $O(\log N)$ w.h.p. The generalization has to manage the (not probable) cases when the "per-step" strategy of Theorem 4 fails. In fact, some instructions could not be completely executed in the given time when several processors try to access different data in the same shared page (*hot spot*). In such a case Ranade technique performed a rehashing of the whole memory while we shall adopt a slightly different technique.

We shall now give the strategy to manage such emulation "errors" and successively prove in section 5, that, with high probability, these hot spots do not influence the overall slowdown of the emulation.

The hot spot can be easily recognized by any node of the hypercube having a not-delivered request in its queue at the end of the "per step" emulation. Similarly to the RA, such node can broadcast that a rehashing is necessary. The only difference with Ranade technique is that we shall rehash only the *active variables*, i.e. those variables involved in the step. Then the instruction is emulated and the updated values of the variables are sent back to the original page of memory.

We point out that, by the RA, the rehashing and the delivery of the updated values of the active variables in an $N$ node hypercube requires time $O(\log N + AV)$ with high probability, where $AV$ is the number of active variables contained in the same shared page.

## 4    Off-line Scenario

Every task $i$ of the program $\mathcal{P}$ is expected to execute a communication to $j$ every $1/f_{i,j}$ computation steps. Let $F_i$ denote the communication frequency of the task $i$, defined as the ratio between the communications required by the task $i$ and the number of instructions of $\mathcal{P}$. It is easy to note that $F_i \leq (N-1) \cdot \max_{j \neq i} f_{i,j}$. Let $F$ be defined as $F = \max_i F_i$. We assume, first, that any communication is probabilistically independent from the others and, second, that any communication at the $i^{th}$ step of $\mathcal{P}$ is independent from the communications in the previous steps. Therefore, the frequency of communication on any link $f_{i,j}$ approximates the probability $p_{i,j}$ of using that link. The *active configuration* $G$ of the parallel program $\mathcal{P}$ in a given step is a "snapshot" of the communications required among tasks during that step and is formally defined as a random graph $G \in \mathcal{G}(N, p)$, where $p \leq \frac{F}{N-1}$. W.l.o.g. in the sequel we will consider $p = \frac{F}{N-1}$.

Let us, now, consider the emulation of a $T_{\text{off}}$-step phase of $\mathcal{P}$ and color the edges used in the $i$-th step with color $i$. Using the previous arguments we can define the $T_{\text{off}}$-*active configuration* as a graph $G'$ in $\mathcal{G}(N, p_1, \ldots, p_{T_{\text{off}}})$, where $p_i = \frac{F}{N-1}$, for $1 \leq i \leq T_{\text{off}}$. On the other hand, as noted in section 2, $G'$ is equivalent to a graph $G$ in $\mathcal{G}(N, p)$, where

$$p = 1 - \prod_{i=1}^{T_{\text{off}}}(1 - p_i) = 1 - \left(1 - \frac{F}{N-1}\right)^{T_{\text{off}}}$$

By Lemma 1 in Section 2, if $p = 1 - \left(1 - \frac{F}{N-1}\right)^{T_{\text{off}}} = \frac{c}{N}$ for $c < \frac{1}{2}$, then a.e. graph in $\mathcal{G}(N, p)$ has no component of size greater than $2 \log n$. Since

$$\left(1 - \frac{F}{N-1}\right)^{T_{\text{off}}} = 1 - \frac{c}{N}$$

$$e^{-\frac{F T_{\text{off}}}{N-1}} \simeq 1 - \frac{c}{N}$$

$$F \simeq \frac{c(N-1)}{N T_{\text{off}}} \simeq \frac{c}{T_{\text{off}}}$$

we can say, by Lemma 1, that if $F T_{\text{off}} < \frac{1}{2}$ then each component of the $T_{\text{off}}$-active configuration can be embedded in a $2 \log N$-node subcube. Joining smaller components in such a way that each component has at least $\log N + 1$ nodes, the total number of components that have to be embedded is at most $\frac{N}{\log N}$ and can be embedded in a hypercube of dimension $\lceil \log N \rceil + 1$ and, therefore, the $N$-task PRAM program is emulated by a $2N$-node hypercube.

The temporary processors for each good phase are pre–computed during the precompilation. The delivery of the partial states to temporary processors can be accomplished along the $2 \log N$-length paths that are also precomputed (see [12]). With these assumptions, we can use the pipelining in order to achieve the delivery of the partial states, of size $O(T_{\text{off}})$, in $2 \log N + O(T_{\text{off}})$ time. Once the partial states of the tasks are present at the corresponding temporary processors, the Ranade's emulation will take time $O(T_{\text{off}} \cdot \log \log N)$ w.h.p. to emulate the $T_{\text{off}}$ steps of the phase. The total time to emulate a good phase ($T_{\text{off}}$ steps in the original program $\mathcal{P}$) is

$$O(T_{\text{off}} \log \log N) + 2 \log N + O(T_{\text{off}}) = O(\log N) \quad \text{for } T_{\text{off}} = \frac{\log N}{\log \log N}$$

and we obtain that $\frac{\log N}{\log \log N}$ steps of the program (corresponding to a good phase) will be emulated with slowdown $O(\log \log N)$ w.h.p..

**Definition 3** *A phase is bad if there is at least a component of size greater than* $2 \log N$.

Every bad phase[5] is executed with slowdown $O(\log N)$ with high probability in the whole hypercube. We can prove the following theorem (proof is omitted due to space limitations).

**Theorem 5** *If the communications between tasks are known before the execution, any $N$-task CRCW PRAM program $\mathcal{P}$ having time complexity $D$ can be executed on a $O(N)$-node hypercube $\mathcal{H}$ with slowdown $O(\log \log N)$ with high probability, provided that the relative frequency of access between any pair of tasks $i$ and $j$ is $f_{i,j} \leq \frac{\log \log N}{2N \log N}$.*

## 5 On–line Scenario

In the previous section, we presented the emulation technique under the unrealistic assumptions that communications among processors are known before the execution of $\mathcal{P}$, and, therefore, the temporary processors and the communication paths can be found off-line.

In this section, we present the Distributed Recombination Algorithm (DRA) which allows each task $i$ to evaluate the temporary processor $\mathcal{TP}(i)$ for the phase. The algorithm is totally distributed: it requires that any task knows the communication requests in the phase ($T_{\text{on}}$ steps long) but no global knowledge is necessary.

---

[5] "Bad" phases correspond to "communication bursts" of the program, typically at the beginning, at the end or in crucial points of the computation.

## 5.1 The Emulation Technique

Given a $T_{on}$-active configuration graph $G$ and a constant integer $\kappa > 0$, we say that a task $v \in G$ has *high degree* (h.d.) if $\deg(v) > \kappa$ and *low degree* otherwise. In the on–line scenario, we say that a phase is good if:

1. the $T_{on}$-active configuration has no component with size greater than $2 \log N$;
2. all the components in the $T_{on}$-active configuration are trees;
3. there are at most $O(\log \log N)$ h.d. nodes in the $T_{on}$-active configuration.

As in the off–line scenario, the $T_{on}$-active configuration can be considered as a random graph in $G \in \mathcal{G}(N, p)$. By Lemma 2, we can say that if $p < \frac{(\kappa-1)^2}{0.72} \cdot \frac{1}{N(\log N - \log \log \log N)}$ then a phase is good with high probability. Using similar arguments as in the off–line scenario, we can prove that if the frequency $F < \frac{(\kappa-1)^2}{0.72(\log N - \log \log \log N)T_{on}}$ then almost any phase will be a good one.

The DRA first verifies if the phase is a good one or not. If the phase is a good one, every component elects a leader, which is in charge for the distribution of subcubes, and, finally, any partial state of the component is delivered to the subcube indicated by component leader; if the phase is a bad one no partial state is delivered. To elect the leader each component is transformed in a constant degree one using a pointer jumping strategy. Furthermore, in a good phase each task has to localize the temporary processors of its neighbors.

During the DRA, communications among tasks are done using the RA defined in the subsection 3.1.1. Every application of the RA takes time $O(\log N)$ time with high probability.

We only sketch here the DRA that can be divided into six parts. A complete scheme and more details can be found in the final version of the paper (see also [2]).

**I – Removing High Degree Nodes.** A distinct node, called the coordinator, can compute in $O(\log N)$ time how many h.d. nodes are in the $T_{on}$-active configuration of the phase.

If there are more than $O(\log \log N)$ h.d. nodes then the coordinator broadcasts a "Bad Phase" message and the emulation will take place in the $N$-node hypercube $\mathcal{H}$. Otherwise the coordinator assigns to each h.d. node a different "slot" of $O(\log N)$ computational steps to transform the star graph consisting of the $i$-th h.d. node and its neighbors in a list. This is based on a broadcasting scheme for the hypercube taking $O(\log N)$ time and a *routing step* (i.e. a successful application of the Ranade algorithm).

Notice that at the end of this phase any low degree node $i$, having degree $d_i$ in the computation graph, will have degree $d'_i = d_i + h_i$, where $h_i$ is the number of h.d. nodes adjacent to $i$. Since $i$ has at most $\kappa$ adjacent nodes, the new graph obtained by removing the h.d. nodes has maximal degree less than $2\kappa$. If there are $O(\log \log N)$ h.d. nodes in the $T_{on}$-active configuration then this part takes time $O(\log N \cdot \log \log N)$ plus the time necessary to execute a step of our Routing Algorithm, otherwise it takes time $O(\log N)$.

**II – Leaders Election.** We define the leader of a connected component a node such that *(a)* it is the *Candidate* of all the nodes of the component, and *(b)* its component is not larger than $2 \log N$ (*anti-trust law*). We want to elect a leader in each component. The election is composed by two steps:

*II.a - Candidate Nomination:* using a pointer jumping technique (see [12]) based on the Eulerian tour, each component nominates Candidate the node having the minimal ID; if the component nodes do not agree on the nomination a bad phase is proclaimed.

*II.b - Anti-trust law:* each Candidate checks the size of its component and proclaims a bad phase if its component has more than $2 \log N$ nodes.

This part requires $O(\log \log N)$ routing steps.

**III – Coordinating the leaders.** Each leader has to know the subcube where the partial states of its component have to be delivered. The new positions are decided by the coordinator once all the information have been gathered in it. The coordinator ensures that no collision between different leaders occurs in the redistribution part. The time complexity is $O(\log N)$.

**IV – Broadcasting leader's decisions.** A leader sends to each node $i$ of its component the ID of $\mathcal{TP}(i)$, where the partial state of $i$ will be sent for the next phase. It can be done in $O(\log \log N)$ routing steps using a pointer jumping technique.

**V – Delivery of the partial states.** Every task sends the partial state to $\mathcal{TP}(i)$. By the Ranade algorithm the transmission takes $O(\log N + T_{on})$ time w.h.p..

**VI – Final Localization.** Each node has to know the addresses of the neighbors in the next (good) phase. This is achieved using a fixed hamiltonian cycle of each subcube: each node sends along the cycle a message including its ID and address. Each node receives the message and recognizes the ID of a neighbor taking note[6] of its address. After a message visited all the nodes in the subcube each node knows the addresses of all its neighbors and the total time is $O(\log N \cdot \log \log N)$. We point out that, if the next phase is a bad one, no localization is needed since task $i$ is executed on processor $i$.

**End Algorithm**

The routing steps required by the DRA are $O(\log \log N)$ for a good phase and $O(T_{on})$ for a bad one. As successively proved in Lemma 6, the time complexity of the DRA is $O(\max\{\log N \cdot \log \log N, \log N + T_{on}\})$ for a good phase and $O(\log^2 N)$ for a bad one (w.h.p.). Therefore, if we set $T_{on} = \log N$ then a good phase will be simulated w.h.p. in time

$$O(T_{on} \log \log N) + O(\max\{\log N \cdot \log \log N, \log N + T_{on}\}) = O(\log N \cdot \log \log N)$$

and, consequently, a good phase will be emulated with high probability with slowdown $S = O(\log \log N)$.

## 5.2 The Analysis

The Routing Algorithm, based on repeated applications of Ranade's algorithm, is used to emulate each routing step within the DRA. We prove in the following

---

[6] It requires $O(\log \log N)$ time to update the received address in its memory.

Lemma that $O(T)$ successive applications of Ranade algorithm are sufficient to correctly route $T$ instances of a routing problem (following proofs are omitted due to space limitations and can be found in [2]).

**Lemma 6** *For any constant $c$, $N$ large enough and $T \to \infty$ as $N$ grows, $T$ routing steps can be emulated by $O(T)$ applications of the Ranade algorithm (according to the RA), with probability greater than $1 - N^{-c}$.*

By Lemma 6, the $O(\log \log N)$ routing steps of the DRA are correctly routed by $O(\log \log N)$ applications of Ranade algorithm.

As a consequence of Theorem 4 we can bound the error probability of the emulation, respectively, for a good and a bad phase [2].

If $D$ it the time complexity of $\mathcal{P}$, during the emulation there are $D/T_{on}$ executions of the DRA and at most $D/T_{on}$ emulations by the subcubes. We can prove that:

**Lemma 7** *Let the $N$-task CRCW PRAM program $\mathcal{P}$ have time complexity $D = O(N^d)$, for a constant $d$. Then:*

1. *the probability $P_{DRA}$ that at least one among the $D/T_{on}$ executions of the DRA, consisting of $T_{on}$ routing steps, is not emulated by $O(T_{on})$ applications of the Ranade algorithm is smaller than $N^{-c}$, for any constant $c$ and $N$ large enough;*

2. *the probability $P_{EM}$ that at least one among the good phases (that are no more than $\frac{D}{T_{on}}$) is not emulated with slowdown $O(\log \log N)$ is smaller than $N^{-c}$, for any constant $c$ and $N$ large enough;*

3. *if the number of bad phases $k$ is such that $k \le c_1 \frac{D}{T_{on}^2} \log \log N$ then the probability $P_{BAD}$ that at least one among the bad phases is not emulated with slowdown $O(\log N)$ is smaller than $N^{-c}$, for any constant $c$ and $N$ large enough.*

We are now ready to prove the following theorem.

**Theorem 8** *Let the $N$-task CRCW PRAM program $\mathcal{P}$ have time complexity $D = O(N^d)$ for any constant $d$ and relative frequency $f_{i,j} = O\left(1/(N \log^2 N)\right)$, for any pair of tasks $i$ and $j$. The slowdown $S$ of the emulation of $\mathcal{P}$ by a hypercube $\mathcal{H}$ according to the emulation technique is $O(\log \log N)$ with high probability.*

PROOF : Let us first suppose that the emulation of each good phase takes time $O(\log N \log \log N)$ and the emulation of each bad phase takes time $O(\log^2 N)$. With this assumption, if $B_m$ is the maximal number of bad phases that our emulation technique can tolerate with a slowdown $O(\log \log N)$, we have that:

$$\left(\frac{D}{\log N} - B_m\right) c_2 \log N \log \log N + B_m c_3 \log^2 N \le c_4 D \log \log N$$

that is, $B_m = c_1 \frac{D}{T_{on}^2} \log \log N$, for a constant $c_1$.

Even if the number of bad phases $k$ is less than $B_m$, it might happen that a bad phase is emulated with a slowdown greater than $O(\log N)$, according Ranade emulation algorithm. It might also happen that a good phase is emulated with slowdown greater than $O(\log \log N)$. However, by Lemma 7, these two events happen with low probability.

We can, now, bound the error probability of the emulation technique:

$$\Pr[S > O(\log \log N)] \leq P_{\text{EM}} + P_{\text{DRA}} + P_{\text{BAD}} + \Pr[k > B_m].$$

When the relative frequency $f_{i,j} \leq c_5 \frac{1}{N \log^2 N}$, for any $i, j$, we have that every $T_{\text{on}}$-active configuration can be considered as a graph in $\mathcal{G}(N, p)$ where $p \leq c_5 \frac{1}{N \log^2 N} < c_6 \frac{1}{N \log N (\log N - \log \log \log N)}$, for $c_6 = \frac{c_5(\kappa-1)^2}{0.72}$ and, by results cited in Section 2, we have that $\Pr[\text{one phase is bad}] < w(N)$ where $w(N)$ tends to 0 as $N$ grows. Therefore we can easily prove that w.h.p. the number of bad phases $k$ is less than or equal to $B_m$. By Lemma 7 we also have that $P_{\text{EM}} \to 0$, $P_{\text{DRA}} \to 0$ and $P_{\text{BAD}} \to 0$ as $N$ grows and the Theorem follows.

∎

With respect to the off-line scenario, the hypercube is no longer able to emulate with slowdown $O(\log \log N)$ w.h.p. the $N$-task PRAM programs with relative frequency of access $\frac{1}{2N \log^2 N} < f_{i,j} \leq \frac{\log \log N}{2N \log N}$. This is due to the computationally hard work of the DRA.

## 6  Conclusions

In this paper we described a general technique to emulate irregularly structured parallel programs with low frequency on hypercubes. Our technique is innovative and, from a theoretical point of view, it is interesting to notice that (under certain limiting, but general, assumptions) sub-logarithmic slowdown emulations can be obtained on hypercubes: our emulation has a slowdown which is exponentially better than previously known results. Moreover, even if (with low probability) our technique would not achieve the $O(\log \log N)$ slowdown, the time complexity is the same, within a constant factor, as Ranade's, both achieving $O(\log N)$ slowdown.

Our theoretical study may also have some practical relevance. We show that if a certain amount of resources (either automatic or human) is taken to keep communication frequency at a low level then a *quantifiable* improvement in performances can be obtained. We consider our result as a first attempt to achieve an exact analysis of improvements that can be obtained on execution time by well-known and widely used clustering techniques. Furthermore, our technique is architecture-independent: it can be easily adapted to any other modular host network where efficient routing and broadcast algorithm are known (such as complete trees, meshes and so on) therefore providing a general framework for executing irregularly structured parallel programs.

Another generalization of our technique is the following. We have defined relative frequency assuming that a communication instruction is executed within the same time of a computation. According to this definition, our technique is suitable for parallel machines where transmission is done according to a "Store

& Forward" model. For parallel machines having particularly fast Routing Units it would be possible to define the relative frequency in a different way (i.e. one could give different weights to the two kinds of instructions) and use again our technique.

**Acknowledgments:** The authors gratefully thank Arnold Rosenberg for his suggestions during many fruitful discussions. Thanks also to Yossi Matias, Bojana Obrenić, Christos Kaklamanis, Pino Persiano and Marc Picquendar for useful discussions. The research was supported by "Progetto Finalizzato Sistemi Informatici e Calcolo Parallelo" of Italian National Research Council (C.N.R.) under grant n. 91.00939.PF69 and by the project "Algoritmi, Sistemi di Calcolo e Strutture Informative" of the Italian Ministry of Universities and Scientific Research.

# References

1. H. ALT, T. HAGERUP, K. MELHORN, F.P. PREPARATA, "Simulation of idealized parallel computers on more realistic ones", Technical Report, University of Saarbrucken (Germany), 1986.

2. V. AULETTA, A. NEGRO, V. SCARANO, "Fast Execution of Irregularly Structured Programs with Low Communication Frequency on the Hypercube", Tech. Rep. 6/95 of Dipartimento di Informatica ed Applicazioni, Universitá di Salerno, Italy (also submitted for publication to *Theoretical Computer Science*, 1995).

3. V. AULETTA, A. NEGRO, V. SCARANO, "Efficient Token Clustering on Hypercubes", Tech. Rep. 5/95 of Dipartimento di Informatica ed Applicazioni, Universitá di Salerno, Italy.

4. B. BOLLOBAS, "Graph Theory. An Introductory Course", Springer-Verlag, 1979.

5. B. BOLLOBAS, "Random Graphs", Academic Press, 1985.

6. A. GERASOULIS, T. YANG, "Dominant Sequence Clustering Heuristic Algorithm for Multiprocessors", Report, 1990.

7. A. GERASOULIS, S.VENUGOPAL, "Linear Clusteering of Linear Algebra Task Graphs for Local Memory Systems", Report, 1990.

8. A. GERASOULIS, S. VENUGOPAL, T. YANG, "Clustering Task Graphs for Message Passing Architectures", Proc. of 1990 International Conf. on Supercomputing, ACM SIGARCH Computer Architecture News, pp.447-456, 1990.

9. C. KAKLAMANIS, D. KRIZANC, S. RAO, "Universal Emulations with Sublogarithmic Slowdown", Proc. of 34th IEEE Annual Symp. on Foundations of Computer Science, 1993.

10. S.J. KIM, "A General Approach to Multiprocessor Scheduling", TR-88-01, Dept. Computer Science, Univ. of Texas at Austin, 1988.

11. R.M. KARP, V. RAMACHANDRAN, "Parallel Algorithms for Shared–Memory Machines", Chapter 17 in *Handbook of Theoretical Computer Science: Algorithms and Complexity*, vol.1, J. Van Leuween ed., Elsevier Publisher, 1990.

12. F.T. LEIGHTON, "Introduction to Parallel Algorithms and Architectures", vol. 1, M.Kauffman Publ. 1992.

13. F.T. LEIGHTON, B. MAGGS, S. RAO, "Universal Packet Routing Algorithms", Proc. of 29th IEEE Annual Symp. on Foundations of Computer Science, 1988.

14. B. MONIEN, H. SUDBOROUGH, "Embedding one Interconnection network in Another", *Computing Supp.*, 7, 1990, pp.257-282.

15. A. RANADE, "How to emulate Shared Memory", Proc. of 28th IEEE Annual Symp. on Foundations of Computer Science, 1987, pp. 185-194.

# Run-time parallelization of irregular DOACROSS loops[*]

V. Prasad Krothapalli[1]     Thulasiraman Jeyaraman[2]     Mark Giesbrecht[2]

[1]Informix Software Inc.
4100 Bohannon Drive, Menlo Park, CA, USA, 94025
email: prasadk@informix.com

[2]Department of Computer Science, University of Manitoba
Winnipeg, MB, Canada, R3T 2N2
email: {tram,mwg}@cs.umanitoba.ca

**Abstract.** *Dependencies between iterations of an irregular DOACROSS loop cannot always be determined at compile-time because they may depend upon input data which is known only at run-time. To parallelize such loops, it is necessary to perform run-time analysis. In this paper, we present a new algorithm to parallelize these loops at run-time. The proposed algorithm handles all types of data dependencies without requiring any special architectural support in the multiprocessor. Our scheme has an inspector which builds the iteration schedule and an executor which uses the schedule to execute the various iterations. Our approach does not require any special synchronization instructions during the inspector stage and the executor can be implemented with or without synchronization support. It allows overlap among dependent iterations and requires very little processor communication. Further, the schedule formed by the inspector can be reused across loop invocations. Our scheme has a consistent performance (i.e., performance does not degrade rapidly with the number of iterations or accesses per iteration) during the inspector stage and ensures good speedup during the executor stage.*

## 1 Introduction

In this paper, we consider run-time parallelization of irregular DOACROSS loops. A generic case of such a loop is presented in Figure 1:

*do i = 1 to M*

    ...

$S_p$:  *A[I1[i]] = ...*

    ...

$S_q$:  *... = A[I2[i]] + ...*

    ...

*enddo*

Figure 1: An irregular DOACROSS loop

* A full version of this paper, including complete performance results, is available via anonymous ftp in ftp.cs.umanitoba.ca:pub/mwg/doacross.ps.Z. This work was supported in part by NSERC grants OGP0155376 and OGP0138482

In the above loop, there are N elements in the index arrays I1 and I2. The entries in arrays I1 and I2 have no restriction and are not available until run-time. Each array can have duplicated values, which implies that all three kinds of data dependencies, namely flow (Read-after-Write), anti- (Write-after-Read) and output- (Write-after-Write) dependencies, could occur between instances of statements $S_p$ and $S_q$. For example, if $I1[1] = I2[3] = I1[4] = I1[5] = x$, then we have the following dependencies: $S_p[1] \xrightarrow{flow} S_q[3] \xrightarrow{anti-} S_p[4] \xrightarrow{output-} S_p[5]$. These accesses form a *dependence (or access) chain*. The entries in the arrays $I1$ and $I2$ are assumed to remain constant during the execution of one invocation of the loop, although they are allowed to change outside the loop.

In order to parallelize the loop, it is necessary to perform run-time analysis, since the inter-iteration dependencies are known only at run-time. Much previous research has been done to design effective run-time parallelization algorithms [1, 2, 3, 4, 5, 6, 7, 9]. The main differences among the schemes proposed are the types of dependence patterns that are handled and the required system or architecture support. In general, run-time parallelization schemes have two stages, namely *inspector* and the *executor* [7, 9, 3, 1]. The inspector determines the dependence relations among the data accesses. The executor uses this information to execute the iterations in parallel in an order that preserves the dependences.

In this paper, we describe and evaluate a new algorithm for the run-time parallelization of DOACROSS loops. We follow the inspector and executor approach. Our scheme handles all types of data dependencies without requiring any special architectural support. It does not require any special synchronization operation during the inspector stage and the executor can be implemented with or without synchronization support. It allows overlap among dependent iterations and requires very little inter-processor communication. The effectiveness of our scheme is evaluated through measurements of parametrized loops on a 8-processor UMA (Uniform Memory Access) shared memory multiprocessor. The results show significant speedups over the serial code with the full overhead of run-time analysis. Our scheme has a consistent performance (ie., the performance does not degrade rapidly with the number of iterations or accesses per iteration) during the inspector stage and ensures good speedup during the executor stage. We organize this paper as follows. Section 2 explains our scheme in detail; Section 3 presents the performance results. Section 4 concludes our study.

## 2  A New Algorithm for Run-time Parallelization

In order to exploit the latent parallelism in the irregular DOACROSS loop in Figure 1, we follow the inspector and executor approach. In the parallel inspector algorithm (Figure 2), the arrays *LastW* and *LastR* record the iteration during which a particular shared array element *A[i]* was last modified and last read respectively. For each one of the shared array references *A[i]* in a particular iteration, the algorithm finds out the different iterations in which they were last modified and last read and then allots an appropriate wavefront number to the particular iteration. Further, the inspector builds an array *L* of linked lists, where *L[j]* contains a list of those iterations in wavefront *j*. This is used during the executor stage to schedule iterations onto different processors.

```
/* There are N elements in the index arrays I1 and I2. There are M iterations
in the loop. There are N elements in the arrays LastW and LastR. Arrays LastR
and LastW are local to the procedure. There are M elements in the array WF. L
is an array of pointers (size M) to linked lists. piece is the size of each section.
P is the number of processors. MAXW[:] has P elements. WF[:], MAXW[:] and
L[:] are shared data structures. They are initialized to zero before the light-weight
threads are activated. Thread id values range from 0 to P-1. */

piece = M/P; Myid = get_myid(); /* get my thread ID */
start = Myid*piece; /* get my share */
if (Myid == (P-1)) { last = M; } else { last = start+piece; }
Max = 0; LastW[:] = 0; LastR[:] = 0;
do i = (start+1) to last
  mywf=0;
  if (LastW[I1] ≠ 0) /* output- dependency */
    { mywf = max(WF[LastW[I1[i]]],mywf); }
  if (LastR[I1] ≠ 0) /* anti- dependency */
    { mywf = max(WF[LastR[I1[i]]],mywf); }
  if (LastW[I2] ≠ 0) /* flow dependency */
    { mywf = max(WF[LastW[I2[i]]],mywf); }
  WF[i] = mywf + 1; /* wavefront allocation */
  LastW[I1[i]] = i; /* update the shadow variables */
  if (WF[LastR[I2]] < WF[i]) { LastR[I2[i]] = i; }
  Max = max(Max,WF[i]); /* record largest wavefront in this section */
enddo
if (Myid == 0) { MAXW[Myid] = Max; }
else
  while(MAXW[Myid-1] == 0); /* Wait until previous section is completed */
  sum = MAXW[Myid-1]; /* Get largest wavefront of all previous sections */
  do i = (start+1) to last
    { WF[i] = WF[i]+sum; } /* Update wavefront numbers in this section */
  MAXW[Myid] = sum+Max;
endif
do i = (start+1) to last /* place the iteration i at the appropriate level */
  { Add_node(L[WF[i]],i); }
```

Figure 2: The Parallel Inspector algorithm

The dependency information thus recorded in the form of wavefronts can be reused for several invocations of the DOACROSS loop, provided the dependencies do not change. The primary advantage of wavefront generation is that it leads to efficient processor scheduling because the wavefronts carry a global picture of the dependence hierarchy. Further, the inspector does not require any *atomic synchronization operations* or *barriers*. In order to parallelize the wavefront computation, *sectioning* [5] is performed on the inspector algorithm.

*Self-scheduling*, unlike *static scheduling*, leads to efficient iteration to processor mapping since the position of iterations in the dependence hierarchy is known only at run-time. The executor can be implemented with either *barrier synchronization* or *busy-wait*. In *barrier sychronization*, a *barrier* condition has to be met whenever all the iterations in a particular wavefront have been scheduled. *The number of barriers required is proportional to the total number of wavefronts.* This obviously reduces the processor utilization since processors tend to idle at the barrier waiting for other processors to complete. One way to get over this problem is to employ the *busy-wait* mechanism. The *busy-wait* mechanism allows overlapped execution of dependent iterations by shifting the dependence granularity from iteration level to the access level and improves processor utilization. It needs some data structures to be set up in order to sequence different accesses. It gives better performance over *barrier sychronization* particularly when the dependence chains are very long; otherwise *barrier synchronization* performs better due to the run-time overheads involved in *busy-wait* mechanism.

## 3  Performance Evaluation

Our experiments are timing runs on a 33 MHz 8-processor SGI shared memory multiprocessor. The machine has 4 CPU boards with 2 CPU's on each board. First level cache hits costs 1 processor cycle; first level misses or second level hits costs 3 processor cycles; second level misses costs 57 cycles to bring 64 bytes. The machine is run in single-user mode for all experiments. In our analysis we use a loop as in Figure 3 as workload. Array $A$ has $N*r$ elements. A *Mostly-Serial Loop* is one with long dependence chains and and a *Mostly-Parallel Loop* is one with shorter dependence chains.

*/* There are N iterations and r accesses per iteration. INDEX contains the actual array references. tmp1 and tmp2 are dummy variables */*

```
do i = 1,N,1
   do j = 1,r,1
      if(odd(j)) tmp1=A[INDEX[i*r+j]]
      else A[INDEX[i*r+j]]=tmp2
      do j = 1,W,1
         dummy loop simulating useful work
      enddo
   enddo
enddo
```

Figure 3: Loop used as experimental workload

A *self-scheduled* form of our executor with *barrier* synchronization and a *pre-scheduled* form of Chen *et al.*'s [1] executor is used for the comparisons. In Chen *et al.*'s scheme both *pre-scheduled* executor and *self-scheduled* executor give very similar performance. We use 8 processors for the experiments and vary the number of iterations ($N$), the iteration grain size ($W$) and the number of references per iteration ($r$). From Table 1, it is obvious that the best results occur when the size of the loop body ($W$) is large and the number of accesses ($r$) is low. Further, the performance is better when the dependence chains are short. From Table 2, it is evident that our algorithm gives superior performance compared to Chen *et al.*'s scheme, largely because our inspector is much faster and efficient, without requiring special synchronization operations and uses very little inter-processor communication. To see how the speedup varies with the number of processors, we also ran several experiments with different types of loops varying the number of processors. With up to 8 processors, we obtain almost linear speedups. We expect the speedup to be scalable to larger number of processors.

| $W$ | $r$ | Mostly-Serial Loop | | | | | Mostly-Parallel Loop | | | | |
|---|---|---|---|---|---|---|---|---|---|---|---|
| | | $N$=1600 | 3200 | 6400 | 12800 | 25600 | $N$=1600 | 3200 | 6400 | 12800 | 25600 |
| | 8 | 3.00 | 3.18 | 3.13 | 3.49 | 3.47 | 3.26 | 3.05 | 3.25 | 3.16 | 3.02 |
| | 4 | 3.60 | 3.81 | 4.14 | 4.41 | 4.36 | 4.36 | 4.36 | 4.44 | 4.33 | 4.22 |
| 160 $\mu s$ | 2 | 3.81 | 4.44 | 4.75 | 4.75 | 4.98 | 5.00 | 4.62 | 5.04 | 5.03 | 5.11 |
| | 1 | 4.29 | 4.65 | 5.24 | 5.22 | 5.44 | 5.00 | 5.22 | 5.58 | 5.52 | 5.60 |
| | 8 | 5.02 | 5.43 | 5.75 | 5.79 | 5.85 | 5.61 | 5.95 | 5.85 | 5.89 | 5.96 |
| | 4 | 5.74 | 6.01 | 5.34 | 6.50 | 6.46 | 6.49 | 6.58 | 6.54 | 6.51 | 6.53 |
| 640 $\mu s$ | 2 | 5.83 | 6.30 | 6.53 | 6.81 | 6.91 | 6.64 | 6.73 | 6.89 | 6.89 | 6.95 |
| | 1 | 6.13 | 6.39 | 6.75 | 6.96 | 7.09 | 7.03 | 6.94 | 7.10 | 7.12 | 7.17 |

Table 1: Speedup of our algorithm over serial execution including *inspector* and *executor* using 8 processors.

| $W$ | $r$ | Mostly-Serial Loop | | | | | Mostly-Parallel Loop | | | | |
|---|---|---|---|---|---|---|---|---|---|---|---|
| | | $N$=1600 | 3200 | 6400 | 12800 | 25600 | $N$=1600 | 3200 | 6400 | 12800 | 25600 |
| | 8 | 3.71 | 10.21 | 26.11 | 76.44 | 194.45 | 18.47 | 66.63 | 229.27 | 560.09 | 1142.25 |
| | 4 | 1.82 | 2.88 | 7.17 | 19.00 | 49.40 | 4.79 | 12.93 | 49.29 | 156.82 | 379.82 |
| 160 $\mu s$ | 2 | 1.25 | 1.67 | 2.41 | 4.70 | 11.44 | 2.17 | 2.88 | 7.88 | 29.42 | 92.64 |
| | 1 | 1.14 | 1.27 | 1.52 | 1.87 | 3.27 | 1.25 | 1.43 | 2.07 | 4.74 | 16.39 |
| | 8 | 2.46 | 5.27 | 13.18 | 33.94 | 86.60 | 8.77 | 33.67 | 107.56 | 268.71 | 584.97 |
| | 4 | 1.62 | 2.14 | 3.71 | 8.17 | 19.83 | 2.41 | 5.53 | 19.20 | 60.29 | 151.33 |
| 640 $\mu s$ | 2 | 1.44 | 1.62 | 1.90 | 2.84 | 5.12 | 1.36 | 1.69 | 3.35 | 10.86 | 32.70 |
| | 1 | 1.41 | 1.47 | 1.58 | 1.77 | 2.25 | 1.15 | 1.14 | 1.33 | 2.19 | 5.90 |

Table 2: Speedup of our algorithm over Chen *et al.*'s scheme including *inspector* and *executor* using 8 processors.

# 4 Conclusions

The dependencies between iterations of an irregular DOACROSS loop cannot always to determined at compile-time. In this paper, we presented and evaluated a new algorithm to parallelize such loops at run-time. Our scheme handles any type of data dependence pattern without requiring any special architectural support. It minimizes inter-processor communication, leads to better processor utilization and allows reuse of the inspector results across several loop invocations. The results shows that the new scheme has a consistent performance (i.e., the performance does not degrade rapidly with the number of iterations or accesses per iteration) during the inspector stage and leads to higher speedups during the executor stage. We have evaluated our algorithm with a set of parametrized loops running on a 8-processor SGI shared memory multiprocessor and varied the loop parameters such as the number of iterations and references. The results show better speedups and they are scalable to higher number of processors.

## Acknowledgements

The authors would like to thank Dr. Derek L. Eager, Professor, Department of Computational Science, University of Saskatchewan, Saskatoon, SK S7N OWO, Canada and Dr. P. Sadayappan, Professor, Department of Computer and Information Science, Ohio State University, Columbus, OH 43210 for their help in the experiments and the anonymous referees for their helpful comments.

## References

1. D.-K. Chen, J. Torrellas and P.-C. Yew, *An Efficient Algorithm for the Run-time Parallelization of DOACROSS Loops* Supercomputing 1994.
2. V. P. Krothapalli *On synchronization and scheduling for Multiprocessors* Ph.D Thesis, The Ohio State University 1990.
3. V. P. Krothapalli and P. Sadayappan, *An approach to synchronization for parallel computing* in ACM Int'l Conf. on Supercomputing, pages 573-581, June 1988.
4. V. P. Krothapalli and P. Sadayappan, *Dynamic scheduling of Doacross loops for multiprocessors* IEEE Parallel Architectures 1991.
5. S.-T. Leung and J. Zahorjan, *Improving the performance of Run-time parallelization* in 4th ACM SIGPLAN Symp. on Principles and Practice of Parallel Programming, pages 83-91, May 1993.
6. S. Midkiff and D. Padua. *Compiler algorithms for synchronization* IEEE Trans. on Computers, C-36(12), December 1987.
7. J. Saltz, R. Mirchandaney and K. Crowley, *Run-time parallelization and scheduling of loops* IEEE Trans. Computers, 40(5):603-612, May 1991.
8. J. Thulasiraman, V. P. Krothapalli and M. Giesbrecht, *Run-time Parallelization of irregular DOACROSS loops*, June 5, 1995, Technical Report No. 95/03, Department of Computer Science, University of Manitoba, Winnipeg, Canada.
9. C.-Q.Zhu and P.-C.Yew, *A scheme to enforce data dependence on large multiprocessor systems* IEEE Trans. on Software Engineering, pages 726-739, June 1987.

# Instruction Scheduling and Global Register Allocation for SIMD Multiprocessors

Benjamin Hao* and David Pearson**

Department of Computer Science
Cornell University, Ithaca, NY 14853 USA
{bhao,pearson}@cs.cornell.edu

**Abstract.** Current trends in system design are pointing to using more and more processing units and storage units in a single system. In order to generate programs for these types of distributed memory machines, the challenge is to coordinate and schedule multiple functional units to perform computations efficiently.

In this paper, we describe how our compiler can automate the process and generate good parallel programs from sequential programs. We show how to turn the straight-line code into a task graph which exhibits maximum parallelism possible. Then we give an algorithm for assigning computation to processors to minimize communication cost. Finally, we give an algorithm to allocate registers across processors using an interference graph.

## 1 Introduction

For SIMD (Single Instruction and Multiple Data) distributed memory multiprocessors, VLIW (Very Long Instruction Word) microprocessors, or ILP (Instruction Level Parallelism) styled machines, to obtain the maximum level of parallelism and the best possible performance, the challenge is to coordinate and schedule the multiple functional (processing) units in the machine to execute desired computations efficiently. Such coordination involves two important tasks: instruction scheduling and global register allocation. Instruction scheduling is the task of mapping computations onto the processing units to achieve maximum parallelism. Global register allocation is the placement of data into each processing unit's local memories such that all processing units executing the same instruction can execute in lock step with all the data ready in the right registers. Instruction scheduling and global register allocation are interrelated. It is impossible to optimize one without any consideration for the other.

---

\* Supported in part by the Advanced Research Projects Agency of the Department of Defense under ONR Contract N00014–92–J–1989, by ONR Contract N00014–92–J–1839, United States—Israel Binational Science Foundation Grant 92–00234 and in part by the U.S. Army Research Office through the Mathematical Science Institute of Cornell University

\*\* Supported by a Fannie and John Hertz Foundation Fellowship

Our goal is to automate the entire optimization process via our compiler and free the programmers from such a tedious task. We concentrate on compiling and parallelizing *straight line scalar code* (SLS code) to run on SIMD multiprocessors (but the techniques developed can be applied to VLIW or any other ILP styled machines with little modifications). We define SLS code as a program segment free of branches, entered at the first statement, and exiting at the last.

We are interested in parallelizing SLS code because: (1) although nested FOR loops are natural for regular problems, irregular problems, large systems of ODE's and so forth can better be handled by synthesized straight-line code for each iteration; (2) statically unrolled loops can give us large basic blocks to explore instruction level parallelism via instruction scheduling across different processing units; (3) removal of conditional branches can be justified in real life through the technique of speculative execution (this technique is often used to keep a high speed super-pipelined RISC processor's pipeline and execution units busy). In other words, we want to keep as many processing units busy as possible to gain maximum parallelism from a sequential program.

We chose to target our compiler for SIMD machines to demonstrate our instruction scheduling and global register allocation algorithms. SIMD was chosen because: (1) SIMD machines have thus far only proved useful for regular problems, but our techniques promise to effectively utilize them on irregular problems as well; (2) they have much more processing and storage units than any other parallel or VLIW processors, hence it is more challenging to manage all of them; (3) they require our algorithms and solutions to be truly scalable to take advantage of all the units; (4) the local memory per node in a SIMD machine is usually very small, thus requires very efficient register allocation.

In this paper, we will present how our compiler performs register allocation and instruction scheduling to generate parallel code from a normal SLS program. But, first we will describe related instruction scheduling and global register allocation studies, and how they are different from ours.

## 2  Prior and Related Work

Instruction scheduling is very important for machines with multiple functional units. Most of the recent studies concentrate on *speculative execution*, the execution of instructions before the conditional branch instruction before them is resolved [1, 2, 3], on VLIW machines. The main goals of these studies are to have superscalar processors looking beyond branch boundaries to achieve more ILP in non-numeric applications, and to be able to recover gracefully from exceptions caused by speculative instructions, instructions being executed during speculative execution. The goal of our compiler-controlled instruction scheduling is, however, to attain maximum possible ILP on SIMD while minimizing overall communication cost.

Recent research on global register allocation [4, 5] focuses on problems of improving existing standard register allocators via clever data structures and integrating these new data structures into other parts of the compiler, especially the instruction scheduler, for better performance. On one hand, our register allocator is similar to theirs because we also try to integrate it better with the instruction scheduler to avoid introducing unnecessary data dependencies that could limit ILP. On the other hand, ours is completely different because we have to contend with the problems of allocating registers across not just one, but many processor.

# 3  Building the Task Graph

The straight-line code we are compiling can be represented as a data-flow graph whose edges represent the values and whose vertices are the operations to be performed. The first task in compilation is to assign execution steps to all these operations, subject to the constraint that all inputs must have been computed before an operation can execute. The SIMD architecture imposes the additional constraint that only one *kind* of operation (e.g. multiplication) can happen at one time (but all the multiplications that are ready to fire can be executed then).

We develop an optimistic schedule in this way, performing all addition operations whose inputs are all ready, then all subtractions, then all multiplications, and so on, cycling through the operations as many times as needed. This schedule can be at most a constant factor slower than the most optimistic schedule for a general PRAM performing the same operations.

This optimistic schedule will later be revised by adding additional time-steps in between the ones assigned. There are two reasons we may need additional steps: First, the optimistic schedule assumes the input values needed are already available at the processor computing some operation, and so we may need extra steps for communication. Second, SIMD requires that all the operations at one time-step all use the same register numbers; our register allocation strategy tries to satisfy this requirement, but when it's impossible, we may need to split one of the time-steps. We discuss these issues in the next two sections.

# 4  Assigning Processor Numbers

We have thus far ignored the problem of assigning computations to processors. We want to do this in a way that minimizes the communication time, which is proportional to the number of hops needed for the value that must move the farthest. We use a simple technique that works well in practice. We proceed sequentially through our preliminary schedule. At each time step, we start with a random processor assignment, then perform local improvements by a hill-climbing algorithm until no further improvements are possible, then move to the next time-step, and so on.

> **Algorithm: Hill Climbing**
> (1) First assign the processors randomly;
> (2) Compute total traveling distance of all the messages
>     between the current and the previous instruction;
> (3) Find the bottleneck communication pair of processors;
> (4) Go down the list of all the processors, and swap each one
>     with the bottleneck processor; the swap can only be carried
>     out when it decreases the bottleneck distance and does not
>     increase the previous message traveling distance of the one
>     being swapped;
> (5) The whole process terminates when after swapping with every
>     other processors, the bottleneck message traveling
>     distance is not decreased.

One swap takes $O(p)$ time, where $p$ is the number of processors. There can be at most $p \log(p)$ swaps per instruction cycle. Therefore, the total running time of hill climbing is at most $O(tp^2 \log(p))$, where $t$ is the total number of parallel instructions.

The worst case running time is not as bad as it seems. Taking up to $O(p \log(p))$ time to swap for each instruction phase, would decrease the message traveling distance drastically. The time we spend now on optimizing the horizontal processor assignment more than pays for itself when we gain back all the time on communication cost in the generated code.

## 5 Register Allocation

Our remaining problem is to assign register numbers to all the data values. In the SIMD setting, each parallel instruction has an opcode, two source registers (S1 and S2) and a destination register. Not only do we have to schedule instructions so that the same operation is performed across all active processors at the same time-step, but we must also ensure that the operations use the same register numbers in each position (S1, S2, and D). This is the job of the register allocator.

We have to slightly modify the concept of a variable lifetime in the parallel setting: define a *thread* to be the lifetime of a variable on a single processor. A thread begins when the value is computed or it is received from another processor, and it ends when the value is last used or transmitted to another processor (although there is potential to gain efficiency by replicating values on more than one processor, we do not do so). A thread corresponds to a register on a single processor, and the register allocator's task is to assign register numbers to threads.

We need to satisfy three constraints:

1. Two threads used in the same position (Source1, Source2, or Destination) by different processors in the same time step must have the same register number.

2. Two threads that are live at the same time in the same processor must have different register numbers.

3. There is a fixed number of registers available (on the CM-2, $\sim$ 128 registers) for all the threads on a given processor.

This is very similar to the register allocation problem for sequential machines, and we use a method that is an extension of the traditional graph-coloring approach that has been so successful in compilers for sequential machines [6]. The only addition is the first constraint.

To allocate registers across all processors, we reduce the task graph to an *interference graph* where each vertex is a thread. The interference graph used here is similar to the one used in a sequential compiler—registers holding different data that are live simultaneously on the same processor are said to interfere with each other. These threads are connected by *interference* edges. Our interference graph, however, has an additional constraint: Threads are from different processors, and they may need to occupy a same physical register on different processors. To represent this new constraint, *equivalence* edges are introduced to connect threads that must be held in same register.

Global register allocation then becomes a problem of coloring the interference graph, each color representing a unique register number. Vertices that interfere (connected by interference edges) need to be assigned different colors, and vertices connected by equivalence edges should have the same color.

Two issues can arise when coloring the interference graph:

1. The graph is not colorable, even with an infinite number of colors;
2. The graph is colorable, but it needs too many colors.

Intuitively, we can reduce the problem to sequential register allocation if we merge all threads connected by equivalence edges into a single vertex. The first problem we call a *self-loop*—it arises if such a vertex has an interference edge with itself, which in turn means that two interfering threads in the interference graph are connected by a path of equivalence edges. Note that this first problem does not arise in sequential register allocation. We present an greedy (non-optimal) algorithm that resolves such conflicts by modifying the task graph while building the interference graph. The resulting interference graph can then be colored.

---

**Algorithm: Building Interference Graph, Resolving Self-loops**

Identify all threads, construct interference edges.
For each time-step do:

  For each thread referenced in this time-step do:
  (1) Connect all threads that appear in the same position in this time-step by equivalence edges;
  (2) If the equivalence edge creates a self-loop then split the time-step if it has not been already. Push the responsible instruction into the new time-step.

---

The second problem above, too many colors, is similar to the sequential case–it means there are not enough local registers for our computation. Our solution is also similar: we *spill* some of the data. Rather than using host memory (which could become a bottleneck), we spill the data to free registers in other processors. When the data is next needed, we generate a sequence of instructions for retrieving it remotely. It is very costly, but we assume it does not happen often enough to degrade the overall performance of generated code.

# 6  Summary and Conclusion

In this paper, we describe how our compiler performs instruction scheduling and global register allocation to generate parallel programs from sequential programs. These generated parallel programs run on SIMD machines. It is quite unusual to explore instruction parallelism on SIMD machines since most SIMD programs only make use of data parallelism. However, this allows us to utilize the massive parallelism that SIMD offers for irregular problems, not just the highly regular problems that SIMD was designed for.

Our limited test results indicate that our approach is effective. Further studies are required to determine if this can be applied to any general sequential programs, and how well our approach applies to other parallel architectures like VLIW.

# References

1. P.P. Chang, S.A. Mahlke, W.Y. Chen, N.J. Warter, and W.W. Hwu, "IMPACT: An Architectural Framework for Multiple-Instruction-Issue Processors" *Proceedings of the 18th International Symposium on Computer Architecture*, pp. 266-275, May 1991
2. S.A. Mahlke, W.Y. Chen, W.W. Hwu, B.R. Rau, and M.S. Schlansker, "Sentinel Scheduling for VLIW and Superscalar Processors" *Proceedings of the 5th International Conference on Architectural Support for Programming Languages and Operating Systems*, pp. 238-259, Sept. 1992
3. K. Ebcioglu, R.D. Groves, K.-C. Kim, G.M. Silberman, and I. Ziv, "VLIW Compilation Techniques in a Superscalar Environment" *Proceedings of the ACM SIGPLAN'94 Conference on Programming Language Design and Implementation*, SIGPLAN notices, pp. 38-48 June 1994
4. S.S. Pinter, "Register Allocation with Instruction Scheduling: a New Approach" *Proceedings of the ACM SIGPLAN'93 Conference on Programming Language Design and Implementation*, SIGPLAN notices, pp. 248-257, June 1993
5. C. Norris and L.L. Pollock, "Register Allocation over the Program Dependence Graph" *Proceedings of the ACM SIGPLAN'94 Conference on Programming Language Design and Implementation*, SIGPLAN notices, pp. 266-277, June 1994
6. G.J. Chaitin, "Register Allocation and Spilling via Graph Coloring" *Proceedings of the ACM SIGPLAN'82 Symposium on Compiler Construction'*, SIGPLAN Notices, pp. 98-105, June 1982

# General Bounds for the Assignment of Irregular Dependency Graphs

Sathiamoorthy Manoharan

Department of Computer Science
University of Auckland
New Zealand.

E-mail: mano@cs.auckland.ac.nz

**Abstract.** Given an irregular dependency graph consisting of inter-dependent tasks, the problem of finding an optimal assignment on a number of parallel execution units is NP-complete. Assignment schemes thus settle for some heuristics that produce sub-optimal solutions. Most popular of these are the work-greedy assignment schemes. This paper presents new bounds on the performance of work-greedy schemes, taking into account the degree of parallelism visible between the tasks and the inter-task communication delays.

**Keywords:** Allocation, Dependency graphs, Instruction-level parallelism, Scheduling, Processor assignment.

## 1  Introduction

A program with multiple tasks can be viewed as a dependency graph: the vertices represent the tasks and the edges represent the dependencies between the tasks. Nothing is assumed about the granularity of the tasks. A task may be a procedure; or it may be an instruction.

Dependency graphs corresponding to arbitrary programs are irregular in their nature. For instance, an arbitrary basic block of a Fortran subroutine will give rise to an irregular instruction dependency graph.

Dependency graphs may have weights associated with their vertices and edges: the weight on a vertex indicates the amount of computation the corresponding task performs, and the weight on an edge indicates the amount of communication between the tasks the edge connects.

Assignment of a dependency graph is a many-to-one mapping function $M : \mathbf{T} \mapsto \mathbf{P}$, which maps the set of tasks $\mathbf{T}$ onto the set of processors $\mathbf{P}$. $M$ is defined for each task of $\mathbf{T}$. In essence, the assignment divides the task set $\mathbf{T}$ into $m$, some possibly empty, ordered subsets or partitions. Here $m$ is the cardinality of the set $\mathbf{P}$. The total time the set of tasks $\mathbf{T}$ takes to execute on the set of processors $\mathbf{P}$ is called the *makespan*. The objective of the assignment is to minimize the makespan.

A naïve approach to solve the assignment problem is to enumerate all the possible assignments and choose the assignment that gives the minimum makespan. However, this approach will take exponential time. It is very unlikely that there would be any cleverer scheme to find the optimal assignment in polynomial time, since even the restricted cases of the assignment problem have been proved to be NP-complete [17, 15]. Practical assignment schemes thus settle for some heuristics that would find sub-optimal assignments in polynomial time [3, 5, 9, 10, 11, 12, 19].

Most of these heuristic schemes are work-greedy: they do not let a processor idle when there is a task the processor could execute. That is, an assignment is work-greedy if no processor remains idle when there is a task the processor could execute. Work-greedy assignments are time-driven: tasks and processors are selected at specific time instances, i.e. when a processor becomes free or when a task finishes its execution.

Work-greedy assignment schemes, in addition to finding *where* to execute a task, attempt to find *when* to execute a task. That is, they always predict the start and finish times of the tasks. This permits computation of bounds on the makespans of work-greedy assignments.

Many work-greedy assignment schemes ignore communication delays. These schemes follow a common basic algorithm.

Tasks are kept in an ordered list. A free processor scans the list from left to right to find the first ready task to be executed. If there is a ready task, the processor executes the task until completion. Otherwise the processor idles until a task becomes ready.

This procedure ensures that the assignment is work-greedy. See [2] for a good account of assignment methods not involving communication delays. See [13] for a review of some work-greedy assignment schemes that do take communication delays into account.

A work-greedy assignment does not guarantee optimality. Yet, it is possible to prove that the makespan of a work-greedy assignment is within a constant factor of the makespan of the optimal assignment. This paper presents some new results bounding the makespans of work-greedy assignments. The bounds are general in the sense that they apply for any task ordering employed and for any irregular dependency graph. Implications of these bounds are discussed in Section 4.

For the purpose of notational convenience, a work-greedy assignment is characterized as an ordered triple $\mathcal{W} = (\beta_1, \beta_2, \beta_3)$, where $\beta_i$ are defined as follows.

1. $\beta_1$ characterizes the execution times of the tasks involved in the assignment.

$$\beta_1 \in \{\text{arbitrary, unit}\}$$

2. $\beta_2$ characterizes the communication time between two tasks assigned to *different* processors.

$$\beta_2 \in \{\text{arbitrary, unit, nil}\}$$

3. $\beta_3$ characterizes the precedence relation between the tasks.

$$\beta_3 \in \{\text{arbitrary, nil}\}$$

Graham et al. [8] and Veltman et al. [18] have used similar notational characterizations.

The rest of this paper is organized as follows. Section 2 presents a bound on the makespan of a work-greedy assignment ignoring the communication delays between tasks. The bound is based on Sarkar's bound [16] and it incorporates the parallelism visible between the tasks. Section 3 extends the results of Section 2 by taking into account the possible communication delays between the tasks. The new bound is an improvement over the bounds presented by Hwang et al. [9] and Lee et al. [11]. Section 4 discusses the implications of these bounds on makespans. The final section concludes with a summary.

## 1.1 Notations

Some notations that need to be used subsequently are defined here. Other notations will be defined in context.

$n$ number of tasks.
$m$ number of processors.
**T** set of tasks $\{ T_0, T_1, \ldots, T_{n-1} \}$.
**P** set of processors $\{ P_0, P_1, \ldots, P_{m-1} \}$.
$\tau_i$ execution time of $T_i$ assumed common on all $P_j$.
$G_T$ task graph depicting tasks and the dependencies among them.
$G_P$ processor graph depicting processors and their interconnections.
$\omega$ the total execution time of $G_T$ on $G_P$ (i.e. the makespan).

## 1.2 Assumptions

The primary architectural considerations are the set of processors and the topology in which the processors are connected. The processor topology is modelled as a graph with vertices representing the processors and weighted edges representing the interconnections between the processors. The weight on a processor graph edge represents the message transfer rate between the processors connected by this edge. All the processors are assumed to be capable of doing the functions required by the tasks.

Task graphs are assumed to be acyclic. A dataflow execution model is assumed for the execution of task graphs. That is, a task can begin its execution when all its inputs are available, and finishes only when it has produced all the required outputs. Communication delay may occur when a task sends its output to its successor tasks. This delay is dependent on the volume of information being transferred and the distance the information needs to travel. Tasks, once scheduled, cannot be preempted. Task replication is not considered, that is, no task can execute on more than one processor.

See Figure 1 for example task and processor graphs. Figure 1(a) shows the task dependency graph corresponding to the evaluation of an expression $z = F(f(x), g(y))$. Figure 1(b) shows a three-processor system where all processors are connected to each other.

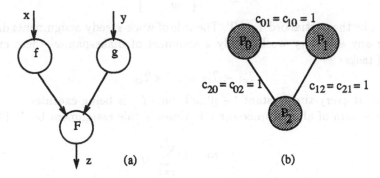

**Fig. 1.** Example task and processor graphs.

## 2   Dependency Graphs with Zero Communication Times

Assignments of dependency graphs with zero communication times are characterized by $\mathcal{W} = $ (arbitrary, nil, arbitrary).

Let $\omega$ denote the makespan of any work-greedy assignment; and let $\tau^*$ be the execution time of the longest chain of the dependency graph; and let $\pi = \sum \tau_i / \tau^*$. Sarkar [16] showed that

$$\max\left[\frac{\sum \tau_i}{m}, \tau^*\right] \leq \omega \leq \frac{1}{m}\left[\sum_i \tau_i + (m-1)\tau^*\right]$$

The following theorem presents an interpretation of this bound using the so-called degree of average software parallelism. Informally, the degree of average software parallelism is a measure of parallelism in a task dependency graph. The bound of Theorem 1 forms the first step towards a bound incorporating communication costs.

**Theorem 1.**

$$\omega'/\omega \leq 1 + (m-1)/\pi \text{ if } m < \pi$$
$$\omega'/\omega \leq 1 + (\pi-1)/m \text{ if } m \geq \pi$$

*where $\omega$ is the length of the optimal makespan, that is not necessarily work-greedy; and $\omega'$ is the makespan of any arbitrary work-greedy assignment.*

**Proof.**

For *any* (and thus, the optimal) assignment of makespan $\omega$, the following inequality holds true:

$$\omega \geq \max\left[\frac{\sum \tau_i}{m}, \tau^*\right] \tag{1}$$

Let $\prec$ be the partial order on **T**. The rule of work-greedy assignments dictates that for any arbitrary work-greedy assignment of makespan $\omega'$ there exists a chain of tasks

$$T_{c1} \prec T_{c2} \prec \ldots \prec T_{cy}$$

such that at every time instant $t \in [0, \omega']$ some $T_{cj}$ is being executed.

Let the sum of all the processor idle times in this assignment be $I$. Then,

$$I \leq (m-1)\sum_{j=1}^{y} \tau_{cj} \tag{2}$$

But for any chain in an assignment, the following inequality holds true:

$$\sum_{j=1}^{y} \tau_{cj} \leq \tau^* \tag{3}$$

Now since

$$\omega' = \frac{1}{m}\left[\sum_i \tau_i + I\right]$$

using (2) and (3) we get,

$$\omega' \leq \frac{1}{m}\left[\sum_i \tau_i + (m-1)\tau^*\right] \tag{4}$$

Note that (4) follows straight from Sarkar's bound. We prove it here so as to make the proof of our next Theorem easy to understand.

When $\sum \tau_i/m \geq \tau^*$, from (1) and (4) we get the bound:

$$\frac{\omega'}{\omega} \leq 1 + \frac{m-1}{\pi} \tag{5}$$

When $\tau^* \geq \sum \tau_i/m$, from (1) and (4) we get the bound:

$$\frac{\omega'}{\omega} \leq 1 + \frac{\pi-1}{m} \tag{6}$$

Both (5) and (6) always hold true. However, when $m \geq \pi$ the bound of (6) is tighter, otherwise the bound of (5) is tighter.

$\square$

$\pi$ is defined to be the degree of average software parallelism. It is a lower bound on the amount of parallelism within a task dependency graph.

Note that, from (1) and (4), we get the following loose bound established by Graham:

$$\frac{\omega'}{\omega} \leq 2 \tag{7}$$

According to Theorem 1, as $m \to \infty$, $\omega'/\omega$ reaches unity (rather than 2 as Graham's bound [7, 6] suggests). This highlights the fact that with unlimited processing resources, any work-greedy assignment is optimal. In practical terms, a work-greedy assignment is optimal if $m \geq n$.

We can also express in terms of $\pi$ a lower bound on the number of processors required to execute the task graph in the minimum possible time.

*A bound on the number of processors.* The number of processors required to finish executing all the tasks in the minimum possible time is bounded below by the ratio of the total execution time requirement of the tasks and the minimum makespan [14]. The total execution time requirement is $\sum \tau_i$ and the minimum possible makespan is $\tau^*$. A lower bound on the number of processors is thus given by

$$\left\lceil \frac{\sum \tau_i}{\tau^*} \right\rceil = \lceil \pi \rceil$$

That is, *any* (not necessarily work-greedy) assignment will require at least $\lceil \pi \rceil$ processors, if it is to execute the task graph in the minimum possible time.

Tighter lower bounds on the number of processors can be found in [4, 1].

## 3 Dependency Graphs with Arbitrary Computation and Communication Times

Assignments of dependency graphs with arbitrary computation and arbitrary communication times are characterized by $\mathcal{W} = $ (arbitrary, arbitrary, arbitrary). The assignment schemes ETF [9], ERT [11], MH [3] and MCP [19] fall under this characterization.

Hwang et al. [9] and Lee et al. [11] proved bounds on the makespans of ETF and ERT. They have proved that

$$\omega' \leq \left(2 - \frac{1}{m}\right)\omega^i + C_x$$

where $\omega'$ is the makespan of the work-greedy assignment (either ETF or ERT), $\omega^i$ is the makespan of the optimal assignment *without* considering communication delays, and $C_x$ is the communication delay along some chain in the task graph.

Expressing $\omega'$ in terms of $\omega^i$ does not reveal much. When giving a guarantee for the makespan of a certain assignment, it is more useful to give a guarantee in terms of $\omega$, the optimal makespan *not ignoring* the communication delay.

As in Theorem 1, the degree of average software parallelism can be incorporated into this bound so that the bound will be tighter.

Moreover, we note that the bound can be generalized for *all* the assignments characterized by $\mathcal{W} =$ (arbitrary, arbitrary, arbitrary). We thus present in the following theorem a generalized bound.

Let $\tau^*$ be the sum of execution times of tasks along the longest chain (ignoring communications) of the dependency graph and $\tau^+$ be $\sum \tau_i$; and let $\pi = \tau^+/\tau^*$. Then we have

**Theorem 2.**

$$\frac{\omega'}{\omega} \leq 1 + \frac{(m-1)}{\pi} + m\,\frac{C_{comm}}{\tau^+} \qquad \text{if } m < \pi$$

$$\frac{\omega'}{\omega} \leq 1 + \frac{(\pi-1)}{m} + \pi\,\frac{C_{comm}}{\tau^+} \qquad \text{if } m \geq \pi$$

*where $\omega$ is the length of the optimal makespan, that is not necessarily work-greedy; and $\omega'$ is the makespan of any arbitrary work-greedy assignment. $C_{comm}$ is the maximum communication delay along some chain of tasks.*

**Proof.**

The proof is similar to the one presented for Theorem 1.

For *any* (and thus, the optimal) assignment of makespan $\omega$, the following inequality holds true:

$$\omega \geq \max\left[\frac{\sum \tau_i}{m}, \tau^*\right] \qquad (8)$$

Let $\prec$ be the partial order on **T**. The rule of work-greedy assignments dictates that for any arbitrary work-greedy assignment of makespan $\omega'$ there exists a chain of tasks

$$T_{c1} \prec T_{c2} \prec \ldots \prec T_{cy}$$

such that at every time instant $t \in B$ some $T_{cj}$ is being executed or is waiting for input from $T_{cj-1}$ (that has finished executing) to start its execution. Here $B$ is the set of all points of time in $[0, \omega']$ for which at least one processor is idle.

Let $proc(T)$ be the processor that has been assigned the task $T$; and let $mtt(P_i, P_j)$ be the maximum time to transfer unit information from processor $P_i$ to processor $P_j$ (possibly via other processors). $C_{comm}$ is calculated as follows:
$$C_{comm} = \sum_{j=1}^{y-1} mtt(proc(T_{cj}), proc(T_{cj+1})) \times v(T_{cj}, T_{cj+1})$$
Let the sum of all the processor idle times in this assignment be $I$. Then,

$$I \leq m\left(\sum_{j=1}^{y} \tau_{cj} + C_{comm}\right) - \sum_{j=1}^{y} \tau_{cj} \qquad (9)$$

But for any chain in an assignment, the following inequality holds true:

$$\sum_{j=1}^{y} \tau_{cj} \le \tau^* \tag{10}$$

Now since

$$\omega' = \frac{1}{m}\left[\tau^+ + I\right]$$

using (9) and (10) we get,

$$\omega' \le \frac{\tau^+}{m} + \frac{(m-1)\tau^*}{m} + C_{comm} \tag{11}$$

When $\tau^+/m \ge \tau^*$, from (8) and (11) we get the bound:

$$\frac{\omega'}{\omega} \le 1 + \frac{m-1}{\pi} + m\,\frac{C_{comm}}{\tau^+} \tag{12}$$

When $\tau^* \ge \tau^+/m$, from (8) and (11) we get the bound:

$$\frac{\omega'}{\omega} \le 1 + \frac{\pi-1}{m} + \pi\,\frac{C_{comm}}{\tau^+} \tag{13}$$

Both (12) and (13) always hold true. However, when $m \ge \pi$ the bound of (13) is tighter, otherwise the bound of (12) is tighter.    □

*Construction of the chain.* The set of all points in time in the interval $[0, \omega']$ is divided into two subsets $A$ and $B$ as follows. $A$ is the set of points in time for which all processors are busy. $B$ is the set of points in time for which at least one processor is idle.

Let $\psi_i$ and $\phi_i$ denote respectively the start and finish times of $T_i$. The following algorithm constructs the chain.

1. Let the chain $C$ be an ordered set of tasks, set to null initially.
2. $T_a \leftarrow$ a task that finishes at time $\omega'$.
3. If $\psi_a \in B$,
   then there exists a processor which for some $\epsilon > 0$ is idle during the time interval $[\psi_a - \epsilon, \psi_a]$. This occurs only when there is a task $T_b$, an immediate predecessor of $T_a$, such that
   $$\phi_b + mtt(proc(T_a), proc(T_b))\, v(T_a, T_b)$$
   is equal to $\psi_a$. Insert $T_a$ into $C$, $T_a \leftarrow T_b$ and go to 3.
4. Let $u = $ l.u.b.[1] $\{x | x < \psi_a \text{ and } x \in B\}$. If $u$ is zero, output $C$ and stop.
5. Find a task $T_b$ such that
   $$\psi_b = \max_i\{\psi_i | T_i \text{ a predecessor of } T_a \text{ and } \psi_i < u\}.$$
   There is a sequence of tasks, $T_c, T_{j1}, \ldots T_{jz}$, such that $T_b \prec T_c \prec T_{j1} \prec \ldots \prec T_{jz} \prec T_a$. Insert $T_c$ into $C$, $T_a \leftarrow T_b$ and go to 3.

---

[1] Least upper bound

The maximum time to transfer information between processors depends as well on the underlying routing strategy and the network contention. These dependencies were ignored in the proof above.

Note that the communication factor that appears in our bound is smaller than those of Hwang et al. and Lee et al. Note also that our bound is applicable to all work-greedy assignments – not just ETF and ERT.

If communication costs can be ignored, then $C_{comm} = 0$. The bounds of Theorems 1 and 2 then match. Note that the value of $C_{comm}$ depends on the assignment. Good assignments will have small values of $C_{comm}$. Now if

$$C^* = \max_{i,j} \left[ mtt(P_i, P_j) \right]$$

$$\times \max_T \left[ \sum_{T_i, T_j \in T'; \ T_j = succ(T_i)} v_{ij} \right]$$

where $\mathbf{T}'$ is any chain in $G_T$ and $v_{ij}$ is the volume of information transfer between $T_i$ and $T_j$, then

$$C_{comm} \leq C^* \quad \text{for any chain.}$$

Thus the bounds of Theorem 2 become

$$\frac{\omega'}{\omega} \leq 1 + \frac{(m-1)}{\pi} + m\,\frac{C^*}{\tau^+} \qquad \text{if } m < \pi \tag{14}$$

$$\frac{\omega'}{\omega} \leq 1 + \frac{(\pi-1)}{m} + \pi\,\frac{C^*}{\tau^+} \qquad \text{if } m \geq \pi \tag{15}$$

These bounds are *not* assignment-dependent.

## 3.1 Dependency Graphs with Unit Computation and Communication Times

Assignments of dependency graphs with unit computation and unit communication times are characterized by $W = $ (unit, unit, arbitrary). For this characterization, Rayward-Smith [15] proves the following upper bound on the makespan $\omega$ of an arbitrary work-greedy assignment:

$$\omega \leq \left( 3 - \frac{2}{m} \right) \omega' - \left( 1 - \frac{1}{m} \right)$$

where $\omega'$ is the makespan of the optimal assignment.

# 4  Implications of the Bounds on Makespans

The hardware parallelism, $m$, and the degree of average software parallelism, $\pi$, have a symmetric relation in the bounds of Theorems 1 and 2. When $m > \pi$, the makespan may be limited by software 'sequentialism'; and when $\pi > m$ the makespan may be limited by hardware inadequacy. Note that, since $\pi$ is only a lower bound on software parallelism, we can find cases where $m \geq \pi$ and yet the makespan is limited by hardware inadequacy.

The loose bound of (7) suggests that, if communication costs can be ignored, the maximum speedup an assignment scheme can achieve is no more than 2. In other words, no assignment scheme can be worse than the optimal scheme by more than a factor of two. The bound by Rayward-Smith suggests that, if communication times are assumed to be unitary and if the computation times are also unitary, this factor of degradation is no more than 3. Thus it is seen that *any* work-greedy assignment scheme can be used for the assignment of

1. independent tasks
2. dependency graphs with zero communication times, and
3. dependency graphs with unit computation and communication times

and still a performance not worse than a small constant factor would be guaranteed.

However, if communication costs are arbitrary, the performance can degrade considerably with bad assignment schemes. In this case, from (14) and (15), we have the following loose bound:

$$\frac{\omega'}{\omega} \leq 2 + \lambda$$

$$\text{where } \lambda = \min(m, \pi) \frac{C^*}{\tau^+} = \frac{C^*}{\tau^+ / \min(m, \pi)}.$$

$\lambda$ signifies the communication to computation ratio along the critical path of the (arbitrary) assignment. Bad assignments will have large values of $\lambda$ and thus they will have a poor performance compared to the optimal assignment. For instance, a work-greedy assignment scheme that ignores the communication costs when the dependency graph *does* have communication requirements may yield a large value of $\lambda$.

## 5   Summary and Conclusions

The heuristics most of the current assignment schemes use is based on satisfying the following rule of thumb: keeping the processors busy leads to a 'good' assignment. Such schemes are said to be work-greedy. Work-greedy assignments are important since most of them provide a solution with a guarantee: it is proved that, when communication costs can be ignored, *any* work-greedy assignment would be close to the optimal assignment by no more than a small constant factor. It is also proved that, should the communication costs be taken into account, this factor may no longer be small. With communication costs, a work-greedy assignment can perform worse than the optimal assignment by a large factor. This factor depends on the communication costs along some path in the task graph. Therefore, if an assignment problem dictates that it involves possible communication delays, then the heuristic assignment schemes must take these delays into account in order to produce good assignments.

## Acknowledgments

To those anonymous referees whose feedback improved this paper.

# References

1. AL-MOUHAMED, M. A. Lower bound on the number of processors and time for scheduling precedence graphs with communication costs. *IEEE Transactions on Software Engineering 16*, 12 (December 1990), 1390–1401.
2. COFFMAN, E. G., Ed. *Computer and Job Shop Scheduling Theory.* John Wiley and Sons, 1976.
3. EL-REWINI, H., AND LEWIS, T. G. Scheduling parallel program tasks onto arbitrary target machines. *Journal of Parallel and Distributed Computing 9* (1990), 138–153.
4. FERNANDEZ, E. B., AND BUSSELL, B. Bounds on the number of processors and time for multiprocessor optimal schedules. *IEEE Transactions on Computers C-22*, 8 (August 1973), 745–751.
5. GERASOULIS, A., VENUGOPAL, S., AND YANG, T. Clustering task graphs for message passing architectures. In *Proceedings of the International Conference on Supercomputing.* ACM Press, Amsterdam, The Netherlands, June 11-15, 1990, pp. 447–456.
6. GRAHAM, R. L. Bounds on the performance of scheduling algorithms. In *Computer and Job Shop Scheduling Theory*, E. G. Coffman, Ed. John Wiley and Sons, 1976, pp. 165–227.
7. GRAHAM, R. L. Bounds on multiprocessing timing anomalies. *SIAM Journal of Applied Mathematics 17*, 2 (March 1969), 416–429.
8. GRAHAM, R. L., LAWLER, E. L., LENSTRA, J. K., AND KAN, A. H. G. R. Optimization and approximation in deterministic sequencing and scheduling: A survey. *Annals of Discrete Mathematics 3* (1979), 287–326.
9. HWANG, J.-J., CHOW, Y.-C., ANGER, F. D., AND LEE, C.-Y. Scheduling precedence graphs in systems with interprocessor communication times. *SIAM Journal of Computing 18*, 2 (April 1989), 244–257.
10. KRUATRACHUE, B., AND LEWIS, T. Duplication scheduling heuristics, a new precedence task scheduler for parallel systems. Tech. Rep. 87-60-3, Computer Science Department, Oregon State University, Corvallis OR, 1987.
11. LEE, C.-Y., HWANG, J.-J., CHOW, Y.-C., AND ANGER, F. D. Multiprocessor scheduling with interprocessor communication delays. *Operations Research Letters 7*, 3 (June 1988), 141–145.
12. MANOHARAN, S., AND THANISCH, P. Assigning dependency graphs onto processor networks. *Parallel Computing 17*, 1 (April 1991), 63–73.
13. MANOHARAN, S., AND TOPHAM, N. P. An assessment of assignment schemes for dependency graphs. *Parallel Computing 21*, 1 (January 1995), 85–1107.
14. MCNAUGHTON, R. Scheduling with deadlines and loss functions. *Management Science 6* (October 1959).
15. RAYWARD-SMITH, V. J. UET scheduling with unit interprocessor communication delays. *Discrete Applied Mathematics 18* (1987), 55–71.
16. SARKAR, V. *Partitioning and Scheduling Parallel Programs for Multiprocessors.* MIT Press, Cambridge MA, 1989.

17. ULLMAN, J. D. Complexity of sequencing problems. In *Computer and Job Shop Scheduling Theory*, E. G. Coffman, Ed. John Wiley and Sons, 1976, pp. 139–164.
18. VELTMAN, B., LAGEWEG, B. J., AND LENSTRA, J. K. Multiprocessor scheduling with communication delays. *Parallel Computing 16* (1990), 173–182.
19. WU, M.-Y., AND GAJSKI, D. D. A programming aid for hypercube architectures. *The Journal of Supercomputing 2*, 3 (November 1988), 349–372.

# A New Scheme for Dynamic Processor Assignment for Irregular Problems

Ranjan k Sen

Indian Institute of Technology

Kharagpur, India

We present an experimental study of a new approach for task assignment for irregularly structured problems under dynamic conditions. Our method is fast and gives solutions that are always close to those obtained for simulated annealing. The target parallel computer we have considered has the Boolean n-cube interconnection structure.

## 1    Introduction

An important phase in parallel computation is the assigning of processors with computational jobs. The overall computational load may be equipartitioned and assigned evenly among the available processors. This results in an even balancing of computational loads. However, the demand for interprocessor communication can considerably influence efficiency. This is particularly so for message oriented distributed memory multi-computers with different interconnection topologies.

Ideally, one would like to match the inter-task communication structure with the processor interconnection topology. A formal graph theory model of this problem was given by Bokhari [9]. The general mapping problem is more difficult than the subgraph isomorphism problem which is known to be NP complete [6]. Several graph embedding schemes for special source and target graphs have been found. For the general case numerous heuristic techniques, that includes randomized techniques such as simulated anealing, have been reported [5,7,10,11,13].

A basic feature of irregularly structured problems that are expected to run on a distributed memory parallel computer is the uncertainty of its structure. In this situation we can use heuristic techniques of the kind mentioned above or randomized techniques such as simualed anealing. The costs of the heuristic solutions are determined through standard benchmarks that are usually not representative of irregular problems. There is not guarnatee of the cost in general. Techniques such as simulated anealing takes considerable processing time and are not suitable for dynamic situations. What we need is a techniques that can ascertain bounded cost solutions in general and take acceptable processing time.

In this paper we propose a mapping scheme for the hypercube target computer that guarantees a bounded cost solution in general. The running time of the scheme is very low. Thus, our scheme is highly suitable for computations with irregular structure. Also, as the running time is low it can be used for remapping for cases that require dynamic mapping [16].

The mapping scheme is based on finding a maximum matching of a graph followed by isometric embedding on an n-cube. The work has been motivated by the availability of bounded error approximation algorithms for obtaining a suboptimal solution of maximum cut [2,3,18]. We focus on an objective function for the mapping that encodes only the cost of interprocessor communication. We assume that an even distribution of computation on to the processing nodes is made (without actual allocation of which processor has which task). The problem then reduces to that of optimzing the allocation of tasks to the processors so that communication overhead is minimized. The volume of interprocessor communication is determined by the extend of communication necessary between the processors. We simplify by assuming this to be unity. We can easily extend this to higher values by assuming parallel edges in the source graph (computational graph). The source graph is an undirected graph which represent the computation after the initial partition with respect to computational load has been made. In using resource costs we have used two simple objective functions. The first is that of maximization of cardinality [9] and the second is the minimization of the average of the lengths of the paths in the n-cube that connects communicating nodes.

## 2 The mapping problem

A parallel computation is characterised by a *problem graph* in which the vertices correspond to the tasks (parts of computation) and the edges to the data communication between the tasks. The weight of a task represents the computational load of the task. Similarly, the weight of an edge gives the relative amount of communication between the two tasks. The parallel computer can also be represented as a graph, called the *host graph*. Both the source and the host graphs are undirected. The vertices in the host graph correspond to the processors and the edges represent communication links. The mapping problem is that of determining a suitable map that assigns the vertices of the problem graph to those of the host graph. One common objective function used in early works on mapping is the maximization of the number of edges of the problem graph that have adjacent images of the end vertices in the host graph (cardinality)[9]. Later, various other objective functions were used [8]. In [12] Shen and Tsai minimizes the maximum turnaround time over all processors. Turnaround time for a processor is given by the sum of the computation and communication load. Another type of objective function used is based on minimization of the communication load over all the processors while the computational load is allowed to vary by a small amount [5]. A widely suggested approach based on computational characteristics inherently assumes an identifiable structure. Techniques of graph transformation, searching for match between data dependencies with stored library communication patterns are known [10].

In general, assume that a parallel computation, comprising of a set P of tasks, is to be run on a parallel computer with $p$ processors. One may first find a partition, $P = \{P_0, P_1, ..P_p\}$. The partition can be guided by an even distribution of the computation load accross the entire system of processors. Corresponding to a mapping $M$, where a block $P_i$ is assigned to processor, say $q$ (formally, $M(P_i) = q$), the computational load associated with processor $q$ is given by $WL_q = \sum_{j \in P_i} w_j$ and $w_j$ is the weight associated with the vertex corresponding to task $j$. The ideal average computational load is $\overline{WL} = (1/p) \times \sum_{i=1}^{p} WL_i$ [5].

In the above formulation communication accross two blocks of a partition is given by the sum of the weights associated with the edges having one end in one block and the other in another. Corresponding to mapping $M$ which associates a block $P_i$ to processor $q$, the communication load is $CL_q(M) = \sum_{i \in P_i, j \in P_j} c_{ij} \times d_{M(i)M(j)}$, where $M(P_i) = q, M(P_j) \neq q$, $c_{ij}$ is the weight associated with edge $(i, j)$, and $d_{pq}$ corresponds to the cost of transmitting between processors $p$ and $q$. In our formulation we assume that $d_{pq}$ depends upon the length of the shortest path between vertices corresponding to processors $p$ and $q$ in the host graph.

Usually, the objective function is given by:

$Cost(M) = k_e \times$ communication overhead $+ k_c \times$ computational load imbalance, where $k_e$ and $k_c$ are respectively parameters used for balancing the computational and communication overheads.

The approach we take is as follows. We partition the computation such that each block represent equivalent (or nearly) computational load. This resolves the problem of load balancing. The problem of balancing communication is treated independently after this. Under this situation the objective function needs to encode the cost of interprocessor communication. Thus, we have for an idealized mapping

$$O = min_M (\sum_q CL_q(M)),$$

subject to the load balancing contraint given by

$$\frac{|WL_q - \overline{WL}|}{\overline{WL}} \leq tol,$$

where, $tol$ is a tolerance limit and $1 \leq q \leq p$.

Suppose that a different mapping $M'$ ensures

$$|\sum_q CL_q(M') - O| \le \beta \times O.$$

where, $\beta < 1$. In this case the communication overhead is more than the minimum that is achievable by solving the optimization problem exactly by factor $\beta$. The crucial observation here is that if one can have a mapping scheme that ensures the above inequality to hold then it may be possible to readjust the computation and communication load properly. This strategy of tolerating a bounded deviation from the optimum communication cost in order to deal with the general mapping problem may be viewed complementary to that of allowing a computing load imbalance as in [5].

## 3 Mapping by simulated annealing

In solving the general mapping problem the simulated annealing technique can be used [14,15]. However, the technique is very time consuming making it impossible to be applied in a dynamic mapping situation. We used a mapping scheme based on simulated annealing in order to compare the results we obtain for the fast bounded quality mapping scheme proposed in this paper.

The simulated annealing algorithm is to provide an efficient simulation of the behavior of a collection of atoms in equilibrium. In each step of this algorithm, an atom is given a small random displacement and the resulting change $\Delta E$, in the energy of the system is computed. If $\Delta E \le 0$, the displacement is accepted and the configuration resulting of this displacement is accepted as the starting point of next step. The case $\Delta E > 0$, is treated probabilistically. The acceptance of the configuration resulting from the acceptance of this uphill move is determined by a probability $\exp(-\Delta E/k_B T)$, which is dependent on the temperature T. This is called Metropolis criterion [15].

The basic simulated annealing algorithm used by us is given below. $\Delta C_{ij}$ is the incremental cost in shifting from configuration $config_i$ to $config_j$.

## Simulated annealing
**begin**
        Initialize; M = 0;
        **repeat**
            **repeat**
                PERTURB($config_i \rightarrow config_j, \Delta C_{ij}$)

```
                if ΔC_ij > 0
                    then accept
                else
                        if exp(-ΔC_ij/c_M) > random(0,1)
                            then accept;
                    if accept
                            then UPDATE(config_j);
                until (equilibrium is almost reached );
                c_{M+1} = f(c_M);
                M = M + 1;
        until (stop_criterion is true);
end
```

An energy state of the system may correspond to a mapping. The process of annealing is simulated by random moves of particles. This has correspondence to a new processor allocation by a random reassignment. The particle movement may take the system to either a higher (uphill) or a lower (downhill) energy state. In the mapping context this corresponds to a higher or lower value of the cost function.

The initial temperature is determined in such a way that all possible uphill moves are accepted with a high probability. This paves the way for a high randomization of the allocation given. We have taken the expected probability of acceptance to be 0.9. A random modification to the processor allocation is made. The uphill moves and downhill moves are counted. If the total number of moves are $m$, with downhill and uphill moves respectively being $m_d$ and $m_u$, and the average increase in the cost for all uphill moves is $\Delta$, the initial temperature $T_i$ is found from: $X = (m_d + \exp(-\Delta/T_i)m_u)/m$, where X is the expected probability of acceptance at temperature $T_i$. The number of possible moves from a given configuration is given as follows. For a transition, we take up a task and a free processor randomly and reassign this task. If we have $|V|$ tasks initially and MAX is the number of processors, we could select a task randomly in $|V|$ ways, and choose a free processor in MAX - $|V|$ ways. The total number of neighboring configurations for a given configuration thus becomes $|V|$ * ( MAX - $|V|$). We make as many number of moves as necessary to reach quasi-equilibrium. Once a quasi-equilibrium is reached, the temperature is reduced by a factor $\alpha$. We took $\alpha$ to be 0.95. The final temperature is chosen in such a way that an uphill move with a cost increase by one is accepted with a very high probability.

# 4 A new mapping scheme

The mapping scheme porposed by us is best viewed as a three-phased heuristic algorithm. The host graph considered is the Boolean n-cube. In the first phase a large bipartite subgraph of the problem graph is obtained. In the second, a mapping of the bipartite graph into the n-cube is made. This gives a set of edges of the problem graph which are not mapped into n-cube edges. In the third phase paths in the n-cube for these edges are obtained. As mentioned before, the chief characteristic of this algorithm is that a bounded cost solution is obtained within a very short time.

## 4.1 Largest bipartite spanning subgraph.

The problem of recognizing the largest bipartite spanning subgraph is the same as that of obtaining a maximum cut where the term largest stands for the maximized sum of the weights of the edges. Finding a maximum cut of a graph is NP complete for general graphs [4,6]. The maximum cut optimization problem is in the MAX SNP class of problems for which it is not possible to design an approximation scheme [1]. Nevertheless, approximation algorithms with constant bound has been developed recently for this problem [2,3,18]. There is a deterministic approach for an approximation algorithm for maximum cut of a graph based on spanning tree [18]. In finding a largest bipartite spanning subgraph we make use of the method based on spanning tree.

Consider the simple maximum cut problem (which is also NP complete [6]) in which the edge weights are one. Each spanning tree defines a set of fundamental cycles corresponding to the non-tree edges. Among all the spanning trees consider one for which the number of odd length fundamental cycles is the minimum. A maximum cut can be obtained simply by deleting the non-tree edges that give the odd length fundamental cycles corresponding to this tree. The approximation algorithm for maximum cut we use is based on finding a spanning tree efficiently for which the number of odd fundamental cycles is close to the minimum. We consider a rooted directed spanning tree $T_u$ of $G$. Let $u$ be the root. Let $d(x,T)$, called the level of vertex $x$ in $T_u$, be the length of the path from $u$ to $x$ in $T_u$. Then, edge $(x,y) \in E(G)$, the edge set of $G$ ($(x,y)$ is a non-tree edge), defines an odd (even) fundamental cycle if and only if $\mid d(x,T_u) - d(y,T_u) \mid$ is even (odd). Call a non-tree edge that gives an even (odd) length fundamental cycle to be lattice (cross) edge.

Given a spanning tree $T_u$, under certain situations, another spanning tree with a lesser number of odd fundamental cycles (in the corresponding set of fundamental cycle) can be generated. Define function $\Delta : V \times T \rightarrow I$, where $T$ is the set of all spanning trees of $G$. For vertex $v$ let $\eta_v$ and $\omega_v$ be the number of even and odd fundamental cycles corresponding to spanning tree $T_u$ that contain vertex $v$. Then, $\Delta(v, T_u) = \omega_v - \eta_v$.

Define matrix $D(T_u) = [d_{ij}]$, where $d_{ij}$, $i \neq j$ and neither $v_i$ nor $v_j$ is a descendant of the other, is the difference of the number of cross and the lattice edges between descendants of $v_i$ and $v_j$ of $T_u$. In case one of the two vertices, say $v_i$, is a descendant of the other, $v_j$, then $d_{ij}$ is the difference of the cross and lattice edges between descendant of $v_i$ and a vertex in $T_j - T_i$, where $T_i$ and $T_j$ represents the subtrees rooted at $v_i$ and $v_j$ respectively. Note, $D$ is a symmetric matrix with $d_{ij} = d_{ji}$. The value of $d_{ii}$ is

$$d_{ii} = \sum_{j \in child(i)} d_{ji} - \sum_{j,j' \in child(i)} d_{jj'} + \sum_{j \in child(i)} d_{jj}.$$

The values of $d_{ii}$ for leaf $v_i$ is 0. The value of $d_{ij}$ where both of $v_i$ and $v_j$ are leaves is 1 or 0 if there is an edge $(v_i, v_j)$ or not respectively.

The weight of the cut (number of edges) corresponding to tree $T_u$ is given by

$$e - \frac{d_{uu} + \mu}{2},$$

and $\mu = e - t + 1$ is the nullity of $G$, where $t$ and $e$ are the number of vertices and edges in the problem graph $G$.

Note that, $\Delta(v, T_u) = d_{vu}$. For vertex $v$ with respect to spanning tree $T_u$, the value of $\Delta(v, T_u)$ is called the weight of $v$ with respect to $T_u$. If

(A) $$\Delta(v, T_u) > w(v, v'),$$

where $v'$ is the parent of $v$ in $T_u$, then $(v, v')$ is interchanged with a cross edge $(i, j)$ where $i$ is in $T_v$ (descendant of $v$ in $T_u$) and $j$ is not. This gives a new spanning tree $T'_u$ in which vertex $v$ has a new parent $j$ ($j$ gets a new child) and vertex $v'$, the initial parent of $v$ in $T_u$, looses child $v$. The matrix $D(T'_u)$ corresponding to the new tree $T'_u$ can be computed in $O(n^2)$ time from the matrix elements of $D(T_u)$.

Note, $D(T'_u) < D(T_u)$. Thus, one can continue to transform a spanning tree to get an improved solution as long as condition (A) is valid for it. This would give an improved solution. When finally, a spanning tree $T_\alpha$ for which condition (A) is no more valid is obtained it gives an approximation solution to the maximum cut. The invalidity of (A) is a necessary condition for the spanning tree to give a maximum cut. In [18] it has been shown that a bounded error sub-optimal solution to maximum cut can be obtained.

In our scheme a breadth-first search tree is used as the initial spanning tree. A breadth-first spanning tree has been chosen because the convergence to the solution is usually fast with it. The level of a vertex in a breadth first spanning tree is one greater than that of its parent. The level of the root is 0. An edge $(i, j)$ in the problem graph is a *cross edge* if and only if the levels of $i$ and $j$ differ by an even number. Similarly, An edge $(i, j)$ in the problem graph is a *lattice edge* if and only if level of $i$ and $j$ differ by an odd number. This makes the computation relatively easier.

Among all vertices that satisfies condition (A) one with maximum weight is selected. Let this vertex be $x$. Now, a cross edge $(i, j)$ going out of subtree $T_x$ is selected where $i \in T_x$. From the spanning tree $T$ the new spanning tree $T'$ is obtained by cyclically interchanging edge $(x, parent(x))$ with $(i, j)$. The spaning tree $T'$ the vertices in $T_x$ are descendants of the vertex $i$.

The spanning trees are repeatedly transformed until a final spanning tree $T_\alpha$ is obtained for which condition (A) does not hold for any vertex in it. The set of cross edges with respect to $T_\alpha$ is denoted by $C(T_\alpha)$. The bipartite graph is given by $G_b = (V, E - C(T_\alpha))$.

## 4.2 Mapping a Bipartite Graph into Boolean n-cube.

A Boolean n-cube is a bipartite graph consisting of $2^n$ vertices labeled 0 through $2^{n-1}$ in binary code. Two vertices of an n-cube are connected by an edge if and only if their labels differ in exactly one bit position. The degree and diameters are $n$ each. The distance between any two vertices of the n-cube is the Hamming distance between the corresponding codes. We could trace the path between any two vertices by starting from the label of one vertex and flipping the differing bits until we get to the label of the other vertex. The intermediate labels are those of the nodes in the path between the two vertices.

Given a graph $G = (V, E)$, let G be called a k-level graph with respect to vertex $u \in V$ if and only if $V$ can be partitioned into $k$ independent sets $V_0, V_1, ...V_{k-1}$, where $V_0 = \{u\}$, $E \subseteq \{(x, y) \mid x \in V_i, y \in V_{i+1}, i = 0, 1, ..k - 2\}$. Let $S_{x,i}$ denote the set $\{A(x) \cap V_{i-1}\}$, where, $x \in V_i$ and $A(x)$ is the neighbors of $x$. Also, $A(B)$ is the union of the neighbors of all the vertices in $B$.

Testing if $G$ is an n-cube or not can be done in $O(n \log n)$ time [17]. A k-level bipartite graph is an n-cube if and only if $k = n + 1$ and $\mid V_i \mid =^n C_i, i = 0, 1, 2, ..n$ and for each $x \in V_{i+1}, i = 1, 2, ...n$, $S_{x,i+1}$ is unique, $\mid S_{x,i+1} \mid = i + 1$ and for each $y, z \in S_{x,i+1}, \mid \{S_{y,i} \cap S_{z,i}\} \mid = 1$.

A label is a string of n bits ( a bit is either a 0 or a 1). $l(x)$ is the label of vertex $x$. The index of a label is the number of 1's in it. The symbol $l(B)$ represents the labels of vertices in set $B$ and $\cup l(B)$ is the OR of these labels. Let $label \in L_p$. Then, $L_q(label), p < q$ is the set of labels in $L_q$ given by $L_q(label) = \{l' \in L_q \mid$ i-th bit of $label = 1$ implies i-th bit of $l' = 1, 1 \le i \le n$} If $q - p = k$ then there are $n-p C_k$ elements in $L_q(label)$. The set $L_q(label)$ can be easily found out. Let $L_i$ be a group of labels, $0 \le i \le n$, containing $^n C_i$ distinct labels as binary strings of index $i$.

Consider a set of vertices $B$ each assigned labels from $L_p$. Let $label \in L_q$, where $p < q$. Then, let $B(label) = \{x \in B \mid$ there is at least one $i, 1 \le i \le n$, where the i-th bit of $l(x)$ is 1 and the i-th bit of label is 0}. Note that $\cup l(B - B(label)) = label$.

The algorithm for mapping a bipartite graph into an n-cube is now given. This algorithm is an extension of the algorithm TEST given in [17] for testing a graph for an n-cube. Let the number of levels in the level representation of the input bipartite graph be $k$, where $k \le n$. The following algorithm assigns labels to the vertices of the bipartite graph iteratively. Initially, all the n labels are assumed to be unassigned to any vertex. The initial value of $n$ (for the n-cube host) is determined by the maximum of the maximum degree of a vertex and the maximum number of vertices in a level $\mid V_i \mid, i = 0, 1, 2, ..k$ of the input bipartite graph.

## Isocube
**begin**

> Initialize; $V_0 := \{u\}$; $l(u) := L_0$; $R := V - \{u\}$;
> **for** $i := 0$ step 1 until $k - 1$ **do**
> $V_{i+1} := A(V_i) \cap R$
>> **if**$\mid V_{i+1} \mid \le \, ^n C_{i+1} \, 0$
>> **then for** each vertex $v \in V_{i+1}$ **do** {assign labels}
>> **begin**
>> $B := A(v) \cap V_i$
>> **if** $\mid B \mid \le i + 1$ **then do**
>> **begin** $label := \cup l(B)$
>> $q := index(label)$
>> **if** $q \le i + 1$ **then if** possible
>> find $label' \in L_{i+1}(label)$ that is not yet
>> assigned to any vertex and assign it to $v$
>> **else** increase dimension of cube
>> **end**
>> **else if** possible find $label'' \in L_{i+1}$
>> which is not yet assigned to any vertex such that
>> $label \in L_q(label'')$. Assign $label''$ to $v$.
>> For each vertex $x \in B(label'')$ put edge $(v, x)$ into RE
>> (Remainder Edge set)

```
        else  increase dimension of cube
        else  increase dimension of cube
        end
    else  increase dimension of cube
    endfor end
```

It is well known that the subgraph isomorphism problem is NP complete for the n-cube. The algorithm given above, however, ensures that a subgraph isomorphic to the n-cube is obtained having at least half the edges in the input bipartie graph.

Consider finding a subgraph of $K_{n,n}$, the completely connected bipartite graph with $n$ vertices in each side of the partition, isomorphic to the n-cube. There are two levels in the level representation of $K_{n,n}$. There is a single vertex in $V_0$, $n$ vertices in $V_1$ and $n-1$ vertices in $V_2$ respectively. There are therefore $n(n-1)$ edges between $V_1$ and $V_2$. According to n-cube characteristics a vertex in $V_2$ can be adjacent to at most two vertices in $V_1$. Moreover, a distinct pair of vertices in $V_1$ is adjacent to a unique vertex in $V_2$. Therefore, there can be at most $n(n-1)/2$ edges put in RE by algorithm Isocube.

# 5   Fast Bounded Mapping

The mapping scheme we present here uses the methods discussed in sections 4.1 and 4.2 respectively to obtain a near maximum bipartite subgraph of the problem graph and a mapping of this bipartite subgraph into an n-cube. The edges of the problem graph in $C(T_\alpha)$ and the subset of the lattice edges that are saved in the set RE are not mapped to any edge of the n-cube. This implies that these edges will have dilation greater than one for the n-cube host graph. Note, the minimum dilation for an edge in $C(T_\alpha)$ and RE are respectively two and three. The maximum dilation is n. The paths can be easily found.

The phases of the mapping algorithm are given below. The overall algorithm is called the 3-phase heuristics.

**Phase 1:**   Obtain a spanning tree. Apply transformations to obtain spanning tree $T_\alpha$.

**Phase 2:**   Form a bipartite subgraph of $G$ by discarding edges in $C(T_\alpha)$ from $G$. Map the bipartite graph into the n-cube.

**Phase 3:** Determine paths in n-cube for edges in $C(T_\alpha)$ and RE directly from allocation in Phase 2.

In phase 1 above the number of edges in $C(T_\alpha)$ is bounded by a constant fraction of the number of edges $e$ in $G$. This is a direct consequence of the approximation algorithm used to obtain the bipartite graph. In phase 2 the number of edges in RE is also bounded. This has been shown to hold for $K_{n,n}$. The analysis can also be done for other bipartite graphs for which this bound is less. The number of edges in RE for $K_{n,n}$ is bounded by .5e. This is also the worst case cardinality cost of the mapping. Now, in phase 3, the dilation in the worst case for a cross or lattice edge in $C(T_\alpha)$ or RE is $n$. This happens when all the $n$ bits of the labels need to be flipped.

The sum of the dilation of the edges of the problem graph $G$ when mapped into the n-cube according to the above mapping algorithm is $\frac{e(1+t)}{2}$, where $t$ and $e$ are the number of vertices and edges in $G$. Since the number of edges in RE is .5e, the average dilation is $.5(1+n)$.

The above worst case results are not at all attractive. However, the results of the experiments with random problem graphs we have run are more encouraging.

# 6  Experimental Results

Table 1 gives the sum of path lengths for random problem graphs with 100 to 200 vertices with differing densities. Table 2 gives the sum of path lengths for random problem graphs of same sizes and densities for the 3-phase heuristics. The running times for the 3-phase heuristics is given in the last column. The corresponding running time for simulated anealing is almost always more than 10,000 times that of the values in this column.

For the 3-phase heuristics the the standard deviation for a random graph of 200 vertices with density 2.0 is 5.85 while that with density 1.5 is as high as 20.87. In case of simulated annealing the corresponding values are 11.39 and 3.94 respectively. If these figures are acceptable the 3-phase heuristics is preferrable to simulated annealing because of its very low running time. Results of a random mapping is given in Table.3. It shows the necessity of systematic mapping schemes.

Table 4 and 5 give the cardinality costs for the simulated annealing and 3-phase heuristics algorithms. In this case the standard deviation is similar. It can be observed that the deviation in cost for the solutions is low for sparser (of lower densities) graphs. For example, for the 200 vertex case it is 15% and about 40% for densities 1.5 and 2.5 respectively. In these cases also the running time for simulated anealing is more than 10,000 times than that for the 3-phase heuristics.

We expect that the main usefulness of the 3-phase heuristics would be in dynamic mapping. We have conducted exhaustive experiments to investigate how does it perform when the input problems graphs are modified by 50%. Table 6 gives the details of errors (compared to simulated annealing) in the solutions initially and after the modifications. The errors seem to remain the same in most cases. In some cases it is reduced by a factor of two to three.

# 7 Conclusion

In this paper we report an experimental study of using a new scheme for processor assignment and compared the solutions with those obtained through simulated annealing. We find that the proposed scheme is very fast and produces solutions that are very close to those obtained by simulated annealing. We have conducted our experiments exhaustively with random graphs of varying densities. We have also conducted experiments with random graphs which varies in structure. We find that the scheme is suitable for irregualr graphs and can be applied when the communication graph dynamically changes in structure.

The experimental results show that the proposed scheme is effective for dynamic computational environments. In particular the 3-phase heuristics scheme guarantees degrated but guaranteed performance for random structures. Further study in this direction is in progress. **References**

1. C.H.Papadimitriou, M. Yannakakis, *Optimization, Approximation and Complexity Classes*, JCSS, 43 (1991), 425-440.

2. M.X.Goemans, D.P.Williamson, *.878-Approximation Algorithm for MAX CUT and MAX 2SAT*, accepted in STOC 94.

3. D.J. Haglin and S.M. Venkatesan, *Approximation and Intractability results for the maximum cut problem and its variants*, IEEE TC, 40 (1991), 110-113.

4. R.M. Karp, *Reducibility among combinatorial problems*, In R.Miller and J. Thatcher, editors, Complexity of Computer Computations, Plenum Press, NY, (1972), 85-103.

5. R. Ercal, J. Ramanujam, R. Sadyappan, *Task Allocation onto a Hypercube by Recursive Mincut Bipartitioning*, JPDC, 10 (1990), 35-44.

6. M.R. Garey, D.H.Johnson, *Computers and Intractability: A guide to the theory of NP-completeness*, W.H.Freeman and Company, (1979).

7. F. Berman, L. Snyder, *On mapping parallel algorithms into parallel architectures*, JPDC, 4 (1987), 429-458.

8. V. Chaudhary, J.K. Aggarwal, *A Generalized Scheme for Mapping Parallel Algorithms*, IEEE PDS, Vol.4. No.3. (1993), 328-346.

9. S.H. Bokhari, *On the mapping problem*, IEEE TC, Vol.C-30, No.3 (1981), 207-214.

10. S.J. Kim, J.C. Browne, *A general approach to mapping of parallel computations upon multiprocessor architectures*, in Prof. Int. Conf. Parallel Processing, (1988), 1-8.

11. K. Efe, *Heuristic models of task assignment scheduling in distributed systems*, IEEE Comput. Mag., Vol.15 (1982), 50-56.

12. C.C.Shen, W.H.Tsai, *A graph matching approach to optimal task assignment in distributed computing systems using a minimax criterion*, IEEE TC, Vol.C-34. No.3. (1985), 197-203.

13. V.M.Lo, *Heuristic algorithms for task assignment in distributed systems*, IEEE TC, Vol.C-37. No.11. (1988), 1384-1397.

14. S.Kirkpatrick, C.D.Gelatt, M.P.Vecchi, *Optimization by simulated annealing*, Science, 220 (1983), 671-680.

15. N. Metropolis, A. Rosenbluth, M. Rosenbluth, A. Teller, E.Teller, *Equation of state calculations by fast computing machines*, J. Chem. Phys., 21 (1953), 1087-1092.

16. D.M. Nicol, *Dynamic remapping of parallel computations with varying resource demands*, IEEE TC, Vol.C-37. No.9. (1988), 1073-1087.

17. K.V.S.Bhat, *On the complexity of testing a graph for a N-cube*, Inf. Prof. Letters, Vol.11. No.1 (1980), 16-19.

18. R.K.Sen, *On maximum Edge Deletion Bipartite Subgraph Problem*, Congressus Numerantum, Vol.74. (1990), 38-54.

**Table 1: Mapping by Simulated annealing for summation of path lengths**

| $|V|$ | $|E|/|V|$ ratio | Cost | | | Std. Deviation |
|---|---|---|---|---|---|
| | | Min | Mean | Max | |
| 100 | 1.5 | 201 | 205 | 213 | 4.61 |
| | 2.0 | 314 | 319 | 327 | 5.34 |
| | 2.5 | 433 | 447 | 454 | 8.57 |
| 140 | 1.5 | 283 | 288 | 292 | 3.81 |
| | 2.0 | 455 | 458 | 461 | 2.35 |
| | 2.5 | 631 | 643 | 659 | 10.05 |
| 170 | 1.5 | 350 | 354 | 358 | 3.77 |
| | 2.0 | 558 | 566 | 579 | 8.26 |
| | 2.5 | 786 | 792 | 798 | 5.32 |
| 200 | 1.5 | 429 | 433 | 439 | 3.94 |
| | 2.0 | 663 | 680 | 691 | 11.39 |
| | 2.5 | 931 | 944 | 953 | 8.03 |

**Table 2: Mapping by 3-phase heuristics for summation of path lengths**

| $|V|$ | $|E|/|V|$ ratio | Cost | | | Std. Deviation | No. of Iterations | Time (sec) |
|---|---|---|---|---|---|---|---|
| | | Min | Mean | Max | | | |
| 100 | 1.5 | 288 | 297 | 307 | 8.79 | 5 | 1 |
| | 2.0 | 446 | 467 | 491 | 16.08 | 5 | 0 |
| | 2.5 | 636 | 648 | 664 | 11.51 | 13 | 1 |
| 140 | 1.5 | 422 | 436 | 450 | 10.01 | 5 | 1 |
| | 2.0 | 679 | 687 | 695 | 6.08 | 7 | 0 |
| | 2.5 | 921 | 946 | 959 | 15.09 | 13 | 3 |
| 170 | 1.5 | 507 | 526 | 544 | 14.57 | 6 | 1 |
| | 2.0 | 831 | 847 | 861 | 11.81 | 16 | 4 |
| | 2.5 | 1188 | 1209 | 1228 | 14.85 | 12 | 3 |
| 200 | 1.5 | 614 | 637 | 671 | 20.87 | 11 | 3 |
| | 2.0 | 1014 | 1023 | 1029 | 5.85 | 12 | 7 |
| | 2.5 | 1420 | 1431 | 1442 | 8.57 | 15 | 6 |

**Table 3: Random mapping**

| $|V|$ | $|E|$ ratio | Cost Cardinality | Cost Summed comn. |
|---|---|---|---|
| 100 | 1.5 | 9 | 624 |
| | 2.0 | 8 | 816 |
| | 2.5 | 6 | 1035 |
| 140 | 1.5 | 6 | 856 |
| | 2.0 | 8 | 1155 |
| | 2.5 | 10 | 1437 |
| 170 | 1.5 | 13 | 1065 |
| | 2.0 | 11 | 1379 |
| | 2.5 | 16 | 1768 |
| 200 | 1.5 | 13 | 1228 |
| | 2.0 | 17 | 1619 |
| | 2.5 | 19 | 2053 |

**Table 4: Mapping by Simulated annealing for cardinality**

| $|V|$ | $|E|/|V|$ ratio | Cost | | | Std. Deviation |
|---|---|---|---|---|---|
| | | Min | Mean | Max | |
| 100 | 1.5 | 114 | 114 | 115 | 0.82 |
| | 2.0 | 131 | 134 | 137 | 2.45 |
| | 2.5 | 143 | 146 | 148 | 1.87 |
| 140 | 1.5 | 156 | 159 | 163 | 2.96 |
| | 2.0 | 174 | 180 | 186 | 4.27 |
| | 2.5 | 198 | 201 | 205 | 3.08 |
| 170 | 1.5 | 189 | 193 | 199 | 4.32 |
| | 2.0 | 216 | 219 | 221 | 1.87 |
| | 2.5 | 238 | 241 | 246 | 3.43 |
| 200 | 1.5 | 216 | 222 | 228 | 4.90 |
| | 2.0 | 253 | 254 | 257 | 1.66 |
| | 2.5 | 271 | 278 | 283 | 4.44 |

**Table 5: Mapping by 3-phase heuristics for cardinality**

| $|V|$ | $|E|/|V|$ ratio | Cost | | | Std. Deviation | No. of Iterations | Time (sec) |
|---|---|---|---|---|---|---|---|
| | | Min | Mean | Max | | | |
| 100 | 1.5 | 94 | 97 | 100 | 2.12 | 5 | 1 |
| | 2.0 | 101 | 101 | 102 | 0.87 | 5 | 0 |
| | 2.5 | 107 | 107 | 109 | 1.12 | 13 | 1 |
| 140 | 1.5 | 126 | 133 | 138 | 4.44 | 5 | 0 |
| | 2.0 | 138 | 139 | 141 | 1.32 | 7 | 1 |
| | 2.5 | 143 | 145 | 148 | 2.06 | 13 | 2 |
| 170 | 1.5 | 163 | 166 | 169 | 2.40 | 6 | 2 |
| | 2.0 | 169 | 171 | 174 | 1.87 | 16 | 4 |
| | 2.5 | 173 | 176 | 179 | 2.24 | 12 | 3 |
| 200 | 1.5 | 187 | 189 | 194 | 3.16 | 11 | 3 |
| | 2.0 | 199 | 200 | 202 | 1.22 | 12 | 6 |
| | 2.5 | 203 | 206 | 208 | 2.12 | 15 | 5 |

**Table 6: Dynamic mapping for cardinality**

| $|V|$ | $|E|/|V|$ | Initially | | | After 50% Modification | | |
|---|---|---|---|---|---|---|---|
| | | Heuristic | SA | %Error | Heuristic | SA | %Error |
| 100 | 1.5 | 97 | 114 | 14.91 | 163 | 192 | 15.90 |
| | 2.0 | 101 | 134 | 24.63 | 167 | 222 | 24.77 |
| | 2.5 | 107 | 146 | 26.71 | 170 | 231 | 26.41 |
| 140 | 1.5 | 133 | 159 | 16.35 | 222 | 254 | 12.60 |
| | 2.0 | 139 | 180 | 22.70 | 238 | 294 | 19.05 |
| | 2.5 | 145 | 201 | 27.86 | 239 | 306 | 21.90 |
| 170 | 1.5 | 166 | 193 | 13.99 | 245 | 254 | 3.54 |
| | 2.0 | 171 | 219 | 21.92 | 256 | 303 | 15.51 |
| | 2.5 | 176 | 243 | 27.57 | 256 | 311 | 17.68 |
| 200 | 1.5 | 189 | 222 | 14.86 | 237 | 256 | 7.42 |
| | 2.0 | 200 | 254 | 21.26 | 244 | 294 | 17.01 |
| | 2.5 | 206 | 278 | 25.90 | 254 | 318 | 20.13 |

# An Efficient Mean Field Annealing Formulation for Mapping Unstructured Domains to Hypercubes

Cevdet Aykanat and Ismail Haritaoglu

Computer Engineering Department, Bilkent University, Ankara, Turkey
aykanat@cs.bilkent.edu.tr

Abstract. We propose an efficient MFA formulation for mapping unstructured domains to hypercube-connected distributed-memory architectures. In the general MFA formulation, $N \times P$ spin variables are maintained and an individual MFA iteration requires $\Theta(q_{av} \cdot P + d^2)$ time for the mapping of a sparse domain graph with $N$ vertices and average vertex degree of $d_{av}$, to a parallel architecture with $P$ processors. The proposed hypercube-specific MFA formulation asymptotically reduces the number of spin variables and the computational complexity of an individual MFA iteration to $N \lg P$ and $\Theta(d_{av} + \lg P)(\lg P)$, respectively, by exploiting the topological properties of hypercubes.

## 1   Introduction

Parallelization schemes for many applications or distributed memory architectures are characterized by the mapping of the problem domain to processor with locality of communication. These schemes employ data parallelism by breaking the data structures supporting a computation into pieces and then assign those pieces to different processors. These decomposition and assignment tasks constitute the domain mapping problem [2]. The objective in the domain mapping is to find a mapping which minimizes the communication overhead while maintaining the same workload for each processor. Problem domain representing the data structure is represented with an undirected graph $G = (V, E)$ referred here as domain graph. Vertices $v \in V$ represent atomic computations (tasks) which can be executed simultaneously and independently. Vertex weight $w_i$ denotes the estimated computational cost of task $i$. Each edge $(i, j) \in E$ denotes the need for the bidirectional interaction between tasks $i$ and $j$. Edge weight $e_{ij}$ denotes the volume of interaction between tasks $i$ and $j$ connected by edge $(i, j) \in E$. This graph usually represents the repeated execution of the computations corresponding to the vertices $i \in V$ intervening partial result exchanges denoted by the edges. An edge incurs interprocessor communication only if the respective pair of computations are mapped to two different processors. Simultaneous single-hop communication between distinct adjacent pairs of processors can be performed concurrently. However, multi-hop communications between distant pairs of processors may require to migration to the interconnection network, thus increasing the communication overhead. Multi-hop

---

This work is partially supported by the Commission of the European Communities, Directorate General for Industry under contract ITDC 204 82366

# An Efficient Mean Field Annealing Formulation for Mapping Unstructured Domains to Hypercubes *

Cevdet Aykanat and İsmail Haritaoğlu

Computer Engineering Department, Bilkent University, Ankara, Turkey
aykanat@cs.bilkent.edu.tr

**Abstract.** We propose an efficient MFA formulation for mapping unstructured domains to hypercube-connected distributed-memory architectures. In the general MFA formulation, $N \times P$ spin variables are maintained and an individual MFA iteration requires $\Theta(d_{avg}P + P^2)$ time for the mapping of a sparse domain graph with $N$ vertices and average vertex degree of $d_{avg}$ to a parallel architecture with $P$ processors. The proposed hypercube-specific MFA formulation asymptotically reduces the number of spin variables and the computational complexity of an individual MFA iteration to $N lg_2 P$ and $\Theta(d_{avg} lg_2 P + P lg_2 P)$, respectively, by exploiting the topological properties of hypercubes.

## 1 Introduction

Parallelization schemes for many applications on distributed memory architectures are characterized by the *mapping* of the problem domain to processors with locality of communication. These schemes employ *data parallelism* by breaking the data structures supporting a computation into pieces and then assigning those pieces to different processors. These decomposition and assignment tasks constitute the *domain mapping* problem [2]. The objective in the domain mapping is to find a mapping which minimizes the communication overhead while maintaining almost the same workload for each processor. Problem domain representing the data structure is represented with an undirected graph $G = (T, I)$, referred here as *domain graph*. Vertices $i, j \in T$ represent atomic computations (tasks) which can be executed simultaneously and independently. Vertex weight $w_i$ denotes the estimated computational cost of task $i$. Each edge $(i, j) \in I$ denotes the need for the bidirectional interaction between tasks $i$ and $j$. Edge weight $e_{ij}$ denotes the volume of interaction between tasks $i$ and $j$ connected by edge $(i, j) \in I$. This graph usually represents the repeated execution of the computations corresponding to the vertices with intervening partial result exchanges denoted by the edges. An edge incurs interprocessor communication only if the respective pair of computations are mapped to two different processors. Simultaneous *single-hop* communications between distinct adjacent pairs of processors can be performed concurrently. However, simultaneous *multi-hop* communications between distant pairs of processors may introduce congestion to the interconnection network, thus increasing the communication overhead. Multi-hop

* This work is partially supported by the Commission of the European Communities, Directorate General for Industry under contract ITDC 204-82166

communications between distant processors are usually routed over the shortest paths of links between the communicating pairs of processors. Hence, multi-hop messages are usually weighted with the distances between the respective pairs of processors in the network, while considering their contribution to the overall communication cost. Here, distance refers to the number of communication links and switching elements along the communication route in *static* and *dynamic* interconnection networks, respectively. Thus, in our communication cost model, an edge $(i, j) \in I$ contributes $e_{ij}d_{M(i),M(j)}$ to the overall communication cost where $M(i) = p$ and $M(j) = q$ denote that processors that tasks $i$ and $j$ are mapped to, respectively, and $d_{pq}$ denotes the distance between processors $p$ and $q$. This model is widely used in the literature [2].

The domain-mapping problem is known to be NP-hard for unstructured domains. Hence, heuristics giving suboptimal solutions are used to solve the problem. Two distinct approaches have been considered in the context of mapping heuristics: *one-phase* and *two-phase*. In one-phase approaches, referred as *many-to-one* mapping, vertices of the domain graph are directly mapped onto the processors. In two-phase approaches, *clustering* phase is followed by *one-to-one* mapping phase. In the clustering phase, vertices of the domain graph are partitioned into $P$ equally weighted clusters while the total number of edges among clusters is minimized. Here, $P$ denotes the number of processors. The problem solved in the clustering phase is identical to the $P$-way graph partitioning problem. In the one-to-one mapping phase, each cluster is assigned to an individual processor so that the total communication overhead is minimized. As expected, two-phase approaches suffer from delaying the processor distance factor to the second phase.

Mean field annealing (MFA) algorithm, proposed for solving combinatorial optimization problems, combines the characteristics of neural networks with the annealing notion of simulated annealing (SA). Previous works on MFA resulted with successful formulation of the algorithm to some classic combinatorial optimization problems including the mapping problem. In MFA, discrete variables, called spins are used for encoding the combinatorial optimization problems. An energy function written in terms of spins is used for representing the cost function of the problem. Then, using the expected values of these discrete variables, a gradient descent type relaxation scheme is used to find a configuration of the spins which minimizes the associated energy function. The MFA formulation proposed for the mapping problem [1] is a general formulation which works for any interconnection topology. In this formulation, $N \times P$ spin variables are maintained and an individual MFA iteration takes $\theta(d_{avg}P + P^2)$ time, for the mapping of a sparse domain graph with $N$ vertices and average vertex degree of $d_{avg}$ to a parallel architecture with $P$ processors. In this work, we propose an efficient MFA formulation for mapping unstructured domains to hypercube-connected distributed-memory architectures. The proposed hypercube-specific MFA formulation asymptotically reduces the number of spin variables and the computational complexity of an individual MFA iteration to $Nlg_2P$ and $\Theta(d_{avg}lg_2P + Plg_2P)$, respectively, by exploiting the topological properties of hypercubes.

# 2 MFA Formulation For Hypercubes

A $D$-dimensional hypercube $H$ consists of $P = 2^D$ processors labeled from 0 to $2^D - 1$ such that there is a direct connection between two processors if and only if the binary representation of their labels differ exactly in one bit. Each processor $p$ is represented by a $D$ bit binary number $(p_{D-1}, \ldots, p_d, \ldots, p_0)$, where $p = \sum_{d=0}^{D-1} p_d 2^d$. A $D$-dimensional hypercube $H$ can be split into two $(D-1)$-dimensional subcubes $H_d^0$ and $H_d^1$ so that each processor of $H_d^0$ is connected to exactly one processor of $H_d^1$. This splitting operation is called *tearing* along dimension (channel) $d$ [5]. Note that there are $D$ such tearings for $d = 0, 1, \ldots, D-1$. Here, $H_d^0$ and $H_d^1$ both contain $P/2$ processors whose $d$th bits are 0 and 1, respectively. The $P/2$ communication links connecting the processors of $H_d^0$ and $H_d^1$ in a one-to-one manner are referred here as channel $d$ for $d = 0, 1, \ldots, D-1$.

In hypercubes, communication distance between a processor pair $p$ and $q$ is equal to the number of bits that differ between their labels. Consider a processor pair $p$ and $q$ with a distance of $k$. Let $\{d_1, d_2, \ldots, d_k\}$ denotes the set of $k$ differing bit positions (dimensions) between processors $p$ and $q$. Then, each differing bit position $d_i$ corresponds to the use of a communication link along channel $d_i$ in the communication route between processors $p$ and $q$, for $i = 1, 2, \ldots, k$. Each differing bit position $d_i$ also means that processors $p$ and $q$ are in different subcubes $H_{d_i}^1$ and $H_{d_i}^0$, or vice-versa, respectively. These properties of hypercube topology can be exploited to decompose the communication cost of each edge $(i, j) \in I$ into its channel components. Let the processor mapping $M(i)$ for a task $i \in T$ be represented as a $D$-bit binary label $M(i) = [m_{D-1}(i), \ldots, m_0(i)]^t$, where $m_d(i)$ represents the $d$th bit of processor $M(i)$. Here, $m_d(i) = 1$ and $m_d(i) = 0$ mean that task $i$ is in the subcubes $H_d^1$ and $H_d^0$, respectively, for a tearing over channel $d$. Using this notation, communication volume contribution of edge $(i, j) \in I$ to channel $d$ is $C_{ij}^d = e_{ij}|m_d(i) - m_d(j)|$ where $|\cdot|$ denotes the absolute value function. Edge $(i, j)$ incurs a communication over channel $d$ only if processors $M(i)$ and $M(j)$ are in different $(D-1)$-dimensional subcubes $H_d^0$ and $H_d^1$. Hence, the total communication cost $C$ can be written as $C = \sum_{(i,j)\in I} C_{ij}$ where $C_{ij} = \sum_{d=0}^{D-1} C_{ij}^d$. Here, $C_{ij}$ denotes the contribution of edge $(i, j) \in I$ to the total communication cost. This communication cost formulation is exploited in this work to propose an efficient encoding scheme for mapping to hypercubes.

## 2.1 Encoding

In the proposed encoding, we assign an Ising spin to each task for each channel. Effectively, we assign $D$ Ising spins $\{s_{id}\}_{d=0}^{D-1}$ to each task $i = 1, 2, \ldots, N$. Here, Ising spin $s_{id}$ corresponds to $m_d(i)$ mentioned earlier. That is, the spin configuration $s_{id} = 1$ ($s_{id} = 0$) means that task $i$ is assigned to one of the $P/2$ processors in the $(D-1)$-dimensional subcube $H_d^1$ ($H_d^0$) defined by the tearing over channel $d$. Note that $M(i) = [s_{i,D-1}, \ldots, s_{i0}]^t$ corresponds to a distinct mapping of task $i$ for each possible configuration of the $D$ spins $\{s_{id}\}_{d=0}^{D-1}$ assigned to task $i$. Hence, the proposed encoding constructs a one-to-one mapping between the configuration space of the problem domain and the spin domain. The proposed encoding requires $N \times D = N lg_2 P$ Ising spins where each Ising spin contains a single spin variable. Hence, the proposed encoding scheme asymptotically reduces the number of spin variables from $N \times P$ of the general MFA formulation to $N lg_2 P$.

## 2.2   Energy Function Formulation

The average (expected) value of each spin is defined as $v_{id} = \langle s_{id} \rangle$. Recall that $s_{id} \in \{0, 1\}$ are two-state discrete variables, whereas $v_{id} \in [0, 1]$ are continuous variables. In order to construct an energy function it is helpful to associate the following meanings to the $v_{id}$ values:

$$v_{id} = \mathcal{P}(\text{task } i \text{ is mapped to } H_d^1) \qquad 1 - v_{id} = \mathcal{P}(\text{task } i \text{ is mapped to } H_d^0) \qquad (1)$$

That is, $v_{id}$ and $(1 - v_{id})$ denote the probabilities of finding task $i$ in a processor in $H_d^1$ and $H_d^0$, respectively. Thus, the formulation of communication cost due to edge $(i, j) \in I$ as an energy term is:

$$E_{ij}^C = \sum_{d=0}^{D-1} E_{ij}^d = e_{ij} \sum_{d=0}^{D-1} [v_{id}(1 - v_{jd})] + [(1 - v_{id})v_{jd}] \qquad (2)$$

Here, $E_{ij}^d$ is the energy term corresponding to $C_{ij}^d$ which denotes the total communication cost of edge $(i, j)$ over channel $d$. Energy formulation for total communication is $E^C = \sum_{(i,j) \in I} E_{ij}^C$. We formulate the energy term corresponding to the imbalance cost term using the same inner product approach adopted in the general formulation [1] as follows

$$E^B = \frac{1}{2} \sum_{i=1}^{N} \sum_{j \neq i}^{N} w_i w_j \sum_{p=0}^{P-1} \mathcal{P}(\text{tasks } i \text{ and } j \text{ are mapped to processor } p)$$

$$= \frac{1}{2} \sum_{i=1}^{N} \sum_{j \neq i}^{N} w_i w_j \sum_{p=0}^{P-1} Z_{ip} Z_{jp} \qquad (3)$$

Here, $Z_{ip}$ denotes the probability of finding task $i$ at processor $p$, i.e.,

$$Z_{ip} = \prod_{d=0}^{D-1} u_{ip}^d, \quad \text{where} \quad u_{ip}^d = \begin{cases} v_{id} & \text{if } p_d = 1 \\ 1 - v_{id} & \text{if } p_d = 0 \end{cases} \qquad (4)$$

Recall that $p_d$ denotes the $d$th bit of the label of processor $p$. Hence, $u_{ip}^d$ is the probability of finding task $i$ in the subcube $H_d^{p_d}$. That is, $u_{ip}^d$ is the probability of finding task $i$ in the subcube $H_d^1$ ($H_d^0$) if $p_d = 1$ ($p_d = 0$). The total energy can be defined in terms of $E^C$ and $E^B$ as $E(\mathbf{V}) = E^C(\mathbf{V}) + \beta E^B(\mathbf{V})$, where $\beta$ is introduced to maintain a balance between the two conflicting optimization objectives of the mapping problem.

## 2.3   Derivation of Mean Field Theory Equations

Using the expression for the proposed energy function, the expression for the mean field experienced by an Ising spin $s_{id}$ can be obtained as

$$\phi_{id} = -\frac{\partial E(\mathbf{V})}{\partial v_{id}} = \phi_{id}^C + \beta \phi_{id}^B \qquad \text{where} \qquad (5)$$

$$\phi_{id}^C = \sum_{j \in Adj(i)} e_{ij}(v_{jd} - 0.5) \qquad \phi_{id}^B = \sum_{j=1, j \neq i}^{N} \sum_{p=0}^{P-1} (-1)^{p_d} w_i w_j Z_{jp} Z_{ip}^d \qquad (6)$$

Here, $\phi_{id}^C$ and $\phi_{id}^B$ denotes the communication cost and imbalance cost components of the mean field $\phi_{id}$. The expression for $Z_{ip}^d$ used in (6) is $Z_{ip}^d = \prod_{c=0,c\neq d}^{D-1} u_{ip}^c$. Note that $Z_{ip}^d$ denotes the probability of finding task $i$ in one of the two processors $p \in H_d^{p_d}$ and $q \in H_d^{1-p_d}$ which are connected by a communication link over channel $d$. Here, $Z_{ip}^d$ can also be interpreted as the probability of finding task $i$ at processor $p \in H_d^{p_d}$ if task $i$ is mapped to $H_d^{p_d}$, i.e., $v_{id} = s_{id} = p_d$.

In the general MFA formulation, updating a single Potts spin updates the expected mapping of the task [1]. However, the MFA formulation proposed for hypercubes, $D = lg_2 P$ Ising spin updates are required to update the expected mapping of a particular task. That is, $D$ Ising spins $\{s_{id}\}_{d=0}^{D-1}$ should be selected for update in order to update the overall mapping of task $i$. Hence, the complexity of $D$ iterations of the proposed hypercube formulation should be compared to the complexity of a single iteration of the general formulation. Thus, the proposed hypercube formulation, together with the efficient implementation scheme proposed in [4], asymptotically reduces the complexity of a simple MFA iteration of the general formulation from $\Theta(d_{avg}P + P^2)$ to $\Theta(d_{avg}lg_2P + Plg_2P)$.

## 3  Experimental Results

This section presents the performance evaluation of the proposed hypercube-specific MFA formulation for the mapping problem, in comparison with the well-known mapping heuristics: general MFA formulation, Simulated Annealing (SA) and Kernighan-Lin (KL). Each algorithm is tested by mapping some test domain graphs to various dimensional hypercubes. Test graphs used for experimentation correspond to the sparse graphs associated with the symmetric sparse matrices selected from *Harwell Boeing sparse matrix test collection* [3]. Weights of the vertices are assumed to be equal to their degrees. These test graphs are mapped to various dimensional hypercubes (D=5, 6, 7, 8).

Table 1 illustrates the performance results of the KL, SA, general and hypercube-specific MFA heuristics for the generated mapping problem instances. In this table, "Gen" and "Hyp" denote the general and hypercube-specific MFA formulations, respectively. Each algorithm is executed 10 times for each mapping instance starting from different, randomly chosen initial configurations. Averages are illustrated in Table 1. Percent computational load imbalance averages of the solutions displayed in this table are computed using $100\times(W_{max} - W_{avg})/W_{avg}$. Here, $W_{max}$ denotes the maximum processor load and $W_{avg}$ denotes the computational loads of processors under perfect load balance conditions. Execution time averages are measured on a SUN SPARC workstation. In Table 1, values displayed in parentheses denote the communication cost and execution time averages normalized with respect to those of the hypercube-specific MFA heuristic. Actual communication cost averages and execution time averages (in seconds) are displayed only for the solutions generated by the hypercube-specific MFA heuristic. In Table 1, bold values indicate the best results for the respective mappings. Table 1 confirms the expectation that hypercube-specific MFA formulation is significantly (36 times on the overall average) faster than general MFA formulation while producing mappings with considerably better qualities. The hypercube-specific MFA heuristic is as fast as the fast KL heuristic while

**Table 1.** Communication cost, percent load imbalance and execution time averages of the solutions found by KL, SA, general MFA and hypercube-specific MFA heuristics for various mapping problem instances. $N$ and $E$ denote the number of vertices and edges in the respective domain graph instances. Values in parentheses denote the communication cost and execution time averages normalized with respect to those of the hypercube-specific MFA heuristic. Bold values represent the best results for the respective mapping instances

| Problem | | | Communication Cost | | | | % Load Imbalance | | | | Execution Time(sec) | | | |
|---|---|---|---|---|---|---|---|---|---|---|---|---|---|---|
| Domain | H | | KL | SA | MFA | | KL | SA | MFA | | KL | SA | MFA | |
| Graph | D | P | | | Gen. | Hyp | | | Gen. | Hyp | | | Gen. | Hyp |
| DWT-1242 | 5 | 32 | (2.13) | **(0.77)** | (1.03) | 2760 | 8.1 | **1.1** | 4.0 | 2.6 | **(0.7)** | (660) | (47.0) | 60 |
| N=1242 | 6 | 64 | (3.53) | (1.09) | (1.50) | **2941** | 8.9 | **2.7** | 5.2 | 4.3 | **(0.6)** | (213) | (29.4) | 201 |
| E=4592 | 7 | 128 | (7.48) | (1.36) | (1.71) | **3605** | 12.1 | **6.1** | 6.6 | 7.2 | (1.1) | (83) | (24.8) | **617** |
| | 8 | 256 | (9.47) | (1.60) | (1.88) | **4829** | 16.3 | **11.9** | 14.0 | 12.4 | (1.5) | (54) | (25.7) | **1247** |
| JAGMESH6 | 5 | 32 | (1.64) | **(0.62)** | (0.87) | 1861 | 6.3 | **1.3** | 3.6 | **1.3** | (0.6) | (530) | 63.52 | 82 |
| N=1377 | 6 | 64 | (2.43) | **(0.86)** | (1.22) | 2298 | 7.4 | **2.4** | 4.1 | 2.7 | (0.5) | (204) | (53.2) | 224 |
| E=3808 | 7 | 128 | (4.95) | (1.07) | (1.59) | **2890** | 12.0 | **4.9** | 5.6 | 5.8 | (0.8) | (102) | (33.7) | 547 |
| | 8 | 256 | (8.01) | (1.27) | (1.67) | **3863** | 13.4 | 11.7 | 12.1 | **10.1** | (2.6) | (60) | (34.4) | **1283** |
| BCSPWR09 | 5 | 32 | (2.56) | **(0.59)** | (1.32) | 1045 | 5.5 | **0.5** | 2.8 | 1.3 | (0.6) | (783) | (15.2) | 97 |
| N=1723 | 6 | 64 | (3.09) | **(0.72)** | (1.37) | 1477 | 10.5 | **1.6** | 5.6 | 3.2 | (0.5) | (350) | (18.7) | 225 |
| E=2394 | 7 | 128 | (5.10) | (1.08) | (1.62) | **1701** | 12.4 | **4.1** | 7.2 | 6.0 | (0.7) | (149) | (20.5) | 637 |
| | 8 | 256 | (8.22) | (1.56) | (1.74) | **2155** | 17.2 | **8.7** | 12.8 | 11.1 | (1.9) | (77) | (26.7) | **1563** |
| LSH2233 | 5 | 32 | (1.60) | **(0.52)** | (0.64) | 3740 | 6.3 | **0.7** | 3.6 | 0.9 | (0.9) | (887) | (26.9) | 112 |
| N=2233 | 6 | 64 | (2.24) | **(0.68)** | (0.99) | 4490 | 8.0 | **1.6** | 3.1 | 2.1 | (0.6) | (332) | (38.1) | 322 |
| E=6552 | 7 | 128 | (3.66) | **(0.84)** | (1.34) | 5375 | 9.4 | **2.9** | 4.4 | 3.6 | (0.9) | (107) | (69.9) | 800 |
| | 8 | 256 | (6.21) | (1.01) | (1.42) | **6865** | 10.2 | **5.3** | 8.8 | 6.8 | (1.8) | (52) | (59.2) | **1783** |
| Overall normalized averages on the basis of number of processors | | | | | | | | | | | | | | |
| | 5 | 32 | (1.98) | **(0.63)** | (0.97) | (1.0) | (4.3) | **(0.6)** | (2.3) | (1.0) | **(0.7)** | (715) | (37.7) | (1.0) |
| | 6 | 64 | (2.82) | **(0.84)** | (1.27) | (1.0) | (2.9) | **(0.5)** | (1.5) | (1.0) | **(0.9)** | (274) | (34.8) | (1.0) |
| | 7 | 128 | (5.30) | (1.10) | (1.57) | **(1.0)** | (2.0) | **(0.8)** | (1.1) | (1.0) | **(0.9)** | (110) | (37.2) | (1.0) |
| | 8 | 256 | (7.97) | (1.36) | (1.68) | **(1.0)** | (1.4) | **(0.9)** | (1.2) | (1.0) | (1.3) | (60) | (36.2) | **(1.0)** |
| Overall normalized averages | | | | | | | | | | | | | | |
| | | | 4.50 | 1.06 | 1.37 | **1.0** | 2.6 | **0.7** | 1.5 | 1.0 | **(0.9)** | (274) | (36.4) | (1.0) |

producing extremely better mappings. The proposed heuristic produces comparable mappings with powerful SA heuristic, however it is drastically (274 times on the average) faster. As is also seen Table 1, the relative quality difference between the mappings produced by hypercube-specific MFA and SA heuristics decreases with increasing number of processors in favor of the proposed heuristic.

# 4  Conclusion

An efficient MFA formulation was proposed for mapping unstructured domains to hypercube-connected distributed-memory architectures. The proposed hypercube-specific MFA formulation asymptotically reduces the number of spin variables and the complexity of the mean filed computations compared to the general MFA formulation. The proposed hypercube-specific MFA heuristic was found to be significantly faster than the general MFA heuristic as was expected.

# References

1. Bultan, T., and Aykanat, C., "A new mapping heuristic based on mean field annealing," *Journal of Parallel and Distributed Computing*, vol. 10, pp. 292-305, 1992.
2. Camp, W.J, Plimpton, S.J, Hendrickson, B.A., and Leland, R.W., "Massively parallel methods for Enineering and Science problem," *Communication of ACM*, vol. 37, no. 4, April 1994.
3. Duff, I.S., and Grius, R.G., "Sparse matrix test problems," *ACM Trans. on Matematical software*, vol. 17, no. 1, pp. 1-14, March 1989.
4. Haritaoglu, I., and Aykanat Cevdet., "An efficient Mean Filed annaealing formulation for mapping unsrtuctured domains " *Technical Report,BU-CEIS-9511*
5. Saad Y. and Schultz M. " Topological Properties of Hypercubes " *IEEE Transaction on Computer*, vol 37, July, 1988

# Partitioning & Mapping of Unstructured Meshes to Parallel Machine Topologies

C. Walshaw, M. Cross, M. G. Everett, S. Johnson, and K. McManus

Parallel Processing Group, Centre for Numerical Modelling & Process Analysis,
University of Greenwich, London, SE18 6PF. E-mail: C.Walshaw@gre.ac.uk

**Abstract.** We give an overview of some strategies for mapping unstructured meshes onto processor grids. Sample results show that the mapping can make a considerable difference to the communication overhead in the parallel solution time, particularly as the number of processors increase.

## 1  Introduction

The use of unstructured mesh codes on parallel machines can be one of the most efficient ways to solve large Computational Mechanics problems. Completely general geometries and complex behaviour can be readily modelled and, in principle, the inherent sparsity of many such problems can be exploited to obtain excellent parallel efficiencies. An important issue for such codes is the problem of distributing the mesh across the memory of the machine at runtime so that the computational load is evenly balanced and the communication overhead is minimised. It is well known that this problem is NP complete, so in recent years much attention has been focused on developing suitable heuristics, and some powerful methods, many based on a graph corresponding to the communication requirements of the mesh, have been devised, e.g. [2].

A pertinent but often ignored factor in parallel processing is the underlying topology of the machine's interconnection network. For example, even on machines with small numbers of processors, it is possible to detect variations between the latencies of processors which are closely linked and those which are 'far apart'. Although most machines now have facilities for 'wormhole routing' (i.e. the passing of messages between two non-adjacent processors without interrupting intermediate processors), high contention of the interprocessor links can result if adjacent partitions are mapped to, say, opposite corners of a processor array. As the trend towards massively parallel machines continues, these effects are likely to be exacerbated and the machine topologies will have an increasingly important effect on the parallel overhead arising from any given partition. Most of the current generation of mesh partitioning algorithms, however, take no account of the topology. The mapping to the machine is either treated as a post-processing step, applied after the data has been partitioned, or even ignored. For some machines with small numbers of processors this may be a legitimate simplification, but as machine sizes increase it is likely that a poor mapping will cause significant performance degradation.

## 1.1 Overview

The strategy employed here to tackle the partitioning/mapping problem is to derive an
initial partition quickly and cheaply as possible and then use powerful optimisation techniques to achieve a high quality solution. This multi-stage approach has been shown to
provide an efficient and flexible approach to partitioning, [6] and is similar to the work of
Vanderstraeten *et al.*, [5], although the techniques vary in that we employ deterministic
heuristics to optimise the partition.

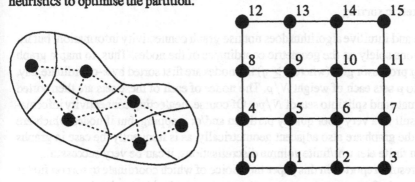

**Fig. 1.** A typical partition with subdomain graph and a $4 \times 4$ processor grid

We use an undirected graph $G(N, E)$, of $N$ nodes & $E$ edges, to represent the data
dependencies arising from the unstructured mesh. Any partition of $G$ induces a subdomain graph $S$ and loosely the mapping problem can be thought of as the placing of this
$S$ onto the processor topology such that the communication overhead is minimised. We
concentrate here on mapping onto a grid topology where we assume that the processors
are connected as a 1D, 2D or 3D array. This is a realistic restriction as grids can be found
in some of the current range of parallel machines such as the Intel Paragon (2D) or Cray
T3D (3D). Figure 1 shows a typical partition, the resulting subdomain graph and a 2D
grid topology.

## 2 The initial partition

The aim of the initial partitioning is to divide up the graph as rapidly as possible prior to
optimisation where most of the work takes place. We use two different initial partitioning
algorithms; the Greedy Algorithm ignores the processor topology completely, whilst the
other, Geometric sorting, does a very crude mapping onto a processor grid.

### 2.1 The greedy algorithm

The Greedy algorithm used here is a simple variant of that originally proposed by Farhat
and fully described in [1]. It derives its name from the way in which it 'bites' into the
mesh; each fresh partition grows out in level sets from a seed node until an appropriate
proportion of the graph has been 'eaten' and the next partition is then seeded (if possible)

from a node on the border of the previous subdomain. This is clearly seen to be the fastest *graph-based* method as it only visits each graph edge once. However, it takes no account of the processor topology except for the fact that two contiguously numbered domains are likely to be (but not necessarily) adjacent. The variant employed here differs from that proposed by Farhat only in that it works solely with a graph rather than the nodes and elements of a finite element mesh.

## 2.2 Geometric sorting

This simple and intuitive algorithm does not use graph connectivity information, but instead partitions solely on the geometric coordinates of the nodes. Thus, to map a graph onto an $p \times q$ processor grid (where $p \geq q$) the nodes are first sorted by $x$-coordinate, say, and split into $p$ sets each of weight $N/p$. The nodes of each of these sets are then sorted by $y$-coordinate and split into sets of $N/pq$. Of course, neglecting connectivity information may result in a very poor quality partition and/or mapping, but if nodes which are adjacent in the graph are also adjacent geometrically, as is frequently the case in graphs arising from finite element/finite volume discretisations, it can be very successful.

For the results reported in this paper the choice of which coordinate to sort on first is left to the user. In fact, using $x$, $y$, $z$-coordinates may not be ideal as it takes no account of the orientation of the mesh and a more successful technique might be to determine the principal axes of inertia of the graph nodes (as in the commonly used Recursive Inertial Bisection – see for example, [4]).

## 3 The optimisation methods

Once the graph is partitioned, optimisation can take place to improve the quality of the partition. The two methods outlined here have different aims; 'uniform optimisation' treats the processor topology as uniform and tries to minimise the number of interprocessor cut-edges. 'Grid optimisation', on the other hand, treats the processor topology as a grid and attempts to optimise the mapping by eliminating non-local communications. Throughout the optimisation, it is assumed that the final partition will not deviate too far from the initial one. Thus, in general, only border nodes are allowed to migrate to neighbouring subdomains.

### 3.1 Uniform optimisation

This algorithm is fully described in [6] where it is seen that a key part of the technique is the way in which each subdomain tries to minimise its own surface energy. In the physical 2D or 3D world the object with the smallest surface to volume ratio is the circle or sphere. Thus the idea behind the subdomain heuristic is to determine the centre of each subdomain (in some graph sense) and to then measure the radial distance from the centre to the edges and attempt to minimise this by migrating nodes which are furthest from the centre.

Determining the 'centre' is relatively easy and can be achieved by moving in level sets inwards from the subdomain border until all the nodes have been visited. The final set defines the centre of the subdomain and, the reverse of this process can then be used to determine the radial distance. Having derived these sets each node can be marked by its radial distance. The code finally decides which nodes to migrate based on a combination of radial distance, load-imbalance and the change in cut-edges.

## 3.2 Grid optimisation

The grid optimisation algorithm is based very much on the uniform optimisation algorithm with some minor changes and a more appropriate method for minimising the surface energy. In summary, the minor changes are that subdomains can only migrate nodes to their neighbours in the *processor grid* and that, when assessing the cost of a partition, interprocessor edges are weighted according to how close together they are in the processor array. We use the square of the number links between the two processors, so that for example, in Figure 1, the cost of an interprocessor edge between 0 and 6 is $9 = (2+1)^2$.

After some experimentation it was found that using the radial distance as a basis for migrating nodes which are far from the subdomain centre was simply not appropriate for achieving a grid mapping, as nodes which are relatively far away from the centre of the subdomain may be well placed for the topology mapping. To see this, consider the partition of the unit square for a 1D processor array where the topology preserving partition is just a series of strips. Migrating nodes which are far away from the centre of the subdomain (i.e. at the extremes of each strip) does not preserve the partition as a 1D array. However, if we attempt to minimise the width of each strip, rather than the radial distance, we do find that the partition can preserve the machine topology. Thus, instead of measuring the radial distance of the subdomain, we measure (in a graph sense) the distance between the borders with processor on the left and the processor on the right.

This technique can also be extended to higher dimensional arrays by each processor classifying the other processors as lying, in the 2D case, to either the north, south, east or west, with processors lying on a diagonal falling into two sets. Thus in Figure 1, relative to 5, processors 0, 4 & 8 are positioned to the west, 2, 3, 6, 7, 10, 11 & 15 to the east, 0, 1 & 2 to the south and 8, 9, 10, 12, 13, 14 & 15 to the north. After measuring the width in each direction border nodes are marked with the maximum of the east/west and north/south distance and in the case where a subdomain does not have nodes on one of the borders (e.g. in Figure 1 processors 0, 1, 2 & 3 do not have a southern border) nodes on the opposite border are simply marked with 0. Nodes are then migrated as for uniform optimisation (as described in [6]).

## 4  Mapping strategies

Table 1 shows the four mapping strategies tested. The *unmapped* partitioning completely ignores processor topology as does the *postmapped*, although it additionally employs a simple processor allocation algorithm at the end. This algorithm continually swaps subdomains between processors until no further improvement in the map cost is possible. The *premapped* partitioning method works the other way round; the graph is initially mapped, albeit crudely, onto the processor grid and then optimised to minimise the number of interprocessor cut-edges. Because the final partition does not deviate *too*

| Strategy | Initial partition | Optimisation | Processor Allocation |
|----------|-------------------|--------------|----------------------|
| Unmapped | Greedy | Uniform | No |
| Postmapped | Greedy | Uniform | Yes |
| Premapped | Geometric sort | Uniform | No |
| Partition mapped | Geometric sort | Grid | No |

**Table 1.** Mapping strategies

*much* from the initial one the resulting subdomain graph still 'fits' reasonably well onto the processor grid. Indeed, although processor allocation was not used for these results, in tests it was very rare that it could find better allocations. The premapping would also be far more attractive than postmapping if the optimisation algorithm were running in parallel as the remapping of a distributed partition can involve a vast exchange of data, with a resulting loss of efficiency. Finally the *partition mapping* strategy acknowledges the processor topology throughout.

## 5   Results

We have tested the mappings using a parallel control volume unstructed mesh flow and stress code developed at Greenwich and described in [3]. The test mesh came from a casting simulation and the resulting graph contains 30,064 nodes and 44,693 edges. The parallel code was run on a Transtech Paramid with i860 processing nodes with an topology can be best modelled by a $p \times 2$ grid.

| Strategy | Partition | | | Time (s) | |
|----------|-----------|------|-------|-----------|----------|
| | $E_c$ | $C$ | $D_a$ | Partition | Solution |
| Unmapped | 939 | 14753 | 4.17 | 5.13 | 154.1 |
| Postmapped | 939 | 2225 | 4.17 | 5.19 | 148.9 |
| Premapped | 982 | 1598 | 3.92 | 6.88 | 144.1 |
| Partition mapped | 1061 | 1069 | 3.17 | 11.39 | 131.7 |

**Table 2.** Results for $P = 24$

Table 2 show some typical partitioning results for $P = 16 := 8 \times 2$. Here $E_c$ is the number of cut edges, $C$ is the partition cost using the distance-squared weighting described in §3.2 and $D_a$ is the average degree of each subdomain. Unfortunately, however, when compared for several values of $P$, none of these measures could really be used to predict the parallel solution time and a future aim is to derive a good cost metric. The timings for the partition come from a Sun 20 workstation and are generally of the same order (although partition-mapping is always more expensive). However, we don't consider these figures particularly relevant as it is intended to parallelise the partition optimisation algorithm. Far more interesting are the parallel solution times and figure 2

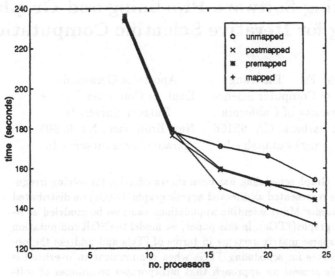

**Fig. 2.** Solution times

shows clearly how much difference a good mapping can make. Although the results are indistinguishable for small numbers of processors, as might be expected, they rapidly separate out for 16 or more.

## 6 Conclusion

The preliminary results of our investigation show that a good mapping can make a considerable difference to the communication overhead in the parallel solution time for unstructured meshes, particularly as the number of processors increases. Future work on this technique will include the parallelisation of the optimisation algorithms and an attempt to derive a meaningful cost function.

## References

1. C. Farhat. A Simple and Efficient Automatic FEM Domain Decomposer. *Comp. & Struct.*, 28:579–602, 1988.
2. C. Farhat and H. D. Simon. TOP/DOMDEC – a Software Tool for Mesh Partitioning and Parallel Processing. Tech. Rep. RNR-93-011, NASA Ames, Moffat Field, CA, 1993.
3. K. McManus, M. Cross, and S. Johnson. Integrated Flow and Stress using an Unstructured Mesh on Distributed Memory Parallel Systems. In *Parallel CFD'94*. Elsevier, 1995.
4. D. Roose and R. Van Driessche. Distributed Memory Parallel Computers and Computational Fluid Dynamics. Rep. TW 186, Dept. Comp. Sci., Katholieke Universiteit Leuven, 1993.
5. D. Vanderstraeten and R. Keunings. Optimized Partitioning of Unstructured Computational Grids. *Int. J. Num. Meth. Engng.*, 38:433–450, 1995.
6. C. Walshaw, M. Cross, and M. Everett. A Parallelisable Algorithm for Optimising Unstructured Mesh Partitions. Tech. Rep. 95/IM/03, University of Greenwich, London SE18 6PF, UK, 1995. (submitted for publication).

# Integrating Software Pipelining and Graph Scheduling for Iterative Scientific Computations

Cong Fu    Tao Yang
Dept. of Computer Science
University of California
Santa Barbara, CA  93106
{cfu,tyang}@cs.ucsb.edu

Apostolos Gerasoulis
Dept. of Computer Science
Rutgers University
New Brunswick, NJ  08903
gerasoulis@cs.rutgers.edu

**Abstract.** Graph scheduling has been shown effective for solving irregular problems represented as directed acyclic graphs(DAGs) on distributed memory systems. Many scientific applications can also be modeled as iterative task graphs(ITGs). In this paper, we model the SOR computation for solving sparse matrix systems in terms of ITGs and address the optimization issues for scheduling ITGs when communication overhead is not zero. We present an approach that incorporates techniques of software pipelining and graph scheduling. We demonstrate the effectiveness of our approach in mapping SOR computation and compare it with the multi-coloring method.

## 1  Introduction

Many irregular computations can be represented as Directed Acyclic Graphs (DAG)[3, 15] and graph scheduling has been shown effective for such computations. There are also a class of problems that can be viewed as the repeated execution of a set of computational tasks and can be modeled by iterative task graphs (ITGs). For example, in the absence of convergence test, the SOR algorithm can be modeled by ITGs. Each iteration contains a set of tasks. Instances of these tasks in different iterations operate on different data and there are data dependencies between task instances within one iteration and between iterations.

Mapping weighted iterative task graphs on message-passing architectures requires the exploration of task and loop parallelism by considering both load balancing and communication optimizations. Using DAG scheduling algorithms (e.g. [20, 23, 28]) for iterative computation is not feasible since the number of iterations may be too large or may not even be known at compile-time. Software pipelining [2, 12, 19, 22] is an important technique proposed for instruction-level loop scheduling on VLIW and superscalar architectures. Loop unrolling or graph unfolding techniques [21] are proposed to explore more parallelism. Our work has been motivated by the above research work but takes into consideration the characteristics of asynchronous parallelism and the impact of communication. We show how software pipelining techniques can be used for mapping iterative task computation on message-passing architectures.

The optimal solution for a special class of ITGs has been studied in  [5]. We are developing heuristic algorithms for general ITGs. Load balancing and communication minimization are the important aspects of optimization. It is known that *data locality* must be explored for reducing unnecessary communication. In task computation model [23, 20], exploring data locality means to localize data communication between tasks by assigning them in the same processor so that tasks could exchange data through local memory to avoid high-cost inter-processor communication. We will demonstrate how such a strategy is used in our algorithm. In [29], we have also considered a method for executing ITG schedules and provided analytic and experimental results on run-time performance of static schedules when static weights are not estimated accurately.

This paper is organized as follows. In Section 2 we will depict how we can model SOR method using ITG to exploit parallelism. Section 3 addresses some difficulties in the ITG scheduling problem and describes how we can overcome them. Sections 4 discusses our approach and the performance analysis. Section 5 presents the experimental results.

## 2 Representation of Iterative Task Computation

### 2.1 The transformed SOR method

The Successive-Over-Relaxation (SOR) method [1] is an iterative method for solving a matrix system $Ax = b$ where $A$ is $n \times n$ coefficient matrix. And at iteration $(k + 1)$, the new value of each variable $x_i$ $(1 \leq i \leq n)$ is updated as:

$$x_i^{(k+1)} = (1 - \omega)x_i^{(k)} + \frac{\omega}{a_{ii}}(b_i - \sum_{j=1}^{i-1} a_{ij}x_j^{(k+1)} - \sum_{j=i+1}^{n} a_{ij}x_j^{(k)})$$

The corresponding SOR algorithm is listed in Fig. 1. In this version, the computation in one iteration of the SOR algorithm with respect to loop $k$ contains statements $(S_i = S_i + a_{i,j} * x_j)$ that update variables $x_i$ $(1 \leq i \leq n)$. When a variable $x_i$ is re-defined at iteration $k$, this value is used in iteration $k$ for computing $x_j$ where $j > i$ and in iteration $k + 1$ for computing $x_j$ where $j < i$. Accordingly, we can divide the computation involved in one iteration of loop $k$ into two parts: NEW$_t$ and OLD$_t$ (See Fig. 2 (a)). The NEW$_t$ part uses the value of $x_i$ produced in iteration $t$ and the OLD$_t$ part uses the value of $x_i$ produced in iteration $t - 1$. For this program, the statements $(S_i = S_i + a_{i,j} * x_j)$ that read the same value $x_j$ are independent. We can rearrange the NEW and OLD parts among iterations, as illustrated in Fig. 2 (b). In this way, the statements that reads the same value of $x_j$ are placed in the same iteration, which allows us to uncover simultaneous reading in the same iteration and hence explore more parallelism. This space re-arrangement corresponds to a program transformation and the result is shown in Fig. 3.

### 2.2 General iterative task graphs

To represent general iterative computations, we introduce the concept of ITGs. An ITG represents a sequence of task computations where each iteration consists of the execution of a set of tasks. There exist task dependencies within an

```
For k=1 to t
    For i=1 to n
        S_i = .0;
        For j=1 to n,j ≠ i
            S_i = S_i + a_{i,j} * x_j;
        EndFor
        x_i = (1 - ω)x_i + ω * (b_i - S_i)/a_{i,i};
    EndFor
EndFor
```

**Fig. 1.** The sequential SOR algorithm.

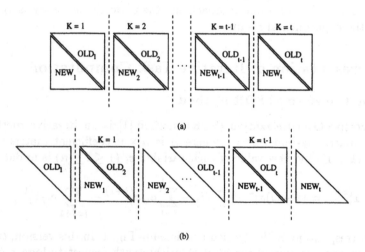

(a)

(b)

**Fig. 2.** Illustration of the transformed SOR computation.

iteration and across iterations. Control dependence is not considered in this paper. Formally, an ITG $G$ contains $v$ tasks $T_1, T_2, \cdots, T_v$, and $e$ data dependence edges. This graph is repeatedly executed for $N$ iterations. Let the instance of task $T_i$ at iteration $k$ be $T_i^k$ $(1 \le k \le N)$. The expanded graph $E(G, N)$ contains all $N * v$ task instances $T_i^k$ $(1 \le i \le v, 1 \le k \le N)$, and these tasks with their dependencies constitute a DAG. Let $(T_i, T_j)$ be a dependence edge from $T_i$ to $T_j$ in $G$, labeled $d_{i,j}$. $d_{i,j}$ is a non-negative integer called dependence distance. Thus task instance $T_j^{k+d_{i,j}}$ depends on $T_i^k$ and it cannot start to execute until $T_i^k$ has completed its computation and the data produced by $T_i^k$ is available at the local memory. Define $Parents(T_i, G)$ to be a set of tasks in $G$ that task $T_i$ depends on.

Each task $T_i$ in an ITG has a computation cost $\tau_i$ and there is a communication cost $c_{i,j}$ for sending a message from task $T_i$ at one processor to task $T_j$ at another processor[9, 25]. The scheduling problem for an ITG is to assign instances of tasks to the given $p$ processors and determine the execution order

```
For i = 1 to n
    Sᵢ = 0;
    For j = i+1 to n
        Sᵢ = Sᵢ + aᵢ,ⱼ * xⱼ;
    EndFor
 EndFor

For k=1 to t-1
    For j = 1 to n
        For i = 1 to n
            If (i ≠ j) Then Sᵢ = Sᵢ + aᵢ,ⱼ * xⱼ;
            Else xᵢ = (1 − ω)xᵢ + ω * (bᵢ − Sᵢ)/aᵢ,ᵢ and Sᵢ = 0;
        EndFor
    EndFor
EndFor

For i = 1 to n
    For j = 1 to i-1
        Sᵢ = Sᵢ + aᵢ,ⱼ * xⱼ;
    EndFor
    xᵢ = (1 − ω)xᵢ + ω * (bᵢ − Sᵢ)/aᵢ,ᵢ;
EndFor
```

**Fig. 3.** The transformed sequential SOR algorithm.

of tasks within each processor. The parallel time is the completion time of the last task instance and the goal of scheduling is to minimize the parallel time.

Fig. 4(a) shows an ITG and the computation weights of all tasks in this ITG are 1 except for task $T_E$ which has $\tau_E = 2$. The communication cost is assumed to be 0.5 between any two processors, for this example. A schedule for this graph when $N = 3$ is depicted in Fig. 4(b). The parallel time is 9.5.

For the SOR method in Fig. 3, we can use the ITG to model the kernel loop $k$. For each element $a_{ij}$ in the matrix, we introduce a task $T_{ij}$. Therefore for a dense matrix $A$, each iteration $k$ contains $n^2$ tasks $T_{i,j}^k$ where $1 \leq i, j \leq n$. And task definitions are shown in Fig. 5. Data dependencies between tasks are specified by the send/receive statements. However, in a sparse matrix system, a lot of tasks which use zero elements for multiplication can be eliminated. The task dependence structure becomes totally irregular. In Fig. 6, we show a sparse matrix in which 'o' indicates a nonzero element. Other unmarked matrix entries are all zeroes. The right side of Fig. 6 shows an ITG based on the SOR method for this matrix, assuming that the convergence test is not conducted in every iteration but every few hundreds of iterations instead. Some of the edges in this graph are marked distance 1, indicating a task depends on data provided by tasks from the previous iteration. The unmarked edges have distance 0, indicating data dependence is within the same iteration. The dependence structure and weights of such graphs are irregular, depending on the nonzero element patterns of sparse matrices.

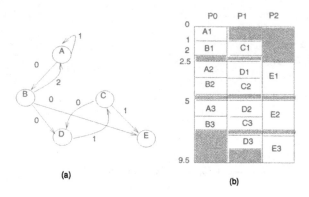

(a)

(b)

**Fig. 4.** (a) An ITG. (b) The Gantt chart of a schedule when $N = 3$.

For tasks $T_{i,j}^k$, $i \neq j$,
  **If** $(j > 1)$ receive($S_i$) from task $T_{i,j-1}^k$;
  **Else** receive($S_i$) from task $T_{i,n}^{k-1}$;
  receive($x_j^k$) from task $T_{j,j}^k$;
  $S_i = S_i + a_{i,j} * x_j^k$;
  **If** $(j < n)$ send($S_i$) to task $T_{i,j+1}^k$;
  **Else** send($S_i$) to task $T_{i,1}^{k+1}$;

Define tasks $T_{i,i}$ as:
  **If** $(i > 1)$ receive($S_i$) from task $T_{i,i-1}^k$;
  **Else** receive($S_i$) from task $T_{i,n}^{k-1}$;
  receive $(x_i)$ from $T_{i,i}^{k-1}$;
  $x_i = (1 - \omega)x_i + \frac{\omega}{a_{i,i}}(b_i - S_i)$;
  $S_i = 0$;
  **If** $(i < n)$ send($S_i$) to task $T_{i,i+1}^k$;
  **Else** send($S_i$) to task $T_{i,1}^{k+1}$;
  broadcast($x_i$) to $T_{r,i}^k$, $r = 1, \cdots, n$, $r \neq i$;

**Fig. 5.** Task definitions for SOR method.

It should be noted that for message-passing architectures, the message transmission overhead is significant and coarse grain partitioning such as submatrix or supernode partitioning for sparse matrix problems should be used. The partitioned SOR method corresponding to Fig. 3 has the matrix/vector-level operations in each statement. For example, $a_{i,j} * x_j$ will be replaced as a multiplication of a submatrix and a vector.

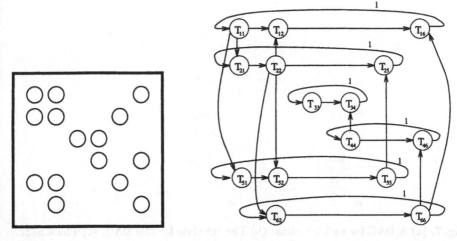

**Fig. 6.** The left part is a sparse matrix and the right side is the ITG based on the SOR method.

## 3    Issues in Scheduling ITGs

In general, the scheduling problem for ITGs is NP-hard. Direct application of DAG algorithms for mapping task instances from all iterations is not feasible. A simple approach to derive a schedule is to use the DAG scheduling algorithm to map the tasks of each iteration, then repeat the same schedule for all iterations. For example, Fig. 7(a) shows the DAG for each iteration by deleting all edges that have a distance larger than 0. A schedule derived for this graph is shown in (b) and then the schedule for the ITG based this DAG schedule is shown in (c). Compared to the schedule of Fig. 4(b), this schedule is much longer. The problem with this approach is that the DAG scheduling algorithm does not consider the overlapping of two or more iterations.

The idea of exploring parallelism within and across iterations has been proposed in software pipelining [2, 19]. In [12], a scheduling algorithm for software pipelining with no communication delay is proposed. We need to extend this result to incorporate communication optimization with load balancing since communication is a major overhead in a message-passing machine. The main optimization in our algorithm is to eliminate unnecessary communication, overlap communication with computation and also have the optimization consistent with the goal of load balancing. We assume that communication between two tasks is zero if these two tasks are mapped to the same processor. Thus placing two tasks together in one processor could eliminate some communication overhead however it might reduce parallelism. A trade-off between parallelization and communication locality must be addressed.

Loop unrolling or graph unfolding techniques [21] are proposed to increase the number of tasks within each iteration so that more parallelism can be explored. Let $f$ be the unfolding factor. When a graph is unfolded $f$ times, the number of

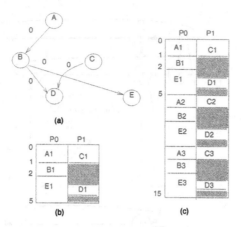

**Fig. 7.** (a) A DAG for each iteration. (b) The schedule for this DAG. (c) The schedule for the ITG.

tasks increases by a factor of $f$ and the number of iterations for the new ITG is $\lfloor N/f \rfloor$. If an ITG is unfolded $N$ times, then the resulting task graph is the expanded graph of $G$, $E(G, N)$. We will integrate the graph unfolding technique in our algorithm and our goal is to derive a small unfolding factor so that tasks from few iterations are examined and the complexity of scheduling is not too high, but still parallelism of the entire iteration space can be explored. In order to derive a schedule which is near optimal, we need to examine the performance of the optimal schedule for this problem. The optimal solution is one that achieves the minimum time for the expanded graph $E(G, N)$. We conduct a comparison of our schedule with an optimal solution. We should emphasize that our analysis measures the asymptotic performance of scheduling and study the competitive ratio of the derived parallel time over the optimal time when $N$ is very large.

## 4 The Heuristic Algorithm

### 4.1 Scheduling model

The starting time of a task $T_i$ at iteration $k$ is modeled as $ST(T_i^k) = \alpha_{p,i} + \beta_p(k - 1)$ where $\alpha_{p,i}$ is called startup delay and $\beta_p$ is the length of the iteration interval. In this model, $T_i^1$ is executed at time $\alpha_{p,i}$, $T_i^2$ is executed at time $\alpha_{p,i} + \beta_p$ and so on. The parallel time is approximately equal to $N * \beta_p$. The goal of the optimization is to minimize $\beta_p$. Notice that $\beta_p$ is uniform for all processors. A non-uniform model is used in [7].

We briefly present an algorithm for scheduling ITGs with dependence cycles on $p$ processors. A detailed description of this algorithm and the algorithm for acyclic ITGs are in [29]. This algorithm first unfolds the graph to increase the number of tasks so that the algorithm has more flexibility in exploring parallelism. Then it transforms the unfolded ITG to a DAG and applies the DAG scheduling techniques. Finally it constructs the ITG schedule based on the DAG schedule. The instances of a task $T_i$ in the unfolded graph are assigned to the same processor.

The overall time complexity of this algorithm is $O(\sqrt{v}e \log^2 \frac{Seq(G)}{\epsilon} + v \log v)$ where constant $\epsilon$ is the desired accuracy to be explained in the algorithm, and $Seq(G) = \sum_{i=1}^{v} \tau_i$. Notice that $v$ is the number of nodes in the task graph and $e$ is the number of dependence edges.

## 4.2 Unfolding the ITG

We unfold the graph in a factor of $f$. In order to determine $f$, we first need to estimate the maximum performance this task graph could achieve. The most important factor is

$$\beta^*(G) = \max_{\text{all cycles } C \text{ in } G} \frac{\tau(C)}{d(C)},$$

where $d(C)$ is the summation of edge distances in this cycle $C$ and $\tau(C)$ is the summation of computation weights of tasks in this cycle. This is the well-known optimal rate (the smallest iteration interval) of the pipelining when the communication cost is zero and there are a sufficient number of processors [22]. To compute this value, we set up the following inequalities for all dependence edges $(T_x, T_y)$ in $G$:

$$\alpha_y - \alpha_x + d_{x,y}\beta \geq \tau_x,$$

where $\alpha_y$ is a non-negative unknown associated with task $T_y$ and $\beta$ is an approximation of $\beta^*(G)$. These inequalities can be solved in a complexity of $O(\sqrt{v}e \log^2 \frac{Seq(G)}{\epsilon})$ using the shortest path algorithm [11] where constant $\epsilon$ is the desired accuracy in finding the minimum value $\beta$ such that $\beta^*(G) \leq \beta \leq \beta^*(G) + \epsilon$.

We need to estimate the granularity of the graph because this value will be useful in computing the performance bound of the produced schedule and the unfolding factor. We use the following value to represent the granularity for a given graph:

$$g(G) = \min_{T_x \in G} \{ \min_{T_y \in Parents(T_x, G)} \frac{\tau_x}{c_{y,x}} \}.$$

Then the graph is unfolded by a factor of $f$ which is $f = \lceil \max(L1, L2) \rceil$ where

$$L1 = \frac{S1(\tau^{max} + \epsilon) + \tau^{max}/g(G)}{(B-1)Seq(G)/p - S1\beta}, \quad L2 = \frac{S1(\tau^{max} + \epsilon) + \tau^{max}/g(G)}{B(\beta - \epsilon) - S1\beta - Seq(G)/p},$$

$$B = S1(1 + \frac{\epsilon}{\max(\beta - \epsilon, Seq(G)/p)}) + 1, \quad S1 = 1 - 1/p + 1/g(G),$$

and $\tau^{max}$ is the maximum task weight in $G$.

This new graph is called $G^f$ which contains $f * v$ nodes. And it needs to be executed $\lfloor N/f \rfloor$ iterations. We use the unfolding algorithm proposed in [21] to construct $G^f$. The analysis in Section 4.6 shows that such a factor $f$ will guarantee that the asymptotic performance of this scheduling is competitive to an optimal solution in a ratio of $B$.

## 4.3 Graph transformation

We transform $G^f$ into a DAG so that the DAG scheduling technique could be applied. Define $DIV(x,y)$ as the largest integer that is less than or equal to $x/y$, i.e. $\lfloor x/y \rfloor$. Define $MOD(x,y) = x - DIV(x,y) * y$. Let the tasks in $G^f$ be renumbered as $T_1, T_2, \cdots, T_{fv}$. We first compute the minimum integer values for $\beta_f$ and $\alpha_i$ $(1 \le i \le fv)$ based on the following inequalities for each dependence edge $(T_i, T_j)$ in $G^f$: $\alpha_j - \alpha_i + \beta_f d_{i,j} \ge \tau_i$, where $\alpha_j$ is a non-negative unknown associated with task $T_j$ in $G^f$ and $\beta_f$ is an approximation of $\beta^*(G^f)$. Since we know that $\beta^*(G^f) = f\beta^*(G)$, it can be shown that $f\beta - f\epsilon \le \beta^*(G^f) \le f\beta$. Thus the value $\beta_f$ can be easily found in this range using the binary searching and the shortest path algorithm. The result satisfies $\beta^*(G) \le \beta_f \le \beta^*(G) + \epsilon$.

For example, edge $(A, B)$ in Fig. 4(a) corresponds to the inequality $\alpha_B - \alpha_A + 0\beta_f \ge 1$. Based on inequalities of all edges, we can produce a solution $\beta_f = 2$, $\alpha_A = 0$, $\alpha_B = \alpha_C = 1$ and $\alpha_D = \alpha_E = 2$.

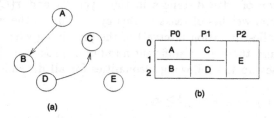

(a)

(b)

**Fig. 8.** (a) A kernel DAG. (b) The schedule for this DAG.

Then we transform the dependence graph $G$ by deleting all edges $(T_i, T_j)$ in the graph $G$ which satisfy: $MOD(\alpha_j, \beta) - MOD(\alpha_i, \beta) < \tau_i$. For example, edge $(C, E)$ of Fig. 4(a) is deleted because its edge weight satisfies $MOD(\alpha_E, \beta) - MOD(\alpha_C, \beta) < \tau_i$.

This transformation was first proposed in [12] for mapping graphs when communication is zero. We can show such a transformation is still valid for our case by carefully designing the ITG schedule in Section 4.5. The dependencies represented by these deleted edges will be satisfied in the final schedule constructed in Section 4.5. It can be verified that the resulting graph after edge deletions is a DAG. We call the transformed graph the kernel DAG $K(G^f)$. For example, the kernel DAG of Fig. 4(a) is in Fig. 8(a).

## 4.4 Mapping the kernel graph

In this step, a DAG schedule is derived for $K(G^f)$. The starting time $\gamma_i$ and the processor assignment $Proc(i)$ of each task $T_i$ are provided. In mapping the kernel DAG, we use two algorithms: one is a multi-stage algorithm designed for the PYRROS system [28], another is a one-stage algorithm. We will choose the smaller one between two solutions produced by these two algorithms. The result of the DAG scheduling is used for constructing the ITG schedule in Section 4.5. We will derive the performance bound for the second algorithm, which will be used in deriving the bound of the ITG schedule. Both algorithms have a complexity $O((v + e) \log v)^1$.

**A multi-stage approach** We apply the DAG scheduling techniques on $K(G^f)$ using the following multi-stage algorithm: 1) Assign tasks to a set of clusters. Tasks in the same cluster will be executed in the same processor. 2) Map the clusters into $p$ processors. 3) Order the execution of tasks within each processor. Multi-stage approaches to scheduling have been advocated in the past works, e.g. [20, 23] due to its lower complexity and competitive performance.

**Clustering:** The goal of clustering is to identify communication-intensive tasks and analyze the impact of communication on global parallel time to decide if sequentialization or parallelization should be used. We use the Dominant Sequence Clustering Algorithm (DSC) [26] for this phase. This algorithm has a complexity of $O((v + e) \log v)$ and it performs a sequence of clustering refinement steps. At each step it identifies a critical edge and tries to assign two end tasks of this edge to the same processor so that the parallel time can be reduced effectively. The DSC algorithm is able to produce optimal solutions for fork DAGs, join DAGs, coarse grain trees and a class of fine grain trees. Notice that the problem of scheduling general fine grain trees or fork-join DAGs is NP-complete [4].

**Mapping clusters to processors:** If the number of clusters is larger than $p$, we need to merge clusters. A merging algorithm which considers load balance but also preserves parallelism has been proposed in [23]. Currently we have used a simple heuristic based on the work profiling method [13] which works well in practice. We first compute the total computational weights for each processor and then use this information to map clusters to processors such that computational load is evenly distributed among processors. This method has a complexity of $O(v \log v)$.

**Task ordering:** For Fig. 8, the ordering of tasks at each processor is fixed due to data dependencies. However, in general tasks in one processor may be independent and the execution order of these tasks affects the starting time of critical tasks at other processors. Thus we further order the execution of tasks within each processor with a goal of overlapping communication with computation to hide communication latency so that the total parallel time is minimized. Finding a task ordering that minimizes the parallel time is NP-hard even for chains of tasks. We have proposed a heuristic algorithm RCP based on the critical-task-first principle and compared its performance with others for randomly generated graphs, and RCP is optimal for fork and join DAGs [27].

This multi-stage approach has been shown practical in mapping large graphs[14, 28]. [14] conducted a comparison with a higher complexity ETF method[18] and

---

[1] The size of the graph increases by $f$ after unfolding. However in practice, we find that $f$ is small, thus $f$ is not included in the complexity term.

found that this approach has a much lower complexity but a competitive performance.

**A one-stage approach** In this approach, we use the idea of the DSC algorithm but limit the number of clusters to $p$. The algorithm first computes the *blevel* value for each task where $blevel(T_x)$ is the length of the longest path from this task $T_x$ to an exit node. The algorithm updates the value of *tlevel* for each unscheduled task where $tlevel(T_x)$ is the length of the longest path from an entry task to this task $T_x$ (the partial order includes the execution order between tasks within the same processors). The algorithm maintains a list of free tasks and at each step it picks one free task $T_1$ with the smallest *tlevel* value and another free task $T_2$ with the biggest $tlevel(T_2) + blevel(T_2)$ value. Then we will try to schedule these two tasks separately through the minimization procedure described in DSC ( [26], page 958). And we will select one of these two tasks that has earlier starting time. If a tie occurs, we will pick the latter one. The *tlevel* value of the selected task will be the latest starting time $\gamma_x$ of this task unless there are no processors available. The minimization procedure reduces the starting time of the selected task by merging one or more parents of this examined task to one processor. In this way the unnecessary communication could be saved. The complexity of this algorithm is $O((v+e)\log v)$. When there is a sufficient number of processors, the algorithm reaches the optimum for fork, join, coarse grained tree DAGs. Also in [29] we show that given a DAG $R$ and $p$ processors, the parallel time produced by this algorithm is bounded by

$$PT(R) \leq (2 - 1/p + 1/g(R))PT_{opt}(R)$$

where $PT_{opt}(R)$ is the optimal solution for this graph $R$. The ETF algorithm [18] has a similar performance bound with a complexity $O(pv^2)$ while our algorithm has a lower complexity $O((v+e)\log v)$.

## 4.5 Constructing an ITG schedule

The DAG scheduling produces processor assignment $Proc(i)$ and the starting time $\gamma_i$ for each task $T_i$ in $K(G^f)$. Next we construct a schedule for the original *ITG* based on the DAG scheduling result. The startup delay of task $T_i$ in the ITG schedule is $\alpha_{p,i} = \gamma_i + \beta_p DIV(\alpha_i, \beta_f)$ and $\beta_p = max(PT(K(G^f)), D)$ where

$$D = \max_{(T_x,T_y)\in G^f, \text{ but } \notin K(G^f)} \left\{ \frac{\gamma_x + \tau_x - \gamma_y + c_{x,y}}{DIV(\alpha_y, \beta_f) - DIV(\alpha_x, \beta_f) + d_{x,y}} \right\}.$$

The processor assignment of instances of $T_i$ in this ITG schedule is the same as $Proc(i)$ derived by the DAG scheduling algorithm. Notice that $c_{x,y} = 0$ if $T_x$ and $T_y$ are assigned to the same processor.

For the kernel DAG of Fig. 8(a) and $p = 3$, the DAG scheduling produces the following solution: $Proc(A) = Proc(B) = 0$, $Proc(C) = Proc(D) = 1$, and $Proc(E) = 2$. And $\gamma_A = \gamma_D = \gamma_E = 0$ and $\gamma_B = \gamma_C = 1$. Thus $\beta_p = 2.5$ and the startup delays for $A, B, C, D, E$ are 0,1,1,2.5,2.5 respectively.

## 4.6 Analysis

We can show that the schedule derived by the above algorithm satisfies the resource and dependence constraints. We also conduct an analysis to compute the unfolding factor that gives a guarantee on the asymptotic performance bound of this heuristic algorithm. Because the result of this analysis is used in the first step of our algorithm, the expression for estimating the unfolding factor can only rely on information from the given graph $G$, not $G^f$. Thus a connection between the characteristics of $G$ and $G^f$ must be constructed.

**Theorem 1** *Let the unfolding factor $f$ be chosen as: $f = \lceil \max(L1, L2) \rceil$ where*

$$L1 = \frac{S1(\tau^{max} + \epsilon) + \tau^{max}/g(G)}{(B-1)Seq(G)/p - S1\beta} \text{ and } L2 = \frac{S1(\tau^{max} + \epsilon) + \tau^{max}/g(G)}{B(\beta - \epsilon) - S1\beta - Seq(G)/p}.$$

*Let $\epsilon \neq \beta - Seq/p$. Then*

$$\lim_{N \to \infty} \frac{PT(G)}{PT_{opt}(G)} \leq B$$

*where*

$$B = S1(1 + \frac{\epsilon}{max(\beta - \epsilon, Seq(G)/p)}) + 1$$

*and $S1 = 1 + 1/g(G) - 1/p$. $PT(G)$ is the solution produced by our algorithm, and $PT_{opt}(G)$ is the optimal solution (by examining the entire iteration space $E(G, N)$).*

This theorem indicates that since $\epsilon$ could be chosen small, the bound is about $S1 + 1 = (1 - 1/p + 1/g(G)) + 1$. When the granularity of the $G$ is not too small, this bound is tight. Notice that our granularity estimation may not be effective when some tasks perform very small computation but receive large messages from others. In practice, the size of data a task communicates is proportional to the amount of computing work it does. On the other hand, the theorem also indicates that the program partitioning we choose to produce ITGs should not make $g(G)$ too small. This is consistent with the previous results [16].

## 5 Experiments

We have tested the performance of sparse SOR ITGs based on submatrix partitioning. The test matrices are the part of the Harwell-Boeing Test Suites [10]. We use matrix BCSSTK14 arising from structural analysis for the roof of Omni Coliseum at Atlanta and matrix BCSSTK15 for Module of an offshore platform. The simulated performance on a nCUBE-2 machine is shown in Fig.9. While the parallelism in a sparse matrix computation is limited, this algorithm is able to explore a decent amount of parallelism.

Our approach for mapping SOR computation is essentially to overlap computation and communication of several SOR iterations. Another approach for parallelizing SOR-based iterative computation is the multi-coloring method [1]. This

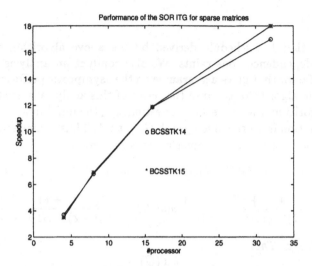

**Fig. 9.** The scheduling performance for BCSSTK14 and BCSSTK15.

scheme performs variable relabeling to increase the amount of exploitable parallelism since nodes with the same color can be computed concurrently. Adams and Jordan [1] have shown that the multi-coloring method is numerically equivalent to performing several SOR iterations simultaneously in the absence of convergence tests. However, in order to preserve inter-color data dependencies, processors must communicate between each computation phase associated with each color. This constitutes a drawback in the implementation of the multi-coloring scheme for message-passing machines as communication and computation cannot be overlapped.

In [8], we conduct the experiments to compare the multi-coloring approach with our approach in solving banded matrix systems. Table 1 shows the megaflops obtained in nCUBE-2 and Intel Paragon machines (vector units are not used). The left part shows the megaflop performance for fixed matrix size $n$ and $p = 64$. The right part is for a fixed matrix band width. The experiments indicate that our approach that overlaps several SOR iterations outperforms the multi-coloring method when many colors are needed. Banded matrices are one type of sparse matrices. For sparse matrices with irregular distribution of nonzero elements, many colors are usually needed [17]. We expect our method performs well but we need to conduct more experiments.

## 6 Conclusions

Our experiments show that the automatic scheduling algorithms for ITGs delivers good performance on the iterative SOR method. In [29], we have presented a method for executing ITG schedules and provided analytic and experimental results to show that run-time performance of static schedules is stable if variations

| | 64 procs n:12,800 | | | |
|---|---|---|---|---|
| | nCUBE-2 | | Paragon | |
| width | color | overlap | color | overlap |
| 21 | 24.5 | 37.3 | 149 | 309 |
| 41 | 26.0 | 41.4 | 165 | 430 |
| 81 | 26.1 | 43.9 | 167 | 537 |
| 161 | 26.5 | 45.3 | 171 | 608 |

| | Width 161, Paragon | | | |
|---|---|---|---|---|
| | n=12800 | | n/p=200 | |
| p (procs) | color | overlap | color | overlap |
| 4 | 22.4 | 41 | 11.1 | 38 |
| 8 | 41.3 | 81 | 22.1 | 76 |
| 16 | 73.9 | 162 | 44.3 | 152 |
| 32 | 121.4 | 314 | 88.9 | 304 |

**Table 1.** The left part is the megaflops obtained with the fixed matrix size and $p = 64$ and the right part is with the fixed matrix bandwidth.

between predicted static weights and actual run-time weights are not significant. We have also discussed a scheduling algorithm for acyclic ITGs with a performance competitive ratio close to $2p/(p + 1)$. Currently we are implementing a run-time support system for efficiently executing irregular ITG schedules.

## Acknowledgement

This was supported in part by NSF RIA CCR-9409695, a startup fund from UCSB and ARPA contract DABT-63-93-C-0064. We thank Vivek Sarkar, Val Donaldson, Jeanne Ferrante and the anonymous referees for their useful comments, and Pedro Diniz for his help in algorithm implementation.

## References

1. L. Adams, and H. Jordan, Is SOR color-blind?, *SIAM J. Sci. Stat. Comp*, 7 (1986), pp 490-506.
2. A. Aiken and A. Nicolau, Optimal Loop Parallelization, *SIGPLAN 88 Conf. on Programming Language Design and Implementation*. pp.308-317.
3. F. T. Chong and R. Schreiber, Parallel sparse triangular solution with partitioned inverses and prescheduled DAGs, Tech Report,MIT, 1994.
4. P. Chretienne, Task Scheduling over Distributed Memory Machines, *Proc. of Inter. Workshop on Parallel and Distributed Algorithms*, (North Holland, Ed.), 1989.
5. P. Chretienne, Cyclic scheduling with communication delays: a polynomial special case. Dec 1993. Tech Report, LITP.
6. M. Cosnard and M. Loi, Automatic Task Graph Generation Techniques, *Proc. of the Hawaii International Conference on System Sciences*, IEEE, Vol II. 1995.
7. V. Donaldson and J. Ferrante, Determining asynchronous pipeline execution times. Tech. Report, UCSD, 1995.
8. P. Diniz and T. Yang. *Efficient Parallelization of Relaxation Iterative Methods for Solving Banded Linear Systems on Multiprocessors*, TRCS94-15, UCSB.
9. T. H. Dunigan, Performance of the INTEL iPSC/860 and nCUBE 6400 Hypercube, ORNL/TM-11790, Oak Ridge National Lab., TN, 1991.
10. I. S. Duff, R. G. Grimes and J. G. Lewis, Users' Guide for the Harwell-Boeing Sparse Matrix Collection, TR-PA-92-86.
11. H. Gabow and R. Tarjan, Faster scaling algorithms for network problems, *SIAM J. Computing*, Oct 1989.

12. F. Gasperoni and U. Schweigelshohn Scheduling Loops on Parallel Processors: A simple algorithm with close to optimum performance. *Proc. of CONPAR 92* , pp. 613-624.

13. A. George, M.T. Heath, and J. Liu, Parallel Cholesky Factorization on a Shared Memory Processor, *Lin. Algebra Appl.*, Vol. 77, 1986, pp. 165-187.

14. A. Gerasoulis, J. Jiao, and T. Yang, A multistage approach to scheduling task graphs. To appear in DIMACS Book Series on Parallel Processing of Discrete Optimization Problems. AMS publisher. Edited by P.M. Pardalos, K.G. Ramakrishnan, and M.G.C. Resende.

15. A. Gerasoulis, J. Jiao and T. Yang, Scheduling of structured and unstructured computation, To appear in DIMACS Book Series, Workshop on Interconnections Networks and Mappings and Scheduling Parallel Computation, 1994, Editors: D. Hsu, A. Rosenberg, D. Sotteau.

16. A. Gerasoulis and T. Yang, On the Granularity and Clustering of Directed Acyclic Task Graphs, *IEEE Trans. on Parallel and Distributed Systems.*, Vol. 4, no. 6, June 1993, pp 686-701.

17. G. Huang and W. Ongsakol, *An Efficient Task Allocation Algorithm and its use to Parallelize Irregular Gauss-Seidel Type Algorithms*, In Proc. of the Eighth International Parallel Processing Symposium, Cancun, Mexico, (1994), pp. 497–501.

18. J. J. Hwang, Y. C. Chow, F. D. Anger, and C. Y. Lee, Scheduling precedence graphs in systems with interprocessor communication times, *SIAM J. Comput.*, pp. 244-257, 1989.

19. M. Lam, Software pipelining: an effective scheduling technique for VLIW machines, *ACM Conf. on Programming Language Design and Implementation*, 1988, 318-328.

20. S.J. Kim and J.C. Browne, A General Approach to Mapping of Parallel Computation upon Multiprocessor Architectures, *Proc. of ICPP*, 1988, V3, 1-8.

21. K. K. Parhi and D. G. Messerschmitt, Static rate-optimal scheduling of iterative dataflow programs via optimum unfolding, *IEEE Trans. on Computers*, 40:2, 1991, pp. 178-195.

22. R. Reiter, Scheduling parallel computations, *J. of ACM*, Oct 1968, pp. 590-599.

23. V. Sarkar, *Partitioning and Scheduling Parallel Programs for Execution on Multiprocessors*, MIT Press, 1989.

24. V. H. Van Dongen, G. R. Gao and Q. Ning A polynomial time method for optimal software pipelining. *Proc. of CONPAR 92*, pp. 613-624.

25. T. Von Eicken, D.E. Culler, S.C. Goldstein, and K. E. Schauser. Active messages: a mechanism for integrated communication and computation, *Proc of 19th Int. Sym. on Computer Architecture*, 1992.

26. T. Yang and A. Gerasoulis. DSC: Scheduling parallel tasks on an unbounded number of processors, *IEEE Transactions on Parallel and Distributed Systems*, Vol. 5, No. 9, 951-967, 1994.

27. T. Yang and A. Gerasoulis. List scheduling with and without communication. *Parallel Computing*, V. 19 (1993) pp. 1321-1344.

28. T. Yang and A. Gerasoulis, PYRROS: Static Task Scheduling and Code Generation for Message-Passing Multiprocessors, *Proc. of 6th ACM Inter. Confer. on Supercomputing*, Washington D.C., 1992, pp. 428-437.

29. T. Yang, C. Fu, A. Gerasoulis and V. Sarkar, Mapping iterative task graphs on distributed-memory machines, Tech. Report 1995. Part of this report will appear in *Proc. of Inter. Conference on Parallel Processing*, 1995.

# Approximation Algorithms for Time Constrained Scheduling

Klaus Jansen[1], Sabine Öhring[2]

[1] Institut für Informatik, Technische Universität, München, Arcisstr. 21, 80 290
München, Germany, email : jansen@informatik.tu-muenchen.de.
[2] Department of Computer Science, University of North Texas, Denton, TX
76203-3886, USA, email : oehring@cs.unt.edu.

Abstract. In this paper we consider the following time constrained
scheduling problem. Given a set of jobs $J$ with execution times $e(j) \in
(0,1]$ and an undirected graph $G = (J, E)$, we consider the problem to
find a schedule for the jobs such that adjacent jobs $(j, j') \in E$ are assigned to different machines and that the total execution time for each
machine is at most 1.

The goal is to find a minimum number of machines to execute all jobs
under this time constraint. This scheduling problem is a natural generalization of the classical bin packing problem. We propose and analyze
several approximation algorithms with constant absolute worst case ratio
for graphs that can be colored in polynomial time.

## 1 Introduction

Let $J$ be a set of jobs with execution times $e(j)$ ($0 < e(j) \leq 1$) and let
$G = (J, E)$ be a conflict graph. We look for a partition of the job set $J$ into
independent sets $U_1, \ldots, U_m$ such that $\sum_{j \in U_i} e(j) \leq 1$ for each $1 \leq i \leq m$. For
each edge $e = (j, j') \in E$ the corresponding jobs $j$ and $j'$ must be processed on
different machines. Each independent set $U_i$ has to be executed by one machine
with total execution time at most 1. The goal of the studied problem is to find
such a partition with a minimum number $m$ of machines.

One application of this scheduling problem is given by Cheadle, Hirschberg
and Wong [6]. The jobs are thought as geographical locations. Finding them in
the same bin corresponds to assigning them to a common facility (computing
service, telephone switching cluster) where each facility is assumed to have a
standard capacity $C$. We desire that locations which are served by the same
facility be close proximity to each other, and therefore we add a conflict edge
between two locations $j$ and $j'$ if the distance $d(j, j')$ is larger than a given limit.
These conflict edges restrict the types of partitions that we allow and yields to
the considered scheduling problem. Another application arises in the production
of e.g. chemical materials. We have conflict edges between jobs $j$ and $j'$ if the
machine preparation times $t(j, j')$ are larger than a given limit.

If $E$ is an empty set, this scheduling problem is equal to the classical bin
packing problem. Furthermore, if $\sum_{j \in J} e(j) \leq 1$ then we obtain the problem to

# Approximation Algorithms for Time Constrained Scheduling

Klaus Jansen[1], Sabine Öhring[2]

[1] Institut für Informatik, Technische Universität München, Arcisstr. 21, 80 290 München, Germany, email : jansenk@informatik.tu-muenchen.de
[2] Department of Computer Science, University of North Texas, Denton, TX 76203-3886, USA, email : oehring@cs.unt.edu

**Abstract.** In this paper we consider the following time constrained scheduling problem. Given a set of jobs $J$ with execution times $e(j) \in (0, 1]$ and an undirected graph $G = (J, E)$, we consider the problem to find a schedule for the jobs such that adjacent jobs $(j, j') \in E$ are assigned to different machines and that the total execution time for each machine is at most 1.
The goal is to find a minimum number of machines to execute all jobs under this time constraint. This scheduling problem is a natural generalization of the classical bin packing problem. We propose and analyse several approximation algorithms with constant absolute worst case ratio for graphs that can be colored in polynomial time.

## 1 Introduction

Let $J$ be a set of jobs with execution times $e(j) \in \mathbb{R}^+$ ($0 < e(j) \le 1$) and let $G = (J, E)$ be a conflict graph. We look for a partition of the job set $J$ into independent sets $U_1, \ldots, U_m$ such that $\sum_{j \in U_i} e(j) \le 1$ for each $1 \le i \le m$. For each edge $e = \{j, j'\} \in E$ the corresponding jobs $j$ and $j'$ must be processed on different machines. Each independent set $U_i$ has to be executed by one machine with total execution time at most 1. The goal of the studied problem is to find such a partition with a minimum number $m$ of machines.

One application of this scheduling problem is given by Chandra, Hirschberg and Wong [5]. The jobs are thought as geographical locations. Putting them in the same bin corresponds to assigning them to a common facility (computing service, telephone switching center) where each facility is assumed to have a standard capacity $C$. We desire that locations which are served by the same facility be close proximity to each other, and therefore we add a conflict edge between two locations $j$ and $j'$ if the distance $d(j, j')$ is larger than a given limit. These conflict edges restrict the types of packings that we allow and yields to the considered scheduling problem. Another application arises in the production of e.g. chemical materials. We have conflict edges between jobs $j$ and $j'$ iff the machine preparation times $t(j, j')$ are larger than a given limit.

If $E$ is an empty set, this scheduling problem is equal to the classical bin-packing problem. Furthermore, if $\sum_{j \in J} e(j) \le 1$ then we obtain the problem to compute the chromatic number $\chi(G)$ of the conflict graph $G$. This means that the time constrained scheduling problem is NP-complete even if $E = \emptyset$ or if $\sum_{j \in J} e(j) \le 1$.

We propose methods which generate approximate solutions for the problem in polynomial time. We define $\omega^H$ to be the number of machines when the jobs are assigned by a heuristic $H$, and $\omega^*$ to be the corresponding optimum number. If independently of the problem instances, $\omega^H \le \rho\omega^*$ holds for a specified constant $\rho$, with $\rho$ as small as possible, then $\rho$ is called the absolute worst case performance ratio of heuristic $H$. The approximation algorithms we propose in this paper work for conflict graphs belonging to graph classes that are easy (i.e. in polynomial time) to color.

We notice that no polynomial time algorithm has an absolute worst case ratio smaller than 1.5 for the bin packing or considered scheduling problem, unless $P = NP$. This is obvious since such an algorithm could be used to solve the partition problem [8] in polynomial time. The scheduling problem for an arbitrary undirected graph is harder to approximate, because Lund and Yannakakis [16] recently proved that unless $P = NP$ there is an $\epsilon > 0$ such that no polynomial time approximation algorithm for the coloring problem can guarantee a worst case ratio better than $|J|^\epsilon$.

The orthogonal problem, called resource constrained scheduling, where the number of machines $m$ is given and where the maximum completion time (called makespan) is minimized was studied before in [2]. In [2] an approximation algorithm is given for the case that we have a priori a $k$-coloring of the conflict graph. The algorithm has the worst case ratio $\frac{k+2}{2}$ for $m \ge k+1$, and when $\frac{m}{k}$ tends to infinity the worst case ratio tends to 2. Moreover, we proved that unless $P = NP$ no approximation algorithm can beat the worst case ratio 2.

Furthermore, in [3] the resource constrained scheduling problem with unit-execution times ($e(j) = \frac{1}{\ell}$ for each job $j \in J$) was studied. In [3] the computational complexity of this problem is studied for different graph classes like bipartite graphs, interval graphs and cographs, arbitrary and constant numbers $m$ and $\ell$.

In this paper, we study seven approximation algorithms for the time constrained problem. The first algorithm is a direct modification of bin-packing heuristics. In Section 2 it is shown that the first algorithm does not have a constant worst case ratio. The other algorithms are based on the composition of two algorithms - a coloring algorithm and bin packing heuristics applied on a part of the conflict graph. The simplest algorithm given in Section 3 uses an optimum coloring and the next-fit heuristic and has the absolute worst case ratio 3. For first-fit the bound becomes 2.7 and for first-fit decreasing the bound lies between 2.691 and 2.7. Applied to bipartite graphs the approximation algorithm generates the ratio 2.

The third algorithm is based on a precoloring method. The main step is to compute a minimum coloring of the conflict graph where the long jobs are separated or colored differently. Based on this method, we obtain an approximation algorithm with worst case ratio $\frac{5}{2}$ for graphs like interval graphs, split graphs, cographs and further graphs; see Section 4. More involved coloring methods are studied in Section 5. We obtain approximation algorithms with worst case bounds $\frac{7}{3}$, $\frac{11}{5}$ and $\frac{15}{7}$. The last algorithm is a general separation method that works for cographs and partial $K$-trees. Based on this separation method we obtain an approximation algorithm with worst case ratio $2 + \epsilon$ for these two graph classes. This result implies approximation with factor $2 + \epsilon$ for any class of graphs with a constant upper bound on the treewidth (e.g. outerplanar graphs, series parallel graphs and Halin graphs).

## 2 Direct bin-packing

In this section we analyse an algorithm that is a direct modification of the bin-packing heuristics. For a survey on the bin packing problem we refer to [6]. First, we describe the bin packing problem and three important approximation algorithms.

The bin packing problem is stated as follows [14]. Let $L = (a_1, \ldots, a_n)$ be a list of real positive numbers $a_i$ $(0 < a_i \leq 1)$. The problem is to place the elements of $L$ into a minimum number $\omega^*(L)$ of bins such that no bin contains numbers whose sum exceeds the capacity 1. We index the bins as $B_1, B_2, \ldots$, initially filled to level zero, and we place the numbers $a_1, \ldots, a_n$ in the given order of the list $L$. The well-known bin-packing heuristics NF (Next Fit), FF (First Fit) and FFD (First Fit Decreasing) can be described as follows:

**Algorithm(NF):** To place $a_i$, take the highest index $j$ such that $B_j$ is filled to level $\beta > 0$. If $\beta + a_i \leq 1$ then place $a_i$ into $B_j$; otherwise place $a_i$ into the next empty bin $B_{j+1}$.

**Algorithm(FF):** To place $a_i$, find the smallest $j$ such that $B_j$ is filled to level $\beta \leq 1 - a_i$ and place $a_i$ into $B_j$.

**Algorithm(FFD):** Arrange the list $L = (a_1, \ldots, a_n)$ into non-increasing order and apply the algorithm (FF) on the derived list.

It is not difficult to show that the number of bins used in the Next Fit packing $\omega^{NF}(L)$ is at most $2\omega^*(L)$. The best bound on the performance of $FF$ is given in [7] where they show that

$$\omega^{FF}(L) \leq \lceil \frac{17}{10}\omega^*(L) \rceil.$$

Currently, the best bound on the performance of $FFD$ has been obtained by Minyi [17] who shows that

$$\omega^{FFD}(L) \leq \frac{11}{9}\omega^*(L) + 1.$$

Therefore, the asymptotic worst case ratio of the $FF$ heuristic is $\frac{17}{10}$ while $FFD$ has an asymptotic worst case ratio of $\frac{11}{9}$. Simchi-Levi [18] studied the absolute worst case ratio of both heuristics and proved that $\omega^{FF}(L)/\omega^*(L) \leq 1.75$ and that $\omega^{FFD}(L)/\omega^*(L) \leq 1.5$.

Now, we describe the first algorithm for the scheduling problem. We index the independent sets $U_1, U_2, \ldots$, initially defined as empty sets and we place the jobs $j \in J$ in the order of a given list $L = (j_1, \ldots, j_n)$.

**Algorithm 1(NF):** To place $j_i$, take the highest index $k$ such that $U_k \neq \emptyset$. If $U_k \cup \{j_i\}$ remains independent and $c(j_i) + \sum_{j \in U_k} c(j) \leq 1$ then place $j_i$ into $U_k$; otherwise place $j_i$ into the next empty set $U_{k+1}$.

**Algorithm 1(FF):** To place $j_i$, find the smallest index $k$ such that $U_k \cup \{j_i\}$ is independent and that $c(j_i) + \sum_{j \in U_k} c(j) \leq 1$ and place $j_i$ into $U_k$.

**Algorithm 1(FFD):** Arrange the list $L = (j_1, \ldots, j_n)$ into non-increasing order $e(j_1) \geq \ldots \geq e(j_n)$ and apply the Algorithm 1(FF) on the derived list.

As abbreviations for the algorithms we use *Alg 1(NF)*, *Alg 1(FF)* and *Alg 1 (FFD)*.

**Theorem 1.** *There is a problem instance $(G = (J, E), e)$ with unit-execution times $e(j) = \frac{1}{k}$ for each job $j \in J$ (with $k = \frac{|J|}{2}$) and a list $L = (j_1, \ldots, j_n)$ such that*

$$\omega^{Alg\ 1(NF)} = \omega^{Alg\ 1(FF)} = \omega^{Alg\ 1(FFD)} = O(|J|) \cdot \omega^*.$$

*Proof.* Let $J$ be $\{a_1, \ldots, a_k\} \cup \{b_1, \ldots, b_k\}$ and let $E$ be $\{\{a_i, b_j\} | 1 \leq i \neq j \leq k\}$. As list $L$ we use $\{a_1, b_1, \ldots, a_k, b_k\}$. Then, Algorithm 1 generates $k$ independent sets $\{a_1, b_1\}, \ldots, \{a_k, b_k\}$. On the other hand, the optimum solution is given by two independent sets $\{a_1, \ldots, a_k\}$ and $\{b_1, \ldots, b_k\}$. Therefore, $\omega^* = 2$ and $\omega^{Alg\ 1(FFD)} = \frac{|J|}{2}$. □

## 3 Coloring method

In this section, we propose a method which generates the constant worst case ratio 2.7 for graphs that can be colored in polynomial time. The algorithm computes in the first step a minimum coloring and applies then a bin-packing heuristic to each color set.

**Algorithm 2:**

**Step 1:** Compute a minimum partition into independent sets $U_1, \ldots, U_{\chi(G)}$ for the conflict graph $G$.

**Step 2:** Apply a bin-packing heuristic (NF, FF, FFD) to each independent set $U_i$, $1 \leq i \leq \chi(G)$.

As above, we denote with *Alg 2(NF)*, *Alg 2(FF)* and *Alg 2(FFD)* the corresponding composed algorithms.

**Theorem 2.**

$$\omega^{Alg\ 2(NF)} \leq 3 \cdot \omega^*.$$

*Proof.* Let $U_i^{(1)}, \ldots, U_i^{(\ell_i)}$ be the independent sets generated by the $NF$ algorithm applied on $U_i$. Each of these independent sets can be processed on one machine with execution time at most 1. We obtain the following (in)-equalities:

(a) $\omega^{Alg\ 2(NF)} = \sum_{i=1}^{\chi(G)} \ell_i$.

(b) $\omega^* \geq \chi(G)$.

(c) $\omega^* > \sum_{i=1, \ell_i > 1}^{\chi(G)} \lfloor \frac{\ell_i}{2} \rfloor$.

The inequality $(c)$ is true, since in the $NF$ algorithm the levels of neighbouring bins $B_i, B_{i+1}$ satisfy: $b_i + b_{i+1} > 1$. We can transform $(c)$ directly into:

(c') $\sum_{i:\ell_i>1} \ell_i < 2\omega^* + \sum_{i:\ell_i>1} 1$.

The (in-) equalities $(a), (b)$ and $(c')$ imply

$$\omega^{Alg\ 2(NF)} = \sum_{i:\ell_i=1} \ell_i + \sum_{i:\ell_i>1} \ell_i$$
$$\leq 2 \cdot \omega^* + \sum_{i:\ell_i \geq 1} 1$$
$$= 2 \cdot \omega^* + \chi(G) \leq 3 \cdot \omega^*.$$

□

We note that there is a set of instances with asymptotically worst case bound 3 for *Alg 2(NF)*.

**Theorem 3.** *If $G = (J, E)$ is a bipartite graph, then $\omega^{Alg\ 2(NF)} \leq 2 \cdot \omega^*$.*

*Proof.* We obtain as above $\omega^{Alg\ 2(NF)} = \ell_1 + \ell_2$. For $\ell_1, \ell_2 > 1$ the inequality $(c)$ implies $\omega^* \geq \lfloor \frac{\ell_1}{2} \rfloor + \lfloor \frac{\ell_2}{2} \rfloor + 1 \geq \frac{\ell_1 + \ell_2}{2}$. In this case $\omega^{Alg\ 2(NF)} = \ell_1 + \ell_2 \leq 2\omega^*$. For $\ell_1 = \ell_2 = 1$ we have $\omega^{Alg\ 2(NF)} = \omega^*$. The remaining case is $\ell_1 = 1$ and $\ell_2 > 1$. Let $b_1, \ldots, b_{\ell_2}$ be the execution times of the constructed independent sets. Since the bin-packing heuristic $NF$ is applied to the large set $U_2$, we get the inequalities

$$b_1 + b_2, b_3 + b_4, \ldots, b_{\ell_2-1} + b_{\ell_2} > 1.$$

We obtain that $\omega^* > \lfloor \frac{\ell_2}{2} \rfloor$. If $\ell_2$ is an even number then $\ell_2 < 2\omega^*$ or $\ell_2 \leq 2\omega^* - 1$. If $\ell_2$ is odd then $\ell_2 < 2\omega^* + 1$. Since $2\omega^* + 1$ is also odd, we have $\ell_2 \leq 2\omega^* - 1$. Therefore, $\omega^{Alg\ 2(NF)} = 1 + \ell_2 \leq 1 + 2\omega^* - 1 \leq 2 \cdot \omega^*$. □

The bound $2 \cdot \omega^*$ can be achieved even for *Alg 2(FFD)*.

**Theorem 4.**
$$\omega^{Alg\ 2(FF)} \leq 2.7 \cdot \omega^*.$$

*Proof.* Let $U_1, \ldots, U_{\chi(G)}$ be a minimum partition of $G$ into independent sets. We define a weighting function $W : [0, 1] \to [0, 8/5]$ as in [7]:

$$W(\alpha) = \begin{cases} 6/5\alpha & \text{for } 0 \leq \alpha \leq 1/6, \\ 9/5\alpha - 1/10 & \text{for } 1/6 < \alpha \leq 1/3, \\ 6/5\alpha + 1/10 & \text{for } 1/3 < \alpha \leq 1/2, \\ 6/5\alpha + 4/10 & \text{for } 1/2 < \alpha \leq 1. \end{cases}$$

Furthermore, let $\bar{W}(U) = \sum_{\alpha \in U} W(e(\alpha))$ and $\bar{W} = \sum_{\alpha \in J} W(e(\alpha))$. Using a result about the weighting function in [7] for each color class, the number of bins generated by $FF$ on a set $U_i$ is bounded by $\bar{W}(U_i) + 1$. This implies that the total number of bins

$$\omega^{Alg\ 2(FF)} \leq \sum_{i=1}^{\chi(G)} \bar{W}(U_i) + 1$$

is at most $\bar{W} + \chi(G)$. Again, we know from [7] that the weight $\bar{W} \leq 1.7 \cdot \omega^*(L)$ where $\omega^*(L)$ is the minimum number of bins in a packing for all jobs without the incompatibility constraint. It is clear that $\omega^*(L) \leq \omega^*(G)$. Therefore, $\omega^{Alg\ 2(FF)} \leq \bar{W} + \chi(G) \leq 1.7 \cdot \omega^*(L) + \chi(G) \leq 1.7\omega^*(G) + \omega^*(G) = 2.7\omega^*(G)$. $\square$

The bound 2.7 can be achieved asymptotically for $Alg\ 2(FF)$ and the worst case ratio for $Alg\ 2(FFD)$ lies between 2.691 and 2.7.

# 4 Precoloring method

In this section, we analyse an approximation method where the "long" jobs $\bar{J} = \{j \in J | e(j) > \frac{1}{2}\}$ are colored differently. We denote with $\chi_{\bar{J}}(G)$ the minimum number of colors in a coloring with this property. This problem is known in the literature as the precoloring extension problem $1 - PrExt$. Given an undirected graph $G = (V, E)$ and $k$ different vertices $v_1, \ldots, v_k \in V$, the problem is to find a minimum coloring $f$ of $G$ such that $f(v_i) = i$ for $1 \leq i \leq k$. This problem is solvable in polynomial time for interval graphs, forests, split graphs, complements of bipartite graphs, cographs, partial $K$-trees and complements of Meyniel graphs [1, 2, 10, 11, 12, 15]. For the definitions of these graph classes we refer to [4, 9]. On the other hand, $1 - PrExt$ is NP-complete for bipartite graphs [2]. Unknown is the computational complexity of $1 - PrExt$ e.g. for chordal graphs [11].

**Algorithm 3:**
**Step 1:** Let $\bar{J}$ be the jobs $j \in J$ with execution time $e(j) > \frac{1}{2}$.
**Step 2:** Compute a partition into independent sets $U_1, \ldots, U_{\chi_{\bar{J}}(G)}$ for the conflict graph $G$ where $|U_i \cap \bar{J}| \leq 1$ for each $1 \leq i \leq \chi_{\bar{J}}(G)$.
**Step 3:** Apply a bin-packing heuristic (NF, FF, FFD) to each independent set $U_i$, $1 \leq i \leq \chi_{\bar{J}}(G)$.

As above, we denote with $Alg\ 3(NF)$, $Alg\ 3(FF)$ and $Alg\ 3(FFD)$ the corresponding composed algorithms. We can apply these algorithms for graph classes, where the graph problem $1 - PrExt$ is solvable in polynomial time. We notice that the set of instances in Theorem 2 generates the ratio 3 for $Alg\ 3(NF)$.

**Lemma 5.** *Let $L$ be a list of positive numbers $a_1, \ldots, a_n \leq 1$ with $a_\ell > \frac{1}{2}$ for at most one index $\ell$, let $B_1, \ldots, B_m$ (with $m > 2$) be the set of bins generated by $FF$ on $L$. If $b_i$ is the level of bin $B_i$ for $1 \leq i \leq m$, then*

$$\sum_{i=1}^{m} b_i \geq \frac{2}{3} \cdot m - \frac{1}{2}.$$

*Proof.* Let $B_k$ be the bin which contains $a_\ell$. If all levels $b_i \geq \frac{2}{3}$ for $1 \leq i < m$, then the sum

$$\sum_{i=1}^{m} b_i \geq \frac{2}{3}(m-2) + 1 > \frac{2}{3}m - \frac{1}{2}.$$

Let us assume that there is an index $j < m$ such that $b_j < \frac{2}{3}$. We choose the smallest index $j$ with this property. It follows that $b_{j'} \geq \frac{2}{3}$ for each $j' < j$. Since $b_j < \frac{2}{3}$, each number $x$ in the bins $B_{j+1}, \ldots, B_m$ is larger than $\frac{1}{3}$. If $m = k$ we define $m' = m - 1$ (otherwise we define $m' = m$). Since $a_i \leq \frac{1}{2}$ for $i \neq \ell$, the bins $B_{j+1}, \ldots, B_{m'-1}$ (with exeception of $B_k$) contain at least two integers and, therefore, the levels $b_{j+1}, \ldots, b_{m'-1}$ (with exception of $b_k$) are larger than $\frac{2}{3}$.

If $k \leq j$, then $b_j + b_m > 1$ and $\sum_{i=1}^{m} b_i > \frac{2}{3}(m-2) + 1$. If $k = m$, the bin levels $b_1, \ldots, b_{j-1}, b_{j+1}, \ldots, b_{m-2} \geq \frac{2}{3}$ and $b_j + b_{m-1} + b_m > \frac{3}{2}$. In this case, the sum $\sum_{i=1}^{m} b_i \geq \frac{2}{3}(m-3) + \frac{3}{2} = \frac{2}{3}m - \frac{1}{2}$. In the remaining case with $j < k < m$, we have $b_j + b_k + b_m > \frac{3}{2}$ and the sum $\sum_{i=1}^{m} b_i$ is again larger than $\frac{2}{3}m - \frac{1}{2}$. $\square$

**Theorem 6.**

$$\omega^{Alg\ 3(FF)} \leq 2.5 \cdot \omega^*.$$

*Proof.* We consider a partition into independent sets $U_1, \ldots, U_{\chi_{\overline{J}}(G)}$ where $\chi_{\overline{J}}(G)$ is the minimum number of colors in a coloring such that the precoloring for $\overline{J}$ is fulfilled. We denote with $k_i$ the number of independent sets generated by $FF$ on $U_i$. Now, we define

$$a = |\{i | 1 \leq i \leq \chi_{\overline{J}}(G), k_i = 1, U_i \cap \overline{J} \neq \emptyset\}|,$$
$$b = |\{i | 1 \leq i \leq \chi_{\overline{J}}(G), k_i = 1, U_i \cap \overline{J} = \emptyset\}|.$$

Lemma 5 implies that the following inequality is true.

$$\omega^* \geq \frac{a}{2} + \sum_{i:k_i=2} 1 + \sum_{i:k_i>2} [\frac{2}{3} \cdot k_i - \frac{1}{2}].$$

This inequality can be transformed into:

$$\sum_{i:k_i>2} k_i \leq \frac{3}{2}\omega^* - \frac{3}{4}a - \sum_{i:k_i=2} \frac{3}{2} + \sum_{i:k_i>2} \frac{3}{4}.$$

Algorithm 3 composed with $FF$ generates

$$\omega^{Alg\ 3(FF)} = a + b + \sum_{i:k_i=2} 2 + \sum_{i:k_i>2} k_i$$
$$\leq \tfrac{3}{2}\omega^* + [\tfrac{1}{4}]a + b + \sum_{i:k_i=2} \tfrac{1}{2} + \sum_{i:k_i>2} \tfrac{3}{4}$$
$$\leq \tfrac{3}{2}\omega^* + a + b + \sum_{i:k_i=2} 1 + \sum_{i:k_i>2} 2$$

Since $a + b + \sum_{i:k_i>1} 1 = \chi_{\overline{J}}(G)$ and $\chi_{\overline{J}}(G) \leq \omega^*$, the last four terms together can be bounded by $\omega^*$. This generates the upper bound 2.5. □

**Corollary 7.** *The algorithm Alg 3(FF) runs in polynomial time and has the absolute worst case ratio 2.5 on the following graph classes:*
*cographs, interval graphs, partial K-trees for constant K, split graphs, complements of bipartite graphs and complements of Meyniel graphs.*

The bound 2.5 can be achieved asymptotically for $Alg\ 3(FF)$ and the worst case ratio for $Alg\ 3(FFD)$ lies between 2.423 and 2.5.

# 5 General coloring methods

In this section, we study three approximation methods for the scheduling problem where the worst case ratio becomes $2 + \tfrac{1}{k}$ with different constants $k = 3, 5$ and 7.

In the first algorithm we consider the job set $\overline{J} = \{j \in J | e(j) > \tfrac{1}{k}\}$ where $k > 1$ is a positive integer. Notice, that an independent set $U$ in a solution of the scheduling problem can have at most $k - 1$ jobs of $\overline{J}$. Therefore, we compute in the first step of the algorithm a coloring of the conflict graph where at most $k - 1$ jobs lie in one color set. Then, in the second step we apply as in the other algorithms a bin packing heuristic.

**Algorithm 4:**
**Step 1:** Let $\overline{J}$ be the jobs $j \in J$ with execution time $e(j) > \tfrac{1}{k}$ (where $k \in \mathbb{N}$ and $k > 1$).
**Step 2:** Compute a minimum coloring with independent sets $U_1, \ldots, U_m(G)$ for the conflict graph $G$ where $|U_i \cap \overline{J}| \leq k - 1, 1 \leq i \leq m$.
**Step 3:** Apply a bin-packing heuristic (NF, FF, FFD) to each independent set $U_i, 1 \leq i \leq m$.

**Lemma 8.** *Let $L$ be a list of positive numbers $a_1, \ldots, a_n \leq 1$ with at most two numbers $a_l, a_{l'} > \tfrac{1}{3}$, let $B_1, \ldots, B_m$ (with $m > 2$) be the set of bins generated by FF on L. If $b_i$ is the level of bin $B_i$ for $1 \leq i \leq m$, then*

$$\sum_{i=1}^{m} b_i \geq \frac{3}{4} \cdot m - \frac{3}{4}.$$

**Theorem 9.** *For $k = 3$*

$$\omega^{Alg\ 4(FF)} \leq 2.\overline{3} \cdot \omega^*.$$

*Proof.* Here, Lemma 8 implies the following inequality:

$$\omega^* \geq \frac{a}{2} + \sum_{k_i=2} 1 + \sum_{k_i \geq 3} [\frac{3}{4}k_i - \frac{3}{4}].$$

Using that the number of independent set $m \leq \omega^*$, we have

$$\omega^{Alg\ 4(FF)} = a + b + \sum_{k_i=2} 2 + \sum_{k_i \geq 3} k_i$$
$$\leq \frac{4}{3}\omega^* + b + \frac{1}{3}a + \sum_{k_i=2} \frac{2}{3} + \sum_{k_i \geq 3} 1$$
$$\leq \frac{4}{3}\omega^* + m \leq \frac{7}{3}\omega^*.$$

$\square$

The bound $2.\overline{3}$ can be achieved for $k \geq 4$ and $Alg\ 4(FF)$.

In the second method, we allow that a color set has at most $\ell$ jobs with execution time in the interval $(\frac{1}{\ell+1}, \frac{1}{\ell}]$ for each $1 \leq \ell \leq k$. We have to compute an optimum coloring such that each color set satisfies this property. In the second step of the approximation algorithm we use again a bin packing heuristic.

**Algorithm 5:**
**Step 1:** Let $\overline{J}_\ell$ be the jobs $j \in J$ with execution time $e(j) \in (\frac{1}{\ell+1}, \frac{1}{\ell}]$ (for each $1 \leq \ell \leq k$).
**Step 2:** Compute a minimum coloring with independent sets $U_1, \ldots, U_m(G)$ for the conflict graph $G$ where $|U_i \cap \overline{J}_\ell| \leq \ell$ for each $1 \leq \ell \leq k$ and $1 \leq i \leq m$.
**Step 3:** Sort the jobs with execution time $e(j) > \frac{1}{k+1}$ in each independent set $U_i$, $1 \leq i \leq m$.
**Step 4:** Apply a bin-packing heuristic (NF, FF, FFD) to each independent set $U_i$, $1 \leq i \leq m$.

**Lemma 10.** *Let $k$ be a positive integer and let $L$ be a list of positive numbers $1 \geq a_1 \geq \ldots \geq a_{n'} > \frac{1}{k+1} \leq a_{n'+1}, \ldots, a_n$ where $|\{j|a_j \in (\frac{1}{\ell+1}, \frac{1}{\ell}]\}| \leq \ell$ for $1 \leq \ell \leq k$. If $B_1, \ldots, B_m$ is the set of bins generated by $FF$ on $L$ and if $b_i$ is the level of bin $B_i$, $1 \leq i \leq m$, then for $m \geq k+1$:*

$$\sum_{i=1}^m b_i \geq \frac{k+1}{k+2} \cdot (m - k - 1) + \frac{k(k-1)}{k+1} + 1.$$

*Moreover, for $m = k \geq 2$ we get:*

$$\sum_{i=1}^k b_i \geq \frac{(k-2)(k-1)}{k} + 1.$$

**Theorem 11.** *For $k = 1, 2, 3, 4$*

$$\omega^{Alg\ 5(FF)} \leq (2 + \frac{1}{k+1}) \cdot \omega^*.$$

*Proof.* The proof works similar as Theorem 6. Here, Lemma 10 implies the following inequalities for $k = 1, 2, 3, 4$:

$$1 : \omega^* \geq \tfrac{a}{2} + \sum_{k_i=2} 1 + \sum_{k_i \geq 3} [\tfrac{2}{3} k_i - \tfrac{1}{3}]$$
$$2 : \omega^* \geq \tfrac{a}{2} + \sum_{k_i=2} 1 + \sum_{k_i \geq 3} [\tfrac{3}{4} k_i - \tfrac{7}{12}]$$
$$3 : \omega^* \geq \tfrac{a}{2} + \sum_{k_i=2} 1 + \sum_{k_i=3} \tfrac{3}{3} + \sum_{k_i \geq 4} [\tfrac{4}{5} k_i - \tfrac{7}{10}]$$
$$4 : \omega^* \geq \tfrac{a}{2} + \sum_{k_i=2} 1 + \sum_{k_i=3} \tfrac{3}{3} + \sum_{k_i=4} \tfrac{5}{2} + \sum_{k_i \geq 5} [\tfrac{5}{6} k_i - \tfrac{23}{30}].$$

With the same method as in Theorem 6, we get as bound for $\omega^{Alg\ 5(FF)} \leq a + b + \sum_{k_i > 1} k_i$ the values 2.5, 2.$\overline{3}$, 2.25 and 2.2 for $k = 1, 2, 3$ and 4, respectively. $\square$

The bound $2 + \frac{1}{5}$ can be achieved for $Alg\ 5(FFD)$ and $k = 5$.

## Algorithm 6:
**Step 1:** Let $\overline{J}_\ell$ be the jobs $j \in J$ with execution time $e(j) \in (\frac{1}{\ell+1}, 1]$ (for each $1 \leq \ell \leq k$).

**Step 2:** Compute a minimum coloring with independent sets $U_1, \ldots, U_m(G)$ for the conflict graph $G$ where $|U_i \cap \overline{J}_\ell| \leq \ell$ for each $1 \leq \ell \leq k$ and $1 \leq i \leq m$.

**Step 3:** Sort the jobs with execution time $e(j) > \frac{1}{k+1}$ in each independent set $U_i, 1 \leq i \leq m$.

**Step 4:** Apply a bin-packing heuristic (NF, FF, FFD) to each independent set $U_i, 1 \leq i \leq m$.

**Lemma 12.** *Let $k$ be a positive integer and let $L$ be a list of positive numbers $1 \geq a_1 \geq \ldots \geq a_n > \frac{1}{k+1}$ where $|\{j | 1 \leq j \leq n, a_j \in (\frac{1}{\ell+1}, 1]\}| \leq \ell$ for $1 \leq \ell \leq k$. If $B_1, \ldots, B_m$ is the set of non-empty bins generated by $FF$ on $L$ and if $b_i$ is the level of bin $B_i, 1 \leq i \leq m$, then*

$$\sum_{i=1}^{m} b_i \geq \begin{cases} 1 & \text{for } m = 2 \\ \frac{7}{4} & \text{for } m = 3 \\ \frac{31}{11} & \text{for } m = 4 \end{cases}$$

**Lemma 13.** *Let $k$ be a positive integer $3 \leq k \leq 10$, let $L$ be a list of positive numbers $1 \geq a_1 \geq \ldots \geq a_{n'} > \frac{1}{k+1} \leq a_{n'+1}, \ldots, a_n$ where $|\{j | a_j \in (\frac{1}{\ell+1}, 1]\}| \leq \ell$ for $1 \leq \ell \leq k$. If $B_1, \ldots, B_m$ is the set of bins generated by $FF$ on $L$ and if $b_i$ is the level of bin $B_i, 1 \leq i \leq m$, then for $m \geq 4$:*

$$\sum_{i=1}^{m} b_i \geq \frac{k+1}{k+2} \cdot (m-4) + \frac{2k}{k+1} + 1.$$

The right sides of the inequalities above have the following values for $k = 3, 4, 5$ and 6. These values will be used later in the proof of the next theorem.

$$k = 3 : \tfrac{4}{5}(m-4) + \tfrac{5}{2} = \tfrac{4}{5}m - \tfrac{7}{10}$$
$$k = 4 : \tfrac{5}{6}(m-4) + \tfrac{13}{5} = \tfrac{5}{6}m - \tfrac{11}{15}$$
$$k = 5 : \tfrac{6}{7}(m-4) + \tfrac{8}{3} = \tfrac{6}{7}m - \tfrac{16}{21}$$
$$k = 6 : \tfrac{7}{8}(m-4) + \tfrac{19}{7} = \tfrac{7}{8}m - \tfrac{11}{14}$$

**Theorem 14.** *For* $k = 1, 2, 3, 4, 5, 6$

$$\omega^{Alg \ 6(FF)} \leq (2 + \frac{1}{k+1}) \cdot \omega^*.$$

*Proof.* Here, Lemma 13 and Lemma 12 imply the following inequalities for $k = 1, 2, 3, 4, 5, 6$:

$$k = 1 : \omega^* \geq \tfrac{a}{2} + \sum_{k_i=2} 1 + \sum_{k_i \geq 3} [\tfrac{2}{3}k_i - \tfrac{1}{3}]$$
$$k = 2 : \omega^* \geq \tfrac{a}{2} + \sum_{k_i=2} 1 + \sum_{k_i \geq 3} [\tfrac{3}{4}k_i - \tfrac{7}{12}]$$
$$k = 3 : \omega^* \geq \tfrac{a}{2} + \sum_{k_i=2} 1 + \sum_{k_i=3} \tfrac{7}{4} + \sum_{k_i \geq 4} [\tfrac{4}{5}k_i - \tfrac{7}{10}]$$
$$k = 4 : \omega^* \geq \tfrac{a}{2} + \sum_{k_i=2} 1 + \sum_{k_i=3} \tfrac{7}{4} + \sum_{k_i \geq 4} [\tfrac{5}{6}k_i - \tfrac{11}{15}]$$
$$k = 5 : \omega^* \geq \tfrac{a}{2} + \sum_{k_i=2} 1 + \sum_{k_i=3} \tfrac{7}{4} + \sum_{k_i \geq 4} [\tfrac{6}{7}k_i - \tfrac{16}{21}]$$
$$k = 6 : \omega^* \geq \tfrac{a}{2} + \sum_{k_i=2} 1 + \sum_{k_i=3} \tfrac{7}{4} + \sum_{k_i \geq 4} [\tfrac{7}{8}k_i - \tfrac{11}{14}]$$

Using the same method as in Theorem 6, we get as bound for $\omega^{Alg \ 5(FF)} = a + b + \sum_{k_i > 1} k_i$ the values $2\tfrac{1}{2}$, $2\tfrac{1}{3}$, $2\tfrac{1}{4}$, $2\tfrac{1}{5}$, $2\tfrac{1}{6}$ and $2\tfrac{1}{7}$ for $k = 1, 2, 3, 4, 5$ and $6$, respectively. □

The bound $2 + \tfrac{1}{7}$ can be achieved for *Alg* $6(FFD)$ and $k = 7$.

## 6 Approximation close 2

In this section, we propose an approximation algorithm to get the worst case ratio $2 + \frac{1}{(k+1)}$ for any constants $k \in \mathbb{N}$. Using this method we obtain approximation algorithms with the worst case bound $2 + \epsilon$ for cographs and partial $K$-trees.

**Algorithm 7:**
**Step 1:** Let $\overline{J}_0 = \{j \in J | e(j) \in (\tfrac{3}{4}, 1]\}$, $\overline{J}_1 = \{j \in J | e(j) \in (\tfrac{1}{2}, \tfrac{3}{4}]\}$ and $\overline{J}_\ell = \{j \in J | e(j) \in (\tfrac{1}{\ell+1}, \tfrac{1}{\ell}]\}$ for each $2 \leq \ell \leq k$.
**Step 2:** Compute a minimum coloring of the confict graph $G$ with independent sets $U_1, \ldots, U_{m}(G)$ where

$$\sum_{\ell=2}^{k} \frac{1}{\ell+1} |U_i \cap \overline{J}_\ell| + \frac{1}{2}|U_i \cap \overline{J}_1| + \frac{3}{4}|U_i \cap \overline{J}_0| < 1 \ (*)$$

for each $1 \leq i \leq m$.
**Step 3:** For each $1 \leq i \leq m$, place the jobs $j \in U_i$ with execution time $e(j) > \frac{1}{k+1}$ into at most two sets $A_i, B_i$ with execution times $e(A_i), e(B_i) \leq 1$.
**Step 4:** For each $1 \leq i \leq m$, apply a bin-packing heuristic (NF, FF, FFD) to $U_i \setminus (A_i \cup B_i)$ where the sets $A_i, B_i$ are placed before into the first and second bin.

**Lemma 15.** *The jobs $j \in U_i$ with execution times $e(j) > \frac{1}{k+1}$ can be placed into at most two bins.*

*Proof.* Let $U$ be an independent set of jobs $j \in J$ with execution times $e(j) > \frac{1}{k+1}$ where the inequality (∗) (see Step 2 of the algorithm) is satisfied.

We show that the sum $\sum_{j \in U} e(j) < \frac{3}{2}$. This inequality implies directly that we can separate the jobs into at most two sets $A$ and $B$ with execution times $e(A), e(B) \le 1$. Let $L = (j_1, \ldots, j_n)$ be a list of the jobs in $U$ and let $i$ be the smallest index such that $\sum_{\ell=1}^{i} e(j_\ell) \ge 1$. If $\sum_{\ell=1}^{i-1} e(j_\ell) \ge \frac{1}{2}$ then we set $A = \{j_\ell | 1 \le \ell \le i-1\}$ and $B = U \setminus A$. Otherwise, if $\sum_{\ell=1}^{i-1} e(j_\ell) < \frac{1}{2}$ then $e(j_i) > \frac{1}{2}$ and we set $A = \{j_i\}$ and $B = U \setminus A$.

Using the inequality (∗), the sum of the execution times can be bounded as follows:

$$
\begin{aligned}
&\sum_{j \in U} e(j) \\
&\le \sum_{\ell=2}^{k} \frac{1}{\ell} |U \cap \bar{J}_\ell| + \frac{3}{4} |U \cap \bar{J}_1| + 1 |U \cap \bar{J}_0| \\
&\le \frac{3}{2} [\sum_{\ell=2}^{k} \frac{1}{\ell+1} |U \cap \bar{J}_\ell| + \frac{1}{2} |U \cap \bar{J}_1| + \frac{3}{4} |U \cap \bar{J}_0|] \\
&< \frac{3}{2} \cdot 1 = \frac{3}{2}.
\end{aligned}
$$

□

**Lemma 16.** *Let $k$ be a positive integer and let $L$ be a list of positive numbers $a_1, \ldots, a_n \le 1$. Let $B_1, \ldots, B_m$ $(m \ge 3)$ be the set of non-empty bins generated by $FF$ on $L$ where the first two bins $B_1$ and $B_2$ are filled with all numbers $a_i > \frac{1}{k+1}$. If $b_i$ is the level of bin $B_i$, $1 \le i \le m$, then*

$$
\sum_{i=1}^{m} b_i \ge \frac{k+1}{k+2} \cdot (m-3) + \frac{k}{k+1} + 1.
$$

*Proof.* If $m = 3$, the last bin $B_3$ contains at least one number $y \le \frac{1}{k+1}$. Then, $b_1, b_2 > \frac{k}{k+1}$ and $b_1 + b_2 + b_3 > 1 + \frac{k}{k+1}$.

Now, let $m > 3$. If all levels $b_3, \ldots, b_{m-1} \ge \frac{k+1}{k+2}$, then the inequality above is true. Therefore, we assume that there is an index $j$, $3 \le j < m$ such that $b_j < \frac{k+1}{k+2}$. Choosing the smallest index $j$ with this property, $b_{j'} \ge \frac{k+1}{k+2}$ for $k + 1 \le j' < j$ and $j < j' < m$. Since $B_j$ contains at least $k+1$ numbers and $b_j < \frac{k+1}{k+2}$, there is one number $y \in B_j$ with $y < \frac{1}{k+2}$. Therefore, we have $b_1, b_2 > \frac{k+1}{k+2}$ and

$$
\begin{aligned}
\sum_{i=1}^{m} b_i &> \frac{k+1}{k+2}(m-2) + 1 \\
&\ge \frac{k+1}{k+2}(m-3) + \frac{k+1}{k+2} + 1 \\
&\ge \frac{k+1}{k+2}(m-3) + \frac{k}{k+1} + 1.
\end{aligned}
$$

□

**Theorem 17.** *For each integer $k \ge 1$:*

$$
\omega^{Alg\ 7(FF)} \le (2 + \frac{1}{k+1})\omega^*.
$$

*Proof.* Again, we consider a partition into independent sets $U_1, \ldots, U_m$ where $m$ is the minimum number of colors in a coloring such that each set $U_i$ satisfies the inequality (*). Lemma 15 implies that the jobs $j \in U_i$ with execution time $e(j) > \frac{1}{k+1}$ can be placed into at most two sets. Therefore, we can apply Lemma 16 and get the following inequality for the optimum value $\omega^*$ of the scheduling problem:

$$\omega^* \geq \frac{a}{2} + \sum_{k_i=2} 1 + \sum_{k_i \geq 3} [\frac{k+1}{k+2} k_i - 3\frac{k+1}{k+2} + \frac{k}{k+1} + 1].$$

This inequality can be transformed into:

$$\sum_{k_i \geq 3} k_i \leq \frac{k+2}{k+1}\omega^* - \frac{k+2}{2(k+1)}a - \sum_{k_i=2} \frac{k+2}{k+1}$$
$$+ \sum_{k_i>2} [3 - \frac{k(k+2)}{(k+1)^2} - \frac{k+2}{k+1}].$$

The algorithm *Alg* 7($FF$) generates at most

$$\omega^{Alg\ 7(FF)} = a + b + \sum_{k_i=2} 2 + \sum_{k_i>1} k_i$$
$$\leq \frac{k+2}{k+1}\omega^* + a[1 - \frac{k+2}{2(k+1)}] + b + \sum_{k_i=2} [2 - \frac{k+2}{k+1}]$$
$$+ \sum_{k_i>2} [3 - \frac{2k^2+5k+2}{k^2+2k+1}].$$

Since $1 - \frac{k+2}{2(k+1)} < 1$, $2 - \frac{k+2}{k+1} < 1$ and $3 - \frac{2k^2+5k+2}{k^2+2k+1} < 1$ for each $k \geq 1$, we obtain

$$\omega^{Alg\ 7(FF)} \leq \frac{k+2}{k+1}\omega^* + m$$
$$\leq \frac{k+2}{k+1}\omega^* + \omega^*$$
$$= (2 + \frac{1}{k+1})\omega^*.$$

$\square$

**Corollary 18.** *The algorithm Alg 7($FF$) runs in polynomial time and has the absolute worst case ratio $2 + \epsilon$ on the following graph classes: cographs and partial $K$-trees for constant $K$.*

# 7 Conclusion

In this paper, we studied the problem of scheduling a set $J$ of jobs with execution times $e(j) \in\ ]0,1]$ and a conflict graph $G = (J, E)$. We were searching for a partitioning of the job set $J$ into independent sets $U_1, \ldots, U_m$ such that $\sum_{j \in U_i} e(j) \leq 1$ for each $1 \leq i \leq m$ and $m$ should be minimal. Set $U_i$ is executed on one machine.

Investigating different methods for approximative solutions to this problem we were able to show the results summarized in Table 1. There, $\omega^H$ is the number of machines required when the algorithm $H$ is used, and $\omega^*$ is the minimal number of machines needed.

The following problems are interesting for further research:

(1) Complexity of $1 - PrExt$ for other graph classes (e.g. chordal graphs).
(2) Approximation algorithms for special graph classes.
(3) Other separation methods to distribute the jobs with long execution times.

Table 1. Summary of the approximation methods

| Algorithm H | $\omega^H$ |
|---|---|
| Direct bin packing $A_1$ | $\omega^{A_1} = O(|J|) \cdot \omega^*$ |
| Coloring $A_2$ | $\omega^{A_2} \leq 2.7 \cdot \omega^*$ |
| Precoloring $A_3$ | $\omega^{A_3} \leq 2.5 \cdot \omega^*$ |
| General Coloring $A_4$ | $\omega^{A_4} \leq (2 + \frac{1}{3}) \cdot \omega^*$ |
| General Coloring $A_5$ | $\omega^{A_5} \leq (2 + \frac{1}{5}) \cdot \omega^*$ |
| General Coloring $A_6$ | $\omega^{A_6} \leq (2 + \frac{1}{7}) \cdot \omega^*$ |
| 2-Approximation $A_7$ | $\omega^{A_7} \leq (2 + \frac{1}{k}) \cdot \omega^*$ |

# References

1. M. Biró, M. Hujter and Z. Tuza, Precoloring extension. I. Interval graphs, *Disc. Math.*, 100 (1991) 267 – 279.
2. H.L. Bodlaender, K. Jansen and G.J. Woeginger, Scheduling with incompatible jobs, Workshop Graph Theoretical Concepts in Computer Science, LNCS 657 (1992) 37 – 49.
3. H.L. Bodlaender and K. Jansen, On the complexity of scheduling incompatible jobs with unit-times, Mathematical Foundations of Computer Science, LNCS 711 (1993) 291 – 300.
4. A. Brandstädt, Special Graph Classes - a Survey. Report SM-DU-199, Universität - Gesamthochschule Duisburg (1991).
5. A.K. Chandra, D.S. Hirschberg and C.K. Wong, Bin packing with geometric constraints in computer network design, Research Report RC 6895, IBM Research Center, Yorktown Heights, New York (1977).
6. E.G. Coffman, Jr., M.R. Garey and D.S. Johnson, Approximation algorithms for bin-packing - an updated survey, *Algorithmic Design for Computer System Design*, G. Ausiello, M. Lucertini, P. Serafini (eds.), Springer Verlag (1984) 49 – 106.
7. M.R. Garey, R.L. Graham, D.S. Johnson and A.C.-C. Yao, Resource constrained scheduling as generalized bin packing, *J. Combin. Theory (A)*, 21 (1976) 257 – 298.
8. M.R. Garey and D.S. Johnson, Computers and Intractability: A Guide to the Theory of NP-completeness, Freeman, San Francisco, 1979.
9. M.C. Golumbic, Algorithmic Graph Theory and Perfect Graphs, Academic Press, London, 1980.
10. M. Hujter and Z. Tuza, Precoloring extension. II. Graph classes related to bipartite graphs, *Acta Math. Univ. Comenianae*, 61 (1993).
11. M. Hujter and Z. Tuza, Precoloring extension. III. Classes of perfect graphs, unpublished manuscript (1993).
12. K. Jansen and P. Scheffler, Generalized coloring for tree-like graphs, Workshop Graph Theoretical Concepts in Computer Science, LNCS 657 (1992) 50 – 59.
13. K. Jansen and S. Öhring, Approximation algorithms for the time constrained scheduling problem, Forschungsbericht, Technische Universität München (1995).

14. D.S. Johnson, A. Demers, J.D. Ullman, M.R. Garey and R.L. Graham, Worst-case performance bounds for simple one-dimensional packing algorithms, *SIAM J. Comput.*, **3** (1974) 256 – 278.

15. J. Kratochvil, Precoloring extension with fixed color bound, *Acta Math. Univ. Comenianae*, **62** (1993) 139–153.

16. C. Lund and M. Yannakakis, On the hardness of approximating minimization problems, 25.th *Symposium on the Theory of Computing* (1993) 286 – 293.

17. Y. Minyi, A simple proof of the inequality $FFD(L) \leq 11/9\,OPT(L) + 1, \forall L$ for the FFD bin-packing algorithm, *Acta Math. Appl. Sinica*, **7** (1991) 321 – 331.

18. D. Simchi-Levi, New worst-case results for the bin-packing problem, *Naval Research Logistics*, to appear.

# On the Scope of Applicability of the ETF Algorithm

Christos Koretz, George Chochia, and Peter Thanisch

Department of Computer Science
The University of Edinburgh
King's Buildings, Edinburgh EH9 3JZ
Scotland
email: {chr,gxc,pt}@dcs.ed.ac.uk

**Abstract.** Superficially, the Earliest Task First (ETF) heuristic [1] is attractive because it models heterogeneous message passing through a heterogeneous network. On closer inspection, however, this is precisely the set of circumstances that can cause ETF to produce seriously sub-optimal schedules. In this paper, we analyse the scope of applicability of ETF. We show that ETF has a good performance in instances are short and the links are fast and a poor performance. For the first application we choose the Diamond DAG with unit execution time for each task and the multiprocessor system in the form of the fully connected network. We show that ETF partitions the DAG into rows each of which is scheduled on the same processor. The analysis reveals that if the communication times between pairs of adjacent tasks in a precedence relation are all less than or equal to unit then the schedule is optimal. If the communication time is equal to the processing time needed to evaluate a row then the completion time is $O(\sqrt{n})$ times more than the optimal one for an $n \times n$ Diamond DAG. For the second application, we choose two joint DAG evaluated by two connected processors.

## 1. Introduction

The problem of scheduling an application onto a set of processors, taking into account communication delays, has been widely studied and is known to be NP-hard except for special cases [11]. One of the forms is the problem of finding an efficient static schedule of a set of partially ordered tasks on a multiprocessor system. Many scheduling heuristics have been proposed to solve this problem and based on the technique employed, the heuristics may be classified in different groups [1], then latter that manipulate the paths between the source node and sink node of the graph are classified as critical path heuristics. Another group of heuristics are the ones which give priorities to the tasks depending on the precedence order and the weights associated to tasks and edges. These algorithms are classified as list scheduling heuristics.

In an attempt to embrace the information about different topologies of real multiprocessors, Hwang et al. [1] proposed the Earliest Task First (ETF), which is a classic greedy strategy, classified as a list scheduling heuristic [1]. ETF schedules a free task to an available processor, in which it can start as early as possible, a task is 'free' when all its immediate predecessors have already been scheduled. It is emphasized that ETF tries to build communication in with computation, leading to the establishment of its performance guarantee.

In [1], an exhaustive analysis of ETF is done and the manner in which the bound is attained by ETF are shown, in order to shed some light to focus on problems that make using ETF when certain relationships hold between the parameters that represent the application and the architecture.

# On the Scope of Applicability of the ETF Algorithm

Cristina Boeres, George Chochia, and Peter Thanisch

Department of Computer Science

The University of Edinburgh

King's Buildings, Edinburgh EH9 3JZ

Scotland

email: {cbx,gac,pt}@dcs.ed.ac.uk

**Abstract.** Superficially, the *Earliest Task First* (ETF) heuristic [1] is attractive because it models heterogeneous messages passing through a heterogeneous network. On closer inspection, however, this is precisely the set of circumstances that can cause ETF to produce seriously sub-optimal schedules. In this paper we analyze the scope of applicability of ETF. We show that ETF has a good performance if messages are short and the links are fast and a poor performance otherwise. For the first application we choose the Diamond DAG with unit execution time for each task and the multiprocessor system in the form of the fully connected network. We show that ETF partitions the DAG into lines each of which is scheduled on the same processor. The analysis reveals that if the communication times between pairs of adjacent tasks in a precedence relation are all less than or equal to unit then the schedule is optimal. If the communication time is equal to the processing time needed to evaluate a row then the completion time is $O(\sqrt{n})$ times more than the optimal one for an $n \times n$ Diamond DAG. For the second application, we choose the join DAG evaluated by two connected processors.

## 1 Introduction

The problem of scheduling an application onto a set of processors, taking into account communication delays, has been widely studied and is known to be NP-hard except for special cases [11]. One of the forms is the problem of finding an efficient static schedule of a set of partially ordered tasks on a multiprocessor system. Many scheduling heuristics have been proposed to solve this problem, and based on the technique employed, the heuristics may be classified in different groups [7]. Heuristics that manipulate the paths between the source node and sink node of the graph are classified as *critical path heuristics*. Another group of heuristics are the ones which give priorities to the tasks, depending on the precedence order and the weights associated to tasks and edges. These algorithms are classified as *list scheduling heuristics*.

In an attempt to include the information about different topologies of real multiprocessors, Hwang *et al.* [1] proposed the *Earliest Task First* (ETF), which is a simple greedy strategy, classified as a *list scheduling heuristic* [2]. ETF schedules a free task to an available processor, in which it can start as early as possible; a task is 'free' when all its immediate predecessors have already been scheduled. It is emphasised that ETF tries to hide communication with computation, leading to the establishment of its performance guarantee.

In [1], an extensive analysis of ETF is done and the makespans of schedules determined by ETF are shown. However, we wish to focus on problems that arise with ETF when certain relationships hold between the parameters that represent the application and the architecture.

In [12], the performance of ETF is compared with the Dominant Sequence Clustering (DSC) algorithm. The number of processors given to ETF is the same as the number of clusters determined by DSC algorithm. Similarities and differences between the two algorithms are described in [12] which examines the ETF property of considering the distance in choosing the best processor to allocate to tasks. Gerasoulis *et al.* point out that ETF gives poor results when scheduling a join *Dag*. In such a case, if the communication cost is sufficiently greater then the computation cost, it is better to execute the tasks in the same processor. However, as ETF schedules the tasks at the earliest time possible, it does not allocates tasks at the same processor even if the communication cost is high.

In [4] an analysis and classification of non-greedy heuristics and greedy heuristics is done. ETF is classified as a greedy heuristic and an extensive set of experiments shows that the DFBN non-greedy heuristic proposed in [3] has a smaller time complexity than greedy algorithms like ETF. However, both ETF and DFBN give bad schedules when considering a join *Dag* as described by Gerasoulis *et al.* [12].

The paper is organized as follows: in Section (2) we give a description of the ETF algorithm. Section (3) contains applications of ETF to the Diamond DAG and the join DAG; we show that the time complexity of ETF can be more than a constant factor times worse than the optimal one. In section (4) we analyze the scope of applicability of ETF and suggest a three stage heuristic which hopefully may improve the situation.

## 2   The ETF Algorithm

The ETF algorithm was developed for scheduling tasks on multiprocessor systems with an arbitrary topology. The interesting feature of the algorithm is that it makes a scheduling decision based on the delay associated with message transfer between any pair of nodes in the network and the amount of data to be transferred between a pair of tasks $t, t'$ such that $t$ is an immediate predecessor of $t'$.

Given a set of tasks $T = \{t_i | i = 1, ..., m\}$ with precedence relation $<$, i.e. where $t, t' \in T$, $t < t'$ means that the evaluation of $t'$ cannot be initiated until the evaluation of the $t$ is complete. $G_T = (T, <)$ is the directed acyclic graph. The function $\mu(t): T \rightarrow Z_0^+$ specifies the evaluation time of the task $t \in T$. Function $\eta(t, t'): T \times T \rightarrow Z_0^+$ is associated with the amount of data to be transferred between $t$ and $t'$. The multiprocessor system is a set of identical processors $P = \{p_i | i = 1, ..., n\}$. For each pair $p, p' \in P$ the function $\tau(p, p'): P \times P \rightarrow Z_0^+$ specifies the delay associated with passing of a message of unit size from processor $p$ to $p'$. The following bound, $\omega_{ETF}$, on the *makespan*, i.e. time to complete the evaluation of any $G_T$, is proved

$$\omega_{ETF} \leq \left(2 - \frac{1}{n}\right)\omega_{opt} + C, \tag{1}$$

where $\omega_{opt}$ is the optimal completion time attainable when communication is ignored and

$$C = \max_{chains} (\tau_{max} \sum_{i=1}^{l-1} \eta(t_{c_i}, t_{c_{i+1}})),$$

where $(t_{c_1}, ..., t_{c_l})$ is a chain of $l$ tasks from $G_T$, and $\tau_{max} = \max_{p,p' \in P} \tau(p, p')$. The maximum is taken over the set of all source to sink chains.

In order to formulate the algorithm it is necessary to introduce the variable *current moment (CM)*, representing the current moment of the event clock, a set of available tasks, $A$, which can be scheduled at time $CM$, and a set $I$ of idle processors at time $CM$. Let $D_t$ and $S_t$ denote, respectively, the sets of immediate predecessors and successors of task $t$. Let $s(t)$ and $f(t)$ denote, respectively, the times when the evaluation of task $t$ begins and finishes. If all immediate predecessors of $t$ are scheduled then function $r(t, p)$

$$r(t,p) = \begin{cases} 0 & \text{if } D_t = \emptyset \\ \max_{t' \in D_t}(f(t') + \eta(t', t)\tau(p(t'), p)) \end{cases}.$$

evaluates the time when the last message from the predecessor task arrives in $p$, i.e. the earliest time at which $t$ may be scheduled on $p$. The function *next(CM)* returns the earliest time after $CM$ at which a processor finishes computing a task. The ETF algorithm is given in Figure 1.

*Initialization:* $I=\{p_1, ..., p_k\}$, $A=\{t \mid D_t = \emptyset\}$, $q= 0$;
$CM=0$, $NM = \infty$, $r(t,p) = 0$, $\forall\, t \in A$, $\forall\, p \in I$; $f(t) = \infty$, $\forall\, t \in T$;
```
0      while q < | T | do
1          while I ≠ ∅ AND A ≠ ∅ do
2              t̂, p̂ :  r(t̂, p̂) = min_{t∈A} min_{p∈I} r(t, p);
3              e_s = max(CM, r(t̂, p̂));
4              if e_s ≤ NM then
5                  p(t̂) = p̂; s(t̂) = e_s; f(t̂) = s(t̂) + μ(t̂);
6                  A = A - t̂; I = I - p̂; q = q + 1;
7                  if f(t̂) ≤ NM then NM = f(t̂) endif
8              else goto 11
9              endif
10         endwhile
11         CM = NM; T_new = {t | f(t) = CM, t ∈ T}; NM = next(CM); A' = ∅;
12         for t ∈ T_new do
13             I = I ∪ p(t);
14             for t' ∈ S_t do
15                 D_{t'} = D_{t'} - 1;
16                 if |D_{t'}| ≡ 0 then A' = A' ∪ t' endif
17             endfor
18         endfor
19         A = A ∪ A';
20         for t' ∈ A do
21             for p ∈ I do
22                 r(t', p) = max_{t∈ D_{t'}}(f(t) + η(t, t') τ(p(t), p))
23             endfor
24         endfor
25     endwhile
```

**Fig. 1. The ETF algorithm**

## 3  Applications of ETF

In this section we consider two applications of ETF. Let $G_T = (T, <)$ be the *diamond DAG* with $n^2$ nodes [8]. The nodes and the edges of the graph can be associated with that of the of $n \times n$ rectangular grid. The nodes are at the grid intersection points and the edges connect nodes at neighbouring intersections. The edges have the orientation from the node with smaller cartesian coordinate to that with larger one. The tasks from $T$ can be identified as $t_{i,j}$, $i, j = 0, ..., n-1$, where the first index is used for the row number, and the second for column number. Choose the multiprocessor system to be a completely connected network of $k \leq n$ processors. Set $\tau(p, p') = 1$ for all $p, p' \in P$ and $\eta(t, t') = \delta$ for all $t, t' \in T$ such that $t < t'$.

**Theorem 1.** *ETF schedules all the tasks in any given row on the same processor so that the task $t_{i,j}$ is scheduled in time $i \cdot (1 + \delta) + j$. Also, at most $\lceil \frac{n}{1+\delta} \rceil$ processors may be involved in the computation simultaneously.*

**Proof.** Apply the induction. At time 0, the set $A$ has one member $t_{00}$ which has no predecessors. The set $I$ consists of all processors in the network. Pick any of them (line 2). The condition in line 4 is true, hence $t_{00}$ will be scheduled on this processor (line 5). The task will be removed from $A$ (line 6) and will never become a member of $A$ in the future. Indeed, the only new members of $A$ are successors of $t_{00}$ (lines from 11 to 19). Hence the theorem holds for time 0. Suppose it holds until time $u$. The set of tasks which were scheduled in time $u$ satisfy the equation $u = i \cdot (1 + \delta) + j$ which has at most one solution for each row $i$. According to the induction hypothesis these are the only tasks which are evaluated. At time $u + 1$, which is *next(u)*, all these processors finish the evaluation of their tasks, thus they will be placed into $I$ again (line 13). Consider any $i = (u - j)/(1 + \delta)$ for some $j = 0, ..., n-2$, such that $t_{i,j}$ is not the last task in that row. Then the task $t_{i,j+1}$ will be placed in the set $A$ of available tasks at time $u + 1$. This task can be scheduled at $u + 1$ on the same processor $p$ as $t_{i,j}$ or at $u + 1 + \delta$ on any other available processor. Thus function $r(t_{i,j+1}, p)$ is minimal for $p$, hence this processor will be selected (line 2). Let $t_{i,j}$ be the task with maximal $i$ satisfying $u = i \cdot (1 + \delta) + j$ at time $u$. Then if $u + 1 = (i + 1) \cdot (1 + \delta)$ the task $t_{i+1,j}$ will be available at time $u + 1$ and it will be scheduled on some (and only one) available processor from $I$. Therefore we have shown that all the tasks in the same row are evaluated by the same processor as the previous task in the row. If $t_{i,j}$ is the last task in the row, i.e. $j = n - 1$ the processor is returned to $I$ i.e. is available again. Hence there could be at most $\lceil \frac{n}{1+\delta} \rceil$ processors involved in the computation simultaneously.  ■

The theorem establishes that the ETF partitions the diamond DAG into lines. It was shown in [6] that for this partitioning, the makespan $\omega_l$ is

$$\omega_l = \frac{n^2}{k} + (k - 1)(1 + \delta) \tag{2}$$

where $k$ is the number of processors. Formally the minimum of (2) is attainable when $k = \frac{n}{\sqrt{1+\delta}}$. However it cannot be reached because of the restriction $k \leq \frac{n}{1+\delta}$ established above. As $\omega_l$ is a decreasing function of $k$ before the formal minimum, the attainable minimum corresponds to maximal $k$, i.e. $k = \frac{n}{1+\delta}$, in which case we obtain

$$\omega_l = n + (n - 1) \cdot (1 + \delta) . \tag{3}$$

Below we prove that (3) is the minimal possible makespan if $0 \leq \delta \leq 1$. Indeed if $\delta$ is within this region the task $t_{i+1,i+1}$ cannot be evaluated earlier than $1 + \delta$ with respect to $t_{i,i}$ for all

$i = 0, ..., n - 2$. Thus the minimal makespan is given by $(n - 1) \cdot (1 + \delta)$ plus the time required to evaluate $n$ tasks $t_{i,i}$, $i = 0, ..., n - 1$ i.e. (3). This is the region where ETF finds the optimal schedule. However this is not the case if $\delta$ is large. If $\delta = n - 1$, then $k = 1$, which means that the DAG will be evaluated by single processor in time $n^2$.

Consider the partitioning of the DAG into stripes [8] of size $\sqrt{n}$. All stripes mapped on different processors. The first processor starts evaluating the first $\sqrt{n}$ tasks in the direction towards the boundary, then communicates with its neighbor proceeding at the same time to the next group of $\sqrt{n}$ tasks, and so on. It is easy to see that the makespan in that case is $2n\sqrt{n}$. Thus the time complexity of the evaluation is $O(\sqrt{n})$ times worse than the optimal one.

For the second application we choose the join DAG, i.e. two level binary tree where tasks $t_1, t_2$ have common successor $t_3$. In [12] it is stated that ETF has a poor performance for this kind of DAG. Let the multiprocessor system consists of two connected processors $p_1$ and $p_2$. Set $\eta(t_1, t_3) = \eta(t_2, t_3) = 1$, $\mu(t_i) = 1$, $i = 1, 2, 3$ and $\tau(p_1, p_2) = \tau$. It is easy to check that both $t_1$ and $t_2$ will be scheduled on $p_1$ and $p_2$ at time 0. The task $t_3$ became available at time $1 + \tau$ and can be scheduled either on $p_1$ or on $p_2$. Hence the makespan is $2 + \tau$. If $0 \leq \tau \leq 1$ then the makespan is optimal, however if $\tau \gg 1$ it is much worse than optimal (equal to 3). In the limiting case $\tau \to \infty$, the ETF makespan is infinitely larger than the optimal one.

## 4   Conclusion and Work in Progress

The results obtained in the previous section are in agreement with the bound stated in [1] for unit execution time (UET) and unit communication time assumptions (UCT), namely

$$\omega_{ETF} \leq \left(3 - \frac{1}{n}\right) \cdot \omega_{opt} - 1 \ .$$

Choose the unit to be $U = min_{t \in T} \mu(t)$. Then the UCT assumption implies that where the tasks $t$ and $t'$ are scheduled on processors $p$ and $p'$, respectively, $max_{t,t' \in T} \eta(t, t') \cdot \tau(p, p')$, is of order $U$. This assumption does not hold in practice if the tasks are the CPU operations like additions and/or multiplication, etc. and the communication between the nodes is organized by means of a message passing interface (MPI). The MPI usually has a large start-up overhead, i.e. the time to initiate the data transfer; this can be of order 10 to 1000 times $U$ depending on the computer and the interface. To model this situation we have to assume that either messages are long or the link is slow. As was demonstrated by the examples above, however, this may result in the inefficient schedules. To improve the situation the DAG must be reorganized in a new one where each node is a cluster of tasks. For the new DAG, the UET, and UCT assumptions must hold.

Another problem with the ETF heuristic is that a pair of functions $\eta(t, t')$ and $\tau(p, p')$ is not sufficient to specify the communication overhead precisely, i.e. there is no parameter associated with the start up overhead $\rho$, which in many cases [5] is dominant over the product $\eta(t, t') \cdot \tau(p, p')$. The start up overhead is the processor activity and hence the processor is busy during this time interval. In case of ETF the communication is allowed to be completely overlapped with computations. In other words ETF simulates the nonblocking message passing with zero startup overhead, whereas real message passing is a mixture of a blocking communication for the period of time $\rho$ and a nonblocking communication for the period of $\eta(t, t') \cdot \tau(p, p')$. In order to overcome this problem we suggest the following three step heuristic. The first two steps are used to produce a new DAG. Each node of the new DAG is a cluster of tasks from $T$ such that a sum of their execution time is approximately equal to $\rho$. In first step Papadimitriou and Yannakakis's heuristic [9] is applied to the original DAG. At this step the number of processors is unspecified. As the second step, we apply the heuristic suggested by Thurimella and Yesha [10]. The number of processors at this step is chosen to be equal to that in the target multiprocessor system. The output is a new DAG with the properties specified above. In the last step we apply the ETF heuristic. The analysis of the schedules is a subject of the work in progress.

# References

1. J.-J. Hwang, Y.-C. Chow, F.D. Anger, and C-Y. Lee. Scheduling precedence graphs in systems with interprocessor communication times. *SIAM J. Comput.*, 18(2):244–257, 1989.
2. A.A. Khan, C.L. McCreary, and M.S. Jones A comparison of multiprocessor scheduling heuristics. Technical Report comparison-ICPP-94, Dept. of Computer Science and Engineering, Auburn University, 1994. Published in the Proceeding of the 8th Int. Parallel Processing Sym. - April, 1994.
3. S. Manoharan and P. Thanisch. Assigning dependency graphs onto processor networks. *Parallel Computing*, 17(1):63–73, 1991.
4. S. Manoharan and N.P. Topham. An assessment of assignment schemes for dependency graphs. *Parallel Computing*, 21(1):85–107, 1995.
5. M.G. Norman, G. Chochia, P. Thanisch, and E. Issman. Predicting the performance of the diamond dag computation. Technical Report EPCC-TR-92-07, Edinburgh Parallel Computing Centre, 1992.
6. M. Norman, P. Thanisch, and G. Chang. Partitioning DAG Computations. In W. Joosen and E. Milgrom, editors, *Parallel Computing: From Theory to Sound Practice*, pages 360–364, Amsterdam, 1992. IOS Press.
7. M.G. Norman and P. Thanisch. Models of machines and computations for mapping in multicomputers. *Computing Surveys*, 25(3):263–302, 1993.
8. C.H. Papadimitriou and J.D. Ullman. A communication-time tradeoff. *SIAM J. Comput.*, 16(4):639–646, 1987.
9. C.H. Papadimitriou and M. Yannakakis. Towards an architecture-independent analysis of parallel algorithms. *SIAM J. Comput.*, 19:322–328, 1990.
10. R. Thurimella and Y. Yesha. A scheduling principle for precedence graphs with communication delay. *J. of Computer and Software Engineering*, 2(2):165–176, 1994.
11. B. Veltman, B.J. Lageweg, and J.K. Lenstra. Multiprocessor scheduling with communication delays. *Parallel Computing*, 16(2-3):173–182, 1990.
12. T. Yang and A. Gerasoulis. DSC: Scheduling parallel tasks on an unbounded number of processors. *IEEE Trans. Paral. Distr. Systems*, 5(9):951–967, Sep 1994.

# Optimal Mapping of
# Neighbourhood-Constrained Systems[*]

Felipe M. G. França
COPPE Sistemas e Computação
Universidade Federal do Rio de Janeiro, Brazil
email: felipe@cos.ufrj.br

Luerbio Faria
Faculdade de Formação de Professores
Universidade Estadual do Rio de Janeiro, Brazil
email: luerbio@cos.ufrj.br.

**Abstract.** The problem of finding the minimum topology of multiprocessing substrates supporting parallel execution of any given neighbourhood-constrained system is proposed and possible optimal strategies are investigated based on the relationship between Barbosa's scheduling by edge reversal - SER - distributed algorithm and the minimum clique covering problem. It is shown that from any given clique covering of length $\lambda$ on a graph $G$, it is possible to obtain a SER trailer dynamics in $G$'s complement that cover $G$ upon $\lambda$ evolutions. It also shown that, conversely, from any given SER dynamics on $G$ in which all of its nodes operate at least once upon $\lambda$ steps, a clique covering of length at most $\lambda$ is defined on $G$'s complement. In addition, a conjecture correlating the length of any minimum clique covering and optimal concurrency in SER- driven systems is stablished.

## 1  Introduction

*Scheduling by edge reversal* - SER - is a powerful parallel and distributed graph-based algorithm developed [BaGa89] [Ba93] for controling concurrent operation amongst the elements of neighbourhood-constrained systems of generic topologies. SER is based on the idea of a population of *processes* executing upon access to shared atomic *resources*. Shared-resouces systems are represented as a finite oriented graph $G = (N, E)$ where processes are the nodes of $G$ and an oriented edge exists between any two nodes whenever they share a resource. In other words a resource is represented by a clique, i.e., a completely conected subgraph in $G$.

SER works starting from any acyclic orientation $\omega$ on $G$. This means that there is at least one sink node. Consider, just for the purpose of this explanation,

---

[*] This work was partially supported by CNPq, CAPES and FAPERJ, Brazilian research agencies.

166

an ideal synchronous environment where according to the beginning of a clock pulse, only sinks are allowed to operate while other nodes remain idle. After operating and before the clock pulse ends, all sinks reverse the orientation of their edges by sending messages to all their neighbours, each one becoming a source It is easy to see that, again, another acyclic orientation, $\omega'$, is formed and a new set of sinks can operate at the next clock pulse [GaBe81]. All subsequent orientations are also acyclic and the scheduling mechanism consists basically of consecutive sets of sinks being defined in $G$ through time.

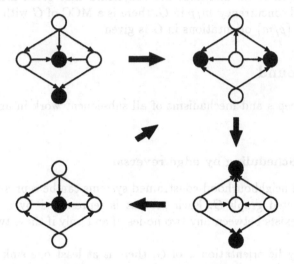

Fig. 1. $m = 1$, $p = 3$, $\gamma^*(G) = 1/3$.

As the number of such acyclic orientations is finite, eventualy a set of orientations will repeat. This defines a period of length $p$ of orientations. It is proved that inside any period every node operates exactly $m$ times. Figure 1 illustrates the SER dynamics. This simple dynamics ensures that no deadlock or starvation will ever occur since at every acyclic orientation there is at least one sink, i.e., one node allowed to operate. The concurrency of a period is defined by the coeficient $m/p$. It is clear that as high is $m/p$, less idle are every node through each period. It is also clear that in any connected system $1/n \leq m/p \leq 1/2$, $n = | N |$ [Ba93]. This implies that if any "optimistic" mapping where one physical processor would host each process of the target shared-resource system, a minimum of half of such processors would be idle at any time. Following the observation that any group of processes belonging to a same clique in $G$ cannot operate simultaneously, the allocation of each of such cliques into distinct physical processors seems a natural policy to reduce idleness.

An optimal mapping of processes of a given neighbourhood constrained system into a processing substract composed by physical processors and communication links, is defined as the minimum number of processors and links necessary to host the target system such that sinks do not share physical processors at any acyclic orientation under any SER dynamics.

The NP-completeness of finding an acyclic orientation which leads to maximum concurrency [BaGa89] and the minimum clique covering - MCC [GaJo79] of the problem are known results. Given a graph $G$ and its complement $\bar{G}$, it is observed that in each acyclic orientation inside any SER dynamics on $\bar{G}$, there is an independent set of sinks which complement is necessarily a clique in $G$ [Fr94].

This work shows that for any given SER dynamics in $\bar{G}$, a clique covering of $G$ exists and, conversely, for any given clique covering in $G$ there is a corresponding SER dynamics in $\bar{G}$. In addition, the conjecture that given a SER dynamics having optimal concurrency $m/p$ in $\bar{G}$, there is a MCC of $G$ with $\lceil p/m \rceil$ cliques obtained from $\lceil p/m \rceil$ orientations in $\bar{G}$ is given.

# 2 Background

The basic concepts and mechanisms of all subsequent work in are explained in this section.

## 2.1 SER - Scheduling by edge reversal

Heavily loaded neighbourhood-constrained systems can be represented as a connected unidirected graph $G$. Each process is represented by a node and one oriented edge exists between any two nodes, if and only if these two nodes share a resource.

For any acyclic orientation $\omega$ of $G$, there is at least one sink node and one source node. By reversing all sinks in $\omega$, a new acyclic orientation $\omega'$ is defined, i.e., $g(\omega) = \omega'$, where $g$ is the function that reverses all sinks of an orientation in a graph $G$. This dinamics is called SER. Eventualy, a sequence of acyclic orientations $(\alpha_0, \ldots, \alpha_{(p-1)})$ such that $\alpha_k = g(\alpha_{(k-1) \bmod p})$, $0 \leq k \leq (p-1)$, is defined and this sequence is called a period of length $p$. SER's fairness is a very important result stated in the following theorem:

**Theorem 2.1** *All nodes become a sink the same number of times in a period.*

The number of times each node becomes a sink during one period is denoted simply by $m$.

## 2.2 Concurrency Measures

A natural way to define the amount of concurrent operation among processes in a distributed system, that consider the average number of times $\gamma_0(\omega)$ that a node becomes a sink from an initial orientation $\omega$ under SER. Another interesting result from Barbosa's work is presented below.

**Theorem 2.4**[BaGa89]*Let $\alpha 0, \ldots, \alpha_{(p-1)}$ be a period in which each node is a sink $m$ times then, $\gamma_0(\omega) = m/p$ for all $\omega \in \Omega(\alpha_0, ..., \alpha_{(p-1)})$.*

Notice that $m$, $p$, and therefore, $\gamma_0(\omega)$, are highly dependent upon an initial $\omega$. It is easy to prove that in a generic connected graph for all $\omega \in \Omega, 1/n \leq \gamma_0(\omega) \leq 1/2$.

Take a distributed resource-sharing system with an arbitrary topology described by $G$: a natural question is how much concurrency $G$ can provide under SER. The answer to this question comes from finding an initial acyclic orientation $\omega$ on $G$ that leads to a period with an optimal amount of concurrency. This number is denoted by $\gamma^*(G)$ such that $\gamma^*(G) = \max\{\gamma_0(\omega)/\omega \in \Omega\}$.

The example of Figure 1 shows that $\gamma_0(\omega) = \gamma^*(G) = 1/3$.

One of the main results of [BaGa89] was to prove that the problem of finding an initial acyclic orientation that maximises concurrency on a generic graph $G$ belongs to the NP-complete class.

## 3 Mapping SER-driven systems

Consider a target neighbourhood-constrained system under SER operation implemented by the conventional processes-into-processors model of distributed and parallel computation. As SER is a fully distributed algorithm, any chosen allocation of the target system into the multiprocessing environment is correct if the latter provides proper low-level inter-process communication services (in order to allow any pair of nodes, each one allocated to any two of the system's processors, to communicate, i.e., to reverse edges).

This means that each set of processes (i.e., nodes of the target system under SER) mapped into any of the environment's physical processors, may have to share this single physical processor as an atomic resource.

In order to give a notion of what would mapping of systems under SER mean, consider the following extreme cases of neighbourhood-constrained systems:

(i) if all processes of the target system share a single atomic resource, i.e., the system is represented by a fully connected graph and only one of the system's nodes can be operating at any time under SER.

(ii) in the case of all processes running without any resource-sharing the system could be represented by a completely unconnected graph in which no edges would exist.

Case (i) demonstrates that the minimum possible topology is enough to host a system with the minimum possible amount of concurrency, i.e., $\gamma_0(\omega) = 1/n$. Case (ii) is the opposite extreme where $n$ processes should be mapped into $n$ distinct processors. The interesting cases are intermediate to (i) and (ii) where arbitrary SER-driven topologies should be mapped having in mind that, ideally, for each set of sinks of each of the acyclic orientations of a SER period, each sink should be assigned to a distinct processor.

Interestingly, SER itself can be a distributed alternative to define generic mappings for SER-driven systems. Notice that each set of sinks of any acyclic orientation belonging to any given SER period on $G$ defines a clique on $\bar{G}$. Mapping cliques of $\bar{G}$ into distinct processors seems a very appropriate policy since nodes belonging to a clique cannot operate simultaneously under SER. Figure 2 illustrates such alternative. The following section presents our results concerning the importance and efficiency of this strategy.

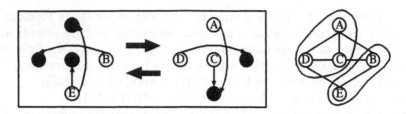

**Fig. 2.** SER running over $\bar{G}$ and defining cliques on $G$.

## 4  MCC through SER

In this section we show that a given SER dynamics on $G$, in which every node is a sink at least once in $\lambda$ orientations, then a clique covering of length at most $\lambda$ on $\bar{G}$ is defined and, conversely, from any given clique covering on $\bar{G}$ resulting in $\lambda$ cliques, it is possible to produce a SER dynamics on $G$ in which every node will be a sink at least once in $\lambda$ orientations.

**Theorem 4.1** *For any given SER dynamics on $G$, in which every node is a sink at least once in $\lambda$ orientations, then it a clique covering of length at most $\lambda$ on $\bar{G}$ is defined.*

**Proof**: As every node of $G$ under SER was a sink at least once during $\lambda$ orientations, this implies that there is a clique covering of length $\lambda$ in $\bar{G}$. If two of those cliques $K_m$ and $K_n$ are such that $N(K_m) \bigcap N(K_n) = K_s$, where $1 < s < m, n$, we get $K_m$ and $K_n - K_s$ as covering components. If $K_n$ is strictly contained in $K_m$ and, say $m \leq n$, it is possible to eliminate $K_n$ as a covering component, in this case the resulting partition will have less than $\lambda$ components.

**Theorem 4.2** *For any given clique covering on $\bar{G}$ resulting in $\lambda$ cliques there is a SER dynamics on $G$, in which every node is a sink at least once in $\lambda$ orientations.*

**Proof**: Let $C$ be a clique covering on $\bar{G}$ such that $C = K_1 , K_2,...,K_\lambda$. Then, for all i, $1 \leq i \leq \lambda$, $K_i$ is an independent set on $G$, so that all $G$'s edges exist only between distinct $K_i$'s. Then it is possible to orient those edges in $G$ according to the following: for all $i, j; i, j \in 1, 2, .., \lambda$, with $i < j$, if $(u, v) \in E(G)$, where $u \in K_i$ and $v \in K_j$, we get the oriented edge $(u, v)$. So in this way an acylic orientation on $G$ is defined. In this orientation, all nodes common to $K_1$ are sinks and all nodes common to $K_\lambda$ are sources. Under SER, all nodes corresponding to $K_1$ will operate first followed by all nodes of $K_2$. Recursevely, up to the $\lambda th$ orientation all nodes will operate at least once.

A considerable number of examples of SER-driven systems under optimal concurrency observed lead us to enunciate the following conjecture:

**Conjecture 4.3** *For any SER dynamics having optimal concurrency $m/p$ in $\bar{G}$, then there is a MCC of $G$ with $\lceil p/m \rceil$ cliques obtained from $\lceil p/m \rceil$ orientations in $\bar{G}$.*

A strong implication of theorem 4.2 is that, from any MCC found for any given graph $G$ it is always possible to define, in linear time, a corresponding trailer of SER dynamics which reproduce such MCC. To reduce the problem of finding an initial acyclic orientation which leads to optimal concurrency to the MCC problem is ongoing work.

# 5 Conclusions

The potential aplicability of this work lies on obtaining minimum multiprocessing substrates offering actual parallel execution customised for any target neighbourhood-constrained system. The main goal of this work is to reinforce the necessity of a deeper investigation on the relationship between the MCC and the optimal mapping of SER-driven systems problems. A number of examples were tested and, far from any definitive proof, they have supported our final conjecture.

# 6 Acknowledgements

The authors would like to thank Priscila M. V. Lima for her important comments to this work and Inês C. Dutra for her help with LaTeX.

# 7 References

[Ba93] Barbosa, V.C. (1993). Massively Parallel Models of Computation, Ellis Horwood, Chichester, UK.

[BaGa89] Barbosa, V.C., and Gafni, E. (1989). "Concurrency in heavily loaded neighborhood-constrained systems", ACM Transactions on Programming Languages and Systems, pp. 562584, vol. 11, no. 4.

[Fr94] França, F.M.G. (1994) Neural Networks as NeighbourhoodConstrained Systems, Ph.D. Thesis, Department of Electric and Electronic Engineering, Imperial College, London, UK.

[GaBe81] Gafni, E.M. and Bertsekas, D.P. (1981). "Distributed algorithms for generating loop-free routes in networks with frequently changing topology", IEEE Transactions on Communications, pp. 11-18, COM-29, no. 1.

[GaJo79] Garey, M.R. and Jonhson, D.S. (1979). Computers and Intractability: A Guide to the Theory of NP- Completeness. Freeman, New York, NY, USA.

# Parallel Processing in DNA Analysis

Charles R. Cantor, Takeshi Sano, Natalia E. Broude, and Cassandra L. Smith

Center for Advanced Biotechnology and Departments of Biomedical Engineering, Biology, and Pharmacology, Boston University, Boston, Massachusetts 02215

## 1 Introduction

Potential analogies exist between the way computers process and analyze data and the way data is handled in biological systems. Biological data is predominantly in the form of DNA. DNA data is at least two-fold redundant, and it is often multi-fold redundant. Thus it is relatively error resistant. A key aspect of DNA data is that the sequence of DNA bases which is the information stored in DNA also provides a way for the specific purification of DNA subsets. Thus, DNA, in principle, can be handled as very complex mixtures of species with the ability to sort things out afterwards. As a result, DNA-based manipulations can sometimes be formulated into highly parallel strategies. In this paper we will introduce the reader to the general properties of DNA and the currently used methods for manipulating and studying DNA molecules. We will emphasize how DNA properties allow parallel strategies to be used for direct biological experiments, and we will also speculate on possible future applications of such strategies which go beyond pure biological applications.

## 2 Basic Properties of DNA

### 2.1 DNA Structure

DNA is one of the most monotonous of all biological molecules. Only four different bases, adenine (A), guanine (G), cytosine (C), and thymine (T) are present, linked by a backbone of alternating deoxyribose sugars and phosphates, called a phosphodiester backbone. Two key structural principles dominate the behavior of DNA. First, there is specific recognition of pairs of bases by hydrogen bonding so that the most stable structure of DNA is a double helix which resembles a circular staircase. Each step of the staircase is either an A-T base pair or a G-C base pair. Second, the base pairs and backbone possess pseudo two-fold rotational symmetry so that a 180-degree rotation in the plane of the base pairs interchanges the two backbones and the two bases. Geometrically the structure of A-T, T-A, G-C, and C-G are virtually identical so that the DNA double helix is nearly a perfectly symmetrical object. While there are complications such as certain periodic sequences which predispose the structure towards bending, as a first approximation we can consider DNA as a regular structure with properties dominated by interactions between bases near-by on the two strands. The information on the two strands is totally redundant. Wherever an A appears on one, a T appears in the corresponding position of the other, and so on.

The order of the bases along a DNA strand is called the sequence. A typical sequence, customarily written in the direction from the 5'-position of a deoxyribose sugar to the 3'-position along the phosphodiester backbone unless otherwise specified, would be ATTGCGAC......... The phosphodiester backbone is directional, and the chemical structure reveals the direction at each point in the structure. Thus the sequences AG and GA refer to totally different chemical structures. The pseudo two-fold rotational symmetry of the DNA double helix means that the two backbone strands run in opposite directions. Thus if we use a constant convention to represent the order of the bases a double helix would be formed by AGGCCACT reacting with AGTGGCCT to form

$$5'-AGGCCACT-3'$$
$$3'-TCCGGTGA-5'$$

where the bottom strand is written from right to left to account for the anti-parallel nature of the strands in the double helix.

## 2.2 DNA Manipulation

Four techniques dominate the ways in which DNA molecules are manipulated in the laboratory; these are chemical synthesis, gel electrophoretic fractionation, hybridization, and *in vitro* amplification.

Automated step-wise chemical synthesis can provide us with essentially unlimited amounts of any DNA sequence up to about 100 bases in length. To form a double-stranded DNA, the two complementary strands are synthesized separately and mixed, whereupon double strand formation is spontaneous. To make longer double strands, the sequences made are offset, and then an enzyme called DNA ligase is used to suture the separate parts together as shown schematically below.

In this way, essentially any arbitrary structure can be synthesized.

DNA molecules can be fractionated according to size by a technique called gel electrophoresis. Here molecules are made to move through the pores of an aqueous gel by the presence of an applied electrical field. The gels used have quasi-random distributions of pore sizes. All DNA molecules have a charge which is proportional to the number of phosphate groups. Larger DNAs can access a smaller fraction of the pores, and thus their velocity in the gel, parallel to the electrical field, is smaller, because their path must be more tortuous. The size resolution of DNA gel electrophoresis is impressive. For single strands, the resolution is one base up to at least 1000 bases. For double strands, the resolution is comparable for short structures, and even structures with a million bases can be fractionated with about 1% length resolution.

All contemporary methods for reading the sequence of DNA bases rely on our ability to fractionate chains by size. In the most widely used current method, a polymerase is used to synthesize a DNA strand complementary to the strand of interest in the presence of chain terminators which stop the synthesis at a specific base. Thus, a target like TGGCCAATACAGACTACGAAT would be used to synthesize the following set of fragments in the presence of a C terminator, C*.

ATTC*
ATTCGTAGTC*
ATTCGTAGTCTGTATTGGC*
ATTCGTAGTCTGTATTGGCC*

Note that these sequences will be copied from right to left along the target DNA because of the anti-parallel nature of the two strands. Such a set of DNA sequences is called a ladder. By measuring the lengths of these fragments; 4, 10, 19 and 20 bases, we can reconstruct the positions of the G's in the original target. The same process is repeated separately for three other base-specific terminators. The resulting sequence is over-determined, and thus the overall process, in the absence of inevitable occasional artifacts with real DNA molecules, is actually quite accurate and robust.

DNA sequences recognize their complements with great specificity. Under carefully controlled conditions, a match of 20 perfect bases can be distinguished from the same structure with a single internal base mismatch, because the latter will be less stable and the strands can be selectively separated by raising the temperature or adding chemical denaturants. End mismatches are much more difficult to distinguish. The double helix is quite fussy about structural perfection, but at the ends of the helix there are clearly structural perturbations allowed that would not be tolerated internally. The shorter a double helix, the more sensitive it is to disruption by an incorrectly paired set of bases. However, short helices are also less stable. In practice to detect a particular DNA sequence, we use complementary strands that usually have at least eight or more bases, and sequence searches with 18 to 20 bases or longer strings are commonplace. Much longer DNA sequences can be used for recognition, but these will recognize approximate matches in addition to perfect matches.

The process of sequence recognition by a complementary DNA strand is called hybridization. The rigor of discrimination between a perfectly matched and a mismatched target is related to the hybridization conditions, and these are called the hybridization stringency. Hybridization is usually carried out by having one DNA strand immobilized on a solid surface. The sequence used for interrogation of the target is called the probe. A radiolabeled or fluorescently labeled probe can be used to detect its complementary sequence in an immobilized target. Alternatively, a labeled target can be analyzed by hybridization to an immobilized, unlabeled probe.

Many variations on the detection of specific DNA sequences by hybridization are used. The most powerful of these are methods called DNA amplification. Here, usually, two different probes are required for the detection of the target. This provides increased discrimination because both probes must simultaneously match corresponding target sequences. In the ligase chain reaction (LCR) [3, 15], two probes are selected to bind at adjacent sites in the target and the enzyme DNA ligase is asked to connect them.

$$X\underline{\hspace{2cm}}Y \qquad X\underline{\hspace{2cm}}Y$$
$$\underline{\hspace{3cm}} \quad --> \quad \underline{\hspace{3cm}}$$

The newly synthesized strand can be removed by heating and the process can be repeated. This leads to an amplification reaction which proceeds linearly with the number of heating cycles. Alternatively, one simultaneously can use the newly synthesized strand as a target for the binding and ligation of two fragments complementary to it. If such a process is repeated, the resulting amplification is exponential since the number of strands doubles with each heating cycle. The synthesis of the new strands is typically detected by what is called a capture color reaction. Here X is a label that can be used for specific affinity capture (such as an antigen for which a corresponding antibody is available), and Y is a signalling system such as a radioisotope, a fluorescent group, or a chemiluminescent group.

The most generally useful DNA amplification scheme is the polymerase chain reaction (PCR) [20]. Here two probes are used to initiate the synthesis of DNA strands complementary to a target molecule. The targets strands are separated, and the probes are complexed with these strands. Then DNA polymerase is used to synthesize new strands as shown below.

$$\underline{\hspace{2cm}} \qquad\qquad \underline{\hspace{3cm}}$$

$$+ \qquad --> \qquad \underline{\hspace{2cm}}$$
$$\underline{\hspace{3cm}} \qquad \underline{\hspace{3cm}}$$

Each cycle of this process doubles the number of strands. By selecting a specific set of initial probes (called primers), one can selectively amplify any substring of the original DNA sequence.

# 3 Parallel Processing in DNA Sequencing

## 3.1 The Need for Large Scale DNA Sequencing

The currently used methods for determining the sequence of DNA have been described above. Each DNA target is converted into four sets of DNA ladders and their lengths are determined by gel electrophoresis. A typical commercial instrument for this task can analyze 12 to 50 samples at once reading up to lengths of 400 in anywhere from 2 to 6 hours. Thus the overall rates of data acquisition are $10^3$ to $10^4$ bases per hour or roughly ten times this per day. A typical gene, the DNA instructions that code for one protein, i.e., one unit of biological function, in a simple organism is 3000 bases long, while in the human or other higher organisms it is ten times this size. Thus contemporary DNA sequencing rates are about one gene per hour per instrument. An average bacterium has a few thousand genes, while in the human there are estimated to be 50,000 to 100,000 genes. Thus, determining the DNA sequence of all of the genes in a single organism is a reasonable but not a trivial task given the scale of the current methods.

The real interest in DNA sequences is not, however, restricted to the properties of single organisms. In the human species, any two randomly-selected individuals are estimated to differ at the DNA sequence level at about 6 million bases. Although many of these differences will lead to no observable functional consequences, others are responsible for the wide range of visible differences (phenotypes) seen in personality, intellect, facial features, fingerprints, and so on. Still other differences are responsible for phenotypes that we call genetic diseases because they interfere materially with the quality of life of an individual or even the viability of that individual. It would clearly be of interest to have sufficient DNA sequencing capability to be able to explore, fully, the diversity of the human species. With the world's current population above 5 billion, even if we had a method of sampling only differences (which we do not have today), this would require the acquisition of a data set with $3 \times 10^{16}$ entries. While such a data set is truly formidable by contemporary computer storage and processing standards, it is not likely to be much of a challenge fifteen years from now, if the rate of improvements in computational capabilities can continue to be extrapolated linearly from the progress over the past few decades.

A second area in which truly large scale DNA sequencing capabilities will be needed is in sampling or monitoring environments. To assess the impact of any human activities on an ecosystem, we need to monitor the organisms present and their state of health. The latter should be revealed, in large part, by their pattern of gene expression. It turns out that the vast majority of organisms in a typical soil sample or other environmental sample cannot be cultured in the laboratory, and so they are unknown to us. The only way we can monitor their presence and their patterns of gene expression is by DNA sequencing (or sequencing of messenger RNAs that are the immediate products of gene expression.) To do this continually and on a large scale will require DNA sequencing capabilities that dwarf those needed for exploration of human diversity.

## 3.2 Sequencing by Hybridization

Dramatically faster speeds for DNA sequencing will be needed if applications like clinical diagnostic sequencing, surveys of human diversity, and ecological and environmental surveys are ever to become realistic pursuits. It does not seem likely that information storage or data analysis will ever be a limiting feature in such studies. At present, the limitation is the actual rate at which DNA sequence data can be obtained experimentally. We are exploring faster ways of DNA sequencing by examining methods like sequencing by hybridization (SBH), which can be executed in a highly parallel fashion so that many samples or probes are analyzed simultaneously.

In sequencing by hybridization as originally proposed [7, 14, 23, 25], a labeled target is hybridized to an array of DNA probes. The pattern of label introduced into the array reveals the content in the target of all of the words complementary to the probes. If eight-base probes are used, a full array would have to contain $4^8$ or about 65,000 elements. While it is practical to make and use arrays of this complexity, it turns out that a far smaller set of probes will lead to accurate reconstruction of the original target sequence, because, by and large, the sequence of a text is largely over-determined by its n-tuple word content. An exception occurs from what are called branch point ambiguities. If the probe word length is n, recurrences of a sequences with length n-1 will lead to degenerate reconstructions of the order of the unique sequences flanking these recurrent sequences. While much has been made of these ambiguities as a basic flaw in SBH strategy, they are easily resolved if small bits of additional information are available about the sequences. Futhermore, for comparative DNA sequencing such as will be needed for ecological or human diversity studies, these branch points will hardly be noticeable.

An alternative form of SBH turns the problem around and uses an array of target samples. Labeled probes are brought to this array, and the presence of the sequence complementary to each probe is revealed in all of the samples at once. A limitation in both this form of SBH and in the form which uses probe arrays is the relative lack of quantitation. Thus a target that had three copies of a given eight-letter word would be detected as positive for that word, but it is not at all clear that an accurate estimate of the number of copies would be available. One way to circumvent this difficulty is to use relatively small targets, whether these are immobilized or delivered from solution. For example, a 250-base target would be unlikely to have many recurrences of 8-base sequences so that plus/minus scoring would provide almost all the sequence data needed. The limitation of this approach is that such a target would detect only a very small subset of a 65,000-element probe array. Thus, using the array in this way would be very inefficient.

The optimal strategy for using a probe array to gain information about a complex DNA target has not been established. A key feature in optimizing such strategies is likely to be data quality. To extract the maximum amount of data from a large sample array requires multiplexed strategies in which many probes or targets are used at once. This is likely to require considerably reducing the cross-talk or cross-hybridization between different samples and probes. Alternatively, probes or targets could be labeled in different ways so that many colors would be available to aid the detection process. With conventional radioactive labels it is hard to get more than three colors; fluorescent labels provide four colors in most current use. However, mass labels, which consist of oligonucleotides chosen so that their molecular masses can be distinguished by mass spectrometry, might allow hundreds of colors to be used.

## 3.3 Positional Sequencing by Hybridization

Supplementing physical hybridization (sequence-specific recognition) with enzymatic steps can increase the rate of data acquisition and also greatly improve the ability to discriminate against mismatches. While such procedures are application to ordinary SBH, we have concentrated on developing them in the context of a variation on SBH which we call positional SBH (PSBH) [6]. The difference between these two methods is shown below schematically, where S indicates an solid surface.

**SBH**

probe

S_____                 —>              S_____                 target

**PSBH**

probe

S_____                 —>              S_____  _____

                                                                    target

In SBH, the probe is single-stranded and the target can be captured at an end or, much more likely, at an internal sequence. In PSBH, the probe is partially double-stranded and the target can be captured only at an end. The special configuration used in PSBH allows 5-base sequences to be used as probes, instead of 8-base sequences. Hence the number of probes required to construct a full array is only 1024. In PSBH, two different enzyme steps can be used to proofread the physical interaction between the probe and the target. As shown below, DNA ligase can be used to seal the target to the probe, while DNA polymerase can be used to copy some of the target sequence as in conventional DNA sequencing or the polymerase chain reaction.

probe

S_____  _____  target

|          Ligation with DNA ligase

S_____|_____

|          Extension with DNA polymerase

S_____|_____|------->

The discrimination of PSBH against mismatched sequences when used with the enzyme proofreading illustrated above is impressive. End mismatches are detected at only about 1% the level of perfect mismatches. Internal mismatches are seen even more infrequently. As a result, it was possible in a pilot study to use a mixture of 25 target molecules and still reconstruct the DNA sequences of the components of this mixture correctly from their hybridization pattern. PSBH has an intrinsic limitation that one can only read the end of the target sequence. Thus the target must be segmented into a set of fragments, in which the distribution of the ends is sufficiently broad in the target sequence, in order to be able to read the entire sequence. However, if the target is converted into a nested set of fragments and the lengths of these fragments can be measured independently (and ways for doing this exist, such as mass spectrometry of the captured target), then PSBH provides very valuable additional information. Besides the identity of five bases detected by hybridization, the length of the particular target fragment that has these bases at its end also provides an idea where this five-base sequence is located within the target. Most branch point ambiguities are readily resolved by such positional information.

## 3.4 Efficient Preparation of Samples for DNA Sequencing

Even with the relatively slow sequencing speeds afforded by contemporarily gel electrophoretic methods, the rate of preparation of the DNA samples needed as input to these instruments is becoming limiting. While conceived as a direct DNA sequencing procedure, PSBH may be even more useful as a device for the rapid preparation of DNA samples for fast serial methods like electrophoresis on arrays of capillaries or mass spectrometry which, for DNA, is essentially electrophoresis in the vapor phase. The PSBH configuration illustrated above would be used in the presence of a specific polymerization terminator like C* [9], discussed earlier. Products of such a reaction would be a family of structures like:

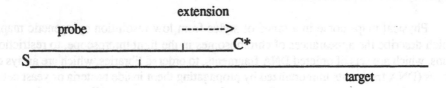

An array of only 1024 probes could capture and then generate sequence ladders from any arbitrary DNA sequence.

There are interesting design issues on how such a capture device could best be used in DNA sequencing. For example, for sequence comparisons, an array could be constructed which would be specifically tailored to the target of interest. Such a target would be fragmented specifically into segments, each of which would be selectively captured by a particular array element. If the target is unknown, it can be fragmented with enzymes that recognize specific short sequences (four to six bases in length) and cut outside these sequences to yield arbitrary single-stranded overhangs that depend on the particular target. The more complex the target or the more frequent these cutting sites, the larger the number of fragments that would be captured by the array. This would lead to a greater utilization of the power of the array to make many ladders in parallel, but as the number of target fragments increases, the probability that two land on the same array element also increases, and when this occurs no sequence data will be obtained from that element at all.

With fast serial methods, the rate of production of arrays of samples may become a limiting step. Because DNA molecules can be replicated, they allow a potentially novel solution to the problem of manufacturing large numbers of arrays. Some of the probe designs we are using would allow direct production of probe arrays by replication of a master array and transfer to a new surface. This would allow the preparation of large numbers of probe arrays, and thus it would facilitate the parallel preparation of many sample arrays.

# 4 Parallel Methods for DNA Physical Mapping

Maps are descriptions of DNA that are less detailed than the full base sequence. There are several different types of maps useful in studying the properties of the DNA molecules that make up the entire genomes of organisms. Genetic markers are DNA sequences that differ in different individuals, and genetic maps give the order of these markers and some estimate of the distance between markers. Genetic maps in the human are made by retrospective examination of the patterns of co-inheritance of pairs of genetic markers. The best markers are highly polymorphic, simple tandemly repeating sequences like $(CA)_n$. The co-inheritance of near-by pairs of genetic markers is imperfect. Sometimes only one marker is passed to an offspring as a result of a process known as meiotic recombination. Genetic maps are a measure of the recombination frequency between pairs of markers.

Physical maps come in a range of styles from low resolution cytogenetic maps, which describe the appearances of chromosomes in the light microscope, to restriction maps, which are sets of ordered DNA fragments, to ordered libraries, which are arrays of clones (DNA fragments immortalized by propagating them inside bacteria or yeast cells) that span large genomic regions. Each of these map types has different applications, advantages, and limitations. The genetic map is the only map that allows the discovery of the approximate location of a genetic trait detectable only by its phenotype. Cytogenetic maps give a rapid genome overview. Restriction maps provide quantitative estimates of distances. Clone libraries are the most powerful type of map, since they provide ready access to DNA that can be used as a source for additional genetic markers, as a target for gene searches, as a source of DNA for hybridization to compare various sets of samples, and ultimately, as a direct source of DNA for sequencing.

As sequencing speeds increase, the rate limiting step is likely to shift from the production of DNA sequence data to the acquisition of samples worth sequencing. In genomic DNA sequencing, the samples needed usually derive from physical maps consisting of contiguous arrays of clones suitable for direct sequence determination. Such a set of samples is called an ordered library. Most past construction of physical maps has involved very tedious top-down or bottom-up strategies. We have shown that more efficient strategies can be developed by using complex mixtures of probes that allow very rapid ordering of overlapping clones.

Until recently, ordered libraries were made by a bottom-up approach, in which individual clones are fingerprinted, by cleavage with sequence specific enzymes, by hybridization, or by partial sequencing, and then overlapping fingerprint patterns are used to assemble contiguous (overlapping) sets of clones. This approach is quite arduous, and it is very difficult to make complete ordered clone sets in this way. Recently, we experimented with a direct top-down approach for clone ordering in which complex DNA probes were used to hybridize to an arrayed library [11]. Ordinary probes used in DNA hybridization range from the eight- to twenty-base sequences described earlier to cloned DNA samples averaging a few thousand to fifty thousand base pairs in length. When such a probe is used to interrogate a large array of DNA samples, usually only a few are observed to hybridize. The resulting information about probe-sample correspondence is quite unambiguous, but the overall strategy results in very inefficient use of the sample array.

To gain efficiency in the interrogation of arrays of clones, we have explored the use of much more complex probes. These can be either large DNA fragments, up to many millions of bases in length, or complex mixtures of small DNA fragments where the mixture, in aggregate, also contains millions of base pairs of total DNA sequence. Such probes detect between 10 and 50% of the samples in the array. This provides a great deal of information from each experiment, but initially most of this information is uninterpretable. To combine the results of successive hybridizations with different complex probes, we have used a likelihood analysis to make estimates of the degree of clone overlap. With only 61 hybridizations, a 1800-clone 5-fold redundant library of the 13.5-Mb genome of the yeast *Schizosaccharomyces pombe* was ordered [11]. This new approach is suitable for any simple genome with a relative paucity of repeating sequences, and it is almost an order of magnitude easier, in terms of the number of experiments required to complete a map, than earlier methods.

To extend the method used on *S. pombe* to the DNA of higher organisms will require methods that remove the effects of the repeating sequences in these genomes, and also reduce the complexity of the starting DNA sample. Selective polymerase chain reaction techniques may prove very useful in achieving these objectives. This will be described in the next section.

## 5 Sequence-specific Manipulation and Purification of DNA

Almost all methods of DNA analysis rely on fractionation. Today, virtually all DNA fractionation is carried out by electrophoretic methods which separate primarily on the basis of DNA size. These methods are simply not sufficient for dealing with very complex mixtures of DNA. We have begun to develop various procedures that allow particular DNA sequences to be selectively captured or amplified. The PSBH technique described earlier is one such approach. Here, several others will be sketched.

## 5.1 Purification of DNA Adjacent to Simple Repeating Sequences

The polymerase chain reaction (PCR) allows the purification of almost any DNA segment by selective amplification. However, in typical PCR applications, known DNA sequence must be available flanking the target of interest. We have developed methods for selective purification of DNA sequences without this prior information. With human samples, one can take advantage of the common interspersed *Alu* repeat to serve as a PCR primer. There are 500,000 to a million copies of this repeat in the human genome. What is amplified are segments flanked by *Alu*'s; hence the method is called inter-*Alu* PCR [18]. If DNA from a monosomic rodent cell containing only a single human chromosome is cut with an enzyme like *Not* I and fractionated by pulsed field gel electrophoresis, inter-*Alu* PCR on individual slices of the gel generates excellent unique sequence DNA probes from specific regions of the human genome [28]. However, a limitation in the inter-*Alu* method is that many regions of the genome do not have a density of *Alu*'s high enough to generate many useful probes. To circumvent this problem, we have recently devised an amplification technique that requires only a single *Alu* sequence [26]. This appears to provide a much higher density of useful DNA probes.

Homopurine-homopyrimidine DNA sequences can form very stable sequence-specific complexes with an additional pyrimidine strand at pH 5 or 6; these complexes can be disrupted at pH 8 or 9. These properties allow very effective sequence-specific capture of such sequences [13]. A variation of the procedure allows selective capture of any DNAs if the sequence at the ends of the duplex is known [12]. Still other variations of this procedure allow the capture of genomic DNA containing specific short tandemly-repeating DNA sequences like (GCC)$_n$ [5]. Such DNA samples are of considerable interest because changes in the lengths of such repeats have been shown to be responsible for a number of inherited neurological diseases.

## 5.2 Total Genome PCR

A problem frequently encountered in work with biological systems is insufficient quantities of sample. This can be particularly severe if the sample is irreplaceable, as in the case of most forensic samples or fossil samples, or if the sample is a single cell, which is required for many biological analyses. To handle such systems it is useful to have a method of preamplification of the entire sample prior to any analysis for specific DNA sequences. Such methods have been termed, generically, whole genome amplification.

A number of different protocols have been developed to try to amplify all of the DNA fragments in sample with no prior knowledge about the sequences they contain. The major challenge in such methods is to generate a product that quantitatively reflects the content and abundance of specific DNA species in the starting sample. This is quite a difficult problem, and it is by no means clear that optimal strategies have been found to do this. A key limitation in PCR, as in most high gain amplification systems, is noise or distortion caused either by stochastic fluctuations or by differential amplification of particular sequences. For example, all else equal, shorter DNA fragments will be preferentially amplified over longer ones, because there is a higher probability in each amplification cycle that a complete new product will be formed from the target.

Our particular protocol for total genome PCR uses a chimeric primer which consists of a constant 18-base DNA tag sequence fused to a variable sequence [10]. For the latter, we used a mixture of all $4^9$ possible sequences of length 9. The initial products of PCR when such primers are used are mostly artifacts, because within the set of primers used are partially complementary pairs which can come together and make short double strands after extension with DNA polymerase. To circumvent this problem, we perform just a few cycles of amplification with this very complex primer mixture. Then the DNA sample is fractionated by size, and all of the artifacts and original primers which are much smaller than typical amplified genomic DNA fragments are removed. The remaining genomic DNA is reamplified by using the constant 18-base tag which becomes incorporated into all species during the initial few cycles of amplification. This procedure results in very effective and representative whole genome amplification.

## 5.3 DNA as a Tag for Other Species

The current status of DNA analysis is quite powerful, and this encourages the use of DNA as a marker to detect other biological analytes. We have developed techniques for detecting antigens by using DNA-tagged antibodies [21]. This method, called immuno-PCR, is much more sensitive than most typical immunoassays. We have also developed a non-enzymatic DNA amplification system, which promises to increase the sensitivity of DNA-based analyses. We have also developed ways of tagging DNA molecules (or other biological macromolecules) with large numbers of many different metals [22]. This raises the possibility of creating highly polychromatic detection systems so that many samples could be analyzed at once.

## 5.4 Future Applications of DNA

The polymerase chain reaction (PCR) allows a subset of DNA molecules to be purified from a complex mixture. When combined with affinity purification of DNA molecules, PCR offers a very powerful way to select a very limited set of molecules from among a set of enormous initial complexity. This kind of purification offers ways to scan large populations of DNAs for those with particular desired properties which may represent DNA reagents for specific applications [8, 24, 27]. For example, it is quite feasible to start with a mixture of $10^{14}$ different DNA sequences which represent a limited set of all variants of a given length. This mixture can be screened for molecules that bind tightly to a given target. The subpopulation that binds tightly is purified and amplified to provide input to a second round of affinity screening. This process is repeated until only a relatively small set of very tight binding DNAs remains in the mixture.

In this way, DNA equivalents of antibodies can be generated. Such molecules are called DNA aptamers. There are several advantages of aptamers over antibodies. They can be generated purely in the test tube. One can start with a greater variety of initial sequences than is available through the biological repertoire of antibodies. The initial mixture of aptamers generated can be studied as a mixture to look for consensus features, or individual components can be cloned and sequenced individually. Test tube evolution methods can then be used to refine and perfect the properties of the original aptamers generated.

Variations on the DNA aptamer approach allow for the *in vitro* selection of DNA or RNA molecules with specific catalytic activity [4, 17, 19]. A whole generation of new materials is likely to result from such approaches. Quite recently, another application of DNA technology which could have considerable importance in the future has been described [2, 16]. It appears that it will be possible to encode, in sets of DNA molecules, problems that are computationally quite intensive. Then the ability to manipulate very large numbers of DNA molecules simultaneously in the test tube and the ability to select or purify from these mixtures molecules with particular preselected sequence or size properties are used to affect an intensely powerful search of DNA sequence space. This approach is at its infancy, and its true power remains to be tested. We have a very elaborate repertoire of methods to manipulate DNA. This article only scratches the surface of what is possible. What combinations of capture, hybridization, amplification and selection will best serve to encode computationally interesting problems in DNA can only be guessed at.

# 6 Parallel Processing Beyond DNA

The human genome project promised to deliver the DNA sequences of the 50,000 to 100,000 genes. As originally contemplated, this was a fifteen-year task with a completion date somewhere around 2004. The original strategy involved making a series of DNA maps as described above and using these maps as samples for DNA sequencing and other gene finding methods. In the past two years, the basic thrust of the human genome project has changed considerably. By searching directly for messenger RNA sequences in a variety of different cell types and tissues, it has turned out that most genes will be found much more rapidly than originally projected. The new methods are called cDNA approaches [1] because they use a complementary DNA (cDNA) copy of the message for actual manipulation and sequencing. Within the next one to two years, we will possess the DNA sequence for most human genes or enough of that sequence that the remainder can be completed easily on a gene-by-gene basis for any gene that appears interesting.

The unexpected speed of gene discovery offers a wonderful opportunity for enhanced biological research but it also poses a number of problems. The original methods proposed for gene finding would have placed them in a geometrical context within the genome; we would have known their approximate location on a chromosome. Now we will have the genes but no idea about their location. Embarrassingly, with existing methods, it will be more effort to locate these genes than it was to discover their DNA sequence. New methods to map large numbers of DNA probes, i.e., the cDNAs being discovered, are badly needed.

A more fundamental problem raised by the explosion of cDNA data is that we will possess all the genes but in most cases they will be accompanied, initially, by very little information about function. In some cases, comparing a cDNA sequence to the available DNA databases provides strong clues about function because very similar sequences with known function already exist. The current DNA databases have more than $2 \times 10^8$ bases of sequence, and this number is increasing rapidly. However, there is a long path between the first hypothesis about gene function to a full understanding of the role a particular gene may play in normal biology and in disease. Past experience has shown that to understand the function of a single gene is a scientific lifetime. We will shortly have 100,000 genes to study, and far fewer people exist trained and committed to study them. What is badly needed is the development of parallel strategies for the study of gene function on the cellular and tissue level so that the momentum gained by the explosion of DNA information is not rapidly dissipated.

# 7. References

1. Adams, M. D. , Kelley, J. M., Gocayne, J. D., Dubnick, M., Polymeropoulos, M. H., Xiao, H., Merril, C. R, Wu, A., Olde, B., Moreno, R. F., Kerlavage, A. R., McCombie, W. R., and Venter, J. C. (1991) Complementary DNA sequencing: expressed sequence tags and human genome project. *Science* **252**, 1651-1656.
2. Adleman, L. M. (1994) Molecular computation of solutions to combinatorial problems. *Science* **266**, 1021-1024.
3. Barany, F. (1991) Genetic disease detection and DNA amplification using cloned thermostable ligase. *Proc. Natl. Acad. Sci. USA* **88**, 189-193.
4. Bartel, D. P. and Szostak, J. W. (1993) Isolation of new ribozymes from a large pool of random sequences *Science* **261**, 1411-1418.
5. Broude, N. E., Chandra, A., Smith, C. L., and Cantor, C. R. (1995) Unpublished data.
6. Broude, N. E., Sano, T., Smith, C. L., and Cantor, C. R. (1994) Enhanced DNA sequencing by hybridization. *Proc. Natl. Acad. Sci. USA* **91**, 3072-3076.
7. Drmanac, R., Drmanac, S., Labat, I., Crkvenjakov, R., Vicentic, A., and Gemmell, A. (1992) Sequencing by hybridization: towards an automated sequencing of one million M13 clones arrayed on membranes. *Electrophoresis* **13**, 566-573.
8. Ellington, A. D. and Szostak, J. W. (1990) *In vitro* selection of RNA molecules that bind specific ligands. *Nature* **346**, 818-822.
9. Fu, D., Broude, N. E., Smith, C. L., Köster, H., and Cantor, C. R. (1995) Unpublished data.
10. Grothues, D., Cantor, C. R., and Smith, C. L. (1993) PCR amplification of megabase DNA with tagged random primers (T-PCR). *Nucleic Acids Res.* **21**, 1321-1322.

11. Grothues, D., Cantor, C. R., and Smith, C. L. (1994) Top-down construction of an ordered *Schizosaccharomyces pombe* cosmid library. *Proc. Natl. Acad. Sci. USA* **91**, 4461-4465.
12. Ito, T., Smith, C. L., and Cantor, C. R. (1993) Affinity capture electrophoresis for sequence-specific DNA purification. *Genet. Anal. Tech. Appli.* **9**, 96-99.
13. Ito, T., Smith, C. L., and Cantor, C. R. (1992) Sequence-specific DNA purification by triplex affinity capture. *Proc. Natl. Acad. Sci. USA* **89**, 495-498.
14. Khrapko, K. R., Lysov, Y. P., Khorlin, A. A., Ivanov, I. B., Yershov, G. M., Vasilenko, S. K., Florentiev, V. L., and Mirzabekov, A. D. (1991) A method for DNA sequencing by hybridization with oligonucleotide matrix. *J. DNA Sequencing Mapping* **1**, 375-388.
15. Landegren, U., Kaiser, R., Sanders, J., and Hood, L. (1988) A ligase-mediated gene detection technique. *Science* **241**, 1077-1080.
16. Lipton, R. J. (1995) DNA solution of hard computational problems. *Science* **268**, 542-545.
17. Lorsch, J. R. and Szostak, J. W. (1994) *In vitro* evolution of new ribozymes with polynucleotide kinase activity. *Nature* **371**, 31-36.
18. Nelson, D. L., Ledbetter, S. A., Corbo, L., Victoria, M., Ramariz-Solis, R., Webster, T. D., Ledbetter, D. H., and Caskey, C. T. (1989) *Alu* polymerase chain reaction: a method for rapid isolation of human-specific sequences from complex DNA sources. *Proc. Natl. Acad. Sci. USA* **86**, 6686-6690.
19. Prudent, J. R., Uno, T., and Schultz, P. G. (1994) Expanding the scope of RNA catalysis. *Science* **264**, 1924-1927.
20. Saiki, R. K., Scharf, S. J., Foloona, F. A., Mullis, K. B., Horn, G. T., Erlich, H. A., and Arnheim, N. (1985) Enzymatic amplification of beta-globin genomic sequences and restriction site analysis for diagnosis of sickle cell anemia. *Science* **230**, 1350-1354.
21. Sano, T., Smith, C. L., and Cantor, C. R. (1992) Immuno-PCR: Very sensitive antigen detection by means of specific antibody-DNA conjugates. *Science* **258**, 120-122.
22. Sano, T., Glazer, A. N., and Cantor, C. R. (1992) A streptavidin-metallothionein chimera that allows specific labeling of biological materials with many different heavy metal ions. *Proc. Natl. Acad. Sci. USA* **89**, 1534-1538.
23. Strezoska, Z., Paunesku, T., Rodasavljevic, D., Labat, I., Drmanac, R., and Crkvenjakov, R. (1991) DNA sequencing by hybridization: 100 bases read by a non-gel-based method. *Proc. Natl. Acad. Sci. USA* **88**, 10089-10093.
24. Szostak, J. W. (1992) *In vitro* genetics. *Trends Biochem. Sci.* **17**, 89-93.
25. Southern, E. M., Maskos, U., and Elder, J. K. (1992) Analyzing and comparing nucleic acid sequences by hybridization to arrays of oligonucleotides: Evaluation using experimental models. *Genomics* **13**, 1008-1017.
26. Tsukamoto, K., Smith, C. L., and Cantor, C. R. (1995) Unpublished data.
27. Tuerk, C. and Gold, L. (1990) Systematic evolution of ligands by exponential enrichment: RNA ligands to bacteriophage T4 DNA polymerase. *Science* **249**, 505-510.
28. Wang, D., Zhu, Y., and Smith, C. L. (1995) A set of inter-*Alu* PCR markers for chromosome 21 generated from pulsed-field gel-fractionated *Not* I restriction fragments. *Genomics* **26**, 318-326.

# Solving Computational Fluid Dynamics Problems on Unstructured Grids with Distributed Parallel Processing

P.W. Grant, M.F. Webster and X. Zhang

Department of Computer Science
University of Wales, Swansea
Swansea SA2 8PP, UK

**Abstract.** This paper describes a distributed parallel implementation of a finite element method for simulating incompressible viscous flow. When applied to unstructured finite element meshes, a conventional implementation of this algorithm becomes particularly space demanding for the storage of system matrices. The parallel implementation not only results in a faster computation but is also potentially capable of solving much larger problems as data and system matrix blocks are distributed. Experimental results demonstrating these key features are presented.

## 1  Introduction

Finite element methods have been frequently used for the numerical solution of partial differential equations. The velocity and pressure in a Newtonian fluid flow can be described as a function of time and spatial location by the Navier-Stokes equations [1]. The particular finite element method described in this paper transforms the solution of the Navier-Stokes equations into a time-stepping solution process on a set of linear equation systems. The associated system matrices are normally sparse.

The essence of finite element methods is to discretise the problem domain into a mesh of finite-elements (usually triangular or rectangular in two space dimensions). A nodal solution vector is then obtained with components at the mesh. Linear interpolation on the shape functions provides the solution at other locations. Triangular elements are used in this implementation. For velocity interpolation, each element is a quadratic function with degrees of freedom defined at six nodes: three vertex nodes and three mid-side nodes. Pressure interpolation is a linear form defined on the three vertex nodes. This provides piecewise continuous interpolation to the solution on the domain. Finite element algorithms are inherently suitable for exploiting data parallelism as data dependency is localised by mesh elements. As a special case, a problem domain can be partitioned into subregions for a distributed parallel solution, requiring only interprocessor communication on subdomain boundaries.

It is often desirable to use the so-called unstructured meshes for the simulation of computational fluid dynamics problems, where for example local flow features, such as boundary layers, shocks or singularity areas, that require fine resolution

# Solving Computational Fluid Dynamics Problems on Unstructured Grids with Distributed Parallel Processing

P.W. Grant, M.F. Webster and X. Zhang

Department of Computer Science
University of Wales, Swansea
Swansea SA2 8PP, UK

**Abstract.** This paper describes a distributed parallel implementation of a finite element method for simulating incompressible viscous flows. When applied to unstructured finite element meshes, a conventional implementation of this algorithm becomes particularly space demanding for the storage of system matrices. This parallel implementation not only results in a faster computation but is also potentially capable of solving much larger problems as data and system matrix blocks are distributed. Experimental results demonstrating these key features are presented.

## 1 Introduction

Finite element methods have been frequently used for the numerical solution of partial differential equations. The velocity and pressure in a Newtonian fluid flow can be described as a function of time and spatial location by the Navier-Stokes equations [1]. The particular finite element method described in this paper transforms the solution of the Navier-Stokes equations into a time-stepping solution process on a set of linear equation systems. The associated system matrices are normally sparse.

The essence of finite element methods is to discretise the problem domain into a mesh of finite-elements (usually triangular or rectangular in two space dimensions). A nodal solution vector is then obtained with components at the mesh nodes; interpolation on the shape functions provides the solution at other locations. Triangular elements are used in this implementation. For velocity interpolation, each element is a quadratic function with degrees of freedom defined at six nodes, three vertex nodes and three mid-side nodes. Pressure interpolation is of a linear form defined on the three vertex nodes. This provides piecewise continuous interpolation to the solution on the domain. Finite element algorithms are inherently suitable for exploiting data parallelism as data dependency is localised by mesh elements. As a special case, a problem domain can be partitioned into subregions for a distributed parallel solution, requiring only interprocessor communication on subdomain boundaries.

It is often desirable to use so-called unstructured meshes for the simulation of computational fluid dynamics problems, where for example local flow features, such as boundary layers, shocks or singularity arise, that require fine resolution in certain subdomains. Since the amount of computation involved in a finite method is generally proportional to the number of mesh elements, this technique allows optimal solution resolution for a given number of elements. An undesirable side effect of this technique is the production of unstructured irregular grids, which for some nodes have high node connectivities or, equivalently, high data dependencies on neighbouring nodes. This has the implication that resultant system matrices, when explicitly assembled, have complex structure and their storage may be overly space demanding. In our implementation, two approaches have been adopted to resolve this difficulty. One is to avoid explicit assembly of system matrices where possible, and the other is to use distributed matrix representation.

## 2 A Taylor-Galerkin/Pressure-Correction Finite Element Scheme

The details of the computational fluid dynamics approach used here are dealt with extensively elsewhere [2, 3] in sequential implementation form. Numerical discretisation and algorithmic approximation issues relating to consistency, correctness and stability are discussed there. Here, in the case of incompressible flows, the Navier-Stokes equations can be discretised by a transient semi-implicit Taylor-Galerkin/pressure-correction (TGPC) finite element scheme [4, 3] of the form:

$$\frac{2\rho}{\Delta t}\mathbf{M}(U^{(n+1/2)} - U^{(n)}) = b_1(U^{(n)}, P^{(n)}) \tag{1}$$

$$\frac{\rho}{\Delta t}\mathbf{M}(U^{(*)} - U^{(n)}) = b_1(U^{(n+1/2)}, P^{(n)}) \tag{2}$$

$$\frac{\Delta t}{2\rho}\mathbf{K}(P^{(n+1)} - P^{(n)}) = b_2(U^{(*)}) \tag{3}$$

$$\frac{2\rho}{\Delta t}\mathbf{M}(U^{(n+1)} - U^{(*)}) = b_3(P^{(n+1)} - P^{(n)}) \tag{4}$$

where $\mathbf{M}$ is an augmented mass matrix, $\mathbf{K}$ a pressure difference stiffness matrix, $U^{(n)}$ the velocity solution vectors, and $P^{(n)}$ the pressure solution vectors. In equations (1), (2) and (4), the right-hand-sides (RHSs) and solutions are *multiple* vectors corresponding to individual velocity components of the continuous solution. The RHS and solution in (3) are, however, *single* vectors representing the scalar pressure variable. The order of computation is to start with (1) and (2) to produce $U^{(*)}$ from $(U^{(n)}, P^{(n)})$, then (3) computes $P^{(n+1)}$ and finally (4) computes $U^{(n+1)}$. Matrices $\mathbf{M}$ and $\mathbf{K}$ are sparse, *symmetric*, and *positive definite* under appropriate imposed boundary conditions.

A Jacobi iterative method [5] is used for the solution of equations (1), (2) and (4) that are all of the same type. This method has been shown to be well-suitable to the solution of such augmented mass matrix equations, due to their favourable conditioning, requiring only a hand-full of iterations [6]. It has two distinctive advantages. Firstly it does not require an explicit assembly of system matrices, making the whole scheme more appropriate for unstructured meshes. Secondly it is highly parallelisable; each vector component of the nodal solution is completely independent of the remainder within a single Jacobi sweep. The matrix **K** arises in the discrete equivalent to a Poisson equation. This is a constant matrix, of relatively small proportions compared with the overall system. Its attributes recommend a direct method of solution for equation (3), such as a Choleski method [7].

The main computation involved in the solution of equations (1)–(4) comprises

- assembly of RHS vectors $b_1$, $b_2$ and $b_3$, accumulating local contributions,
- implicit assembly of system matrix **M** (very similar to that of RHSs) convoluted with
- the Jacobi iteration, and
- the Choleski solution.

The Choleski method requires the factorisation of the system matrix **K**. This factorisation along with the assembly of **K** need only be performed once during the start-up period of this finite element scheme and is therefore not a major consideration in the over computation procedure.

Among these computation activities, the assembly processes and Jacobi iteration are highly parallelisable; unfortunately this is not true for the Choleski solution process. It is our experience that the amount of storage space for Choleski factors imposes a major limitation on the size of problems solvable on a single computer which is perhaps more critical than computation speed. By distributing the subblocks of a Choleski factor to various storage locations, this limitation can be significantly relaxed. In the implementation described here, strategies have been devised to perform efficient distributed storage and computation.

## 3 A Distributed Parallel Implementation

### 3.1 Domain Decomposition

Although finite element methods are inherently parallelisable according to their localised data dependency, an arbitrary distribution of computation does not normally result in a satisfactory parallel performance on distributed platforms as communication among processors is unlikely to be minimised. A simple and sensible way to distribute workload is to partition spatial problem domains into subblocks and assign mesh elements within a connected region to the same processor. In this way, interprocessor communication will only occur in the boundary areas of subblocks. Loadbalancing can be achieved by varying the size of the subblocks. There are many techniques which partition spatial domains, the one used here is a Recursive Spectral Bisection (RSB) method [8]. RSB attempts to minimise the total length of subblock boundaries and therefore reduces interprocessor communication.

## 3.2 Assembly Process and Jacobi Iteration

The main computation involved in the TGPC algorithm is the assembly of RHSs and system matrices. In the RHS assembly case, each RHS vector entry is associated with a specific mesh node. Each entry is formed by accumulating contributions from elements to which the corresponding node is attached. The assembly can be performed in two different ways, either element or node-oriented. The one used in this implementation is element-oriented. This implies that each time a small vector (of size six , or three) of contributions from a particular element is computed, this contribution is accumulated into corresponding entries of a global vector.

The fundamental computations in a Jacobi iteration are system matrix and vector multiplications. Similar to the RHSs, the system matrix $M$ can be viewed as an accumulation of many element matrices of size $6 \times 6$. The system matrix and vector multiplication can therefore be performed as the summation of multiplications of element matrices and vectors of size six. As an element matrix and vector multiplication only produces a vector of size six, there is no need to allocate a large amount of space for matrix $M$, avoiding undesirable storage implications for unstructured meshes.

Clearly, the assembly process and matrix and vector multiplication in a Jacobi iteration are all element-based. They only differ in how element vectors are produced from individual elements. There is no data dependency between any such element operation and these processes are therefore highly parallelisable. The parallelisation technique based on domain decomposition (described in the last section) is employed here, and static loadbalancing is straightforward to achieve. As all elements require the same amount of computation, all subdomains are partitioned with equal numbers of elements.

One issue which has not been discussed is how contributions to boundary nodes may be accumulated. To facilitate this operation, an extra boundary processor is instigated. In this context, a processor accumulates contributions sent from all subdomains by using message passing and then broadcasts the results to the subdomains concerned. The advantage of using an extra processor is that the number of interprocessor communication connections is the same as the number subdomains, this being the smallest we can expect. The computation on boundary nodes is performed prior to that on internal nodes so that the communication cost may be hidden and the boundary processor can operate in parallel with subdomain processors.

A Jacobi iteration also involves vector addition and subtraction, and diagonal matrix and vector multiplication. These operations are node-oriented, and distributed according to whichever subdomain a node belongs to.

There are several other parallelisation approaches which are also appropriate for this TGPC algorithm. These include node-oriented parallel assembly, parallelisation over degrees of freedom, and subdomain contraction Jacobi iteration [9].

## 3.3 Choleski Solution

There are two major difficulties here: explicit storage of Choleski factors and accessing coarse-grained parallelism suitable for workstation clusters.

For structured meshes, a standard fixed bandwidth storage scheme is a reasonable choice as it is simple and can be space efficient. For unstructured meshes, a variable bandwidth, or profile, storage scheme is preferred as, in this case, the minimum bandwidths of assembled system matrices tend to be large. The matrix profile can normally be significantly reduced by adopting a profile reduction scheme such as that proposed by Sloan [10].

Here, it is appropriate to use a distributed parallel computation scheme for Choleski forward/backward substitutions which marries with the concept of domain decomposition. A certain amount of coarse-grained parallelism is accessible if a Choleski factor is devised of the following block form

$$
\begin{bmatrix}
L_{11} & & & \\
& L_{22} & & \\
& & \cdot & \\
& & \cdot & \\
L_{m1} & L_{m2} & \cdot\cdot & L_{mm}
\end{bmatrix}.
\tag{5}
$$

Then forward/backward substitutions on blocks $\{L_{ii}, L_{mi}\}, i = 1, 2, ..., m - 1$ can be performed in parallel. This formation is not difficult to achieve when we take advantage of a domain decomposition procedure. Conceptually, just as with the parallel assembly process described in the last section, it is possible to carry out forward/backward substitutions in inner areas of subdomains in parallel as these areas are not directly connected. This suggests that, for a partition with $m - 1$ subdomains, block $L_{ii}$ should only be associated with internal nodes of the $i$th subdomain. Operationally, this formation can be achieved by using the following domain node numbering scheme:

1. number all internal nodes before any subboundary node, and
2. number nodes in the same subdomain consecutively.

As a result, $L_{mi}$ will represent the dependencies between internal and boundary nodes within the $i$th subdomain, and $L_{mm}$ the dependencies among all boundary nodes.

Fortunately, this numbering scheme is not in conflict with that required for Sloan's profile reduction scheme, and a combined form is adopted that economises on storage [11]. By employing Sloan's heuristics function, this scheme first numbers all internal nodes and then numbers all boundary nodes.

The block $\{L_{ii}, L_{mi}\}$, together with the associated computation, is distributed to the $i$th parallel processor and $L_{mm}$ is distributed to the boundary processor. Again, only $m - 1$ communication connections are required. This is not as parallelisable as the assembly processes and Jacobi iteration, as communication and forward (or backward) substitution on boundary nodes can only start after (or before) the same operation has finished (or is started) on internal nodes. It should be noted that, of the overall computation, the Jacobi component is the dominant part. This storage scheme can be viewed as a distributed version of Liu's generalized envelope method [12] with the exception that nodes are not ordered by a minimum degree node numbering scheme. Liu's method provides a convenient way to exploit all zero entries in a Choleski factor using a conventional variable bandwidth storage scheme. In our case, this means all zero entries will be removed from storage when all entries on the second diagonal of $L_{ii}$ are non-zero.

In this implementation, the same domain partition used for the assembly processes and Jacobi iteration is adopt. Since forward/backward substitutions are not element-oriented operations, such a partition does not necessary lead to a balanced computation. Actually, the amount of computation required on a subdomain is governed by the profile of its corresponding matrix block $\{L_{ii}, L_{mi}\}$. For unstructured meshes, although a subdomain containing nodes with higher connectivities tends to have less columns in block $\{L_{ii}, L_{mi}\}$, this is likely to be denser; a self-balancing mechanism exists here.

# 4  Experimental Results and Concluding Remarks

A network of nineteen diskless Sun Sparc-1 workstations has been used as a test platform and the PVM library has been used for network message passing. These workstations run a SunOS (UNIX) operating system, and are interconnected by an Ethernet network.

| | type | # elements |
|---|---|---|
| Mesh 1 | structured | 1600 |
| Mesh 2 | unstructured | 1535 |
| Mesh 3 | structured | 6400 |
| Mesh 4 | unstructured | 5764 |

Table 1. Test mesh parameters

Simulations of steady Newtonian fluid flows past a rigid sphere in a tube have been conducted. Structured and unstructured two dimensional meshes of approximately 1600 and 6000 elements have been used. The parameters for these meshes are given in Table 1 and their central portions are plotted in Figure 1.

First the main components of this algorithm, RHS assembly, Jacobi solver, and Choleski solver, are individually tested and relative performance together with ideal performance are plotted in Figure 2. For the RHS assembly (RHS) and Jacobi solver (Jacobi), the ideal performance is linear and this is very well approached for both types of meshes. For the Choleski forward/backward substitution component (Choleski), the performance is far from favourable due to

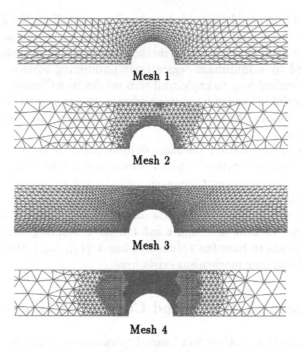

Mesh 1

Mesh 2

Mesh 3

Mesh 4

**Fig. 1.** Test meshes

the nature of the solver. However both predicted and actual performance improves when mesh size increases. These results are very close to the outcome of a theoretical prediction (**Cho_ideal**) discounting communication cost (discussed later) for smaller partition numbers. As expected, all performances tend to depart from the ideal for larger partition numbers with the Choleski component being the most severe (this is understandable as communication cost cannot be hidden in this component). This deficiency may be attributed to the number of separate messages generated during a unit time period, rather than the total message volume in the period. The total volume is far short of the bandwidth of Ethernet and more messages tend to introduce a longer delay to resolve message collision on a shared physical communication channel.

Figure 3 shows the overall relative speed between an $n$ domain partition and a case with no subpartitioning ($n = 1$). Approximately linear speedup has been achieved and there is little performance difference for the structured and unstructured meshes. The overall speed performance of the algorithm has not been affected in any significant way by the Choleski component as forward/backward substitutions are computationally insignificant in overall run time (for three dimension flows, this situation may well alter and further investigation is planned). Such a speedup performance is considered very satisfactory, bearing in mind the moderate size of test problems.

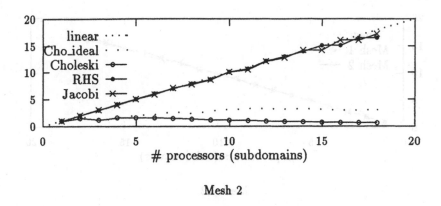

Mesh 2

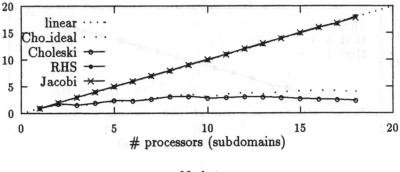

Mesh 4

**Fig. 2.** Relative speed of individual components

Figure 4 displays the run profiles for Choleski factor blocks where $n$ is the number of subdomains, **ave** and **max** indicate the average and maximum numbers of entries in $\{L_{ii}, L_{mi}\}$ respectively, symbol $L_{mm}$ the size of $L_{mm}$, and c/n the size of the complete Choleski factor for $n = 1$, $c$, divided by $n$. In Figure 4, both the average and maximum profiles of $\{L_{ii}, L_{mi}\}$ follow closely the inverse ratio of $n$. The consistent peak at $n = 3$ is due to the fact that there is a significant $L_{mi}$ profile increase at this point. The profile of $L_{mm}$ is a major factor that influences the scalability of this implementation, and in both test cases, the run profiles for $L_{mi}$ increase linearly.

As the profiles in Figure 4 indicate the amount of computation required to perform forward/backward substitutions, this information can be used to predict ideal parallel computation speed with zero communication cost by computing the normalised total profile of $L_{mm}$ and the maximum profile of $\{L_{ii}, L_{mi}\}$. The

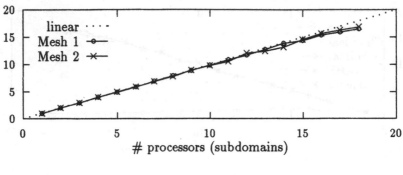

Mesh 1,2

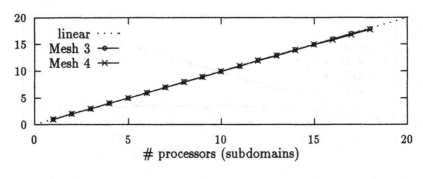

Mesh 3,4

**Fig. 3.** Overall relative speed

performance prediction for the Choleski component shown in Figure 2 is based on this ideal prediction, which is observed to be accurate for smaller numbers of subdomains. The best actual performance is only about 3%. For lager numbers of subdomains, the actual performance departs from the ideal prediction due to obviously the congestion on the network.

We can also observe from Figure 4 the loadbalance of the subblock tasks associated with the forward/backward computations by noting the difference between the maximum and average profiles of $\{L_{ii}, L_{mi}\}$. Compared with the structured mesh case, the unstructured mesh case is less balanced, but not significant enough to seriously affect the general performance.

In conclusion, this parallel implementation is satisfactory for two dimension test cases and advantage has been taken of methods that prove themselves to be insensitive to the use of unstructured meshes. The implementation needs further testing particularly with regard to additional parallelisation aspects and

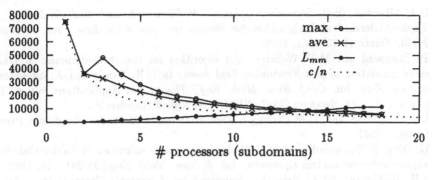

Mesh 3

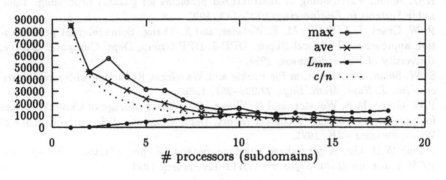

Mesh 4

**Fig. 4.** # entries of Choleski factor blocks

for three dimension problems, where the forward/backward substitution step may prove of greater computational significance.

## 5 Acknowledgements

This research has been supported by a grant from the UK EPSRC (GR/J12321).

## References

1. R. Temam. *Navier-Stokes Equations: Theory and Numerical Analysis*. North-Holland Publishing Company, Amsterdam, 1977.
2. H.R. Tamaddon-Jahromi, P. Townsend, and M.F. Webster. Numerical solution of unsteady viscous flows. *Computer Methods in Appliend Mechanics and Engineering*, 95:301–315, 1992.

3. D.M. Hawken, H.R. Tamaddon-Jahromi, P. Townsend, and M.F. Webster. A Taylor-Galerkin-based algorithm for viscous incompressible flow. *Int. J. Num. Meth. Fluids*, 10:327–351, 1990.

4. P. Townsend and M.F. Webster. An algorithm for the three-dimensional transient simulation of non-Newtonian fluid flows. In G.N. Pande and J. Middleton, editors, *Proc. Int. Conf. Num. Meth. Eng.: Theory and Applications*, volume II, pages T12/1–11, Swansea, 1987. NUMETA, Nijhoff, Dordrecht.

5. L.A. Hageman and D.M. Young. *Applied Iterative Methods*. Academic Press, London, 1981.

6. D. Ding, P. Townsend, and M.F. Webster. Iterative solutions of Taylor-Galerkin augmented mass matrix equations. *Int. J. Num. Meth. Eng.*, 35:241–253, 1992.

7. J.H. Wilkinson and C. Reinsch. *Handbook for Automatic Computation, Linear Algebra*, volume II. Springer-Verlag, New York, 1971.

8. H.D. Simon. Partitioning of unstructured problems for parallel processing. *Computer Systems in Engineering*, 2:135–148, 1991.

9. P. W. Grant, J. A. Sharp, M. F. Webster, and X. Zhang. Some relevant parallelisation approaches. Technical Report DPP-3, DPP Group, Dept. Computer Science, University of Wales, Swansea, 1994.

10. S. W. Sloan. An Algorithm for Profile and Wavefront Reduction of Sparse Matrices. *Int. J. Num. Meth. Eng.*, 23:239–251, 1986.

11. P.W. Grant, M.F. Webster, and X. Zhang. Distributed storage of Choleski factors for parallel computing. Technical report, Dept. Computer Science, University of Wales, Swansea, UK, 1995.

12. Joseph W.H. Liu. A generalized envelope method for sparse factorization by rows. *ACM Trans. on Math. Software*, 17:112–129, March 1991.

# Parallel Decomposition of Unstructured FEM-Meshes *

## Ralf Diekmann, Derk Meyer, and Burkhard Monien

Department of Mathematics and Computer Science
University of Paderborn, Germany **

**Abstract.** We present a massively parallel algorithm for static and dynamic partitioning of unstructured FEM-meshes. The method consists of two parts. First a fast but inaccurate sequential clustering is determined which is used together with a simple mapping heuristic to map the mesh initially onto the processors of a massively parallel system.

The second part of the method uses a massively parallel algorithm to remap and optimize the mesh decomposition taking several cost functions into account. It first calculates the amount of nodes that have to be migrated between parts of clusters in order to obtain an optimal load balancing. In a second step, nodes to be migrated are chosen according to cost functions optimizing the amount and necessary communication and other measures which are important for the numerical solution method (like for example the aspect ratio of the resulting domains).

The parallel parts of the method are implemented in C under Parix to run on the Parsytec GCel system. Results on up to 64 processors are presented and compared to those of other existing methods.

**Keywords:** Parallel Adaptive Finite Element Simulations, Parallel Mesh Decomposition, Parallel Graph Partitioning, Remapping/Repartitioning, Dynamic Mapping

## 1. Introduction

Finite difference (FDM), finite element (FEM) and boundary element (BEM) methods are probably the most important techniques for numerical simulation in mechanical and electrical engineering, physics, chemistry and biology. The finite element method is used for stability calculations as in many areas e.g. car and plane construction and construction engineering. 50% of all stability proofs in engine production use FEM. Simulations of heat conduction, fluid dynamics, diffusion, sound and earthquake wave propagation and chemical reactions make use of finite element or boundary element methods.

* This work was partly supported by the EC, Sonderforschungsbereich 1511 "Massive Parallelität, Algorithmen, Entwurfsmethoden, Anwendungen", by the Esprit Basic Research Action Nr. 7141 (ALCOM II) and the EC HC&M Project MAP.
** WWW: http://www.uni-paderborn.de/fachbereich/AG/monien/

# Parallel Decomposition of Unstructured FEM-Meshes *

Ralf Diekmann, Derk Meyer, and Burkhard Monien

Department of Mathematics and Computer Science
University of Paderborn, Germany **

**Abstract.** We present a massively parallel algorithm for static and dynamic partitioning of unstructured FEM-meshes. The method consists of two parts. First a fast but inaccurate sequential clustering is determined which is used, together with a simple mapping heuristic, to map the mesh initially onto the processors of a massively parallel system.
The second part of the method uses a massively parallel algorithm to remap and optimize the mesh decomposition taking several cost functions into account. It first calculates the amount of nodes that have to be migrated between pairs of clusters in order to obtain an optimal load balancing. In a second step, nodes to be migrated are chosen according to cost functions optimizing the amount and necessary communication and other measures which are important for the numerical solution method (like for example the aspect ratio of the resulting domains).
The parallel parts of the method are implemented in C under Parix to run on the Parsytec GCel systems. Results on up to 64 processors are presented and compared to those of other existing methods.

**Keywords:** Parallel Adaptive Finite Element Simulations, Parallel Mesh Decomposition, Parallel Graph Partitioning Remapping/Repartitioning, Dynamic Mapping

## 1 Introduction

Finite difference (FDM), finite element (FEM) and boundary element (BEM) methods are probably the most important techniques for numerical simulation in mechanical and electrical engineering, physics, chemistry and biology. The finite element method is used for stability calculations in many areas, e.g. car and plane construction and construction engineering. 95% of all stability proofs in engine production use FEM. Simulations of heat conduction, fluid dynamics, diffusion, sound and earthquake wave propagation and chemical reactions make use of finite element or boundary element methods.

* This work was partly supported by the DFG Sonderforschungsbereich 1511 "Massive Parallelität: Algorithmen, Entwurfsmethoden, Anwendungen", by the Esprit Basic Research Action Nr. 7141 (ALCOM II) and the EC HC&M Project MAP.
** WWW: http://www.uni-paderborn.de/fachbereich/AG/monien/

The core of all of these methods is the discretization of the domain of interest into a mesh of finite elements. The partial differential equation used to describe the physical problem is approximated by a set of simple functions on these elements. One of the major disadvantages of FEM is the high amount of computation time required to simulate problems of practical size with sufficient accuracy, especially in the 3D case. For typical applications in computational fluid dynamics (CFD) for example, the mesh can reach sizes of several millions of elements. Therefore there are strong efforts to use modern supercomputers for such kinds of simulations in order to reduce computation times to reasonable magnitudes and to provide sufficiently large amounts of memory.

The domain decomposition method embodies large potentials for a parallelization of FEM methods. In this data-parallel approach, the domain of interest is partitioned into smaller subdomains, either before the mesh generation or afterwards (mesh partitioning). The subdomains are assigned to processors that calculate the corresponding part of the approximation.

The mesh decomposition and assignments of subdomains to processors can be modeled as graph embedding problem where a large graph (the mesh) has to be mapped onto a smaller one (the processor network) [19]. Unfortunately, this mapping problem is *NP*-complete and there exist almost no efficient sequential or parallel heuristics solving it sufficiently [6]. With growing performance of interconnection networks and especially with the establishment of independent routing networks, it is appropriate to reduce the mapping problem to the task of partitioning the graph (the FEM-mesh) into as many equal sized (or weighted) clusters as there are numbers of processors and to minimize the number of edges crossing the partition boundaries.

For the special application of partitioning FEM-meshes heuristics have to be flexible with respect to the measures they optimize. Graph partitioning in general is a combinatorial optimization problem. Normal partitioning heuristics minimize the total *cut size*, i.e. the number of edges crossing partition boundaries. This makes sense in order to reduce the amount of necessary communication of the parallel FEM-simulation. But there are several other measures that are often much more important than cut size and that depend very much on the numerical solution method used for the simulation [8]. Examples are the *aspect ratio* of subdomains (i.e. the ratio between the length of the longest and the shortest boundary-segment, where a segment is a part of the boundary leading to a single neighbor), or their convexity.

Some of the most efficient numerical methods use adaptively refining meshes which change their structure during runtime in order to adapt to the characteristics of the physical problem [1]. Parallel adaptive environments have to include the ability to cope with these changing meshes.

*The new method:* The heuristic described in this paper tries to optimize the shape of subdomains in addition to communication amounts. It is build in a modular way in order to allow the replacement of certain parts, like for example the cost functions which are optimized. It is embedded in a larger research project which aims to design an efficient and flexible frame for the development of massively parallel adaptive finite element simulation codes. Such completely parallel FEM-codes consist of parallel mesh generation, parallel partitioning and load balancing and parallel numerical solvers. Thus the parallel partitioning plays an important role within such a code and is a determining factor for the overall efficiency.

The method consists of two parts. The first one simulates a parallel mesh generation and had to be designed because there are currently no parallel mesh generators available. It performs a fast but inaccurate sequential clustering of the mesh and maps the resulting clusters to the processors of a parallel system. We implemented several clustering and mapping strategies in order to simulate the behavior of different parallel mesh generators and evaluated the influence of the initial clustering on the following parallel partitioning algorithm.

The second part of the method consists of a massively parallel algorithm which takes the clustering as input (or the output of a parallel mesh generator, if available) and optimizes the load distribution together with several other measures resulting from the numerical solution method kept in mind. The parallel phase again consists of two steps. The first one calculates the amount of nodes (or elements) of the mesh that have to be migrated between pairs of subdomains. The second step performs the physical node (or element) migration optimizing communication demands and subdomain shapes. It is followed by a node-exchange phase which further tries to optimize the decomposition. If the numerical solver is using adaptive meshes then this second phase can be used after each refinement/derefinement to restore an optimal load balancing.

*Related work:* A large number of efficient graph partitioning heuristics have been designed in the past, most of them for recursive bisection but also some for direct $k$-partitioning. See [5, 7, 12, 14, 16] for overviews of different techniques. Many of the most efficient methods have been collected into the *Chaco* library by Hendrickson and Leland [13].

Farhat describes in [8] a simple and efficient sequential algorithm for the partitioning of FEM-meshes. This front-technique is a breath-first-search based method which is widely used by engineers and influenced the development of a number of other partitioning tools [9, 17]. We describe it in more detail in Section 2.1, as it is, among others, used within our mesh-generation simulation.

*Recursive Orthogonal Bisection (ROB)* and *Unbalanced Recursive Bisection (URB)* use node-coordinates to partition a mesh and neglect the graph structure [15]. Both methods are fast and easy to implement whereas URB offers larger flexibility. There are ways to parallelize both methods but the parallelization requires to hold the coordinates of all nodes on each processor. Both parallel versions can be used in an adaptive environment.

Walshaw and Berzins apply *Recursive Spectral Bisection (RSB)* which was introduced by Simon et. al. [21, 22] to adaptive refining meshes by combining the method with a contraction scheme [24]. The sequential algorithm performs a remapping taking the existing clustering into account.

The partitioning algorithm included in the *Archimedes* environment [2] is based on a geometric approach where a $d$-dimensional mesh is projected onto a $(d + 1)$-dimensional sphere and partitioned by searching for a center point and cutting hyper-planes. This sequential method uses global information on the node coordinates as well as the graph structure to obtain good partitions. Currently there are no parallel versions available and the use in an adaptive simulation is not directly possible.

The *PREDIVIDER* [17] uses the Farhat front-technique starting from several randomly chosen points and optimizes the decomposition afterwards by a node-exchange strategy. The method is neither parallel nor used in an adaptive environment.

*PUL-SM* and *PUL-DM* are software tools designed at the EPCC to support parallel unstructured mesh calculations [23]. The partitioning with *PUL-DM* is done sequentially and there is currently no support for adaptive refining meshes.

Ou and Ranka introduce *Index Based Partitioning (IBP)* [20] where they reduce the partitioning problem to index sorting which is solved by a parallel version of Sample-Sort. Like ROB and URB this method ignores structural information but can be used to handle adaptive refining meshes.

Hammonds *Cyclic Pairwise Exchange (CPE)* heuristic [12] maps the mesh randomly on a hypercube and optimizes the embedding by a pairwise exchange of nodes until a local minimum of a cost function counting the amount of resulting communication is achieved.

Finally Walshaw et. al. designed the software tool *JOSTLE* [25] which is able to support adaptively changing meshes. The method uses Farhat's algorithm for a sequential clustering, tries to optimize the subdomain shapes, restores an optimal load balancing and finally tries to minimize the communication demands (cut size) by a parallelizable version of the KL-algorithm. The last three steps can be applied if adaptive numerical methods are used and can also be implemented in parallel. A sequential version of the method performs well compared to existing methods and is often faster. Currently there is no parallel implementation available.

The heuristic described here is implemented in a massively data-parallel environment. It is able to perform static partitioning as well as dynamic repartitioning and can therefore be used to handle adaptively changing meshes within a completely parallel FEM-code. The following section describes the different sequential algorithms for initial clustering we tested together with some mapping strategies. Section 3 describes the parallel heuristic and is followed by a section with results compared to existing heuristics.

## 2  Emulating Parallel Mesh-Generation

In a completely parallel FEM-code the mesh generation is done in parallel, too. But if the mesh generation is performed sequentially or if existing meshes are supposed to be used, the elements have to be distributed over the processors of the massively parallel system (which is supposed to be a distributed memory machine) prior to any parallel partitioning algorithm. This requires a first and fast initial mapping of the mesh to the processor graph. In some applications this mapping is done randomly [12] but as the mesh contains a lot of structure it is recommended to use this additional information in order to help the following parallel partition optimization phase.

In our method the initial assignment of elements to processors is done in two steps: first a clustering of the mesh is determined and afterwards the clusters are mapped, one-to-one, onto the processor graph.

## 2.1  Fast Initial Clustering

In principle, any sequential graph partitioning algorithm can be used to calculate the initial clustering. We decided to use three different methods which are fast, differ in their general behavior (i.e. in the characteristics of their output) and take benefit from the geometric information available with the node coordinates.

We rate the methods according to the *load* (i.e. variance in cluster size), *shape* of subdomains, *cut size*, *connection* of subdomains (i.e. each subdomain should consist of only one connected component) and *degree* and *structure* of the resulting cluster graph they produce (the cluster graph contains a node for each cluster and edges expressing dependencies between clusters).

**Box Decomposition:** The *Box* method is an iterative variant of recursive orthogonal bisection (ROB) (cf. Sec. 1 and [15]). It determines the smallest surrounding box of the domain and partitions it into $n_x \cdot n_y \cdot n_z = P$ (no. of processors) "subboxes". The number of boxes in each direction is variable but it is recommended to choose them according to the ratio of the side-length of the surrounding box. The boxes are determined in a way that each box contains the same number of nodes of the mesh. The method generates equal sized clusters, well shaped subdomains which are not necessarily connected, often bad cut size and a well structured cluster graph.

**Voronoi-Diagrams:** The *Voronoi* method determines the Voronoi-diagram to $P$ nodes of the mesh. Each of the Voronoi-cells then represents one subdomain. The choice of the $P$ nodes uses two strategies: Feder's and Green's method to determine a set of points with largest geometrical distance between each other *(farthest point method)* [10] and a pure random choice. Experiments showed for this application a slightly better cut size if random choice is used. The method produces a non-balanced clustering with good cut size, well shaped subdomains (although they need not be convex) which are not necessarily connected and an irregular structured cluster graph.

**Farhat's Algorithm:** Farhat's algorithm [8, 9] uses a BFS-like front technique to determine the clusters one after another. Starting from non-clustered nodes connected to the boundary of partition $i - 1$ it inserts nodes into cluster $i$ according to their number of external edges, i.e. according to the number of edges leading to non-clustered nodes. The algorithm produces compact and balanced partitions which are not necessarily connected, a reasonable cut size and an irregular structured cluster graph.

## 2.2 Mapping to the Parallel Machine

The parallel machine is supposed to be a distributed memory MIMD-system with two- or three-dimensional grid interconnection network.

The assignment of clusters to processors turns out to be a 1:1-mapping problem of an arbitrary graph (the cluster graph) to a 3D grid. Minimizing the dilation of such an embedding is still *NP*-complete [6].

**GEOM MAP:** With *GEOM MAP* we introduce a simple, coordinate based, mapping heuristic of geometric graphs to grids. The coordinates of the nodes of the cluster graph correspond to the centers of gravity of the clusters. A 2D- or 3D-box system corresponding to the size (and dimension) of the processor topology is mapped over the cluster graph and the box boundaries are adjusted until each box contains exactly one node.

Figure 1 shows an example for the mapping of an eight node cluster graph onto a $4 \times 2$–grid and the resulting communication structure.

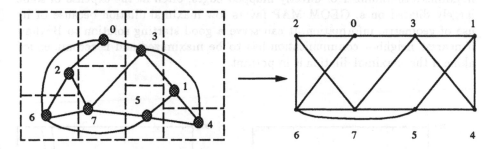

**Fig. 1.** The GEOM MAP algorithm.

**Bokhari's Algorithm:** Bokhari introduces an iterative improvement heuristic for graph mappings [3]. The heuristic repeatedly exchanges pairs of nodes increasing the number of dilation-1-edges of the embedding until no further improvement is possible. It then permutes $\sqrt{P}$ randomly chosen nodes and applies the hill climbing search again. If no further improvement is achieved, the algorithm terminates. The method is fairly slow if the processor network is large $(O(P^3))$. It has to be applied starting on an initial mapping. We chose the identity and the solution of GEOM MAP as starting solution.

## 2.3 First Comparison

Figure 2 shows the resulting communication structure if the graph *airfoil1_dual* is clustered into 64 parts using the Voronoi-method and mapped onto an $(8 \times 8)$-grid using the different mapping algorithms.[3]

---

[3] For a description of the different input graphs, see Appendix A

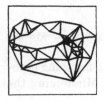   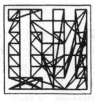

**Fig. 2.** Results of the different mapping variants: The cluster graph of a 64-partitioning of *airfoil1_dual* using the Voronoi-method and the embeddings of Identity + Bokhari, GEOM MAP and GEOM MAP + Bokhari.

Figure 3 shows the dilation and the amount of nearest neighbor communication (i.e. edges mapped without dilation) achieved by the different mapping algorithms. It can be observed that GEOM MAP produces the lowest maximal dilation of all methods whereas the combination of GEOM MAP and Bokhari results in the largest amount of directly mapped edges. Bokhari's algorithm maximizes the number of directly mapped edges, often at the expense of some largely dilated ones. GEOM MAP favors low maximal dilation because of its use of geometric information. It can serve a good starting solution to Bokhari if nearest neighbor communication has to be maximized and is recommended alone if the maximal dilation is important.

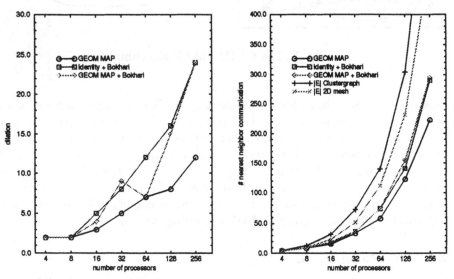

**Fig. 3.** Dilation and amount of nearest neighbor communication produced by different mappings applied to the clustering of the Voronoi method.

# 3 Parallel Remapping

The parallel partition optimization heuristic is the most important part of the whole method. It can be used within a completely parallel FEM environment optimizing the decomposition of parallel mesh generators and especially with adaptive simulations if the mesh (and therefore the load distribution) changes during runtime.

The heuristic consists of two different parts, a balancing flow calculation and a node migration phase. The migration phase again splits into a number of steps.

## 3.1 Flow Calculation

The balancing flow calculation uses the *Generalized Dimension Exchange (GDE)* method which was introduced by Xu and Lau in 1991 (see e.g. [27, 28]). The method is completely parallel and local. It requires no global information and converges on certain networks like e.g. grids very fast.

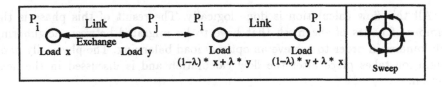

**Fig. 4.** The basic operation of the GDE algorithm.

Figure 4 shows the basic operation of the GDE algorithm. In each step two processors $P_i$ and $P_j$ balance their load over their common edge according to an exchange parameter $\lambda$. A collection of steps in which each edge of the network is included once is called a *sweep*. It was shown [27] that the expected number of sweeps on grid networks is very low, if an appropriate value of $\lambda$ is chosen.

Unfortunately, the optimal $\lambda$-values are not known for arbitrary graphs and wrong values lead to decreased convergence rates. But if the algorithm is applied on the processor network (grid) it can happen that it determines a flow between processors whose clusters are not direct neighbors in the cluster graph.

Figure 5a) shows such an example. The grid-edges between clusters 0 and 7 and between 3 and 5 do not belong to the cluster graph (cf. Fig. 1). A migration of nodes between such clusters would lead to bad subdomain shapes and to non-connected clusters.

We overcome this problem by transferring the flow on grid edges which do not belong to the cluster graph to cluster edges on shortest paths between the corresponding subdomains. In Fig. 5b) the flow on grid-edge $7 \rightarrow 0$ is transferred to the path $7 \rightarrow 3 \rightarrow 0$ in the cluster graph and $3 \rightarrow 5$ is transferred to $3 \rightarrow 4 \rightarrow 5$. The transfer of the flow to the cluster graph can result in cyclic flow which is eliminated in order to reduce the number of necessary node migrations (cf. Fig. 5c)).

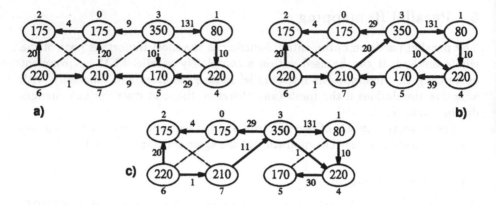

**Fig. 5.** a): The example of Fig. 1 with artificial load and the flow calculated by the GDE-method. b): Transfer of the flow to the cluster-graph. c): Elimination of cycles.

All this flow calculation is done logically. The result of this phase is the number of nodes of the mesh that have to be migrated between neighboring subdomains in order to achieve an optimal load balancing. The physically node migration takes place after the flow calculation and is discussed in the next section.

## 3.2 Node Migration

The node migration phase again consists of four different steps which have to be applied iteratively. Only the second one realizes the balancing flow, the others try to optimize the shape and communication demands of the decomposition.

**Constructing Connected Subdomains:** The initial clustering can result in subdomains containing non-connected parts of the mesh. This first step tries to construct clusters which consist of only one connected component each. Every processor calculates in parallel the connected components of his part of the mesh. To each such component the longest common boundary to components on other processors is determined. The smallest components are then moved to the corresponding processors which contain the clusters with the longest common boundary and merged with these clusters.

This phase results in an increased load deviation between processors but improves the cut size, the shape of subdomains and the degree of the cluster graph.

**Realizing the Flow:** The flow calculation determines the number of nodes to move over each edge of the cluster graph. The nodes to be migrated are chosen iteratively according to their benefit in cut size and subdomain shape. The cost function used to value the nodes consists of two parts, one counting the cut size and one measuring the change of the shape if a node is moved.

Let $D_1, \ldots, D_P$ be the subdomains assigned to the $P$ processors. For a node $v \in D_i$ let $g(v, D_j)$ be the change in cut size if $v$ is moved to cluster $D_j$. We define $\delta_i$ to be the center of gravity of cluster $D_i$, i.e. $\delta_i$ is the mean of all node coordinates in subdomain $D_i$. Let $d(v, w)$ be the geometrical distance between two arbitrary points $v$ and $w$. The *radius* of a subdomain $D_i$ is defined as $r_i = \sqrt{|D_i|/\pi}$ in the 2D-case and $r_i = \sqrt[3]{3|D_i|/(4\pi)}$ in the 3D-case. In this measure, the size (area or volume) of a cluster is approximated by its number of nodes. The idea to optimize the shape is based on a migration of nodes lying far away from the center of gravity. We normalize the distance of a node from the center of its cluster by the radius of the corresponding subdomain [4] and set the change in shape to the changing value of this measure for the originating and the destinating cluster of a node:

$$f(v, D_j) = \frac{d(\delta_i, v)}{r_i} - 1 + \frac{d(\delta_j, v)}{r_j} - 1$$

Then the benefit $b(v, D_j)$ of a migration of node $v \in D_i$ to cluster $D_j$ is a weighted combination of $f$ and $g$:

$$b(v, D_j) = \omega_1 \cdot g(v, D_j) + \omega_2 \cdot f(v, D_j)$$

The processors determine the nodes to be moved to neighboring clusters according to this cost function step by step, i.e. they perform movements of single nodes updating the radius of the subdomains after each movement.

Several problems occur if the node migration takes place in an asynchronous parallel environment. Besides of some inconsistencies in node placement information the structure of the cluster graph may change and sometimes a cluster may split into disconnected components. These problems can be avoided by a careful choice of nodes to be migrated. The details are technical and will appear in the full paper.

**Eliminating Node-Chains:** Near domain boundaries, especially near inner boundaries but sometimes also between subdomain boundaries, the described node migration strategies may produce small node "offshoots". This is mainly because they overweight cut size in comparison to domain shape if the mesh is very irregular.

To avoid such chains which worsen the shape very much we use an extra search for these cases. The chains are easy to detect because they consist of nodes on subdomain boundaries which are only connected to nodes also lying on boundaries. The detected chains are moved in order to optimize the shape. The resulting load imbalance can be removed by a second flow calculation and migration.

**Improving the Shape:** After the first three steps have produced balanced and connected subdomains, the fourth phase uses a hillclimbing approach to further optimize the decomposition. All processors determine in parallel pairs of nodes that can be exchanged to improve the costs of the partition. This node exchange is done very carefully to avoid the generation of node-chains or disconnected components.

## 3.3   The Parallel Algorithm

```
Procedure Par²
    Obtain initial clustering;
    REPEAT
        Construct connected subdomains;
        REPEAT
            Determine balancing flow;              /* GDE /*
            Realize flow;
        UNTIL (Partition balanced);
        IF (first loop)   Eliminate node chains;
    UNTIL (second loop);
    Improve partition;
```

**Fig. 6.** The structure of the parallel heuristic.

Figure 6 shows the overall structure of the parallel partition optimization heuristic $Par^2$. It constructs connected components and then repeats to calculate and realize a flow of nodes between subdomains until the partition is balanced. This repetition is necessary because in some cases a determined flow can not be realized directly (if for example during the node migration a cluster would become empty, the node movement is stopped).

After the first balanced partition is achieved, the algorithm searches for node chains and eliminates them. This makes a further flow calculation and node migration phase necessary.

Finally the algorithm tries to further improve the partition by node exchanges.

The next section shows the benefits of the four different steps and a comparison of results to those obtained by existing methods.

## 4   Results

### 4.1   Cost Functions

In literature, the quality of obtained partitions is measured by several different cost functions. We chose the most important ones to compare the results of $Par^2$ to other partitioning heuristics. Note that $Par^2$ optimizes the cost function shown in Sec. 3.2 and not directly those shown here.

| Function | Description | Ref. |
|----------|-------------|------|
| $\Gamma_1$ | Total cut size | [5, 7, 11, 15, 20, 21, 22, 26] |
| $\Gamma_2$ | Maximal cut size | [11] |
| $\Gamma_3$ | Degree of cluster graph | [11] |
| $\Gamma_4$ | Aspect ratio | |
| $\Gamma_5$ | Shape | |

The total cut size ($\Gamma_1$) is the sum of all mesh edges connecting different subdomains. It is a measure for the total amount of data that has to be transferred in each step of the numerical algorithm. $\Gamma_2$ is the maximal number of external edges of one cluster and corresponds to the largest single data transfer in each communication step. The maximal degree of the cluster graph ($\Gamma_3$) is equal to maximal number of communications that have to be initiated by a single processor. In some hardware topologies this time dominates the message transfer time (if messages are small) and is therefore very important.

$\Gamma_4$ and $\Gamma_5$ measure the shape of subdomains. The aspect ratio of a cluster is (in this case) defined as the ratio between its longest and shortest boundary segment. A segment is a part of the boundary leading to a single neighboring cluster. For $\Gamma_4$ its length is measured in numbers of nodes. The aspect ratio of the partition ($\Gamma_4$) then gives the maximum aspect ratio of all subdomains. $\Gamma_5$ determines the difference between the area (or volume) of the largest inner circle (or ball) and the area (or volume) of the smallest outer circle (or ball) of a domain. This measures the similarity of the shape of a domain to the ideal shape (circle or ball).

## 4.2 Influence of Initial Clustering

| Measure: $\Gamma_1$ | k | Box | | Farhat | | Voronoi | |
|---|---|---|---|---|---|---|---|
| airfoil1_dual | 8 | 207 | (272) | 329 | (423) | 238 | (230) |
| crack_dual | 8 | 463 | (556) | 437 | (611) | 426 | (421) |
| big_dual | 8 | 535 | (709) | 719 | (848) | 494 | (519) |
| airfoil1_dual | 32 | 666 | (870) | 639 | (684) | 619 | (630) |
| crack_dual | 32 | 1154 | (1405) | 1146 | (1483) | 1150 | (1143) |
| big_dual | 32 | 1478 | (1950) | 1384 | (1454) | 1525 | (1375) |

**Table 1.** Comparison of achieved cut sizes after different initial data distributions. Values in brackets indicate the initial cut size after clustering, other values the best cut size after parallel optimization.

Table 1 shows the best cut sizes for various test graphs obtained by $Par^2$ after initial clustering with one of the presented algorithms (cf. Sec. 2). It can be seen that balanced $k$-partitions resulting from the Box resp. Farhat method have been improved significantly. This shows that $Par^2$ is able to optimize even balanced decompositions. The best initial data distribution depends very much on the problem structure, the number of subdomains and the considered cost function. The last fact can be observed from Table 2 which shows results of the different measures if the parallel heuristic is started on the three initial clusterings. The Voronoi method produces in general very good results which could often hardly be improved. But note that it also produces very unbalanced partitions which cause large node movements.

| Initial | k | Graph: *crack_dual* | | | | | | | | |
|---|---|---|---|---|---|---|---|---|---|---|
| | | $\Gamma_1$ | | $\Gamma_2$ | | $\Gamma_3$ | | $\Gamma_4$ | | $\Gamma_5$ |
| Farhat | 8 | 437 | (611) | 171 | (211) | 6 | (6) | 4.8 | (15.4) | 0.8 (2.6) |
| Box | 8 | 463 | (556) | 164 | (197) | 4 | (4) | 79.0 | (82.0) | 0.6 (0.6) |
| Voronoi | 8 | 426 | (421) | 152 | (155) | 6 | (6) | 11.8 | (13.5) | 0.6 (0.6) |
| Farhat | 64 | 1634 | (2121) | 79 | (130) | 7 | (21) | 21.0 | (25.0) | 0.2 (1.3) |
| Box | 64 | 1653 | (1925) | 98 | (160) | 9 | (8) | 22.0 | (34.0) | 0.1 (0.5) |
| Voronoi | 64 | 1674 | (1663) | 76 | (94) | 8 | (8) | 21.0 | (20.0) | 0.2 (0.2) |

**Table 2.** Comparison of several cost functions after different data distributions. Numbers in brackets denote the initial value after clustering, other numbers the value after parallel optimization.

### 4.3 Comparison to other Heuristics

We compare the performance of $Par^2$ to a number of other efficient and often used partitioning heuristics. The HS-heuristic [7] is our own implementation, the versions of KL, the Inertial method (In), the Spectral method (SP) and the Multilevel method (ML) are implemented in the Chacolibrary of partitioning algorithms [13]. The results of Farhat's algorithm are obtained by an own implementation which is also used to determine one of the initial clusterings.

Table 3 shows results of the different methods if the benchmark graphs are split into 16 parts and cut size is counted. The results of $Par^2$ are the best achieved with any of the different initial clusterings. The results of the partitioning heuristics are obtained by recursive bisection with the best found parameter settings.

| Graph | KL | HS | In | In +KL | SP | SP +KL | ML +KL | Farhat | $Par^2$ |
|---|---|---|---|---|---|---|---|---|---|
| grid2_dual | 357 | 350 | 432 | 330 | 373 | 328 | 317 | 406 | 379 |
| | 0.96 | 0.61 | 0.10 | 1.02 | 5.42 | 6.61 | 2.89 | 0.38 | 8.2 |
| airfoil1_dual | 860 | 764 | 503 | 400 | 372 | 309 | 325 | 491 | 382 |
| | 0.48 | 0.16 | 0.20 | 0.86 | 21.29 | 21.20 | 2.98 | 0.76 | 20.5 |
| whitaker3_dual | 1733 | 2224 | 696 | 623 | 729 | 615 | 657 | 654 | 651 |
| | 7.11 | 0.58 | 0.37 | 1.76 | 70.83 | 72.12 | 6.02 | 1.73 | 33.2 |
| crack_dual | 1738 | 2162 | 797 | 639 | 671 | 577 | 615 | 1010 | 660 |
| | 1.75 | 0.69 | 0.45 | 2.03 | 74.14 | 82.60 | 6.47 | 1.53 | 47.1 |
| big_dual | 1875 | 1543 | 1219 | 995 | 863 | 675 | 605 | 1050 | 913 |
| | 2.00 | 0.62 | 1.05 | 3.31 | 124.8 | 131.34 | 8.05 | 2.26 | 22.5 |

**Table 3.** Comparison of achieved cut sizes with different partitioning heuristics for $k = 16$ (small numbers indicate running times in seconds on SS10/50 for sequential heuristics and 16 T805 for $Par^2$).

212

It can be observed that the efficient combinations of global and local heuristics like SP+KL and ML+KL outperform all other methods. The pure local methods KL and HS behave poor on the last four meshes. This is because the maximal degree of these graphs is three (cf. Appendix A).

The results of $Par^2$ are convincing, always better than those of Farhat's algorithm and comparable to SP or IN+KL. The timing results seem to be poor, but this is mainly due to the differing architectures of the sequential and parallel machines. All sequential measurements were taken on Sun SS10/50 workstations, the parallel algorithm ran on a network of T805 Transputers. We show no further time measurements because $Par^2$ is not designed to obtain speedups but to produce high quality clusterings in a massively parallel environment.

| Cost-function | Graph: airfoil1_dual, k = 8 | | | |
|---|---|---|---|---|
| | $Par^2$ | SP | In+KL | HS |
| $\Gamma_1$ | 207 | 251 | 259 | 379 |
| $\Gamma_2$ | 65 | 86 | 95 | 309 |
| $\Gamma_3$ | 4 | 4 | 5 | 5 |
| $\Gamma_4$ | 1.0 | 1.4 | 1.4 | 1.6 |
| $\Gamma_5$ | 5.5 | 5.2 | 8.2 | 72.0 |

**Table 4.** Comparison of different cost functions.

Table 4 shows results of the different cost functions if the mesh *airfoil1_dual* is partitioned into 8 clusters using $Par^2$, Spectral, Inertial with KL and HS. In nearly all measures the parallel heuristic is able to produce improved results. Note that especially $\Gamma_2$ and $\Gamma_3$, expressing the structure of the cluster graph, are not directly optimized by $Par^2$ but the results are nevertheless significantly better than those of the other methods. The values of $\Gamma_4$ and $\Gamma_5$ are indirectly taken into account by the cost function of the parallel method. Regarding the aspect ratio, $Par^2$ is able to achieve an optimal result. To be fair we have to mention that all the other methods are pure graph partitioning heuristics which optimize cut size only. But the example shows that cut size is not the only important measure.

## 5 Conclusions

We presented the parallel partitioning heuristic $Par^2$ for unstructured FEM-meshes. The data-parallel heuristic runs in an asynchronous massively parallel environment and is able to optimize mesh-mappings and to solve the load balancing problem if adaptively refining/derefining meshes are used.

Measurements using several benchmark FEM-meshes together with different initial placements of meshes to processors showed that $Par^2$ produces results in cut size which are comparable to many other existing methods. If the shape of subdomains and the structure of the resulting cluster graph is considered, the new method generates results which are significant improvements compared to those of pure partitioning heuristics. This is mainly due to the fact that $Par^2$ optimizes not only cut size but also partition shapes.

$Par^2$ is implemented in C under Parix to run on the Parsytec GCel and GC/PP systems. Currently we are working on an integration into a completely parallel FEM-code.

## Acknowledgments

This work would not have been possible without the help of many of our colleagues. We would especially like to thank Horst Buchholz, Hinderk van Lengen and the rest of the structural mechanics group in Paderborn who gave us, together with Wolfgang Borchers and Uwe Dralle, some insight into the demands of FEM-simulations. Cheng-Zhong Xu provided lots of help on the GDE method during his stay in Paderborn. The code of the Chaco[4] library was provided by Bruce Hendrickson and Robert Leland. Horst Simon, Alex Pothen and Steven Hammond made additional tools and FEM-meshes available. Finally we want to thank our colleagues Reinhard Lüling, Jürgen Schulze, Robert Preis, Ralf Weickenmeier and Carsten Spräner for many helpful discussions.

## References

1. P. Bastian: *Parallel Adaptive Multigrid Methods.* Tech. Rep., IWR Heidelberg 1993
2. G.E. Blelloch, A. Feldmann, O. Ghattas, J.R. Gilbert, G.L. Miller, D.R. O'Hallaron, E.J. Schwabe, J.R. Shewchuk, S.-H. Teng: *Automated Parallel Solution of Unstructured PDE problems.* CACM, to appear
3. S.H. Bokhari: *On the Mapping Problem.* IEEE TOC 30(3), 1981, pp. 207-214
4. N. Chrisochoides, C.E. Houstis, E.N. Houstis, S.K. Kortesis, J.R. Rice: *Automatic Load Balanced Partitioning Strategies for PDE Computations.* Proc. of ACM Int. Conf. on Supercomputing, 1989, pp. 99–107
5. R. Diekmann, R. Lüling, B. Monien, C. Spräner: *A parallel local-search Algorithm for the k-Partitioning Problem.* Proc. of the 28th Hawaii Int. Conference on System Sciences (HICSS '95), vol. 2, pp. 41-50
   http://www.uni-paderborn.de/fachbereich/AG/monien/PERSONAL/diek.html
6. R. Diekmann, R. Lüling, A. Reinefeld: *Distributed Combinatorial Optimization.* Proc. of Sofsem'93, Czech Republik 1993, pp. 33-60
7. R. Diekmann, B. Monien, R. Preis: *Using Helpful Sets to Improve Graph Bisections.* Tech. Rep. tr-rf-94-008, CS-Dept., Univ. of Paderborn, 1994
   To Appear in: DIMACS Series in Discrete Mathematics and Theoretical Computer Science, American Mathematical Society 1995
8. C. Farhat: *A Simple and Efficient Automatic FEM Domain Decomposer.* Computers & Structures, Vol. 28(5), 1988, pp. 579-602

---

[4] Chaco is copyrighted by Sandia National Laboratories. Its use is granted under License Agreement No. 93-N00053-021.

9. C. Farhat, H.D. Simon: *TOP/DOMDEC - a Software Tool for Mesh Partitioning and Parallel Processing.* Tech. Rep. RNR-93-011, NASA Ames 1993

10. T. Feder, D.H. Greene: *Optimal Algorithms for Approximate Clustering.* ACM Symp. on Theory of Computing (STOC), 1988

11. N. Floros, J. R. Reeve, J. Clinckemaillie, S. Vlachoutsis, G. Lonsdale: *Comparative Efficiencies of Domain Decompositions.* Tech. Rep. Univ. of Southampton, 1994

12. S.W. Hammond: *Mapping Unstructured Grid Computations to Massively Parallel Computers.* Tech. Rep. No. 92.14, RIACS, NASA Ames, June 1992

13. B. Hendrickson, R. Leland: *The Chaco User's Guide.* Technical Report SAND93-2339, Sandia National Laboratories, Nov. 1993

14. B. Hendrickson, R. Leland: *An Improved Spectral Graph Partitioning Algorithm for Mapping Parallel Computations.* SIAM J. on Scientific Computing, Vol. 16, No. 2, pp. 452-469, 1995.

15. M.T. Jones, P.E. Plassmann: *Parallel Algorithms for the Adaptive Refinement and Partitioning of Unstructured Meshes.* Preprint, Argonne National Laboratory 1994

16. G. Karypis, V. Kumar: *A Fast and High Quality Multilevel Scheme for Partitioning Irregular Graphs.* Techn. Rep. 95-035, Dept. of Comp. Science, University of Minnesota, 1995.

17. H. van Lengen, J. Krome: *Automatische Netzeinteilungsalgorithmen zum effektiven Einsatz der parallelen Substrukturtechnik.* R. Flieger, R. Grebe (ed.): Parallele Datenverarbeitung aktuell: TAT '94 IOS Press, 1994, S. 327-336 (in German)

18. O.C. Martin, S.W. Otto: *Partitioning of Unstructured Meshes for Load Balancing.* Techn. Rep. CSE-94-017, Oregon Grad. Inst. of Science & Technology 1994,

19. B. Monien, R. Diekmann, R. Feldmann, R. Klasing, R. Lüling, K. Menzel, T. Römke, U.-P. Schroeder: *Efficient Use of Parallel & Distributed Systems: From Theory to Practice.* To appear in: J. van Leeuwen (ed.) *Trends in Computer Science,* Springer LNCS 1000, 1995.

20. C.-W. Ou, S. Ranka: *Parallel Remapping Algorithms for Adaptive Problems.* Tech. Rep. CRCP-TR94506, Rice University, 1994

21. A. Pothen, H.D. Simon, K.P. Liu: *Partitioning Sparse Matrices with Eigenvectors of Graphs.* SIAM J. on Matrix Analysis and Applications 11/3, 1990, pp. 430-452

22. H.D. Simon: *Partitioning of unstructured problems for parallel processing.* Comput. Syst. Eng. 2, 1991, pp. 135-148

23. S. Trewin: *PUL-DM Prototype User Guide.* Tech. Rep., Edinburgh Parallel Computing Center, 1993

24. C. Walshaw, M. Berzins: *Dynamic Load-balancing for PDE solvers on apative unstructured meshes.* Concurrency: Practice and Experience 7(1), 1995, pp. 17-28

25. C. Walshaw, M. Cross, M.G. Everett: *A Parallelisable Algorithm for Optimising Unstructured Mesh Partitions.* Math. Res. Rep., Univ. of Greenwich, London, 1995

26. R.D. Williams: *Performance of Dynamic Load Balancing Algorithms for Unstructered Mesh Calculations.* Concurrency 3, 1991, pp. 457-481

27. C. Xu, F. Lau: *The Generalized Dimension Exchange Method for Load Balancing in k-ary n-cubes and Variants.* J. Par. Distr. Comp. 24(1), 1995, pp. 72-85
    http://www.uni-paderborn.de/fachbereich/AG/monien/PERSONAL/czxu.html

28. C. Xu, B. Monien, R. Lüling, F. Lau: *An Analytical Comparison of Nearest Neighbor Algorithms for Load Balancing in Parallel Computers.* Proc. of 9th International Parallel Processing Symposium (IPPS '95), 1995.

# A    The Benchmark Suite

| mesh | $|V|$ | $|E|$ | deg | #Elm. | Elm. Deg | Dim |
|---|---|---|---|---|---|---|
| grid2 | 3296 | 6432 | 5 | 3136 | 4 | 2 |
| airfoil1 | 4253 | 12289 | 9 | 8034 | 3 | 2 |
| whitaker3 | 9800 | 28989 | 8 | 19190 | 3 | 2 |
| crack | 10240 | 30380 | 9 | 20141 | 3 | 2 |
| big | 15606 | 45878 | 10 | 30269 | 3 | 2 |

**Table 5.** The benchmark suite

Table 5 shows important characteristics of the graphs chosen as benchmark suite. The same meshes are used as test graphs in several other publications [2, 5, 7, 12, 13, 21, 22].

Given are the number of nodes ($|V|$), number of edges ($|E|$), maximal node degree, number of elements, type of elements (number of nodes belonging to one element, all meshes are homogeneous in their type of elements), and the geometric dimension.

For most of our measurements we chose to partition the dual graphs (or element-graph) to the above given. Such a dual graph consists of one node per element of the original mesh connected to all nodes representing neighboring elements. The number of nodes of the dual graph therefore equals the number of elements of the original one, its degree corresponds to the element type.

The choice of dual graphs results from the requirements of most numerical simulation methods to split along element boundaries.

# Massively Parallel Approximation of Irregular Triangular Meshes with G¹ Parametric Surfaces

Miguel Angel Garcia

Division of Robotics and Artificial Intelligence
Institute of Cybernetics
Polytechnic University of Catalonia / Spanish Council for Scientific Research
Diagonal 647, planta 2, 08028 Barcelona, SPAIN
fax: +34 3 401 66 05, e-mail: garcia@ic.upc.es

Abstract. A new data parallel algorithm for reconstructing smooth surfaces defined by arbitrary 3D triangular meshes is presented. The obtained surfaces are composed of triangular patches that join with first order geometric continuity. Every patch is generated by a parametric function that approximates the vertices of each control triangle of the mesh. A coarse granularity for integration of those functions, in which each triangular patch is generated on a separate processor, yields the best performance as when no communication among processors occurs. The data distribution to attain such an independent task-farm topology is studied. The algorithm has been implemented on a Connection Machine CM-200 system, achieving linear scaling in the number of processors. The simplicity and inherent parallelism of this technique allow its implementation on a wide variety of other parallel and vector architectures.

## 1. Introduction

Triangular meshes are widely used to represent either synthetically or sensorially generated object surfaces in a large variety of fields where scattered information is handled. Computer graphics, geographic information systems (GIS) and robotics are some examples. The availability of techniques for estimating the original surfaces represented by such triangular meshes is of great interest to all these fields. On the other hand, the task of surface reconstruction is frequently associated with tight timing constraints due to real-time requirements of many of the applications that demand this kind of processes. In order to satisfy those constraints, the utilization of parallel computers is likely to be beneficial.

The problem of generating smooth surfaces through interpolation or approximation of control meshes of arbitrary topology does not fit the regular structure of most parallel architectures. Thus, it is not surprising that previous works [3][7][8][10] have focused on the problem of parallel generation of tensor product splines, such as Bézier or B-splines, since they approximate or interpolate surfaces defined by rectangular meshes of control points. Unfortunately, rectangular meshes cannot represent surfaces of arbitrary topology directly.

The author has been supported by the Government of Spain under an FPI fellowship and the CICYT project 'TAP93-0415'. A complementary grant has been received from the Polytechnic University of Catalonia.

# Massively Parallel Approximation of Irregular Triangular Meshes with $G^1$ Parametric Surfaces

Miguel Angel García

Division of Robotics and Artificial Intelligence
Institute of Cybernetics
Polytechnic University of Catalonia / Spanish Council for Scientific Research
Diagonal 647, planta 2. 08028 Barcelona, SPAIN
fax: +34 3 401 66 05, e-mail: garcia@ic.upc.es

**Abstract.** A new data-parallel algorithm for reconstructing smooth surfaces defined by arbitrary 3D triangular meshes is presented. The obtained surfaces are composed of triangular patches that join with first order geometric continuity. Every patch is generated by a parametric function that approximates the vertices of each control triangle of the mesh. A coarse granularity implementation of those functions, in which each triangular patch is generated on a separate processor, yields the best performances when no communication among processors occurs. The data distribution to attain such an independent task-farm topology is studied. The algorithm has been implemented on a Connection Machine CM-200 system, achieving linear scaling in the number of processors. The simplicity and inherent parallelism of this technique allow its implementation on a wide variety of other parallel and vector architectures.

## 1 Introduction

Triangular meshes are widely used to represent either synthetically or sensorially generated object surfaces in a large variety of fields where scattered information is handled. Computer graphics, geographic information systems (GIS) and robotics are some examples. The availability of techniques for estimating the original surfaces represented by such triangular meshes is of great interest to all those fields. On the other hand, the task of surface reconstruction is frequently associated with tight timing constraints due to real-time requirements of many of the applications that demand this kind of processes. In order to satisfy those constraints, the utilization of parallel computers is likely to be beneficial.

The problem of generating smooth surfaces through interpolation or approximation of control meshes of arbitrary topology does not fit the regular structure of most parallel architectures. Thus, it is not surprising that previous works [1][7][8][10] have focused on the problem of parallel generation of tensor-product splines, such as Bézier or B-splines, since they approximate or interpolate surfaces defined by rectangular meshes of control points. Unfortunately, rectangular meshes cannot represent surfaces of arbitrary topology directly.

The author has been supported by the Government of Spain under an FPI fellowship and the CICYT project TAP93-0415. A complementary grant has been received from the Polytechnic University of Catalonia.

This work presents a novel application of SIMD architectures to the problem of approximation of arbitrary triangular meshes of control points. A parallel implementation of a geometric model previously developed by the author is described. This model was originally proposed as a Graphics tool [2] for approximating triangular meshes of control points with smooth parametric surfaces yielding first order geometric continuity $G^1$. Later on, the model was proposed as an efficient tool for surface reconstruction through geometric fusion of neighborhoods of noisy points obtained by sensing [3]. A further extension [4] included interpolation capabilities and was applied to the reconstruction of terrain surfaces in GIS allowing for uncertainty. The model fulfills a set of valuable properties [5] that make it suitable for the efficient representation of complex surfaces of arbitrary topology and genus.

Every surface generated with this technique is composed of as many triangular surface patches as triangles in its associated control mesh. Each patch is generated by a parametric function that approximates the 3D positions of the control points of a triangle. Two parametric functions, $S_{ABC}(P)$ and $G_{ABC}(P)$, are defined. The first function produces triangular surface patches that join with $C^0$ continuity. The second function generates triangular surface patches that join with first order geometric continuity $G^1$ (tangent plane continuity). $G_{ABC}(P)$ is directly obtained from $S_{ABC}(P)$ by modifying the three borders of the latter with cubic Bézier curves calculated to yield the desired continuity.

In a preliminary work [6], three parallel implementations of $S_{ABC}(P)$ on a Connection Machine CM-200 were analyzed considering different degrees of granularity. A coarse granularity implementation, in which each surface patch is generated on a single processor, produced the best results when no communication among processors occurred. Efficiencies close to 100% were obtained.

This paper presents a parallel implementation of the whole geometric model at coarse granularity, including the $G_{ABC}(P)$ functions. The data distribution among processors in order to attain an independent task-farm topology that guarantees maximum efficiency is also analyzed and experimental results are given. The next section summarizes the geometric model. Section three describes the parallel algorithm. Section four gives experimental results of this technique on two CM-200 systems of 4K and 16K processors. Finally, conclusions are given and future lines suggested in section five.

## 2 Geometric Approximation of Triangular Meshes

A triangular mesh $\Delta$ is defined as the set $\Delta = \{ CP, T \}$, where $CP$ is a set of 3D control points and $T$ is a description of the mesh topology as a triangulation of those points. Each control point $X$ is defined by three spatial coordinates and a weighting factor: $X = \{ (x_X, y_X, z_X), W_X \}$. The weighting factor $W_X$ represents the attraction exerted by that point upon the surface. The mesh topology is represented as a set of *polygonal patches* associated with each control point. A polygonal patch associated with a point $X$ lists the identifiers of the control points adjacent to $X$ in counter-clockwise order. According to this definition, every control triangle is associated with three polygonal

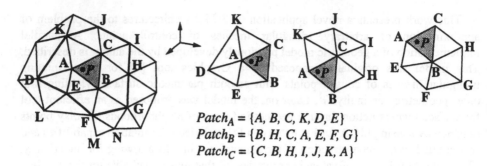

$Patch_A = \{A, B, C, K, D, E\}$
$Patch_B = \{B, H, C, A, E, F, G\}$
$Patch_C = \{C, B, H, I, J, K, A\}$

**Fig. 1.** 3D polygonal patches associated with a control triangle *ABC*.

patches. For instance, Fig. 1 shows the three polygonal patches associated with a control triangle *ABC*.

Each control triangle, in general denoted as *ABC*, is the definition domain of a parametric surface patch $S_{ABC}(P)$ that approximates the three vertices of *ABC*. This approximation takes into account all the control points that belong to the three polygonal patches that contain *ABC*. The parameter *P*, referred to as the *evaluation point*, represents the position inside *ABC* where the function is evaluated. The evaluation point is represented by its *barycentric coordinates* $(b_A, b_B, b_C)$ with respect to the vertices of *ABC*: $P = b_A \, A + b_B \, B + b_C \, C$.

The current definition of $S_{ABC}(P)$ does not ensure derivative continuity between adjacent surface patches. In order to yield first order geometric continuity $G^1$ between them, a second parametric function $G_{ABC}(P)$ is defined. $G_{ABC}(P)$ modifies the three borders of $S_{ABC}(P)$ using cubic Bézier curves such that adjacent patches join with the same tangent plane. This local process guarantees that the overall shape defined by the first function along with its properties are preserved.

Those aspects of the definition of $S_{ABC}(P)$ and $G_{ABC}(P)$ with repercussion on the proposed parallel implementation are summarized below. Further details are omitted owing to space limitations and can be found in [2][3].

## 2.1 Definition of $S_{ABC}(P)$

Let *ABC* be a control triangle that belongs to a given triangular mesh. This section summarizes the definition of a parametric function $S_{ABC}$ that maps each evaluation point *P* contained in *ABC* to a point $S_{ABC}(P)$ lying on a triangular surface patch. That patch approximates the vertices of *ABC* taking into account the vertices themselves and their surrounding control points.

First, each triangular patch, roughly a 3D irregular polygon, is normalized onto a 2D regular polygon circumscribed in a circle of unitary radius. This regular polygon is called the *polar representation* of the original polygonal patch and only depends on the topology of the patch. Hence, it can be computed before the approximation stage.

Polar representations will be considered to be part of the input information supplied to the parallel algorithm along with the control points and the set of polygonal patches.

Three successive stages are necessary to compute $S_{ABC}(P)$: (1) computation of topological influences, (2) generation of surface subpatches and (3) merging of surface subpatches. According to them, the algorithmic complexity to evaluate $S_{ABC}(P)$ is $O(d)$, with $d$ being the mesh degree or maximum number of control points adjacent to any control point.

## Computation of Topological Influences

The topological influence $Inf_{ABC}(X, P)$ of a control point $X$ upon the evaluation point $P$ denotes how much $X$ affects the position of the approximating surface that corresponds to $P$, taking only the mesh topology into account. According to the current formulation, only the control points that belong to the three polygonal patches that contain $ABC$ affect the surface patch which approximates $ABC$.

Three groups of topological influences are computed independently. Each corresponds to the influences upon $P$ of the control points that belong to one of the polygonal patches that contain $ABC$. For instance, the topological influences associated with $Patch_A$ are calculated as follows. First, the polar representation $P_A$ of the evaluation point in $Patch_A$ is determined as

$$P_A = b_A \, \mathbf{A}_A + b_B \, \mathbf{A}_B + b_C \, \mathbf{A}_C \qquad (1)$$

where $\mathbf{A}_A$, $\mathbf{A}_B$ and $\mathbf{A}_C$ are the 2D polar representations of $A$, $B$ and $C$ in $Patch_A$ [2]. Then, the topological influence upon $P$ of each $X$ belonging to $Patch_A$ is the result of applying a bell-shaped function $\mathcal{B}$ to the Euclidean distance between $P_A$ and $\mathbf{A}_X$, where $\mathbf{A}_X$ is the polar representation of $X$ in that patch: $Inf_{ABC}(X, P) = \mathcal{B}(\|P_A, \mathbf{A}_X\|)$ That function is a second degree polynomial obtained by translation and scaling of the quadratic basis B-spline function [2].

## Generation of Surface Subpatches

The topological influences corresponding to all the control points of a same polygonal patch $Patch_A$ are combined to produce a surface subpatch $S_A(P)$,

$$S_A(P) = \frac{\displaystyle\sum_{X \in Patch_A} Inf_{ABC}(X, P) \; W_X \, \mathbf{X}}{\displaystyle\sum_{X \in Patch_A} Inf_{ABC}(X, P) \; W_X} \qquad (2)$$

$W_X$ is the weighting factor associated with control point $X$, and $\mathbf{X}$ the 3D coordinates of the latter. Three subpatches $\{S_A(P), S_B(P), S_C(P)\}$ are thus generated, each corresponding to one of the polygonal patches that contain $ABC$.

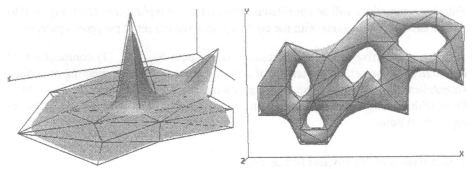

**Fig. 2.** Examples of open and closed meshes and reconstructed $C^0$ surfaces. All the weighting factors $W_X$ are equal to 100.

## Merging of Surface Subpatches

The final triangular approximant $S_{ABC}(P)$ is obtained by merging the three previous subpatches as

$$S_{ABC}(P) = \alpha(P) \, S_A(P) + \beta(P) \, S_B(P) + \gamma(P) \, S_C(P) \tag{3}$$

where $\alpha(P)$, $\beta(P)$ and $\gamma(P)$ are scalar functions that determine the influence of each subpatch in the final result. Those coefficients are calculated such that one of the patches will prevail over the other two as $P$ approaches the central vertex of that patch.

Fig. 2 shows the application of $S_{ABC}(P)$ approximants to the reconstruction of both an open and a closed mesh of arbitrary topology.

## 2.2 Definition of $G_{ABC}(P)$

The $S_{ABC}(P)$ patches defined above can be locally modified to guarantee first order geometric continuity $G^1$ (tangent plane continuity) between adjacent patches. A new patch $G_{ABC}(P)$ is defined based on the previous one and preserving its general shape. In summary, a narrow band along the three borders of $S_{ABC}(P)$ is modified using cubic Bézier curves that are calculated in such a way that those curves that belong to adjacent patches join with the same direction. The evaluation of $G_{ABC}(P)$ has linear complexity $O(d)$ since it requires the evaluation of $S_{ABC}(P)$ a fixed number of times. Three steps are necessary in order to define the new function.

### Computation of Normal-Vector Fields

In order that adjacent patches join with tangent plane continuity, it is necessary to define a field of normal vectors along the three boundaries of $S_{ABC}(P)$. These vectors express the orientation of the tangent planes at each point along the boundaries (Fig. 3). A normal vector field is defined for each boundary of $S_{ABC}(P)$ independently.

In order to compute those normal fields, it is necessary to evaluate $S_{ABC}(P)$ and the three patches that may be adjacent to it. This requirement affects the data distribution of the parallel implementation.

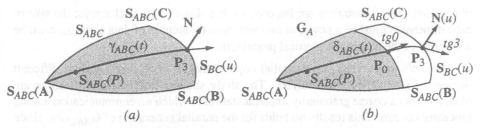

*(a)*  *(b)*

**Fig. 3.** Generation of subpatches. *(a)* Original curve $\gamma_{ABC}(t)$ calculated on $S_{ABC}$ that passes through points $S_{ABC}(A)$ and $S_{ABC}(P)$. *(b)* Piecewise curve $\delta(t)$ that reaches $S_{BC}(u)$ being perpendicular to the normal field $N(u)$ evaluated at $P_3$.

**Generation of Surface Subpatches**

Once three normal vector fields are defined along the boundaries of $S_{ABC}(P)$, three subpatches { $G_A(P), G_B(P), G_C(P)$ } are determined. Each subpatch modifies one of the borders of $S_{ABC}(P)$ with a narrow band of cubic Bézier curves that reach the boundary curve of that border being orthogonal to the normal vector field calculated for that boundary (Fig. 3b). This process only considers information associated with the corresponding surface patch. Hence, no neighboring patches must be evaluated.

**Merging of Surface Subpatches**

The three subpatches calculated above are merged to produce the final approximant $G_{ABC}(P)$ by using a convex combination formulation similar to (3). In this case though, the three coefficients are calculated as a variation of a *discrete transfinite interpolant* proposed by Nielson [2]. The final result is a triangular patch that interpolates the boundary curves defined by $S_{ABC}(P)$ ensuring that orientations of the tangent planes at those boundaries agree with the normal vector fields calculated before. Since adjacent patches share a same normal field, they join with tangent plane continuity.

## 3 Data-Parallel Approximation of Triangular Meshes

This section describes a parallel implementation of the whole geometric model described above on a Connection Machine CM-200. The CM-200 is an SIMD array processor designed to exploit data parallelism [9] by means of a parallel processing unit that embodies thousands of 1-bit serial processors. This unit can process vector data (array data, in general) in parallel. Every data element is associated with an individual processor. Each array operation is transmitted from a host serial computer to the parallel processing unit, where the operation is executed by all processors at the same time.

Each physical processor can emulate several *virtual processors* through sequential execution. The number of virtual processors (processors hereafter) associated with a single physical processor is referred to as the *VP ratio*. A single array data structure is called a *parallel array*. The CM-200 supports parallel arrays of arbitrary number of dimensions. Two constraints are imposed on the shape of parallel arrays: the size of each dimension must be a power of two and the total number of data elements must be a multiple of the number of physical processors.

In a preliminary work [6], a parallel implementation of $S_{ABC}(P)$ at three different degrees of granularity was analyzed. The study showed that best performances are obtained with a coarse granularity implementation in which no communication among processors occurs. This result also holds for the parallel generation of $G_{ABC}(P)$, since its definition is based on $S_{ABC}(P)$.

## 3.1 Granularity Analysis

Three parallel implementations of $S_{ABC}(P)$ at different granularities (fine, medium, coarse) were analyzed in [6]. Those implementations assumed a maximum number of sixteen control points per polygonal patch. This means a mesh degree $d$ equal to sixteen.

The fine granularity implementation was devised with the aim of obtaining an iteration-free algorithm that achieves constant run-time complexity $O(1)$ given $O(dT)$ processors, with $d$ being the mesh degree and $T$ the number of control triangles. That is the solution that yields maximum parallelism. Each processor executes the computations associated with a single control point. This means that each processor calculates (1) and a single term of both the numerator and denominator of (2). The sums and quotient in (2) and the sum in (3) involve the exchange of information among processors using *reduction* operations [6].

The medium granularity implementation assigns the computations associated with a same polygonal patch to a single processor. This means that each processor calculates (1), (2) and one of the terms in (3). The final sum in (3) is obtained through a reduction operation applied to each group of three processors. Thus, the computation of a surface point for all the triangles of the control mesh has linear time complexity $O(d)$ with $O(T)$ processors.

The coarse granularity implementation assigns the computations associated with a same triangle to a single processor. Therefore, an *independent task-farm topology* is attained in which each processor calculates (1), (2) and (3) with no need for communication with other processors. The computation of a surface point for all the triangles of the control mesh has linear time complexity $O(d)$ with $O(T)$ processors. In this case though, the proportionality constant is three times larger than in the medium granularity implementation.

Although the three versions are codified in C* with independence of the underlying architecture of the CM-200 system, the two constraints about the shape of parallel arrays affect the final efficiency. Specifically, the fine granularity version defines 3D parallel arrays of *4* (patches/triangle) x 16 (*d*) x *T* data elements. This means that the computation of each control triangle involves 4x16 processors. Note that four patches per triangle are defined although only three of them are required. The fourth one is necessary to make the size of that dimension be a power of two. Similarly, the medium granularity version defines 2D parallel arrays of 4x*T* data elements, with four

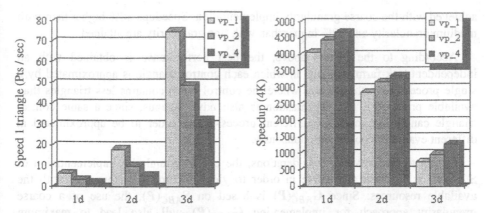

**Fig. 4.** (*left*) Number of approximated points per second and triangle for different VP ratios on a 4K CM-200. (*right*) Global speedup versus granularity for different VP ratios on a 4K CM-200 at full load. The speed on a single processor was measured for VP=1.

processors associated with a single triangle. Finally, the coarse granularity version assigns a single processor per control triangle. In this case no idle processors are necessary.

Fig. 4(*left*) shows the speed of approximation of a single triangle considering a full loaded CM-200 with 4K physical processors and three different VP ratios. The coarse granularity implementation (1d), in which each triangle is associated with a single processor, yields the slowest speed with 6.45 approximated points per second and triangle. The medium granularity implementation (2d), with four processors per triangle, achieves a speed of 17.92 points per second and triangle. This is 2.8 times larger than in the previous case. The fine granularity implementation (3d), with sixty-four processors per triangle, yields the best result, with a speed of 74.66 points per second and triangle. This is 11.6 times faster than in the coarse version. Logically, VP ratios larger than one slow down the speed of approximation since each processor must deal with several triangles sequentially.

Obviously, higher degrees of parallelism lead to individual triangles being approximated faster. However, since more resources (processors) are devoted per triangle, fewer triangles can be approximated at the same time on a single machine. Therefore, in order to obtain a better estimation about the overall performance of the parallel machine, it is necessary to study global speeds, in the sense of total number of points per second that may be approximated.

Fig. 4(*right*) shows the global speedups for the coarse (1d), medium (2d) and fine (3d) granularity versions, considering a full loaded CM-200 with 4K physical processors and three different VP ratios. Note that speedups beyond the number of physical processors only have sense considering that the speed of the sequential implementation of $S_{ABC}(P)$ running on a single CM-200's processor (6.45 points/sec.) was obtained for a VP equal to one. Experiments show that best performances are achieved with the coarse granularity implementation. Speedups 30% higher than with medium granularity and 82% higher than with fine granularity are attained.

According to the results above, the best performance is obtained with an independent task-farm topology in which each control triangle is approximated by a single processor. In those cases where the control mesh contains less triangles than available processors, this organization is also advantageous, since a same control triangle can be replicated on different processors in order to be approximated at different evaluation points simultaneously.

Owing to the previous considerations, the coarse granularity implementation of $S_{ABC}(P)$ is the best alternative in order to yield maximum performance with the available resources. Since $G_{ABC}(P)$ is based on $S_{ABC}(P)$, the use of a coarse granularity approach for implementing $G_{ABC}(P)$ will also lead to maximum performances.

## 3.2 Data Distribution

Section 3.1 shows that a coarse granularity implementation of both $S_{ABC}(P)$ and $G_{ABC}(P)$ yields maximum performance when each control triangle is approximated by an independent processor avoiding interprocessor communication. This section describes how a control mesh is distributed among the processors in order to attain such an independent task-farm topology.

### Data Distribution for $S_{ABC}(P)$ Patches

Let us assume that each triangle of the given control mesh is associated with a specific processor of the parallel processing unit. This mapping is arbitrary and does not affect the final result. Let us consider a control triangle $ABC$ with three adjacent triangles as shown in Fig. 5a.

Let $Patch_X$ be a closed polygonal patch centered at an arbitrary control point $X$, $Patch_X = \{X_0, X_1, ..., X_n\}$, where $X_0 = X$. Let $\Delta_X$ represent the number of control triangles contained in that patch: $\Delta_X = n_x$. Throughout this section, data distributions will be analyzed for the general case of closed polygonal patches. Data distributions involving open patches are restrictions of the general case.

The evaluation of an $S_{ABC}(P)$ patch that approximates a control triangle $ABC$ requires the information associated with the three polygonal patches that contain $ABC$. Therefore, the processor associated with $ABC$ must hold all the triangles adjacent to $ABC$ (including it) and all the control points associated with those triangles (Fig. 5b). Quantitatively, the maximum number of control points that must be stored in a single processor is

$$CP/Proc = 6 + (n_a - 4) + (n_b - 4) + (n_c - 4) = n_a + n_b + n_c - 6 \qquad (4)$$

and the maximum number of control triangles associated with a single processor

$$\Delta/Proc = 4 + (\Delta_A - 3) + (\Delta_B - 3) + (\Delta_C - 3) = \Delta_A + \Delta_B + \Delta_C - 5 \qquad (5)$$

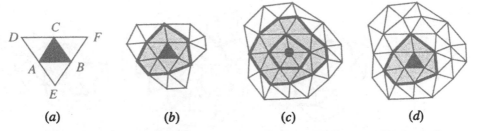

**Fig. 5.** Data distribution for $S_{ABC}(P)$ patches. (*a*) Control triangle *ABC* with three adjacent neighbors. (*b*) Control points and triangles associated with a single processor. (*c*) Processors containing a control point. Each processor contains a shaded triangle. (*d*) Processors containing a control triangle.

Each control point *X* participates in the approximation of the triangles that surround it and all the triangles adjacent to the previous ones (Fig. 5*c*). Thus, the maximum number of processors that require a given control point *X* is

$$Proc/CP = \Delta_{X_0} + n_x + \sum_{i=1}^{n_x} \left( \Delta_{X_i} - 4 \right) = \sum_{i=0}^{n_x} \Delta_{X_i} - 3n_x \qquad (6)$$

Alternatively, since each control triangle participates in the approximation of all its neighbors (Fig. 5*d*), the maximum number of processors that may need a certain triangle *ABC* coincides with the maximum number of triangles associated with a single processor as defined in (5): $Proc/\Delta = \Delta/Proc$.

### Data Distribution for $G_{ABC}(P)$ Patches

Considering the structure shown in Fig. 6*a*, the computation of $G_{ABC}(P)$ requires the evaluation of four control triangles: $S_{ABC}(P)$, $S_{FCB}(P)$, $S_{DAC}(P)$ and $S_{EBA}(P)$. Therefore, in order that a processor evaluates $G_{ABC}(P)$ independently from other processors, it must keep all the polygonal patches that contain those four triangles. Thus, all the information associated with the patches centered at *A*, *B*, *C*, *D*, *E* and *F* must be stored in every processor's local memory. Consequently, in order to compute $G_{ABC}(P)$, the set of triangles and control points necessary to compute $S_{ABC}(P)$ must be complemented now with new points and triangles necessary for the evaluation of its adjacent patches.

The shaded area of Fig. 6*b* encompasses the control triangles and points that intervene in the computation of $G_{ABC}(P)$ considering the same example of Fig. 5*b*. Note that all control points and triangles belonging to $Patch_D$, $Patch_E$ and $Patch_F$ are now included. The maximum number of control points associated with a single processor is

$$CP/Proc = (n_a + n_b + n_c - 6) + (n_d - 4) + (n_e - 4) + (n_f - 4)$$
$$= n_a + n_b + n_c + n_d + n_e + n_f - 18 \qquad (7)$$

while the maximum number of control triangles associated with a single processor is

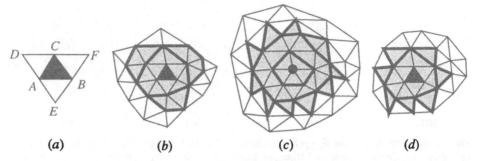

**Fig. 6.** Data distribution for $G_{ABC}(P)$ patches. (a) Control triangle $ABC$ with three adjacent neighbors. (b) Control points and triangles associated with a single processor. (c) Processors containing a control point. (d) Processors containing a control triangle.

$$\Delta/Proc = (\Delta_A + \Delta_B + \Delta_C - 5) + (\Delta_D - 3) + (\Delta_E - 3) + (\Delta_F - 3)$$
$$= \Delta_A + \Delta_B + \Delta_C + \Delta_D + \Delta_E + \Delta_F - 14 \tag{8}$$

Alternatively, each control point increments its influence scope with new processors according to the pattern shown in Fig. 6c. A pattern alike with respect to Fig. 5d is obtained considering the processors influenced by a single control triangle (Fig. 6d).

Thus, the maximum number of processors associated with a control point $X$ is

$$Proc/CP = \Delta_{X_0} + n_x + 2\sum_{i=1}^{n_x}\left(\Delta_{X_i} - 4\right) = \Delta_{X_0} + 2\sum_{i=1}^{n_x}\Delta_{X_i} - 7n_x \tag{9}$$

while the maximum number of processors associated with a control triangle is

$$Proc/\Delta = 4 + 2(\Delta_A - 3) + 2(\Delta_B - 3) + 2(\Delta_C - 3) = 2(\Delta_A + \Delta_B + \Delta_C) - 14 \tag{10}$$

## 4 Results

The parallel algorithms described above have been implemented in C* on two Connection Machines CM-200 of 4K and 16K 1-bit physical processors respectively. Each physical processor runs at 10MHz and contains one megabit of local memory. Configurations with 8K physical processors are also supported by the 16K version. For simplicity, the parallel processors were loaded sequentially from the front-end.

As introduced in section 3.1, experiments have consisted of the approximation of as many control triangles as available processors. Different VP ratios have also been tested by assigning more than a single triangle per processor. Results show that the coarse granularity implementation of $S_{ABC}(P)$ yields best results, with efficiencies around 99.5% for VP=1, Fig. 7(*left*). Interestingly enough, better performances are even got for VP ratios between two and under thirty-two, basically owing to the

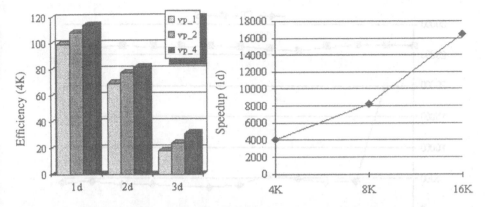

**Fig. 7.** (*left*) Efficiency versus granularity for different VP ratios on a 4K CM-200 at full load. The speed on a single processor was measured for VP=1. (*right*) Speedup versus number of physical processors for VP=1.

pipelined structure of the floating point processors of the CM-200. Efficiencies over 100% have sense considering that a unitary VP ratio was used for the measurement of the approximation speed on a single physical processor. On the other hand, experiments with 4K, 8K and 16K configurations show that the algorithm scales linearly in the number of physical processors, Fig. 7(*right*).

Similar experiments have been carried out for the approximation of $G_{ABC}(P)$ patches, obtaining speedups, efficiencies and scalabilities equivalent to the ones presented above. Fig. 8 compares the speed of evaluation (in points per second) of the $G^1$ patches $G_{ABC}(P)$ versus the $C^0$ ones $S_{ABC}(P)$ on a 4K CM-200 at full load. The horizontal axis represents the number of evaluation points that have been considered in each case. Those points are uniformly distributed over each triangle.

In general, the $G^1$ approximant is between four and six times slower than the $C^0$ one. Fluctuations along the $G^1$ curve depend on the number of evaluation points, owing to the different percentages of those points that require the modification of zero, one or two borders of $S_{ABC}(P)$ in order to yield the $G^1$ patches. This effect is due to the piecewise definition of $G_{ABC}(P)$ (Section 2.2).

# 5 Conclusions

This paper presents a novel application of SIMD architectures to the reconstruction of smooth surfaces defined by 3D triangular meshes of arbitrary topology and genus. These surfaces are composed of two types of triangular patches that may join with $C^0$ or $G^1$ continuity respectively. Parallel implementations of those patches show that a coarse granularity approach, where each control triangle is approximated by an independent processor, yields maximum performance and scales linearly in the number of processors. The data distribution to attain an independent task-farm

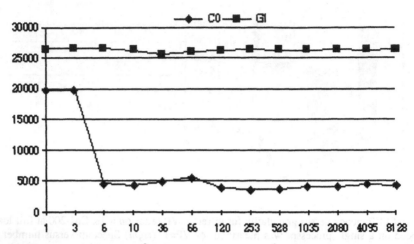

**Fig. 8.** Speed of evaluation of $C^0$ patches ($S_{ABC}(P)$) and $G^1$ patches ($G_{ABC}(P)$) on a 4K CM-200 at full load with coarse granularity versus number of evaluation points.

topology has been studied and experimental results on two CM-200 data-parallel computers have been reported.

This technique is currently being extended to the parallel reconstruction of scalar data (e.g., temperature, pressure) associated with 3D surfaces. This will represent a new application of parallel architectures to the problem of *surface on surface* modeling. Another interesting line of research is the development of parallel algorithms for detecting intersections between surfaces generated with this technique. Those issues will be the subject of future works.

## Acknowledgments

I thank Prof. Basañez for the help he has provided. Jan Rosell helped me in implementing the visualization programs using GL. Special thanks are due to the European Center for Parallelism of Barcelona (CEPBA) for providing me with access to a CM-200 with 4K physical processors. I am in debt with Christophe Caquineau from INRIA at Sophia-Antipolis for running the different experiments for me on a CM-200 with 16K physical processors.

## References

1.  F. Chen and A. Goshtasby. A parallel B-spline surface fitting algorithm. ACM Transactions on Graphics, vol.8, no.1, 1989, 41-50.

2.  M.A. García. Smooth Approximation of Irregular Triangular Meshes with G1 Parametric Surface Patches. Int. Conf. on Computational Graphics and Visualization Techniques, Alvor, Portugal, 1993, 380-389.

3. M.A. García. Efficient Surface Reconstruction from Scattered Points through Geometric Data Fusion. IEEE Int. Conf. on Multisensor Fusion and Integration for Intelligent Systems. Las Vegas, USA, 1994, 559-566.

4. M.A. García. Terrain Modelling with Uncertainty for Geographic Information Systems. Int. Society for Photogrammetry and Remote Sensing Commission III Symposium, Munich, Germany, 1994, 273-280.

5. M.A. García. Reconstruction of Visual Surfaces from Sparse Data using Parametric Triangular Approximants. IEEE Int. Conf. on Image Processing. Austin, USA, 1994, 750-754.

6. M.A. García. Fast Generation of Free-Form Surfaces by Massively Parallel Approximation of Triangular Meshes of Arbitrary Topology. Technical Report, Institute of Cybernetics, January 1995, 15 pags.

7. W. Jiaye, Z. Caiming and W. Wenping. Parallel algorithm for B-spline surface interpolation. Int. Conf. on Computer-Aided Design and Computer Graphics. 1989, 260-262.

8. B. Pham and H. Schroder. Parallel algorithms and a systolic device for cubic B-spline curve and surface generation. Computers & Graphics (Pergamon), vol.15, no.3, 1991, 349-354.

9. Thinking Machines Corporation. The Connection Machine System, CM-2 User's Guide, V6.1, October 1991.

10. A. Valenzano, P. Montuschi and L.Ciminiera. Systolic accelerator for parametric surface modelling. IEE proceedings-E, vol.138, no. 4, july 1991.

# Distributed Symbolic Computation with DTS

T. Bubeck*    M. Hiller    W. Küchlin**    W. Rosenstiel

W. Schickard Institute for Informatics
University of Tübingen
Sand 13, D-72076 Tübingen, Germany
EMail: {bubeck,hiller,kuechlin,rosen}@informatik.uni-tuebingen.de
http://www-ti.informatik.uni-tuebingen.de/dts

**Keywords:** Parallel and Distributed Computing, Threads, Algebraic and Symbolic Computing, Irregular Load Balancing.

**Abstract.** We describe the design and implementation of the *Distributed Threads System* (DTS), a programming environment for the parallelization of irregular and highly data-dependent algorithms. DTS extends the support for *fork/join* parallel programming from shared memory threads to a distributed memory environment. It is currently implemented on top of PVM, adding an asynchronous RPC abstraction and turning the net into a pool of anonymous compute servers. Each node of DTS is multi-threaded using the C threads interface and is thus ready to run on a multiprocessor workstation. We give performance results for a parallel implementation of the RSA cryptosystem, parallel long integer multiplication, and parallel multi-variate polynomial resultant computation.

## 1 Introduction

### 1.1 Motivation

Our work has two main motivations, a concrete one and a more abstract one. The concrete motivation is to parallelize SAC-2 [10], a large library of symbolic algebra (Computer Algebra) codes.[3] The parallel library, PARSAC-2 [19, 23], also covers symbolic algorithms in automated theorem proving, specifically variants of Knuth-Bendix completion of term-rewriting systems [5, 6]. Both Symbolic and Algebraic algorithms are typically extremely data-dependent; in this paper, we only consider the algebraic part.

PARSAC-2 was developed first for shared memory machines, using multi-threaded C code with *S-threads* [22], a custom threads enhancement for symbolic computation. The original purpose of developing DTS was to logically extend the fork/join functionality of threads to the network as far as possible. If PARSAC-2 is run on a network of multi-processor workstations, we want to be able to

---

* Research supported by DFG through SFB 382/C6
** Research supported by DFG under grant Ku 966/2
[3] We use SAC-2 in its C variant SACLIB [3].

execute a suitable subclass of threads transparently across the network instead of on the local node. Of course, these *network-threads* must be heavy enough, side-effect free, and able to copy their parameters transparently across the net.

The more abstract goal of developing the network component DTS was to explore the hypothesis that our fork/join programming style, developed for parallel symbolic computation on shared memory, is useful also in a far broader sense, both outside of symbolic computation and on distributed memory. The general condition under which we believe this style of parallelization, supported by DTS, to be useful, is *irregularity*. The fundamental observation is that elaborate low-level code optimizations are frequently impossible or impractical if parallel code is to be used in a changing environment. More specifically, we can discern the following cases:

- Irregularity of control flow, e.g. data dependency.
- Irregularity of usage, such as for library code used in different hardware and software contexts.
- Irregularity of source code, i.e. instability due to ongoing algorithm and software development.
- Irregularity of hardware, i.e. running the same code on different or dynamically changing machines.

All these conditions make it hard or impractical, even if theoretically feasible, to craft highly optimized parallel code. We believe this to be especially the case in day-to-day software development on workstation networks.

A partial solution has been provided by portable parallelization environments such as the Parallel Virtual Machine (PVM) [32]. PVM is rapidly emerging as one de facto standard for distributed computation and thus becomes important for scientific applications. PVM supports the distributed creation of computation tasks (UNIX processes) and the communication of messages and data between them. The suggested programming model is to write a single program which is replicated many times on the computation nodes and exploits data parallelism with little and regular communication. For non data-parallel problems such as the symbolic algebra applications described below, the alternative is to write a set of independent programs which are placed on the computation nodes and engage in complex communication. In practice, this is hard to handle for lack of a cohesive programming model. Message passing code is also difficult to use in libraries and to use sequentially or in changing hardware conditions.

Our DTS system adds a layer of functionality to PVM, providing more flexibility and enabling a more abstract and coherent programming model by extending the fork/join paradigm across the network. As always, there is a price in efficiency. Our empirical data in Section 3 show for a significant algorithm in algebraic computation that this price may be relatively small.

## 1.2 The Programming Model

The user writes a single program and is allowed to fork (and join) subroutines, resulting in SPMD parallelism. The suggested way to deal with data-dependent parallelism in this model is to use a divide-and-conquer style of (mainly functional) programming, where multiple recursive calls provide logical parallelism.

Parallel programs created this way can be used on different architectures. The forks, providing only logical parallelism, can be interpreted in different ways, changing even dynamically at run-time, to create real parallelism. They are naturally executed on Threads systems on shared memory machines. If the forked subroutines need no shared memory, carrying all parameters with them, they can also be executed across a network, e.g. using DTS. In extreme cases, e.g. for debugging purposes or on a loaded system, they can also be interpreted as procedure calls. On a network of multiprocessor workstations, only the heaviest tasks should be executed across the network, the medium level should be distributed over the processors of a node, and the lightest tasks should be executed as procedure calls by the joining task.

If the environment uses *lazy task creation*, it can be arranged that only the heavy tasks from high up in the call tree get converted into real parallelism, while the small-grained low-level tasks are executed otherwise. In the shared memory part of PARSAC-2, lazy task creation is already supported by the *virtual threads* enhancement of S-threads [24]. Practical experience with this scheme is excellent. In the course of a few minutes, hundreds of thousands of virtual tasks can be created and mapped onto the few available processors [5]. Virtual tasks are however not yet available for DTS; the experiments reported in Section 3 confirm the basic validity of our assumption that efficient parallel execution of non-trivial tasks is possible on such a high level of programming abstraction.

## 1.3 PARSAC System Architecture

PARSAC-2 contains three major bodies of software:

- The *S-threads* system for parallel symbolic computation in C
- Sequential libraries for CA (SACLIB) and term-rewriting (ReDuX)
- Parallelized sequential code and new parallel algorithms.

Figure 1 illustrates the system architecture. The application level consists of both sequential and parallel code; the term-rewriting part is called PaReDuX.[7] The clear separation into system environment and application provides for modularity and portability. Both parts have been developed simultaneously, S-threads responding to the needs of the application, and the application testing the system.

## 1.4 DTS Overview

The Distributed Threads System (DTS), implemented on top of PVM, was designed to provide a higher level of programming abstraction for the highly data-dependent and recursive algorithms of symbolic algebra. DTS supports essentially an SPMD parallel functional style of programming (in C), centered around the fork/join paradigm. Function calls forked by the application are placed on

# PARSAC

| | | |
|---|---|---|
| Term Rewriting ReDuX | Computer Algebra SAC-2 | **Application** |
| List and Symbol Processing | | |
| S-threads | DTS | S-threads | |
| C Threads | PVM | C Threads | **System** |
| (hardware blocks) | | **Hardware** |

**Fig. 1.** The architecture of PARSAC-2.

the net by the DTS load manager, which also provides for load balancing and recovery after node failures. These function calls are concurrent threads of control within the application program; therefore we will call them *network threads*. Another way to think about them is to regard them as asynchronous remote procedure calls into a pool of servers formed by the copies of the application program on the net. Of course, network threads cannot access shared memory and have to carry a copy of their parameters with them across the net (or access them via a network file system). The pool of servers includes the client, as the load manager may decide that the most effective way to execute the fork is for the client to do it himself. Carrying input parameters together with the function name is similar to active messages as implemented by Nexus [13]. In contrast to DTS, Nexus is designed as a compiler target and is therefore more flexible but also harder to use. In addition to [13], we also balance the jobs and recover them in case of crashes.

In our programming model, we view network threads as a logical extension of conventional threads, now called *node threads* for distinction. To allow this integration, DTS incorporates a threads system on each node of the network, using operating systems threads if possible. Multi-threading each node also serves to overlap communication and computation. Using PVM, DTS replicates a program on the network, intercepts fork/join calls and calls user-supplied routines for marshalling parameters, and executes forks across the network; all low-level communication is handled transparently by PVM.

The implementation used in our experiments contained a preemptively scheduled threads package based on the SunOS LWP facility on each single processor of our SPARC network. Single- and Multiprocessor SPARC's running Solaris

2.x now use Solaris threads instead. Node threads have two uses: *computation threads* are used to execute (serve) network threads coming from the outside or service forks coming from the same node but ineligible to go across the net. *DTS system threads* execute DTS functions concurrently with the computation; at present, each node contains a *node manager* thread which handles network fork/joins and a *heartbeat* thread whose heartbeat is used by the load manager to determine whether the node is alive. The load manager is currently realized by a single process executing on some node (in addition to the server process). Techniques described in [33] can be used to decentralize load managing if it ever becomes a bottleneck.

## 1.5  Symbolic Algebra

Symbolic algebraic algorithms find increasing application in scientific computation [12]. An important problem in Computer Algebra with a great many applications in the Sciences is finding the exact solutions of a set of non-linear polynomial equations. Algorithms such as Gröbner Basis computation, polynomial factorisation, polynomial resultant and g.c.d. computation, and fast integer arithmetic are important methods for this purpose. (For an overview and detailed information of algebraic algorithms see [15].) If these tasks can be speeded up through parallelization, bigger systems of equations can be solved.

While many methods employed in symbolic algebra, such as the computation with multiple homomorphic images, are naturally parallel, the parallelism is highly data dependent, of mixed grain-size, and frequently comes from parallel recursive calls. The multivariate polynomial resultant algorithms of Section 3.2 must work for polynomials in any number of variables, with any degree, coefficients of any length, and any degree of sparseness (percentage of zero coefficients). We have to cover all these cases with a single parallel program. In addition, since we are building a library of parallel subroutines rather than a stand-alone application, we have no compile-time information about the number of processors or the amount of parallelism generated elsewhere in the system. Precomputation of parallelization and task and data placement schedules are largely out of the question.

It has been observed [28] that task placement may be aided by cost prediction functions based on the asymptotic analysis available for most algebraic algorithms, usually dependent on the degree and coefficient lengths of polynomials. This scheme may produce good results for simple algorithms such as polynomial multiplication. However, only an exact order ($\Theta$) analysis will yield a precise cost prediction. More complex algorithms may have large differences between best and worst cases. Their run-time may be influenced by additional input parameters such as sparseness in a way which is difficult to analyse formally, or by parameters such as the number of common roots which are impossible to determine easily.

Due to the data-dependent nature of algebraic algorithms, MIMD computers are the preferred architecture for parallelization. The case of a network of workstations is especially important for most practical uses of computer algebra systems. Since the inputs and outputs of parallel subtasks are typically small with respect to the run-time of the computation it is therefore possible to move tasks over a network. However, workstations are rapidly becoming shared-memory parallel machines, and the additional fine-grained parallelization of symbolic algebra tasks is important in order to homogenize the irregular grain-sizes of the heavy tasks that can move across the net.

Our use of divide-and-conquer parallelization and the S-threads environment goes back to [19]; the work on DTS and its application goes back to [1, 16]. Several other parallel Computer Algebra systems are also under construction. The PACLIB system [29] for shared memory machines has been influenced by Parsac; it has been used for parallel resultant computation [18]. DSC [11] for distributed symbolic computation is built directly upon TCP/IP; it has been used for very coarse-grained parallelization. PAC [27] was built on Transputers and used static assignment of tasks to processors. PAC++ [14] is more similar to our work, using a divide-and-conquer parallelization style and a kernel structure. Its task placement is aided by cost prediction functions [28]. For a more complete overview of related work see [23].

## 2  Design and Implementation of DTS

In this section, we describe the basic properties of DTS [2] which provides a framework to parallelize a program on a number of workstations. They are connected in a way, that the programmer sees one single computer consisting of multiple processors.

DTS consists of a run-time environment and some library functions (mainly dts_fork() and dts_join()). They can be used in standard programming languages, like C or FORTRAN and are implemented on top of a message passing system and a thread package (see figure 2). The message passing system (currently PVM 3.3.7 [32]) is used to exchange data between different machines easily, whereas the thread package (depending on the computer archi-

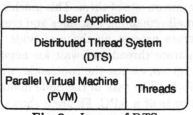

Fig. 2.: Layers of DTS

tecture e. g. Solaris threads) is used to achieve local parallelism at each machine.

On computers with *shared* memory the programming model of threads has become prevalent in the last few years [33]. The programming model of *distributed* memory machines (like workstation clusters) should be similar in order to allow an uniform usage of parallelism on both architectures and to enable the system to decide on its own whether to map a parallel part onto a local thread or an remote computer system. Running a procedure as a local thread makes sense if the machine is a multiprocessor and the thread is executed on another processor. But even if it is no multiprocessor the time necessary for communication can be overlapped by useful computation if more than one thread runs.

Following the programming pattern of thread packages, the user of DTS is able to submit a procedure call using `dts_fork()`. This procedure runs in parallel to the caller and gets normally executed on one of the hosts in a user-defined pool of worker machines. In contrast to Remote Procedure Call (RPC), the calling program does *not* block until the result is returned. Instead it is possible for the program to create further jobs. After starting all parallel tasks, the caller typically waits for the running procedures to complete and gets each result using `dts_join()`.

A cluster of workstation can be seen as a distributed memory machine and therefore each machine holds its own memory. The change of any memory data is therefore not done on all machines. This means that only procedures without any side-effects, which do not rely on global data, can be parallelized through DTS in a straight-forward way.

DTS follows the SPMD model (*single program, multiple data*), which means that all machines run an identical program and have the same functionality. Each can make arbitrary parallel procedure calls which get executed on another machine. DTS decides at a given time, which job should be executed on which machine and tries to keep all machines busy (see section 2.2). But although DTS uses the SPMD model, it is still able to work on heterogeneous workstation clusters, because it translates all values (procedure pointers and user data) between the different representations. It is currently implemented on Sun workstations with one or more processors (under SunOS 4.1.x or Solaris 2.x), Solbourne multiprocessors, and on IBM RS/6000 and PowerPC under AIX 3.2.x. It is easy to port to other architectures, relying on UNIX, PVM, and a threads package.

## 2.1 Implementation

Before running a DTS application, the user selects a number of workstations to use for parallel execution and starts the program on one of them. This machine is called *root node*. DTS starts the program on all remaining machines and creates the *load balancer process (LBP)* as a separate process on the root node. All nodes launch their node managers in a separate thread and wait for network threads. They do not continue the main program, except the root node, which starts parallel execution by doing the first forks. The task of the node manager is similar to the dispatcher of the server process of a RPC. Figure 3 shows the state of three machines after initialization.

Starting a forked job on the executing machine through the node manager means receiving the procedure name and input parameters, starting this procedure in a separate thread, and sending the results back to the caller. Running the called procedures in separate threads allows the execution of more than one called procedure on each machine, because the node manager can listen for more incoming jobs, after starting the first job. The result of a forked procedure is received by the node manager on the calling machine, which stores the result, until the caller requests it with `dts_join()`.

Figure 4 shows the six necessary steps to start a procedure on a remote host. First of all, a node—named *caller*—calls `dts_fork(p,a)`, where p is the

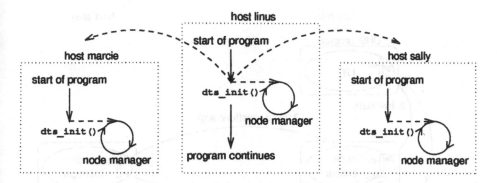

**Fig. 3.** Three machines after initialization

procedure to execute in parallel and **a** are its arguments. Then DTS sends a request to the LBP to ask for the executing machine. After sending this request—even before the answer arrives—the caller can continue, because all following steps will be handled by the independent node managers. This leads to more parallelism and increases the usage of the machine. The LBP returns the ID of the least loaded machine to the node manager, which translates p and a and sends them to the executer. There the node manager receives them and forks the called procedure in a newly created thread, to immediately watch for the next request. After executing the procedure, the result is sent back to the caller, received and stored in a safe place by the node manager. The next message sent to the LBP is used to indicate that this job is finished and should be deleted from its queues. If the caller asks for the result with dts_join(), the local node manager returns the previously received value.

## 2.2 Load Balancing

In order to achieve good performance, parallel systems must balance the jobs on the processors. DTS uses the LBP to decide which job should be executed on which machine. Following the taxonomy of [8] our load balancing scheme could be characterized as adaptive physically non-distributed dynamic global scheduling with one-time assignment.

Each node periodically sends its load (in general the number of running jobs) to the LBP. This enables the LBP to select one of the available machines for execution of a forked job by looking at the loads of the different machines.

Ideally *all* machines should have work until the end of the computation, where all should stop at the same time. The situation where nearly all machines have finished and are waiting for the last machine to complete its jobs should be avoided.

The LBP tries to achieve this by *not* immediately starting all forked procedures. Instead it runs only MAXJOBS on each machine and keeps the remaining jobs in a queue. Running more than one task per machine has the advantage that most communication can be overlapped by useful computation. On the other

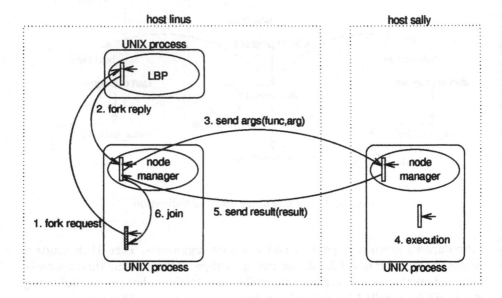

**Fig. 4.** The execution of an `dts_fork()`

hand, not too many jobs should be started on each machine to avoid the risk of unbalanced workload or overloading a single machine. Otherwise efficiency will go down because of paging and other unwanted activities.

Every time a job finishes on a particular machine, the LBP starts a new job on this machine. This job is taken from the queue of pending jobs. If the queue gets smaller and the possible end of the computation arrives, the number of running jobs at each node is even more reduced, by not starting a new job on a therefore "overloaded" machine. Fewer jobs per machine reduce the probability of an unbalanced job distribution and is therefore very important at the end.

The maximum number of jobs on each node is limited by the LBP through $l(\# \ of \ items \ in \ queue) = \min(\texttt{MAXJOBS}, \lceil \frac{\# \ of \ items \ in \ queue}{\# \ of \ hosts} \rceil)$, where MAXJOBS as 5 has produced good results on different test cases.

## 2.3 Fault Tolerance

As stated above, all nodes periodically (every $t$ seconds) send their load to the LBP. A hardware or software crash of a machine can be registered by the LBP, if one does not send its load for a time greater than $t$. To make sure that a running but heavily loaded machine is not considered broken, the LBP recognizes a machine only as broken if it does not send a message for more than $5*t$ seconds.

If the LBP registers the crash of a machine, it automatically restarts all jobs executed on the crashed host on another machine, without concern or knowledge by the user program. In addition, all jobs forked by the crashed host will be deleted from the queue of pending jobs. Restarting jobs is possible, because the LBP enters the ID of the machine executing an job in its job queue.

The *recovery* ensures that the application continues, even if some machines go down. If a dropped machine restarts, it is automatically integrated again. This mechanism also allows to delete or add machines during run-time, without the need to stop the computation.

# 3 Empirical Results

We present empirical results from two important parallel algebraic algorithms, the RSA cryptosystem and multivariate polynomial resultant computation.

The experiments were conducted on up to 13 machines of type Sun ELC (4/25) running SunOS 4.1 and PVM 3.1.4. The system was *DTS_PARSAC* as described in [16], integrating DTS [1] with *PARSAC-2* [19].

All measurements were done using wall clock time. The sequential and parallel algorithms were realized in separate programs and were measured separately. All reported run-times are the average of 5 single runs. The measurements were done at night, on an almost empty network.

## 3.1 The RSA Cryptosystem

First we want to show the behavior of DTS with the RSA [26] cryptosystem. This problem is irregular in the sense that the input data is treated in blocks of a certain size depending on the key length. Additionally, the size of the input data determines the number of blocks en- and decrypted. The computation weight of each block en- or decryption on the other hand is virtually the same. So the load balancing of a distributed RSA algorithm is clearly regular. The run-times, speedup and efficiency graphs of an example measure are shown in figure 5.

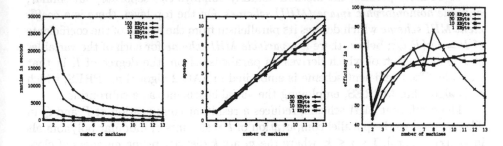

**Fig. 5.** Run-times, speedup and efficiency of RSA

The run-time for two machines is higher than that of the sequential case. This is due to the fact that the distributing machine does not en- or decrypt any blocks, so we effectively just have one worker. The case with 1 KByte big input data shows us the theoretical behavior of unsatisfying parallelism. In that case we have certain steps of speedups, which is due to the pigeon-hole-principle.

As long as we have enough parallelism we are near to the theoretical maximum as given by Amdahl's law. We even achieved an efficiency over 90 percent when running only one computation thread per machine.

## 3.2 Multivariate Polynomial Resultants

Multivariate Polynomial Resultants can be used for solving non-linear systems of polynomials symbolically, following classical elimination theory. Given two $r$-variate polynomials $P, Q \in \mathbb{Z}[x_1, \ldots, x_r]$, we are interested in their common roots. The resultant $R(P, Q)$ is a polynomial in $r - 1$ variables with the property that $P = P(x_r)$ and $Q = Q(x_r)$ have a non-constant g.c.d. (and hence common roots), if $x_1, \ldots, x_{r-1}$ are such that $R(x_1, \ldots, x_{r-1})$ is zero. The resultant computation thus "eliminates" one variable from the equation solving problem. Starting with a system of $r$ polynomials and using repeated elimination, together with algorithms for the computation of g.c.d.'s and the isolation of real roots of univariate polynomials, we get a method for solving systems of equations. For an introduction to resultants and their use in equation solving, see [15]; the modular resultant algorithm parallelized here is due to Collins [9].

The *modular method* recursively maps the multivariate resultant computation to multiple resultant computations of homomorphic images, and, using the Chinese Remainder Algorithm, lifts the image resultants back up to the originally desired resultant. In the base case of univariate polynomials, the resultant may be computed using a polynomial remainder sequence. Most of the images are created by evaluating the polynomials at $d^{v-1}$ points, where $d$ is a bound on the degree of the resultant and $v$ is the number of variables. The complexity of the algorithm is exponential in the number of variables and polynomial in the degree of $P$ and $Q$. This process therefore contains a large amount of parallelism at several levels of granularity.

To be more precise, the method actually employs two separate, but similar, *multiple homomorphic image (MHI) schemes*. On the top level, there is a *coefficient MHI scheme* which derives its parallelism from the length of the coefficients of $R = \mathrm{res}(P, Q)$; below, there is a *variable MHI scheme* for each of the variables of $P$ and $Q$, each of which derives its parallelism from the degree of $R$ in that variable. The coefficient scheme is embodied in SAC-2 algorithm IPRES, which calls algorithm MPRES, employing the variable scheme, as a subroutine.

The coefficient MHI scheme, reduces a resultant computation of $P$ and $Q$ in $\mathbb{Z}[x_1, \ldots, x_r]$ to the parallel computation of $k$ resultants of modular polynomials in $\mathbb{Z}_{p_i}[x_1, \ldots, x_r]$, $1 \le i \le k$, where the $p_i$ are $k$ distinct prime numbers of close to machine word size. The homomorphisms involved here *reduce* all coefficients modulo the prime. The lifting process repeatedly applies the Chinese Remainder Algorithm (CRA) to the modular results, with coefficients in $\mathbb{Z}_{p_i}$, in order to retrieve the correct coefficients of the resultant in $\mathbb{Z}$ (the resultant is now a polynomial in $\mathbb{Z}[x_1, \ldots, x_{r-1}]$).

In the multivariate case, the variable MHI scheme reduces each resultant computation of $P$ and $Q$ in $\mathbb{Z}_{p_i}[x_1, x_2, \ldots, x_r]$ to multiple parallel recursive resultant computations of the homomorphic images of $P$ and $Q$ in $\mathbb{Z}_{p_i}[x_2, \ldots, x_r]$.

Each result is a polynomial $R \in \mathbb{Z}_{p_i}[x_2, \ldots, x_{r-1}]$, and is itself the homomorphic image of the true resultant of $P$ and $Q$. The homomorphisms involved here *substitute* variable $x_1$ by $d + 1$ distinct values, where $d$ is a bound on the degree of the resultant. In this case the lifting process consists of polynomial interpolation which reconstructs the true result in $\mathbb{Z}_{p_i}[x_1, x_2, \ldots, x_{r-1}]$ from the homomorphic images of the result. Lifting may become a bottleneck if $k$ is large. It can be parallelized, too, but the grain-size is too small in our examples for computation over the network. For completeness we mention that in the base case of modular univariate polynomials, the resultants are computed by polynomial remainder sequences.

This modular method of computing resultants is structurally very similar to the modular method of computing polynomial g.c.d.'s which was also parallelized in PARSAC-2 [20, 21].

## 3.3 IPRES

IPRES is irregular in the sense that the number of distributed MPRES calls and the primes used for transformation depend on the input polynomials. It should theoretically be regular regarding its computation weight. This might be not true due to side effects of the underlying Computer Algebra system.

This algorithm was already distributed on a net of workstations by Seitz [30, 31]. His system, called DSAC-2, uses hand-crafted low-level communication in the context of the Computer Algebra system SAC-2 and its implementation language ALDES [25].

Our approach was to rely on standard communication systems, like PVM, and to build a distribution system also applicable to other languages and applications.

We tested IPRES with 7 cases, varying the number of variables, the degree of the polynomials and their coefficient length. Due to that also the number of MPRES calls changes. Table 1 shows the test cases. The SAC-2 function IPRAN() generates an integral random polynomial. The first argument determines the number of variables, the second the coefficient length, the third the possibility that the polynomial has non-null coefficients and the last argument states the maximal degrees.

Figure 6 shows the run-times of the test cases. Unlike with RSA or MPRES, we also achieve speedup with just two machines. This is due to the enormous weight of the Chinese Remainder Algorithm. In this case, one machine computes the modular resultants and the other is engaged in lifting. If lifting is itself a heavy task, we will see a speed-up. On the other hand, the computational weight of lifting is also responsible for the limit in speed-up, which presents a practical case of Amdahl's law.

Further we notice that the graphs ascend as we have more machines. This could be due to irregularities of our measures, like in MPRES. Seitz [30, 31] in his measures of IPRES also observes such a behavior in the case where the parent waits for the children in a predetermined order instead of using join_any().

| Case | Polynomial A | Polynomial B | # MPres |
|------|--------------|--------------|---------|
| 1 | IPRAN(3,64,1/2,(8,6,4)) | IPRAN(3,64,1/2,(7,5,3)) | 36 |
| 2 | IPRAN(3,128,1/2,(5,4,3)) | IPRAN(3,128,1/2,(5,4,3)) | 47 |
| 3 | IPRAN(3,64,1/2,(5,4,3)) | IPRAN(3,64,1/2,(5,4,3)) | 24 |
| 4 | IPRAN(5,64,1/2,(3,3,2,2,1)) | IPRAN(5,64,1/2,(2,2,1,1,1)) | 12 |
| 5 | IPRAN(3,32,1/2,(5,4,3)) | IPRAN(3,32,1/2,(5,4,3)) | 13 |
| 6 | IPRAN(4,64,1/2,(3,3,3,3)) | IPRAN(4,64,1/2,(2,2,2,2)) | 12 |
| 7 | IPRAN(3,64,1/2,(3,4,5)) | IPRAN(3,64,1/2,(2,4,5)) | 12 |

**Table 1.** Polynomials and number of MPRES calls of the IPRES test cases

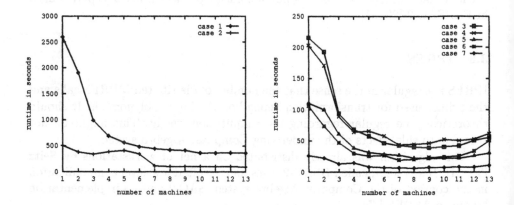

**Fig. 6.** Run-times of IPRES

Due to the complexity of the software involved, it is difficult to give a definitive explanation at this time.

Figure 7 shows the graphs of the achieved speed-ups, where we note that the graphs indicate partial super-linear speed-ups, probably due to the increasing memory with more machines. Our cases don't match the one from Seitz exactly, but we can see that the speed-ups are in the same range.

Until reaching the limit given by the Chinese Remainder Algorithm we achieve very good efficiencies (see figure 7) of up to over 90 percent. To achieve even better run-times the Chinese Remainder Algorithm should be parallelized. This has been done successfully on shared-memory machines, for the closely related case of multivariate polynomial gcd calculation. [20, 21].

## 3.4 MPRES

MPRES is irregular in the way, that the number of distributed MPRES calls and the values used for evaluation depend on the input polynomials. It should theoretically be regular regarding its computation weight. Our measures show, that in practice the distributed calls have different run-times. This seems to be due to side effects of the underlying Computer Algebra system.

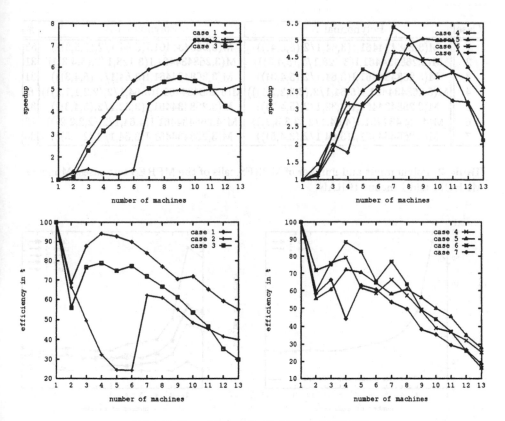

**Fig. 7.** Speedup and efficiency of IPRES

We did only create parallel jobs on the first level of recursion of MPRES. All remaining calls were computed on the local processor, according to the sequential execution.

The recursive algorithm MPRES was used with seven different polynomials as input. These were exactly the polynomials as created by *IPRES*. This allowed the investigation, whether MPRES is useful for any *further* parallelization of already parallel algorithms. The used polynomials were relatively fine-grained which is a disadvantage for parallel execution on distributed memory systems. Anyhow, we did not choose more coarse-grained polynomials because MPRES is normally used as a part of other algorithms. The test cases are shown in table 2.

Figure 8 shows the run-times of the different polynomials. The time mentioned for one machine is the time of the sequential execution.

The machine which created all parallel calls to MPRES was not used for computation of these jobs. Therefore the time needed for two machines was higher than the time for sequential execution, because we have the additional work for job distribution, but still only one machine to compute on. On more than 2 machines, the run-time is going down and soon levels off with increasing

| Case | Polynomial A | Polynomial B | # |
|------|--------------|--------------|---|
| 1 | M(3,268434461,I(3,64,1/2,(8,6,4))) | M(3,268434461,I(3,64,1/2,(7,5,3))) | 53 |
| 2 | M(3,268434461,I(3,128,1/2,(5,4,3))) | M(3,268434461,I(3,128,1/2,(5,4,3))) | 31 |
| 3 | M(3,268434461,I(3,64,1/2,(5,4,3))) | M(3,268434461,I(3,64,1/2,(5,4,3))) | 31 |
| 4 | M(5,268434461,I(5,64,1/2,(3,3,2,2,1))) | M(5,268434461,I(5,64,1/2,(2,2,1,1,1))) | 6 |
| 5 | M(3,268434461,I(3,32,1/2,(5,4,3))) | M(3,268434461,I(3,32,1/2,(5,4,3))) | 31 |
| 6 | M(4,268434461,I(4,64,1/2,(3,3,3,3))) | M(4,268434461,I(4,64,1/2,(2,2,2,2))) | 13 |
| 7 | M(3,268434461,I(3,64,1/2,(3,4,5))) | M(3,268434461,I(3,64,1/2,(2,4,5))) | 26 |

**Table 2.** Polynomials and number of MPRES calls of the MPRES test cases. M means MPHOM and I means IPRAN.

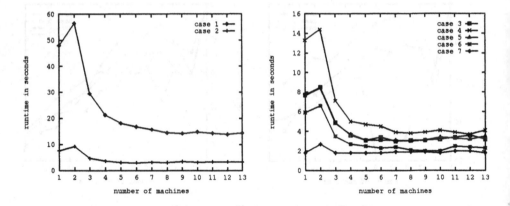

**Fig. 8.** Run-times of MPRES

number of machines. An exception is polynomial #7, whose computation could not made faster through parallelization, because the created polynomials were too light-weight. A closer examination of the created polynomials showed, that the time used for computation differs a lot. Therefore some machines do much more jobs than others. With an increasing number of machines, the most heavy-weight job will become dominant. Further, the speedup was slowed down by the time needed for sequential interpolation of the computed results on the forking machine.

Some polynomials showed an increasing run-time when executed on a lot of machines. This may be due to inexact timings, slightly different machine types, or other influences. Polynomial #4 created only 6 parallel calls to MPRES, which should lead to the best performance, if 7 machines were used. Actually the best run-time was reached with 12 machines, going up and down a little between 7 and 12. This is not possible without other hidden influences, because additional machines, which do not take part in computation in any kind, could not change the run-time of the program.

The speedups for the run-times are shown in figure 9.

According to the run-times the diagram first states a slowdown followed by

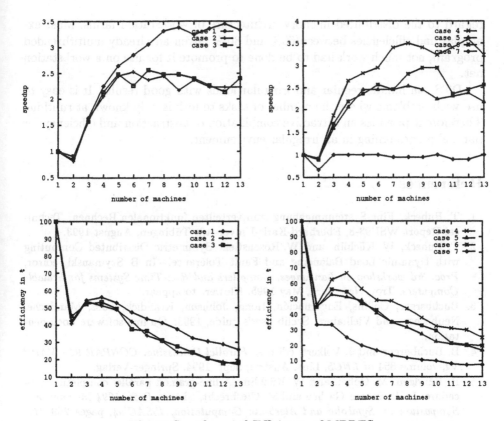

**Fig. 9.** Speedup and Efficiency of MPRES

increasing speedups which finally stagnate. The corresponding part of the graph should be parallel to the x-axis. Its different form is due to load influences. Last we want to take a look on the efficiency of the algorithm in figure 9.

We achieved good efficiencies even for lightweight polynomials. Nearly all computations achieve values between 40 and 60 percent up to about 6 machines. Then the efficiency decreases slowly. Taken by them selves these results might have looked better. By taking heavier polynomials we surely could have presented better results. But we wanted to see, if polynomials that result from distributed computations of real world IPRES evaluations could be distributed with success. This seems to be possible, because our tests stated sufficient efficiency while not overloading the machines.

# 4 Conclusion

We presented DTS, an environment for parallel computing on a cluster of work-stations. Further we showed run times of some irregular applications using DTS. We achieved good program speedups, even for relatively light-weight jobs with regard to the distributed memory architecture of workstation farms. Most examples had efficiencies between 60% and 80%. Given an already multithreaded program, not much work had to be done to promote it for use on a workstation net.

DTS can handle regular and irregular loads with good results. It is easy to use with problems where the number of tasks to fork is only known at runtime. Therefore it provides an attractive combination of abstraction and efficiency for parallel programming in an irregular environment.

# References

1. T. Bubeck. Eine Systemumgebung zum verteilten funktionalen Rechnen. Technical Report WSI-93-8, Eberhard-Karls-Universität Tübingen, August 1993.
2. T. Bubeck, W. Küchlin, and W. Rosenstiel. Symmetric Distributed Computing with Dynamic Load Balancing and Fault Tolerance. In B. Szymanski, editor, *Proc. 3rd workshop on Languages, Compilers and Run-Time Systems for Scalable Computers*, Troy, New York, May 1995. Kluwer. to appear.
3. Buchberger, Collins, Encarnación, Hong, Johnson, Krandick, Loos, Mandache, Neubacher, and Vielhaber. Saclib user's guide, 1993. On-line software documentation.
4. B. Buchberger and J. Volkert, editors. *Parallel Processing: CONPAR 94—VAPP VI*, volume 854 of *LNCS*, Linz, Austria, Sept. 1994. Springer-Verlag.
5. R. Bündgen, M. Göbel, and W. Küchlin. A fine-grained parallel completion procedure. In J. von zur Gathen and M. Giesbrecht, editors, *Proc. 1994 International Symposium on Symbolic and Algebraic Computation: ISSAC'94*, pages 269–277, Oxford, England, July 1994. ACM Press.
6. R. Bündgen, M. Göbel, and W. Küchlin. Multi-threaded AC term rewriting. In Hong [17], pages 84–93.
7. R. Bündgen, M. Göbel, and W. Küchlin. Parallel ReDuX → PaReDuX. In J. Hsiang, editor, *Rewriting Techniques and Applications, 6th Intl. Conf., RTA-95*, volume 914 of *LNCS*, pages 408–413, Apr. 1995. Springer-Verlag.
8. T. L. Casavant and J. G. Kuhl. A Taxonomy of Scheduling in General-Purpose Distributed Computing Systems. *IEEE Transactions on Software Engineering*, 14(2):141–154, Feb 1988.
9. G. E. Collins. The calculation of multivariate polynomial resultants. *J. ACM*, 19:515–532, 1971.
10. G. E. Collins and R. Loos. Specification and index of SAC-2 algorithms. Technical Report WSI-90-4, Universität Tübingen, Germany, 1990.
11. A. Diaz, E. Kaltofen, K. Schmitz, and T. Valente. DSC: A system for distributed symbolic computation. In Watt [34], pages 323–332.
12. J. Fleischer, J. Grabmeier, F. Hehl, and W. Küchlin, editors. *Computer Algebra in Science and Engineering*, Bielefeld, Germany, Aug. 1994. World Scientific.
13. I. Foster, C. Kesselman, and S. Tuecke. The Nexus task-parallel runtime system. In *Proc. 1st Intl Workshop on Parallel Processing*, Bangalore, 1994.
14. T. Gautier and J. L. Roch. PAC++ system and parallel algebraic numbers computation. In Hong [17], pages 145–153.
15. K. O. Geddes, S. R. Czapor, and G. Labahn. *Algorithms for Computer Algebra*. Kluwer Academic Publishers, Boston, MA, 1992.

16. M. Hiller. Verteiltes symbolisches Rechnen mit PARSAC-2. Master's thesis, W.-Schickard-Institut für Informatik, Universität Tübingen, Sept. 1993.

17. H. Hong, editor. *First Intl. Symp. Parallel Symbolic Computation PASCO'94*, volume 5 of *LNSC*, Sept. 1994. World Scientific.

18. H. Hong and H. W. Loidl. Parallel computation of modular multivariate polynomial resultants on a shared memory machine. In Buchberger and Volkert [4], pages 325–336.

19. W. W. Küchlin. PARSAC-2: A parallel SAC-2 based on threads. In S. Sakata, editor, *Applied Algebra, Algebraic Algorithms, and Error-Correcting Codes: 8th International Conference, AAECC-8*, volume 508 of *LNCS*, pages 341–353, Tokyo, Japan, Aug. 1990. Springer-Verlag.

20. W. W. Küchlin. On the multi-threaded computation of integral polynomial greatest common divisors. In Watt [34], pages 333–342.

21. W. W. Küchlin. On the multi-threaded computation of modular polynomial greatest common divisors. In H. Zima, editor, *Parallel Computation (1st Internatl. ACPC Conf.)*, volume 591 of *LNCS*, pages 369–384, Oct. 1991. Springer-Verlag.

22. W. W. Küchlin. The S-threads environment for parallel symbolic computation. In Zippel [35], pages 1–18.

23. W. W. Küchlin. PARSAC-2: Parallel computer algebra on the desk-top. In Fleischer et al. [12].

24. W. W. Küchlin and J. A. Ward. Experiments with virtual C Threads. In *Proc. Fourth IEEE Symp. on Parallel and Distributed Processing*, pages 50–55, Dallas, TX, Dec. 1992. IEEE Press.

25. R. G. K. Loos. The algorithm description language ALDES (Report). *ACM SIGSAM Bull.*, 10(1):15–39, 1976.

26. R. L. Rivest, A. Shamir, and L. Adleman. A Method for Obtaining Digital Signatures and Public-Key Cryptosystems. *Communications of the ACM*, 21(2):120–126, February 1978.

27. J.-L. Roch. PAC: Towards a parallel Computer Algebra co-processor. In J. Della Dora and J. Fitch, editors, *Computer Algebra and Parallelism*, Computational Mathematics and Applications, pages 33–50. Academic Press, London, 1989.

28. J. L. Roch, A. Vermeerbergen, and G. Villard. A new load-prediction scheme based on algorithmic cost functions. In Buchberger and Volkert [4], pages 878–889.

29. W. Schreiner and H. Hong. The design of the PACLIB kernel for parallel algebraic computation. In J. Volkert, editor, *Parallel Computation (2nd Internatl. ACPC Conf.)*, volume 734 of *LNCS*, pages 204–218, Gmunden, Austria, Oct. 1993. Springer-Verlag.

30. S. Seitz. *Verteiltes Rechnen in SAC-2*. PhD thesis, Universität Tübingen, 1990.

31. S. Seitz. Algebraic computing on a local net. In Zippel [35], pages 19–32.

32. V. S. Sunderam. PVM: A framework for parallel distributed computing. *Concurrency: Practice and Experience*, 2(4):315–339, Dec. 1990.

33. A. S. Tanenbaum. *Modern Operating Systems*. Prentice-Hall, Englewood Cliffs, NJ 07632, 1992.

34. S. M. Watt, editor. *Proc. 1991 International Symposium on Symbolic and Algebraic Computation: ISSAC'91*, Bonn, Germany, July 1991. ACM Press.

35. R. Zippel, editor. *Computer Algebra and Parallelism*, volume 584 of *LNCS*, Ithaca, NY, Mar. 1992. Springer-Verlag.

# A Parallel Processing Paradigm for Irregular Applications

A. Das,[1] L. E. Moser[2] and P. M. Melliar-Smith[2]

Nanyang Technological University, Singapore[1]
University of California, Santa Barbara[2]

**Abstract.** We present a simple and elegant model of computation particularly well-suited to irregularly structured applications in which it is difficult to map the algorithms and data onto a parallel architecture. Unlike other parallel processing paradigms, there is no need to map the application onto the parallel architecture. Nevertheless, an efficient implementation, the Intersecting Broadcast Machine, exists for this model of computation in which the data are mapped entirely at random onto the array of processors. Simulation results for this architecture for a parallel term-matching algorithm indicate high processor and bus utilizations and excellent load balancing characteristics.

## 1 Introduction

Parallel processing has made much progress over the last two decades. Its impact has been felt in the solution of partial differential equations, in the solution of matrix equations, in digital signal processing, and in image processing. All of these applications have the common feature that the problem has an inherent regular structure.

We present a parallel processing paradigm that is specifically aimed at irregularly structured applications. These applications include symbolic computation, such as automated theorem provers, knowledge-based systems, and interpreters for logic programs.

The paradigm aims to address three important problems of parallelizing irregular applications: mapping the application onto the parallel processor, balancing the load, and reducing the communication overhead. These problems are addressed by the use of randomization in the allocation of the data to the processors and in the operations that are performed by the processors.

## 2 The Model of Computation

The model of computation consists of a set of processors, a set of rules, and a set of objects called the *object space*. The *state* of the object space at any given time is determined by the objects that have been created using the given set of rules up to that time. Processors apply rules to objects in the object space in a completely asynchronous manner and independent of the application of other rules. The choice of a rule to be executed is made nondeterministically, subject to the condition that each rule is executed infinitely often.

A *rule* consists of a *guard*, a set of conditions that determines to which of the objects in the object space the rule is to be applied, and a *create* statement that creates one or more new objects. An object is accessed by its content, rather than by a specific name or address. Once an object is created, it is never changed or destroyed. Thus, the object space is monotonically nondecreasing in size.

An *algorithm* is defined by a set of rules. An *execution* of an algorithm is the closure of the application of the rules to the object space. An *execution step* is an application of a rule that results in a change of the state of the object space. An execution reaches a *fixed point* if the application of each rule leaves the object space unchanged, *i.e.* no more new objects are created. Termination of an algorithm corresponds to reaching a fixed point.

The model of computation has a *progress property* which requires that, if one or more objects satisfies the guard of some rule, then that rule will be applied and one or more new objects will be created within a finite amount of time. This property guarantees that, if there is any finite sequence of execution steps leading to the termination of the algorithm, then the algorithm will terminate in a finite amount of time. It also ensures that a rule will be applied to every object that (ever) satisfies the guard of that rule.

The model of computation is fairly general and is functionally complete and, thus, is quite difficult to implement. With a particular implementation in mind, we propose the following restriction of the model. The only functions that can be computed are those with at most two arguments, *i.e.* the functions are monadic, dyadic, or constants. Since any function of multiple arguments can be expressed as a composition of binary and/or unary functions (*cf.* currying), this is a purely syntactic restriction, and does not restrict the power of the model.

## 3  An Architectural Implementation

The Intersecting Broadcast Machine [2], illustrated in Figure 1, is a novel parallel architecture that implements the above model of computation for irregularly structured applications. The most unusual aspect of the Intersecting Broadcast Machine is that the data are not assigned to processors by a preplanned mapping but, rather, are distributed among the processors at random. Likewise, the operations to be performed by each processor are not scheduled in advance but, instead, are determined at each processor by the presence of the data necessary to carry out those operations. At least two processors are guaranteed to receive the data required for each operation to be performed.

In considering the computational costs of implementing an algorithm on the Intersecting Broadcast Machine, it is important to recognize that many of these costs are not "pure overhead" but are often a necessary part of the execution of the algorithm. For example, a parallel sorting algorithm that we have devised for this architecture incurs the smallest number of interprocessor messages as well

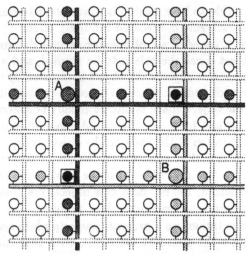

Fig. 1.: The formation of intersections. The broadcasting of two objects, *A* and *B*, from random locations in the array results in at least two processors at the intersections of the broadcasts, where the next stage of the computation can be performed.

as the smallest number of comparisons of any known parallel sorting algorithm, including comparisons required to select applicable rules [1].

The Intersecting Broadcast Machine is an MIMD array processor architecture; however, it differs radically from conventional mesh-connected processors. The architecture consists of two orthogonal sets of broadcast buses with processors located at the intersections of the buses. Each processor has two interfaces, one connecting to each of the two buses at its intersection. An arbitration mechanism for each bus allocates the bus among contending processors.

The allocation of data to processors in the array and the activities at each processor are random; consequently, the communication among processors is also random. Processing at a particular processor takes place only when the relevant data objects are available. Each new object resulting from the processing is then broadcast along one row and one column, and is stored by the processors along those two buses for possible use in future computations. Although a processor might never use a data object it receives, it must still store that object until the program establishes that it will never need that object again.

The architecture implements the model of computation as follows. All of the rules that define the program are stored at every processor. A processor applies a rule to a pair of objects when those objects become available. Initially, the objects are broadcast by random processors in the array on pairs of orthogonal buses. Subsequently, an application of a rule to a pair of objects results in the generation of a new object that is broadcast on a pair of orthogonal buses. The local object space of a processor consists of the objects that are broadcast to it on the pair of orthogonal buses that form the intersection at which the processor is located. In an $n \times n$ array of processors, $2n - 1$ copies of an object exist until a processor removes that object from its local object space.

The Intersecting Broadcast Machine provides two types of broadcast:

- A *primary* broadcast contains the identity and value of a data object. These are not necessarily distinct; in many cases, a subset of the fields of an object serves to identify the object.
- An *auxiliary* broadcast contains only the identity of an object and, thus, is generally smaller than a primary broadcast.

Now consider an arbitrary processor in the array that has created a data object $A$, as shown in Figure 1. That processor broadcasts $A$'s value and $A$'s identity on the two buses to which it is connected (shown by shading), and every processor along those two buses receives and stores the object $A$. Another processor, which does not share a bus with the processor that broadcast object $A$ creates an object $B$, which is similarly broadcast over two orthogonal buses and stored by the processors along those buses (shown by lighter shading). Now there are two processors, at the intersections of those buses, that have both data objects and that can perform a computation $f(A, B)$. There is no need to plan or even to know in advance where the objects are created. The design thus lends itself to complex calculations for which such planning would be difficult.

Assuming no intent to provide fault tolerance, each computation should be done only once in the array and, thus, one of the two processors at the intersections must be selected to perform the computation. The selection can be done algorithmically or, as described here, by a race. Each processor enqueues the operation along with other operations it must perform and, when the operation has been completed, the result $f(A, B)$ is broadcast on the two buses to which the processor is connected. One of the processors wins the race and broadcasts its result. Broadcasting $f(A, B)$ not only communicates the result, but it also informs the processors that had computed and broadcast $A$ and $B$ that the result has been computed. These two processors then generate auxiliary broadcasts on the orthogonal buses that inform the fourth processor that the result $f(A, B)$ has been computed and broadcast and, consequently, that there is no need for it to broadcast that result as well. This mechanism works quite efficiently provided that all processors are heavily loaded, which reduces the probability that the second processor has calculated the result before it can be inhibited.

The main and auxiliary broadcasts also serve another function. Along each bus there are many processors that have received and stored one of the two objects and are waiting for the second object, which they will never receive. Receipt of the main or auxiliary broadcast of $f(A, B)$ indicates that such processors will not be required to compute $f(A, B)$ and that, therefore, they can invoke storage management algorithms. The race strategy for selecting processors has the desirable effect that it helps to maintain the data and the computational load uniformly but randomly across the array. This is established in [2], where an extension of the basic architecture to provide fault tolerance is also given.

## 4 Simulation Results

The performance of the Intersecting Broadcast Machine, and the effectiveness of the parallel processing paradigm it implements, was evaluated by a discrete

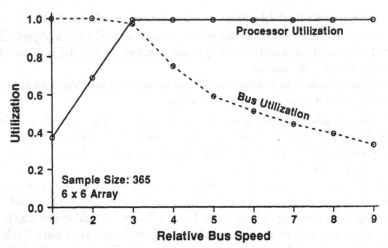

Fig. 2.: The processor and bus utilizations for various ratios of mean bus speed to mean processor speed.

event simulation, programmed in the C++ programming language and run on a Sun SPARCstation. We summarize here the results from a sample simulation for a parallel term matching algorithm.

In term matching, we are given two terms, a pattern term that contains function and variable symbols and a subject term that contains only function symbols. The problem is to determine an assignment to the variables of the pattern that will make the two terms identical or to determine that no such assignment exists. Term matching is an irregularly structured problem in that a function can have an arbitrary number of arguments, and each argument can have arbitrary complexity.

The performance of the architecture depends critically on the relative speeds of the processors and the buses, as represented by the ratio of mean bus speed to mean processor speed. The mean processor speed is the average rate at which new data objects are generated by a processor, and the mean bus speed is the average rate at which data objects are transferred over a bus. Figure 2 shows the processor and bus utilizations for the term matching algorithm for a $6 \times 6$ processor array as a function of the ratio of mean bus speed to mean processor speed. When the buses are only slightly faster than the processors, processor utilization suffers; for faster buses, excellent processor utilization is achieved.

The simulation showed that very high processor utilizations correspond to high utilizations for all processors. Consequently, we also investigated the utilizations of individual processors in a system with slow buses and fast processors, and thus relatively low processor utilizations. Figure 3 shows the utilizations of individual processors in a $6 \times 6$ processor array under these conditions. As is evident, excellent load balancing is achieved with all processors active most of the time, which demonstrates the robustness of the random allocation, even for an irregular application. These processor utilizations should be compared with the processor utilizations below 10% achieved by tree architectures for similar applications.

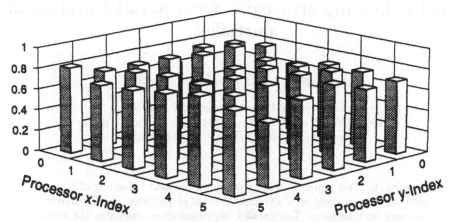

**Fig. 3.:** Utilizations for individual processors, showing excellent load balancing under difficult conditions with slow buses and fast processors.

## 5 Conclusion

We have presented a novel parallel processing paradigm that is intended for complex irregularly structured applications. In our model, an algorithm is described by a set of rules, each of which consists of a create statement and a guard. Conceptually, processors apply the rules to objects in the object space asynchronously until a fixed point is reached.

The model of computation can be implemented efficiently in a novel MIMD array processor, the Intersecting Broadcast Machine, with no need for shared memory. This architecture has the unusual feature that it is not necessary to preplan the allocation of data and operations to processors in the array; rather the data are distributed at random across the array.

Randomization seldom yields optimal performance, as might be achieved for a regular problem on a mesh architecture. However, because randomization is insensitive to the structure of the application, programmability and performance do not deteriorate as the structure of the application becomes more complex and difficult to map onto the array. Thus, the randomization employed by our parallel processing paradigm is particularly appropriate for irregular problems, and achieves excellent performance for a wide range of applications.

## References

1. A. Das, L. E. Moser and P. M. Melliar-Smith, "A parallel sorting algorithm for a novel model of computation," *International Journal of Parallel Programming*, vol. 20, no. 5, October 1991, pp. 403-419.
2. P. M. Melliar-Smith, L. E. Moser, A. Das and C. Ye, "The Intersecting Broadcast Machine: A regular architecture for irregular applications," *Journal of Computer and Software Engineering*, vol. 2, no. 4, December 1994, pp. 349-376.

# Load balancing strategies for a parallel system of particles

Serge Miguet and Jean-Marc Pierson *

Laboratoire de l'Informatique du Parallélisme
ENS-LYON, 46 Allée d'Italie, 69364 Lyon Cedex 07, France
email : [jmpierso,miguet]@lip.ens-lyon.fr

**Abstract.** This paper presents a study on the load balancing of a parallel implementation of a dynamic system of particles on distributed memory architectures. The parallel implementation simulates the temporal evolution and behavior of a general system of particles. Long range interactions with the environment as well as short range interactions between particles are fairly handled.

In order to deal with these constraints, a complexe data structure has been implemented. An important study on load balancing is developed for a simple case. Difficulties to theorically calculate the relocation of datas (depending upon simulation and architecture) is shown, and an heuristic is proposed for the general cases. Some results on MIMD architectures and on a network of workstations are finally briefly presented.

## 1 Introduction

Studying and displaying the dynamics of a system of particles is today an important task in domains such as Molecular Physics, Chemistry and even scientific popularization or special effects in the domain of the movie industry ([9],[6]). The ArSciMed company [2] has produced a sequential software called *Dexter* which studies the temporal behavior of a general system of particles, where particles can be as different as quarks, gluons, drops or grains of sand. The interactions of the particles with the environment (wind, ...), obstacles, forces (gravitation, electric and magnetic fields, ...) are taken into account. Moreover, elementary particles can collide and possibly create new kinds of particles. Short range interactions between particles are handled, and permanent long range interactions, such as a point of attraction or a magnetic field, are also computed. These constraints imply to have a knowledge of the neighborhood of all particles and are handled by a complex data structure in the sequential program. In a general case, the space is sparsely filled with particles. In order to minimize the memory utilisation, only those regions of the space where particles can be located are represented.

As the number of particles present in such simulations gets very high, computations are very CPU and memory consuming leading naturally to parallel

---

* This work was supported by the Région Rhône-Alpes, by the Stratagème project of the MESR and the Esprit BRA 6632 NANA2 of the EEC

[2] ARSCIMED, ARt SCIence MEDia, 100 rue du Faubourg Saint-Antoine, 75012 Paris, FRANCE

implementations. The basic idea of our approach is to use a space-based allocation together with dynamic partitions of the space allowing to keep the workload as well balanced as possible. Studies on 2D and 3D partitioning [12], [1] as well as the necessity to keep neighborhood locality and to adopt an efficient load balancing strategy led us to map the 3D world to a one-dimensional space. The processors are virtually connected as a linear network and the 3D world is distributed along an axis, called *partitioning axis* in the following. The originality of this approach resides in the facts that the interactions between particles are taken into account, and that a load balancing strategy is proposed. The main goal of this paper is to explain our load balancing technique and to derive the optimal load balancing strategy. To do this, we validate a model for the cost of balancing the load, and compare it with the cost of having unbalanced executions.

Interested readers will refer to [7] where the sequential part of the project, some related works on other parallel implementations ([11], [5], [10], [3]), our distribution scheme of datas and some extended numerical results are fully presented. This paper will focus on a study of our load balancing strategy. Some performances on several commercial MIMD architectures and comparisons with a network of workstations are also presented.

## 2  Load balancing

A strategy of dynamic load balancing has been developed, based on the so called "elastic" technique, presented in [8]. The elastic allocation scheme is especially done for balancing the load by the help of dynamic data redistributions. It is the most useful when the computations involving an elemental data item strongly depend on some neighborhood of this data item. Each data item (a particle in our case) is associated by a projection function $\Pi$ with an integer of $[L, R[$, where $L$ and $R$ denote the left and right indices of the partitionning and correspond in our application to the extents of the particles along the partitioning axis. We assume that the $P$ processors are (at least virtually) connected as a linear network. Each processor $q$ is responsible for an interval $[l_q, r_q[$ of $[L, R[$.

We won't detail here the original "elastic" algorithm but we will focus on the improvement done on it. Computing the workload of each data item, the cumulative workload of items and the ideal elementary workload, we find the frontier indices $l_q, r_q$ for each processor $q$, where the different intervals form a partition of the domain $[L, R[$, that is $r_q = l_{q+1}$ and $l_q \neq r_q$: each processor has at least one data item, and each data item belongs to only one processor. The asumptions made are that each data item has a positive load and that each processor always keeps at least one data item in its local memory. These are no longer true in our application, in the case for instance of two independant sets of particles separated by empty space or in the very first iterations of the algorithm, where there are less particles than the number of processors. For these two reasons, we proposed a new way of determining the frontier indices, and a slight modification of the redistribution algorithm, leading to the concept of ParList presented in [4].

Let us consider a (possibly multiple) frontier index $l_q$ computed as above. The fact that $l_q$ is a frontier index means that data $l_q - 1$ should be mapped to a processor different of the one of data $l_q$, because the cumulated load $CW(l_q)$ has crossed value $qEW$, where $EW$ is the elementary workload. The point is that the cumulated load $CW(l_q)$ of $l_q$ can be closer of $qEW$ than $CW(l_q-1)$. If it is the case, then we have better to choose $l'_q = l_q + 1$ as the $q^{th}$ frontier index, such that the processor $q-1$ gets the data item $l_q$. Else, we keep $l'_q = l_q$. This small test added to the computation of the indices allows to handle all particular cases that appeared before. See figure 1 for a particular example.

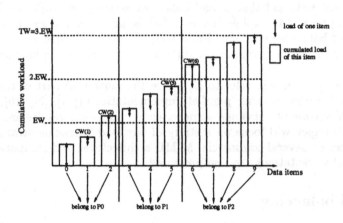

**Fig. 1.** Cumulative histogram of workload

We have 3 processors and 10 data items to distribute. The data item number 2 is allocated to processor 0 although its cumulated workload $CW(2)$ has crossed the elementary workload $EW$, because it is closer to it than $CW(1)$. In other words, the frontier index $l_1$ is chosen to be 3 rather than 2. In an opposite way, data item number 6 belong to processor 2 because $CW(6)$ has crossed $2.EW$ and $CW(5)$ is closer to $2.EW$ than $CW(6)$. Ence we have kept to $l_2$ the value of 6.

As the load balance is time consuming, it must not be done at each step of the algorithm, but only when the cost of the dis-balance is higher than the cost of the load balance phase.

## 3   Study on load-balance

It is very difficult to predict the optimal number of steps between two consecutive load-balances because it hardly depends upon the scene treated, that means the number of particles, of sources, and of forces applied to the particles. Suppose we want to load balance every $r$ iterations, and try to find the best compromise on r, for a simulation during $k$ iterations. We understand intuitively that we will have to find a compromise for the load balancing strategy: the smaller $r$, the bigger the overhead for computing the optimal distribution, but the best balanced the computations. On the other hand, the larger $r$, the less time is spent in the load balancing code, but the most disbalance will appear. We will exhibit some results in a very simple case and the difficulties of such an approach in the general case for which we propose an heuristic.

## 3.1 A simple simulation

We have first considered a very simple simulation, and tried to find the best $r$ for it. Let us consider a scene where only one source of particles is present at the origin, on processor 0, giving $N$ particles an initial velocity along the x-axis (chosen as the partitioning axis) at each time step. Assume we have $P$ processors and suppose we have $M.P$ particles equally distibuted onto the processors at step $t_0$.

Let us assume that the velocity of the particles is such that, during the next step, $N$ particles will move from processor 0 to processor 1, $N$ also from processor 1 to processor 2, ..., and $N$ particles from processor $P-2$ to processor $P-1$. That means that processor $P-1$ will have $M+N$ particles to process at step $t_0+1$, whereas all other processors will have only $M$ particles.

As you can see, this case is basic. We have computed the optimal $r$ by computing the total time of execution on the last processor $P-1$. Indeed, this processor is the most loaded of the linear network, because it will receive $N$ particles from its left neighbour $P-2$ at each time step.

The result (proved in [7]) is that the total time can be expressed as follows :

$$T = ar + \frac{b}{r} + c \tag{1}$$

where $a, b, c$ are constant with $r$, and depends on the characteristics of the machine, the numbers $N$ and $M$ of particles, and the total number of iteration $k$.

This function admits a minimum $r_{opt}$ which is

$$r_{opt} = \sqrt{\frac{2T_q}{\tau_a}} \tag{2}$$

where $T_q$ is the time to compute a parallel prefix sum among the processors, and $\tau_a$ the arithmetic time to process a particle (update velocity, acceleration, transformation...). If we know the characteristics of the machine, we are able to compute precisely this $r_{opt}$ ($r_{opt} = 3$ for the Intel Paragon).

## 3.2 An heuristic for general cases

As illustrated in the previous section, determining in advance when to call the load-balancing routine is complicated and very dependant of the scene we simulate. Thus we propose a scene-independant heuristic, that can be used when we don't have any informations about the scene. Again, we are looking for an order of magnitude of the redistribution frequency $r$.

To the question "when should I call the load-balancing routine?", an intuitively natural answer could be: "Suppose I call it now. After $r$ iterations, the time I have spent in redistributing the data will be rentabilized because I have done $r$ iterations better balanced than if I didn't have done the redistribution".

Comparing the time to perform the $r$ unbalanced iterations and the time to perform the load balancing then $r$ balanced iterations led to the following result:

$$r \geq \frac{\max(N, O)\tau_c}{N\tau_a}$$

where $N$ is the overload of the most loaded processor compared to the average load $M$, $O$ the lack of the less loaded and $\tau_c$ the communication time of one particle, including its integration in data structure.

The favorable case, which is the most likely to happen is $N \geq O$: Most of the times, the imbalance involves one or some processors on which particles accumulate. In these cases, we obtain thus:

$$r \geq \frac{\tau_c}{\tau_a} \tag{3}$$

The numerical experiments give a ratio around 5 for the Intel Paragon.

If it could happen that one processor has suddenly much less particles than the average, then load balancing shouldn't be performed so often: The limit case is when $O = M$ (all the particles of one given processor have disappeared). In this case, the redistribution takes so much time that it is only rentable after $k = \frac{M\tau_c}{N\tau_a}$ iterations, that can be as large as $p\frac{\tau_c}{\tau_a}$. But again, this shouldn't be a frequent case.

## 4 Results

The parallel implementation of the program has been developed with the help of PPCM, which stands for Parallel Portable Communication Module. It is a set of functionalities which makes programs totally independent of the target architecture (see [2] for further details on what is available in PPCM). PPCMX is an extension to PPCM, which permits to all the processors of a parallel machine to execute graphics output in a X window on the front-end. It is a distributed elementary visualisation system. This extension has made possible the display on-the-fly of the different steps of the evolution of the particle system.

We have experiment that for different simulations our asumptions have been verified. Indeed, using the iPSC or the Paragon of Intel, as well as a network of workstations with PVM, for simulations varying from 10000 to 25000 particles, the optimal redistribution was $r_{opt} = 5$.

Concerning the speedup of the application, it varies a lot with the target parallel machine. Using PVM on a network of workstations gave a limited speedup of 3 with a number of processors from 2 to 8. On iPSC, we obtained 3.7 for 4 processors while we got 6.5 with 8 processors and 9.5 with 16 processors on the Intel Paragon machine. On these machines, the network is very efficient and most of the time is spent in computation. The communication part is almost completely masked by the computations. Moreover, on a network of workstations, communications are almost serialized because only one medium is available for all processors.

# 5 Conclusion

We have presented in this article an important study on the load balancing strategy used in our parallel approach on a MIMD architecture of the computation of the dynamic evolution of a system of particles. Our paper tries to give some intuitive idea about the approach of load balance study and it reveals also the difficulty to conduce such a study in general cases. A good heuristic proposes a compromise between the cost of the redistribution and the one of the unbalance.

An approach where the number of iterations between two redistributions could change during the process should be interesting. Indeed, after a given number of iterations depending upon the scene, it may reach a point where the spatial distribution does not vary a lot during the process, so that redistribution would be unusefull.

# References

1. Krishna P. Belkhale and Prithviraj Banerjee. Recursive partitions on multiprocessors. In Q. F. Stout D. W. Walker, editor, *The Fifth Distributed Memory Computing Conference*, volume 2, pages 930–938, April 1990.
2. Henri-Pierre Charles. Ppcm: A portable parallel communication module. Technical Report 92-04, Laboratoire de l'Informatique du Parallélisme, June 1992.
3. Greg Eisenhauer and Karsten Schwan. MD - A Flexible Framework for High-Speed Parallel Molecular Dynamics. In Tentner and Stevens, editors, *Proceedings of the Conference on High Performance Computing '94*, 1994.
4. Fabien Feschet, Serge Miguet, and Laurent Perroton. *CAPA : Parallélisme et Applications Irrégulières*, volume 2, chapter ParList : une structure de donnée parallèle pour l'équilibrage des charges. HERMES, 1995. to be published.
5. Kazuyuki Katsuragi and Yukihiko Inoue. Study on vector and parallel and highly parallel algorithm of the lattice gas cellular automaton. In Tentner and Stevens, editors, *Proceedings of the Conference on High Performance Computing '94*, 1994.
6. Lucasfilm Ltd. The Adventures of Andre and Wally B. (film), August 1984.
7. Serge Miguet and Jean-Marc Pierson. Dynamic load balancing in a parallel particle simulation. In *Proceedings of HPCS'95*, Montréal, July 1995.
8. Serge Miguet and Yves Robert. Elastic load balancing for image processing algorithms. In H.P. Zima, editor, *Parallel Computation*, Lecture Notes in Computer Science, pages 438–451, Salzburg, Austria, September 1991. 1st International ACPC Conference, Springer Verlag.
9. Paramount. Star Trek II: The Wrath of Kahn. Genesis Demo, also in SIGGRAPH Video Review, 1982.
10. Steve Plimpton and Tim Bartel. Parallel particle simulations of low-density fluid flows. In Tentner and Stevens, editors, *Proceedings of the Conference on High Performance Computing '94*, 1994.
11. Karl Sims. Particle animation and rendering using data parallel computation. *Computer Graphics*, 24(4):405–413, August 1990.
12. Lawrence Snyder and David G. Socha. An algorithm producing balanced partitionings of data arrays. In Q. F. Stout D. W. Walker, editor, *The Fifth Distributed Memory Computing Conference*, volume 2, pages 867–875, April 1990.

# A Reconfigurable Parallel Algorithm for Sparse Cholesky Factorization

A. Benaini, D. Laiymani          G.R. Perrin

LIB                                    ICPS
Université de Franche-Comté Université Strasbourg I
25030 Besancon Cedex          F-67400 Illkirch
France                                France

## Abstract

This paper describes an efficient multi-phase parallel algorithm for sparse Cholesky factorization. The algorithm is simple in its concept and takes ideas from Kumar and Gupta [13] and Roman [18]. We adapt the sub-tree to sub-cube mapping strategy introduced by George et al [9] to reconfigurable parallel machines which allows an improvement in communication performances. In the case of regular grid problems our algorithm incurs less communication overhead and is more scalable that the known parallel sparse Cholesky factorization [9, 13]. Furthermore, we extend our algorithm to the case of the block Cholesky factorization. The different simulation results confirm our analysis and produce good speedup.

## 1 Introduction

Computing the solutions of sparse linear systems arises in various scientific applications. Quite often, the $N \times N$ system matrix is symmetric positive definite and the Cholesky factorization can be used to find a lower triangular matrix $L$ such that $A = LL^T$ in order to solve the linear system $Ax = b$.

The factorization process involves three steps: the *reordering step*, the *symbolic factorization* and the *numerical factorization* [2, 15]. The problems of implementing an ordering algorithm and performing the symbolic factorization procedure are outside the scope of this paper. Here, we propose a parallel algorithm for the numerical step of the Cholesky factorization. This algorithm is dedicated to parallel reconfigurable machines i.e. machines in which the interconnection network can be altered during the execution of an application. When the number of communication links per processor is equal to $d$, the machine is called $d$-reconfigurable. The algorithmic model used is the *multi-phase* model [1]. This model relies on the idea that a parallel algorithm can be decomposed into series of elementary data movements. So, this algorithm is implemented as a series of phases, so that, each phase is efficiently executed on the processor graph (of degree $d$) that exactly reflects the need of the current data transfer pattern [4]. Phases are assumed to be separated from one to another, by synchronization-reconfiguration points.

It appears difficult to obtain analytical expressions for the number of arithmetic or communication operations in the Cholesky factorization of a general sparse matrix [13]. Indeed, computation and fill-in during the factorization of a sparse matrix are functions of the number and positions of the nonzero elements in the original matrix. Nevertheless, in the case of adjacency matrices of graphs whose $N$-node sub-graphs have $O(\sqrt{N})$-node separtors, very interesting works have been done in [9, 13]. This class of matrices includes sparse matrices arising out of all two-dimensional finite difference and finite elements problems. In [10] George et al propose a simple algorithm with columns partitionning of an $N \times N$ matrix of this type on $p$ processors and results in $O(Np \log N)$ total communication cost. Using a different way for mapping columns to processors George et al [9] improve the previous algorithm and obtain an $O(Np)$ communication volume. In [19, 20] Rothberg et al propose two-dimensional partionning algorithms and the best of them present an $O(N\sqrt{p} \log p)$ communication volume. Recently Gupta and Kumar [13] describe a parallel algorithm with a communication overhead of $O(N\sqrt{p})$. Note that this last work is based on the multifrontal method [7] for the Cholesky factorization and is dedicated to hypercube supercomputers.

In this paper, we describe a parallel algorithm for factoring an $N \times N$ sparse matrix on a $d$-reconfigurable machine with $p$ processors. The total communication overhead of our algorithm is $O(N \log p)$ if the matrix satisfies the separator criterion. The algorithm is simple in its concept and is based on the sub-tree to sub-cube mapping strategy introduced by George et al [9]. We also exploit the works done by Kumar and Gupta in [13] and by Desprez [6] in order to overlap communications by computations. Finally, we show that our algorithm is scalable and we extend it to the block Cholesky factorization using ideas proposed by Roman in [18].

An outline of the paper is as follows. Section 2 contains some background results on the sparse $LL^T$ factorization. In section 3 we present the multi-phase algorithm and section 4 exposes the communication overhead and the scalability analysis. In section 5 we show how to express the algorithm for the block Cholesky factorization. Finally section 6 concludes and presents some experimentals results.

## 2 Sparse Cholesky factorization

In what follows, $A$ is a parse matrix of size $N \times N$ and $LL^T$ is its Cholesky factorization. Let's introduce some notations. Let $Struct(L_{j*})$ be the set of column subscripts of nonzeros elements in row $j$ of $L$ and $Struct(L_{*j})$ be the set of row subscripts of nonzero elements in column $j$ of $L$ [14]. These sets are computed during the symbolic factorization step. The sparse column-Cholesky factorization is presented in figure 1. It is well known that during this factorization process some zero elements in $A$ are nonzero in $L$. The reduction of this fill-in phenomenon depends on the ordering of $A$. In the example of figure 2, fill-in elements are denoted by $\otimes$ and non-zero elements by $\times$.

```
For j := 1 to n do
        < Tcol(j) : For k ∈ Struct(L_{j*}) ∪ {j} do
                < cmod(j,k) : For i ∈ Struct(L_{*j}) do
                                    l_{ij} = l_{ij} - l_{ik} * l_{jk}
                        Endfor
        >
            Endfor

        < cdiv(j) : l_{jj} = √(l_{jj})
                    For i ∈ Struct(L_{j*}) do
                            l_{ij} = l_{ij}/l_{jj}
                    Endfor
      > >
    Endfor
```

**Fig. 1.** Column-Cholesky factorization for sparse matrices

$$
A = \begin{pmatrix}
1 & & & & & & \times & \\
 & 2 & \times & & & & & \\
 & \times & 3 & & & \times & & \\
 & & & 4 & \times & & & \\
 & & & & 5 & \times & & \times \\
 & & \times & \times & 6 & \times & & \\
\times & \times & & & \times & 7 & \times \\
 & & & & \times & & \times & 8
\end{pmatrix}
\quad
L = \begin{pmatrix}
1 & & & & & & & \\
 & 2 & & & & & & \\
 & \times & 3 & & & & & \\
 & & & 4 & & & & \\
 & & & & 5 & & & \\
 & & \times & \times & 6 & & & \\
\times & \times & & & \times & 7 & \\
 & & & & \times & \otimes & \times & 8
\end{pmatrix}
$$

**Fig. 2.** Column-Cholesky factorization: example of matrices structure

Let $Tcol(j)$ be the task that computes the $j$-th column of $L$. Each such task is composed of the two sub-tasks:

- $cmod(j,k)$: update column $j$ by column $k$ (for all $k \in Struct(L_{j*})$) and
- $cdiv(j)$: division of column $j$ by $\sqrt{l_{jj}}$.

The precedence relation graph is built on the basis of dependences constraints that exist between the $cdiv()$ and $cmod()$ operations: $cdiv(j)$ cannot begin before $cmod(j,k)$ for all $k \in Struct(L_{j*})$ and $cmod(j,k)$ cannot be executed before $cdiv(k)$.

However, $cmod()$ operations for different columns can be performed concurrently. Figure 3 shows the dependence graph of the example of figure 2. For example, after the computation of $cdiv(6)$, $cmod(7,6)$ and $cmod(8,6)$ could be executed in parallel.

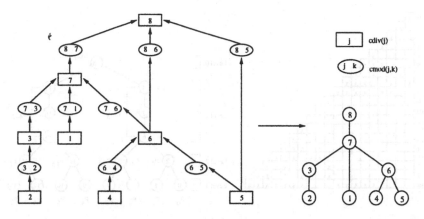

**Fig. 3.** Dependence constraint graph and elimination tree for the matrix of figure 2

It is shown in [10] that the column-Cholesky factorization is well suited for medium to coarse grain parallel implementations. So, it is relevant to packed both $cdiv()$ and $cmod()$ operations. Then a task $Tcol(j)$ is defined as:

$$Tcol(j) = \{cmod(j, k) \; k \in Struct(L_{j*})\} \cup cdiv(j)$$

Thus, some precedence vertices becomes redundant and the simplified graph is the well known *elimination tree* of $L$ [17] (see figure 3 for an example).

Elimination trees provide a precise information about columns dependencies. Indeed, operations $cdiv(j)$ cannot be executed before the computation of $cdiv(i)$ for all nodes $i$ descendant of node $j$ in the elimination tree.

So, trees that are short and wide are well suited for parallel computations because if node $i$ and $j$ belong to the same level of the tree and if their descendant nodes have been already computed, then tasks $Tcol(j)$ and $Tcol(i)$ will be performed independently. Such trees are provided by orderings such as the *minimum degree* algorithm [12] or the *nested dissection* algorithm [11].

## 3 A Multi-phase parallel algorithm

**Definition 1** *[13] A supernode is a group of consecutive nodes in the elimination tree that own one child.*

Any references to levels or depth of the tree will be with respect to supernodes. Figure 4 presents a supernodal tree and illustrates the notion of supernodal level. For the sake of simplicity we assume that the supernodal tree is a binary tree. Gupta and Kumar [13] state that any elimination tree can be converted to a binary supernodal tree by a simple pre-processing step.

Our parallel algorithm is based on the standard *sub-tree* to *sub-cube* task assignment strategy introduced in [9]. The two sub-trees of the root are assigned

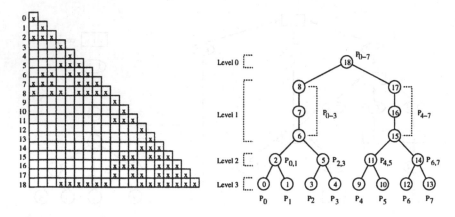

**Fig. 4.** Supernodal tree and sub-tree task assignement (from [12])

to sub-cubes of $p/2$ processors each. Each sub-tree is then partitionned recursively using the same strategy. So, at a level $\log p$, the $p$ remaining sub-trees are assigned to individual processors. Figure 4 illustrates this task assignement for $p = 8$ processors. In this figure, $P_{i-j}$ means that the corresponding nodes are computed by processors $P_i, P_{i+1}, \ldots P_j$. In fact, our allocation strategy is quite different. Indeed, for a level $s < \log p$ the different nodes of a supernode are assigned to an unique processor, the *root processor*. The remaining ones will be used for the computations associated with this supernode. In this way, the total computation load will be well balanced. Furthermore, with a reconfigurable machine, the notion of sub-cubes is useless. That's why sub-trees are assigned to *sub-sets* of processors. Here, we do not focus on how these processors are interconnected.

As presented above, each sub-tree at level $\log p$ is assigned to individual processors. So, all the computations of these sub-trees i.e. $Tcol()$ operations, are performed in parallel without any communications. Here, the algorithm processes the elimination tree supernodal levels by supernodal levels. Consider a supernode at level $s < \log p$. This supernode is assigned to $q$ processors. Note that any two supernodes at level $s$ are assigned to two disjoint sub-sets of processors. So they can be performed concurrently. A supernode is root of two sub-trees and the different columns, needed for the computation of this supernode, result from these sub-trees. Furthermore, according to the task assignment described above, each sub-tree is allocated to a unique processor.

The root processor must compute all the nodes of a supernode i.e. the tasks $Tcol(j)$ for $j \in Supernode$. So we derive three processes for the computation of a supernode (as shown in figure 5)

- The root processor receives all the columns, say $k$, such $cmod(j, k)$ are needed for computing $Tcol(j)$, $j \in Supernode$.
- In order to share the workload, the different columns $j$, $j \in Supernode$

will be partitionned and distributed among the remainder of the sub-set of processors assigned to the current supernode.

- The root processor sends the different columns $k$ and, in a pipeline way $cmod(j, k)$ and $cdiv(j)$ operations are performed. After the computation of a task $Tcol(j)$ i.e. each processor has performed the $cdiv(j)$ operation on its sub-block, these sub-blocks are send to the root processor.

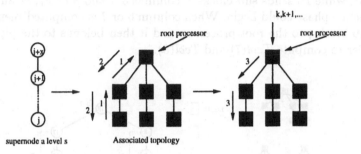

supernode a level s       Associated topology

1. Reception of columns k
2. Distribution of columns j
3. Computation of cmod() and cdiv() operations

**Fig. 5.** The computation of $cmod()$ and $cdiv()$ operations for a supernode at level $s$

If $q$ is the number of processors assigned to the current supernode, and if the target parallel machine is $d$-reconfigurable, then the three previous processes can be computed on a $d$-ary tree of $q$ processors.

Let's explain in more details the last step of the algorithm. The root processor initializes the pipeline process by sending a column $k$, required for the computation of columns $j \in Supernode$, to its soons processors. Then, these processors can compute the $cmod(j, k)$ operations on their sub-blocks of columns $j$ and send the column $k$ to their own soons (the two processes of computing and sending can be done in parallel). It is clear that during the previous computations it is possible for the root processor to process a new column $k$. In this way it is possible to overlap communications by computations.

When, for a column $j$, all the $cmod()$ operations have been computed, each processor performed the $cdiv(j)$ operations and a reduction opertaion is performed in order to place the column $j$ in the pipeline queue. This operation is done in parallel with the pipeline of columns $k$, if the communication links are bidirectional.

So, after the entire computations on $q$ processors of a supernode at level $s$, at supernode level $s - 1$, the number of processor assigned to each supernode is $2q$ and the induced topologies will be some $d$-ary trees of $2q$ processors and so on. In fact, the topologies of a supernode at level $s+1$ are obtained by merging the topologies of the two supernodes at level $s$ in order to built a $d$-ary tree.

After $\log p$ steps the algorithm ends. So the multi-phase algorithm requires $\log p$ phases (or steps) and each phase is decomposed in three elementary processes. Figure 6 illustrates this multi-phase algorithm with the elimination tree given in figure 4. According to the matrix of this figure, at supernodal level 1, processor $P_0$ must compute $Tcol(6), Tcol(7)$ and $Tcol(8)$. But $P_0$ already holds columns $0, 1, 2, 6, 7$ and 8 and $P_2$ holds columns $3, 4$ and 5. So $P_2$ sends these columns to $P_0$ while $P_0$ sends sub-blocks of columns $6, 7$ and 8 to $P_1, P_2$ and $P_3$. Now the pipeline phase could begin. When column 6 or 7 is computed then it is sends, by sub-blocks, to the root processor, and it then belongs to the pipeline queue in order to compute $Tcol(7)$ and $Tcol(8)$.

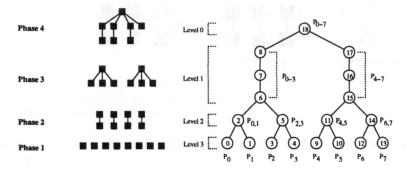

**Fig. 6.** Illustration of the multi-phase algorithm

## 4 Communication overhead and scalability analysis

In this section, we analyse the communication cost and the scalability of our multi-phase algorithm on a $d$-reconfigurable machine. These results hold for sparse matrices resulting from a finite difference operator on regular two-dimensional grids ordered by a nested dissection algorithm.

Note that the nested dissection algorithm used in the previous sections and in our experiments is quite different from the one we assume in the following analysis. Nevertheless, within small constant factors, the analysis remains the same as the standard nested dissection algorithm [8].

In general, given a $\sqrt{N} \times \sqrt{N}$ grid, we consider *cross-shaped separators* [9], called level-0 separator, composed of $2\sqrt{N} - 1$ nodes. These nodes partitionned the square grid, say level-0 grid, in four sub-grids, say level-1 sub-grids, of size $(\sqrt{N} - 1)/2 \times (\sqrt{N} - 1)/2$. These sub-grids are further recursively partitionned in the same way.

The supernodal elimination tree generated by this ordering is such that each non-leaf supernode has four child supernodes. At level 0 the supernode has

$2\sqrt{N} - 1$ nodes and at level $s$ the size of a supernode is half than the size of a supernode at level $s - 1$. Furthermore, the size of a level-$s$ sub-grid is approximatively $\sqrt{N}/2^s \times \sqrt{N}/2^s$. The number of nodes in a level-$s$ separator is approximatively $2\sqrt{N}/2^s$ and hence, following [13] at level $s$ of the supernodal elimination tree, the length of a supernode is approximatively $2\sqrt{N}/2^s$. It is shown in [9] that the number of nonzeros associated with a $m \times m$ sub-grid that are required by nodes on a separator is bounded by $km^2$ where $k = 341/12$. Moreover, the number of nonzeros associated with the first level of cross-shaped separators of this sub-grid is bounded by $\bar{k}m^2$ with $\bar{k} = 31/4$. Thus we can state the two following lemmas [13, 9]:

**Lemma 1** *On a level-$s$ sub-grid the number of non-zero elements required by the separator nodes is bounded by $\frac{kN}{4^s}$*

**Lemma 2** *The number of non-zeros elements associated with the first level of cross-shaped seperators of a level-$s$ sub-grid is bounded by $\frac{\bar{k}N}{4^s}$*

### 4.1 Communication overhead

We begin by stating the following obvious lemma:

**Lemma 3** *If a reduction operation has to merge a message of size m distributed among q processors, the communication overhead of this procedure on a d-ary tree is bounded by $O(m \log_d q)$*

Now consider the level $s$ of the supernodal elimination tree. Each supernode is assigned to sub-sets of $p/4^s$ processors. In the first process of the algorithm and according to lemma 1, at most $\frac{kN}{4^s}$ non-zeros are required by the root processor. Following lemma 3, on a $d$-ary tree this operation has a communication overhead of $O(\frac{kN}{4^s} \log_d (p/4^s))$. Recall that this operation is processed $\log p$ times (at each supernodal level), then the communication overhead of process 1 is $O(N \log p)$. The same analysis holds for the process 2 of the algorithm because, according to lemma 2, at level $s$, $\frac{\bar{k}N}{4^s}$ non-zeros elements (those that are associated with the nodes of the supernode) are to be send to $p/4^s$ processors on a $d$-ary tree. Thus the total communication overhead of process 2 is $O(N \log p)$. Now in the pipeline phase $\frac{kN}{4^s} + \frac{\bar{k}N}{4^s}$ nonzeros are to be send to $p/4^s$ processors on a $d$-ary tree. The total communication overhead of process 3 is again $O(N \log p)$.

**Proposition 1** *Factoring an $N \times N$ sparse matrix associated with an $\sqrt{N} \times \sqrt{N}$ regular finite difference grid ordered by a nested dissection algorithm produces a communication overhead of $O(N \log p)$.*

Note that in the state of the art of parallel direct solutions of sparse linear systems, the best results are obtained by Gupta and Kumar [13], who propose a parallel algorithm for the Cholesky factorization whose communication overhead is $O(N\sqrt{p})$.

## 4.2   Scalability analysis

The scalability of a parallel algorithm on a parallel architecture, refers to the capacity of the algorithm to keep a given efficiency while the number of processors grows [5, 16].

Following the notations given by Gupta and Kumar [16], let $W(N)$ be the serial run time of the sparse Cholesky factorization and $T_p(N, p)$ be the parallel execution time on $p$ processors. The overhead function is

$$T_o(N, p) = pT_p(N, p) - W(N)$$

and the efficiency of a parallel system is given by

$$E = W(N)/(W(N) + T_o(N, p)) = 1/(1 + T_o(N, p)/W(N))$$

For a fixed problem size, $E$ decreases as $p$ increases and for a fixed $p$, if $N$ is increased then $E$ increases too. So, for a parallel system, the efficiency can be kept at a desired value for increasing $p$, provided $N$ is also increased.

In order to maintain a fixed efficiency, the following relation must be satisfied:

$$W(N) = \gamma T_o(N, p)$$

where $\gamma$ is constant depending on the efficiency to be maintened. This equation is used to determine the isoefficiency function of a parallel algorithm/architecture.

The total work involved in factoring the adjacency matrix of an $N$-node graph with $O(\sqrt{(N)})$-node separator using a nested dissection ordering, is $O(N^{1.5})$. Furthermore, the total communication overhead of our algorithm is $O(N \log p)$. Thus, from equation 1, a fixed efficiency can be maintened if and only if

$$N^{1.5} \propto N \log p$$

and hence

$$N^{1.5} = W(N) \propto (\log p)^3$$

So, the problem size must be increased as $O(\log^3 p)$ to maintain a constant efficiency as $p$ grows.

The best known isoefficiency function for the sparse Cholesky factorization is produced by Gupta and Kumar scheme [13] for an hypercube topology and is equal to $O(p^{1.5})$. This shows the advantage of reconfigurable machines in terms of scalability.


## 5   Block analysis

In this section, we extend our algorithm to the sparse block Cholesky factorization. In the remainder we use the block decomposition given by Roman in [18].

## 5.1 Exchanges graph and block elimination tree

Following [18], $L$ is decomposed into rectangular blocks of non uniform size. Diagonal blocks are with non-zero elements (full blocks) while other blocks are either zero either dense (with nonzero rows). The size of each sub-diagonal block is determined as a function of the size of diagonal blocks (see the example of figure 7). In [18] Roman shows how to decompose $L$ in a such manner. Let $Bcol(k)$ be the set of column blocks subscripts $i > k$ of $L$ modified by the column block $k$. $BRow(k)$ is the set of column blocks subscripts $j < k$ of $L$, which modified the column block $k$.

The *block elimination tree* is the graph with nodes $\{1, 2, \ldots N\}$ and such that $\forall k = 1, \ldots N$, the father of $k$ is $min(BCol(k))$. The local computation of a column block $k$ and the modifications of column blocks of $BCol(k)$ can be done only after the modifications of $k$ by the column blocks $BRow(k)$. The elements of $BCol(k)$ are in the ancestry of $k$ and those of $BRow(k)$ in its descent (see figure 7).

The block elimination tree is equivalent to the supernodal elimination tree presented in section 3. In fact, a supernode is now a column block and it represents a vertex in the block elimination tree.

## 5.2 Multi-phase analysis

The computations associated with the column block $k$ can be decomposed in the following way:

- a task $(k, k)$ of local computation which consists in factoring the diagonal block and modified the sub-diagonal blocks.
- a task $(k, i)$, $i \in BCol(k)$ which updates the blocks of $BCol(k)$.

As in the non-block case, this formulation shows an important parallelism. Indeed, tasks $(k, i)$ for different column blocks $i$ can be performed concurrently (for more details see [18]).

So, the multi-phase algorithm presented above is naturally extended to the block Cholesky factorization. We use the *sub-tree to sub-set of processors* mapping of the block elimination tree and at each level $s$, $s > \log p$, the three steps of the non-block algorithm are applied and the different topologies remain the sames. Nevertheless, the algorithm differs in the necessity of factorizing every diagonal blocks. This factorization is, in fact, a dense Cholesky factorization and can be easily and efficiency implemented on $2D$-grid topology, with a wrap-around mapping of the columns to the processors. The communication overhead of this algorithm is bounded by $O(N\sqrt{p})$ if $N$ is the size of the matrix to factorize and $p$ is the number of available processors.

The Cholesky factorization of a dense matrix of size $M \times M$ (which corresponds to a diagonal block of $A$) on a 2D grid of $p$ processors, processes as follows. Each processor own $\frac{M}{p}$ columns. After the computation of a column $k$, this column $k$ is broadcasted to the other processors in order to compute the

$cmod(j, k)$ operations for $j > k$. Here, it is possible to overlap communications by computations [6]. We decompose a column $k$ (of size $M - k$) in blocks of size $\frac{M-k}{r}$. Assume that the *store and forward* communication protocole is used. Then the communication time of message of size $L$, between two processors physically connected is given by $\alpha + L\tau$ where $\alpha$ is known as the start-up time and $\tau$ is the propagation time of a byte. Then, the communication time of a block is

$$T_{com}(k) = \alpha + \frac{M - k}{r}\tau$$

Between two physically processors, if we want to overlap communications by computations, we have to minimize the following function:

$$T = T_{com}(k) + T_{comp}(k + 1)$$

where $T_{comp}(k)$ is the computation time required for a processor to performed the $cmod(j, k)$ operations on the columns $j$ that it owns. A processor own, in fact, $\frac{M}{p}$ columns $j$ and processes, at least, one column because of the wrap-around mapping. So, we can write the previous equation as:

$$T = r(\alpha + \frac{M - k}{r}\tau) + \frac{M - k}{r}\beta$$

where $\beta$ is the time of a floating point operation. By deriving $T$ we get,

$$\frac{\partial T}{\partial r} = \alpha - \frac{(M - k)\beta}{r^2}$$

The optimum $T$ is obtained when $\frac{\partial T}{\partial r} = 0$ and $\frac{\partial^2 T}{\partial r^2} > 0$. We find:

$$r_{opt} = \sqrt{\frac{(M - k)\beta}{\alpha}}$$

Note that the dense Cholesky factorization must be applied only when the diagonal blocks are large enough.

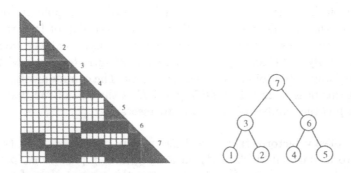

**Fig. 7.** Column block partionning, and block elimination tree

In the case of sparse matrices resulting from a finite difference operator on regular two-dimensional grids ordered by a nested dissection algorithm the block column approach is well suited [18]. Indeed, the distribution of the non-zeros elements do not create column blocks of small size. Furthermore, the communication overhead analysis is the same as in the non-block case. Indeed, the decomposition is such that a supernode node represents a column block. So, the multi-phase algorithm will require $\log p$ steps and at each step the amount of communicated data is again bounded by lemma 1 and lemma 2.

Nevertheless, in terms of communication cost, the most penalizing procedure is the dense Cholesky factorization. According to lemma 2, this factorization is applied on matrices of size $\frac{kN}{4^s}$ for a level $s$ of the block elimination tree. Thus, at level $s$ the communication overhead induced by the dense Cholesky factorization is bounded by $O(N\sqrt{\frac{p}{4^s}})$. Recall that this operation is applied $\log_4 p - 1$ times, we get a communication overhead of $N\sqrt{p}\sum_{s=0}^{\log_4 p-1}\frac{1}{2^s}$ which is bounded by $O(N\sqrt{p})$.

# 6 Experimental results and concluding remarks

We report some experimental results of the multi-phase algorithm for the non-block Cholesky factorization previously exposed. These results arise from simulations on a conventional computer.

Our set of experiments were conducted on $k \times k$ grid problems of varying size, using a nested dissection ordering, and for $d$-reconfigurable machines with various numbers of processors $p$. The multiprocessor system is assumed to be dynamically reconfigurable and using the multi-phase algorithmic model [1]. In order to make comparisons with existing architectures like nCUBE2, the number of links per processors is set such $p = 2^d$. It is clear that the greater is $d$, the shallower are the tree topologies and the better is the algorithm. Our simulations are based on computation and communication characteristics of Transputers and we do not focus on the time needed to configure the interconnection network after each $\log p$ phases [3]. Indeed, different tests have shown that this time is negligible with respect to the total execution time.

Experimental results are presented in figure 8. It appears that our algorithm provides good speedups even on moderate problem sizes. As the number of processors grows, the multi-phase algorithm is applied to more supernodal levels ($\log p$) and consequently the communication time increased. This explains the evolution of our speedups when $p$ grows.

Even if our results arise from simulations, they give a good indication on the behavior of our algorithm. In particular, speedups are better than those exposed by George [9]. This is clearly explained by the fact that our multi-phase algorithm has a $O(N\log p)$ communication overhead while George algorithm produces a $O(Np)$ communication overhead. The same remarks hold for Kumar [13] implementation which generates a total communication overhead of $O(N\sqrt{p})$.

We have not tested our algorithm in the case of the block Cholesky factorization. Nevertheless, in this case, it would be interesting to determine the size

273

| p | N=225 | | N=961 | | N=3969 | |
|---|---|---|---|---|---|---|
| | Speedup | Efficiency | Speedup | Efficiency | Speedup | Efficiency |
| 2 | 1.8 | 90% | 1.94 | 97% | 1.99 | 99.5% |
| 4 | 2.9 | 72.5% | 3.9 | 97.5% | 3.9 | 97.5% |
| 8 | 3.9 | 48.75% | 7.7 | 96.25% | 7.8 | 97.5% |
| 16 | 6.4 | 40% | 9.1 | 56.87% | 15 | 93.75% |
| 32 | 6.6 | 20.6% | 17.20 | 53.75% | 21.3 | 66.5% |
| 64 | 6.7 | 10.46% | 17.5 | 27.34% | 37.2 | 58.12% |

**Fig. 8.** Speedup and efficiency results for the multi-phase parallel algorithm

from which the factorization of the diagonal blocks must be parallelized. These different tests will confirm the interest of reconfigurable machines, in terms of communication performances and scalability.

# 7 Acknowledgments

We wish to express our sincere thanks to the referees for their many helpful comments and suggestions.

# References

1. J-M. Adamo and L. Trejo. Programming Environment for Phase-reconfigurable Parallel Programming on Supernode. *Journal of Parallel and Distributed Computing*, 23:278–292, 1994.
2. A. Benaini. The $WW^T$ factorization of dense and sparse matrices. *Intern. J. Computer Math.*, 56:219–229, 1995.
3. A. Benaini and D. Laiymani. A Multi-phase Gossip Procedure : Application to Matrices Factorization. In *Int. Conf. Software for Multiprocessors and Supercomputers*, pages 426–434, 1994.
4. A. Benaini and D. Laiymani. Parallel Block Generalized WZ Factorization on a Reconfigurable Machine. In *Proc. of International Conference on Parallel and Distributed Systems*. IEEE Computer Society, December 1994.
5. M. Cosnard. A comparison of parallel machine models from the point of view of scalability. In *Proc. of MPCS'94*, pages 258–267. IEEE Computer Society, 1994.
6. F. Desprez. *Procédure de Base pour le Calcul Scientifique sur Machines Parallèles a Mémoire Distribuée*. PhD thesis, Institut National Polytechnique de Grenoble, 1994.
7. I. Duff. Parallel implementation of multifrontal schemes. *Parallel Computing*, pages 193–204, 1986.
8. A. George and J.W-H. Liu. *Computer Solution of Large Sparse Positive Definite Systems*. Prentice-Hall, 1981.
9. A. George, J.W-H Lui, and E. Ng. Communication results for parallel sparse Cholesky factorization on a hypercube. *Parallel Computing*, 10:287–298, 1989.

10. J.A. George, M.T. Heath, J.W-H. Liu, and E.G-Y. Ng. Sparse Cholesky factorization on a local-memory multiprocessor. *SIAM J. Sci. Statis. Comput.*, 8:327–340, 1988.

11. J.A. George and J.W-H. Lui. An Automatic Nested Dissection Algorithm of Irregular Finite Element Problems. *SIAM J. Numerical Analysis*, 15:1053–1069, 1978.

12. J.A. George and J.W-H. Lui. A Fast Implementation of the Minimum Degree Algorithm Using Quotient Graphs. *ACM Trans. Math. Software*, 6:337–358, 1980.

13. A. Gupta and V. Kumar. A Scalable Parallel Algorithm for Sparse Cholesky Factorization. In *Proc. of Supercomputing '94*, 1994.

14. M. Hahad, J. Erhel, and T. Priol. A New Approach to Parallel Sparse Cholesky Factorization on Distributed Memory Parallel Computers. Technical Report 2081, INRIA, 1993.

15. J.W-H. Liu. The role of elimination trees in sparse factorization. *SIAM J. Matrix Anal. Appl.*, 11:134–172, 1990.

16. A. Gupta nad V. Kumar. Analysing Scalability of Parallel Algorithms and Architectures. Technical Report 91-54, Department of Computer Science - University of Minnesota - Minneapolis, 1991.

17. A. Pothen. The Complexity of Optimal Elimination Trees. Technical Report CS-88-16, Pennsylvania State University, 1988.

18. J. Roman. Partitionnement algorithmique des données pour la factorization de cholesky par bloc de grands systèmes linéaires creux sur des calculateurs mimd. *Calculateurs Parallèles*, 6:115–120, 1994.

19. E. Rothberg. Performance of panel and block approaches to sparse Cholesky factorization on the ipsc/860 and paragon multicomputers. In *Proceedings of the 1994 Scalable High Performance Computing Conference*, May 1994.

20. E. Rothberg and A. Gupta. A efficient block-oriented approach to parallel sparse Cholesky factorization. In *Supercomputong '92 Proceedings*, 1992.

# Adapted wavelet analysis on moderate parallel distributed memory MIMD architectures *

Andreas Uhl

Research Institute for Softwaretechnology, Salzburg University, Austria

**Abstract.** Among other adaptive wavelet analysis methods, wavelet packet best basis selection has become a popular method in image compression. This paper introduces a subband based parallelization of the decomposition and the best basis selection. This approach overcomes most of the difficulties of a straightforward parallel version of the sequential algorithm. Beside the higher efficiency the algorithm is easier to implement than its classical version. Results are presented that are achieved through an implementation on a workstationcluster using PVM.

## 1 Introduction

One of the ironies to come out of image compression research is that as the data rates come down the computational complexity of the algorithms increases. This leads to the problem of long execution times to compress an image or image sequence, which shows immediately the 'need for speed' in image and video compression. Unfortunately many compression techniques demand execution times that are not possible using a single serial microprocessor, which leads to the use of general purpose high performance computers for such tasks (beside the use of DSP chips or application specific VLSI designes).

Parallel architectures and algorithms suitable for application in image processing represent special challenges, especially for distributed memory architectures where each processor has fast access only to a rather small local memory. The difficulties are mainly a consequence of the large amount of data involved in this kind of applications. The main problem is how to perform an efficient mapping of tasks and data to the processor nodes which raises the questions of load balancing, data distribution and communication minimization.

Image coding methods that use wavelet transforms have been successful in providing high rates of compression while maintaining good image quality and have generated much interest in the scientific community as competitors to e.g. JPEG [23] and fractal image coding [2]. Even superior to these techniques are methods based on wavelet packet decompositions, which represent an adaptive generalization of multiresolution decompositions and comprise the entire family of subband coded tree decompositions. This superiority has to be paid with an increase of complexity from $O(N)$ in the wavelet case to $O(N \log(N))$ in the wavelet packet case, which can be overcome by using parallel methods.

* This work was partially supported by the Austrian BMWF, PACT-project, contract no. 308.929/1-IV/3/93

# 2   Wavelet image compression

A wide variety of wavelet-based image compression schemes have been reported in the literature, ranging from simple entropy coding to more complex techniques such as vector quantisation [1], adaptive transforms ([9],[22]), tree encoding [18] and edge-based coding [11]. In all these schemes compression is accomplished by applying a wavelet transform to decorrelate the image data, quantizing the resulting transform coefficients and coding the quantized values. In this paper we restrict our attention to the transform part.

The fast wavelet transform (which is used in signal and image processing) can be efficiently implemented by a pair of appropriatly designed Quadrature Mirror Filters (QMF). Therefore, wavelet based image compression can be viewed as a form of subband coding [24]. A 1-D wavelet transform of a signal $s$ is performed by convolving $s$ with both QMF's and downsampling by 2; since $s$ is finite, one must make some choice about what values to pad the extensions with. This operation decomposes the original signal into two frequency-bands (calles subbands), which are often denoted coarse scale approximation and detail signal. Then the same procedure is applied recursively to the coarse scale approximations several times (see figure 1).

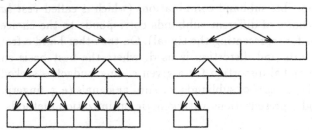

Figure 1: Wavelet packet and wavelet decomposition tree

The classical 2-D transform is performed by two seperate 1-D transforms, resulting at each decomposition step in a low pass image (the coarse scale approximation) and three detail images (see figure 2).

# 3   Wavelet packets and best basis selection

Wavelet packets represent a generalisation of the method of multiresolution decomposition and comprise the entire family of subband coded (tree) decompositions [17], [24]. Whereas in the wavelet case the decomposition is applied recursively to the coarse scale approximations (leading to the well known (pyramidal) wavelet decomposition tree), in the wavelet packet decomposition the recursive procedure is applied to all the coarse scale approximations **and** detail signals, which leads to a complete binary tree (figure 1) and more flexibility in frequency resolution. Higher dimensional wavelet packets are produced by analogy to wavelets. Wavelet packet decomposition leads in the general $s$-dimensional case to $2^{sl}$ subbands at decomposition level $l$.

After having generated the whole decomposition tree, there are several possibilities how to use this big set of subbands for representing the signal (figure 2): the wavelet representation (left), the short time fourier representation (mid) and an unnamed inhomogenous scheme (right).

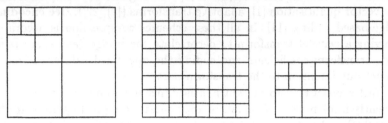

Figure 2: 2-D wavelet, short time fourier und unnamed decomposition scheme

There are also several possibilities how to determine the subbands suited well for a coding application. On the one hand an additive information-cost functional on sequences is defined and a search is performed for its minimum over all possible decomposition depths (which is a generalisation of traditional subband coding methods and is called *best level selection* [8]) or over the entire collection of possible subband combinations (which is called *best basis selection* [7], since the choice of different subbands corresponds to the choice of different basis functions for representing the signal). On the other hand a framework that includes both rate and distortion is used, where the best basis subtree which minimizes the global distortion for a given coding budget is seeked [17]. Other methods use fixed bases of subbands for similar signals (e.g. fingerprints [12]) or search for good representations with genetic optimization methods [3].

When best basis selection should be performed, a cost function on sequences (of transform-coefficients) is defined, which measures the 'information cost' in the sense of the concentration of information. Such a cost function should give large values when the coefficients are roughly the same size and small values when all but a few coefficients are negligable, e.g.:

**Entropy**: Let $X = (x_0, x_1, x_2, \ldots)$ be the sequence of coefficients. An additive analogon to Shannon — Weaver entropy is $\lambda(x) = -\sum_j x_j^2 \log(x_j^2)$, minimizing the latter minimizes the former.

For best basis selection first the costfunctions of all nodes in the decomposition tree are evaluated. Beginning at the bottom of the tree, the cost function of each parent node is compared to the sum of the cost functions of his children nodes. If the parents' cost is higher, this decomposition has to be performed and the information cost of the children is assigned to the parent. If the childrens' cost is higher this decomposition has to be avoided. This procedure is applied recursively at each level of the tree until the topmost node of the tree (the root) is reached. Obviously this method requires additive cost-functions.

# 4 Parallel wavelet packet decomposition and best basis selection

There has been already some work done on parallelizing the wavelet transform: general investigations [19] and implementations on SIMD - machines ([14] – a 1D transform on a MasPar, [10] – a 2D transform on a CM-2 and on a SYMPATI 2) and on Hypercubes ([13] – a 2D transform) are reported. In [15] a 2D Gabor transform is parallelized, which is not the kind of wavelet transform we treat here (in fact, the main computational load in that case is a 2D FFT). A wavelet packet decomposition is implemented on a hypercube in [16] for purposes of parallel numerical linear algebra.

Though the high degree of data locality of the wavelet packet decomposition suggests a fine–grained parallel approach, massively parallel machines are a scarce resource. We introduce an algorithm for efficient 2-D parallel wavelet packet decomposition and best basis selection on moderate parallel distributed memory MIMD architectures up to 16 processors ($16 = 4^2$, which is the number of subbands after two steps of decomposition). This algorithm is suited also for shared memory computers but the gain in efficiency is much higher for distributed memory architectures. In case of up to 4 or more than 16 processors are available, the technique may be adapted easily. Generally spoken the efficiency decreases the more processors are being used, since the parallelization is subband oriented und the number of subbands is limited by $4^l$ at decomposition level $l$.

The straightforward way to parallelize the two-dimensional decomposition scheme [16] is to divide the image into blocks of rows (or columns) and to decompose each segment independently on its own processor. This method suffers from some serious drawbacks:

1) Wavelettransforms need some sort of zero-padding, periodization, reflection [21] or especially designed filters [6] at the borders of the data – performing the convolutions seperatly on each processor will induce artefacts in the transform where the convolutions near divisions in data will artificially overlap with zeros or the periodized/reflected data or will be performed artificially with the border filters. Clearly we will need to provide some extra data to each processor to avoid this effect. There are two possible ways to handle this border data [19]:

   (a) The data swapping approach: the necessary border data is exchanged between the processors while the decomposition is carried out.

   (b) The overlapping data method: all necessary data to compute the desired levels is sent to the processors initially.

For distributed memory architectures data swapping is rather ineffective since it induces synchronization and causes a big amount of communication at each step of the decomposition. Even for shared memory architectures it has been shown [19] that the overlapping data method is superior. So the only way the decomposition can be done efficiently is the overlapping data approach, which suffers from the fact, that as the number of levels grows, the amount of extra data and thus extra computations grows as a power of two.

2) A complete decomposition (in the sense of full decomposition depth) cannot be performed in parallel like this – when we reach one approximation/detail point per processor, the data has to be redistributed completely.

3) The evaluation of the costfunction causes much communication, best basis selection is difficult to implement and the decomposition into the best basis is difficult to balance.

Memory requirements can be quite big for the whole decomposition scheme, therefore it may be impractical or even impossible to store all wavelet packet coefficients. This problem can be overcome by trading off space for time, namely discarding the computed coefficients as soon as their information cost has been stored.

## Parallel decomposition and best basis selection

Wavelet packet decomposition is a local, data independent operation which is therefore relatively easy to balance. The data is mapped in equalsized blocks of rows (or columns) onto the processors including the necessary border data for two decomposition levels. These two initial decomposition steps are performed by calculating the coefficients in breath-first order and the information cost is computed. (If architectures with up to 4 or more than 16 processors are used, either one or at least three initial decomposition steps should be performed – on the one hand the number of initial steps should be kept to a minimum, on the other hand it should be avoided to result in more processors than subbands after the initial step(s)). In the following the data is redistributed in a way, that each processor is assigned one (or more) subbands (depending on the number of processors) of the wavelet packet decomposition scheme (see figure 3: in case of the availability of up to four processors, only one decomposition level is performed before redistribution). Since the data has to be redistributed any way, we even save communication amount, because at this stage of the decomposition redistribution is easier to organize.

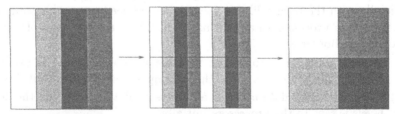

Figure 3: Equally coloured regions are assigned to the same processor:
data partitioning, decomposition and redistribution

Now the decomposition can be continued without need of extra border data, down to any decomposition level and the costfunctions can be evaluated without communication indpendently on each processor. When the decomposition is completed, the best basis is chosen independently on each processor for 'its subbands' up to the two topmost levels – at this point of the calculation the need for synchronization comes in: one processor has to collect the results and evaluate the best basis for the last two levels.

If all coefficients could be stored, the calculation is completed, otherwise a decomposition into the best basis is necessary (see below). If the calculation takes place in an environment with unpredictable load situation, dynamic load balancing may be applied easily for both the initial steps (e.g. a pool of tasks consisting of small blocks of the data) and the further subband based decomposition (e.g. a pool of tasks consisting of the subbands).

**Parallel decomposition into the best basis**

Since the decomposition into the best basis is a data dependent operation, we use a run-time data distribution technique for load balancing (inhomogenous bases may appear where the workload is concentrated on the decomposition of a few subbands which leads to an unbalanced load situation in our subband based parallelization – see figure 2 left and right scheme). The first two decomposition steps are performed exactly like it was done before with respect to the avoidance of the decomposition of unnecessary subbands. Now data has to be redistributed. This can be done in an adaptive way, since the amount of work that has to be done on an arbitrary subband can be easily evaluated. Moreover dynamic load balancing techniques may be applied (e.g. a pool of tasks method).

# 5 Experimental Results

We have implemented the algorithm on a homogeneous workstation cluster consisting of 8 DEC AXP 3000/400 (interconnected by FDDI) using the parallel programming environment PVM [20]. Such a configuration can be viewed as a special kind of didtributed memory MIMD architecture with high communication cost. The algorithm is applied to satellite images with 4096x4096 pixels.

A problem is how to handle the huge amount of data in general when using a workstation cluster – an image with $4096^2$ pixels needs about 64 MB memory, summed up to 768 MB when storing 12 decomposition levels. When using PVM we must take into account, that before sending data it is copied into a buffer, what can double the memory requirements. This is why the transforms have to be carried out in place, which results in the need for two decomposition runs (as explained before). We use a master-slave technique, since for best basis selection global decisions have to be made (e.g. basis choice of the two topmost levels, which is done by the masterprocess) and data distribution can be handled easier.

Since this application is very memory intensive, other applications running on the cluster might cause swapping. This is why we assume to be the only user of the machines, which results in a static load balancing scheme (beside the run-time data distribution). Of course it would be possible to use dynamic load balancing (e.g. pool of tasks methods) for all decomposition levels – but on the one hand the amount of extra border data and computation rises with a finer partition of the rows (only for the two topmost levels), on the other hand such a method is limited due to the small memory capacities of the workstations.

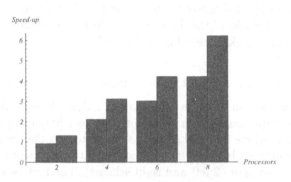

Figure 4: Speedup over DEC AXP 7000/710

Figure 4 shows speedup with 2, 4, 6 and 8 machines of the straightforward parallelization and the algorithm introduced here over a sequential implementation on a DEC/AXP 7000/710 with 500 MB memory, on which satellite image processing is performed commercially.

## 6 Conclusion

In this paper a subband based parallelization of a 2-D wavelet packet decomposition and best basis selection suited for image coding is introduced. Experimental results show a higher speedup compared to a traditional block-based parallel implementation of the sequential algorithm. Moreover the subband based parallelization is much easier to implement due to less communication and synchronization demand.

## References

1. M. Antonini, M. Barlaud, P. Mathieu, and I. Daubechies. Image coding using wavelet transform. *IEEE Trans. on Image Process.*, 1(2):205–220, 1992.
2. M.F. Barnsley and L.P. Hurd. *Fractal image compression*. AK Peters Ltd., Wellesley, Massachusetts, 1992.
3. C.H. Chu. Genetic algorithm search of multiresolution tree with applications in data compression. In H.H. Szu, editor, *Wavelet Applications, Proc. SPIE 2242*, pages 950–958, 1994.

4. C. K. Chui, editor. *Wavelets: A Tutorial in Theory and Applications*. Academic Press, San Diego, 1992.

5. C. K. Chui, L. Montefusco, and L. Puccio. *Wavelets: Theory, Algorithms and Applications*. Academic Press, San Diego, 1994.

6. A. Cohen, I. Daubechies, and P. Vial. Wavelets on the interval and fast wavelet transforms. *Appl. Comput. Harmon. Anal.*, 1(1):54–81, 1994.

7. R. R. Coifman and M. V. Wickerhauser. Entropy based methods for best basis selection. *IEEE Trans. on Inf. Theory*, 38(2):719–746, 1992.

8. R.R. Coifman, Y. Meyer, S. Quake, and M.V. Wickerhauser. Signal processing and compression with wavelet packets. In Y. Meyer and S. Roques, editors, *Progress in wavelet analysis and applications, Proceedings of the International Conference "Wavelets and Applications", Toulouse, 1992*, pages 77–93. Editions Frontieres, 1993.

9. P. Desarte, B. Macq, and D.T.M. Slock. Signal-adapted multiresolution transform for image coding. *IEEE Trans. on Inf. Theory*, 38(2):897–904, 1992.

10. H. Essafi and M.M. Pic. Application of parallel computing to wavelet transform. In Y. Meyer and S. Roques, editors, *Progress in wavelet analysis and applications, Proceedings of the International Conference "Wavelets and Applications", Toulouse, 1992*, pages 683–687. Editions Frontieres, 1993.

11. J. Froment and S. Mallat. Second generation compact image coding. In [4], pages 655–678.

12. T. Hopper. Compression of gray-scale fingerprint images. In H.H. Szu, editor, *Wavelet Applications, Proc. SPIE 2242*, pages 180–187, 1994.

13. T.L. Huntsberger and B.A. Huntsberger. Hypercube algorithm for image decomposition and analysis in the wavelet representation. In Walker and Stout, editors, *Proceedings of the 5th Distributed Memory Conference*, pages 171–175. IEEE Computer Society Press, 1990.

14. H.J. Lee, J.C. Liu, A.K. Chan, and C.K. Chui. Parallel implementation of wavelet decomposition/reconstruction algorithms. In A.F. Laine, editor, *Mathematical Imaging: Wavelet Applications in Signal and Image Processing, Proc. SPIE 2034*, pages 248–257, 1993.

15. M. Misra and V. K. Prasanna. Parallel computation of 2-D wavelet transforms. In *Proc. of the 11th IAPR Int. Conference on Pattern Recognition*, volume IV, pages 111–114. IEEE Comput. Soc. Press, 1992.

16. L. Bacchelli Montefusco. Parallel numerical algorithms with orthonormal wavelet packet bases. In [5], pages 459–494.

17. K. Ramchandran and M. Vetterli. Best wavelet packet bases in a rate-distortion sense. *IEEE Trans. on Image Process.*, 2(2):160–175, 1993.

18. J.M. Shapiro. Embedded image coding using zerotrees of wavelet coefficients. *IEEE Trans. on Signal Process.*, 41(12):3445–3462, 1993.

19. S. Sullivan. Vector and parallel implementations of the wavelet transform. Technical report, Center for Supercomputing Research and Development, University of Illinois, Urbana, 1991.

20. V.S. Sunderam, G.A. Geist, J. Dongarra, and R. Manchek. The PVM concurrent computing system: evolution, experiences, and trends. *Parallel Computing*, 20:531–545, 1994.

21. C. Taswell and K.C. McGill. Wavelet transform algorithms for finite-duration discrete-time signals. *ACM Transactions on Mathematical Software*, 20(3):398–412, 1994.

22. A. Uhl. Compact image coding using wavelets and wavelet packets based on non-stationary and inhomogeneous multiresolution analyses. In A.F. Laine and M. Unser, editors, *Mathematical Imaging: Wavelet applications in signal and image processing II, Proc. SPIE 2303*, pages 378–388, 1994.

23. G.K. Wallace. The JPEG still picture compression standard. *Communications of the ACM*, 34(4):30–44, 1991.

24. J. Woods and S.D. O'Neil. Subband coding of images. *IEEE Trans. on Acoust. Signal Speech Process.*, 34(5):1278–1288, 1986.

# A New Parallel Approach to the Constrained Two-Dimensional Cutting Stock Problem

Stefan Tschöke and Norbert Holthöfer

University of Paderborn
Department of Computer Science
33095 Paderborn, Germany
email: stefan@uni-paderborn.de
http://www.uni-paderborn.de/fachbereich/AG/monien/index.html

Abstract. In this paper we present a new parallelization of an efficient best-first branch-and-bound algorithm to solve the constrained two-dimensional single stock guillotine cutting stock problem (C2P) to optimality.

The underlying sequential branch-and-bound algorithm is based on an exact version of Wang's heuristic suggested by Viswanathan and Bagchi. In our algorithm we improve the upper bound and introduce duplicate pruning.

For an efficient parallelization we developed a special communication structure, as due to the unusual branching strategy and detection of duplicates a standard parallelization of the branch-and-bound approach cannot be applied to this problem. This structure allows a dynamic and fully distributed load-balancing using a direct neighbor strategy.

Computational results on two different parallel systems are presented. The implementation is system-independent using the portable parallel branch-and-bound library (PPBB-LIB) developed in Paderborn and can easily be ported to other systems.

Keywords: two-dimensional cutting, parallel branch-and-bound, combinatorial optimization

## 1    Introduction

The efficient solution of large combinatorial optimization problems is highly important for many applications in the field of research and engineering. Using today's technology and algorithmic methods it is often not possible to give optimal solutions for real-world problems. The use of parallel computers increases the problem size which can be solved optimally.

Many problems of operations research and artificial intelligence can be defined as combinatorial optimization problems. Among these the area of cutting problems has been intensively studied in the past. Here an overview see

This work was partly supported by the EU Human Capital and Mobility Project SCOOP: Solving Combinatorial Optimization Problems in Parallel and by the PARABOR Project of Federal German Ministry of Research (BMBF).

# A New Parallel Approach to the Constrained Two-Dimensional Cutting Stock Problem *

Stefan Tschöke and Norbert Holthöfer

University of Paderborn
Department of Computer Science
33095 Paderborn, Germany
e-mail: sts@uni-paderborn.de
http://www.uni-paderborn.de/fachbereich/AG/monien/index.html

**Abstract.** In this paper we present a new parallelization of an efficient best-first branch-and-bound algorithm to solve the constrained two-dimensional single stock guillotine cutting stock problem (CSP) to optimality.

The underlying sequential branch-and-bound algorithm is based on an exact version of Wang's heuristic suggested by Viswanathan and Bagchi. In our algorithm we improve the upper bound and introduce duplicate pruning.

For an efficient parallelization we developed a special communication structure, as due to the unusual branching strategy and detection of duplicates a standard parallelization of the branch-and-bound approach cannot be applied to this problem. This structure allows a dynamic and fully distributed load-balancing using a direct neighbor strategy.

Computational results on two different parallel systems are presented. The implementation is system-independent using the portable parallel branch-and-bound library (PPBB-LIB) developed in Paderborn and can easily be ported to other systems.

**Keywords:** two-dimensional cutting, parallel branch-and-bound, combinatorial optimization

## 1  Introduction

The efficient solution of large combinatorial optimization problems is highly important for many applications in the field of science and engineering. Using today's technology and algorithmic methods, it is often not possible to give optimal solutions for real-world problems. The use of parallel computers increases the problem size which can be solved optimally.

Many problems of operations research and artificial intelligence can be defined as combinatorial optimization problems. Among these the area of the cutting problems has been intensively studied in the past. For an overview see

* This work was partly supported by the EU Human Capital and Mobility Project: "SCOOP: Solving Combinatorial Optimization Problems in Parallel" and by the PARALOR Project of Federal German Ministry of Research (BMBF)

[2, 10]. Cutting stock problems have many applications in production processes in paper, glass, metal and timber cutting industries. Many different versions of cutting problems exist as there are one-, two- and three dimensional cuttings with or without several constraints. We present a branch-and-bound algorithm to solve the constrained two-dimensional cutting stock problem which guarantees optimal solutions. Two-dimensional cutting with branch-and-bound has been studied earlier by Cristofides and Whitlock [1], Wang [14] and Viswanathan and Bagchi [13]. These authors, however, have only solved relatively small instances or did not solve the problem to optimality. By proposing a new sharper upper bound and an efficient parallelization we are able to solve larger instances than they did.

Branch-and-bound is a well-known technique for solving combinatorial search problems. Its basic scheme is to reduce the problem search space by dynamically pruning unsearched areas which cannot yield better results than already found. Execution of a branch-and-bound algorithm in parallel is to accelerate the search process further by decomposing the search space into numerous subspaces and assigning the searches of subspaces across multiple processors.

In parallel branch-and-bound computations, a load distribution algorithm is needed to distribute the subproblems among the processors at run-time so that they can be executed in parallel. For an overview of different load-balancing strategies in branch-and-bound algorithms see Gendron and Grainic [3]. Our approach is based on the direct neighbor load-balancing approach by Tschöke, Lüling, and Monien [6, 11]. For cutting stock problems only few parallel algorithms are known (see [5]).

Previous parallel programming of branch-and-bound algorithms was machine-dependent. In addition to problem-dependent branch-and-bound procedures, programmers were also responsible for architecture-dependent load distribution, termination detection and input/output operations. To relieve the programmers of architecture-dependent parallelization tasks and to ensure the efficiency of parallel implementation automatically, Tschöke et. al. proposed a parallel portable branch-and-bound library, PPBB-LIB (see [12]). It subsumes the architecture-dependent features and provides heap management, termination detection, and load distribution in a distributed manner. With the support of the PPBB-LIB, programmers only need to implement the branching and the bounding procedures. The cutting stock problem was implemented using the PPBB-LIB. Computational results on two different parallel systems were shown.

## 2 The Sequential Algorithm

### 2.1 Problem formulation

In this paper, we will consider the constrained single stock two-dimensional cutting stock problem. Given is one stock rectangle of size L x W which must be cut in an optimal way into demanded smaller rectangles by orthogonal guillotine cuts (i. e. all cuts must run from one side of the rectangle to the other and be parallel to the other two edges; without loss of generality the cuts are infinitesimally thin). The number $n$ of smaller rectangles $r_i$ $(1 \leq i \leq n)$, their sizes $l_i * w_i$, their values $v_i$, and their demand constraints $c_i$ (the maximum number of times that a piece may appear) are given as well. The task is to find a feasible cutting pattern with $a_i$ pieces of type $i$ which maximizes the value of the stock under these constraints:

$$\text{Maximize} \sum_{i=1}^{n} a_i v_i \quad \text{subject to } a_i \leq c_i, \ a_i \text{ integer.}$$

## 2.2 A best-first branch-and-bound algorithm

We are going to present a best-first branch-and-bound algorithm adapted from Wang's idea in [14] and improved versions by Oliveira and Ferreira in [9] and Viswanathan and Bagchi in [13]. The main idea to get an optimal cutting pattern for the stock is to combine successively rectangles to larger rectangles in two ways: Horizontal and vertical combinations, which are the only meaningful ways for guillotine cuts (see figure 1, the cut loss is shaded). Both the initially n small rectangles and the generated new rectangles are called *meta rectangles* subsequently. The sequence of the combination process of meta rectangles is determined by upper bounds for the meta rectangles: For each meta rectangle m of size a x b a bound on the maximum value of the stock is computed if m is placed at the bottom left side of the stock. One way to compute such a bound is shown in [4], improved version can be found in [13]: Initially the maximum value for the free area outside the meta rectangle of size a x b at the bottom left side is computed once and then accessible by a table look-up for all reasonable sizes a x b. The upper bound for a meta rectangle of size a x b is then computed as the sum of this expected value of the free area outside a x b and the *value* of this meta rectangle which is the sum of the values of the small rectangles inside a x b. We managed to further improve this upper bound.

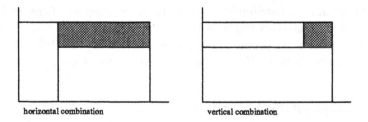

horizontal combination      vertical combination

**Fig. 1.** possible combination

The sequential algorithm works as follows: All meta rectangles, initially the n small rectangles, are stored in a heap, OPEN, which contains the open subproblems ordered by their upper bounds. Successively, the subproblem r with the highest upper bound is taken from OPEN and copied to an extra list, BEST, of best subproblems and combined vertically and horizontally with all meta rectangles already belonging to BEST (including r). All combinations c that do not violate the stock dimensions and the demand constraints are put to OPEN if their upper bounds are larger than the *lower bound lb* which is the highest value found for a meta rectangle up to now. This is the branching step. The degree of the search tree increases as the size of list BEST. If the value of c is even greater than lb we have a new lower bound and all elements from OPEN whose upper bound does not exceed lb can be removed from OPEN. This is the branching step. The algorithm stops as soon as OPEN is empty and the found best pattern, an optimal solution for the problem, is presented. For easiness and quick reference, this is the informal algorithm:

| | |
|---|---|
| OPEN: | heap of open subproblems, ordered by their upper bounds |
| BEST: | list of stored best subproblems |
| r, m: | meta rectangles (subproblems) |
| ub(m): | upper bound of considered meta rectangle m |
| value(m): | sum of the values $v_i$ of small rectangles $r_i$ contained in m |
| best, lb: | present meta rectangle with highest value lb; lb = value(best) |

```
begin
    lb = 0;
    OPEN = {r₁, r₂, r₃, ..., rₙ};
    BEST = {};
    while OPEN ≠ {}
        r = get_first(OPEN)
        BEST = BEST ∪ {r};
        ∀m ∈ B :
            build feasible horizontal and vertical combinations c of (r, m)
            if ub(c) ≥ lb then
                OPEN = OPEN ∪ c;          /* store c in OPEN (branching) */
            if value(c) > lb then
                best = c; lb = value(c);                /* update best and lb */
                remove all elements from OPEN with ub ≤ lb;   /* bounding */
    output best;                              /* best is an optimal solution */
end.
```

The correctness of the algorithm is shown in [13]. The iterative combination process generates all necessary cutting patterns to find an optimal solution. The best-first characteristic saves time and memory, the combination of growing meta rectangles achieves fast solutions which are good lower bounds. Simple spatial permutations of small rectangles are prevented directly by the algorithm but with increasing size and number of combination processes the growth of generated permutations of meta rectangles is dramatic. Many permutations take place due to the fact that any small rectangle in a guillotine cutting pattern can always be positioned at the bottom left corner of the pattern without changing its composition of demanded small rectangles (compare [13]). Paragraph 2.3

discusses ways to hinder this exponential growth. This algorithm for the cutting stock problem resembles A* algorithms (see [8]) which perform a best-first search for an optimal solution in a state space graph also using two lists, OPEN and CLOSED. Here, the second list is only employed to store best taken subproblems from OPEN for (later) duplicate pruning.

## 2.3 Detection of duplicates

Consider the patterns in figure 2. Pattern 2 is a spatial permutation of pattern 1. Pattern 3 has the same size as pattern 1 but less consumption of one small rectangle. Pattern 4 needs more space for the same consumption as pattern 1. Patterns 3 and 4 have worse upper bounds than pattern 1 but might be taken to BEST even in a sequential run if the stock is large enough. In a parallel run all patterns might be generated and be sent on the ring to all processing nodes.

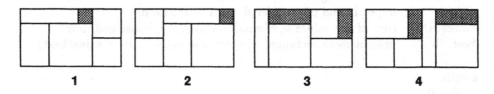

**Fig. 2.** types of duplicates

If pattern 1 has already been generated we call patterns 2 - 4 duplicates of pattern 1 and define generally:

**Definition 1.** Pattern Q is called a duplicate of pattern P if
1. $l_Q \geq l_P$ and
2. $w_Q \geq w_P$ and
3. $cons_i(Q) \leq cons_i(P)$ for all small rectangles $i$, $1 \leq i \leq n$.

Here, $l_P$ and $w_P$ mean the length and width of a pattern P and $cons_i(P)$ is the number of small rectangles of type $i$ in P.

Duplicates cause exponential growth both in the OPEN heaps and in the BEST lists because duplicates generate further duplicates and so on. These duplicates resemble duplicates in A* algorithms. A duplicate Q of a pattern P is deleted if

1. one weak inequality in definition 1 is a strong one or
2. all inequalities are weak and
   (a) Q and P are in the same BEST list and P has been put to BEST before Q (temporal preference) or
   (b) Q and P are in different BEST lists and the processor identity PID of the processor on which Q has been generated is less than that of P (structural preference).

Rules to prevent duplicates in the combining process without loosing necessary patterns can just be formulated for easy combinations. For example in figure 3 the horizontal combination of meta rectangles P and Q for Q turned or not is only meaningful in the second case because $l_Q \leq w_P$, $w_Q \leq w_P$, and $l_Q \leq w_Q$. For vertical combinations similar rules can be formulated.

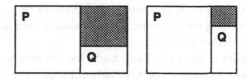

**Fig. 3.** a simple duplicate

To avoid more complex duplicates we store all selected best subproblems in a reduced form (consumption vector only) in a data structure which consists of lists of the subproblems ordered two-dimensionally by length and width. This data structure allows an easy check of the conditions of definition 1. The best elements from all processors have to be stored in this reduced form on each node to guarantee the quality of the duplicate detection with an increasing number of processors. To scan the OPEN heaps for duplicates would be time and memory consuming and is usually unnecessary because of their sizes and the fact that most elements of them are bounded anyway. Thus the combination with duplicates in the BEST lists - the source of the exponential growth of the patterns - is hindered.

For practical instances (restricted stock area and therefore restricted number of rectangles per pattern) the detection of duplicates reduces the sizes of the OPEN heaps and the BEST lists and time requirements by more than 60 % on average.

More sophisticated duplicate detection measures have been tested but resulted just in a slight decrease of subproblems and in a low increase of run time because of the more complicated detection.

## 3 Parallelization

### 3.1 The parallel algorithm

The main task of the sequential branch-and-bound algorithm is to combine the most promising open subproblem in OPEN with all inspected best subproblems in BEST again and again.

In standard branch-and-bound algorithms a parallelization is easy because all open elements can be evaluated individually and independently. Furthermore the heap of open subproblems can be distributed and balanced among the different processing nodes. Contrary to the standard case, here we have a second list, BEST, whose elements are to be combined with all chosen best subproblems on all processing nodes. One single and central list BEST causes a bottleneck for storage of and for access to the best elements. Maintaining a copy of the dynamically growing list BEST on all processing nodes squanders space and time for copying and necessitates complicated measures for keeping track of completed and still indispensable combinations.

We present a parallel algorithm with distributed lists OPEN and BEST and with a refined way to insure all necessary combinations to guarantee optimality on the one hand and to prevent combinations that would not take place in a sequential run on the other hand.

Consider the model in figure 4. Each node has its own local heap OPEN of open subproblems and list BEST of best subproblems. The distribution of elements between the different heaps is managed by an appropriate load-balancing mechanism (see [6], [7], and [11]). For example the weight function for distribution is determined by the number of elements in and the upper bounds of the first elements of each heap.

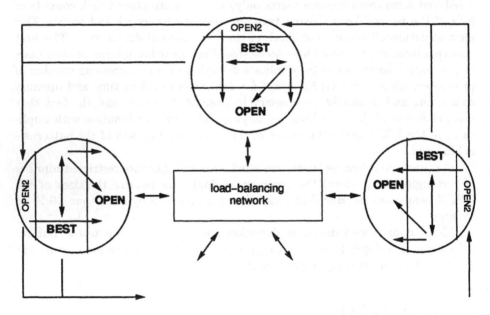

**Fig. 4.** structure of the distributed data management

The algorithm on each processor resembles the sequential case: The first element of the OPEN heap is moved to BEST and combined with all of its elements. To guarantee that each combination is performed as in the sequential case the elements which are copied to and combined with the local BEST list have to be sent to all other processing nodes for combination with their BEST lists as well. Therefore, a ring as a virtual topology between all processors for sending these elements is established. Why we choose a ring for broadcasting the new local BEST list elements and not a topology with higher troughput is explained in the following. Each node receives a second heap, OPEN2, for copies of the cycling best elements (the name OPEN2 is chosen because this data structure has the role of a second heap for each node). When asking for one new element the one with the higher upper bound from OPEN and OPEN2 is taken. This rule at least locally keeps the upper bound criterion of taking the next element for combination.

An unpleasant phenomenon takes place if, at the same time, an element e from the heap of processor 1 and f from the heap of processor 2 reach the ring. e is combined with f in 2 and f with e in 1 vice versa. A duplicate is generated which would not be produced in the sequential version. In the worst case (duplicates generate further duplicates) an exponential growth of elements is the result. Elements of 1 which pass 2 before f is sent do not cause problems (they are just combined in 1) and elements that leave 1 after f has passed and been copied in 1 do no harm as well (they are just combined with f in 2).

Therefore, each cycling element e that is copied to a local OPEN2 heap gets two local stamps. They indicate the positions of the first and last local element of BEST which are still on the ring at that time. These cycling elements, which have not returned to their origin processor when e is copied to the OPEN2 heap, are called *critical* for e because only the combination with these elements might cause duplicates which would not be produced in the sequential run. These still cycling local BEST elements are called the *critical region* for e.

As an example, consider the following situation (figure 5):

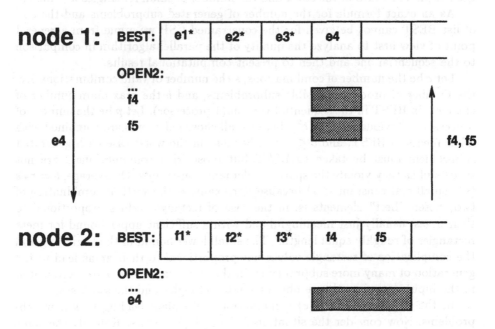

**Fig. 5.** critical regions

Element e4 in processing node 1 is taken from the OPEN heap into BEST, combined, copied, and sent to node 2 whose BEST list elements f3 and f4 have not returned on e4's arrival. Therefore f3 and f4 are critical for e4. On the other hand, on arrival of f3 and f4 at 1 at least element e4 could not have returned because the ring as a topology for broadcasting keeps the order of sent elements. This is the reason why a ring is chosen. There f3 and f4 have critical regions including e4 (elements from other processors extending the critical regions are not considered).

As all elements know their critical combination partners by the stamps, generation of duplicates is hindered for example by a random number assigned to each element at its generation time. In a conflict the smaller number wins and combines (in case of equal numbers a structural preference of the smaller processor ID will help).

The process of taking the best element from the heaps and combining it with local BEST elements continues until all heaps are empty.

The overall termination detection, queue management, and load-balancing algorithms as well as the copying and sending of best elements are done by a second process on each processor. For a description of the load-balancing algorithms see [11] and [12].

## 3.2 Analysis of the Parallelization

That the cutting stock problem is NP-hard is easily proven by a reduction to the knapsack problem. In the case of an unconstrained CSP solutions polynomial in the length and width of the stock and the number of small rectangles are known.

As an exact formula for the number of generated subproblems and the size of list BEST cannot be given for the constrained CSP we argue from a general point of view first to analyze the quality of the parallel algorithm in comparison to the sequential one and then to present computational results.

Let $c$ be the number of combinations, $s$ the number of valid combinations, i. e. the number of produced feasible subproblems, and $b$ the maximum number of elements in BEST in the sequential version (1 processor). Let $p$ be the number of processors. Obviously $c = O(b^2)$, because all chosen elements are combined with all elements in BEST, and $b \leq s < c$, because in the worst case each generated subproblem must be taken to BEST but most tried combinations $c$ are not successful as they violate the spatial or demand constraints. On average, $b = r*s$ ($r$ a small real constant $< 1$) because, for example, the vertical combination of two chosen "best" elements is, in the case of rectangle values proportional to their areas, usually just meaningful and with a sufficient upper bound for meta rectangles of roughly equal lengths. The small lower bound in the beginning and the complication of rectangle values not proportional to their areas lead to the generation of many more subproblems. In the worst case $c$ and $b$ are exponential in the input data, i. e. the number of small rectangles and the stock size.

In the sequential run $O(c)$ combinations take place leading to $s$ new subproblems. Now consider the situation for $p > 1$ processors: Roughly the same combinations as in the sequential case are carried out (just the sequence is lost and some additional unnecessary combinations due to the delayed arrival of new lower bounds from other processors might happen). The appropriate load-balancing insures a harmonious equal distribution of approximately $s/p$ subproblems on each node. Also local list BEST will have only about $b/p$ elements. As arriving best elements from other processors cannot be processed immediately, heap OPEN2 might have the size of $(p-1)/p*b$ but as BEST elements from other processors tend to price out locally produced ones the size is much less in practice. Furthermore, the duplicate detection needs memory $O(b)$. Altogether, node i has storage requirements of $O(s/p+b/p+(p-1)/p*b+b) = O(s/p+b)$ elements.

Similarly, the time analysis shows a time consumption of $c = O(b^2)$ combinations for the sequential algorithm and $O(c/p) = O(b^2/p)$ combinations of the altogether $b$ best subproblems with the $b/p$ locally best subproblems. Additionally, time $O(b^2)$ for the administration of the second heap OPEN2 leads to a time consumption of $O(b^2/p + b)$. The communication costs are not considered in this analysis.

## 3.3  The portable parallel branch-and-bound library PPBB-LIB

PPBB-LIB is a portable parallel branch-and-bound library [12] developed to relieve the programmers of architecture-dependent parallelization tasks and ensure the efficiency of parallel implementation automatically. It subsumes the architecture-dependent features and provides heap management, termination detection, and a decentralized mechanism for load distribution. Specifically, a parallel implementation of branch-and-bound algorithms includes seven main components:

- heuristic for the computation of an initial solution and other approximative solutions
- branching procedure
- bounding procedure
- methods to reduce the solution space
- functions for data input and output (i/o)
- queue management for the subproblems
- load distribution

The first four parts are application-dependent, and are programmed by users as a application process. The last three components are encapsulated in a communication process of PPBB-LIB. An application process is coupled with a communication process through a so-called branch-and-bound interface, as illustrated in Figure 6.

The communication process provides runtime support for application processes. Architecture-dependent communication primitives as provided by PVM or PARIX are encapsulated in the kernel of the communication process. They are transparent to the user.

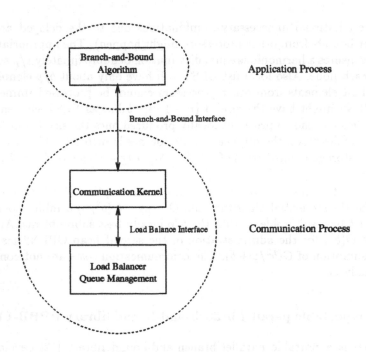

**Fig. 6.** process structure

In a distributed computing environment, each processing node concurrently executes both an application process and a communication process. The application process repeatedly fetches subproblems for expansion from the queue managed by the local communication process and returns those newly generated subproblems. In addition to queue management, the communication process also provides a dynamic load-balancing mechanism. Subproblems are migrated among processors through a communication kernel, which is transparent to the application process. Figure 7 presents an overview of the PPBB-LIB architecture in a distributed computing environment.

In the figure, the pair of processes with index 0 is a special one. Its communication process is connected to an additional i/o process and an additional monitor process. The i/o process runs the extracted and collected i/o functions of the original branch-and-bound algorithm and does the i/o of data for all other processes. Solid lines represent communication channels between processors, through which communication processes exchange load information, and transfer subproblems for load-balancing. Dashed lines represent a virtual ring used in distributed termination detection and I/O data transportation.

Currently, the PPBB-LIB has been implemented under PARIX on Parsytec SC320, GCel 1024 (both T805 Transputer systems) and on POWERGC-PP with 48 nodes (96 Motorola MPC601 processors). Sequential versions were also tested on Sun SPARCstation 10. The performance of Sun Sparc 10 50 MHz can be compared with one MPC 601 processor. In our application the Sun is about

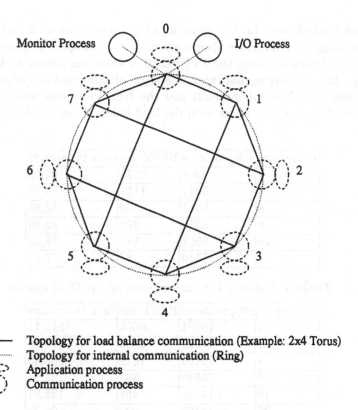

Monitor Process

I/O Process

—— Topology for load balance communication (Example: 2x4 Torus)
············ Topology for internal communication (Ring)
Application process
Communication process

**Fig. 7.** the parallel process system of the PPBB-Library

15% slower than the MPC 601. The T805 is about 17 times slower than an MPC 601.

## 4 Computational Results

Our CSP algorithm has been implemented on two different parallel systems (the Motorola PowerPC 601-based GC/PP system and the Transputer T805-based GCel system) using the portable parallel branch-and-bound library PPBB-LIB. For four representative examples, which can be found in the appendix, we give computational results. Examples 1 and 3 are taken from [1]. As they are too small when the orientation of the small rectangles is fixed it is allowed to turn them by 90 degrees such complicating the complexity of the NP-hard problem enormously. In fact the number n of small rectangles is doubled. Results for other randomly generated problems as problems 2 and 4 were similar. See Appendix for the detailed decription of the instances. The following tables show the number of generated subproblems, the size of list BEST on average, and the CPU time in seconds for the different problems in dependence on the number of processors.

The results which vary for the same input because of random factors in the load-balancing mechanism are always given as the average of 10 runs.

For load-balancing using the PPBB-LIB a torus was chosen as the virtual topology. The underlying hardware topology of our parallel systems is a 2-dimensional grid. The subproblems and the BEST elements were distributed equally on the processing nodes with the load-balancer described in [11].

| Processors | subproblems | BEST list | time in seconds |
|---|---|---|---|
| 1 | 5296 | 2275 | 102,56 |
| 2 | 5241 | 1117 | 54,89 |
| 4 | 5311 | 549 | 32,85 |
| 8 | 5317 | 272 | 22,89 |
| 16 | 5501 | 142 | 18,08 |
| 32 | 5510 | 87 | 17,50 |

**Table 1.** Instance 1: measurements on the GCel system

| Processors | subproblems | BEST list | time in seconds |
|---|---|---|---|
| 1 | 15081 | 6666 | 1315,11 |
| 2 | 14329 | 3222 | 676,76 |
| 4 | 13155 | 1612 | 353,40 |
| 8 | 13630 | 807 | 193,31 |
| 16 | 14020 | 408 | 125,91 |
| 32 | 13123 | 222 | 92,38 |

**Table 2.** Instance 1 with duplicate detection switched off on GCel

| Processors | subproblems | BEST list | time in seconds |
|---|---|---|---|
| 1 | 6796 | 1193 | 177,38 |
| 2 | 5680 | 565 | 78,44 |
| 4 | 4911 | 301 | 47,63 |
| 8 | 6647 | 158 | 27,46 |
| 16 | 7210 | 78 | 18,09 |
| 32 | 7873 | 38 | 13,65 |

**Table 3.** Instance 2: measurements on GCel

**Interpretation:**

For one processor there is no necessity for load-balancing and sending elements on the ring. Yet the transition to two processors often saves more than half the time.

| Processors | subproblems | BEST list | time in seconds |
|---|---|---|---|
| 1 | 65876 | 13359 | 172,93 |
| 2 | 65903 | 6401 | 81,48 |
| 4 | 64903 | 3426 | 50,46 |
| 8 | 64280 | 1802 | 34,12 |
| 16 | 58211 | 964 | 23,21 |

**Table 4.** Instance 3: measurements on the GC/PowerPlus

| Processors | subproblems | BEST list | time in seconds |
|---|---|---|---|
| 1 | 77741 | 15014 | 152,11 |
| 2 | 63375 | 6832 | 75,54 |
| 4 | 62486 | 3264 | 43,01 |
| 8 | 55813 | 1616 | 30,91 |
| 16 | 53712 | 823 | 22,16 |

**Table 5.** Instance 4: measurements on the GC/PowerPlus

With an increasing number of processing nodes the initial distribution and the load-balancing of subproblems become more complex and time consuming for still relatively small instances. At the beginning of the combination process some processing nodes carry out bad combinations of meta rectangles which would not take place on less nodes and send local BEST subproblems with bad upper bounds on the ring. The load of the ring and of the load-balancing network slightly increases with the number of nodes.

A major reason for larger networks being less efficient is the relatively small computational effort of combining two meta rectangles. Most combinations fail just due to the restricted stock size and too small upper bounds of the combinations, i. e. a few comparisons suffice to disqualify a combination. On the one hand, the parallelization makes it necessary to send all BEST subproblems onto the ring for post combinations, i. e. each processor has to make a copy of each BEST subproblem from each other processor. The disproportion of the primary task to combine (which is well distributed) and the secondary tasks to balance load, copy, and send (which are sequential factors) bring about a decline in efficiency especially for problems which are too small and for networks too large for a problem. On the other hand the distributed storage of the heaps of open subproblems enables the user to solve problems with high memory demands.

# 5 Conclusion

The algorithm proposed in this paper efficiently solves large instances of the two-dimensional single stock guillotine cutting stock problem to optimality. Our sequential algorithm with its improved upper bounds and duplicate pruning is faster than known other algorithms and produces much less subproblems. The parallelization makes it possible to solve much larger problems and is effective as long as the problem is large enough in comparison to the number of processors in most cases. The described detection of duplicate patterns reduces time both in sequential and parallel runs enormously.

# References

1. N. Christofides, C. Whitlock. *An Algorithm for Two-Dimensional Cutting Problems.* Operations Research 25 (1977), pp. 30-44.
2. H. Dyckhoff. *A typology of cutting and packing problems.* European Journal of Operational Research 44 (1990), pp. 145-159.
3. B. Gendron and T. G. Crainic. *Parallel branch-and-bound algorithms: survey and synthesis.* Operations Research 42 (1994), pp. 1042-1066.
4. P. C. Gilmore and R. E. Gomory. *The Theory and Computation of Knapsack Functions.* Operations Research 14 (1966), pp. 1045-1075.
5. B. Kröger, O. Vornberger. *A Parallel Branch-and-Bound Approach for Solving a two-dimensional Cutting Stock Problem.* Osnabrücker Schriften zur Mathematik, September 1990.
6. R. Lüling and B. Monien. *Load Balancing for distributed branch and bound algorithms.* Proceedings of 6th International Parallel Processing Symposium, pp. 543-548, March 1992.
7. R. Lüling and B. Monien. *A dynamic distributed load balancing algorithm with provable good performance.* Proceedings of 5th ACM Symposium on Parallel Algorithms and Architectures, pp. 164-173, 1993.
8. D. S. Nau, Vipin Kumar and L. Kanal. *General Branch-and-Bound and its Relation to A\* and AO\*.* Artificial Intelligence, Vol. 23, 1984.
9. J. F. Oliveira and J. S. Ferreira. *An improved version of Wang's algorithm for two-dimensional cutting problems.* European Journal of Operational Research 44 (1990), pp. 256-266.
10. Paul E. Sweeney and Elizabeth Ridenour Paternoster. *Cutting and Packing Problems: A Categorized, Application-Oriented Research Bibliography.* Journal of the Operational Research Society 43 (1992), pp. 691-706.
11. S. Tschöke, R. Lüling, and B. Monien. *Solving the traveling salesman problem with a distributed branch-and-bound algorithm on a 1024 processor network.* Proceedings of International Parallel Processing Symposium, 1995.
12. S. Tschöke and T. Polzer. *Portable parallel branch-and-bound library: User manual.* Technical report, University of Paderborn, 1995.
13. K. V. Viswanathan and A. Bagchi. *Best-first Search Methods For Constrained Two-Dimensional Cutting Stock Problems.* Operations Research 41 (1993), pp. 768-776.
14. P. Y. Wang. *Two Algorithms for Constrained Two-Dimensional Cutting Stock Problems.* Operations Research 31 (1983), pp. 573-586.
15. C.-Z. Xu, R. Lüling, B. Monien, and F. C. M. Lau. *An analytical comparison of nearest neighbor algorithms for load balancing in parallel computers.* Proceedings of 9th International Parallel Processing Symposium, 1995.

# Appendix

| | Problem 1 | Problem 2 | Problem 3 | Problem 4 |
|---|---|---|---|---|
| opt. solution | 1920 | 4620 | 2901 | 9750 |
| L | 40 | 55 | 40 | 99 |
| W | 70 | 85 | 70 | 99 |
| n | 20 | 30 | 10 | 20 |
| turnable | yes | no | yes | yes |
| (l, w, c, v) | (09, 17, 1, 140) | (10, 20, 2, 190) | (09, 24, 3, 216) | (14, 16, 1, 228) |
| | (15, 24, 1, 240) | (11, 21, 1, 220) | (09, 35, 3, 315) | (14, 31, 2, 406) |
| | (15, 24, 2, 240) | (12, 22, 2, 240) | (10, 14, 1, 140) | (15, 17, 3, 235) |
| | (16, 25, 4, 260) | (12, 40, 2, 450) | (11, 13, 3, 143) | (17, 19, 3, 303) |
| | (17, 27, 2, 280) | (13, 23, 3, 280) | (12, 08, 3, 094) | (18, 19, 2, 333) |
| | (19, 11, 4, 160) | (14, 24, 1, 390) | (13, 07, 3, 090) | (20, 34, 2, 650) |
| | (21, 12, 3, 180) | (15, 25, 4, 360) | (14, 08, 3, 110) | (20, 39, 3, 775) |
| | (22, 32, 3, 340) | (15, 26, 3, 350) | (21, 22, 1, 582) | (21, 29, 2, 648) |
| | (23, 14, 4, 220) | (16, 28, 2, 450) | (30, 07, 2, 210) | (25, 25, 2, 610) |
| | (24, 34, 4, 380) | (17, 14, 1, 250) | (31, 13, 1, 403) | (27, 27, 3, 729) |
| | (25, 35, 3, 400) | (18, 27, 2, 460) | | (29, 34, 2, 937) |
| | (26, 36, 4, 410) | (19, 15, 3, 250) | | (30, 25, 2, 750) |
| | (27, 37, 3, 420) | (20, 30, 2, 570) | | (30, 27, 3, 799) |
| | (28, 38, 4, 440) | (21, 13, 2, 250) | | (33, 30, 2, 968) |
| | (29, 18, 3, 300) | (22, 25, 1, 600) | | (35, 30, 2, 1052) |
| | (29, 39, 4, 460) | (22, 32, 3, 660) | | (37, 27, 4, 999) |
| | (30, 41, 2, 480) | (23, 14, 4, 310) | | (38, 49, 2, 1877) |
| | (31, 21, 3, 320) | (24, 30, 2, 720) | | (40, 25, 2, 1025) |
| | (31, 43, 4, 500) | (24, 34, 4, 790) | | (43, 28, 4, 1204) |
| | (33, 23, 4, 360) | (25, 30, 2, 760) | | (44, 34, 4, 1499) |
| | | (25, 35, 3, 840) | | |
| | | (26, 36, 4, 900) | | |
| | | (26, 40, 2, 1000) | | |
| | | (27, 37, 3, 980) | | |
| | | (28, 38, 3, 1010) | | |
| | | (29, 19, 5, 550) | | |
| | | (29, 39, 4, 1050) | | |
| | | (30, 10, 1, 280) | | |
| | | (31, 21, 3, 630) | | |
| | | (31, 43, 4, 1320) | | |

The data of the four examples is given in the following form: Length L and width W of the stock, number n of small rectangles, the turnability of the small rectangles, and the small rectangles with (length, width, constraint, value). For comparison, the value of the optimal solution of the problem is given in the second row.

# Using the PROSET-Linda Prototyping Language for Investigating MIMD Algorithms for Model Matching in 3-D Computer Vision

W. Hasselbring[1] and R. B. Fisher[2]

[1] Dept. of Computer Science, University of Dortmund
Informatik 10 (Software Technology), D-44221 Dortmund, Germany
Telephone: 49-(231)-755-4712, Fax: 49-(231)-755-2061
email: willi@ls10.informatik.uni-dortmund.de

[2] Dept. of Artificial Intelligence, University of Edinburgh
5 Forrest Hill, Edinburgh EH1 2QL, Scotland, United Kingdom
Telephone: 44-(31)-650-3098, Fax: 44-(31)-650-6899
email: rbf@aifh.ed.ac.uk

**Abstract.** This paper discusses the development of algorithms for parallel interpretation-tree model matching for 3-D computer vision applications such as object recognition. The algorithms are developed with a prototyping approach using PROSET-Linda. PROSET is a procedural prototyping language based on the theory of finite sets. The coordination language Linda provides a distributed shared memory model, called tuple space, together with some atomic operations on this shared data space. The combination of both languages, viz. PROSET-Linda, is designed for prototyping parallel algorithms.

The classical control algorithm for symbolic data/model matching in computer vision is the *Interpretation Tree* search algorithm. Parallel execution can increase the execution performance of model matching, but also make feasible entirely new ways of solving matching problems. In the present paper, we emphasize the *development* of several parallel algorithms with a prototyping approach. The expected improvements attained by the parallel algorithmic variations for interpretation-tree search are analyzed.

**Keywords:** model-based vision, object recognition, parallel search, prototyping parallel algorithms.

## 1 Introduction

Three-dimensional computer vision is commonly divided into several levels. In the research investigated at Edinburgh, low-level vision is concerned with processing range data acquired by a laser range scanner to eliminate noise [10]. Medium-level vision is concerned with identifying geometric surfaces [22]. High-level vision tries, for example, to identify the shape and position of data objects using matched given model features. In the high-level component, first the model invocation process pairs likely model and data features for further consideration [7]. Model matching then uses the candidate matches proposed by the invocation to form consistent groups of matches.

The classical control algorithm for symbolic model matching in computer vision is the *Interpretation Tree* search algorithm [13]. The algorithm searches a tree of potential model-to-data correspondences, such that each node in the tree represents one correspondence and the path of nodes from the current node back to the root of the tree is a set of simultaneous pairings. This model matching algorithm is a specialized form of the general AI tree search technique, where branches are pruned according to a set of consistency constraints according to some (geometric) criterion. The goal of the search algorithm is to maximize the set of consistent model-to-data correspondences in an efficient manner. Finding these correspondences is a key problem in model-based vision, and is usually a preliminary step to object recognition, pose estimation, or visual inspection.

Unfortunately, this algorithm has the potential for combinatorial explosion. To reduce the complexity, techniques for pruning the trees have been developed, thus limiting the number of candidate matches considered [13]. However, even with these effective forms of pruning, the algorithms still can have exponential complexity, making the standard interpretation-tree search algorithms unsuitable for use in scenes with many features.

Parallel execution can increase the execution performance of model matching, but also allow entirely new ways of solving matching problems. As has been observed, it is only from new algorithms that orders of magnitude improvements in the complexity of a problem can be achieved [3]. Thus, rapid prototyping of parallel algorithms may serve as the basis for developing parallel, high-performance applications. **In this paper, we present a methodology for the *development* of parallel high-level vision algorithms using a PROSET-Linda based prototyping approach.**

Parallelism in low- and medium-level computer vision is usually programmed in a *data-parallel* way, for instance based on the computational model of cellular automata [14]. For high-level symbolic computer vision, the data-parallel approach is not appropriate, as symbolic computations have an irregular control flow depending on the actual input data.

Data parallelism is opposed to *control parallelism*, which is achieved through multiple threads of control, operating independently. The data-parallel approach lets programmers replace iteration (repeated execution of the same set of instructions with different data) with parallel execution. It does not address a more general case, however: performing many interrelated but *different* operations at the same time. This ability is essential for developing algorithms for high-level symbolic computer vision. The data-parallel programming model is based on the *single-program/multiple-data* (SPMD) model as opposed to the *multiple-instruction/multiple-data* (MIMD) model.

Developing parallel algorithms is in general considered an awkward undertaking. The goal of the PROSET-Linda approach is to partially overcome this problem by providing a tool for prototyping parallel algorithms [15]. To support prototyping parallel algorithms, a prototyping language should provide simple and powerful facilities for dynamic creation and coordination of parallel processes.

Section 2 gives a brief introduction to the tool for implementing the parallel variations of the interpretation-tree search algorithm, viz. PROSET-Linda for prototyping parallel algorithms. Section 3 takes a general look at parallel interpretation-tree search. We do not parallelize the standard interpretation-tree algorithm, but the non-wildcard and best-first alternatives in Sects. 4 and 5, respectively. Section 6 evaluates the investigated algorithms. Section 7 discusses the transformation of prototypes into efficient implementations and Sect. 8 draws some conclusions.

# 2 Prototyping Parallel Algorithms with PROSET-Linda

Before presenting the implementation of the parallel interpretation-tree model matching algorithms, we have a look at PROSET-Linda as the language used for implementation. The procedural, set-oriented language PROSET [5] is a successor to SETL [20]. PROSET is an acronym for PROTOTYPING WITH SETs. The high-level structures that PROSET provides qualify the language for prototyping. Refer to [4] for a full account of prototyping with set-oriented languages and to [6, 18] for case studies for prototyping using SETL.

## 2.1 Basic Concepts

PROSET provides the data types atom, integer, real, string, Boolean, tuple, set, function, and module. PROSET is weakly typed, i.e., the type of an object is in general not known at compile time. Atoms are unique with respect to one machine and across machines. They can only be created and compared for equality. Tuples and sets are compound data structures, the components of which may have different types. Sets are unordered collections while tuples are ordered. There is also the undefined value om which indicates undefined situations.

As an example consider the expression [123, "abc", true, {1.4, 1.5}] which creates a tuple consisting of an integer, a string, a Boolean, and a set of two reals. This is an example of what is called a *tuple former*. As another example consider the *set forming* expression {2*x: x in [1..10] | x>5} which yields the set {12, 14, 16, 18, 20}. The quantifiers of predicate calculus are provided (∃, ∀). The control structures have ALGOL as one of its ancestors.

## 2.2 Parallel Programming

Process communication and synchronization in PROSET-Linda is reduced to concurrent access to a shared data pool, thus relieving the programmer from the burden of having to consider all process inter-relations explicitly. The parallel processes are decoupled in time and space in a simple way: processes do not have to execute at the same time and do not need to know each other's addresses (as it is necessary with message-passing systems). Linda is a coordination language which extends a sequential language by means for synchronization and communication through so-called *tuple spaces* [12]. Synchronization and communication in PROSET-Linda are carried out through several atomic operations: addition, removal, reading, and updates of individual tuples in tuple space. Linda and PROSET both provide tuples; thus, it is quite natural to combine both models to form a tool for prototyping parallel algorithms. The access unit in tuple space is the tuple. Reading access to tuples in tuple space is associative and not based on physical addresses, but rather on their expected content described in *templates*. This method is similar to the selection of entries from a data base. PROSET supports multiple tuple spaces. Several PROSET-Linda library functions are provided for handling multiple tuple spaces dynamically.

PROSET provides three tuple-space operations. The **deposit** operation deposits a tuple into a tuple space:

```
deposit [ "pi", 3.14 ] at TS end deposit;
```

TS is the tuple space at which the tuple [ "pi", 3.14 ] has to be deposited. The **fetch** operation tries to fetch and remove a tuple from a tuple space

```
fetch ( "name", ? x |(type $(2) = integer) ) at TS end fetch;
```

This template only matches tuples with the string **"name"** in the first field and integer values in the second field. The symbol $ may be used like an expression as a placeholder for the values of corresponding tuples in tuple space. The expression $(i) then selects the ith element from these tuples. Indexing starts with 1. As usual in PROSET, | means *such that*. The optional *l*-values specified in the formals (the variable x in our example) are assigned the values of the corresponding tuple fields, provided matching succeeds. Formals are prefixed by question marks. The selected tuple is removed from tuple space. The **meet** operation is the same as **fetch**, but the tuple is not removed and may be changed:

```
meet ( "pi", ? x ) at TS end meet;
```

Changing tuples is done by specifying expressions **into** which specific tuple fields will be changed. Consider

```
meet ( "pi", ? into 2.0*3.14 ) at TS end meet;
```

where the second element of the met tuple is changed into the value of the expression 2.0*3.14. Tuples which are met in tuple space may be regarded as shared data since they remain in tuple space irrespective of changing them or not.

## 3 Parallel Interpretation-Tree Search

Parallelism in a tree search algorithm can be obtained by searching the branches of a tree in parallel. A simple approach would be to spawn a new process for each subtree to be evaluated. This approach would not work well since the amount of parallelism is determined by the input data and not by, for instance, the number of available processors.

The programs which will be presented in the following sections are master-worker applications (also called *task farming*). In a master-worker application, the task to be solved is partitioned into independent subtasks. These subtasks are placed into a tuple space, and each process in a pool of identical workers then repeatedly retrieves a subtask description from the tuple space, solves it, and puts the solutions into a tuple space. The master process then collects the results. An advantage of this programming approach is easy load balancing because the number of workers is variable and may be set to the number of available processors.

Similar to sequential tree search, it is in general not necessary to search the entire tree: *bounding rules* avoid searching the entire tree.

## 4 Parallel Non-wildcard Search Tree Algorithms

As many of the nodes in the standard interpretation tree algorithm arise because of the use of *wildcards*, an alternative search algorithm explores the same search space, but it does not use a wildcard model feature to match otherwise unmatchable data features [8]. The tree in Fig. 1 displays an example non-wildcard interpretation tree. In a sequential algorithm, the tree is searched depth-first following the leftmost branches first (no pruning is shown here to illustrate the shape of the tree). The tuple $\Omega$ is the output of model invocation.

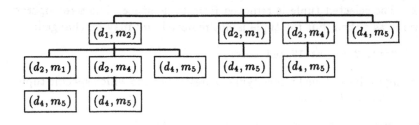

**Fig. 1.**
An example interpretation tree for $\Omega = [(d_1, m_2), (d_2, m_1), (d_2, m_4), (d_4, m_5)]$. The $d_i$ are data features and the $m_i$ are model features. The root of the interpretation tree has no pairings. Each data feature appears (in order) at most once in a branch. At each node at level $k$ in the tree, therefore, there is a hypothesis with $k$ features matched.

Section 4.1 presents a parallel non-wildcard complete search algorithm which finds all satisfactory matches. A match is satisfactory when the termination number of matched features has been reached.

The sequential non-wildcard search tree algorithm stops when the first satisfactory match has been found [8]. It does not search for *all* solutions. Section 4.2 presents a parallel non-wildcard search tree algorithm which stops when the first satisfactory match has been found.

## 4.1 Parallel Complete Search Tree Algorithm

This section discusses a parallel master-worker implementation of the non-wildcard search tree algorithm which provides all satisfactory matches.

Model invocation uses model and data properties to pair likely model and data features for further consideration [7]. It produces a sorted list of consistent model-to-data pairs ($model_i, data_i, A_i$) where $A_i$ is the compatibility measure (plausibility) of the features $model_i$ and $data_i$. The pair list is initially sorted with larger $A_i$ values at the top. The hypotheses from the model invocation are stored as a tuple in the variable **Hypotheses**.

Figure 2 displays the coarse structure of the master-worker program. Arrows indicate access to the tuple spaces. These access patterns are only shown for one of the identical worker processes.

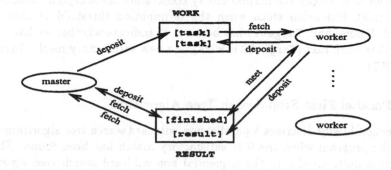

**Fig. 2.** The coarse structure of the master-worker program.

In this paper, only small parts of the code can be presented. Refer to [16] for the complete description. We use two tuple spaces. One for the work tasks (**WORK**) and one for the results (**RESULT**). The number of worker processes **NumWorker** is an argument to the main program. This could be, for instance, the number of available processors. The termination threshold for satisfactory matches is the next argument to the main program. The master (the main program) spawns **NumWorker** worker processes to do the work and puts the initial task tuples into tuple space **WORK**. These initial tasks represent the nodes at the first level of the interpretation-tree. Then, the master initializes a shared counter for the number of finished workers at tuple space **RESULT** and waits until all workers have done their work (by executing a blocking fetch until the number of finished worker processes equals **NumWorker**). Then the master fetches the possible matches from **RESULT**.

This was a sketch of the implementation of the master process (the main program). Now let us look at the worker procedure. Each worker executes in a loop in which it first checks whether there are more task tuples in tuple space **WORK**, and terminates when there is no more work to do. Before termination, the shared counter for the number of finished workers in **RESULT** is incremented to indicate the termination to the master.

Each extension of a branch in the interpretation-tree is formed by appending new entries from $\Omega$, subject to the constraints that (1) each data feature appears at most once on a path through the tree and (2) the data features are used in order (with gaps allowed). The condition in the following **for** loop of the worker ensures that these constraints are satisfied:

```
for Entry in Hypotheses | (forall x in MyPath | (Entry(1) > x(1))) do
   if Consistent (MyPath, Entry) then
      deposit [MyPath + {Entry}] at TargetTS end deposit;
   end if;
end for;
```

The set of pairs **MyPath** represents the current partial branch in the tree. The condition **Entry(1) > x(1)** enforces the data feature ordering constraint. Only extensions that satisfy the normal binary constraints are accepted (**Consistent** checks this). Extension stops when the termination threshold of matches is reached. Beforehand, **TargetTS** has been set to indicate whether we have a new incomplete work task (**TargetTS** is **WORK**) or a new satisfactory result (**TargetTS** is **RESULT**).

## 4.2 Parallel First-Stop Search Tree Algorithm

This section briefly describes a parallel non-wildcard search tree algorithm which stops the program when the first satisfactory match has been found. This algorithm is quite similar to the sequential non-wildcard search tree algorithm, but the tree is searched in a non-deterministic order and *not* depth-first following the leftmost branches first.

Synchronization between the master and the workers is achieved when the first satisfactory match has been found. Provided that there exist at least one consistent match, the master need not wait until all tasks are evaluated as is the case with the parallel non-wildcard complete search tree algorithm of Sect. 4.1. The master waits for the first satisfactory match to be deposited by a worker at **RESULT**. For a detailed discussion of this program refer to [16].

# 5  Parallel Best Search Tree Algorithms

The best-first search tree algorithm [8] assumes that it is possible to evaluate how well sets of model features match sets of data features (based on the plausibilities from the invocation and consistency measures as the set sizes grow). As any real problem is likely to provide some useful heuristic ordering constraints, the potential for speeding up the matching process is large.

In contrast to the non-wildcard algorithms (see Sect. 4), with the best-first algorithms we are interested in both the cost of a path to a solution (i.e. we wish to minimize the time to finding a solution) as well as the quality of the solution. Both algorithms use the same tree structure (see Fig. 1), but the portion explored may be different.

Section 5.1 presents a parallel search tree algorithm which provides the optimal match where each data feature is mapped to a model feature when considering plausibilities for the data/model feature pairs. The sequential best-first search tree algorithm searches for the first plausible solution (usually not the optimal solution). Section 5.2 presents a parallel best-first search tree algorithm.

## 5.1 Parallel Optimum Search Tree Algorithm

One parallel search tree algorithm finds the *optimal* match where a satisfactory number of data features is mapped to model features when considering plausibilities for the data/model feature pairs.

In addition to putting the initial task tuples into WORK, and initializing a shared counter for the number of finished workers at WORK, the master initializes an empty result set with plausibility 0.0 at tuple space RESULT (the current optimum). After spawning the workers, the master waits until all workers have done their work, and then fetches the optimal match from RESULT.

The algorithm assumes that the plausibility evaluation is monotonically decreasing as the path length increases. First the worker computes the plausibility of its own path of matches and reads the plausibility of an already known satisfactory match from RESULT, and compares it with the plausibility of its own (not yet satisfactory) match. If its own plausibility is lower than the plausibility of an already known satisfactory match, the worker continues to fetch another task tuple (according to the bounding rule). Otherwise, the worker checks whether the length of its partial match is already a satisfactory match but one. If so, it changes the optimal match in RESULT to its own evaluated match (extended to a satisfactory match). This algorithm is essentially a *branch-and-bound* algorithm [19]. For a detailed discussion of the task evaluation refer to [16].

## 5.2 Parallel Best-First Search Tree Algorithm

An alternative parallel best-first search tree algorithm terminates at the first satisfactory match. The central data structure is a distributed priority queue of entries of the following form, sorted by the estimated evaluation of the next potential extension:

$$(S_i = \{pair_{i_1}, pair_{i_2}, \ldots pair_{i_n}\}, g(S_i), m, f(S_i \cup \{pair_m\}))$$

where $S_i$ is a set of $n$ mutually compatible model-to-data pairs (a partial branch in the tree), $g(S_i)$ is the *actual* evaluation of $S_i$, $m$ indicates that $pair_m$ is the next extension of $S_i$ to be considered, and $f(S_i \cup \{pair_m\})$ is the *estimated* evaluation of that extension. The priority queue is sorted with larger $f()$ values at the top.

In addition to putting the initial task tuples into tuple space WORK, and initializing a shared counter for the number of finished workers, the master initializes the top of the priority queue at tuple space WORK with components $(\{\}, 1.0, 1, A_1)$:

```
deposit [ 1, 0, {}, 1.0, 1, Hypotheses(1)(3) ] at WORK end deposit;
```

Each entry of the priority queue is stored as a tuple in WORK. The first component indicates the *pointer* to the corresponding entry. The integer 1 indicates the top of the queue. The second component *points* to the next entry. The integer 0 indicates the end of the queue. Figure 3 illustrates the structure of this queue.

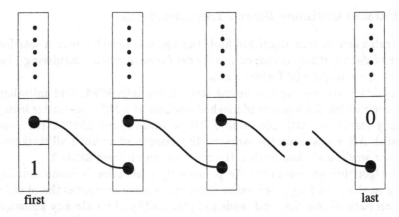

**Fig. 3.** The distributed priority queue for parallel best-first search.
The integer values 1 and 0 are used to indicate the top and the end of the queue, respectively. The intermediate entries are *identified* by the contained atoms. We use black circles to represent the atoms. A link between two atoms means that these two atoms are equal. Note, that the atoms are not the *addresses* of the respective entries, but rather the *identification* of the entries (distributed pointers which are independent of memory addresses to allow access from different processors).

The expression Hypotheses(1)(3) selects the plausibility for the highest rated hypothesis from the model invocation (this is $A_1$). The hypotheses are initially sorted by the model invocation.

Again, each worker executes in a loop and first pops the top of the priority queue $(S_i, g(S_i), m, f(S_i \cup \{pair_m\}))$ at tuple space WORK:

```
fetch ( 1, ? second, ? S_i, ? g, ? m, ? f ) at WORK end fetch;
if second /= 0 then
  -- The second entry becomes the first one through a changing meet:
  meet ( ? into 1, ?, ?, ?, ?, ? | $(1)=second ) at WORK end meet;
end if;
```

After popping the top of the priority queue, other worker processes can work in parallel on the tail of the queue to allow parallel access to the distributed queue, provided that there exists a tail.

If not rejected by consistency checks, early termination or non-existence of further hypotheses, the worker generates the next descendant of the successful extension:

$$(S_i \cup \{pair_m\}, g(S_i \cup \{pair_m\}), m+1, f(S_i \cup \{pair_m\} \cup \{pair_{m+1}\}))$$

plus the next descendant of the parent:

$$(S_i, g(S_i), m+1, f(S_i \cup \{pair_m\}))$$

to be inserted into priority queue.

Insertion of the next descendant of the successful extension is done by the **Insert** function, which enters the new node into the appropriate priority position, provided that the priority queue contained more than one entry:

```
if second /= 0 then
  Insert (1, S_i + {Hypotheses(m)}, g, m+1, f);
else
  next := newat(); -- A new 'distributed pointer'
  deposit [1, next, S_i + {Hypotheses(m)}, g, m+1, f] at WORK end deposit;
end if;
```

If the priority queue contained only the popped entry (the variable **second** indicates this), we directly deposit the new entry as the top of the priority queue. The next entry then obtains the atom **next** as its identity. PROSET's built-in function **newat** returns a new atom. The next descendant of the parent is inserted accordingly.

The algorithm needs two evaluation functions, $f()$ for the estimated new state evaluation and $g()$ for the actual state evaluation. The $f()$ evaluation function gives longer branches higher evaluations to direct the workers to search the tree depth-first. As with the first-stop algorithm (see Sect. 4.2), the master waits for the first satisfactory match to be deposited by a worker at RESULT.

The priority queue is stored as a *distributed data structure* [17] in tuple space WORK. Distributed data structures may be examined and manipulated by multiple processes simultaneously. In this case, multiple processes can work independently on different partitions of the queue. The individual entries are *linked* together by means of PROSET's atoms. PROSET does not support *pointers* as they are known in Modula, C or similar procedural languages. As mentioned in Section 2.1, atoms are unique with respect to one machine and across machines (they contain the host and process identification, creation time, and an integer counter). Atoms can only be created and compared for equality. We use them as *distributed pointers* which are independent of the processor's memory addresses. Note, that multiple processes can work independently on different partitions of the queue. The insertion procedure of new entries into the distributed priority queue **Insert** is presented in [16]. A variety of other data structures, such as distributed priority sorted heaps or distributed sorted trees, could be used to implement the priority queue.

# 6 Evaluation

**The parallel complete search tree algorithm.** The parallel non-wildcard complete search tree algorithm provides all satisfactory matches. If we neglect pruning of inconsistent branches, the number of evaluated nodes is proportional to $H^T$ where $H$ is the number of hypotheses from the model invocation and $T$ is the termination threshold. The time to evaluate these nodes with the sequential algorithm is proportional to $H^T$, whereas the time to evaluate these nodes with the parallel algorithm is proportional to $\frac{H^T}{W}$ where $W$ is the number of worker processes, since the worker processes evaluate the branches of the tree in parallel. However, the actual amount of parallelism may be restricted by the branching factor of the tree and contention caused by competing access to the tuple spaces. In principle, the situation for the above calculation does not change when considering pruning of inconsistent branches

With the non-wildcard algorithm, the second and third levels of the search tree represent matches that use several non-wildcard pairings. The binary constraints eliminate almost all false pairings quickly [8]. The trade-off is that the branching factor of the non-wildcard tree is $H$ instead of the number of data features as with the standard interpretation-tree algorithm, but the depth of the tree for any false sets of matches is usually very shallow. Therefore, the parallel non-wildcard complete search algorithm allows a high amount of parallelism because of the large branching factor of the tree.

**The parallel first-stop search algorithm.** The parallel first-stop search algorithm is quite similar to the sequential non-wildcard search tree algorithm. The tree is not searched depth-first following the leftmost branches first, but in parallel in a non-deterministic order.

For the sequential algorithm, the time to find the first match is highly data dependent. If, for instance, the left-most branch represents a satisfactory match, the sequential algorithm will probably be faster than the parallel algorithm, because the parallel algorithm will probably not follow the left-most branch first. The parallel algorithm *may* find a satisfactory match earlier, but this is not definite since the evaluation order is non-deterministic. However, the mean time to finding a solution is improved in proportion to the number of workers. Since the non-wildcard algorithms do not consider any valuation for the data/model feature pairs, nothing can *guide* the workers to follow the most promising branches.

This raises the question whether it pays to parallelize the tree search when we are only interested in obtaining *any* satisfactory match. If there are many possible solutions, then this parallel algorithm is unlikely to make dramatic improvements; however, if there are few solutions, then the speedup should be nearly linear in the number of workers. The situation changes to some extent when we are interested in obtaining a *good* satisfactory match.

**The parallel optimum search algorithm.** This algorithm searches in parallel the same tree as a similar sequential branch-and-bound algorithm would

312

search. The bounding rules apply to parallel search in the same way as they apply to sequential search (branch-and-bound). Therefore, the parallel optimum search algorithm can be compared to a similar sequential branch-and-bound algorithm in much the same way as the parallel non-wildcard complete search tree algorithm of Sect. 4.1 can be compared to a sequential non-wildcard algorithm which provides all satisfactory matches (see above).

**The parallel best-first algorithm.** For testing this algorithm, the output from the low- and medium-level components of the IMAGINE2 system [9] for the range image of a workpiece is used. Some experimental results for the parallel best-first search algorithm are displayed in Fig. 4. Figure 4a shows the number of visited nodes in relation to the number of workers and Fig. 4b shows the number of visited nodes per worker in relation to the number of workers. $T$ is the termination threshold for satisfactory matches. The zigzag line is due to non-determinism, but the tendency is obvious. The number of visited nodes per worker converges to approximately $\frac{T}{2}$ as the number of workers increases. Therefore, the addition of worker processes increases the search space.

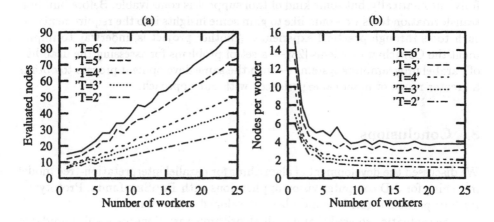

**Fig. 4.** The experimental results for the parallel best-first search algorithm.

The parallel best-first algorithm appears to be a good compromise between the parallel optimum search algorithm and the sequential best-first algorithm. It is not necessarily much faster than the sequential best-first algorithm, but can produce better results within the same or even a shorter time. The $f()$ function for the estimated new state evaluations directs the workers to search the tree depth-first, which increases the probability of finding a satisfactory match earlier. The workers are *guided* by the plausibilities to follow the most promising branches.

# 7 Transforming the Prototype Implementation into an Efficient Implementation

As a consequence of our evaluation, in a successor project the prototype of the parallel best-first algorithm will be transformed into an efficient implementation. In a first step, the PROSET-Linda prototype is transformed into a C-Linda implementation [21]. With Linda, it is easy to program with different styles, e.g. with distributed data structures, active data structures and message passing [2]. The C-Linda implementation will be programmed in a message-passing style to serve as a preliminary step for a message-passing implementation with an MPI library (Message Passing Interface [11]). We then use the CHIMP/MPI (Common High-Level Interface to Message Passing) [1] implementation at the Edinburgh Parallel Computing Centre, which is an efficient implementation of the MPI standard. CHIMP/MPI supports Sun, Silicon Graphics, IBM, and DEC workstations as well as Sequent Symmetry and Meiko Transputer/i860/SPARC Computing Surfaces. This CHIMP/MPI implementation will be used to compare performance of the algorithm on different parallel computing systems.

Note that this transformation is done by hand and not supported by a compiler or other tools. We do not believe that such transformations can be done fully automatically, but some kind of tool support is conceivable. Before building transformation tools we would like to gain some insights into the requirements on such tools through practical experience. Another project is underway to implement the Cowichan Problems [23] — a set of problems for assessing the usability of parallel programming systems — with the same development process to obtain a greater range of practical experiences with our approach.

# 8 Conclusions

We discussed the development of algorithms for parallel interpretation-tree model matching for 3-D computer vision applications with PROSET-Linda. Prototypes for four parallel algorithms have been developed and evaluated.

The evaluation showed that not all algorithmic variations are good candidates for parallelization. An application area for prototyping is to carry out *feasibility studies*. If we had implemented the algorithms directly with a production language, for example C with extensions for message passing, the implementation effort would have been higher. However, the exact savings in time cannot be presented: This would require a similar project without prototyping for comparison.

The other main observation to make at this point is: because the sequential variations of interpretation-tree model matching algorithm were presented in a *set-oriented* way [8], it was quite straightforward to implement them and the alternative parallel implementations in PROSET and then compare them, in only a few weeks. The four presented programs are complete executable prototypes for the developed algorithms. They could be regarded as *executable specifications*.

One of the goals of the successor project will be to compare performance of the algorithm with that predicted by the prototype. This is what prototyping is about: experimenting with ideas for algorithms and evaluating them to make the right decisions for the next steps in the development. Purely theoretic evaluations are often not possible in practice. The main contribution of this paper are the presented techniques for parallelization of interpretation-tree model matching and the evaluation of these techniques. It is also a case study for prototyping of parallel algorithms.

## Acknowledgments

This work has been supported by the TRACS program funded by the Human Capital and Mobility program of the European Commission (contract number ERB-CHGE-CT92-0005), and the Universities of Dortmund and Edinburgh.

The authors would like to thank Andrew Fitzgibbon for the help with the IMAGINE2 system, Philippe Fillatreau and Josef Hebenstreit for the discussions on object recognition, Peter Maccallum and Neil MacDonald for support with the Edinburgh Parallel Computing Centre facilities, and Henri Bal and Peter Maccallum for the comments on drafts of this paper.

## References

1. R. Alasdair, A. Bruce, J.G. Mills, and A.G. Smith. CHIMP/MPI User Guide. Technical Report EPCC-KTP-CHIMP-V2-USER 1.2, Edinburgh Parallel Computing Centre, Edinburgh, UK, June 1994.
2. N. Carriero and D. Gelernter. *How to write parallel programs*. MIT Press, 1990.
3. J. Cocke. The search for performance in scientific processors. *Communications of the ACM*, 31(3):249–253, 1988.
4. E.-E. Doberkat and D. Fox. *Software Prototyping mit SETL*. Leitfäden und Monographien der Informatik. Teubner-Verlag, 1989.
5. E.-E. Doberkat, W. Franke, U. Gutenbeil, W. Hasselbring, U. Lammers, and C. Pahl. PROSET — A Language for Prototyping with Sets. In N. Kanopoulos, editor, *Proc. Third International Workshop on Rapid System Prototyping*, pages 235–248, Research Triangle Park, NC, June 1992.
6. K.A. Faigin, S.A. Weatherford, J.P. Hoeflinger, D.A. Padua, and P.M. Petersen. The Polaris Internal Representation. *International Journal of Parallel Programming*, 22(5):553–586, 1994.
7. R.B. Fisher. Model invocation for three dimensional scene understanding. In J. McDermott, editor, *Proc. 10th International Joint Conference on Artificial Intelligence*, pages 805–807. Morgan Kaufmann, 1987.
8. R.B. Fisher. Best-first and ten other variations of the interpretation-tree model matching algorithm. DAI Research Paper No. 717, Dept. of Artificial Intelligence, University of Edinburgh, Edinburgh, UK, September 1994.
9. R.B. Fisher, A.W. Fitzgibbon, M. Waite, E. Trucco, and M.J.L Orr. Recognition of complex 3-D objects from range data. In S. Impedovo, editor, *Proc. 7th International Conference on Image Analysis and Processing*, pages 509–606, Monopoli, Bari, Italy, September 1993.

10. R.B. Fisher, D.K. Naidu, and D. Singhal. Rejection of spurious reflections in structured illumination range finders. In *Proc. 2nd Conference on Optical 3D Measurement Techniques*, Zurich, Switzerland, October 1993.

11. Message Passing Interface Forum. MPI: A Message-Passing Interface Standard. Technical Report CS-94-230, University of Tennessee, Computer Science Department, Knoxville, TN, May 1994. (published in the International Journal of Supercomputing Applications, Volume 8, Number 3/4, 1994).

12. D. Gelernter. Generative communication in Linda. *ACM Transactions on Programming Languages and Systems*, 7(1):80–112, January 1985.

13. W.E.L. Grimson. *Object Recognition By Computer: The Role of Geometric Constraints*. MIT Press, 1990.

14. W. Hasselbring. CELIP: A cellular language for image processing. *Parallel Computing*, 14(5):99–109, May 1990.

15. W. Hasselbring. Prototyping parallel algorithms with PROSET-Linda. In J. Volkert, editor, *Parallel Computation (Proc. Second International ACPC Conference)*, volume 734 of *Lecture Notes in Computer Science*, pages 135–150, Gmunden, Austria, October 1993. Springer-Verlag.

16. W. Hasselbring and R.B. Fisher. Investigating parallel interpretation-tree model matching algorithms with PROSET-Linda. DAI Research Paper No. 722, University of Edinburgh, Dept. of Artificial Intelligence, Edinburgh, UK, December 1994. (also available as Software-Technik Memo Nr. 77, University of Dortmund).

17. M.F. Kaashoek, H.E. Bal, and A.S. Tanenbaum. Experience with the distributed data structure paradigm in Linda. In *USENIX/SERC Workshop on Experiences with Building Distributed and Multiprocessor Systems*, pages 175–191, Ft. Lauderdale, FL, October 1989.

18. P. Kruchten, E. Schonberg, and J.T. Schwartz. Software prototyping using the SETL programming language. *IEEE Software*, 1(4):66–75, October 1984.

19. E.L. Lawler and D.E. Wood. Branch-and-bound methods: a survey. *Operations Research*, 14(4):699–719, July 1966.

20. J.T. Schwartz, R.B.K. Dewar, E. Dubinsky, and E. Schonberg. *Programming with Sets – An Introduction to SETL*. Springer-Verlag, 1986.

21. Scientific Computing Associates, New Haven, CT. *C-Linda User's Guide & Reference Manual*, 1992.

22. E. Trucco and R.B. Fisher. Computing surface-based representations from range images. In *Proc. IEEE International Symposium on Intelligent Control (ISIC-92)*, pages 275–280, Glasgow, UK, August 1992.

23. G.V. Wilson. Assessing the usability of parallel programming systems: The Cowichan problems. In *Proc. IFIP WG10.3 Working Conference on Programming Environments for Massively Parallel Distributed Systems*, Monte Verita, Ascona, Switzerland, April 1994. Birkhäuser Verlag AG.

# Parallel Search for Combinatorial Optimization: Genetic Algorithms, Simulated Annealing, Tabu Search and GRASP *

P. M. Pardalos¹, L. Pitsoulis¹, T. Mavridou¹ and M. G.C. Resende²

¹ Center for Applied Optimization and Department of Industrial and Systems
  Engineering, University of Florida, Gainesville, FL 32611-6595 USA.
² AT&T Bell Laboratories, Room 2D-152, 600 Mountain Avenue, Murray Hill, NJ
  07974-2070, USA.

Abstract. In this paper we review parallel search techniques for approximating the global optimal solution of combinatorial optimization
problems. Recent developments on parallel implementation of genetic
algorithms, simulated annealing, tabu search, and greedy randomized
adaptive search procedures (GRASP) are discussed.

Key words: Parallel Search, Heuristics, Genetic Algorithms, Simulated
Annealing, Tabu Search, GRASP, Parallel Computing.

## 1. Introduction

Search techniques are fundamental problem-solving methods in computer science
and operations research. Search algorithms have been used to solve many classes
of problems, including path-finding problems, two-player games and constraint
satisfaction problems. Classical examples of path-finding problems include many
combinatorial optimization problems (e.g. integer programming) and puzzles
(e.g. Rubik's cube, 8-tile Puzzle). Chess, backgammon, and othello belong to
the class of two player games, while a classic example of a constraint satisfaction
problem is the eight-queens problem.

For NP-hard combinatorial optimization problems, exact search algorithms
such as branch and bound, may degenerate to complete enumeration. For that
reason, exact approaches limits us to solve only moderately sized problem instances, due to the exponential increase in CPU time when problem size increases. Therefore, in practice, heuristic search algorithms are necessary to
find sub-optimal solutions to these problems. For large-scale problems, one of
the main implications of heuristic search is its computational complexity. Efficient parallel implementation of search algorithms can significantly increase the

* Invited paper, Workshop on "Parallel Algorithms for Irregularly Structured Problems, Lyon, France (September 4-6, 1995).

Etymologically, the word heuristic comes from the Greek word heuriskein, meaning
the Greek mathematician and inventor Archimedes (ca. 287 B.C.) is known for the
famous Heureka! when he discovered a method for determining the purity of gold.

# Parallel Search for Combinatorial Optimization: Genetic Algorithms, Simulated Annealing, Tabu Search and GRASP *

P. M. Pardalos[1], L.Pitsoulis[1], T. Mavridou[1], and M. G.C. Resende[2]

[1] Center for Applied Optimization and Department of Industrial and Systems Engineering, University of Florida, Gainesville, FL 32611-6595 USA
[2] AT&T Bell Laboratories, Room 2D-152, 600 Mountain Avenue, Murray Hill, NJ 07974-2070 USA

**Abstract.** In this paper, we review parallel search techniques for approximating the global optimal solution of combinatorial optimization problems. Recent developments on parallel implementation of genetic algorithms, simulated annealing, tabu search, and greedy randomized adaptive search procedures (GRASP) are discussed.
Key words: Parallel Search, Heuristics, Genetic Algorithms, Simulated Annealing, Tabu Search, GRASP, Parallel Computing.

## 1  Introduction

Search techniques are fundamental problem-solving methods in computer science and operations research. Search algorithms have been used to solve many classes of problems, including *path-finding problems, two-player games* and *constraint satisfaction problems*. Classical examples of path-finding problems include many combinatorial optimization problems (e.g. integer programming) and puzzles (e.g. Rubic's cube, Eight Puzzle). Chess, backgammon, and othello belong to the class of two player games, while a classic example of a constraint satisfaction problem is the eight-queens problem.

For $\mathcal{N}P$-hard combinatorial optimization problems, exact search algorithms, such as branch and bound, may degenerate to complete enumeration. For that reason, exact approaches limit us to solve only moderately sized problem instances, due to the exponential increase in CPU time when problem size increases. Therefore, in practice, heuristic [3] search algorithms are necessary to find sub-optimal solutions to these problems. For large-scale problems, one of the main limitations of heuristic search is its computational complexity. Efficient parallel implementation of search algorithms can significantly increase the

---

* invited paper, Workshop on "Parallel Algorithms for Irregularly Structured Problems" Lyon, France (September 4–6, 1995)

[3] Etymologically the word *heuristic* comes from the Greek word *heuriskein* to discover; the Greek mathematician and inventor Archimedes (287–212 B.C.) is known for the famous *Heureka!* when he discovered a method for determining the purity of gold.

size of the problems that can be solved. While there is a large body of work on search algorithms, work on parallel search algorithms is relatively sparse.

In this paper, we explore different approaches of parallel heuristic search for solving combinatorial optimization problems. We focus on issues of parallelizing genetic algorithms, simulated annealing, tabu (or taboo) search, and GRASP (greedy randomized adaptive search procedures). These heuristic methods have been used to approximately solve a wide spectrum of combinatorial optimization problems.

## 2 Parallel Genetic Algorithms

In the 1960's, biologists began to use digital computers to perform simulations of genetic systems. Although these studies were aimed at understanding natural phenomena, some were not too distant from the modern notion of a genetic algorithm (GA). Genetic algorithms, as they are used today, were first introduced by John Holland [23]. Genetic algorithms try to imitate the development of new and better populations among different species during evolution, just as their biological counterparts. Unlike most standard heuristic algorithms, GAs use information of a population of individuals (solutions) when they conduct their search for better solutions and not only information from a single individual. GAs have been applied to a number of problems in combinatorial optimization. In particular, the development of parallel computers has made this an interesting approach.

A GA aims at computing sub-optimal solutions by letting a set of random solutions undergo a sequence of unary and binary transformations governed by a selection scheme biased towards high-quality solutions. Solutions to optimization problems can often be coded to strings of finite length. The GAs work on these strings [23]. The encoding is done through the structure named *chromosomes*, where each chromosome is made up of units called *genes*. The values of each gene are binary, and are sometimes called *alleles*. The problem is encoded by representing all its variables in binary form and placing them together in a single chromosome. A fitness function evaluates the quality of a solution represented by a chromosome.

There are several critical parts which strongly affect the success of genetic algorithms:

- Representation of the solutions.
- Generation of the initial population.
- Selection of individuals in an old population that will be allowed to affect the individuals of a new population. In terms of evolution, this relates to the selection of suitable parents in the new population.
- Genetic operators, such as crossover and mutation, i.e. how to recombine the genetic heritage from the parents in the previous generation.

If $P(t)$ denotes the population at time $t$, the GA can be described as in Figure (1).

---

**Layout of Genetic Algorithm**

**Input:** *A problem instance*

**Output:** *A (sub-optimal) solution*

1. $t = 0$, initialize $P(t)$, and evaluate the fitness of the individuals in $P(t)$

2. **while** (termination condition is not satisfied) **do**
   (a) $t = t + 1$
   (b) Select $P(t)$, recombine $P(t)$ and evaluate $P(t)$

3. Output the best solution among all the population as
   the (sub-optimal) solution.

---

**Fig. 1.** Layout of Genetic Algorithm

$P(0)$ is usually generated at random. The evaluation of a population $P(t)$ involves computing the fitness of the individuals and checking if the current population satisfies certain termination conditions. Types of termination rules include:

– A given time limit which is exceeded.
– The population is dominated by a few individuals.
– The best objective function value of the populations is constant over a given number of generations.

Due to their inherent parallel properties, GAs have been successfully implemented on parallel computers, introducing this way a new group of GAs, *Parallel Genetic Algorithms* (PGAs). In a PGA, the population is divided into subpopulations and an independent GA is performed on each of these subpopulations. Furthermore, the best individuals of a local population are transferred to the other subpopulations. Communication among the subpopulations is established to facilitate the operations of selection and recombination. There are two types of communication [34]: (1) *among all nodes* where the best string in each subpopulation is broadcasted to all the other subpopulations, and (2) *among the neighboring nodes*, i.e. only the neighboring subpopulations receive the best strings.

The most important aspects of PGAs, which result in a considerable speedup relative to sequential GAs, are the following [25]:

– *Local selection*, i.e. a selection of an individual in a neighborhood is introduced, in contrast with the selection in original GAs which is performed by considering the whole population.

- *Asynchronous behavior* which allows the evolution of different population structures at different speeds, possibly resulting in an overall improvement of the algorithm in terms of CPU time.
- *Reliability* in computation performance, i.e. the performance of one processor does not affect the performance of the other processors.

Jog et al. [25] consider two basic categories of *parallel genetic algorithms*:

1. The *coarse-grained* PGAs, where subpopulations are allocated to each processor of the parallel machine. The selection and recombination steps are performed within a subpopulation.
2. The *fine-grained* PGAs, where a single individual or a small number of individuals are allocated to each processor.

In the same reference, a review of parallel genetic algorithms applied to the *traveling salesman problem* (TSP) is presented. A PGA developed by Suh and Gucht [51], has been applied to TSPs having 100–1000 cities. PGAs without selection and crossover, so called *independent strategies* were used. These algorithms consist of runing an "unlimited" number of independent sequential local searches in parallel. PGAs with *low amount of local improvement* were used and performed better in terms of quality solution than the independent strategies. In terms of computational time, the PGA showed nearly a linear-speedup for various TSPs, using up to 90 processors. The algorithms were run on a BBN Butterfly.

Another implementation of a PGA applied to the TSP can be found in [21], where an asynchronous PGA, called ASPARAGOS, is presented in detail. An application of ASPARAGOS was also presented by Muhlenbein [33] for the *quadratic assignment problem* (QAP) using a polysexual voting recombination operator. The PGA was implemented on QAPs of size 30 and 36 and for TSPs of size 40 and 50 with known solutions. The algorithm found a new optimum for the Steinberg's problem (QAP of size 36). The numbers of processors used to run this problem were 16, 32, and 64. The 64 processor implementation (on a system with distributed memory) gave by far the best results in terms of computational time.

Furthermore, Battiti and Tecchiolli [5] presented parallelization schemes of genetic algorithms and tabu search for combinatorial optimization problems and in particular for *quadratic assignment* and *N-k problems* giving indicative experimental results.

Tanese [53] presents a parallel genetic algorithm implemented on a 64-processor NCUBE/six hypercube. Each processor runs the algorithm on each own subpopulation (coarse-grained PGA), and sends in an adjustable frequency a portion of good individuals to one of its neighboring processors. Each exchange takes place along a different dimension of the hypercube. The PGA is applied to a function optimization problem and its performance is compared with the corresponding GA, which is found to be similar. In addition, the PGA achieves comparable results with near linear-speedup.

Pettey et al. [43] proposed an "island model" that restricts the communication among the subpopulations to some adjacent interconnected subpopulations [30]. The PGA was tested on four of DeJong's testbed of functions [14]. Population sizes of 50 to 800 were used, with the best answer in terms of quality solution corresponded to a population of size 50, which is approximately the theoretical optimal population size. The algorithm was implemented on an Intel *iPSC*, a message-based multiprocessor system with a binary *n-cube* interconnection network.

More recently, Lee and Kim [30] developed PGAs, based on the island model, for solving job scheduling problems with generally weighted earliness and tardiness penalties (GWET), satisfying specific properties, such as the *V-shaped schedule* around the due date. A binary representation scheme is used to code the job schedules into chromosomes. A GA is developed by parallelizing the population into subgroups, each of which keeps its distinct feasible schedules. The initial population is constructed so that the resulting genotype sequence satisfies the *V-shaped schedule*. Two different reproduction methods are employed, the *roulette wheel selection* and the *N-best selection method*. Also, the *crossover* and *mutation* operators are implemented in parallel. Several instances of problems with subpopulations of 30 chromosomes (jobs) and total population size of 100 to 200 where used to evaluate the efficiency of the PGA. The authors report that the roulette wheel selection scheme performs far better than the *N*-best selection in terms of quality solution, though the *N*-best selection gives good results in terms of CPU time. The mutation operator seems to improve the performance of the PGA. The paper concludes, showing the superior performance of the parallel algorithm when compared to the sequential GA. In terms of CPU time, the parallelization of the population into several groups speeds up the convergence of the GAs as the size of the problem increases.

Parallel genetic algorithms have been applied to the graph partition problem [29], scheduling problems [11], and global optimization problems [49].

## 3   Parallel Simulated Annealing

Since the simulated annealing method (SA) was proposed several years ago by Kirkpatrick et al. [27], based on the pioneering work of Metropolis et al. [32], much research has been accomplished regarding its implementation (sequential and parallel) to solve a variety of difficult combinatorial optimization problems. Simulated annealing is based on the analogy between statistical mechanics and combinatorial optimization. The term *annealing* refers to the process of a thermal system by first melting at high temperatures and then lowering the temperature slowly based on an annealing schedule, until the vicinity of the solidification temperature is reached, where the system is allowed to reach the *ground state* (the lowest energy state of the system). Simulated annealing is a simple Monte Carlo approach to simulate the behavior of this system to achieve thermal equilibrium at a given temperature in a given annealing schedule. This analogy has been applied in solving combinatorial optimization problems. Given an objective function $f(x)$ over a feasible domain $D$, a generic simulated annealing algorithm for finding the global minimum of $f(x)$ is given in Figure 2.

---

## Layout of Simulated Annealing

**Input:** *A problem instance*

**Output:** *A (sub-optimal) solution*

1. Generate an initial solution at random and initialize the temperature $T$.

2. **while** $(T > 0)$ **do**
   (a) **while** (thermal equilibrium not reached) **do**
      (i) Generate a neighbor state at random and evaluate the change in energy level $\Delta E$.

      (ii) If $\Delta E < 0$ update current state with new state.

      (iii) If $\Delta E \geq 0$ update current state with new state with probability $e^{\frac{-\Delta E}{K_B T}}$, where $K_B$ is a constant.

   (b) Decrease temperature $T$ according to annealing schedule.

3. Output the solution having the lowest energy.

---

**Fig. 2.** Layout of Simulated Annealing

An introduction to general concepts of parallel simulated annealing techniques can be found in Aarts and Korst [1]. Several parallel algorithms based on SA have been implemented for a variety of combinatorial optimization problems. In the context of annealing, a parallel implementation can be presented in two forms [47]: (1) *functional parallelism*, which uses multiple processors to evaluate different phases of a single move, (2) *data parallelism*, which uses different processors or group of processors to propose and evaluate moves independently. The second form has the advantage of "easily scaling the algorithm to large ensembles of processors."

The *standard-cell approach* is a semi-custom designing method in which functional building blocks, called *cells*, are used to construct a part of, or an entire, VLSI chip [47]. Two basic approaches have been applied to the placement problem [47] – *constructive* methods and *iterative* methods. The SA technique belongs to the second group, as an approach that uses probabilistic hill climbing to avoid local minima. The `TimberWolf` program has been proposed as a version of SA implemented for the cell placement problem. It has been shown to provide enormous chip area savings compared to the already existed standard methods of cell layout. Jones and Banerjec [26] developed a parallel algorithm based on `TimberWolf`, where multiple cell moves are proposed and evaluated by using pairs of processors. The algorithm was implemented on a iPSC/1 Hypercube. Rose et al. [45] presented two parallel algorithms for the same problem. The *Heuristic Spanning* approach replaces the high temperature portion of simulated annealing, assigning cells to fixed sub-areas of the chip. The *Section Annealing* approach is used to speed-up the low temperature portion of simulated annealing. The placement here is geographically divided and the pieces are assigned to separate processors. Other parallel algorithms based on SA and implemented for the cell placement problem can be found in [8, 47, 55].

Greening [22] examines the *asynchronous parallel* SA algorithm in relation with the effects of calculation errors resulting from the parallel implementation or an approximate cost function. More specifically, in Greening's work, the effects of *instantaneous* and *accumulated* errors are analyzed. The first category contains the errors which result as the difference between the true and inaccurate costs computed at a given time. An accumulated error is the sum of a stream of instantaneous errors. The author proves a direct connection between the accumulated errors measured in previous research work, and annealing properties.

Most recently, Boissin and Lutton [6] proposed a new SA algorithm that can be efficiently implemented on a massively parallel computer. A comparison to the sequential algorithm has been presented by testing both algorithms on two classical combinatorial optimization problems: (1) the *quadratic sum assignment problem* and (2) the *minimization of an unconstrained 0–1 quadratic function*. The numerical results showed that the parallel algorithm converges to high-quality suboptimal solutions. For the problem of minimization of quadratic functions with 1000 variables, the parallel implementation on a 16K Connection Machine was 3.3 times faster than the sequential algorithm implemented on a SPARC 2 workstation, for the same quality of solution.

# 4  Parallel Tabu Search

Tabu search (TS), first introduced by Glover [18, 19], is a heuristic procedure to find good solutions to combinatorial optimization problems. A *tabu list* is a set of solutions determined by historical information from the last $t$ iterations of the algorithm, where $t$ is fixed or is a variable that depends on the state of the search, or a particular problem. At each iteration, given the current solution $x$ and its corresponding neighborhood $N(x)$, the procedure moves to the solution in the neighborhood $N(x)$ that most improves the objective function. However, moves that lead to solutions on the tabu list are forbidden, or are tabu. If there are no improving moves, TS chooses the move which least changes the objective function value. The tabu list avoids returning to the local optimum from which the procedure has recently escaped. A basic element of tabu search is the *aspi-*

*ration* criterion, which determines when a move is admissible despite being on the tabu list. One *termination* criterion for the tabu procedure is a limit in the number of consecutive moves for which no improvement occurs. Given an objective function $f(x)$ over a feasible domain $D$, a generic tabu search for finding an approximation of the global minimum of $f(x)$ is given in Figure 3.

---

**Layout of Tabu Search**

**Input:** *A problem instance*

**Output:** *A (sub-optimal) solution*

1. Initialization:
    (a) Generate an initial solution $x$ and set $x^* = x$;
    (b) Initialize the tabu list $T = \emptyset$;
    (c) Set iteration counters $k = 0$ and $l = 0$;

2. **while** $(N(x) \setminus T \neq \emptyset)$ **do**
    (a) $k = k + 1; l = l + 1$;
    (b) Select $x$ as the best solution from set $N(x) \setminus T$;
    (c) If $f(x) < f(x^*)$ then update $x^* = x$ and set $l = 0$;
    (d) If $k = \overline{k}$ or if $l = \overline{l}$ go to step 3;

3. Output the best solution found $x^*$;

---

**Fig. 3.** Layout of Tabu Search

A more detailed description of the main features, aspects, applications and extensions of tabu search, can be found in [20]. Several implementations of parallel algorithms based on TS have been developed for classical optimization problems, such as TSP and QAP, which will be discussed below.

Taillard [52] presents two implementations of parallel TS for the quadratic assignment problem. Computational results on instances of size up to 64 are reported. The form of TS considered is claimed to be more robust than earlier implementations, since it requires less computational effort and uses only the basic elements of TS (moves to neighboring solutions, tabu list, aspiration function). The neighborhood used is *2-exchange*. The tabu list is made up of pairs $(i, j)$ of interchanged units both of which are placed at locations they had occupied within the last $s$ iterations, where $s$ is the size of tabu list. The size $s$ changes its value randomly within some specified interval during the search. The *aspiration criterion* is introduced to allow the tabu moves to be chosen, if both interchanged units are assigned to locations they have not occupied within the $t$ most recent iterations. In the first method, the neighborhood is divided into $p$ parts of approximately the same size. Each part is distributed for evaluation to one of $p$ different processors. Using a number of processors proportional to the size of the problem (precisely $p = n/10$), the complexity is reduced by a factor of $n$, where $n$ is the size of the problem. Moreover, the computational results showed improvement to the quality of solution for many large problems and the best published solutions of other problems have been found. The second method performs independent searches, each of which starts with a different initial solution. The parallel algorithm was implemented on a ring of 10 transputers (T800C-G20S). The computational complexity of this algorithm is less than that of earlier TS implementations for QAP by a factor $n$.

Another parallel tabu search algorithm for solving the quadratic assignment problem has been developed by Chakrapani and Skorin-Kapov [9]. The algorithm includes elements of TS, such as aspiration criterion, dynamically changing tabu list sizes and long-term memory [18]. A new intensification strategy is proposed, based on the intermediate term memory, restricting the searches in a neighborhood. This results in less amount of computational effort during one iteration since the procedure does not examine the entire neighborhood. A massively parallel implementation was tested on the Connection Machine CM-2 for large QAPs of size ranging from $n = 42$ to $100$, using $n^2$ processors. The new tabu strategy gave good results in terms of quality of solutions. For problems up to size $n = 90$, it obtained the best known solutions or close to those. For size $n = 100$, every previously best solution found was improved upon.

Battiti and Tecchiolli [5] describe a parallelization scheme for tabu search called *reactive* tabu scheme, and apply it to the quadratic assignment problem and the $N$-$k$ problem with the objective of achieving a speedup in the order of the number of processors. In the reactive tabu search, each processor executes an independent search. Furthermore, the same problems are solved by a parallel genetic algorithm in which the interaction between different search processes is strong because the generation of new candidate points depends on the consideration of many members of the population.

A tabu search for the traveling salesman problem has been proposed by Fiechter [17], and was tested on instances having 500 to 10000 vertices. A new estimation of the asymptotic normalized length of the shortest tour through points uniformly distributed in the unit square is given. Numerical results and speedups obtained by the implementation of the algorithm on a network of transputers show the efficiency of the parallel algorithm.

## 5 Parallel GRASP

A GRASP [16] is an iterative process for finding approximate solutions to combinatorial optimization. Let, as before, $f(x)$ denote the objective function to be minimized over a feasible domain $D$. A generic layout of GRASP is given in Figure 4. The GRASP iterations terminate when some stopping criterion, such

---

**Layout of GRASP**

**Input:** *A problem instance*

**Output:** *A (sub-optimal) solution*

1. Initialization: set $x^* = \infty$;
2. **while** (stopping criterion not satisfied) **do**
   (a) Construct a greedy randomized solution $x$;
   (b) Find local minimum $\tilde{x}$ in neighborhood $N(x)$ of $x$;
   (c) If $f(\tilde{x}) < f(x^*)$ then update $x^* = \tilde{x}$;
3. Output the best solution found $x^*$;

---

**Fig. 4.** Layout of GRASP

as maximum number of iterations, is satisfied. Each iteration consists of a construction phase, and a local search phase. If an improved solution is found, then the incumbent is updated. A high-level description of these two phases is given next.

In the construction phase, a feasible solution is built up, one element at a time. The choice of the next element to be added is determined by ordering all elements in a candidate list with respect to a greedy function. An element from the candidate list is randomly chosen from among the best candidates in the list, but is not necessarily the top candidate. Figure 5 displays a generic layout for the construction phase of a GRASP. The solution set $S$ is initialized empty, and the construction iterations are repeated until the solution is built. To do this, the restricted candidate list is setup. This candidate list contains a subset of candidates that are well ordered with respect to the greedy function. A candidate selected from the list at random is added to the solution. The greedy function is adapted to take into account the selected element.

The solutions generated in the construction are not guaranteed to be locally optimal and therefore local search is applied to produce a locally optimal solution. Figure 6 illustrates a generic local search procedure.

GRASP can be easily implemented on an MIMD multi-processor environment. Each processor can be initialized with its own copy of the procedure, the problem data, and independent pseudo-random number sequences. The GRASP iterations are then independently executed in parallel and the best solution found over all processors is the GRASP solution. This approach was implemented by Pardalos, Pitsoulis, and Resende [39] to approximately solve instances of the QAP of dimension up to $n = 128$. On a Kendall Square KRS-1 parallel computer with 128 processors (of which only 64 were utilized), the authors were able

---

**Layout of GRASP Construction Phase**

**Input:** *A problem instance and pseudo random number stream*

**Output:** *A (sub-optimal) solution*

1. Initialization: set solution $S = \emptyset$;
2. **while** (solution construction not done) **do**
   (a) Using greedy function, make restricted candidate list (RCL);
   (b) At random, select element $s$ from RCL;
   (c) Place $s$ in solution, i.e. $S = S \cup \{s\}$;
   (d) Change greedy function to take into account updated $S$;
3. Output the solution $x$ corresponding to set $S$;

---

**Fig. 5.** Layout of GRASP Construction Phase

---

**Layout of GRASP Local Search Phase**

**Input:** *A problem instance, solution $x$, neighborhood $N(x)$*

**Output:** *A locally-optimal solution $\tilde{x}$*

1. **while** ($x$ not locally optimal) **do**
   (a) Find $\tilde{x} \in N(x)$ with $f(\tilde{x}) < f(x)$;
   (b) Update $x = \tilde{x}$;
3. Output the locally optimal solution $\tilde{x}$;

---

**Fig. 6.** Layout of GRASP Local Search Phase

to achieve on average a speedup factor of 62 and speedup factors of 130 and 221 on single instances of dimensions $n = 30$ and $n = 22$, respectively.

Another approach to implement GRASP in parallel was proposed by Feo, Resende, and Smith [15], where the problem being optimized is decomposed into many smaller problems, and each processor is given a set of small problems, that are solved with GRASP one after the other. Using this approach to approximately solve large instances of the maximum independent set problem, the authors were able to achieve almost linear speedup on an eight processor Alliant FX/80 MIMD computer.

# 6 Concluding Remarks

In the last ten years, we have witnessed an explosion and availability of parallel, multiprocessing computers. Since most of the interesting combinatorial optimization problems are $\mathcal{N}P$-hard, it is quite natural to consider implementing algorithms on such environments. In this brief survey, we summarized recent developments in parallel implementations of several classes of new heuristics for combinatorial optimization.

# References

1. E. AARTS AND J. KORST, *Simulated Annealing and Boltzmann Machines – A Stochastic Approach to Combinatorial Optimization and Neural Computing*, John Wiley and Sons, 1989.
2. S.G. AKL, D.T. BARNARD AND R.J. DORAN, *Design, Analysis, and Implementation of a Parallel Tree Search Algorithm*, IEEE Transactions on Pattern Analysis and Machine Intelligence, Vol. PAMI-4 (1982), pp. 192–203.
3. I. ALTH, *A Parallel Game Tree Search Algorithm with a Linear Speedup*, Journal of Algorithms 15 (1993), pp. 175–198.
4. G.Y. ANANTH, V. KUMAR AND P. M. PARDALOS, *Parallel Processing of Discrete Optimization Problems*, In Encyclopedia of Microcomputers Vol. 13 (1993), pp. 129–147, Marcel Dekker Inc., New York.
5. R. BATTITI AND G. TECCHIOLLI, *Parallel Biased Search for Combinatorial Optimization: Genetic Algorithms and TABU*, Microprocessors and Microsystems 16 (1992), pp. 351–367.
6. N. BOISSIN AND J.-L. LUTTON, *A Parallel Simulated Annealing Algorithm*, Parallel Computing, 19 (1993), pp. 859–872.
7. R.J. BROUWER AND P. BANERJEE, *A Parallel Simulated Annealing Algorithm for Channel Routing on a Hypercube Multiprocessor*, Proceedings of 1988 IEEE International Conference on Computer Design, pp. 4–7.
8. A. CASOTTO AND A. SANNGIOVANNI-VINCENTELLI, *Placement of Standard Cells Using Simulated Annealing on the Connection Machine*, Proceedings ICCAD, 1987, pp. 350–352.
9. J. CHAKRAPANI AND J. SKORIN-KAPOV, *Massively Parallel Tabu Search for the Quadratic Assignment Problem*, Annals of Operation Research, 41 (1993), pp. 327–341.
10. R.D. CHAMBERLAIN, M.N. EDELMAN, M.A. FRANKLIN AND E.E. WITTE, *Simulated Annealing on a Multiprocessor*, Proceedings of 1988 IEEE International Conference on Computer Design, pp. 540–544.
11. G.A. CLEVELAND AND S.F. SMITH, *Using Genetic Algorithms to Schedule Flow Shop Releases*, Proceeding of the Third International Conference on Genetic Algorithms, (1990), Morgan Kaufmann, Los Altos, CA.
12. J.P. COHOON, S.U. HEGDE, W.N. MARTIN AND D. RICHARDS, *Punctuated Equilibria: A Parallel Genetic Algorithm*, Proceedings of the Second International Conference on Genetic Algorithms and their Applications, J.J. Grefenstette (editor), July 1987, pp. 148–154.
13. D. CVIJOVIC AND J. KLINOWSKI, *Taboo Search: An Approach to the Multiple Minima Problem*, Science, 267 (1995), pp. 664–666.

14. K.A. DE JONG, *An Analysis fo the Behavior of a Class of Genetic Adaptive Systems*, Doctoral dissertation, Department of Computer and Communication Sciences, University of Michigan, 1975.

15. T.A. FEO, M.G.C. RESENDE AND S.H. SMITH, *A Greedy Randomized Adaptive Search Procedure for Maximum Independent Set*, Operations Research, 42 (1994), pp. 860–878.

16. T.A. FEO AND M.G.C. RESENDE, *Greedy Randomized Adaptive Search Procedures*, Journal of Global Optimization, 6 (1995), pp. 109–133.

17. C.-N. FIECHTER, *A Parallel Tabu Search Algorithm for Large Traveling Salesman Problems*, Discrete Applied Mathematics, 51 (1994), pp. 243–267.

18. F. GLOVER, *Tabu Search. Part I*, ORSA J. Comput., 1 (1989), pp. 190–206.

19. F. GLOVER, *Tabu Search. Part II*, ORSA J. Comput., 2 (1990), pp. 4–32.

20. F. GLOVER, E. TAILLARD AND D. DE WERRA, *A User's Guide to Tabu Search*, Annals of Operation Research, 41 (1993), pp. 3–28.

21. M. GORGES-SCHLEUTER, *ASPARAGOS: A Parallel Genetic Algorithm and Population Genetics*, Lecture Notes on Computer Science, Vol. 565 (1989), pp. 407–518.

22. D.R. GREENING, *Asynchronous Parallel Simulated Annealing*, Lectures in Complex Systems, Vol. 3 (1990), pp. 497–505.

23. J.H. HOLLAND, *Adaptation in Natural and Artificial Systems*, University of Michigan Press, Ann Arbor, MI, 1975.

24. S. R. HUANG AND L.S. DAVIS, *Speedup Analysis of Centralized Parallel Heuristic Search Algorithms*, Proceedings of the International Conference on Parallel Processing, Vol. 3. Algorithms and Applications (1990), pp. 18–21.

25. P. JOG, J.Y. SUH AND D. VAN GUCHT, *Parallel Genetic Algorithms Applied to the Traveling Salesman Problem*, SIAM Journal of Optimization, 1 (1991), pp.515–529.

26. M. JONES AND P. BANERJEE, *Performance of a Parallel Algorithm for Standard Cell Placement on the Intel Hypercube*, Proceedings of the 24th Design Automation Conference, 1987, pp. 807–813.

27. S. KIRKPATRICK, C.D. GELLAT JR. AND M.P. VECCHI, *Optimization by Simulated Annealing*, Science, 220 (1983), pp. 671–680.

28. V. KUMAR AND L.N. KANAL, *Parallel Branch-and-Bound Formulations for AND/OR Tree Search*, IEEE Transactions on Pattern Analysis and Machine Intelligence, Vol. PAMI-6 (1984), pp. 768–778.

29. G. VON LASZEWSKI, *Intelligent Structural Operators for K-Way Graph Partitioning Problem*, Proceeding of the Fourth International Conference on Genetic Algorithms, (1991), Morgan Kaufmann, San Mateo, CA.

30. C.Y. LEE AND S.J. KIM, *Parallel Genetic Algorithms for the Earliness-Tardiness Job Scheduling Problem with General Penalty Weights*, Computers & Ind. Eng., 28 (1995), pp. 231–243.

31. A. MAHANTI AND C.J. DANIELS, *A SIMD Approach to Parallel Heuristic Search*, Artificial Intelligence, 10 (1993), pp. 243–282.

32. N. METROPOLIS, A. ROSENBLUTH, M. ROSENBLUTH, A. TELLER AND E. TELLER, *Equation of State Calculations by Fast Computing Machines*, Journal of Chemical Physics, 21 (1953), pp. 1087–1092.

33. H. MUHLENBEIN, *Parallel Genetic Algorithms, Population Genetics and Combinatorial Optimization*, Lecture Notes in Computer Science, Vol. 565 (1989), pp. 398–406.

34. H. MUHLENBEIN, M. SCHOMISCH AND J. BORN, *The Parallel Genetic Algorithm as Function Optimizer*, Proceedings on an International Conference on Genetic Algorithms, (1991).

35. T.A. MARSLAND AND F. POPOWICH, *Parallel Game-Tree Search*, IEEE Transactions on Pattern Analysis and Machine Intelligence, Vol. PAMI-7 (1985), pp. 442–452.

36. P. M. PARDALOS, Y. LI AND K. A. MURTHY, *Computational Experience with Parallel Algorithms for Solving the Quadratic Assignment Problem*, In Computer Science and Operations Research: New Developments in their Interface, O. Balci, R. Sharda, S.A. Zenios (eds.), Pergamon Press, pp. 267–278 (1992).

37. P. M. PARDALOS, AND G. GUISEWITE, *Parallel Computing in Nonconvex Programming*, Annals of Operations Research 43 (1993), pp. 87–107.

38. P. M. PARDALOS, A. T. PHILLIPS AND J. B. ROSEN, *Topics in Parallel Computing in Mathematical Programming*, Science Press, 1993.

39. P. M. PARDALOS, L. S. PITSOULIS AND M.G.C. RESENDE, *A Parallel GRASP Implementation for the Quadratic Assignment Problem*, In *Solving Irregular Problems in Parallel: State of the Art* (Editors: A. Ferreira and J. Rolim), Kluwer Academic Publishers (1995).

40. P.M. PARDALOS, M.G.C. RESENDE, AND K.G. RAMAKRISHNAN (Editors), *Parallel Processing of Discrete Optimization Problems*, DIMACS Series Vol. 22, American Mathematical Society, (1995).

41. P.M. PARDALOS AND H. WOLKOWICZ (Editors), *Quadratic Assignment and Related Problems*, DIMACS Series Vol. 16, American Mathematical Society (1994).

42. C. PETERSON, *Parallel Distributed Approaches to Combinatorial Optimization: Benchmark Studies on Traveling Salesman Problem*, Neural Computation, Vol. 2, (1990), pp. 261–269.

43. C.B. PETTEY, M.R. LEUZE AND J.J. GREFENSTETTE, *A Parallel Genetic Algorithm*, Proceedings of the Second International Conference on Genetic Algorithms and their Applications, J.J. Grefenstette (editor), July 1987, pp. 155–161.

44. C. POWLER, C. FERGUSON AND R. E. KORF, *Parallel Heuristic Search: Two Approaches*, In Parallel Algorithms for Machine Intelligence and Vision, V. Kumar, P.S. Gopalakrishnan and L.N. (eds.), Springer-Verlag, pp. 42–65 (1990).

45. J.S. ROSE, W.M. SNELGROVE AND Z.G. VRANESIC, *Parallel Standard Cell Placement Algorithms with Quality Equivalent to Simulated Annealing*, IEEE Transactions on Computer-Aided Design, Vol. 7 (1988), pp. 387–396.

46. sc A.V. Sannier and E.D. Goodman, *Genetic Learning Procedures in Distributed Environments*, Proceedings of the Second International Conference on Genetic Algorithms and their Applications, J.J. Grefenstette (editor), July 1987, pp. 162–169.

47. J.S. SARGENT, *A Parallel Row-Based Algorithm with Error Control for Standard-Cell Placement on a Hypercube Multiprocessor*, Thesis, University of Illinois, Urbana-Illinois, 1988.

48. B. SHIRAZI, M. WANG AND G. PATHAK, *Analysis and Evaluation of Heuristic Methods for Static Task Scheduling*, Journal of Parallel and Distributed Computing 10 (1990), pp. 222–232.

49. P.S. DE SOUZA, *Asynchronous Organizations for Multi-Algorithm Problems*, Ph.D. Thesis, Department of Electrical and Computer Engineering, Carnegie Mellon University, 1993.

50. R. SHONKWILER AND E.V. VLECK, *Parallel Speed-Up of Monte Carlo methods for Global Optimization*, Journal of Complexity 10 (1994), pp. 64–95.

51. J. SUH AND D. VAN GUCHT, *Distributed genetic Algorithms*, Tech. Report 225, Computer Science Department, Indiana University, Bloomington, IN, July 1987.

52. E. TAILLARD, *Robust Taboo Search for the Quadratic Assignment Problem*, Parallel Computing, 17 (1991), pp. 443–445.

53. R. TANESE, *Parallel Genetic Algorithm for a Hypercube*, Proceedings of the Second International Conference on Genetic Algorithms and their Applications, J.J. Grefenstette (editor), July 1987, pp. 177–183.

54. N.L.J. ULDER, E.H.L. AARTS, H. -J. BANDELT, P.J.M. VAN LAARHOVEN AND E. PESCH, *Genetic Local Search Algorithms for the Traveling Salesman Problem*, In **Lecture Notes in Computer Science**, Parallel Problem Solving from Nature-Proceedings of 1st Workshop, PPSN 1, Vol. 496 (1991), pp. 109–116.

55. C.-P. WONG AND R.-D. FIEBRICH, *Simulated Annealing-Based Circuit Placement on the Connection Machine System*, Proceedings of International Conference on Computer Design (ICCD '87), 1987, pp. 78–82.

# Better Algorithms for Parallel Backtracking

Peter Sanders

University of Karlsruhe, 76128 Karlsruhe, Germany
Email: sanders@ira.uka.de

**Abstract.** Many algorithms in operations research and artificial intelligence are based on the backtracking principle, i.e., depth first search in implicitly defined trees. For parallelizing these algorithms, an efficient load balancing scheme is of central importance.

Previously known load balancing algorithms either require a message for each tree node or they only work efficiently for large search trees. This paper introduces new randomized dynamic load balancing algorithms for tree structured computations, a generalization of backtrack search. These algorithms only need to communicate when necessary and have an asymptotically optimal scalability for hypercubes, butterflies and related networks, and an improved scalability for meshes and hierarchical networks like fat trees.

Keywords: Analysis of randomized algorithms, depth first search, distributed memory, divide and conquer, load balancing, parallel backtracking.

## 1 Introduction

Load balancing is one of the central issues in parallel computing. Since for many applications it is almost impossible to predict how much computation a given subproblem involves, dynamic load balancing strategies are needed which are able to keep the processors (PEs) busy without incurring an undue overhead.

We discuss this in the following context (for a more detailed explication refer to Section X.Y). There are $n$ PEs which interact by exchanging messages through a network of diameter $d$. The problems to be load balanced are tree shaped computations. Initially, there is only one large root problem. Subproblems can be represented by splitting existing problems into two independent subproblems; nothing is known about the relative size of the two parts. Furthermore, a subproblem can be worked on sequentially. The only thing the load balancer knows about a subproblem is whether it is exhausted or not. The performance analysis is based on the total sequential execution time $T_{seq}$ and a bound $h$ on the height of the binary tree defined by splitting the root problem into atomic pieces.

One application domain for which this is a useful model is parallel depth first tree search (backtracking). Search trees are often very irregular and the size of a subtree is hard to predict, but it is easy to split the search space into two parts (even if the underlying tree is not binary). Note that backtrack search is a central aspect of many AI and OR applications and of parallel functional and logical programming languages.

# Better Algorithms for Parallel Backtracking

Peter Sanders

University of Karlsruhe, 76128 Karlsruhe, Germany
Email: sanders@ira.uka.de

**Abstract.** Many algorithms in operations research and artificial intelligence are based on the backtracking principle, i.e., depth first search in implicitly defined trees. For parallelizing these algorithms, an efficient load balancing scheme is of central importance.
Previously known load balancing algorithms either require sending a message for each tree node or they only work efficiently for large search trees. This paper introduces new randomized dynamic load balancing algorithms for *tree structured computations*, a generalization of backtrack search. These algorithms only need to communicate when necessary and have an asymptotically optimal scalability for hypercubes, butterflies and related networks, and an improved scalability for meshes and hierarchical networks like fat trees.

**Keywords:** Analysis of randomized algorithms, depth first search, distributed memory, divide and conquer, load balancing, parallel backtracking.

## 1 Introduction

Load balancing is one of the central issues in parallel computing. Since for many applications it is almost impossible to predict how much computation a given subproblem involves, dynamic load balancing strategies are needed which are able to keep the processors (PEs) busy without incurring an undue overhead.

We discuss this in the following context (for a more detailed explication refer to Section 2.1): There are $n$ PEs which interact by exchanging messages through a network of diameter $d$. The problems to be load balanced are *tree shaped computations*: Initially, there is only one large root problem. Subproblems can be generated by splitting existing problems into two independent subproblems; nothing is known about the relative size of the two parts. Furthermore, a subproblem can be worked on sequentially. The only thing the load balancer knows about a subproblem is whether it is exhausted or not. The performance analysis is based on the total sequential execution time $T_{seq}$ and a bound $h$ on the height of the binary tree defined by splitting the root problem into atomic pieces.

One application domain for which this is a useful model is parallel depth first tree search (backtracking). Search trees are often very irregular and the size of a subtree is hard to predict, but it is easy to split the search space into two parts (even if the underlying tree is not binary.) Note that backtrack search is a central aspect of many AI and OR applications and of parallel functional and logical programming languages.

We now go on by describing *receiver induced tree splitting*, a simple and successful scheme for parallelizing tree shaped computations in Section 1.1 which is compared to other approaches found in the literature in Section 1.2. An overview of the remainder of the paper concludes this introduction.

## 1.1 Receiver induced tree splitting

The basic principle of *Receiver induced tree splitting* is that a PE only works on a single subproblem at a time and only activates the load balancer when this subproblem is exhausted. The load balancer supplies new subproblems by requesting other PEs to split their subproblem. Idle PEs receiving a request either reject the request or redirect it to another PE. Figure 1 shows pseudocode for such a generic tree splitting algorithm.

```
put the root problem on PE 0
DOPAR on all PEs
    WHILE not finished DO
        IF subproblem is empty THEN
            get new work from load balancer
        WHILE subproblem is not empty DO
            IF there is a load request THEN
                split subproblem
                send one part to the initiator of the request
            do some work on subproblem
```

**Fig. 1.** Receiver induced tree splitting.

This approach has proved useful under a variety of circumstances [6, 14, 5, 22, 15, 25, 2, 11, 26, 7]. A major advantage of receiver induced tree splitting is that load balancing only takes place when necessary. If the sequential execution time $T_{seq}$ is large, the average size of a transmitted subproblem is also fairly large (i.e. it represents a large execution time). Productive work done on a migrated subproblem therefore makes up for the expense of communication. For sufficiently large problem sizes, most receiver induced tree splitting schemes can achieve efficiencies arbitrarily close to 1, i.e., the parallel execution time $T_{par}$ can be bounded by $(1 + \epsilon)\frac{T_{seq}}{n} + ($ lower order terms) for arbitrary $\epsilon > 0$. However, in practice it is crucial how the problem size has to be scaled with the number of PEs in order to achieve a desired efficiency. In this respect there are large differences between different load balancing strategies. We use the behavior of the lower order terms as a measure for the *scalability* of an algorithm – the smaller these terms the smaller is the problem size required for good efficiency.

In [14] it is shown that sending requests to neighboring PEs has a quite poor scalability except for the combination of low diameter interconnection networks (e.g. hypercubes) and a work splitting function which produces subproblems of nearly equal size. The basic problem of these *neighborhood polling* schemes is that highly loaded PEs are quickly surrounded by a cluster of busy PEs and are therefore unable to transmit work; subproblem transmissions at the border of these clusters only involve small subproblems which are not worth the effort of communicating them.

In [14, 15] a variety of other partner selection schemes is analyzed. There seems to be a dilemma between schemes based on local information on the one hand which may produce many vain requests to idle PEs, and global selection schemes on the other hand which incur additional message traffic and often suffer from contention at centralized schedulers. But *random polling*, i.e., selecting communication partners uniformly at random is identified as a promising scheme. Good speedups are reported for up to 1024 PEs. In [25] it is proved that random polling works in time $(1+\epsilon)\frac{T_{\text{seq}}}{n}+O(dh)$ with high probability for crossbars, butterflies, meshes and many other architectures. This is asymptotically optimal for networks with constant diameter because the sequential component for following the maximum depth branch implies a lower bound of

$$T_{\text{par}} \in \Omega\left(\frac{T_{\text{seq}}}{n}+h\right). \tag{1}$$

In [26] the asymptotic influence of message lengths and atomic grain sizes of subproblems is also investigated. Most other authors assume it to be constant. We also start with this assumption in order to free the analysis from rather uninteresting details. But in Section 6 we discuss consequences of a more detailed model. In [2] random polling is generalized to *fully strict multithreaded computations* allowing certain interactions between subproblems. An expected execution time in $O\left(\frac{T_{\text{seq}}}{n}+T_{\infty}\right)$ is proved for fully connected networks. ($T_{\infty}$ denotes the sequential component of a problem.)

On SIMD computers, load balancing is done in separate load balancing phases initiated by some triggering condition [22, 27, 11]. The best schemes use the ability of many SIMD computers to quickly compute prefix-sums: Communication partners can be matched by enumerating the busy and idle PEs respectively. Good speedups have been observed for up to 32K PEs.

## 1.2  Other related work

Another family of algorithms which are applicable to tree shaped computations are *dynamic tree embedding* algorithms [19, 23, 10]. Using our terminology, these algorithms are based on splitting the root problem into a maximum number of atomic subproblems. The tree generated by this process is on-line embedded into the interconnection network.

Building on results from [19], it is shown in [23] how randomized dynamic tree embedding algorithms can be used to perform backtracking on butterflies and hypercubes in time $O\left(\frac{T_{\text{seq}}}{n}+h\right)$ with high probability. These algorithms achieve constant efficiency for problems of size $\Omega(nh)$ meeting the lower bound from Equation (1). However, if communicating an atomic subproblem is expensive compared to solving it, the efficiency of these algorithms is limited to a quite small constant value and this figure does not improve for larger subproblems where algorithms like random polling can achieve very high efficiencies.

The situation is even worse if tree embedding is to be used on meshes because this is not possible with constant dilation. In [10], it is demonstrated how trees with $O(n)$ leaves can be deterministically embedded into an $r$-dimensional mesh in time $O\left(\sqrt[r]{nh}\right)$. It is not clear however, how useful the methods used there are for larger problem sizes.

On the other side of the spectrum, load balancing can be done with very little communication by broadcasting the root problem to all PEs and locally splitting it into individual pieces based on the PE number. Applied in a straightforward way, this technique leads to poor load balancing [3], but using it as an initialization for dynamic load balancers can yield a significant improvement. In [28], it is shown that for certain search trees with $h \in O(\log T_{\text{seq}})$ the combination of a randomized initialization scheme and a variant of random polling on meshes achieves execution times in $(1 + \epsilon)\frac{T_{\text{seq}}}{n} + O(n^{1/r})$ on the average. For $T_{\text{seq}} \in \Omega(dn)$ this is asymptotically optimal. By randomly chopping the tree into much more pieces than PEs it is even possible to devise an efficient static load balancing scheme for tree shaped computations which uses a single broadcast of the root problem as the only nonlocal operation. (Plus collecting results.)

## 1.3 Overview

The goal of this paper is to present receiver induced tree splitting algorithms which are as scalable as dynamic tree embedding schemes but retain the advantage of low communication overhead. The emphasis is on algorithms which are not only interesting from a theoretical point of view but also simple and efficient in practice.

We start by introducing a simple yet realistic model of the machine and the application in Section 2 which is later generalized in Section 6. Then, Section 3 presents a hypercube based algorithm. The PEs perform receiver induced tree splitting; communication is done with neighboring PEs. By iterating through the dimensions of the hypercube, it can be guaranteed that the load remains evenly distributed as long as "fresh" dimensions of the hypercube are available. When all dimensions are exhausted, the subproblems are randomly permuted and the cycle can start again. Execution times are in $(1 + \epsilon)\frac{T_{\text{seq}}}{n} + O(h)$ with high probability.

The algorithm is adapted to butterflies (and related constant degree networks), $r$-dimensional meshes and hierarchical networks like fat trees in Section 4. Execution times are in $(1 + \epsilon)\frac{T_{\text{seq}}}{n} + O(h)$, $(1 + \epsilon)\frac{T_{\text{seq}}}{n} + O(h)\frac{n^{1/r}}{\log n}$ and $(1 + \epsilon)\frac{T_{\text{seq}}}{n} + O(h)\sqrt{\log n}$ respectively with high probability.

Section 5 shows how the expensive random permutations can be avoided as long as PE utilization is good. A sufficiently accurate estimate of the global load can be maintained with very little communication: A PE falling idle only informs a supervising PE with probability $O(1/n)$. Finally, Section 7 summarizes the results and compares them to known lower bounds.

## 2  Notation

### 2.1  Machine and Application Model

We consider a message passing MIMD computer with $n$ PEs numbered 0 through $n-1$. The PEs operate asynchronously but for simplicity we assume the existence of a global time. A message packet can be communicated to a neighboring PE in unit time. We assume the packet switching model of communication, i.e., sending a packet to a PE $k$ hops away takes time $k$. The network diameter is denoted by $d$.

Initially, a data structure describing the entire problem (the root problem) is located on PE 0. Let $T_{\text{seq}}$ denote the root problem's sequential execution time or *size*. We do not want to look at very small problems; we assume that $T_{\text{seq}} \in \Omega(n)$. Any subproblem can be worked on sequentially such that after working on a subproblem of size $T$ for time $t$ we get a subproblem of size $T - t$.

The *splitting function* is able to split a subproblem $S$ of size $T$ into two subproblems $S_1$ and $S_2$ of size $T_1$ and $T_2$ in unit time. For the analysis we assume that $T_1 + T_2 = T$ regardless when and where the subproblems are processed. The *generation* gen$(S)$ of a subproblem is inductively defined by gen(root problem) = 0 and gen$(S_1)$ = gen$(S_2)$ = gen$(S)$ + 1. A subproblem $S$ with gen$(S) \geq h$ must be guaranteed to be reduced to a constant atomic size $T_{\text{atomic}}$ or smaller. An immediate consequence of the above definitions is that

$$h \in \Omega(\log n) \ .$$

($\log n$ means $\log_2 n$ throughout this paper.) Splitting an atomic subproblem yields the same subproblem plus an empty subproblem. All other properties of the splitting function can be chosen by an adversary. We do not discuss termination detection and reporting results because they are not a bottleneck if implemented properly. Finally, we assume that a description of a subproblem fits into a single network packet.

### 2.2  Randomized Algorithms

The analysis of the randomized algorithms described here is based on the notion of behavior *with high probability*. Among the various variants of this notions we have adopted the one from [8].

**Definition 1.** A positive real valued random variable $X$ is in $O(f(n))$ *with high probability* – or $X \in \tilde{O}(f(n))$ for short – iff

$$\forall \beta > 0 : \exists c > 0, n_0 > 0 : \forall n \geq n_0 : \mathbf{P}\left[X > cf(n)\right] \leq n^{-\beta} \ ,$$

i.e., the probability that $X$ exceeds the bound $f$ by more than a constant factor is polynomially small. In this paper, the variable used to express high probability is always $n$ – the number of PEs.

A keystone of many probabilistic proofs are the following *Chernoff bounds* which give quite tight bounds on the probability that the sum of 0/1-random variables deviates from the expected value by some factor.

**Lemma 2 Chernoff bounds.** *Let the random variable $X$ represent the number of heads after $n$ independent flips of a loaded coin where the probability for a head is $p$. Then [18]:*

$$\mathbf{P}\left[X \le (1 - \epsilon)np\right] \le e^{-\epsilon^2 np/3} \text{ for } 0 < \epsilon < 1 \tag{2}$$

$$\mathbf{P}\left[X \ge \alpha np\right] \le e^{\left(1 - \frac{1}{\alpha} - \ln \alpha\right)\alpha np} \text{ for } \alpha > 1 \tag{3}$$

# 3 Hypercube poll-and-shuffle

## 3.1 The basic algorithm

Consider a $\log n$-dimensional hypercube network. Every PE performs receiver induced tree splitting. Computation time is partitioned into *phases* of constant length $T_{\text{phase}}$. Idle PEs are only allowed to send requests after a phase. After phase number $i$, requests go to the neighbor along dimension $i$ (i.e. PE $k$ sends a request to PE $k$ **xor** $2^i$). When we have reached phase $\log n$, we are out of fresh dimensions for communication. Therefore, we randomly permute the subproblems (we say that idle PEs contain empty subproblems) and start a new *cycle* by resetting the phase counter to 0. Figure 2 shows this partitioning of the time line for $n = 2^4$ and 2 cycles.

time

| i | local computation phase    ▨ neighborhood polling    ▮ random permutation

**Fig. 2.** Two cycles of hypercube poll-and-shuffle for $n = 2^4$.

Using this schedule, we can guarantee that after "most" phases with low PE utilization subproblems have a certain likelihood of receiving a request:

**Lemma 3.** *For any $\gamma \in (0, 1)$, for any subproblem $S$, and for any phase with a number $i$ less than $\log n - \log \frac{2}{\gamma}$, if at any point during this phase at least $\gamma n$ PEs are idle, then after this phase $S$ receives a request with a probability of at least $\gamma/2$.*

*Proof.* Due to space constraints, we can only outline this and all subsequent proofs and have to refer to the full paper for details. During the current cycle, $S$ can only have interacted with $2^i < \frac{\gamma}{2}n$ PEs. Sufficiently many of the remaining PEs will issue a request and with probability $\geq \gamma/2$ one of these PEs will be $S's$ neighbor along dimension $i$. This is shown by partitioning the set of all possible permutations into equivalence classes of equal size – one class for each pairing of $S$ with another subproblem. ∎

Building on this we can bound the number of phases necessary to reduce all subproblems to atomic size.

**Lemma 4.** *For any constant* $\gamma > 0$, $\tilde{O}(h)$ *phases with at least* $\gamma n$ *idle PEs and a phase number less than* $\log n - \log \frac{2}{\gamma}$ *are sufficient such that every existing subproblem $S$ has* $gen(S) \geq h$.

*Proof.* By viewing the event that a subproblem is hit by a request as a Bernoulli trial with success probability at least $\gamma/2$, we can use Chernoff bounds to show that the probability that a particular subproblem receives less than $h$ requests after $O(h)$ phases is polynomially small. Since taking the minimum over all subproblems only increases this probability by a factor at most $n$, the same is true for all subproblems together. ∎

So, at the end of each cycle there is a constant number of phases about which we cannot say very much. The other phases either do productive work or they reduce the size of the remaining subproblems. Furthermore, if we make the phases sufficiently long, the time for doing productive work and issuing requests will dominate the time for routing the random permutations. Based on this observation we can bound the parallel execution time:

**Theorem 5.** *Let* $T_{\mathrm{par}}$ *denote the execution time of the hypercube poll-and-shuffle algorithm. For every* $\epsilon > 0$ *there is a choice of the phase length* $T_{\mathrm{phase}}$ *such that*

$$T_{\mathrm{par}} \in (1 + \epsilon)\frac{T_{\mathrm{seq}}}{n} + \tilde{O}(h) \ .$$

Hypercube poll-and-shuffle is asymptotically optimal because its execution time meets the lower bound of Equation (1). The algorithm is better than any known tree embedding scheme because efficiencies arbitrarily close to 1 are possible even if $T_{\mathrm{atomic}} \ll 1$, and it is better than previously known tree splitting algorithms because the lower order term $\tilde{O}(h)$ is smaller than the $\tilde{O}(h \log n)$ term for random polling.

## 3.2 Random permutations

Choosing a permutation uniformly at random is not as easy as it sounds. $\Omega(n \log n)$ random bits are necessary to define a random permutation. Although this can be done in time $O(\log n)$ if we assume an independent source of random bits in every PE, we still need to coordinate the information in such a way that every PE knows where to send its information.

One possibility works as follows: First, every PE chooses a PE number uniformly at random and sends its subproblem to this PE. From the analysis of randomized routing algorithms (e.g. [18]) we know that the maximum number of subproblems destined for the same PE is in $\tilde{O}(\log n)$. Now, every PE sequentially permutes the locally present subproblems in time $\tilde{O}(\log n)$. We then enumerate the subproblems using a parallel prefix sum of the number of subproblems in each PE (time $O(\log n)$). Finally, every subproblem is sent to the PE defined by its number (time $\tilde{O}(\log n)$).

In practice, it might be better to replace this quite expensive procedure by some kind of pseudorandom permutations. For example, it is common practice in computational group theory [21] to precompute a small set of random permutations which have the property of generating the entire group (in this case the symmetric group $S_n$ of all permutations over PE numbers). Then, a pseudorandom permutation is constructed by combining a small randomly selected sample of these precomputed permutations.

## 4    Other Networks

Our starting point is the idea to adapt the hypercube poll-and-shuffle algorithm to other networks by embedding a hypercube into the real network in such a way that poll-and-shuffle works efficiently.

This is quite easy for *hypercubic networks* in the sense of [18] (e.g. butterflies, cube-connected-cycles, perfect shuffle, DeBruijn) because poll-and-shuffle uses the hypercube dimensions one after the other. Using the quite general results from [17] on routing and [18, Section 3.3.3] on emulating *normal* hypercube algorithms we can conclude:

**Theorem 6.** *Hypercube poll-and-shuffle can be adapted to constant degree hypercubic networks in such a way that*

$$T_{\text{par}} \in (1 + \epsilon)\frac{T_{\text{seq}}}{n} + \tilde{O}(h) \ .$$

*Proof.* Neighborhood polling and permutation routing takes a constant factor longer than on the hypercube. But this can be compensated by making $T_{\text{phase}}$ correspondingly larger. Everything else is completely analogous to the proof of Theorem 5. ∎

By introducing some minor modifications into the poll-and-shuffle concept we can also derive good algorithms for meshes and hierarchical networks like fat trees.

## 4.1 Meshes

Consider an $r$-dimensional mesh ($n$ a power of 2, $d = r2^{\lceil \log n/r \rceil} - r$ and $r$ constant). A hypercube can be embedded in such a way that every $j$-dimensional subcube is embedded into a submesh of diameter $r2^{\lceil j/r \rceil} - r$ (e.g. [15, Figure 6.11]). Using this embedding, a simple calculation shows that the communication necessary for $\log n$ phases of poll-and-shuffle can be performed in time $O(n^{1/r})$. Routing can also be performed in time $O(n^{1/r})$ [18].

The only complication we have to deal with is that the proof of Theorem 5 only works for phases of equal length. In fact, if we used a phase length proportional to the communication expense it would be conceivable that the short phases have good PE utilization and the long phases have low PE utilization, resulting in a poor overall efficiency. The solution is quite simple: We omit the last $r \log \log n$ phases of each cycle and set $T_{\text{phase}} := c\frac{n^{1/r}}{\log n}$, that is, a constant times the communication expense of the most expensive remaining phase. (The embedding of a $\log n - r \log \log n$-dimensional subcube has diameter $r2^{\lceil \frac{\log n - r \log \log n}{r} \rceil} - r \in O\left(\frac{n^{1/r}}{\log n}\right)$):

**Theorem 7.** *Let $T_{\text{par}}$ denote the execution time of the hypercube poll-and-shuffle algorithm simulated on an $r$-dimensional mesh with the last $r \log \log n$ phases of each cycle omitted. For every $\epsilon > 0$ there is a choice of the constant $c$ such that*

$$T_{\text{par}} \in (1 + \epsilon)\frac{T_{\text{seq}}}{n} + \tilde{O}\left(h\frac{n^{1/r}}{\log n}\right) .$$

*Proof.* Analogous to the proof of Theorem 5. $r \log \log n$ takes the role of $\log \frac{2}{\gamma}$ and we have to substitute the appropriate execution times for polling and random permutations. ∎

Using the results from [1] on emulating mesh algorithms on the mesh of trees network we can conclude that same performance is possible on meshes of trees.

## 4.2 Fat trees

We can use a similar approach as for meshes in order to derive a fairly good load balancing algorithm for fat trees [20]. We partition the network into sub fat trees of height $\sqrt{\log n}$ (with $2^{\sqrt{\log n}}$ PEs each). Setting $T_{\text{phase}}$ to $c\sqrt{\log n}$, we can perform $\sqrt{\log n}$ poll-phases in time $O(\log n)$. Since routing is also possible in logarithmic time, we get:

**Theorem 8.** *Let $T_{\text{par}}$ denote the execution time of the hypercube poll-and-shuffle algorithm simulated on a fat tree performing only $\sqrt{\log n}$ phases per cycle. For every $\epsilon > 0$ there is a choice of the constant $c$ such that*

$$T_{\text{par}} \in (1 + \epsilon)\frac{T_{\text{seq}}}{n} + \tilde{O}\left(h\sqrt{\log n}\right) .$$

*Proof.* Similar to proof of Theorem 7. This time we need a factor $O(\sqrt{\log n})$ more cycles than for the hypercube case. But a cycle takes no more time than in the hypercube case. ∎

The same pattern can be applied to any network: If possible, embed subcubes into subnetworks in such a way that intra-subnetwork routing is faster than global routing. If the saving is sufficiently large to make up for the random permutations, we get an algorithm superior to random polling.

## 5 Adaptively initiating permutations

The periodically invoked random permutation is a quite expensive operation during which no work on the subproblems is possible. In addition, there is actually no reason to redistribute subproblems as long as the PE utilization is good. A simple approach to avoiding unnecessary work is to determine the average number of idle PEs during a cycle and to trigger a random permutation only if PE utilization is low. For example, we can trigger when the average number of idle PEs raises above $\gamma n$ for some appropriate constant $\gamma$. More sophisticated triggering conditions, which take the current cost for load balancing and the past development of PE utilization into account, are described in [22, 11].

A simple way to implement this idea is to count the number of idle phases during a cycle on each PE and to determine the average number of idle PEs by globally adding all these values after each cycle. But although a global add may be considerably cheaper than migrating all subproblems, we would still have an expensive global operation which is invoked periodically even though PE utilization may be fairly stable.

Counting can be made more adaptive by letting idle PEs notify a monitoring PE (say PE 0) about their idleness. (Refer to [16] for another approach to adaptively determining global load changes which is used in the context of balancing independent work packets.) However, if *every* idle PE sent a message, the monitoring PE would become a terrible bottleneck. Here, randomization comes to the rescue again: Whenever a PE becomes idle or an idle PE enters a new phase, it notifies PE 0 with probability[1] $\frac{c}{n}$ (for some constant $c$ still to be determined). If PE 0 receives $m$ notifications during $k$ phases, the average number of idle PEs can be estimated to be $\frac{mn}{ck}$. (The effect of message latency is compensated by only using notifications from phases sufficiently far back such that all their messages must have arrived with high probability.)

We first show that the arrival rate of notifications is sufficiently low in order to avoid contention at PE 0.

**Lemma 9.** *The number of notifications sent during* $\log n$ *phases is in* $\tilde{O}(\log n)$.

---

[1] For fat trees, the probability needs to be set to $c\sqrt{\log n}/n$ in order to achieve the right balance of messages. For meshes we can choose some higher probability in $O(n^{1/r})$ without creating a hot spot.

*Proof.* Using Chernoff bounds by viewing the decisions whether a notification is sent as independent Bernoulli trials with success probability $\frac{c}{n}$. ■

Since $\log n \in O(d(n))$ for all the networks we are considering, the contention at PE 0 will not asymptotically change the message latency.

We go on by showing that a significant underestimation of the fraction of idle PEs is improbable.

**Lemma 10.** *Let $\bar{\gamma}$ denote the average fraction of idle PEs over $\alpha \log n$ phases $(\alpha > 0)$. Let $\hat{\gamma}$ denote the estimate of $\bar{\gamma}$ based on the notifications sent by idle PEs. For every $\epsilon > 0$ there is a choice of the constant $c$ such that $\hat{\gamma} \geq \bar{\gamma} - \epsilon$ with probability at least $1 - \frac{1}{n}$.*

*Proof.* Similar to the proof of Lemma 9. ■

Finally, the effect of overestimations of the number of idle PEs can be compensated by never initiating random permutations after less than $\log n$ phases. We now have all the required components for analyzing a variant of poll-and-shuffle which bases triggering decisions on the estimate of the fraction of idle PEs.

**Theorem 11.** *Let $T_{\text{par}}$ denote the execution time of the poll-and-shuffle algorithm with probabilistic triggering of shuffling. For every $\epsilon > 0$ there is a choice of the phase length $T_{\text{phase}}$, the constant $c$, and a triggering policy such that*

$$T_{\text{par}} \in (1 + \epsilon)\frac{T_{\text{seq}}}{n} + \tilde{O}(h) \ .$$

*Proof.* Due to message latencies there is a fraction of the current cycle about which PE 0 is not informed. $T_{\text{phase}}$ must be sufficiently large such that this fraction is small. $c$ must be sufficiently large such that the number of phases needed to accumulate sufficiently many notifications is small compared to $\log n$. Lemma 9 shows that contention of notification messages at PE 0 is not an issue if $c \ll T_{\text{phase}}$. We can use Lemma 10 in order to show that with high probability only a small number of cycles with low PE utilization will go undetected. A possible strategy for triggering permutations is to trigger whenever the estimate for the number of idle PEs exceeds $\frac{\epsilon}{2}n$. In order to avoid an accumulation of estimation errors, outdated information has to be discarded from time to time, for example by considering only the last $\alpha \log n$ phases for some appropriate $\alpha$. ■

## 6  Generalizing the problem model

In Section 2 we made a lot of simplifying assumptions about the machine and problem model in order to concentrate on load balancing, irregularity and locality. Now we want to outline how relaxing some of these assumptions affects the performance of our algorithms. For example, the global time can be replaced by local synchronization between the phases. (for details refer to the full paper.)

## 6.1 Message lengths

For many backtracking applications our assumption of constant message lengths is quite realistic: Requests, rejections and other control information only need a constant number of machine words. And, if we initially broadcast the root problem to all PEs, subproblems can often be represented by sequences of $O(h)$ bits indicating how to derive the subproblem from the root problem by subsequent split operations (e.g. [12]). Under the usual assumption that $O(\log n)$ bits fit into a machine word our assumption is strictly justified for the frequent case [15] $h \in O(\log T_{seq})$ and $T_{seq}$ polynomial in $n$ (Larger problems are easy to load balance anyway).

Still, in other cases it is better to treat the message length as an additional variable of the problem.[2] Let us assume that $l$ is an upper bound on the length of the representation of a subproblem depending on the root problem only. If we stick to packet routing, we can easily adapt our analysis by charging $O(dl)$ instead of $O(d)$ time for transmitting a message. But we might be able to do better by using cut-through routing [15] (i.e. chopping messages into constant size pieces) which makes it possible to send a subproblem in time $O(l + d)$ as long as there is no network contention. For networks with a high bisection width of $\Omega(n)$ (e.g. hypercubes, fat trees, multi-stage butterflies) and long messages ($l \in \Omega(d)$) poll-and-shuffle now has no advantage over random polling since the transmission time is in $\tilde{O}(l)$ regardless of the distance between communication partners. (Refer to [26] for a discussion why the network traffic is sufficiently uniform to justify this conclusion.)

However, for networks with limited bisection width like meshes or butterflies, cut-through routing has no asymptotic advantage over packet routing when the network is highly loaded. And indeed, any efficient receiver induced tree splitting algorithm must sometimes handle $\Omega(nh)$ load transfers which is a constant fraction of the total number of messages for random polling and poll-and-shuffle. (For details refer to the full paper.)

This observation has a consequence of some practical importance. One might be tempted to regard poll-and-shuffle as only of theoretical interest since many contemporary machines with mesh architecture have a low latency hardware router such that the physical *distance* between communication partners is only of secondary importance for the case of low network load. But poll-and-shuffle can nevertheless yield a significant improvement on these machines because the usable *bandwidth* per message is higher than for random polling: For example, consider the poll-and-shuffle algorithm for $r$-dimensional meshes from Section 4.1. During every phase of a cycle at least $\Omega(n^{\frac{r-1}{r}} \log n)$ PEs can communicate in parallel via cut-through routing without any contention while for random polling the figure is only $O(n^{\frac{r-1}{r}})$.

---

[2] Note that the tree embedding schemes from Section 1.2 can only achieve an efficiency in $O\left(\frac{1}{l}\right)$ for nonconstant message lengths.

## 6.2   The splitting function

In Section 2 we assumed that the splitting function is able to split a subproblem of size $T$ into two subproblems of size $T_1$ and $T_2$ in unit time such that that $T_1 + T_2 = T$ regardless when and where the subproblems are processed.

Relaxing the assumption that the splitting function takes unit time does not yield anything new as long as splitting a subproblem does not take longer than communicating it. For example, this is always the case if $T_{\text{split}} \in O(l)$, i.e., splitting is linear in the length of a the representation of a subproblem. Similarly, the effect that splitting often performs productive work on the ancestor problem in order to find an acceptable place for splitting is quite uninteresting.

However, $T_1$ and $T_2$ can be quite dependent on the order of subproblem evaluation in general. Usually, the reason is that the evaluation of one subproblem yields information which can be used to prune (or reduce in size) other subproblems. The resulting *speedup anomalies* are a complex issue by themselves. For some classes of problems, large superlinear speedups (compared to sequential depth first search) can be achieved [4, 24], others show wildly varying speedups over several orders of magnitude [29] and search algorithms with strong pruning heuristics like game tree search are very hard to parallelize efficiently [5, 7]. We did not incorporate these effects into our model because they are quite application dependent and because we wanted to concentrate on the load balancing aspect of parallel search.

Also, there are many applications for which our model is quite accurate: All but the last iteration of iterative deepening search algorithms like IDA* [13] are independent of the evaluation order, and in the last iteration it is a quite good approach to work on several randomly selected subproblems until the first solution is found [9, 4, 24].

A practically useful application of branch-and-bound is to verify that a known (heuristic) solution is within a certain percentage of the optimum. In this case the search tree does not depend on the execution order. Similarly, in many applications optimal solutions are usually found quickly but verifying their optimality takes very long such that our assumption holds for the main part of the search.

## 6.3   Problem granularity

If we consider $T_{\text{atomic}}$ to be an additional problem variable, we trivially get an additional lower bound $T_{\text{par}} \in \Omega(T_{\text{atomic}})$ and it is quite simple to change the analysis of our algorithms to show that there is simply an additional $O(T_{\text{atomic}})$ term in the upper bound for the parallel execution time if $T_{\text{seq}} \in \Omega(nT_{\text{atomic}})$. (For random polling this has been done in [26].)

# 7   Conclusion

The load balancing algorithms for tree shaped computations presented in this paper are a promising family of algorithms. For low diameter networks they achieve efficiencies arbitrarily close to 1 for a per PE load in $O(h)$. This is asymptotically optimal since the sequential component of the problem instances is of the same order. Therefore, the new algorithms are at the same time asymptotically as scalable as tree embedding techniques and have the same communication economy as earlier tree splitting based algorithms which require larger problem sizes for good efficiency.

For meshes, the algorithms have a better scalability (by a factor $O(\log n)$) than the best previously known algorithms. In the important case of logarithmic depth trees ($h \in O(\log n)$), the PE load of $O(d)$ required for constant efficiency is asymptotically optimal. The new algorithms for fat trees are by a factor $\sqrt{\log n}$ better than the best previously known ones.

In fact, the algorithms turn out to be optimal in so many cases that we were tempted to title this paper "Towards asymptotically optimal algorithms for parallel backtracking." However, the discussion in Section 6 shows that optimality is so dependent on the underlying model that such a title would be misleading.

# 8  Acknowledgements

I would like to thank H. Rust, A. C. Achilles, H. Fernau, T. Minkwitz and T. Worsch for many constructive discussions which helped to shape the algorithms and their analysis.

# References

1. A.-C. Achilles. Optimal emulation of meshes on meshes-of-trees. In *EURO-PAR International Conference on Parallel Processing*, 1995.
2. R. D. Blumofe and C. E. Leiserson. Scheduling multithreaded computations by work stealing. In *Foundations of Computer Science*, 1994.
3. O. I. El-Dessouki and W. H. Huen. Distributed enumeration on between computers. *IEEE Transactions on Computers*, C-29(9):818–825, September 1980.
4. W. Ertel. *Parallele Suche mit randomisiertem Wettbewerb in Inferenzsystemen.* Dissertation, TU München, 1992.
5. R. Feldmann, P. Mysliwietz, and B. Monien. Studying overheads in massively parallel min/max-tree evaluation. In *ACM Symposium on Parallel Architectures and Algorithms*, pages 94–103, 1994.
6. R. Finkel and U. Manber. DIB— A distributed implementation of backtracking. *ACM Trans. Prog. Lang. and Syst.*, 9(2):235–256, Apr. 1987.
7. H. Hopp and P. Sanders. Parallel game tree search on SIMD machines. In *Workshop on Algorithms for Irregularly Structured Problems*, LNCS, Lyon, 1995. Springer.
8. D. Ierardi. 2d-bubblesorting in average time $O(\sqrt{N \lg N})$. In *ACM Symposium on Parallel Architectures and Algorithms*, 1994.
9. V. K. Janakiram, E. F. Gehringer, D. P. Agrawal, and R. Mehotra. A randomized parallel branch-and-bound algorithm. *International Journal of Parallel Programming*, 17(3):277–301, 1988.

10. C. Kaklamanis and G. Persiano. Branch-and-bound and backtrack search on mesh-connected arrays of processors. In *ACM Symposium on Parallel Architectures and Algorithms*, 1992.
11. G. Karypis and V. Kumar. Unstructured tree search on SIMD parallel computers. *IEEE Transactions on Parallel and Distributed Systems*, 5(10):1057–1072, 1994.
12. J. C. Kergommeaux and P. Codognet. Parallel logic programming systems. *ACM Computing Surveys*, 26(3):295–336, 1994.
13. R. E. Korf. Depth-first iterative-deepening: An optimal admissible tree search. *Artificial Intelligence*, 27:97–109, 1985.
14. V. Kumar and G. Y. Ananth. Scalable load balancing techniques for parallel computers. Technical Report TR 91-55, University of Minnesota, 1991.
15. V. Kumar, A. Grama, A. Gupta, and G. Karypis. *Introduction to Parallel Computing. Design and Analysis of Algorithms*. Benjamin/Cummings, 1994.
16. T. Lauer. *Adaptive dynamische Lastbalancierung*. PhD thesis, Max Planck Institute for Computer Science Saarbrücken, 1995.
17. F. T. Leighton, B. M. Maggs, A. G. Ranade, and S. B. Rao. Randomized routing and sorting on fixed-connection networks. *Journal of Algorithms*, 17:157–205, 1994.
18. T. Leighton. *Introduction to Parallel Algorithms and Architectures*. Morgan Kaufmann, 1992.
19. T. Leighton, M. Newman, A. G. Ranade, and E. Schwabe. Dynamic tree embeddings in butterflies and hypercubes. In *ACM Symposium on Parallel Architectures and Algorithms*, pages 224–234, 1989.
20. C. E. Leiserson. Fat trees: Universal networks for hardware efficient supercomputing. In *International Conference on Parallel Processing*, pages 393–402, 1985.
21. T. Minkwitz. Personal communication. Department of Informatics, University of Karlsruhe, 1995.
22. C. Powley, C. Ferguson, and R. E. Korf. Depth-fist heuristic search on a SIMD machine. *Artificial Intelligence*, 60:199–242, 1993.
23. A. Ranade. Optimal speedup for backtrack search on a butterfly network. *Mathematical Systems Theory*, pages 85–101, 1994.
24. V. N. Rao and V. Kumar. On the efficiency of parallel backtracking. *IEEE Transactions on Parallel and Distributed Systems*, 4(4):427–437, April 1993.
25. P. Sanders. Analysis of random polling dynamic load balancing. Technical Report IB 12/94, Universität Karlsruhe, Fakultät für Informatik, April 1994.
26. P. Sanders. A detailed analysis of random polling dynamic load balancing. In *International Symposium on Parallel Architectures Algorithms and Networks*, pages 382–389, Kanazawa, Japan, 1994. IEEE.
27. P. Sanders. Massively parallel search for transition-tables of polyautomata. In *Parcella 94, VI. International Workshop on Parallel Proccessing by Cellular Automata and Arrays*, pages 99–108, Potsdam, 1994.
28. P. Sanders. Randomized static load balancing for tree shaped computations. In *Workshop on Parallel Processing*, TR Universität Clausthal, Lessach, Austria, 1994.
29. A. P. Sprague. Wild anomalies in parallel branch and bound. Technical Report CIS-TR-91-04, CIS UAB, Birmingham, AL 35294, 1991.

# Parallel Game Tree Search on SIMD Machines

Holger Hopp and Peter Sanders

University of Karlsruhe, 76 128 Karlsruhe, Germany
E-mail: {hopp,sanders}@ira.uka.de

Abstract. We describe an approach to the parallelization of game tree search on SIMD machines. It turns out that the single-instruction restriction of SIMD machines is not a big obstacle for achieving efficiency. We achieve speedups up to 3660 on a 16K processor MasPar MP-1. If the search trees are sufficiently large and if there are no strong move ordering heuristics. To our best knowledge, the largest speedups previously reported (usually on MIMD machines) are more than an order of magnitude smaller.

Keywords: Parallel game tree search, load balancing, program transformations for SIMD.

## 1    Introduction

Two player games with complete information like chess have always been an active area of research in artificial intelligence because they constitute a nontrivial but easy to specify problem area. Since the same tree search algorithms used for most game implementations are very computation intensive, games are also an interesting "benchmark" application for parallel computing.

The main challenge for parallelization is that the strong tree pruning heuristics like α-β-search used in the sequential case produce very irregular search trees with little or no immediately available parallelism. Early work on parallel game tree search was therefore not able to achieve speedups above 5–10 (e.g. [3]). More recent work is able to exploit todays MIMD machines with up to 1024 processor elements [1, 9]. However, a lot of special tuning appears to be necessary and it is not clear how far the current techniques will lead. Using even larger scale parallelism as available on SIMD machines has largely failed so far [4].

A principal objective of the work described here is to investigate how game tree search can be parallelized on even larger numbers of PEs. In addition, we use α-β-search as a case study how algorithms with relatively complex control flow can be implemented by an efficient data parallel program. Since the performance of real games like chess or Othello depends on many application specific details not directly related to the α-β-algorithm, we restrict ourselves to synthetic game trees. By changing the parameters of the tree generating process, we are able to model a wide spectrum of possible scenarios.

# Parallel Game Tree Search on SIMD Machines

Holger Hopp and Peter Sanders

University of Karlsruhe, 76128 Karlsruhe, Germany
E-mail: {hopp,sanders}@ira.uka.de

**Abstract.** We describe an approach to the parallelization of game tree search on SIMD machines. It turns out that the single-instruction restriction of SIMD-machines is not a big obstacle for achieving efficiency. We achieve speedups up to 5850 on a 16K processor MasPar MP-1 if the search trees are sufficiently large and if there are no strong move ordering heuristics. To our best knowledge, the largest speedups previously reported (usually on MIMD machines) are more than an order of magnitude smaller.

**Keywords:** Parallel game tree search, load balancing, program transformations for SIMD.

## 1  Introduction

Two-player games with complete information like chess have always been an active area of reasearch in artificial intelligence because they constitute a nontrivial but easy to specify problem area. Since the game tree search algorithms used for most game implementations are very computation intensive, games are also an interesting "benchmark" problem for parallel computing.

The main challenge for parallelization is that the strong tree pruning heuristics like $\alpha\beta$-search used in the sequential case produce very irregular search trees with little or no immediately available parallelism. Early work on parallel game tree search was therefore not able to achieve speedups above 5–10 (e.g. [6]). More recent work is able to exploit todays MIMD machines with up to 1024 processor elements (PEs) [4, 9]. However, a lot of special tuning appears to be necessary such that it is not clear how far the current techniques will lead. Using even larger scale parallelism as available on SIMD-machines has largely failed so far [2].

A principal objective of the work described here is to investigate how game tree search can be parallelized on even larger numbers of PEs. In addition, we use $\alpha\beta$-search as a case study how algorithms with relatively complex control flow can be implemented by an efficient data parallel program. Since the performance of real games like chess or Othello depends on many application specific details not directly related to the $\alpha\beta$-algorithm, we restrict ourselves to synthetic game-trees. By changing the parameters of the tree generating process, we are able to model a wide spectrum of possible scenarios.

The structure of this paper is as follows: In section 2 we line out how sequential $\alpha\beta$-search can be implemented on a SIMD machine without incurring a large overhead to the synchronous control flow. Section 3 describes the key parts of the parallel implementation with a strong emphasis on load balancing. Then, we experimentally evaluate some of the more important aspects of our algorithm in section 4. Finally, section 5 summarizes and discusses the key results.

## 2 Sequential $\alpha\beta$-Search on SIMD Machines

We now decribe how a recursive function with a highly data dependent control flow such as $\alpha\beta$-search can be decomposed into simple operations which can effectively be executed on a SIMD machine like the MasPar MP-1. The MP-1 consists of a central control unit for computing global values and broadcasting instructions and a large number of simple 4-bit processing elements (PEs) with a local memory. (As opposed to some other SIMD machines, each PE is able to use locally generated addresses). The PEs are interconnected by a router which is able to route arbitrary permutations, a 2D-mesh and a broadcast bus. In addition, the system programming language MPL (an extension of ANSI-C) offers micro-coded primitives for collective operations like reductions and (segmented) prefix operations [14, 15]. We use a configuration with 16384 PEs with 16 KB of memory each.

```
FUNCTION αβ (position J; integer α,β): integer;
    VAR j,w,value: integer;
BEGIN
    determine successors J.1 ... J.w;
    IF w = 0
        THEN RETURN g(J);          (* leaf evaluation *)
    END ;
    value := α;
    FOR j:=1 TO w DO
        value := max (value, -αβ(J.j, -β, -value));
        IF value ≥ β
            THEN RETURN value;      (* cut *)
        END ;
    END ;
    RETURN value;
END ;
```

**Fig. 1.** $\alpha\beta$-algorithm (negamax-variant)

Figure 1 shows pseudocode for the negamax-variant of recursive $\alpha\beta$-search (closely following [17]). Inputs are a position in the game and a range of results $(\alpha, \beta)$ (*search window*) which can still influence the overall result (Initially

$(-\infty, \infty)$). Output is the quality of the position (Its *value*). The value of a leaf (a final position or a position at some maximal search depth) is its heuristic evaluation. The value of an interior node is the value of the position after making the "best" move which can be found by evaluating the successors from the point of view of the opponent. Once this value exceeds the upper bound $\beta$, no additional search can influence the overall result and we can *prune* the remaining subtrees by returning immediately. The search windows of the recursive calls are set according to the old search window and the best move found so far.

In our parallel algorithm every PE at a SIMD machine shall run the $\alpha\beta$-algorithm working on different subtrees. Then it makes no sense to use an $\alpha\beta$-function like figure 1 directly. We first eliminate recursion by explicitly managing a search stack. Then, we must make sure that the program contains only a single loop nest. Else, PEs which have finished executing an interior loop would always have to wait for the last PE to finish – resulting in a very high SIMD overhead. This can be done by decomposing the control flow into *elementary operations* containing no loops which depend on local data. For $\alpha\beta$, we have chosen the following operations:

**Leaf evaluation (LE):** Make a heuristic evaluation of a leaf.
**Node Generation (NG):** Generate successors of an interior node.
**Tree Movement ($\alpha\beta$):** Move up and down the tree by popping and pushing the stack and perform maximization.

The top level control flow is now managed by a *state* variable indicating which operation has to be performed next. If every operation properly sets *state* at its end, the control flow can be implemented by a single synchronous *test loop*.

**WHILE** not finished **DO**
    **IF** state = LE **THEN** Leaf evaluation
    **IF** state = NG **THEN** Node generation
    **IF** state = $\alpha\beta$ **THEN** Move in tree
**END**

There is still some SIMD overhead left but a PE waiting for a particular operation must wait for at most two tests.

Additionally, we are free to choose any sequence of tests and we can test cheap or important operations more frequently. It turns out that carefully scheduling the test loop makes it possible to considerably reduce SIMD overhead. For a general discussion of this technique refer to [19]. Additional implementation details are reported in section 3.5 after we have introduced the remaining operations used for load balancing and other purposes.

## 3 The Parallel Algorithm

The basis of our approach to parallelize game tree search is that every PE executes a sequential $\alpha\beta$-algorithm, but different subtrees of the search tree. Then, the main task of parallelization is to find a load balancing strategy which is able to supply the PEs with subtrees which are relevant for finding the overall result.

In the load balancing procedure a set of PEs (*masters*) send work to other PEs (*slaves*) always using point to point communication. In order to follow the philosophy of creating elementary operations, the load balancing procedure is small and so each master sends only a single subtree to a slave. To distribute two or more subtrees to slaves, the elementary operation "load balancing" must be performed twice or more.

Distributing every possible subtree immediately to other PEs in order to exploit as much parallelism as possible expands lots of nodes, which are pruned by the sequential $\alpha\beta$-algorithm. The ratio $N_{par}/N_{seq}$ where $N_{par}, N_{seq}$ denote the number of nodes expanded by the parallel respectively the sequential algorithm defines the *search overhead*. The main problem of parallel game tree search is to keep the search overhead small *and* achieve good processor utilization. So, in this paper we first describe methods how to decrease the search overhead while achieving high parallelism (section 3.1 and 3.2) and then discuss the choice of connections between masters and slaves (section 3.3).

If the parallel expansion of right subtrees begins too early, they are searched with the completely open search window $(-\infty, \infty)$. In the sequential $\alpha\beta$-algorithm these subtrees are searched with a smaller $\beta$-value, which allows more cutoffs. This can be explained with Knuth and Moore's node types [11]:

**Definition 1.** The **node type** of a node J in a game tree is defined as:

$$type(\epsilon) := 1$$

$$type(J.i) := \begin{cases} 1 & \text{if } type(J) = 1 \text{ and } i = 1 \\ 2 & \text{if } type(J) = 1 \text{ and } i > 1 \\ 3 & \text{if } type(J) = 2 \text{ and } i = 1 \\ 2 & \text{if } type(J) = 3 \\ \text{undefined else} \end{cases}$$

The nodes with defined node types are the nodes of the *minimal tree*. This tree contains those nodes that must always be visited by the sequential $\alpha\beta$-algorithm. Type-1-nodes are searched with the open search window $(-\infty, \infty)$, type-2-nodes with a search window $(-\infty, -v)$, and type-3-nodes with a search window $(v, \infty)$. The nodes with undefined node type are searched with a search window $(v, w)$, which leads to cutoffs if $v \geq w$ $(v, w \neq \pm\infty)$.

Expanding a node in parallel before knowing $\alpha, \beta$-bounds will make this subtree much larger than in the sequential case, because there are less opportunities for cutoffs. For example, expanding a right successor of the root (a type-2 node) in parallel with a search window $(-\infty, \infty)$ will effectively change this node to a type-1-node, and it also changes all (indirect) successor node types accordingly.

## 3.1 The Young Brothers Wait Concept

In order to decrease the search overhead, we adopt the *Young Brothers Wait Concept* (YBWC) introduced in [4, 5]: A successor $v.J$ of a node $v$ must not be expanded before the leftmost brother $v.1$ is completely evaluated. The YBWC significantly reduces the search overhead, but it decreases the available parallelism.

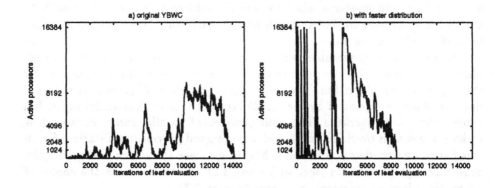

**Fig. 2.** Active processors

For example, figure 2 a) shows the number of active PEs while expanding a width 7, depth 15 synthetic game tree. In this example, the YBWC reduces the search overhead from 236.4 to 2.9, but it also reduces the average processor utilization from 95.2% to 18.8%. The reason is that the YBWC only generates sufficient parallelism in the last phases of the search. When the minimax value of a type-1-node is evaluated, only one PE is active. These nodes are called *synchronization nodes*. Other nodes produce weaker synchronizations, resulting in an overall utilization curve like figure 2 a).

The second approach in [4], the YBWC-1-2, slightly relaxes YBWC. It only delays the parallel expansion at type-1, type-2 and some type-undefined nodes. This increases the average processor utilization, but it also increases search overhead. YBWC-1-2 does not avoid synchronization nodes. The synchronizations are necessary to expand the right successors of a type-1 node with a defined $\beta$-value.

## 3.2 Faster Distribution at Synchronization Nodes

It is important to reactivate all inactive PEs immediately after a synchronization node. A good choice is to distribute all branches of the *right minimal tree* – the unsearched subtree of the minimal tree rooted at the synchronization node. The right minimal tree can be distributed quickly, without communication. Each PE generates the subtree for which it is responsible using only the root node and its PE number [3].

The root's negamax value is evaluated in several sequential phases, one phase for each synchronization node (bottom-up, shown in figure 3). Parallelism is only used within the phases. A preceding phase has evaluated the negamax value of the preceding synchronization node. The current phase evaluates the negamax value of the current synchronization node as follows: The right minimal tree of the synchronization node is distributed to the PEs without communication. After this initialization, the main loop with the dynamic load balancing routine takes over until the negamax value of the synchronization node is known.

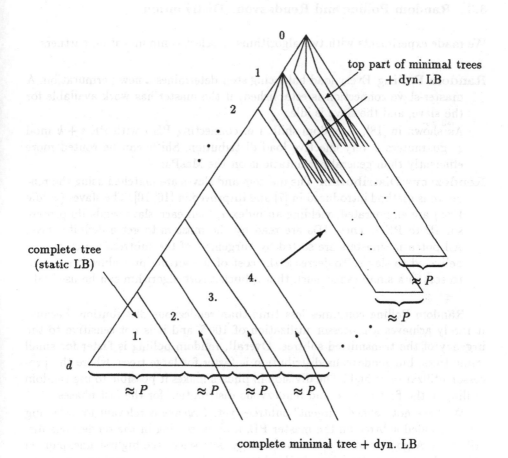

**Fig. 3.** Phases of the parallel algorithm with faster distribution

In the first phases the right minimal trees (symbolized by the trapezoids in figure 3) are very small. We can distribute the complete minimax tree for the first few phases at once (the triangle in figure 3) and compute its value using a sequence of segmented prefix-min/max-operations. In intermediate phases we can at least distribute the right minimal tree. Later, we distribute the right minimal tree up to a certain depth. The complete algorithm is more complex, for a more detailed description refer to [8].

The faster distribution at synchronization nodes has reduced the number of iterations in the example in figure 2 from 14144 to 8487. The average processor utilization increased from 18.8% to 34.7%. The search time was 39% shorter compared to the pure YBWC.

## 3.3 Random Polling and Rendezvous Distribution

We made experiments with two algorithms to select communication partners:

**Random Polling** Every load balancing step determines a new permutation. A master-slave connection is established, if the master has work available for the slave, and the slave is idle.

As shown in [18], a random shift, i.e. connecting PE $i$ with PE $i + k$ mod $P$ guarantees a very effective load distribution. Shifts can be routed more efficiently than general permutations on the MasPar.

**Rendezvous Distribution** The masters and slaves are matched using the rendezvous method introduced in [7] and improved in [16, 10]. The slaves (= idle PEs) are enumerated, yielding an index $i$, then each slave sends its processor ID to PE $i$. These IDs are read by the masters to get a definite slave. All potential masters are sorted by "urgency" of the subtrees which can be delivered to slaves. To decrease the cost of the sorting procedure it is useful to sort in a small range, such that a bucket sort algorithm can be used [8].

Random Polling consumes less time than rendezvous distribution, because it rarely achieves a processor utilization of 100% and it is not sensitive to the urgency of the transmitted subtree. Overall, random polling is faster for small game trees, but rendezvous distribution is faster for large trees, where the processor utilization is high. The division in phases makes it possible to use random polling in the first phases, and rendezvous distribution for the last phases.

We have not defined "urgent" subtrees yet. *Urgency* is relevant for selecting a unexpanded subtree on the master PE, and for sorting in the rendezvous distribution. A good subtree selection strategy is to select the highest unexpanded subtree in the game tree. If several subtrees on the same tree level are available, take the leftmost one. This method achieves good load sharing, but it expands a lot of nodes which are not expanded by the sequential $\alpha\beta$-algorithm. YBWC distinctly decreases this speculative computation, but does not even come close to eliminating it.

Other simple urgency functions besides "top-down, left-right" failed in our experiments. The selection strategy "bottom-up, left-right" reduces the number of expanded nodes by 30–40%, but it is slower by about 50% since it generates too little, and only very fine grained parallelism. The selection strategy "left-right, top-down", which prefers left subtrees regardless of their tree level, incurs more node expansions (7%) as well as a higher run time (50%).

## 3.4 Further Improvements

This subsection briefly explains additional elementary operations used for improving the performance. For a more detailed description of these algorithms refer to [8].

The elementary operation "passing $\alpha,\beta$-values" sends new $\alpha,\beta$-values to slave PEs. This makes more cutoffs possible and frees PEs working on pruned subtrees. For all but very small game trees this operation decreases the runtime.

The second improvement is only rarely useful. The *stack merging* operation is used to decrease the number of waiting PEs. A PE has the state *waiting*, if it has fully expanded its subtree and must wait for other PEs which expand other subtrees. The operation merges stacks of waiting PEs to the PEs they are waiting for and frees the waiting PEs for new work. This operation is very expensive, so a low testing frequency in the main loop is necessary. In very large game trees this operation decreases the run time by 0–2%, for smaller and normal-sized game trees stack merging is useless. In experiments, the maximum number of waiting PEs was only 700 (of 16384) – too small a number to make this operation useful.

## 3.5 Scheduling of elementary operations

What elementary operations are necessary for a SIMD game tree search? We need operations to implement the sequential $\alpha\beta$-algorithm (*search operations*) and operations to implement the parallel parts (*management operations*), which use communication between PEs.

We splitted the sequential parts into three elementary operations (section 2): *node generation* (NG), *leaf evaluation* (LE), and *moving within the game tree* ($\alpha\beta$). For management we mentioned the elementary operations *load balancing* (LB), *passing $\alpha,\beta$-values* (PV), and *stack merging* (SM). The forth management operation *report result* (RR) sends results from the slaves to their masters.

The relative frequency of NG and LE strongly depends on the kind of the game tree to be searched. Narrow and well ordered game trees need more node generations, others need more leaf evaluations. It is also important whether the search depth is even or odd, particularly for wide game trees. The third criterion is the ratio of execution times of NG and LE. The more expensive operation should be tested less frequently.

The tree moving operation $\alpha\beta$ is very short, so it is a good choice to increase its testing frequency. For example, for some classes of wide trees the sequence

NG; $\alpha\beta$; $\alpha\beta$; LE; $\alpha\beta$; $\alpha\beta$; LE; $\alpha\beta$; $\alpha\beta$;

was a good choice, but for a narrower tree a sequence with two times more NGs than LEs was good. For very wide trees it was favorable to test LE up to four times more often than NG.

A testing sequence with NG, LE, and $\alpha\beta$ is called *basic sequence*. Finding an optimal basic sequence is an important part of SIMD game tree search. Its choice can change the run time by a factor of 2–3. Fortunately, for real game trees it is usually known how wide or how well ordered they are. A good basic sequence can be found with a few experiments. The influence of the tree depth on performance is very small, the influence of the tree width and the NG/LE execution time ratio is larger.

Now a complete testing sequence is created by combining the basic sequence with the management operations. The RR operation is cheap and should be tested often. The YBWC-blocking and deblocking demands a frequent load balancing. In our experiments it was a good choice to call the LB operation every 1-5 basic sequences (*BS*), depending on the game tree size and shape. This is such a high frequency, that more adaptive strategies for triggering [16, 10] are not worth the additional expense for counting active PEs. The PV and SM operations should be tested more rarely. A complete testing sequence looks like

**LOOP** *BS*; RR; *BS*; RR; LB; *BS*; RR; *BS*; RR; PV; LB; **END** .

## 4 Experimental Results

In this section we present some experimental results with synthetic game trees. We look at *regular* trees with fixed depth $d$ and width $w$ for every node. This model is frequently used in the literature [17].

The *leaf value distribution* should simulate successor ordering heuristics with different strength. Two leaf value distributions are used here: *Uniformly distributed* trees simulate game trees without heuristics for ordering successor nodes. The probability that successor $J.k$ is the best is the same for all successors, $f(k) = \frac{1}{w}$. *Geometrically distributed* trees simulate game trees with node ordering heuristics. The probability that successor $J.k$ is the best is

$$f(k) = \begin{cases} p(1-p)^{k-1} & \text{if } 1 \le k < w, \\ (1-p)^{k-1} & \text{if } k = w, \end{cases}$$

where $p$ is a value in the range [0..1]. The higher $p$, the higher the quality of ordering. Minimal trees are generated with $p = 1.0$. These synthetic game trees are slightly more ordered than $p$-ordered trees [17] or strongly ordered trees [13], but the performance results are similar. We used algorithms' similar to those in [17] to generate these synthetic game trees.

Speedup and efficiency are measured in relation to the sequential $\alpha\beta$-algorithm on the MasPar. The sequential execution times for larger trees are extrapolated from sequential times on a fast sequential machine. If not otherwise mentioned, all 16K PEs are used.

Figure 4 shows speedups for uniformly distributed trees of width 7. To achieve high speedups, very large trees must be searched. Some data about a w7d22 tree (width 7, depth 22): The MasPar expands $7.4 \cdot 10^{10}$ nodes in parallel in 1:45 hours, a SPARC 5 (85 MHz) needs 47:24 hours for $6.6 \cdot 10^{10}$. nodes. The MasPar was 27 times faster than the SPARC, but a single PE of the MasPar was 220 times slower than the SPARC. The right curve in figure 4 shows the reasons for the relatively good (for SIMD game tree search) efficiency of 36%. The search overhead is small for the large trees (w7d22: 1.12). The main reason for the small

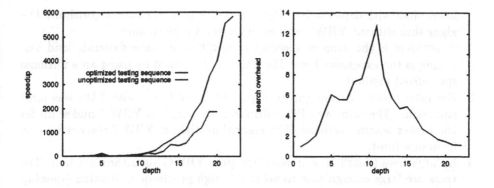

**Fig. 4.** Uniformly distributed trees (width 7)

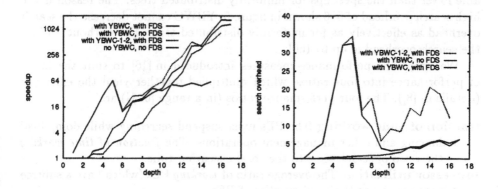

**Fig. 5.** 0.9-geometrically distributed trees (width 7)

speedups for small trees is the low processor utilization (figure 2), but also the high search overhead of up to 13 (figure 4).

The second speedup curve in figure 4 shows the detrimental effect of suboptimal testing sequences. The low curve is optimized for 0.9-geometrically distributed trees with a more complex leaf evaluation function.

Figure 5 shows speedups for 0.9-geometrically distributed trees of width 7 using different load balancing techniques (logarithmic scale!!). The curves can be divided into four classes of tree sizes:

1. For very small search depths (up to depth 5) it is possible to distribute all leafs to the PEs and evaluate the negamax value with scans, which is done by the faster distribution at synchronization nodes (FDS) from section 3.2. This is an order of magnitude faster than the purely dynamic algorithms.
2. For small search depths (depth 6 to 10) the distribution procedure cannot exhaust the search tree without dynamic load balancing. The speedups are

lower than with depth 5, but higher than for pure dynamic algorithms. The algorithm without YBWC still achieves good performance.

A problem is the drop of speedup at depth 6, because dynamic load balancing is too expensive here. The gap could be filled by using an additional specialized method.

3. For intermediate depths (up to depth 14) YBWC-1-2 with FDS was most successful. The improved PE utilization compared to YBWC makes up for the higher search overhead. The algorithm without YBWC reaches its performance limit.

4. In large trees (depth 15 and more) the pure YBWC algorithms are best. The trees are large enough now to achieve a high processor utilization (speedup w7d17: 1650).

Unfortunately, the speedups for geometrically distributed trees are considerable lower than the speedups for uniformly distributed trees. The reason is the high search overhead of 5–6 shown in figure 5. YBWC cannot decrease the search overhead as effectively as for uniformly distributed trees. But without YBWC the search overhead is up to 160!

We adopt the performance measures introduced in [16] to split the losses of performance into four ratios, which multiplied together yield the efficiency (details in [8]). The four performance ratios (in a range [0..1]) are

**fraction of time working** The PEs must suspend searching while doing load balancing and other management operations. The *fraction of time working* is the ratio of search time to the total execution time.

**processor utilization** The average ratio of *working* PEs (which have a subtree for expansion) to the total number of PEs.

**raw speed ratio** The *raw speed ratio* reflects the inefficiencies of SIMD calculations. Some PEs are inactive in conditional statements, but they are still called working.

**work ratio** This is the reciprocal of search overhead. It describes performance losses incurred by the expansion of nodes which are not expanded by the sequential algorithm.

Table 1 shows the four performance ratios of four example trees (* = estimated). The losses due to search overhead (work ratio) are the main problem, the SIMD overhead (raw speed ratio) is smaller than one might expected.

Using less than 16K PEs leads to speedups comparable with speedups achieved on MIMD machines. Even for the difficult geometrically distributed trees (w7d13, $p = 0.9$) we achieved a speedup of 141 on 1024 PEs, ignoring the SIMD effects this is comparable with MIMD results [4].

# 5  Conclusions

The YBWC as an approach to parallel game tree search does have the potential for large scale parallelism. But the game trees have to be very large if redundant

**Table 1.** Ratios and measures

| leaf value distribution | uniform | | 0.9-geometrical | |
|---|---|---|---|---|
| tree size | w7d16 | w7d22 | w7d13 | w7d17 |
| processor utilization | 0.762 | 0.902 | 0.577 | 0.851 |
| fraction of time working | 0.825 | 0.88* | 0.790 | 0.90* |
| work ratio | 0.253 | 0.893 | 0.137 | 0.169 |
| raw speed ratio | 0.441 | 0.50* | 0.743 | 0.78* |
| efficiency | 0.070 | 0.357 | 0.046 | 0.101 |
| speedup | 1150 | 5852 | 761 | 1650 |

work shall not limit the efficiency too much. This problem is particularly severe if the game tree is strongly ordered. Therefore, finding good heuristics for keeping the balance between sufficient parallelism and low search overhead will be a key issue in future research. For real games, additional problems are likely to occur due to hard to parallelize heuristics. For example, transposition tables are so communication intensive that they can only be used in the upper levels of the search trees [4, 9].

A not so severe problem is keeping the PEs busy. The first phases of the search which contain little parallelism due to synchronization nodes can be accelerated using the specialized distribution methods described in section 3.2. This optimization is even more important if a real game is implemented using iterative deepening techniques. The later phases of search contain enough parallelism to be load balanced using standard methods like random polling which are also used in other circumstances [18, 1, 12].

Using SIMD machines for parallel game tree search turned out to be not so much different from using MIMD machines. The negamax variant of $\alpha\beta$-search can be broken down into few simple operations. By carefully scheduling these operations together with the required communication operations, the SIMD overhead can be kept quite small. As long as the node evaluation function does not have a very complex structure, we expect this experience to transfer to real games. However, a philosophy behind SIMD, namely to achieve maximal raw performance by employing massive amounts of slow but cheap PEs is not very successful for game tree search. For difficult to parallelize problems, it is more cost effective to employ fewer but faster PEs even if the theoretical peak performance is lower.

# References

1. R. D. Blumofe and C. E. Leiserson. Scheduling multithreaded computations by work stealing. In *Foundations of Computer Science*, 1994.
2. V. Cung and L. Gotte. A first step towards the massively parallel game-tree search. In *International Workshop on Parallel Processing for Artificial Intelligence*, pages 88–93, Chambery, 1993. Elsevier.

3. O. I. El-Dessouki and W. H. Huen. Distributed enumeration on between computers. *IEEE Transactions on Computers*, C-29(9):818–825, September 1980.

4. R. Feldmann. *Game Tree Search on Massively Parallel Systems*. PhD thesis, Universität Paderborn, August 1993.

5. R. Feldmann, P. Mysliwietz, and B. Monien. Studying overheads in massively parallel min/max-tree evaluation. In *ACM Symposium on Parallel Architectures and Algorithms*, pages 94–103, 1994.

6. R. Finkel and J. Fishburn. Parallelism in alpha-beta search. *Artificial Intelligence*, 19:89–106, 1982.

7. W. D. Hillis. *The Connection Machine*. Series in Artificial Inteligence. MIT Press, Cambridge, MA, 1985.

8. H. Hopp. Parallele Spielbaumsuche auf SIMD-Rechnern. Diplomarbeit, Universität Karlsruhe, Feb. 1995.

9. C. F. Joerg and B. C. Kuszmaul. Massively parallel chess. In *Third DIMACS parallel implementation challenge workshop*, pages 299–308. Rutgers University, 1994.

10. G. Karypis and V. Kumar. Unstructured tree search on SIMD parallel computers. *IEEE Transactions on Parallel and Distributed Systems*, 5(10):1057–1072, 1994.

11. D. Knuth and W. Moore. An analysis of alpha-beta pruning. *Artificial Intelligence*, 6(4):293–326, 1975.

12. V. Kumar, A. Grama, A. Gupta, and G. Karypis. *Introduction to Parallel Computing. Design and Analysis of Algorithms*. Benjamin/Cummings, 1994.

13. T. A. Marsland and M. Campbell. Parallel search of strongly ordered game trees. *ACM Computing Surveys*, 14(4):533–551, Dec. 1982.

14. MasPar Corporation. *MasPar System Overview*, July 1992.

15. MasPar Corporation. *MPL Reference Manual*, May 1993.

16. C. Powley, C. Ferguson, and R. E. Korf. Depth-fist heuristic search on a SIMD machine. *Artificial Intelligence*, 60:199–242, 1993.

17. A. Reinefeld. *Spielbaum-Suchverfahren*. Informatik-Fachberichte, Band 200. Springer-Verlag, 1989.

18. P. Sanders. A detailed analysis of random polling dynamic load balancing. In *International Symposium on Parallel Architectures Algorithms and Networks*, pages 382–389, Kanazawa, Japan, 1994. IEEE.

19. P. Sanders. Efficient emulation of MIMD behavior on SIMD machines. Technical Report IB 29/95, Universität Karlsruhe, Fakultät für Informatik, 1995.

# Asynchronous Parallel Branch and Bound and Anomalies

A. de Bruin, G.A.P. Kindervater, H.W.J.M. Trienekens

Department of Computer Science, Erasmus University,
P.O. Box 1738, 3000 DR Rotterdam, The Netherlands
email {arie, ggak, harry}@cs.few.eur.nl.

Abstract. The parallel execution of branch and bound algorithms can result in seemingly unreasonable speedups or slowdowns. Almost never the speedup is equal to the increase in computing power. For synchronous parallel branch and bound, these effects have been studied extensively. For asynchronous parallelizations, only little is known.

In this paper, we derive sufficient conditions for examples that, at any time, asynchronous parallel branch and bound algorithm (with elimination by lower bound tests and dominance) will be at least as fast as its sequential counterpart. The technique used for obtaining the results seems to be more generally applicable.

The essential observations are that, under certain conditions, the parallel algorithm will always work on at least one node that is eliminated too by the sequential algorithm, and that the parallel algorithm, after elimination of all such nodes, is able to conclude that the optimal solution has been found.

Finally, some of the theoretical results are brought into connection with a few practical experiments.

## 1. Introduction

In many cases, enumeration is the last (and only) resort to obtain a solution to hard problems that do not contain much internal structure upon which a solution method can capitalize. Branch and bound implements a form of enumeration, whereby it is tried to avoid to devote energy to reaches of the solution space to be searched, that turn out to be irrelevant for obtaining the desired solution. Due to the nature of the problems in question, it is hard, if not impossible, to predict which direction the search should take in order to confine as much as possible the work to be done.

The fact that the problems under investigation are hard, inspires to use parallelization. However, as parallel versions of sequential branch and bound show an irregular behavior, unexpected effects with respect to the efficiency of the parallelizations have to be dealt with. The search space of a

This work was partially supported by the former Esprit Basic Working project SCOOP — Solving Combinatorial Optimization Problems in Parallel — of the European Union

# Asynchronous Parallel Branch and Bound and Anomalies

A. de Bruin, G.A.P. Kindervater, H.W.J.M. Trienekens

Department of Computer Science, Erasmus University
P.O. Box 1738, 3000 DR Rotterdam, The Netherlands
email: {arie, gapk, harryt}@cs.few.eur.nl

**Abstract.** The parallel execution of branch and bound algorithms can result in seemingly unreasonable speedups or slowdowns. Almost never the speedup is equal to the increase in computing power. For synchronous parallel branch and bound, these effects have been studied extensively. For asynchronous parallelizations, only little is known.

In this paper, we derive sufficient conditions to guarantee that an asynchronous parallel branch and bound algorithm (with elimination by lower bound tests and dominance) will be at least as fast as its sequential counterpart. The technique used for obtaining the results seems to be more generally applicable.

The essential observations are that, under certain conditions, the parallel algorithm will always work on at least one node, that is branched from by the sequential algorithm, and that the parallel algorithm, after elimination of all such nodes, is able to conclude that the optimal solution has been found.

Finally, some of the theoretical results are brought into connection with a few practical experiments.

## 1   Introduction

In many cases, enumeration is the last (and only) resort to obtain a solution to hard problems that do not contain much internal structure upon which a solution method can capitalize. Branch and bound implements a type of enumeration, whereby it is tried to avoid to devote energy to regions of the solution space to be searched, that turn out to be irrelevant for obtaining the desired solution. Due to the nature of the problems in question, it is hard, if not impossible, to predict which direction the search should take in order to reduce as much as possible the work to be done.

The fact that the problems under investigation are hard, suggests to use parallelization. However, as parallel versions of enumerative methods like branch and bound show an irregular behavior, unexpected effects with respect to the efficiency of the parallelizations have been detected. One would expect (or could

This work was partially supported by the Human Capital and Mobility project SCOOP — Solving Combinatorial Optimization Problems in Parallel — of the European Union.

hope) that attacking a problem with $p$ processors instead of one, results in a speedup close to $p$, but in the examination of parallelizations of branch and bound algorithms, so called anomalies have been observed: *detrimental* anomalies (speedup less than 1), and *acceleration* anomalies (speedup greater than $p$).

For synchronous parallel branch and bound, this type of anomalous behavior has been extensively theoretically studied [Burton, Huntbach, McKeown & Rayward-Smith, 1983; Lai & Sahni, 1984; Lai & Sprague, 1985, 1986; Li & Wah, 1984, 1986]. Typical results are properties that the rules applied by the branch and bound algorithm should have in order to ensure that no detrimental anomaly can occur, while leaving open the possibility of an acceleration anomaly.

For the asynchronous case, we only know of work by Corrêa & Ferreira [1995a, 1995b], who have obtained interesting results for a very broad class of branch and bound algorithms. The effect is, that their analysis leads to rather loose upper bounds on the execution time needed.

In this paper, we investigate asynchronous parallelizations, where the algorithm exploits a global active set (i.e., a pool of nodes to be investigated for finding an optimal solution). We do not only cover the case where elimination is implemented by lower bound tests, we also treat dominance. Our results are obtained by a new technique for analyzing branch and bound executions, of which we expect that it can be applied to other kinds of parallelizations as well.

In our analysis, parallel executions are compared with the corresponding sequential algorithm. To do so, we need the notion of *primary nodes*, i.e., nodes that are branched from by the sequential algorithm. We will postulate properties of the rules and tests applied by the branch and bound algorithm, from which we can derive results like the following:

- If during execution of the parallel algorithm no primary nodes are around any more, the algorithm must have obtained an optimal solution, and may terminate.
- At each point during execution of the parallel algorithm, at least one primary node is being handled.
- The elimination of primary nodes is possible during the parallel execution of the algorithm.

The first two results ensure that the parallel algorithm cannot run slower than the sequential algorithm executed on the slowest processor in the parallel system. In the last situation, acceleration anomalies may be observed, since such an anomaly can only occur if primary nodes are eliminated.

The rest of the paper is laid out as follows. In Section 2, we present the standard rules and ideas of (sequential) branch and bound, together with some definitions that we will need in the sequel. Moreover, we will define the class of parallelizations that we will consider. In Section 3, we will derive the results as sketched above. Section 4 relates the results to preventing or enabling anomalies. One of the observations is that it might be dangerous to extend a parallel system with a processor, that is appreciably less powerful than the other ones, because it increases the theoretical upper bound on the execution time. That this effect is not only of theoretical nature is illustrated in Section 5, where an experiment is described in which adding a slow processor results in a significant slowdown. In the last section, we present our conclusions.

## 2 The branch and bound algorithm

Branch and bound algorithms solve optimization problems by partitioning the solution space, i.e., the original problem is repeatedly decomposed into smaller subproblems until a solution has been obtained. Throughout the paper, we will assume that all optimization problems are posed as minimization problems, and that solving a problem is tantamount to finding a feasible solution with minimal value. If there are several such solutions, it does not matter which one is found.

Let $P_0$ be the minimization problem to be solved. The way $P_0$ is repeatedly decomposed into smaller subproblems can be represented by a finite rooted tree, called *problem tree*. We denote the problem tree by $T = (P, A)$, where $P$ is the set of nodes, and $A$ is the set of arcs. There is a one-to-one correspondence between the nodes of the problem tree and the subproblems generated. The *root* of the problem tree is $P_0$. If node $P_j$ is generated by decomposition from node $P_i$, then $(P_i, P_j) \in A$. We say that $P_i$ is the *parent* of $P_j$, and that $P_j$ is a *child* of $P_i$. The part of the problem tree that is actually generated by the branch and bound algorithm is called the *search tree*.

Branch and bound algorithms can be characterized by four rules [Mitten, 1970; Ibaraki, 1976]: a *branching rule* stating how nodes can be decomposed, a *bounding rule* for the computation of a lower bound on the optimal solution value of a node, a *selection rule* defining which node to branch from next, and an *elimination rule* stating how to recognize and eliminate nodes that cannot yield an optimal solution to the original problem. We will call these four rules the *basic rules* of the branch and bound algorithm.

In the following, we will discuss the basic rules in detail, and identify important properties of the rules with respect to termination and correctness of branch and bound algorithms. We treat the rules in the same order as their definition.

Let $f(P_i)$ be the optimal solution value of node $P_i$, and let $P_i$ be decomposed into $P_{i_1}, P_{i_2}, \ldots, P_{i_m}$ by the branching rule. Then, we must have:

$$f(P_i) = \min_{k=1,\ldots,m} f(P_{i_k}).$$

In other words, the optimal solution value of a node can be obtained by evaluating its children. In practice, branching rules are such that each feasible solution to a parent node is also a solution of at least one of its children.

Let $g(P_i)$ be a lower bound on the optimal solution value of node $P_i$ computed by the bounding rule, and let $L$ be the set of leaf nodes that can be solved without decomposition. We postulate the following properties of the lower bound function:

$$g(P_i) \leq f(P_i), \text{ for } P_i \in P,$$

$$g(P_i) = f(P_i), \text{ for } P_i \in L, \text{ and}$$

$$g(P_i) \leq g(P_j), \text{ for } (P_i, P_j) \in A.$$

The properties state respectively that $g$ is a lower bound estimate of $f$, that $g$ is exact when $P_i$ can be solved without decomposition, and that lower bounds never decrease when traversing down the problem tree.

The concept of *heuristic search* provides a framework to compare all kinds of selection rules, for example, depth first, breadth first, or best bound [Ibaraki 1976]. In heuristic search, a *heuristic search function* $h$ is defined on the set of nodes. It governs the order in which the nodes are branched from. The branch and bound algorithm always branches from the node with the smallest heuristic value.

A heuristic search function $h$ is *injective* if and only if it assigns a unique value to each node, i.e.,

$$h(P_i) \neq h(P_j), \text{ if } P_i \neq P_j.$$

Injectivity is no severe restriction because each noninjective heuristic search function can be easily transformed into an injective one by extending a heuristic value with the unique path number of its argument as an additional component, and by defining a lexicographic order on these tuples. As all path numbers are unique, all heuristic values of the nodes will be unique. Notice that an injective heuristic search function induces a complete order on the nodes.

A heuristic search function $h$ is *nonmisleading* if and only if the heuristic value of a node is not less than the heuristic value of its parent, i.e.,

$$h(P_i) \leq h(P_j), \text{ for } (P_i, P_j) \in A.$$

Note that the most common search strategies, like depth first and best bound search, are nonmisleading by nature.

The last rule to be considered is the elimination rule. It consists of three types of tests for eliminating nodes.

Firstly, the *feasibility test*: a node can be discarded from further examination if it can be proven not to have a feasible solution.

Secondly, the *lower bound test*: a node, of which the lower bound is no less than the value of a known feasible solution, cannot produce a better solution, and can be eliminated. The *incumbent* represents the best solution obtained so far, together with its value.

Finally, a node may be discarded by the *dominance test*. We say that a node $P_i$ dominates a node $P_j$ if it can be proven that $f(P_i) \leq f(P_j)$. If $P_j$ has a feasible solution, $P_i$ must produce as least as good a solution as $P_j$. However, if $P_j$ is infeasible, $P_i$ may be infeasible as well. In both cases, $P_j$ does not have to be investigated any more. The dominance test is based upon a dominance relation $\mathcal{D}$. If the dominance relation holds for a given pair of nodes $P_i$ and

$P_j$, denoted by $P_i \mathcal{D} P_j$, then $P_i$ dominates $P_j$. According to Ibaraki [1977], a dominance relation $D$ should satisfy the next properties:

$\mathcal{D}$ is a partial order (a reflexive, antisymmetric, and transitive relation),

$P_i \mathcal{D} P_j \Rightarrow P_j$ is not a proper descendant of $P_i$, and

$(P_i \mathcal{D} P_j$ and $P_i \neq P_j) \Rightarrow P_i \mathcal{D} P_{j\bullet}$, for all descendants $P_{j\bullet}$ of $P_j$.

In this paper, we assume that all dominance relations possess the above properties. Because the dominance relation is a partial order, it is possible that for some $P_i$ and $P_j$ neither $P_i \mathcal{D} P_j$ nor $P_j \mathcal{D} P_i$ holds. If a dominance relation is *weak*, most of the nodes are incomparable. A node $P_i$ is said to be a *currently dominating node* if it has been generated and has not been dominated so far. Due to the transitivity of the dominance relation, for each dominated node there exists a currently dominating node at any point in time of the execution of the branch and bound algorithm. So, for efficiently implementing the dominance test, the branch and bound algorithm only has to keep track of all currently dominating nodes. Note that the lower bound test can be viewed upon as a special case of the dominance test.

At this point, we will introduce some notions and definitions, which we need in the remainder of the paper.

A function $f$ is said to be *consistent* with a function $f^*$, if

$$f(P_i) \leq f(P_j) \Rightarrow f^*(P_i) \leq f^*(P_j), \text{ for all } P_i, P_j \in P.$$

A dominance relation $\mathcal{D}$ is said to be *consistent* with a function $f$, if

$$P_i \mathcal{D} P_j \Rightarrow f(P_i) \leq f(P_j), \text{ for all } P_i, P_j \in P.$$

An *active node* is a node that has been generated and hitherto neither has been completely branched from nor eliminated. The active nodes can be divided into two categories: those that are currently being branched from, and the others. In each stage of the computation, there exists an *active set*, i.e., the set containing all active nodes that are not being branched from at that moment.

A *critical node* is a node with lower bound less than the optimal solution value.

## 2.1 A sequential implementation

In sequential branch and bound algorithms, there is a main loop in which the basic rules are repeatedly applied in some predefined order. We consider the following implementation of the loop.

Using the selection rule, a node in the active set is chosen to branch from. The node is extracted from the active set, and decomposed according to the branching rule. For each of the children thus generated the bounding rule is applied to calculate a lower bound. If during the computation of the bound the child node is solved, i.e., the optimal solution to the node is found, the incumbent will be updated, depending on whether the newly found solution value is better than the one found so far. If a child node is not solved during computation of the bound, it is added to the active set. Finally, the elimination rule is used to prune the active set.

The computation continues until the active set is empty. If so, the incumbent represents an optimal solution to the original problem.

## 2.2 A parallel implementation

In this paper, we will focus on parallelizations where iteration steps of the same type as in the sequential algorithm are executed concurrently and asynchronously by several processes, called workers. There is one global data structure, the *extended active set*, which is the active set, augmented by the incumbent. If no confusion can arise, we will drop the adjective extended.

The data structure can be considered as an abstract data type, on which two operations are defined: `insert` and `select`. The `insert` operation takes as parameters a possibly empty set of nodes, and an optional solution. The effect of the operation will be equivalent to an insertion of the given nodes into the active set, followed by a replacement of the incumbent by the newly offered solution, if the latter one is better, and by an elimination of those nodes in the active set that can be removed by the elimination rule. The `select` operation will only succeed if the active set contains at least one node, in which case it will extract a node using the selection rule. If there is no node in the set, a special value `empty` is delivered.

The above description does not prescribe that the active set is actually implemented as indicated. It only formulates the effect of the operations. Furthermore, we do not indicate whether the active set must be implemented as a separate process, or in a distributed fashion, e.g., distributed over the worker processes.

The `insert` and `select` operations can be executed concurrently. We demand from the active set that the operations are implemented as atomic transactions. Executing the operations in parallel must have the same effect as executing an interleaving of the operations, i.e., a sequential execution in some unspecified order. Consequently, the active set maintains the following invariant, that is true before and after each operation (i.e., in the interleaving): the active set contains, in addition to the incumbent, only nodes that have been submitted to the `insert` operation, it contains no nodes that can be removed by the elimination rule, and if the set is nonempty, the `select` operation will succeed in extracting a node from it.

The worker processes execute a loop. Each iteration starts with a `select` operation on the active set, which will be repeated until the result is not `empty`, i.e., a node is extracted from the active set. Having obtained a node, the worker branches from it, and performs an `insert` operation on the results of the branching.

Finally, we will have to deal with termination. The parallel computation will be finished when all workers receive only `empties` on their `select` operations. In that case, the active set will contain an optimal solution to the original problem.

Termination detection can be implemented by letting the active set keep track of the number of workers trying to extract a node from the active set. If this number equals the total number of workers, the active set can notify the workers that the computation has completed.

For the proofs to follow, we will have to specify the notions of *being branched from*, *active node*, and *active set*, in order to avoid ambiguity in the parallel case. A node is being branched from, if it has been extracted by the `select` operation, and the `insert` operation on the results of the branching has not completed yet. An active node is a node that is either being branched from, or that has been inserted in the active set, and has not yet been selected or eliminated. The active set contains the set of active nodes that are currently not being branched from.

As a final remark, note that a parallelization with only one worker is equivalent to the sequential algorithm described in the previous subsection. We will call this algorithm the *corresponding sequential branch and bound algorithm*. The *sequential solution* is defined as the optimal solution yielded by the corresponding sequential branch and bound algorithm.

## 3 Properties of primary nodes

In this section, we investigate the properties of primary nodes. We will prove the results as indicated in the introduction. The first theorem deals with the elimination of nodes.

**Theorem 1.** Let $\mathcal{D}$ be a dominance relation, consistent with the lower bound function. If during execution of the parallel algorithm, an optimal solution is known, and there are no active primary nodes around any more, all active nodes can be eliminated.

**Proof.** Consider an active node. As there are no primary nodes around any longer, it must be a nonprimary node. In the sequential case, the node itself or one of its ancestors may have been eliminated, for two reasons. In both situations, we will show that the active node can be eliminated by the parallel algorithm too.

First, if the active nonprimary node, or one of its ancestors, was killed by a lower bound test, it can now be eliminated by a lower bound test as well, as an optimal solution is known.

Second, if the active nonprimary node, or one of its ancestors, was eliminated by a dominance test, the sequentially dominating node, or one of its ancestors, must have been eliminated, because it cannot have not been generated (the active nonprimary node would then have been eliminated) and will not be generated in the future (its father must be a primary node, and there are no more primary nodes nor can they be generated any more). Again, there are two cases. If the sequentially dominating node, or one of its ancestors, has been eliminated by a lower bound test, the active nonprimary node can be eliminated by a lower bound test as well, due to the consistency of $\mathcal{D}$ with the lower bound function. Similarly, if the sequentially dominating node, or one of its ancestors, has been eliminated by a dominance test, the active nonprimary node can also be eliminated by a dominance bound test due to the transitivity of $\mathcal{D}$ and Ibaraki's third condition on dominance relations. $\square$

The consequence of Theorem 1 is that the parallel algorithm, after having obtained an optimal solution, will terminate when all primary nodes have been branched from or eliminated. The next theorem states sufficient conditions to ensure that the parallel algorithm will actually have found an optimal solution when no primary nodes are around any more, and that during the process at least one primary node is being branched from.

**Theorem 2.** Let $\mathcal{D}$ be a dominance relation, consistent with the lower bound function, such that primary nodes are not dominated by any other node, and let $h$ be an injective, nonmisleading heuristic search function. If during execution of the parallel algorithm, no active primary nodes are around any more, an optimal solution must have been found. Furthermore, if during execution of the parallel algorithm a nonprimary node is being selected, some worker process is currently branching from a primary node.

**Proof.** We start with the first part of the theorem. If there are no primary nodes around, new primary nodes cannot be generated any more. It follows that either the corresponding sequential solution has been generated, or that it, or one of its ancestors has been eliminated by a dominance test. The last part is due to the assumptions on $\mathcal{D}$ that guarantee that the nodes on the path from to root to the sequential solution (they are all primary nodes) cannot be eliminated by a dominance test. Hence, either the sequential solution or an alternative one has been found.

The second part of the theorem is a bit more complicated. Suppose that there is currently no primary node being branched from, and let nonprimary node $P_{np}$ be the node with lowest heuristic value in the active set. In the corresponding sequential algorithm $P_{np}$ has not been branched from, and, therefore, $P_{np}$, or one of its ancestors, must have been eliminated. Let $P_{np}^{seq}$ be the node that eliminates $P_{np}$, or one of its ancestors, either by a lower bound or a dominance test, and let $P_f$ be the father of $P_{np}^{seq}$.

As $P_{np}^{seq}$ has been generated in the sequential algorithm, $P_f$ must be a primary node. Because $P_{np}^{seq}$ eliminates $P_{np}$, $P_f$ must have been branched from before the sequential algorithm would select $P_{np}$. Due to the fact that the heuristic search function $h$ is injective and nonmisleading, the sequential algorithm branches from nodes in increasing order of their $h$-values, which implies that $h(P_f) < h(P_{np})$. We have to consider three situations with respect to the parallel algorithm.

First, $P_f$ has been branched from, and $P_{np}^{seq}$ has been generated. If $P_{np}^{seq}$ has eliminated $P_{np}$ by a lower bound test, the current incumbent, which must be at least as good as $P_{np}^{seq}$, can eliminate $P_{np}$. On the other hand, if $P_{np}^{seq}$ has eliminated $P_{np}$ by a dominance test, the node that currently dominates $P_{np}^{seq}$ also dominates $P_n$.

Second, $P_f$, or one of its ancestors, has been eliminated. Let $g$ be the lower bound function, and let $v_{inc}$ denote the value of the incumbent. We now have that $v_{inc} \leq g(P_f) \leq g(P_{np}^{seq}) \leq g(P_{np})$, where the first inequality stems from the fact that primary nodes can only be eliminated by a lower bound test, and the last inequality is true irrespective whether $P_{np}^{seq}$ eliminates $P_{np}$ by a lower bound or a dominance test. Hence, $P_{np}$ can be eliminated by a lower bound test.

Third, because of the assumption that currently no primary node is being branched from, the last possibility is that $P_f$, or one of its ancestors, is a member of the active set. If this is the case, $h(P_f)$ must be greater than $h(P_{np})$, because $P_{np}$ has the lowest $h$-value in the active set. We have, however, $h(P_f) < h(P_{np})$, proving that $P_f$, or one of its ancestors, cannot be a member of the active set. □

The last theorem of this section is concerned with the elimination of primary nodes.

**Theorem 3.** There exist heuristic search functions and dominance relations such that primary nodes may be eliminated by the parallel algorithm.

**Proof.** Assume that no primary nodes are eliminated by a dominance test. We have to make a distinction between critical and noncritical nodes. Critical nodes cannot be eliminated by a lower bound test. Consequently, if the parallel algorithm is able to eliminate primary nodes, the sequential algorithm must branch from noncritical nodes. Almost every heuristic search function may allow for branching from noncritical nodes. Some examples are depth first search, breadth first search, but even best bound search (if there are nodes with lower bound equal to the optimal solution value [Fox, Lenstra, Rinnnooy Kan & Schrage, 1978]). □

## 4    Exploiting properties of primary nodes

While designing parallel branch and bound algorithms, one wishes to prevent detrimental anomalies, while leaving open the possibility of acceleration anomalies. We will show how the theorems from the previous section can be used to reach this goal.

In our presentation, we will not consider the time needed for communication and the like. We will only take into account the effect of parallelism on the search tree generated. Detrimental and acceleration anomalies are defined by comparing the execution of the parallel algorithm with the execution of the corresponding sequential algorithm. The sequential algorithm is continuously branching from primary nodes. Hence, the anomalies may only happen if the search tree in the parallel case is different from the search tree generated by the sequential algorithm. In other words, an anomaly is induced by the (in)efficiency of either version of the algorithm. In the next subsection, however, we will show that certain inefficiencies are harmless, and do not cause detrimental anomalies to happen.

Unproportional acceleration or deceleration of a parallel branch and bound algorithm may also be observed when extending a parallel architecture with an additional processor. We do not deal with this situation from a theoretical point of view, but only mention an example from Lai & Sahni [1984], in which almost doubling the number of processors still leads to a slowdown of the parallel algorithm, where the search tree remains the same.

## 4.1 Preventing detrimental anomalies

Under the conditions of Theorems 1 & 2, the parallel algorithm will always work on a primary node, and it terminates as soon as there are no primary nodes around any more. Hence, there will be no detrimental anomaly.

Without dominance relations, the use of an injective and nonmisleading heuristic search function will be sufficient. The presence of dominance relations complexifies the situation. It is most of the time impossible to check whether or not a primary node can be eliminated by a dominance test in the parallel algorithm. However, we know of two examples from the literature which state conditions that prevent detrimental anomalies. We will show that they ensure that no primary nodes are eliminated by a dominance test, i.e., they can be seen as special cases of our theorems.

**Li & Wah [1984].** In their paper, in which they develop a synchronous version of the global active set branch and bound algorithm, Li & Wah show that no detrimental anomaly occurs if (a) the heuristic search function is injective, non-misleading, and consistent with the lower bound function, and (b) the dominance relation is consistent with the heuristic search function.

**Theorem 4.** Let the heuristic search function $h$ be injective, nonmisleading, and consistent with the lower bound function $g$, and let the dominance relation $\mathcal{D}$ be consistent with $h$. Under these conditions, no primary node can be eliminated by a dominance test.

**Proof.** Let primary node $P_1$ be dominated by node $P_2$. We have that

$$P_2 \mathcal{D} P_1 \Rightarrow h(P_2) \leq h(P_1) \Rightarrow g(P_2) \leq g(P_1), \text{ i.e.,}$$

$\mathcal{D}$ is consistent with $g$. Consider the sequential algorithm. Since $h(P_2) \leq h(P_1) \Rightarrow h(P_2) < h(P_1)$, the father of $P_2$, with an even a smaller $h$-value than $P_2$, cannot be a primary node. Otherwise, $P_2$ would have been generated and would have caused an elimination of primary node $P_1$. In the same way as in Theorem 2, we can now show that the elimination of the father of $P_2$, or one of its ancestors, leads to an elimination of $P_1$ as well, which is a contradiction since $P_1$ is assumed to be primary node. $\square$

**Trienekens [1990].** The conditions posed by Trienekens are more or less the same as those from Li & Wah. Trienekens shows that no detrimental anomaly occurs if (a) the heuristic search function is injective, nonmisleading, and strictly consistent with the lower bound function (i.e., $\leq$ is replaced by $<$), and (b) the dominance relation is consistent with the lower bound function.

**Theorem 5.** Let the heuristic search function $h$ be injective, nonmisleading, and strictly consistent with the lower bound function $g$, and let the dominance relation $\mathcal{D}$ be consistent with $g$. Under these conditions, no primary node can be eliminated by a dominance test.

**Proof.** We will prove the theorem by showing that the dominance relation $\mathcal{D}$ is consistent with the heuristic search function $h$, in which case we can apply the previous theorem. Let node $P_1$ be dominated by a node $P_2$. It follows that $g(P_2) \leq g(P_1)$. However, if $h(P_1) < h(P_2)$, then $g(P_1) < g(P_2)$, which is in contradiction with the previous statement. Hence, $h(P_2) \leq h(P_1)$, and the dominance relation $\mathcal{D}$ is consistent with the heuristic search function $h$. Now, we can apply Theorem 4 for our proof. $\square$

We will end our discussion on the prevention of detrimental anomalies by giving an upper bound on the execution time needed by the parallel algorithm, if Theorems 1 & 2 can be applied.

Let $T_{par}(I)$ denote the time needed to solve problem instance $I$ with the given parallel branch and bound algorithm on the given machine, let $T_{seq}(I)$ denote the time needed to solve problem instance $I$ with the corresponding sequential branch and bound algorithm on the least powerful processing element of the given parallel machine, and let $T_{max}$ be an upper bound on the time needed to branch from a single node by the least powerful processing element of the given parallel machine.

**Theorem 6.** If the dominance relation is consistent with the lower bound function, such that primary nodes are not dominated by any other node, and if the heuristic search function is injective and nonmisleading, then $T_{par}(I) \leq T_{seq}(I) + T_{max}$.

**Proof.** Trivial. $\square$

The bound on $T_{par}$ is, or course, rather loose, because it assumes that all essential work is performed by the slowest processor element. It is, however, all that can be guaranteed.

## 4.2 Allowing acceleration anomalies

Acceleration anomalies may only occur if the search tree generated by the parallel algorithm is smaller than the one generated by the corresponding sequential algorithm. Consequently, they only happen if primary nodes are eliminated.

First, suppose primary nodes may be eliminated by a dominance test. If so, the Theorems 1 & 2 cannot be applied, and allowing for acceleration anomalies in this way may result in the opposite: a slowdown of the algorithm.

Second, suppose primary nodes may not be eliminated by a dominance test. For an acceleration anomaly to occur, it is necessary that primary nodes are eliminated by a lower bound test. As critical nodes have to be branched from at all times, the sequential algorithm must branch from other nodes as well. In Lai & Sahni [1984], examples are given that show that the heuristic search strategies indicated in Theorem 3 indeed may effect an acceleration anomaly. Unfortunately, we also have the next theorem.

**Theorem 7.** Let the heuristic search function $h$ be injective, nonmisleading, and consistent with the lower bound function $g$, and let the dominance relation be such that it cannot cause elimination of primary nodes. If the lower bound cannot attain the optimal solution value, except for nodes representing an optimal solution, no primary nodes can be eliminated at all.

**Proof.** The sequential algorithm branches from nodes in increasing order of their $h$-value, and due to the consistency of the heuristic search function with the lower bound function, in nondecreasing order of their $g$-value. Hence, the sequential algorithm only branches from critical nodes. Because these critical nodes cannot be eliminated by a dominance test, the parallel algorithm must branch from them too. □

For counter examples (in the absence of dominance relations) if either one of the conditions is dropped, we refer to Lai & Sahni [1984] and Burton, Huntbach, McKeown & Rayward-Smith [1983].

## 5   Anomalies in the real world

Acceleration anomalies of parallel branch and bound algorithms have been observed in practice, whereas detrimental anomalies don't seem to happen very often. See, for instance, McKeown, Rayward-Smith & Rush [1992].

In a number of computational experiments, in which we solved the traveling salesman problem (TSP) on a loosely coupled network of workstations with the branch and bound algorithm that we are considering in this paper, we encountered an unexpected behavior of the algorithm. As the results are interesting, we will deal with them briefly. For a complete description of the experiments, we refer to Trienekens [1990].

In the experiments, we repeatedly enlarged the loosely coupled network by adding processing elements. All the processing elements, except one, were of equal processing power. The one exception had significantly less power. Because the asynchronism of the branch and bound algorithm introduces nondeterminism, we solved each instance of the traveling salesman problem several times.

Most of the time, adding a processing element of equal power decreased the time needed to solve the problem instance. Sometimes, the time didn't change significantly, but it never increased noticeably. The situation changed when we added the less powerful processing element. Next to a greater fluctuation in execution times, also deceleration of the algorithm could be observed. Figure 1

| worker processes on | fastest time (in minutes) | number of nodes | slowest time (in minutes) | number of nodes |
|---|---|---|---|---|
| 2 pyramids | 29.65 | 260 | 29.82 | 260 |
| 3 pyramids | 20.35 | 260 | 20.40 | 260 |
| 4 pyramids | 15.82 | 260 | 15.85 | 260 |
| 5 pyramids | 13.93 | 260 | 14.05 | 260 |
| 2 pyramids + 1 sun | 26.78 | 260 | 27.03 | 260 |
| 3 pyramids + 1 sun | 18.90 | 260 | 19.03 | 260 |
| 4 pyramids + 1 sun | 15.02 | 260 | 15.10 | 260 |
| 5 pyramids + 1 sun | 13.30 | 260 | 13.75 | 260 |

(a) Results on a 75 city instance.

| worker processes on | fastest time (in minutes) | number of nodes | slowest time (in minutes) | number of nodes |
|---|---|---|---|---|
| 2 pyramids | 0.82 | 12 | 0.85 | 12 |
| 3 pyramids | 0.80 | 15 | 0.88 | 14 |
| 4 pyramids | 0.72 | 20 | 0.90 | 17 |
| 5 pyramids | 0.82 | 24 | 0.88 | 24 |
| 2 pyramids + 1 sun | 0.92 | 13 | 1.70 | 25 |
| 3 pyramids + 1 sun | 0.82 | 17 | 1.05 | 19 |
| 4 pyramids + 1 sun | 0.97 | 21 | 1.18 | 29 |
| 5 pyramids + 1 sun | 0.80 | 26 | 1.18 | 27 |

(b) Results on a 50 city instance.

**Fig. 1.** Results from the parallel algorithm for the TSP.

shows some typical outcomes. Looking at primary nodes and Theorem 6, we can explain what happened.

If at a given point in time during execution, the current number of processing elements is not large enough to handle all presently active primary nodes at the same time, the addition of a processing element has the effect that more primary nodes can be handled in parallel and, therefore, the time needed to handle all primary nodes will decrease.

However, if there are not enough primary nodes for the available processing elements, the processing elements start branching from nonprimary nodes. As long as the relatively fast processing elements work on primary nodes, and the slow ones on nonprimary nodes, everything is still under control. But if it is the other way around, it may happen that the computation is hold up, because the results from the slow processing elements are delayed. The numbers from Figure 1 show that both situations occur when adding a slow processing element.

We conclude that it can be dangerous to increase the processing power of a system by adding a less powerful processing element. Only if there is enough parallelism in the problem instance to be solved, this will decrease the execution time. Otherwise, the execution time may increase.

# 6 Conclusions

Our research on the anomalies that can occur during the execution of parallel branch and bound algorithms has yielded sufficient conditions to prevent detrimental anomalies. The conditions are stated as properties concerning the problem instance to be solved, and not in terms of the branch and bound algorithm used for solving the problem instance. Hence, the results are valid for all (parallel) branch and bound algorithms, as long as these algorithms comply to the conditions under which the properties are valid.

The conditions derived contain the ones already known for synchronous branch and bound algorithms as a special case.

The conditions for preventing detrimental anomalies are all worst case conditions. They do not state anything about the average performance of branch and bound algorithms.

Acceleration anomalies may occur, and indeed do occur, under certain conditions. The presence of 'nasty' dominance relations imply that allowing for acceleration anomalies may also imply the occurrence of detrimental anomalies.

In practice, a potential detrimental anomaly may be obscured by an acceleration anomaly, and the other way around. The extension of a parallel architecture with some relatively slow processor has to be done with some care.

# References

1. F.W. Burton, M.M. Huntbach, G.P. McKeown, V.J. Rayward-Smith (1983). *Parallelism in Branch-and-Bound Algorithms*, Report CSA/3/1983, University of East Anglia, Norwich.
2. R. Corrêa, A. Ferreira (1995a). A distributed implementation of asynchronous parallel branch-and-bound. A. Ferreira & J. Rolim (eds.). *Solving Irregular Problems in Parallel: State of the Art*, Kluwer, Boston, to appear.
3. R. Corrêa, A. Ferreira (1995b). Modeling parallel branch-and-bound for asynchronous implementations. *1994 DIMACS Workshop on Parallel Processing of Discrete Optimization problems*, DIMACS, Piscataway, to appear.
4. B.L. Fox, J.K. Lenstra, A.H.G. Rinnnooy Kan, L.E. Schrage (1978). Branching from the largest upper bound: folklore and facts. *European J. Oper. Res. 2*, 191–194.
5. T. Ibaraki (1976). Theoretical comparisons of search strategies in branch-and-bound algorithms. *Int. J. Comput. Inform. Sci. 5*, 315–344.
6. T. Ibaraki (1977). The power of dominance relations in branch-and-bound algorithms. *J. Assoc. Comput. Mach. 24*, 264–279.
7. T.-H. Lai, S. Sahni (1984). Anomalies in parallel branch-and-bound algorithms. *Comm. ACM 27*, 594–602.
8. T.-H. Lai, A. Sprague (1985). Performance of parallel branch-and-bound algorithms. *IEEE Trans. Comput. C-34*, 962–964.
9. T.-H. Lai, A. Sprague (1986). A note on anomalies in parallel branch-and-bound algorithms with one-to-one bounding functions. *Inform. Process. Lett. 23*, 119–122.
10. G.-J. Li, B.W. Wah (1984). *Computational Efficiency of Parallel Approximate Branch-and-Bound Algorithms*, Report TR-EE 84-6, Purdue University, West Lafayette.

11. G.-J. Li, B.W. Wah (1986). Coping with anomalies in parallel branch-and-bound algorithms. *IEEE Trans. Comput. C-35*, 568–573.
12. G.P. McKeown, V.J. Rayward-Smith, S.A. Rush (1992). Parallel branch-and-bound. L. Kronsjoe, D. Shumsheruddin (eds.) *Advances in Parallel Algorithms*, Advanced Topics in Computer Science 14, Blackwell, Oxford, 111–150.
13. L.G. Mitten (1970). Branch-and-bound methods: general formulation and properties. *Oper. Res. 18*, 24–34.
14. H.W.J.M. Trienekens (1990). *Parallel Branch and Bound Algorithms*, Ph.D. thesis, Erasmus University, Rotterdam.

# Fast Priority Queues for
# Parallel Branch-and-Bound

Peter Sanders

University of Karlsruhe, 76128 Karlsruhe, Germany
Email: sanders@ira.uka.de

**Abstract.** Currently used parallel best first branch-and-bound algorithms either suffer from contention at a centralized priority queue or can only approximate the best first strategy. Both fast strategy for parallel priority queues are known but they cannot be implemented very efficiently on contemporary machines.

We present quite simple randomized algorithms for parallel priority queues on distributed memory machines. For branch-and-bound they are asymptotically as efficient as previously known PRAM algorithms with high probability. The simplest versions require not much more communication than the approximated branch-and-bound algorithm of Karp and Zhang.

**Keywords:** Analysis of randomized algorithms, distributed memory, load balancing, median selection, parallel best first branch-and-bound, parallel priority queue.

## 1 Introduction

Branch-and-bound search is an important technique for many combinatorial optimization problems. Since it can be a quite time consuming technique, parallelization is an important issue.

This paper presents a new technique for parallelizing best first branch-and-bound. It is based on a randomized implementation of a distributed priority queue which supports fast collective access to the globally best elements. The new algorithm expends as few nodes as implementations based on centralized priority queues, which suffer from a severe communication bottleneck. Our algorithm is asymptotically not more communication intensive than approaches which can only coarsely approximate the global best first strategy. (Preliminary results of this research have been presented in[26].)

For simplicity the methods presented here are described in a branch-and-bound context, but the algorithm contains generally useful subroutines which constitute improved algorithms for parallel priority queues and give a new insight into parallel median selection.

We go on by introducing models for the parallel machine, the analysis of randomized algorithms and branch-and-bound in Section 2. Section 3 surveys

# Fast Priority Queues for
# Parallel Branch-and-Bound

Peter Sanders

University of Karlsruhe, 76128 Karlsruhe, Germany
Email: sanders@ira.uka.de

**Abstract.** Currently used parallel best first branch-and-bound algorithms either suffer from contention at a centralized priority queue or can only approximate the best first strategy. Bottleneck free algorithms for parallel priority queues are known but they cannot be implemented very efficiently on contemporary machines.

We present quite simple randomized algorithms for parallel priority queues on distributed memory machines. For branch-and-bound they are asymptotically as efficient as previously known PRAM algorithms with high probability. The simplest versions require not much more communication than the approximated branch-and-bound algorithm of Karp and Zhang.

**Keywords:** Analysis of randomized algorithms, distributed memory, load balancing, median selection, parallel best first branch-and-bound, parallel pritority queue.

## 1 Introduction

Branch-and-bound search is an important technique for many combinatorial optimization problems. Since it can be a quite time consuming technique, parallelization is an important issue.

This paper presents a new technique for parallelizing best first branch-and-bound. It is based on a randomized implementation of a distributed priority queue which supports fast collective access to the globally best elements. The new algorithm expands as few nodes as implementations based on centralized priority queues which suffer from a severe communication bottleneck. Our algorithm is asymptotically not more communication intensive than approaches which can only coarsly approximate the global best first strategy. (Preliminary results of this research have been presented in [26].)

For simplicity, the methods presented here are described in a branch-and-bound context, but the algorithm contains generally useful subroutines which constitute improved algorithms for parallel priority queues and give some insights into parallel median selection.

We go on by introducing our models for the parallel machine, the analysis of randomized algorithms and branch-and-bound in Section 2. Section 3 surveys some relevant approaches to parallel branch-and-bound together with basic results about their efficiency. The main body of this paper is Section 4; it describes and analyses a randomized synchronous global best first branch-and-bound algorithm which can be described quite concisely and which turns out to be asymptotically very efficient. These results are complemented by Section 5 where we present enhancements which make the algorithm more effective on contemporary machines with asynchronous behavior, preference for coarse grained communication and a high penalty for collective operations. The conclusions in Section 6 summarize and discuss the results.

# 2 The Model

We first describe our model of a parallel machine in Section 2.1, and then define measures for randomized algorithms and some tools for their analysis in Section 2.2. Section 2.3 introduces branch-and-bound algorithms.

## 2.1 The Parallel Machine

We consider a MIMD computer with $n$ processors (PEs) which interact by exchanging messages through a network of diameter $d$. Messages are assumed to fit into a single network packet. The PEs work asynchronously. When we describe algorithms in a data parallel, synchronized style we do this in such a way that synchronization is not a bottleneck.

We do not assume a specific network topology. Instead, the algorithms are based on the following set of building blocks:

**Routing** Every PE either sends up to $k$ messages to randomly determined receivers, or receives up to $k$ messages from randomly determined senders ($k$ constant).

**Broadcast** One PE sends a message to all other PEs.

**Reduction** Given value $v_i$ on PE $i$ determine $v_0 \oplus v_1 \oplus \cdots \oplus v_{n-1}$ for an associative commutative operator $\oplus$. (We use min, max, and +).

**Prefix** For $v_i$ and $\oplus$ as above determine $v_0 \oplus v_1 \oplus \cdots \oplus v_i$ on PE $i$.

**Sort$^{\frac{1}{2}}$** Sort (or rank) a sample of $n^{\frac{1}{2}}$ values located on different PEs.

The analysis can focus on finding the number of necessary basic operations. The execution time for a particular network is then easy to determine by multiplying the counts with the execution times $T_{\text{Routing}}$, $T_{\text{Broadcast}}$, $T_{\text{Reduction}}$, $T_{\text{Prefix}}$ and $T_{\text{Sort}^{\frac{1}{2}}}$. However, in order to simplify the discussion, we assume that $\{T_{\text{Broadcast}}, T_{\text{Reduction}}, T_{\text{Prefix}}, T_{\text{Sort}^{\frac{1}{2}}}\} \cup O(\log n) \subseteq O(d)$ with high probability. This assumption is justified for many network, e.g., $r$-dimensional meshes, hypercubes and related constant degree networks (butterfly, perfect shuffle, ...) or a combination of a multistage network for routing and a tree network for collective operations. All the necessary results can be found in [14].

## 2.2 Analysis of Randomized Algorithms

The analysis of the randomized algorithms described here is based on the notion of behavior *with high probability*. Among the various variants of this notions we have adopted the one from [8].

**Definition 1.** A positive real valued random variable $X$ is in $O(f(n))$ *with high probability* – or $X \in \tilde{O}(f(n))$ for short – iff

$$\forall \beta > 0 : \exists c > 0, n_0 > 0 : \forall n \geq n_0 : \mathbf{P}[X > cf(n)] \leq n^{-\beta} ,$$

i.e., the probability that $X$ exceeds the bound $f$ by more than a constant factor is polynomially small. In this paper, the variable used to express high probability is always $n$ – the number of PEs.

One advantage of the high probability approach is that there are quite simple rules combining results about simpler problems into more complex results. In this paper we need the following results which we present without proof because they are based on quite straightforward elementary probability theory.

**Lemma 2.** *Let* $X_1 \in \tilde{O}(f_1), \ldots, X_k \in \tilde{O}(f_k)$ *be random variables (k constant).*

$$\bigotimes_{i=1}^{k} X_i \in \tilde{O}\left(\bigotimes_{i=1}^{k} f_i\right) \text{ for } \bigotimes \in \left\{\max, \sum, \prod\right\} \tag{1}$$

**Lemma 3.** *Let* $\{X_1, \ldots, X_m\} \subseteq \tilde{O}(f)$ *be a set of identically distributed random variables (m at most polynomial in n).*

$$\max_{i=1}^{m} X_i \in \tilde{O}(f) \tag{2}$$

$$\sum_{i=1}^{m} X_i \in \tilde{O}(mf) \tag{3}$$

A keystone of many probabilistic proofs are the following *Chernoff bounds* which give quite tight bounds on the probability that the sum of 0/1-random variables (Bernoulli Experiments) deviates from the expected value by some factor.

**Lemma 4 Chernoff bounds.** *Let the random variable* $X$ *represent the number of heads after* $n$ *independent flips of a loaded coin where the probability for a head is p. Then [14]:*

$$\mathbf{P}[X \leq (1-\epsilon)np] \leq e^{-\epsilon^2 np/3} \text{ for } 0 < \epsilon < 1 \tag{4}$$

$$\mathbf{P}[X \geq (1+\epsilon)np] \leq e^{-\epsilon^2 np/2} \text{ for } 0 < \epsilon < 1 \tag{5}$$

$$\mathbf{P}[X \geq \alpha np] \leq e^{\left(1-\frac{1}{\alpha}-\ln \alpha\right)\alpha np} \text{ for } \alpha > 1 \tag{6}$$

## 2.3 Branch-and-Bound

We adopt the model of Karp-Zhang [9]. Let $H$ denote the search tree with a set of nodes $V$. Node degrees are bounded by a constant. All node costs $c(v)$ are assumed to be different[1] and $c(v)$ is monotonously increasing on any path from the root to a leaf. (When we compare nodes, we actually compare their costs.) We are looking for the leaf $v^*$ with minimal cost. Let $\tilde{V} = \{v \in V : v \leq v^*\}$ and let $\tilde{H}$ be the subtree of $H$ containing the nodes $\tilde{V}$. Let $m = |\tilde{V}|$ and $h$ the length of the longest root-leaf path in $\tilde{H}$. Clearly $\tilde{V}$ is a set of nodes which have to be expanded by any algorithm which wants to find $v^*$ together with a proof that there cannot be better solutions. We do not want to look at very small problems and therefore assume that $m \in \Omega(n \log n)$.

```
VAR F = {root node}                                    (* frontier set *)
VAR c* = ∞                                             (* best solution so far *)
WHILE F ≠ ∅ DO
    select some v ∈ F and remove it
    IF c(v) < c* THEN
        IF v is a leaf node THEN process new solution; c* := c(v)
        ELSE insert successors of v into F
```

**Fig. 1.** Abstract branch-and-bound algorithm.

Most branch-and-bound algorithms can be viewed as a variant of the abstract algorithm depicted in Figure 1. The processor cyclically selects a node $v$ from the *frontier* set $F$ and expands it. A node with a higher value than the best one investigated so far cannot lead to a solution and is pruned. The remaining inner nodes are expanded and their successors are inserted into the frontier set. Leaf nodes are solution candidates. When $F$ becomes empty, we know that the best leaf node found so far is the solution. For the analysis, we assume that expanding a node (i.e. generating its successors) takes time $T_x$; all other operations on nodes, node values and solutions take unit time.

If the best first selection strategy is used, i.e., $F$ is organized as a priority queue, the algorithm expands the (optimal) number of $m$ nodes. Selection and insertion can be done in time $O(\log m)$, e.g., by using a heap implementation of $F$. (log denotes the base 2 logarithm throughout this paper.) So, for sequential best first branch-and-bound we get the execution time

$$T_{\text{seq}} \in m(T_x + O(\log m)) \ .$$

---

[1] We can assume this without loss of generality because we could always append a unique node identification to the least significant digits of a node cost.

# 3  Approaches to Parallelization

Most parallelizations of branch-and-bound are based on executing the algorithm from Figure 1 on multiple (usually all) PEs in parallel. The main challenge is to implement the frontier set $F$ in such a way that the PEs perform useful work without incurring an undue communication overhead. Henceforth, we restrict the discussion to approximations of sequential *best first* branch-and-bound.

## 3.1  Global Best First Branch-and-Bound

In terms of node expansions, the best we can do is *global best first branch-and-bound*: $F$ is a global data structure and selections find the globally best nodes which are present in $F$. In spite of this rigid requirement, we may have to expand nodes outside $\tilde{H}$ if we want to exploit any parallelism at all. If we neglect communication and queue maintenance costs, global best first takes time

$$T_{\mathrm{par}} \in \Theta\left(T_{\mathrm{x}}\left(\frac{m}{n} + h\right)\right) \ .$$

The lower bound is easy to understand since every branch and bound algorithm must expand at least $m$ nodes and has a sequential component of $h$ node expansions. The upper bound holds for a synchronous algorithm where the $n$ best nodes are expanded in each iteration [9]: For every iteration, if $|F \cap \tilde{V}| \geq n$ all PEs get nodes from $\tilde{H}$. In all other iterations, the maximum path length to a leaf in $\tilde{H}$ is reduced. So, the synchronous algorithm needs at most $\frac{m}{n} + h$ iterations.

However, if we do take the queue maintenance cost into account, we see the difficulties of global best first search. If $F$ is implemented as a centralized priority queue [13] this implies an additional sequential component such that $T_{\mathrm{par}} \in \Omega\left(m \log m\right)$. Besides being a bottleneck, the queue manager's memory might be the limiting factor for the maximal possible problem size. The situation gets only slightly better by pipelining up to $O\left(\log m\right)$ priority queue accesses [24] because the head of the priority queue is still a bottleneck such that $T_{\mathrm{par}} \in \Omega\left(m\right)$. In practice these algorithms appear to perform worse than a centralized approach [24].

Better results are possible by exploiting a property of synchronous global best first: insertions and deletions can be performed collectively for $\Omega(n)$ elements at a time. By using a heap which contains multiple elements in each heap node and by substituting the compare and exchange operations of the usual heap algorithm by parallel sorting and merging operations, $n$ insertions and deletions can be performed in time $O(\log m)$ on EREW PRAMs [4] and on *pipelined hypercubes* [3][2]. However, these algorithms are quite complex and are based on difficult to implement sorting and merging algorithms. Furthermore, the results are less favorable on weaker (and more realistic) models of parallel computations. On single-ported hypercubes and meshes, timings of $O\left(\log m \log n\right)$ respectively $O\left(\sqrt{n} \log m\right)$ have been achieved [6, 23].

---

[2] This algorithm requires newly inserted elements to be sorted, so we must add another $O(\log n \log \log n)$ or $\tilde{O}\left(\log n\right)$ term for the sorting operation.

## 3.2 Local Best First Branch-and-Bound

In order to reduce communication overhead, most current approaches to parallel best-first branch-and-bound use local priority queues in combination with a load balancer which tries to approximate global best first by exchanging nodes between PEs.

A very simple approach is used in [9, 22]. Every new node is inserted into the local queue of a PE determined uniformly at random. For $m \in \Omega(n \log n)$, it is shown that $\tilde{O}\left(\frac{m}{n} + h\right)$ parallel branch-and-bound iterations are sufficient. In our more detailed model this results in execution times of

$$T_{\mathrm{par}} \in \tilde{O}\left(\left(\frac{m}{n} + h\right)(T_x + d + \log m)\right) .$$

The problem with this algorithm is that it is still too communication intensive for fine grained problems (i.e. small $T_x$) and that the random placement can lead to a considerable load imbalance – the best known bounds from [22] indicate a constant factor overhead above $2e \approx 5.4$. In practice, more adaptive load balancing algorithms are often preferred which exchange only some nodes. This can be done using global communication [17, 16, 12] local communication [15, 2, 17, 18, 29, 7, 28, 30] or using separate load balancing phases [5]. These algorithms appear to work quite well for many practical applications and there are a number of results about the achieved quality of load balancing. But little is known about how many nodes outside $\tilde{H}$ have to be expanded. One exception are specialized models of branch-and-bound which imply that there are many nodes with the same value [5]. This property can be exploited by specialized load balancers which are not very good for the general case however. Also, depth first search or iterative deepening search might also be a good approach for this class of problems.

# 4 A First Algorithm and its Analysis

We now describe and analyze an efficient synchronous algorithm for global best first branch-and-bound. The description starts with an overview of the basic algorithm in Section 4.1. We then elaborate probabilistic bounds on the sizes of some intermediate data structures in Section 4.2 which play a key role in the analysis of the algorithm. After investigating a nontrivial subroutine in Section 4.3 we can finally integrate the pieces into an analysis of the full algorithm in Section 4.4.

## 4.1 The Basic Algorithm

Our basic idea is to use Karp-Zhang's approach of local queues with random placement of nodes as an underlying data structure, but to extract the *globally* best nodes in each iteration. Figure 2 shows pseudocode for the algorithm. The local queue is stored in two parts; a sorted array $F_0$ which acts as a buffer for fast access to the smallest nodes, and a heap $F_1$ for the remaining nodes. Let

```
VAR c* = ∞: Number                           (* best solution value so far *)
VAR i = 0: Integer                           (* iteration counter *)
FORALL PEs DOPAR synchronously
    VAR F₀ = ∅: Sorted Array of Node         (* buffer *)
    VAR F₁ = ∅: Heap of Node                 (* main queue *)
    IF PENum = 0 THEN F₁ := {root node}
    WHILE not all queues empty DO
        i := i + 1; IF i ≡ 0 mod log n THEN F₁ := F₀ ∪ F₁; F₀ := ∅ FI
        WHILE |{v ∈ F̌₀ : v < min F̌₁}| < n DO F₀ := F₀ ∪ {deleteMin(F₁)}
        extract the n smallest nodes in F̌₀
        v := one of these on each PE
        branch-and-bound node expansion of v
        send successors of v to randomly determined PEs
        insert received nodes into F₀
```

**Fig. 2.** Synchronous global best first branch-and-bound.

the $\breve{\cdot}$-accent denote the global union operation, e.g., $\breve{F}_0$ denotes the union of all buffers. Every $\log n$ iterations of the main loop (we call this a *cycle*), the buffer $F_0$ is emptied into $F_1$. In Section 4.2 we show that this measure is sufficient to keep $F_0$ small ($|F_0| \in \tilde{O}(\log n)$) most of the time. The extraction of the $n$ best nodes proceeds in two phases. First, nodes are moved from $F_1$ to $F_0$ until the smallest $n$ nodes must be in the buffers[3]. This can be checked by counting the buffer nodes smaller than the minimum node in $\breve{F}_1$. Then, a distributed algorithm to be described in Section 4.3 finds the $n$ smallest nodes in $\breve{F}_0$. These nodes are removed and used for a synchronous branch-and-bound step (as in Algorithm 1). Newly generated nodes are then sent to other PEs determined uniformly at random and independently of each other. At their destination they are inserted into the local buffers.

## 4.2 Queue Sizes

**Lemma 5.** *The maximum number of new nodes to be inserted into $F_0$ on any PE after an iteration is in* $\tilde{O}\left(\frac{\log n}{\log \log n}\right)$.

*Proof.* Let $X_i$ denote the number of new nodes to be inserted on PE $i$. Since the search tree $H$ has constant degree, there is a constant $k$ such that $kn$ is a bound for the overall number of new nodes. The placements of nodes can be viewed as independent Bernoulli experiments with success probability $\frac{1}{n}$. (We count the placement of a node at PE $i$ as a success). Therefore, we can apply the Chernoff

---

[3] In order to avoid tedious discussions of special cases we assume throughout this paper that deleting nodes form empty queues returns dummy nodes with value ∞.

bound (6): Let $c$ be some constant we are free to choose.

$$\mathbf{P}\left[X_i \geq c\frac{\log n}{\log\log n}\right] \leq \exp\left[\left(1 - \frac{1}{\frac{c\log n}{k\log\log n}} - \log\frac{c\log n}{k\log\log n}\right)\frac{c\log n}{k\log\log n}k\right]$$

$$\leq \exp\left[\left(1 - \log\frac{c\log n}{k\log\log n}\right)c\frac{\log n}{\log\log n}\right]$$

$$= n^{-\frac{c}{\ln 2}\left(1 - \frac{\log\log\log n + \log(k/c) + 1}{\log\log n}\right)} \leq n^{-\beta}$$

for sufficiently large $n$ and an appropriate choice of $c$. Using the maximum rule (2) we conclude that $\max_{i=0}^{n-1} X_i$ is also in $\tilde{O}\left(\frac{\log n}{\log\log n}\right)$. ∎

Using similar techniques we can also derive the following bounds:

**Lemma 6.** *The maximum number of new nodes to be inserted into $F_0$ on any PE during a cycle is in $\tilde{O}(\log n)$.*

**Lemma 7.** *The maximum number of nodes moved from $F_1$ to $F_0$ on any PE during a cycle is in $\tilde{O}(\log n)$.*

**Lemma 8.** *At any moment, globalMax$|F_0| \in \tilde{O}(\log n)$.*

**Lemma 9.** *At any moment, globalMax$|F_1| \in \tilde{O}\left(\frac{m}{n}\right)$.*

*Proof.* Similar to the proof of Lemma 5. For Lemmata 6 and 9, we change the number of Bernoulli trials to $kn\log n$ and $m \in \Omega(n\log n)$ respectively. For Lemma 7 observe that during a cycle the $n\log n$ globally best nodes are expanded. In the worst case they all have to be extracted from $\check{F}_1$. But since they have been placed randomly, no PE will have more than $\tilde{O}(\log n)$ of them. Lemma 8 ist a consequence of the Lemmata 6 and 7, and of the summation rule (1). ∎

### 4.3 Extracting Nodes

We want to remove the $n'$ smallest nodes from $\check{F}_0$. (In our case $n' = n$.) Figure 3 lines out an efficient probabilistic algorithm for doing this. We maintain a candidate set $F'$ (initially $F_0$) and a set of nodes $F_{\text{out}}$ known to belong to the smallest ones. $m'$ is the size of $\check{F}'$. The algorithm is related to the well known sequential quicksort-like median selection algorithm [1, Section 10.2]. However, instead of choosing a single pivot for partitioning the remaining candidates, we try to partition $F'$ into three parts; nodes which are certain to belong to the smallest nodes, those which are certain *not* be among the smallest ones, and a (hopefully small) set of remaining candidates for the next iteration.[4]

---

[4] We would like to thank an anonymous referee for pointing out that very similar algorithms are also described in [25, 21].

**FORALL** PEs **DOPAR** synchronously

$F' := F_0$                                           (* solution candidates *)

$m' := |\breve{F}'|$                                 (* number of remaining candidates *)

$F_{\text{out}} := \emptyset$                                       (* nodes already found *)

**WHILE** $n' > 0 \wedge m' > n^{\frac{1}{2}} \wedge m' > n'$ **DO**

    randomly select $n^{\frac{1}{2}}$ samples from $\breve{F}'$ with replacement

    let $s_i$ denote the the $i$-th smallest sample                   (* sort them *)

        $(s_i = -\infty$ for $i \leq 0$, $s_i = \infty$ for $i > n^{\frac{1}{2}})$

    $u := s_{\frac{n'}{m'}n^{\frac{1}{2}}+n^{\frac{1}{4}+\epsilon}}$                               (* upper pivot *)

    $l := s_{\frac{n'}{m'}n^{\frac{1}{2}}-n^{\frac{1}{4}+\epsilon}}$                               (* lower pivot *)

    **IF** $|\{v \in \breve{F}' : v < u\}| \geq n'$ **THEN** $F' := F' \setminus \{v \in F' : v \geq u\}$

    **IF** $|\{v \in \breve{F}' : v \leq l\}| \leq n'$ **THEN** $F' := F' \setminus \{v \in F' : v \leq l\}$

        $F_{\text{out}} := F_{\text{out}} \cup \{v \in F' : v \leq l\}$; $n' := n' - |\{v \in \breve{F}' : v \leq l\}|$**FI**

    $m' := |\breve{F}'|$

**IF** $m' \leq n'$ **THEN** $F_{\text{out}} := F_{\text{out}} \cup F'$

**ELSE IF** $n' > 0$ **THEN**            (* $m' \leq n^{\frac{1}{2}}$; sorting is easy now *)

    sort $\breve{F}'$ and insert the $n'$ smallest nodes into their local $F_{\text{out}}$

**Fig. 3.** Finding the $n$ best nodes from $\breve{F}_0$.

First, a random sample of size $n^{\frac{1}{2}}$ is selected. (It simplifies the analysis to assume that this is done with replacement, i.e., nodes may be selected for multiple samples). We then rank the sample nodes and choose two pivots $u$ and $l$, spaced by $n^{\frac{1}{4}+\epsilon}$ from an estimate for a node with a rank close to $n'$. $0 < \epsilon < \frac{1}{4}$ is a small constant we are free to choose. We prove that with high probability at least $n'$ nodes will be smaller than $u$ such that nodes larger than $u$ can be excluded from consideration and that there are no more than $n'$ nodes smaller than $l$ such that those that *are* smaller can savely be selected. This randomized partitioning process is repeated until a trivial case occurs.

**Lemma 10.** *There is a choice of $\epsilon > 0$ such that the number of partitioning iterations is in $\tilde{O}(1)$.*

Due to space constraints we omit the proof which is again based on Chernoff bounds and on the fact that for an appropriate choice of $\epsilon$ the number of elements between $l$ and $u$ is small with high probability. Very similar arguments can also be found in [25, 21].

**Lemma 11.** *Extracting the $n$ smallest nodes from $F_0$ takes time $\tilde{O}(d)$.*

*Proof.* An iteration involves the following communication operations:

- A prefix sum for enumerating the nodes in $F'$.

- Routing randomly selected samples to different PEs. Since the elements have been placed randomly, the samples will be evenly distributed over the PEs such that routing them is possible in time $\tilde{O}(d)$.
- Sorting the samples.
- A constant number of reductions and broadcasts for counting nodes and disseminating pivots.

All other operations are performed locally. By representing $F'$ and $F_{\text{out}}$ as two indices into the sorted array $F_0$, the local operations can be performed in time $O(\log \text{globalMax}|F_0|) \subseteq O(\log m') \subseteq O(\log n)$ using binary search. All operations inside the loop can be performed in time $\tilde{O}(d + \log n) \subseteq \tilde{O}(d)$. The same is true for the operations outside the loop. Since the number of iterations is in $\tilde{O}(1)$ we can conclude that the total time for selection is in $\tilde{O}(d + \log n) \subseteq \tilde{O}(d)$ (using the product rule (1)). ∎

## 4.4 Putting the Pieces Together

We now have all the required results to come back to the analysis of Algorithm 2.

**Theorem 12.** *One cycle (log n iterations) of global best first branch-and-bound using Algorithm 2 takes time* $\left(T_x + \tilde{O}\left(d + \log \frac{m}{n}\right)\right) \log n$.

*Proof.* Since $\text{globalMax}|F_0| \in \tilde{O}(\log n)$ (Lemma 6), emptying $F_0$ into $F_1$ takes time $\tilde{O}\left(\log \frac{m}{n} \log n\right)$. Due to Lemma 7, there are only $\tilde{O}(\log n)$ iterations of the while loop (per cycle) for moving nodes from $F_1$ to $F_0$ each of which involves two reductions and one priority queue access (time $O\left(d + \log \frac{m}{n}\right)$). The remaining operations have to be counted for each iteration (i.e. $\log n$ times): Extracting the $n$ best nodes takes time $\tilde{O}(d)$ (Lemma 11), and assigning these nodes to the PEs can be done using a prefix sum and a routing operation (time $O(d)$). Node expansions take time $T_x$ and $\tilde{O}\left(\frac{\log n}{\log\log n}\right)$ new nodes (Lemma 6) can be inserted into $F_0$ in time $\tilde{O}(\log n)$ by first sorting them (e.g. by heap-sort) and then merging them with $F_0$. Summing all this together (Relations (1,3)) yields time $\left(T_x + \tilde{O}\left(d + \log \frac{m}{n}\right)\right) \log n$. ∎

**Theorem 13.** *The parallel execution time of the branch-and-bound algorithm 2 is*

$$T_{\text{par}} \in \left(\frac{m}{n} + h\right)\left(T_x + \tilde{O}\left(d + \log \frac{m}{n}\right)\right) .$$

*Proof.* Since Algorithm 2 is a global best first algorithm, $\frac{m}{n} + h$ iterations are sufficient to complete the search. For $m$ polynomial in $n$ the theorem is an immediate consequence of Lemma 12 and the summation rule (3). Else, we must additionally exploit that the execution times of different cycles are independent of each other because a cycle deterministically removes the $n \log n$ best nodes without moving the other nodes. Therefore, with high probability, only a polynomially small fraction of the cycles will require a time exceeding the limit from

Lemma 12. These "slow" cycles cannot significantly change the total execution time because the worst case time for a cycle involves only a polynomial number of operations. ■

## 5 Refinements

Algorithm 2 is mainly designed for simplicity and analyzability. We now describe improvements which might be useful for a real implementation. After introducing some simple enhancements, we show how the number of communication operations can be reduced at the cost of slightly increasing message sizes in Section 5.1, and we explain how an asynchronous machine can be used more efficiently in Section 5.2. Finally, we line out a very simple algorithm variant which uses a minimal number of communication operations at the cost of slightly deviating from the global best first principle.

As a first improvement note that the loop in Algorithm 2

**WHILE** $|\{v \in \breve{F}_0 : v < \min \breve{F}_1\}| < n$ **DO** $F_0 := F_0 \cup \{\mathsf{deleteMin}(F_1)\}$

yields two kinds of information that can be used to speed up the subsequent extraction process. While the condition is true, all nodes smaller than $\min \breve{F}_1$ can savely be selected. When it is false, nodes larger than $\min \breve{F}_1$ can be excluded from consideration for this iteration.

Queue maintenance costs can be reduced by using the *leftist tree* variant for representing $F_1$ and $F_0$ [11]. Emptying $F_0$ into $F_1$ can then be performed in time $O(\log m)$ by merging the two trees. Furthermore, those nodes which are immediately fetched back into $F_1$ after the beginning of a cycle can be retrieved in constant time using this representation.

Furthermore, if sending nodes involves long messages we will only put $c(v)$ and a reference to the node in $F$. Since most nodes are never really expanded in many branch-and-bound applications, this measure will considerably reduce the message traffic.

### 5.1 Using Coarser Grained Communication

Algorithm 2 employs a relatively large number of fine-grained communication operations per iteration. On many contemporary machines, it is better to use more coarse grained but fewer operations. For example, we can coalesce several iterations of the while loop for moving nodes from $F_1$ to $F_0$ into two vector operations for minimum determination and counting.

Similarly, the number of iterations of the selection procedure 3 can be reduced by sorting a larger sample or using more than two pivots at a time. A particularly interesting scheme for choosing pivots is to use $u_i = s_{\frac{n'}{m}n^{\frac{1}{2}}+2^i}$, $l_i = s_{\frac{n'}{m}n^{\frac{1}{2}}-2^i}$ ($i = 1, \ldots, \log n/2$). The number of pivots is quite moderate, we will always be able to do some partitioning and the pivots lie very dense around the estimate for the $n'$-th smallest node. Also, there are no tuning parameters (like $\epsilon$) which we would have to adapt for maximal performance.

## 5.2 Asynchronous Operation

If node expansion times vary, it is wasteful to synchronize all PEs for every parallel node expansion. In addition, if new nodes are inserted as early as possible, the number of expanded nodes can be reduced. These advantages can be exploited by an algorithm where every PE hosts a worker process which asynchronously iterates through the branch-and-bound loop of Figure 1. A load balancing process is responsible for managing the priority queue accesses. In order to retain the economy of accessing the queue collectively, "delete-min"-requests are delayed until a sufficient number of requests have accumulated.

If a dedicated communication processor can be programmed to host the load balancing process, we can afford to start a load balancing phase immediately after the last one has finished. Else, there is a tradeoff between starting the access procedure too often, making the per-node access time very high and starting it too rarely, making many PEs wait. Simple strategies are starting load balancing periodically [7] or when the number of requests (found by periodically counting the requests) exceeds a fixed bound. More sophisticated strategies try to optimize the overall runtime based on the history of the computation [20, 10]. In [27] we describe a randomized adaptive triggering scheme which does not require periodic counting of requests. Finally, the waiting time can be partially hidden by running several branch-and-bound processes on each PE. Note however, that this measure can significantly increase the number of expanded nodes for small problems.

Asynchronous operation also gives some additional opportunities for optimizing the priority queue access. The selection algorithm 3 spends a considerable fraction of its time finding the last few nodes among the $n'$ smallest ones. Now we can break the process when a fixed fraction $\alpha > \frac{1}{2}$ of the desired nodes are found. If we prefer PEs which did not get a node the last time, some requests will be delayed by a factor $\leq 2$ but most accesses are accelerated.

## 5.3 A Minimalistic Variant

On many contemporary machines, collective operations for prefix sum, reduction and broadcast are so expensive that it pays to minimize their use; even if the quality of the algorithm is decreased. In our algorithm there are a lot of opportunities for this:

- Just keep $|F_0| = \alpha \log n$ fixed without checking if it actually contains the $n'$ smallest nodes. By choosing the constant $\alpha$ appropriately, this will work with high probability. If it fails, we leave the global best first strategy but we can still hope to have a good approximation.
- Select only a single sample from $F_0$. Since $|F_0|$ is the same everywhere and the nodes have been placed randomly we can use a simplified selection strategy where a predetermined set of $n^{\frac{1}{2}}$ PEs randomly selects one of their local nodes.

– Sort the sample and immediately enumerate the nodes with $v < s_{\frac{n'}{\alpha n \log n} n^{\frac{1}{2}} - \gamma n^{\frac{1}{4}+\epsilon}}$. For sufficiently large $n$, with high probability, these nodes belong to the $n'$ smallest ones in $\check{F}_0$ and their number is close to $n'$. ($\gamma$ is some constant we have to choose appropriately.) If this procedure enumerates more than $n'$ nodes, we simply choose an arbitrary subset – again deviating from the global best first strategy.

The only remaining collective operations are: Triggering a load balancing phase, sorting $n^{\frac{1}{2}}$ numbers, broadcasting a pivot, and enumerating requesting PEs and selected nodes.

# 6 Conclusions

The approach to parallelize branch-and-bound using a global best first strategy may be more practicable than previously believed. If the minimal search tree consists of $m \in \Omega(nh)$ nodes and the node expansion time $T_x$ is sufficiently coarse grained, $T_x \in \Omega\left(d + \log \frac{m}{n}\right)$, we expect linear speedup

$$T_{\text{par}} \in \left(\frac{m}{n} + h\right)\left(T_x + \tilde{O}\left(d + \log \frac{m}{n}\right)\right)$$

using our randomized parallel priority queues ($n$: number of PEs, $d$: network diameter, $h$: search tree depth). Efficiencies arbitrarily close to one are possible when $T_x \gg d + \log \frac{m}{n}$ and $\frac{m}{n} \gg h$. This is a significant improvement compared to Karp-Zhang's local best first algorithm which has maximum efficiency $\frac{1}{2e}$. For problems with a finer granularity we still have to resort to approximations of global best first. Applications with a very coarse granularity ($T_x \in \Omega(n \log n)$) can use the simpler and more work efficient centralized approach as long as the priority queue fits into the limited memory of a single PE. However, these applications often contain additional parallelism in the node evaluation function. (For example linear programming as a node evaluation for integer linear programming.) In this case, our algorithm gives us more freedom to exploit both sources of parallelism at once.

Although we have tied the description of the parallel priority queue algorithm to branch-and-bound, we can easily adapt it to other applications. As long as the initiators of "insert" and "delete-min" requests do not introduce additional contention, $O(n)$ operations of any kind can be completed in

$$\tilde{O}\left(d + \log \frac{m}{n}\right)$$

amortized time. (Where $m \in \Omega(n \log n)$ is the number of elements in the queue.) For hypercubes, constant degree hypercubic networks like butterflies, CCC, perfect shuffle or DeBruijn, and combinations of multistage networks with tree networks, this is in $\tilde{O}(\log m)$ and therefore as efficient as the priority queue algorithms on PRAMS and pipelined hypercubes. In addition, our algorithm is relatively simple and adapted to the properties of real machines. In particular, if we use the enhancements and simplifications from Section 5.

An equally interesting but slightly more complicated idea is to derive a general median selection algorithm from Algorithm 3. The assumption that the locally present elements are sorted, can be lifted without making the local operations very expensive. But if the largest elements are unevenly distributed, the sampling operations in the later iterations may have to get many values from the same PE thereby introducing considerable contention. (In fact, based on this argument a lower bound of $\Omega\left(\frac{m}{n}\log\log n\right)$ for deterministic algorithms on many interconnection networks is proved in [19].) Nevertheless, we conjecture that

$$T_{\text{par}} \in O\left(\frac{m}{n} + d\right)$$

will hold on the average (where $m$ is the number of elements) yielding efficiencies close to one for $\frac{m}{n} \gg d$. (For sufficiently large $n$ and a careful implementation of the local operations, few elements will be moved more than once and few elements will have to be compared more than twice.)

# References

1. T. H. Cormen, C. E. Leiserson, and R. L. Rivest. *Introduction to Algorithms.* McGraw-Hill, 1990.
2. G. Cybenko. Dynamic load balancing for distributed memory multiprocessors. *Journal of Parallel and Distributed Computing*, 7:279–301, 1989.
3. S. K. Das, M. C. Pinotti, and F. Sarkar. Optimal parallel priority queues in distributed memory hypercubes. Technical Report CRPDC-94-23, University of North Texas, Denton, December 1994.
4. N. Deo and S. Prasad. Parallel heap: An optimal parallel priority queue. *The Journal of Supercomputing*, 6(1):87–98, Mar. 1992.
5. M. Dion, M. Gengler, and S. Ubeda. Comparing two probabilistic models of the computational complexity of the branch and bound algorithm. In *CONPAR/VAPP*, LNCS, pages 359–370, Linz, 1994. Springer.
6. A. K. Gupta and A. G. Phoutiou. Load balanced priority queue implementations on distributed memory parallel machines. In *Sixth International Conference on Parallel Architectures and Languages Europe*, number 817 in LNCS, pages 689–700, Athens, July 1994. Springer.
7. D. Henrich. *Lastverteilung für Branch-and-bound auf eng-gekoppelten Parallelrechnern*. Dissertation, Universität Karlsruhe, 1994.
8. D. Ierardi. 2d-bubblesorting in average time $O(\sqrt{N}\lg N)$. In *ACM Symposium on Parallel Architectures and Algorithms*, 1994.
9. R. M. Karp and Y. Zhang. Parallel algorithms for backtrack search and branch-and-bound. *Journal of the ACM*, 40(3):765–789, 1993.
10. G. Karypis and V. Kumar. Unstructured tree search on SIMD parallel computers. *IEEE Transactions on Parallel and Distributed Systems*, 5(10):1057–1072, 1994.
11. D. E. Knuth. *The Art of Computer Programming — Sorting and Searching*, volume 3. Addison Wesley, 1973.
12. T. Lauer. *Adaptive dynamische Lastbalancierung*. PhD thesis, Max Planck Institute for Computer Science Saarbrücken, 1995.

13. P. S. Laursen. Simple approaches to parallel branch and bound. *Parallel Computing*, 19:143–152, 1993.

14. T. Leighton. *Introduction to Parallel Algorithms and Architectures*. Morgan Kaufmann, 1992.

15. F. C. Lin and R. M. Keller. The gradient model load balancing method. *IEEE Transactions on Software Engineering*, 13(1):32–38, 1987.

16. R. Lüling and B. Monien. A dynamic load balancing algorithm with provable good performance. Technical report, Universität Paderborn, 1994.

17. R. Lüling, B. Monien, and F. Ramme. Load balancing in large networks: A comparative case study. In *3th IEEE Symposium on Parallel and Distributed Processing*. IEEE, 1991.

18. G. P. McKeown, V. J. Rayward-Smith, and S. A. Rush. Parallel branch-and-bound. In *Advances in Parallel Algorithms*, pages 349–362. Blackwell, 1992.

19. C. G. Plaxton. On the network complexity of selection. In *Foundations of Computer Science*, pages 396–401. IEEE, 1989.

20. C. Powley, C. Ferguson, and R. E. Korf. Depth-fist heuristic search on a SIMD machine. *Artificial Intelligence*, 60:199–242, 1993.

21. S. Rajasekaran. Randomized parallel selection. In *Tenth Conference on Foundations of Software Technology and Theoretical Computer Science*, number 472 in LNCS, pages 215–224, Bangalore, 1990. Springer.

22. A. Ranade. A simpler analysis of the Karp-Zhang parallel branch-and-bound method. Technical report, University of California Berkeley, 1990.

23. A. Ranade, S. Cheng, E. Deprit, J. Jones, and S. Shih. Parallelism and locality in priority queues. In *Sixth IEEE Sypmposium on Parallel and Distributed Processing*, pages 97–103, October 1994.

24. V. N. Rao and V. Kumar. Concurrent access of priority queues. *IEEE Transactions on Computers*, 37(12):1657–1665, 1988.

25. R. Reischuk. Probabilistic parallel algorithms for sorting and selection. *SIAM Journal on Computing*, 14(2):396–409, 1985.

26. P. Sanders. Flaschenhalsfreie parallele Priority queues. In *PARS Workshop, Potsdam*, volume 13 of *PARS Mitteilungen*, pages 10–19, 1994.

27. P. Sanders. Better algorithms for parallel backtracking. In *Workshop on Algorithms for Irregularly Structured Problems*, LNCS, Lyon, 1995. Springer.

28. J. Song. A partially asynchronous and iterative algorithm for distributed load balancing. *Parallel Computing*, 20:853–868, 1994.

29. M. H. Willebeek-LeMair and A. P. Reeves. Strategies for dynamic load balancing on highly parallel computers. *IEEE Transactions on Parallel and Distributed Systems*, 4(9), 1993.

30. C. Xu and F. C. Lau. Optimal parameters for load balancing with the diffusion method in mesh networks. *Parallel Processing Letters*, 4(1):139–147, 1994.

# A Parallel Formulation for General Branch-and-Bound Algorithms*

Ricardo Corrêa**

LMC-IMAG, 46 av. Felix Viallet, 38031, Grenoble Cédex, France
Ricardo.Correa@imag.fr

Abstract. We consider in this paper the problem of searching for an (sub)optimal solution in a discrete solution space and we formulate the method called branch-and-bound. It is shown that the formulation is general to X-state-spaces and CP-based branch-and-bound and branch-and-cut. It includes a parallel data structure that can express a large variety of parallel strategies used in parallel branch-and-bound. The general formulation can be used underlying libraries that make accessible the parallelism to the operations research community.

## 1  Introduction

In a wide class of problems arising in operations research and artificial intelligence, one searches for an optimal solution among all vectors in a solution space $X$ that satisfy a set of constraints (which defines a possibly very large discrete domain $X$). The term (discrete) constrained optimization problem will be used in this text to investigate this class of problems, abstractly stated as follows.

Constrained Optimization Problem. Given a discrete set $X$ of feasible solutions, each feasible solution having a value given by an objective function $f: W \rightarrow \Re$, and an optimal solution $x^* \in X$, for which $f^* = f^*(x^*) = f(x^*)$, such that for all $x \in X$, $f^* \leq f(x)$, if $X = W$ then the optimal solution is *undefined*.

The method called branch-and-bound is an iterative search algorithm often used in this context. Its principle lies in successive splitting of the original problem in small subproblems, until it is enumerated that a feasible solution found during the search is optimal. Applying this principle in a naive way would imply the enumeration of all feasible solutions. The aim of a branch-and-bound algorithm is to limit the number of feasible solutions that need to be explicitly enumerated in order to demonstrate that a given feasible solution is optimal. In several industrial, research or other real-world environments, unsaturated programmers must face up to intractable instances of increased importance.

*This work was partially supported by TRACS - the project Programme of the French CNRS and the Human Capital and Mobility project SCOOP - Solving Combinatorial Optimization Problems in Parallel - of the European Union.
**Partially supported by a CNPq (Brazil) fellowship, grant 201121/92-5 (BC)

# A Parallel Formulation for General Branch-and-Bound Algorithms[*]

Ricardo Corrêa[**]

LMC – IMAG, 46, av. Félix Viallet, 38031, Grenoble Cedex, France
Ricardo.Correa@imag.fr

**Abstract.** We consider in this paper the problem of searching for an *(sub)optimal solution* in a discrete solution space and we formulate the method called *branch-and-bound*. It is shown that the formulation is general to $A^*$, *state-space* and *LP-based branch-and-bound* and *branch-and-cut*. It includes a parallel data structure that can express a large variety of parallel strategies used in parallel branch-and-bound. The general formulation can be used in designing libraries that make accessible the parallelism to the operations research community.

## 1 Introduction

In a wide class of problems arising in operations research and artificial intelligence, one searches for an *optimal solution* among all vectors in a solution space $W$ that satisfy a set of constraints (which defines a possibly very large discrete domain $X$). The term *(discrete) constrained optimization problem* will be used in this text to designate this class of problems, abstractly stated as follows.

**Constrained Optimization Problem:** *Given a discrete set $X$ of feasible solutions, each feasible solution having a value given by an objective function $f : W \rightarrow Y$, find an optimal solution $x^* \in X$, for which $f^* = f^*(X) = f(x^*)$, such that for all $x \in X$, $f^* \leq f(x)$. If $X = \emptyset$, then the optimal solution is "undefined."*

The method called *branch-and-bound* is an iterative search algorithm often used in this context. Its principle lies in successive splittings of the original problem in smaller subproblems until it is demonstrated that a feasible solution found during the search is optimal. Applying this principle in a naïve way would imply the enumeration of all feasible solutions. The aim of a *branch-and-bound* algorithm is to limit the number of feasible solutions that need to be explicitly enumerated in order to demonstrate that a given feasible solution is optimal. In several industrial, research or other real-world environments, mathematical programmers must face up to moderate instances of constrained optimization

---

[*] This work was partially supported by DRET, the project Stratagème of the French CNRS, and the Human Capital and Mobility project SCOOP - Solving Combinatorial Optimization Problems in Parallel - of the European Union.

[**] Partially supported by a CNPq (Brazil) fellowship, grant 201421/92-5 (BC).

problems for which an *exact optimal solution* is highly desirable. In such circumstances, parallel processing can drastically the time of solution. *Branch-and-bound* algorithms have also been formulated as a general method which is able to provide a *suboptimal solution*. A *suboptimal solution* is any feasible solution that is not demonstrated to be non-optimal. There are many cases for which the average time complexity of *branch-and-bound* algorithms is polynomial (eventually finding a suboptimal solution). Consequently, parallel processing gives us the perspective of efficiently solving relatively large instances in these cases.

The contribution of this paper is a parallel formulation for general branch-and-bound as a single meta-algorithm with which a great variety of algorithms and parallelization strategies used to solve constrained optimization problems can be expressed. The algorithm works by operating over a list of subproblems and produces a sequence of increasingly better feasible solutions. The (parallel) formulation consists of the definition of the (parallel) list and the operators. It is shown that the formulation is general to $A^*$, *state-space* and *LP-based branch-and-bound*, and *branch-and-cut*, but other methods could also be considered [9].

The basis of the parallel formulation is *distributed memory* parallel systems, which are composed of a set of connected processors, which communicate exclusively by exchange of messages. We consider the *high level* parallelization, which uses the set of processors to concurrently split several subproblems at each iteration. The processors interact by operating a *parallel multilist*, which is a parallel data structure that can express a large variety of parallel strategies for implementing *branch-and-bound algorithms* in parallel. For this reason, the parallel formulation can be used in the design of branch-and-bound libraries that incorporate the knowledge available in the domain of parallelizing search algorithms. Such a library makes accessible the parallelism to the operations research and artificial intelligence communities and, due to its potential for facilitating the task of developing parallel software using different parallel strategies, it facilitates algorithmic research and model development.

Other formulations of general branch-and-bound algorithms have been reported in the literature. Mitten [14] formulated a sequential branch-and-bound where pruning by lower bounding and relaxation are imposed (see our ordinary branch-and-bound, section 5). Other sequential formulation was proposed by Ibaraki in some published papers. In [6] dominance relations are studied, and in [7] a sequential decision process is used for state-space representations. Nau et al. [15] proposed a general sequential formulation which uses a *representation scheme* (see section 2). Turning to parallel processing, Eva and Wah [18] and Finkel and Manber [5] conceived distributed and more general formulations. Finally, McKeown et al. [13] formulated parallel branch-and-bound for state-space representation as a higher-order function.

Besides this introductory section, the remainder of the paper is organized as follows. The parallel formulation will be firstly presented in its mathematical definitions and, then, in its computational architecture. The general formulation is described in section 2. In section 3, some special instantiations of the general formulation are presented, where *branch-and-cut* is formulated as its instantiation. In sections 4 the parallel multilist permitting the parallel implementations are presented. Finally, some comments on the applications of this formulation and some conclusions are presented.

## 2 A General Formulation of Branch-and-Bound

In this section, a variation of the general formulation of Nau et al. is described as our highest level of abstraction in branch-and-bound algorithms [15]. The sequential algorithm consists of a sequence of *iterations* in which subproblems in a *list* $\mathcal{L}$ are solved to optimality or split. This *list* is only accessed and modified via *general operators*, namely, *selection*, *pruning* and *insertion*, which are the operators modifying $\mathcal{L}$, and *evaluation*, which is the only general operator that modifies a subproblem. Eventually, more than one list can be considered. The formulation is described by defining the general operators and the sequential algorithm; the sequential list operators; and the paradigms used to parallelize the sequential algorithm, including the parallel data structure used to implement these paradigms.

In order to respect the principle of generality of the formulation, *representation schemes* for the subproblems are used instead of the subproblems themselves. A *representation scheme* is a pair $(R, \rho)$, where $R$ is a set of *representations* and $\rho : R \to 2^W$ is a *representation function*. For a representation $r$, the representation function $\rho(r)$ is the corresponding subset $w$ of $W$. The use of a unique representation scheme in the definition of the operators avoids situations where different representations for a same subproblem yield different behaviors of the operator [15].

### 2.1 The sequential algorithm

The execution of the algorithm starts with the list $\mathcal{L}$ containing $r_0$, the representation of a subset of $W$ that includes $X$. At the end of the execution, the algorithm returns an $x^*$ and the corresponding $f^*$, if one searches for an exact optimal solution, or, otherwise, a feasible solution whose value is an acceptable approximation of $f^*$. For the sake of simplicity, for any operator defined in the sequel in this subsection, we have $operator(\emptyset) = \emptyset$. Therefore, given a representation (set of representations) $r$ $(R)$, we denote $f^*(r)$ $(f^*(R))$ the value of the optimal solution of $r$ $(R)$.

Since a branch-and-bound algorithm enumerates representations, it is desirable to visit representations in such a way that for every two representations $r_1, r_2$ such that $f^*(r_1) > f^*(r_2)$, then $r_1$ is not visited before $r_2$. This principle would assure that the representations not containing an optimal solution would be avoided. Unfortunately, $f^*$ is not known beforehand and we are constrained to approximate the order of enumeration by assigning a *heuristic priority* $\omega(r)$ to each representation $r$ (e.g. best-first, depth-first [8]). We say that a representation $r_1$ is *better* than another representation $r_2$ if $\omega(r_1) > \omega(r_2)$. This heuristic priority is used in the first operator of an iteration, *selection*.

**Definition 1 Selection.** The *selection* operator deletes and returns the representation of highest priority from $\mathcal{L}$.

Following a *selection*, the operator applied is *evaluation*.

**Definition 2 Evaluation.** The *evaluation* operator, applied to a representation $r$, returns a set of new representations, where each new representation is a strict subset of $r$, and, eventually, a representation of a suboptimal solution such that one of the following conditions holds:

1. the value of at least one new representation equals $f^*(R)$; or
2. the value of the suboptimal solution returned equals $f^*(R)$.

There are two differences between the operator *evaluation* just defined and the *splitting* defined by Nau et al. in [15]. *Evaluation* is more general because feasible solutions can be eliminated, and suboptimal solutions can be found in two manners: first, an *evaluation* tries to solve, heuristically, each selected representation to optimality; second, an *evaluation* may generate representations simple enough to be solved to optimality directly, determining a feasible solution.

The goal of the third operation, *pruning*, is to allow an intelligent search that avoids considering representations known not to be essential to the search of an (sub)optimal solution of $X$.

**Definition 3 Pruning.** Let $R$ be a set of representations. The *pruning* operator deletes a set of representations from $R$ such that $f^*(R') = f^*(R)$, where $R'$ is the set $R$ after the pruning.

The last operation in an iteration is the *insertion* operator.

**Definition 4 Insertion.** Let $R$ be a set of representations. The *insertion* operator includes the representations of $R$ in $\mathcal{L}$.

Finally, three functions are also defined. A boolean function must be provided in order to determine that the quality criteria for a suboptimal solution is satisfied: *SearchIsFinished*. A function that returns the (sub)optimal solution found must also be provided: *OptimalSolution*. A boolean function that compares two representations $r_1, r_2$, named *BetterRep*, returns $TRUE$ if $r_1$ is better than $r_2$, and $FALSE$ otherwise. The algorithm in figure 1 describes the sequence of iterations. In this algorithm, $r_{opt}$ represents the suboptimal solution at every point of the execution. The correctness of similar branch-and-bound formulations has already been demonstrated by several authors, which can be easily adapted to our formulation. For more details, see [14, 15].

## 2.2 List operators

The list operators allowing the implementations of the general operators of the previous subsection are briefly described in this subsection. In section 4, parallel versions of these list operators are defined. Suppose we are given a list of representations $\mathcal{L}$.

```
 1.  list L;
 2.  representation r_opt;
 3.  /* L is initially empty */
 4.  /* r_opt is a representation of a suboptimal solution */
 5.  /* or ''undefined.'' */
 6.  algorithm branch - and - bound(r_0):
 7.  list SPL;
 8.  representation r;
 9.  insertion({r_0});
10.      /* the termination depends on the state of L, */
11.      /* on the definition of the problem */
12.      /* and on the best solution found */
13.      while not (SearchIsFinished(r_0)) do
14.          r ← selection();
15.          /* evaluation can found a suboptimal solution */
16.          (r, SPL) ← evaluation(r);
17.          /* updates the best solution found */
18.          if BetterRep(r, r_opt) then r_opt ← r;
19.          /* prunes representations in SPL or L */
20.          pruning(SPL);
21.          insertion(SPL);
22.      /* returns ρ(r_opt) */
23.      return OptimalSolution(r_opt);
```

**Fig. 1.** General sequential branch-and-bound.

**Put:** given a set of representations, this list operator puts all the representations of this set in $L$ using the function $BetterRep$ to compare representations. It is useful to implement the general operator *insertion*.

**GetMax:** this list operator gets the highest priority representation in $L$. It is useful to implement the general operator *selection*.

**DelWorseSubList:** this list operator deletes a set of representations from $L$ that are worse than a given suboptimal solution, using the function $BetterRep$ to compare representations. It is useful to implement the general operator *pruning*.

**GetWorseRep:** this list operator receives a representation $r$. It searches for an equivalent representation $r'$ in $L$. If the search fails, it returns $r$. Additionally, if $r$ is better than $r'$, it returns $TRUE$; otherwise, it returns $FALSE$. It uses the function $BetterRep$ to compare representations, and it is useful to implement the general operator *pruning* by *dominance* (see section 3).

**EmptyList:** this list operator checks whether $L$ is empty. It is useful to implement the boolean function $SearchIsFinished$ (see section 3).

## 2.3 Parallel formulation paradigms

Suppose we are given a set of processors in a distributed memory environment. The parallel formulation for general branch-and-bound algorithms is derived modifying the sequential formulation such that each processor has its own list of representations and executes the algorithm in figure 1. These modifications are three: first, in step **9.**, only one processor inserts $r_0$, and the others insert nothing; second, in step **13.**, the boolean function $SearchIsFinished$ becomes parallel, expressing a global state of the processors; third, in step **18.**, all processors must be informed of the updates of $r_{opt}$. In this parallel formulation, the processors interact by operating a *parallel multilist* $\mathcal{M}$ of representations (we postpone the details until section 4). The operators of parallel multilists defined in section 4 allow the implementation of the following *processor interaction* and *synchronization* paradigms.

*Parallel multilists* Essentially, a *multilist* is a forest corresponding to a set of lists of representations arranged in rooted tree structures. Each *node* in these trees contains a list of representations, and each leaf is connected to exactly one processor. Equivalently, to each processor corresponds a leaf node and, consequently, a tree of $\mathcal{M}$. The processors operate $\mathcal{M}$ addressing operation requests (or representations) to the leaf corresponding to it, and each node can sends/receives operation requests to/from its parent/children. The execution of one operation in a node may yield the transfer of representations from/to this node to/from any other node. A multilist can be abstractly seen as a way to express different levels of common knowledge of its lists. A *parallel multilist* is a parallel version of a multilist, where the nodes of the multilist are distributed over the processors.

*Processor interaction paradigms* The processors can interact following two different paradigms, namely *distributed data* and *shared data* paradigms [2, 3]. The *distributed data* paradigm is a fully distributed approach, where each processor works on different and disjoint lists. Given that the structure of the searched space is not known beforehand, and since subproblems are generated and selected in an unpredictable way, irregularities appear during the parallel search. Consequently, special techniques for deciding about migrations of representations from one list of $\mathcal{M}$ to another must be used to address the problems related to the irregularity of the searched space or of the parallel search process [8].

In the *shared data* paradigm, every two processors can interact *exclusively* through a common node in $\mathcal{M}$. In this case, each processor can only access the lists in the nodes of $\mathcal{M}$ located in the path from its corresponding leaf to the root of its tree. Using this paradigm, the structure of the searched space is not taken into account, avoiding the troubles inherent to irregularity, possibly yielding implicit qualitative and quantitative workload sharing [2].

*Synchronization paradigms* We define two different synchronization paradigms, namely *synchronized* or *asynchronous* [2, 3, 10, 11, 12, 18]. In the *synchronized* formulation, the processor interaction paradigm used is shared data and step

**14.** of figure 1 is synchronized, determining that *a selection is not performed before all the insertions of the previous iteration have finished.* Such a behavior severely restricts the set of possible optimizations in the implementation of the operations of $\mathcal{M}$, being only useful with a few processors or if the computation time for one decomposition operation is much longer than the communication time to transfer one subproblem from one node of $\mathcal{M}$ to another.

Contrary to synchronized branch-and-bound, the main characteristic of an *asynchronous* algorithm is that the processors do not have to wait at predetermined points for predetermined data to become available. The objective is to allow reduction of the synchronization penalty and overlap between communication and computation. On the other hand, the algorithm may select more unnecessary representations, and the detection of termination tends to be somewhat more difficult to implement [2].

# 3  Special Instantiations

In this section, the generality of the formulation is illustrated by using particular methods for constrained optimization problems as instantiations of the general formulation. Due to space restrictions, the formal demonstrations are left to another paper. For a parallel version of the examples in this section, each list should be replaced by a parallel multilist.

## 3.1  A*

This kind of search algorithm is used when the searched space is represented by a *state-space graph* [15, 17]. Given a subproblem $v$ in this case, a *partial solution* is a sequence of elementary decisions leading the original problem to $v$. A *state* is the additional information assigned to the representation of $v$ that explicitly defines the remaining subproblems to be explored from $v$. If two subproblems have the same state but different partial solutions then they are different, but *equivalent*. The implementation of the general operators is shown in the algorithm of figure 2. It employs two lists of representations and three more specific operators defined in the following.

**Definition 5 Branching.** The *branching* operator, applied to any representation $r$, returns the following:

1. a set of new representations, where each new representation is $r$ plus one elementary decision; or
2. a representation of a suboptimal solution if $r$ is a parent of a suboptimal solution.

The representation of each subproblem includes its *lower bound*, which is used in order to implement a best-first search strategy.

**Definition 6 Lower Bounding.** Let $R$ be a set of representations. The *lbounding* operator, applied to any $R$, calculates the *lower bound* $l(r)$, for all $r \in R$, such that:

1. $l(r) \leq f^*(r)$;
2. $l(r) = f(x)$, if $\rho(r) = \{x\}$ and $x$ is a feasible solution; and
3. $l(r') \leq l(r)$, if $r$ is generated by the branching of $r'$.

In $A^*$ algorithms, the lower bound of each representation $r$ is written as $l(r) = g(r) + h(r)$, where $g(r)$ is the additive cost of the partial solution of $\rho(r)$ and $h(r)$ is an estimate of the best solution of the state of $\rho(r)$. For $h(r)$, the conditions imposed to the lower bound also apply. The pruning is by *dominance*. In general terms, if the available information on the representation of subproblems can be used to show that a subproblem $v_j$ cannot includes a better feasible solution for $X$ than that obtainable from another subproblem $v_i$, then $v_j$ can be eliminated of the search [6].

**Definition 7 Dominance.** Let $r$ be a representation. Then, $r$ is eliminated from the search if there exists a representation $r'$ such that:

1. $r$ and $r'$ are equivalent; and
2. $l(r) \leq l(r')$.

## 3.2 State-space branch-and-bound

The *state-space branch-and-bound* is a variation of $A^*$ used in *tree search* with an additional type of pruning, and other two specific operators: *infeasibility* and *local_bounding* [6, 13]. They are defined in the sequel (see figure 3).

**Definition 8 Infeasibility.** Let $R$ be a set of representations. The *infeasibility* operator, applied to $R$, deletes the representations of $R$ that contains no feasible solution.

The second type of pruning is by *bounding*, which prunes representations that cannot lead to a feasible solution which is better than the current best known suboptimal solution [7].

**Definition 9 Local Bounding.** Let $R$ be a set of representations. The *local_bounding* operator deletes the representations $r$ of $R$ such that $f(r_{opt}) < l(r)$.

A more powerful dominance relation than definition 7 can be defined. For details, see [6].

```
1.  instantiation LP-branch-and-bound(r₀):
       ⋮

2.      operator lbounding(R):
3.          r₁ ← null;
4.          for every r ∈ R
5.              r₁ ← solution of r;
6.              if r₁ is feasible then
7.                  keep r₁ if it is the best found in R;
8.                  discard r;
9.              else l(r) ← f(r₁);
10.         return r₁;
11.     operator evaluation(r):
12.         (r, SPL) := branching(r);
13.         if (SPL ≠ ∅) then
14.             infeasibility(SPL);
15.             r = lbounding(SPL);
16.             ubounding(r, SPL);
17.             return (r, SPL);
18.     operator local_bounding(R):
19.         if there is a new rₒₚₜ then
20.             for every r ∈ R
21.                 if l(r) ≥ f(rₒₚₜ) then discard r;
22.             DelWorseSubList(rₒₚₜ);
23.     operator pruning(R):
24.         local_bounding(SPL);
25.         dominance(R);
```

Fig. 4. LP-based branch-and-bound.

## 3.4 Branch-and-Cut

In *branch-and-cut* algorithms, the search is guided by structural information in order to drastically decrease the number of subproblems enumerated, based on *relaxations, cutting* and *dominance relations*. The key aspect here is to be able to generate a relatively small set of constraints which, when added to the relaxed problem, substantially reduces the gap between the value of their optimal solutions. However, complete knowledge of all necessary constraints is rarely available, being the reason for successive splittings in the hope of simplifying the determination of constraints. In this way, a new operator is defined, *cutting*. Eventually, if *lbounding* determines a relaxed optimal solution which is infeasible, then *cutting* tries to cut this particular infeasible solution from the relaxed representation [16].

**Definition 13 Cutting.** Let $R$ be a set of representations. The *cutting* operator, applied to any $R$, returns a set of new representations such that:

1. each new representation is a subset of some representation of $R$; and
2. feasible solutions are not discarded.

The following algorithm (figure 5) illustrates a branch-and-bound algorithm.

```
1.  instantiation branch-and-cut(r₀):
        ⋮
2.      operator evaluation(r):
3.          while cut(SPL) do
4.              infeasibility(SPL);
5.              r = lbounding(SPL);
6.              cutting(SPL);
7.              ubounding(r, SPL);
8.              return branching(r);
9.          operator local_bounding(R):
10.             if there is a new r_opt then
11.                 for every r ∈ R
12.                     if l(r) ≥ f(r_opt) then discard r;
13.                 DelWorseSubList(r_opt);
14.         operator pruning(R):
15.             local_bounding(SPL);
16.             dominance(R);
```

**Fig. 5.** Branch-and-cut.

# 4 Parallel Multilist Operators

In the next subsections, we describe some parallel multilist operators and give some properties. Suppose we are given a parallel multilist $\mathcal{M}$. The operation requests are performed by the processors specifying one *accessible node* as the *destination node* of the operation. An *accessible node* is a node from its corresponding leaf to the root of its tree. The subtree rooted at the destination node is the *operation subtree*. The request follows in the operation subtree from the leaf corresponding to the processor until it reaches the destination node. The three following operations are common to the synchronized and asynchronous paradigms.

**EmptyList:** this multilist operator checks if the operation subtree is empty.

**DelWorseSubList:** for each node that receives this request from a child $n$, it applies *DelWorseSubList* to its list, then it sends the same request to all children except $n$, and, finally, if it is not the destination node, it sends the request to its parent.

**DelWorseRep:** for each node in the operation tree receiving this request from a child $n$, it applies the list operator *DelWorseRep* in its list. If it succeeds, it returns the result to $n$. Otherwise, it sends the request to its children except $n$ and, if it is not the destination node, it sends a *DelWorseRep* request to its parent. For each node receiving the request from its parent, it tries the corresponding list operation locally and, if it fails, it sends the request to its children (if it is not a leaf node). For each node, it applies *DelWorseRep* in its list and returns the result to the node having requested the operation. Finally, when each non-leaf node $n$ receives all the results, it sends a combined result to the node having requested the operation to $n$.

## 4.1 Synchronized operations

The principle is that all processors operate $M$ as it was a single list. In all cases, once an operation request has been issued to $M$, the corresponding processor remains idle due to the *latency time* associated to $M$.

**Put:** each leaf put the representations received from the corresponding processor in its list. Then, if the leaf node is not the destination node, it gets a number of representations in its list and sends them to its parent. The number of representations sent equals the number of leaves in the operation subtree. For each node non-leaf that is not the destination node in the operation subtree, it blocks the operation until all its children has sent their representations, before getting from its list and sending to its parent. Finally, the destination node inserts the representation it receives in its list.

**GetMax:** each leaf node receives a request from its corresponding processor, which are propagated until the destination node. When the destination node receives the request from all its children, it sends a number of the best representations in its list to each child. The number of representations returned to each child equals the number of leaf nodes in the subtree rooted on this child. The other nodes successively receives from its parent, puts the received representations in its list, gets the best representations in its list and sends one of them to each child.

## 4.2 Asynchronous operations

The principle of the asynchronous operators is that each processor can work in its own pace by speculative computation. There are no synchronizations, and nodes do not wait for results from other nodes to send a result.

**Put:** similar to the synchronized case, except that each intermediate node does not block, sending the best nodes immediately to its parent.

**Get:** similar to the synchronized case, except that each intermediate node does not block, sending the best nodes to the child and the request to its parent.

**PutGetMax:** avoids thrashing effects. The nodes puts locally, sends the better downward and putgetmax upward.

### 4.3  Implementing the parallel formulation paradigms

A parallel multilist (and its operators) is a powerful data structure that is able to implement a wide variety of parallel branch-and-bound strategies (for a survey of parallel implementations, see [4]). It must be configured in terms of the desired parallel strategy. This configuration determines the number and the shape of the trees. The configurations range from a set of distributed lists to a centralized list.

The implementation of the different processor interaction paradigms depends on the configuration as well. For implementing the shared data paradigm, the parallel multilist is configurated a unique tree, and the processors must be connected to leaf nodes. The distributed data paradigm is implemented definig the parallel multilist as a set of disconnected lists. Finally, we note that shared data operations and distributed data operations may be combined, illustrating the flexibility of the data structure.

### 4.4  Some properties of shared data paradigms

The first property concerns the synchronized paradigm.

**Property 1** *If only synchronized operations are used, then the several representations selected at one node n of $M$ are guaranteed to be the current representations with highest priority in the subtree $M$ rooted at n.*

In the more general asynchronous case, we have the following property.

**Property 2** *Whenever a representation r is selected from a node n of $M$, there is no other representation with smaller priority than r that was inserted in n and not yet selected.*

## 5  Conclusions

In this paper, we described a general formulation of sequential and parallel branch-and-bound. This general formulation is able to express a wide variety of search algorithms for constrained optimization problems. This general formulation includes a parallel data structure that can express a large variety of parallel strategies used in high level parallel branch-and-bound. It presents flexibility, i.e., the use of different data structures and parallelization techniques are possible. The main application of this general application is parallel branch and bound libraries.

# Acknowledgments

I would like to thank the substantial help granted by Gregory Mounié and Afonso Ferreira, and the suggestions provided by the anonymous refeeres.

# References

1. E. Beale. Branch and bound methods for mathematical programming systems. *Annals of Discrete Mathematics*, 5:201–219, 1979.
2. R. Corrêa and A. Ferreira. A distributed implementation of asynchronous parallel branch-and-bound. In A. Ferreira and J. Rolim, editors, *Solving Irregular Problems in Parallel: State of the Art*. Kluwer Academic Publisher, Boston (USA), 1995.
3. R. Corrêa and A. Ferreira. On the effectiveness of synchronous branch-and-bound algorithms. *Parallel Processing Letters*, 1995. To appear.
4. R. Corrêa and A. Ferreira. Parallel best-first branch-and-bound in discrete optimization: a framework. Tec. Rep. 95–03, DIMACS, Rutgers Univ., March 1995.
5. R. Finkel and U. Manber. DIB – A distributed implementation of backtracking. *ACM Transactions on Prog. Lang. and Syst.*, 9(2):235–256, April 1987.
6. T. Ibaraki. The power of dominance relations in branch-and-bound algorithms. *Journal of the ACM*, 24(2):264–279, April 1977.
7. T. Ibaraki. Branch-and-bound procedure and the state-space representation of combinatorial optimization problems. *Inf. and Control*, 36:1–27, 1978.
8. V. Kumar, A. Grama, A. Gupta, and G. Karypis. *Introduction to Parallel Computing: Design and Analysis of Algorithms*. The Benjamin/Cummings Publishing Company, Inc., 1994.
9. V. Kumar and L. Kanal. A general branch-and-bound formulation for understanding and synthesizing And/Or tree search procedures. *Artificial Intelligence*, 21:179–198, 1983.
10. T. Lai and S. Sahni. Anomalies in parallel branch-and-bound algorithms. *Communications of the ACM*, 27:594–602, 1984.
11. T. Lai and A. Sprague. Performance of parallel branch-and-bound algorithms. *IEEE Transactions on Computers*, C-34(10):962–964, October 1985.
12. G. Li and B. Wah. Coping with anomalies in parallel branch-and-bound algorithms. *IEEE Transactions on Computers*, C-35(6):568–573, June 1986.
13. G. McKeown, V. Rayward-Smith, and H. Turpin. Branch-and-bound as a higher-order function. *Annals of Operations Research*, 33:379–402, 1991.
14. L. Mitten. Branch-and-bound methods: General formulation and properties. *Operations Research*, 18:24–34, 1970. Errata in *Operations Research* 19 (1971), 550.
15. D. Nau, V. Kumar, and L. Kanal. General branch and bound, and its relation to A* and AO*. *Artificial Intelligence*, (23):29–58, 1984.
16. M. Padberg and G. Rinaldi. A branch and cut algorithm for the solution of large-scale symmetric traveling salesman problem. *SIAM Review*, 33:60–100, 1991.
17. J. Pearl. *Heuristics - Intelligent Search Strategies for Computer Problem Solving*. Reading, MA: Addison-Wesley, 1984.
18. B. Wah and Y. Eva. MANIP - A multicomputer architecture for solving combinatorial extremum-search problems. *IEEE T. on Comp.*, C-33(5):377–390, 1984.

# Springer-Verlag
# and the Environment

We at Springer-Verlag firmly believe that an international science publisher has a special obligation to the environment, and our corporate policies consistently reflect this conviction.

We also expect our business partners – paper mills, printers, packaging manufacturers, etc. – to commit themselves to using environmentally friendly materials and production processes.

The paper in this book is made from low- or no-chlorine pulp and is acid free, in conformance with international standards for paper permanency.

# Lecture Notes in Computer Science

For information about Vols. 1–903

please contact your bookseller or Springer-Verlag